Less managing. More **D0128915** *arning.*

 ## INSTRUCTORS...

Would you like your **students** to show up for class more **prepared**? *(Let's face it, class is much more fun if everyone is engaged and prepared...)*

Want ready-made application-level **interactive assignments,** student progress reporting, and auto-assignment grading? *(Less time grading means more time teaching...)*

Want an **instant view of student or class performance** relative to learning objectives? *(No more wondering if students understand...)*

Need to **collect data and generate reports** required for administration or accreditation? *(Say goodbye to manually tracking student learning outcomes...)*

Want to **record and post your lectures** for students to view online?

 ## With **McGraw-Hill's** *Connect® Plus Management,*

INSTRUCTORS GET:

- Interactive Applications – **book-specific interactive assignments** that require students to APPLY what they've learned.

- Simple **assignment management,** allowing you to spend more time teaching.

- **Auto-graded** assignments, quizzes, and tests.

- **Detailed Visual Reporting** where student and section results can be viewed and analyzed.

- Sophisticated **online testing** capability.

- A **filtering and reporting** function that allows you to easily assign and report on materials that are correlated to accreditation standards, learning outcomes, and Bloom's taxonomy.

- An easy-to-use **lecture capture** tool.

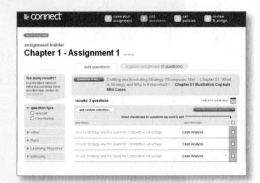

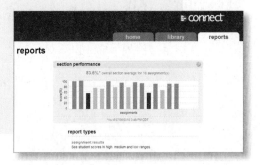

Want an online, **searchable version** of your textbook?

Wish your textbook could be **available online** while you're doing your assignments?

Connect® Plus Management eBook

If you choose to use *Connect® Plus Management*, you have an affordable and searchable online version of your book integrated with your other online tools.

Connect® Plus Management eBook offers features like:

- Topic search
- Direct links from assignments
- Adjustable text size
- Jump to page number
- Print by section

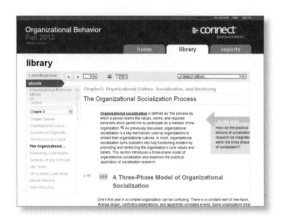

Want to get more **value** from your textbook purchase?

Think learning management should be a bit more **interesting**?

Check out the STUDENT RESOURCES section under the *Connect®* Library tab.

Here you'll find a wealth of resources designed to help you achieve your goals in the course. You'll find things like **quizzes, PowerPoints, and Internet activities** to help you study. Every student has different needs, so explore the STUDENT RESOURCES to find the materials best suited to you.

essentials of
STRATEGIC
MANAGEMENT

The Quest for Competitive Advantage

Third Edition

John E. Gamble
University of South Alabama

Arthur A. Thompson, Jr.
The University of Alabama

Margaret A. Peteraf
Dartmouth College

McGraw-Hill
Irwin

ESSENTIALS OF STRATEGIC MANAGEMENT: THE QUEST FOR COMPETITIVE ADVANTAGE
Published by McGraw-Hill/Irwin, a business unit of The McGraw-Hill Companies, Inc., 1221 Avenue of the Americas, New York, NY, 10020. Copyright © 2013, 2011, 2009 by The McGraw-Hill Companies, Inc. All rights reserved. Printed in the United States of America. No part of this publication may be reproduced or distributed in any form or by any means, or stored in a database or retrieval system, without the prior written consent of The McGraw-Hill Companies, Inc., including, but not limited to, in any network or other electronic storage or transmission, or broadcast for distance learning.

Some ancillaries, including electronic and print components, may not be available to customers outside the United States.

This book is printed on acid-free paper.

1 2 3 4 5 6 7 8 9 0 DOW/DOW 1 0 9 8 7 6 5 4 3 2

ISBN 978-0-07-802928-8
MHID 0-07-802928-7

Vice president and editor-in-chief: *Brent Gordon*
Editorial director: *Paul Ducham*
Executive editor: *Michael Ablassmeir*
Executive director of development: *Ann Torbert*
Editorial coordinator: *Andrea Heirendt*
Vice president and director of marketing: *Robin J. Zwettler*
Marketing director: *Amee Mosley*
Executive marketing manager: *Anke Braun Weekes*
Marketing specialist: *Elizabeth Steiner*
Vice president of editing, design, and production: *Sesha Bolisetty*
Lead project manager: *Harvey Yep*
Buyer II: *Debra R. Sylvester*
Senior designer: *Matt Diamond*
Senior photo research coordinator: *Keri Johnson*
Photo researcher:
Senior media project manager: *Bruce Gin*
Media project manager: *Suresh Babu, Hurix Systems Pvt. Ltd.*
Cover design: *Cara Hawthorne*
Interior design: *Pam Verros*
Typeface: *10.5/13 Palatino Roman*
Compositor: *Laserwords Private Limited*
Printer: *R. R. Donnelley*

Library of Congress Cataloging-in-Publication Data

Gamble, John (John E.)
    Essentials of strategic management : the quest for competitive advantage/John E. Gamble, Arthur A. Thompson, Jr., Margaret A. Peteraf.—3rd ed.
       p. cm.
    Includes index.
    ISBN 978-0-07-802928-8 (alk. paper)—ISBN 0-07-802928-7 (alk. paper)
    1. Strategic planning. 2. Business planning. 3. Competition. 4. Strategic planning—Case studies. I. Thompson, Arthur A., 1940- II. Title.
    HD30.28.G353 2013
    658.4'012—dc23
                                                          2011046965

www.mhhe.com

ABOUT THE AUTHORS

John E. Gamble is currently a Professor of Management in the Mitchell College of Business at the University of South Alabama. His teaching specialty at USA is strategic management and he also conducts a course in strategic management in Germany, which is sponsored by the University of Applied Sciences in Worms.

Dr. Gamble's research interests center on strategic issues in entrepreneurial, health care, and manufacturing settings. His work has been published in various scholarly journals and he is the author or co-author of more than 50 case studies published in an assortment of strategic management and strategic marketing texts. He has done consulting on industry and market analysis for clients in a diverse mix of industries.

Professor Gamble received his Ph.D. in management from The University of Alabama in 1995. Dr. Gamble also has a Bachelor of Science degree and a Master of Arts degree from The University of Alabama.

Arthur A. Thompson, Jr., earned his B.S. and Ph.D. degrees in economics from The University of Tennessee, spent three years on the economics faculty at Virginia Tech, and served on the faculty of The University of Alabama's College of Commerce and Business Administration for 25 years. In 1974 and again in 1982, Dr. Thompson spent semester-long sabbaticals as a visiting scholar at the Harvard Business School.

His areas of specialization are business strategy, competition and market analysis, and the economics of business enterprises. In addition to publishing over 30 articles in some 25 different professional and trade publications, he has authored or co-authored five textbooks and six computer-based simulation exercises that are used in colleges and universities worldwide.

Dr. Thompson spends much of his off-campus time giving presentations, putting on management development programs, working with companies, and helping operate a business simulation enterprise in which he is a major partner.

Dr. Thompson and his wife of 49 years have two daughters, two grandchildren, and a Yorkshire terrier.

Margaret A. Peteraf is the Leon E. Williams Professor of Management at the Tuck School of Business at Dartmouth College. She is an internationally recognized scholar of strategic management, with a long list of publications in top management journals. She has earned myriad honors and prizes for her contributions, including the 1999 Strategic Management Society Best Paper Award recognizing the deep influence of her work on the field of Strategic Management. Professor Peteraf is on the Board of Directors of the Strategic Management Society and has been elected as a Fellow of the Society. She served previously as a member of the Academy of Management's Board of Governors and as Chair of the Business Policy and Strategy Division of the Academy. She has also served in various editorial roles and is presently on nine editorial boards, including the *Strategic Management Journal,* the *Academy of Management Review,* and *Organization Science.* She has taught in Executive Education programs around the world and has won teaching awards at the MBA and Executive level.

Professor Peteraf earned her Ph.D., M.A., and M.Phil. at Yale University and held previous faculty appointments at Northwestern University's Kellogg Graduate School of Management and at the University of Minnesota's Carlson School of Management.

BRIEF CONTENTS

The standout features of this Third Edition of *Essentials of Strategic Management* are its concisely written and robust coverage of strategic management concepts and its compelling collection of cases. The text presents a conceptually strong treatment of strategic management principles and analytic approaches that features straight-to-the-point discussions, timely examples, and a writing style that captures the interest of students. This edition also includes the important contributions of our newest member of the author team, Margie Peteraf. The author team's overriding objectives for this revision were to strengthen linkages to the latest research findings and modify the coverage and exposition as needed to ensure squarely on-target content. As in any substantive revision, coverage was trimmed in some areas and expanded in others. New material has been added here and there. The presentations of some topics were recast, others fine-tuned, and still others left largely intact. Also, scores of new examples have been added, along with fresh Concepts & Connections illustrations, to make the content come alive and to provide students with a ringside view of strategy in action. The fundamental character of the Third Edition of *Essentials of Strategic Management* is very much in step with the best academic thinking and contemporary management practice. The chapter content continues to be solidly mainstream and balanced, mirroring *both* the penetrating insight of academic thought and the pragmatism of real-world strategic management.

Complementing the text presentation is a truly appealing lineup of 16 diverse, timely, and thoughtfully crafted cases. All of the cases are tightly linked to the content of the 10 chapters, thus pushing students to apply the concepts and analytical tools they have read about. Twelve of the 16 cases were written by the coauthors to illustrate specific tools of analysis or distinct strategic management theories. The four cases not written by the coauthors were chosen because of their exceptional linkage to strategic management concepts presented in the text. We are confident you will be impressed with how well each of the 16 cases in the collection will work in the classroom and the amount of student interest they will spark.

For some years now, growing numbers of strategy instructors at business schools worldwide have been transitioning from a purely text-cases course structure to a more robust and energizing text-cases-simulation course structure. Incorporating a competition-based strategy simulation has the strong appeal of providing class members with *an immediate and engaging opportunity to apply the concepts and analytical tools covered in the chapters in a head-to-head competition with companies run by other class members.* Two widely used and pedagogically effective online strategy simulations, *The Business Strategy Game* and *GLO-BUS*, are optional companions for this text. Both simulations, like the cases, are closely linked to the content of each chapter in the text. The Exercises for Simulation Participants, found at the end of each chapter, provide clear guidance to class members in applying the concepts and analytical tools covered in the chapters to the issues and decisions that they have to wrestle with in managing their simulation company.

Through our experiences as business school faculty members, we also fully understand the assessment demands on faculty teaching strategic management and business policy courses. In many institutions, capstone courses have emerged as the logical home for assessing student achievement of program learning objectives. The Third Edition includes a set of Assurance of Learning Exercises at the end of each chapter that link to the specific Learning Objectives appearing at the beginning of each chapter and highlighted throughout the text. *An important new instructional feature of this edition is the linkage of selected chapter-end Assurance of Learning Exercises and 10 cases to the publisher's web-based assignment and assessment platform called Connect.* Your students will be able to use the online *Connect* supplement to (1) complete two of the Assurance of Learning Exercises appearing at the end of each of the 10 chapters, (2) complete chapter-end quizzes, and (3) enter their answers to a select number of the suggested assignment questions for 10 of the 16 cases in this edition. With the exception of some case exercises, all of the *Connect* exercises are automatically graded, thereby enabling you to easily assess the learning that has occurred.

In addition, both of the companion strategy simulations have a built-in Learning Assurance Report that quantifies how well each member of your class performed on nine skills/learning measures *versus tens of thousands of other students worldwide* who completed the simulation in the past 12 months. We believe the chapter-end Assurance of Learning Exercises, the all-new online and automatically graded Connect exercises, and the Learning Assurance Report generated at the conclusion of *The Business Strategy Game* and *GLO-BUS* simulations provide you with easy-to-use, empirical measures of student learning in your course. All can be used in conjunction with other instructor-developed or school-developed scoring rubrics and assessment tools to comprehensively evaluate course or program learning outcomes and measure compliance with AACSB accreditation standards.

Taken together, the various components of the Third Edition package and the supporting set of Instructor Resources provide you with enormous course design flexibility and a powerful kit of teaching/learning tools. We've done our very best to ensure that the elements comprising this edition will work well for you in the classroom, help you economize on the time needed to be well prepared for each class, and cause students to conclude that your course is one of the very best they have ever taken—from the standpoint of both enjoyment and learning.

DIFFERENTIATION FROM OTHER TEXTS

Five noteworthy traits strongly differentiate this text and the accompanying instructional package from others in the field:

1. *Our coverage of resource-based theory of the firm in the Third Edition is unsurpassed by any other leading strategy text* . RBV principles and concepts are

prominently and comprehensively integrated into our coverage of crafting both single-business and multibusiness strategies. In Chapters 3 through 8 it is repeatedly emphasized that a company's strategy must be matched *not only* to its external market circumstances *but also* to its internal resources and competitive capabilities. Moreover, an RBV perspective is thoroughly integrated into the presentation on strategy execution to make it unequivocally clear how and why the tasks of assembling intellectual capital and building core competencies and competitive capabilities are absolutely critical to successful strategy execution and operating excellence.

2. *Our coverage of business ethics, core values, social responsibility, and environmental sustainability is unsurpassed by any other leading strategy text.* Chapter 9, "Strategy, Ethics, and Corporate Social Responsibility," is embellished with fresh content so that it can better fulfill the important functions of (1) alerting students to the role and importance of ethical and socially responsible decision making and (2) addressing the accreditation requirements of the AACSB International that business ethics be visibly and thoroughly embedded in the core curriculum. Moreover, discussions of the roles of values and ethics are integrated into portions of Chapters 2 and 10 to further reinforce why and how considerations relating to ethics, values, social responsibility, and sustainability should figure prominently into the managerial task of crafting and executing company strategies.

3. *The caliber of the case collection in the Third Edition is truly top-notch* from the standpoints of student appeal, teachability, and suitability for drilling students in the use of the concepts and analytical treatments in Chapters 1 through 10. The 16 cases included in this edition are the very latest, the best, and the most on-target that we could find. The ample information about the cases in the Instructor's Manual makes it effortless to select a set of cases each term that will capture the interest of students from start to finish.

4. Especially useful is the publisher's trailblazing *web-based assignment and assessment platform called Connect* to gauge class members' prowess in accurately completing (a) selected chapter-end exercises, (b) chapter-end quizzes, and (c) the creative author-developed exercises for 10 of the cases in this edition.

5. The two cutting-edge and widely used strategy simulations—*The Business Strategy Game* and *GLO-BUS*—that are optional companions to the Third Edition give you unmatched capability to employ a text-case-simulation model of course delivery.

ORGANIZATION, CONTENT, AND FEATURES OF THE THIRD EDITION TEXT CHAPTERS

The following rundown summarizes the noteworthy features and topical emphasis in this new edition:

• Chapter 1 focuses on the central questions *"Where are we now?" "Where do we want to go from here?"* and *"How are we going to get there?"* In putting these questions into the context of business strategy, we introduce students to the primary approaches to building competitive advantage and the key elements of business-level strategy. Following Henry Mintzberg's pioneering research, we also stress why a company's strategy is partly planned and partly reactive and why this strategy tends to evolve over time. The chapter also discusses why it is important for a company to have a *viable business model* that outlines the company's customer value proposition and its profit formula. This brief chapter is the perfect accompaniment to your opening day lecture on what the course is all about and why it matters.

- Chapter 2 delves more deeply into the managerial process of actually crafting and executing a strategy—it makes a great assignment for the second day of class and provides a smooth transition into the heart of the course. The focal point of the chapter is the five-stage managerial process of crafting and executing strategy: (1) forming a strategic vision of where the company is headed and why, (2) developing strategic as well as financial objectives with which to measure the company's progress, (3) crafting a strategy to achieve these targets and move the company toward its market destination, (4) implementing and executing the strategy, and (5) monitoring progress and making corrective adjustments as needed. Students are introduced to such core concepts as strategic visions, mission statements and core values, the balanced scorecard, and business-level versus corporate-level strategies. There's a robust discussion of why *all managers are on a company's strategy-making, strategy-executing team* and why a company's strategic plan is a collection of strategies devised by different managers at different levels in the organizational hierarchy. The chapter winds up with a section on how to exercise good corporate governance and examines the conditions that led to recent high-profile corporate governance failures.

- Chapter 3 sets forth the now-familiar analytical tools and concepts of industry and competitive analysis and demonstrates the importance of tailoring strategy to fit the circumstances of a company's industry and competitive environment. The standout feature of this chapter is a presentation of Michael Porter's "five forces model of competition" *that has long been the clearest, most straightforward discussion of any text in the field* .

- Chapter 4 presents the resource-based view of the firm and convincingly argues why a company's strategy must be built around its most competitively valuable resources and capabilities. We provide students with a simple taxonomy for identifying a company's resources and capabilities and frame our discussion of how a firm's resources and capabilities can provide a sustainable competitive advantage with the *VRIN model*. We introduce the notion of a company's *dynamic capabilities* and cast SWOT analysis as a simple, easy-to-use way to assess a company's overall situation in terms of its ability to seize market opportunities and ward off external threats. There is solid coverage of value chain analysis, benchmarking, and competitive strength assessments—standard tools for appraising a company's relative cost position and customer value proposition vis-à-vis rivals.

- Chapter 5 deals with the basic approaches used to compete successfully and gain a competitive advantage over market rivals. This discussion is framed around the five generic competitive strategies—low-cost leadership, differentiation, best-cost provider, focused differentiation, and focused low-cost.

- Chapter 6 deals with the *strategy options* available to complement a company's basic competitive strategy and improve its market position. The advantages and disadvantages of offensive strategies (including the benefits of a blue ocean strategy), defensive strategies, first-mover, fast-follower, and late-mover strategies are discussed. The chapter features sections on what use to make of vertical integration strategies; outsourcing strategies; strategic alliances and collaborative partnerships; and merger and acquisition strategies.

- Chapter 7 explores the full range of strategy options for competing in international markets: export strategies; licensing; franchising; establishing a subsidiary in a foreign market; and using strategic alliances and joint ventures to build competitive strength in foreign markets. There's also a discussion of how to best tailor a company's international strategy to cross-country differences in market conditions and buyer preferences, how to use international operations to improve overall competitiveness, and the unique characteristics of competing in emerging markets.

- Chapter 8 introduces the topic of corporate-level strategy—a topic of concern for multibusiness companies pursuing diversification. This chapter begins by explaining why successful diversification strategies must create shareholder value and lays out the three essential tests that a strategy must pass to achieve this goal (*the industry attractiveness, cost of entry, and better-off tests*). Corporate strategy topics covered in the chapter include methods of entering new businesses, related diversification, unrelated diversification, combined related and unrelated diversification approaches, and strategic options for improving the overall performance of an already diversified company. The chapter's analytical spotlight is trained on the techniques and procedures for assessing a diversified company's business portfolio— the relative attractiveness of the various businesses the company has diversified into, the company's competitive strength in each of its business lines, and the *strategic fit* and *resource fit* among a diversified company's different businesses. The chapter concludes with a brief survey of a company's four main postdiversification strategy alternatives: (1) sticking closely with the existing business lineup, (2) broadening the diversification base, (3) divesting some businesses and retrenching to a narrower diversification base, and (4) restructuring the makeup of the company's business lineup.

- Chapter 9 reflects the very latest in the literature on (1) a company's duty to operate according to ethical standards, (2) a company's obligation to demonstrate socially responsible behavior and corporate citizenship, and (3) why more companies are limiting strategic initiatives to those that meet the needs of consumers in a manner that protects natural resources and ecological support systems needed by future generations. The discussion includes approaches to ensuring consistent ethical standards for companies with international operations. The contents of this chapter will definitely give students some things to ponder and will help to make them more *ethically aware* and conscious of *why all companies should conduct their business in a socially responsible and sustainable manner*. Chapter 9 has been written as a "stand-alone" chapter that can be assigned in the early, middle, or late part of the course.

- Chapter 10 is anchored around a pragmatic, compelling conceptual framework: (1) building dynamic capabilities, core competencies, resources, and structure necessary for proficient strategy execution; (2) allocating ample resources to strategy-critical activities; (3) ensuring that policies and procedures facilitate rather than impede strategy execution; (4) pushing for continuous improvement in how value chain activities are performed; (5) installing information and operating systems that enable company personnel to better carry out essential activities; (6) tying rewards and incentives directly to the achievement of performance targets and good strategy execution; (7) shaping the work environment and corporate culture to fit the strategy; and (8) exerting the internal leadership needed to drive execution forward. The recurring theme throughout the chapter is that implementing and executing strategy entails figuring out the specific actions, behaviors, and conditions that are needed for a smooth strategy-supportive operation—the goal here is to ensure that students understand that the strategy-implementing/strategy-executing phase is a make-it-happen-right kind of managerial exercise that leads to operating excellence and good performance.

We have done our best to ensure that the 10 chapters convey the best thinking of academics and practitioners in the field of strategic management and hit the bull's-eye in topical coverage for senior- and MBA-level strategy courses. The ultimate test of the text, of course, is the positive pedagogical impact it has in the classroom. If this edition sets a more effective stage for your lectures and does a better job of helping you persuade students that the discipline of strategy merits their rapt attention, then it will have fulfilled its purpose.

THE CASE COLLECTION

The 16-case lineup in this edition is flush with interesting companies and valuable lessons for students in the art and science of crafting and executing strategy. There's a good blend of cases from a length perspective—about one-half are under 15 pages, yet offer plenty for students to chew on; about a fourth are medium-length cases; and the remaining one-fourth are detail-rich cases that call for more sweeping analysis.

At least 12 of the 16 cases involve companies, products, people, or activities that students will have heard of, know about from personal experience, or can easily identify with. The lineup includes at least four cases that will provide students with insight into the special demands of competing in industry environments where technological developments are an everyday event, product life cycles are short, and competitive maneuvering among rivals comes fast and furious. Twelve of the cases involve situations where the role of company resources and competitive capabilities in the strategy-making, strategy-executing scheme is emphasized. Scattered throughout the lineup are seven cases concerning non-U.S. companies, globally competitive industries, and/or cross-cultural situations; these cases, in conjunction with the globalized content of the text chapters, provide abundant material for linking the study of strategic management tightly to the ongoing globalization of the world economy. You'll also find four cases dealing with the strategic problems of family-owned or relatively small entrepreneurial businesses and 11 cases involving public companies and situations where students can do further research on the Internet.

Nine of the 16 cases have accompanying videotape segments—Competition among the North American Warehouse Clubs, Netflix, Redbox, Blue Nile, Google, Sara Lee, Southwest Airlines, Starbucks, and Cash Connection.

THE TWO STRATEGY SIMULATION SUPPLEMENTS: *THE BUSINESS STRATEGY GAME* AND *GLO-BUS*

The Business Strategy Game and *GLO-BUS: Developing Winning Competitive Strategies*—two competition-based strategy simulations that are delivered online and that feature automated processing and grading of performance—are being marketed by the publisher as companion supplements for use with the Third Edition (and other texts in the field). *The Business Strategy Game* is the world's most popular strategy simulation, having been used in courses involving over 600,000 students at 700+ university campuses in more than 40 countries. *GLO-BUS*, a somewhat simpler strategy simulation introduced in 2004, has been used at 400+ university campuses worldwide in courses involving over 120,000 students. Both simulations allow students to apply strategy-making and analysis concepts presented in the text and may be used as part of a comprehensive effort to assess undergraduate or graduate program learning objectives.

The Compelling Case for Incorporating Use of a Strategy Simulation

There are *three exceptionally important benefits* associated with using a competition-based simulation in strategy courses taken by seniors and MBA students:

- *A three-pronged text-case-simulation course model delivers significantly more teaching and learning power than the traditional text-case model.* Using *both* cases and a strategy simulation to drill students in thinking strategically and applying what they read in the text chapters is a stronger, more effective means of helping them connect theory with practice and develop better business judgment. What cases do that a simulation cannot is give class members broad exposure to a variety of companies and industry situations and insight into the kinds of strategy-related problems managers face. But what a competition-based strategy simulation does far better than case analysis is thrust class members squarely into *an active, hands-on managerial role* where they are totally responsible for assessing market conditions, determining how to respond to the actions of competitors, forging a long-term direction and strategy for their company, and making all kinds of operating decisions. Because they are held fully accountable for their decisions and their company's performance, *co-managers are strongly motivated* to dig deeply into company operations, probe for ways to be more cost-efficient and competitive, and ferret out strategic moves and decisions calculated to boost company performance. *Consequently, incorporating both case assignments and a strategy simulation to develop the skills of class members in thinking strategically and applying the concepts and tools of strategic analysis turns out to be more pedagogically powerful than relying solely on case assignments—there's stronger retention of the lessons learned and better achievement of course learning objectives.*

- *The competitive nature of a strategy simulation arouses positive energy and steps up the whole tempo of the course by a notch or two.* Nothing sparks class excitement quicker or better than the concerted efforts on the part of class members each decision round to achieve a high industry ranking and avoid the perilous consequences of being outcompeted by other class members. Students really enjoy taking on the role of a manager, running their own company, crafting strategies, making all kinds of operating decisions, trying to outcompete rival companies, and getting immediate feedback on the resulting company performance. Co-managers become *emotionally invested* in running their company and figuring out what strategic moves to make to boost their company's performance. All this stimulates learning and causes students to see the practical relevance of the subject matter and the benefits of taking your course.

- *Use of a fully automated online simulation reduces the time instructors spend on course preparation, course administration, and grading.* Since the simulation exercise involves a 20- to 30-hour workload for student-teams (roughly 2 hours per decision round times 10-12 rounds, plus optional assignments), simulation adopters often compensate by trimming the number of assigned cases from, say, 10 to 12 to perhaps 4 to 6. This significantly reduces the time instructors spend reading cases, studying teaching notes, and otherwise getting ready to lead class discussion of a case or grade oral team presentations. Course preparation time is further cut because you can use several class days to have students meet in the computer lab to work on upcoming decision rounds or a three-year strategic plan (in lieu of lecturing on a chapter or covering an additional assigned case). Not only does use of a simulation permit assigning fewer cases, but it also permits you to eliminate at least one assignment that entails considerable grading on your part. Grading one less written case or essay exam or other written assignment saves enormous time. With *BSG* and *GLO-BUS*, grading is effortless and takes only minutes; once you enter percentage weights for each assignment in your online grade book, a suggested overall grade is calculated for you. You'll be pleasantly surprised—and quite pleased—at how little time it takes to gear up for and to administer *The Business Strategy Game* or *GLO-BUS*.

In sum, incorporating use of a strategy simulation turns out to be *a win-win proposition for both students and instructors.* Moreover, a very convincing argument can be made that a competition-based strategy simulation is *the single most effective teaching/learning tool that instructors can employ to teach the discipline of business and competitive strategy, to make learning more enjoyable, and to promote better achievement of course learning objectives.*

Administration and Operating Features of the Two Simulations

The Internet delivery and user friendly designs of both *BSG* and *GLO-BUS* make them incredibly easy to administer, even for first-time users. And the menus and controls are so similar that you can readily switch between the two simulations or use one in your undergraduate class and the other in a graduate class. If you have not yet used either of the two simulations, you may find the following of particular interest:

- Setting up the simulation for your course is done online and takes about 10 to 15 minutes. Once setup is completed, no other administrative actions are required beyond that of moving participants to a different team (should the need arise) and monitoring the progress of the simulation (to whatever extent desired).

- Participant's Guides are delivered electronically to class members at the website—students can read it on their monitors or print out a copy, as they prefer.

- There are two- to four-minute Video Tutorials scattered throughout the software (including each decision screen and each page of each report) that provide on-demand guidance to class members who may be uncertain about how to proceed.

- Complementing the video tutorials are detailed and clearly written Help sections explaining "all there is to know" about (a) each decision entry and the relevant cause-effect relationships, (b) the information on each page of the Industry Reports, and (c) the numbers presented in the Company Reports. *The Video Tutorials and the Help screens allow company co-managers to figure things out for themselves, thereby curbing the need for students to ask the instructor "how things work."*

- Built-in chat capability on each screen enables company co-managers to collaborate online in the event that a face-to-face meeting to review results and make decision entries is not convenient (or feasible, as is usually the case for class members taking an online course). Company co-managers can also use their cell phones to talk things over while online looking at the screens.

- Both simulations are quite suitable for use in distance-learning or online courses (and are currently being used in such courses on numerous campuses).

- Participants and instructors are notified via e-mail when the results are ready (usually about 15 to 20 minutes after the decision round deadline specified by the instructor/game administrator).

- Following each decision round, participants are provided with a complete set of reports—a six-page Industry Report, a one-page Competitive Intelligence report for each geographic region that includes strategic group maps and bulleted lists of competitive strengths and weaknesses, and a set of Company Reports (income statement, balance sheet, cash flow statement, and assorted production, marketing, and cost statistics).

- Two "open-book" multiple choice tests of 20 questions are built into each simulation. The quizzes, which you can require or not as you see fit, are taken online and automatically graded, with scores reported instantaneously to participants and automatically recorded in the instructor's electronic grade book. Students are automatically provided with three sample questions for each test.

- Both simulations contain a three-year strategic plan option that you can assign. Scores on the plan are automatically recorded in the instructor's online grade book.

- At the end of the simulation, you can have students complete online peer evaluations (again, the scores are automatically recorded in your online grade book).

- Both simulations have a Company Presentation feature that enables each team of company co-managers to easily prepare PowerPoint slides for use in describing their strategy and summarizing their company's performance in a presentation either to the class, the instructor, or an "outside" board of directors.

- *A Learning Assurance Report provides you with hard data concerning how well your students performed vis-à-vis students playing the simulation worldwide over the past 12 months.* The report is based on nine measures of student proficiency, business know-how, and decision-making skill and can also be used in evaluating the extent to which your school's academic curriculum produces the desired degree of student learning insofar as accreditation standards are concerned.

For more details on either simulation, please consult Section 2 of the Instructor's Manual accompanying this text or register as an instructor at the simulation websites (www.bsg-online.com and www.glo-bus.com) to access even more comprehensive information. You should also consider signing up for one of the webinars that the simulation authors conduct several times each month (sometimes several times weekly) to demonstrate how the software works, walk you through the various features and menu options, and answer any questions. You have an open invitation to call the senior author of this text at (205) 722-9145 to arrange a personal demonstration or talk about how one of the simulations might work in one of your courses. We think you'll be quite impressed with the cutting-edge capabilities that have been programmed into *The Business Strategy Game* and *GLO-BUS*, the simplicity with which both simulations can be administered, and their exceptionally tight connection to the text chapters, core concepts, and standard analytical tools.

RESOURCES AND SUPPORT MATERIALS FOR THE THIRD EDITION FOR STUDENTS

Key Points Summaries

At the end of each chapter is a synopsis of the core concepts, analytical tools, and other key points discussed in the chapter. These chapter-end synopses, along with the core concept definitions and margin notes scattered throughout each chapter, help students focus on basic strategy principles, digest the messages of each chapter, and prepare for tests.

Two Sets of Chapter-End Exercises

Each chapter concludes with two sets of exercises. The Assurance of Learning Exercises can be used as the basis for class discussion, oral presentation assignments, short written reports, and substitutes for case assignments. The Exercises for Simulation Participants are designed expressly for use by adopters who have incorporated use of a simulation and wish to go a step further in tightly and explicitly connecting the chapter content to the simulation company their students are running. The questions in both sets of exercises (along with those Concepts & Connections illustrations that qualify as "mini cases") can be used to round out the rest of a 75-minute class period should your lecture on a chapter only last for 50 minutes.

A Value-Added Website

The student version of the Online Learning Center (OLC) or website www. mhhe.com/gamble3e contains a number of helpful aids:

- 20-question self-scoring chapter tests that students can take to measure their grasp of the material presented in each of the 10 chapters.
- A "Guide to Case Analysis" containing sections on what a case is, why cases are a standard part of courses in strategy, preparing a case for class discussion, doing a written case analysis, doing an oral presentation, and using financial ratio analysis to assess a company's financial condition. We suggest having students read this guide prior to the first class discussion of a case.
- PowerPoint slides for each chapter.

The Connect Management Web-based Assignment and Assessment Platform

Beginning with this edition, we have taken advantage of the publisher's innovative *Connect* assignment and assessment platform and created several features that simplify the task of assigning and grading three types of exercises for students:

- There are self-scoring chapter tests consisting of 20 multiple choice questions that students can take to measure their grasp of the material presented in each of the 10 chapters.

- Connect Management includes interactive versions of two Assurance of Learning exercises for each chapter that drill students in the use and application of the concepts and tools of strategic analysis.

- The *Connect Management* platform also includes author-developed interactive application exercises for 10 of the 16 cases in this edition that require students to work through answers to a select number of the assignment questions for the case; these exercises have multiple components and include calculating assorted financial ratios to assess a company's financial performance and balance sheet strength, identifying a company's strategy, doing five forces and driving forces analysis, doing a SWOT analysis, and recommending actions to improve company performance. The content of these case exercises is tailored to match the circumstances presented in each case, calling upon students to do whatever strategic thinking and strategic analysis is called for to arrive at pragmatic, analysis-based action recommendations for improving company performance.

All of the Connect exercises are automatically graded (with the exception of a few exercise components that entail student entry of essay answers), thereby simplifying the task of evaluating each class member's performance and monitoring the learning outcomes. The progress-tracking function built into the *Connect Management* system enables you to

- View scored work immediately and track individual or group performance with assignment and grade reports.

- Access an instant view of student or class performance relative to learning objectives.

- Collect data and generate reports required by many accreditation organizations, such as AACSB.

FOR INSTRUCTORS

Online Learning Center (OLC)

In addition to the student resources, the instructor section of www.mhhe.com/gamble3e includes an Instructor's Manual and other support materials. Your McGraw-Hill representative can arrange delivery of instructor support materials in a format-ready Standard Cartridge for Blackboard, WebCT, and other web-based educational platforms.

Instructor's Manual

The accompanying IM contains:

- A section on suggestions for organizing and structuring your course.
- Sample syllabi and course outlines.
- A set of lecture notes on each chapter.
- Answers to the chapter-end Assurance of Learning Exercises.
- A copy of the test bank.

- A comprehensive case teaching note for each of the 16 cases—these teaching notes are filled with suggestions for using the case effectively, have very thorough, analysis-based answers to the suggested assignment questions for the case, and contain an epilogue detailing any important developments since the case was written.

Test Bank and EZ Test Online

There is a test bank containing over 700 multiple choice questions and short-answer/essay questions. It has been tagged with AACSB and Bloom's Taxonomy criteria. All of the test bank questions are also accessible within a computerized test bank powered by McGraw-Hill's flexible electronic testing program EZ Test Online (www.eztestonline.com). Using EZ Test Online allows you to create paper and online tests or quizzes. With EZ Test Online, instructors can select questions from multiple McGraw-Hill test banks or author their own, and then either print the test for paper distribution or give it online.

PowerPoint Slides

To facilitate delivery preparation of your lectures and to serve as chapter outlines, you'll have access to approximately 350 colorful and professional-looking slides displaying core concepts, analytical procedures, key points, and all the figures in the text chapters.

Instructor's Resource CD

All of our instructor supplements are available on disk; the disk set includes the complete Instructor's Manual, Computerized Test Bank (EZ Test), accompanying PowerPoint slides, and the Digital Image Library with all of the figures from the text. It is a useful aid for compiling a syllabus and daily course schedule, preparing customized lectures, and developing tests on the text chapters.

The Business Strategy Game and *GLO-BUS* Online Simulations

Using one of the two companion simulations is a powerful and constructive way of emotionally connecting students to the subject matter of the course. We know of no more effective way to arouse the competitive energy of students and prepare them for the challenges of real-world business decision making than to have them match strategic wits with classmates in running a company in head-to-head competition for global market leadership.

ACKNOWLEDGMENTS

We heartily acknowledge the contributions of the case researchers whose case-writing efforts appear herein and the companies whose cooperation made the cases possible. To each one goes a very special thank-you. We cannot overstate the importance of timely, carefully researched cases in contributing to a substantive study of strategic management issues and practices. From a research standpoint, strategy-related cases are invaluable in exposing the generic kinds of strategic issues that companies face in forming hypotheses about strategic behavior and in drawing experienced-based generalizations about the practice of strategic management. From an instructional standpoint, strategy cases give students essential practice in diagnosing and evaluating the strategic situations of companies and organizations, in applying the concepts and tools of strategic analysis, in weighing strategic options and crafting strategies, and in tackling the challenges of successful strategy execution. Without a continuing stream of fresh, well-researched, and well-conceived cases, the discipline of strategic management would lose its close ties to the very institutions whose strategic actions and behavior it is aimed at explaining. There's no question, therefore, that first-class case research constitutes a valuable scholarly contribution to the theory and practice of strategic management.

A great number of colleagues and students at various universities, business acquaintances, and people at McGraw-Hill provided inspiration, encouragement, and counsel during the course of this project. Like all text authors in the strategy field, we are intellectually indebted to the many academics whose research and writing have blazed new trails and advanced the discipline of strategic management.

We also express our thanks to Todd M. Alessandri, Michael Anderson, Gerald D. Baumgardner, Edith C. Busija, Gerald E. Calvasina, Sam D. Cappel, Richard Churchman, John W. Collis, Connie Daniel, Christine DeLaTorre, Vickie Cox Edmondson, Diane D. Galbraith, Naomi A. Gardberg, Sanjay Goel, Les Jankovich, Jonatan Jelen, William Jiang, Bonnie Johnson, Roy Johnson, John J. Lawrence, Robert E. Ledman, Mark Lehrer, Fred Maidment, Frank Markham, Renata Mayrhofer, Simon Medcalfe, Elouise Mintz, Michael Monahan, Gerry Nkombo Muuka, Cori J. Myers, Jeryl L. Nelson, David Olson, John Perry, L. Jeff Seaton, Charles F. Seifert, Eugene S. Simko, Karen J. Smith, Susan Steiner, Troy V. Sullivan, Elisabeth J. Teal, Lori Tisher, Vincent Weaver, Jim Whitlock, and Beth Woodard. These reviewers provided valuable guidance in steering our efforts to improve earlier editions.

As always, we value your recommendations and thoughts about the book. Your comments regarding coverage and contents will be taken to heart, and we always are grateful for the time you take to call our attention to printing errors, deficiencies, and other shortcomings. Please email us at jgamble@usouthal.edu, or athompso@cba.ua.edu, or margaret.a.peteraf@tuck.dartmouth.edu.

John E. Gamble
Arthur A. Thompson
Margaret A. Peteraf

CONTENTS

CHAPTER 9   STRATEGY, ETHICS, AND CORPORATE SOCIAL RESPONSIBILITY   187

>> PART TWO: CASES IN CRAFTING AND EXECUTING STRATEGY

GUIDED TOUR

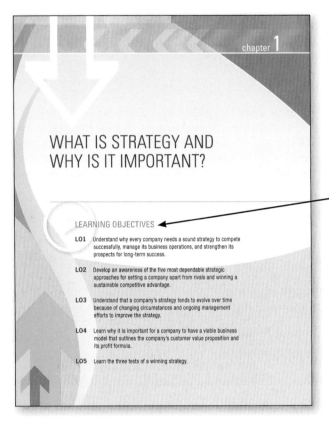

Learning Objectives are listed at the beginning of each chapter; corresponding numbered indicators in the margins show where learning objectives are covered in the text.

Concepts & Connections appear in boxes throughout each chapter to provide in-depth examples, connect the text presentation to real-world companies, and convincingly demonstrate "strategy in action." Some are appropriate for use as mini cases.

Margin Notes define core concepts and call attention to important ideas and principles.

We provide these with a dedication to the highest quality of customer satisfaction delivered with a sense of warmth, friendliness, fun, individual pride, and company spirit.

Note that Trader Joe's mission statement does a good job of conveying "who we are, what we do, and why we are here," but it provides no sense of "where we are headed."

An example of a well-stated mission statement with ample specifics about what the organization does is that of the Occupational Safety and Health Administration (OSHA): "to assure the safety and health of America's workers by setting and enforcing standards; providing training, outreach, and education; establishing partnerships; and encouraging continual improvement in workplace safety and health." Google's mission statement, while short, still captures the essence of what the company is about: "to organize the world's information and make it universally accessible and useful." An example of a not-so-revealing mission statement is that of Microsoft. "To help people and businesses throughout the world realize their full potential" says nothing about its products or business makeup and could apply to many companies in many different industries. A well-conceived mission statement should employ language specific enough to give the company its own identity. A mission statement that provides scant indication of "who we are and what we do" has no apparent value.

> **CORE CONCEPT**
> A well-conceived **mission statement** conveys a company's purpose in language specific enough to give the company its own identity.

Ideally, a company mission statement is sufficiently descriptive to:

- Identify the company's products or services.
- Specify the buyer needs it seeks to satisfy.
- Specify the customer groups or markets it is endeavoring to serve.
- Specify its approach to pleasing customers.
- Give the company its own identity.

Occasionally, companies state that their mission is to simply earn a profit. This is misguided. Profit is more correctly an *objective* and a *result* of what a company does. Moreover, earning a profit is the obvious intent of every

The managerial process of crafting and executing a company's strategy consists of five integrated stages:

1. *Developing a strategic vision* that charts the company's long-term direction, a *mission statement* that describes the company's business, and a set of *core values* to guide the pursuit of the strategic vision and mission.
2. *Setting objectives* for measuring the company's performance and tracking its progress in moving in the intended long-term direction.
3. *Crafting a strategy* for advancing the company along the path to management's envisioned future and achieving its performance objectives.
4. *Implementing and executing the chosen strategy* efficiently and effectively.

▶FIGURE 2.1 **The Strategy-Making, Strategy-Executing Process**

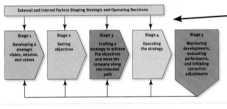

Figures scattered throughout the chapters provide conceptual and analytical frameworks.

▶▶▶ KEY POINTS

The strategic management process consists of five interrelated and integrated stages:

1. *Developing a strategic vision* of where the company needs to head and what its future product-customer-market-technology focus should be. This managerial step provides long-term direction, infuses the organization with a sense of purposeful action, and communicates to stakeholders management's aspirations for the company.

2. *Setting objectives* and using the targeted results as yardsticks for measuring the company's performance. Objectives need to spell out *how much of what kind of performance by when.* A *balanced scorecard* approach for measuring company performance entails setting both *financial objectives and strategic objectives.*

3. *Crafting a strategy to achieve the objectives* and move the company along the strategic course that management has charted. The total strategy that emerges is really a collection of strategic actions and business approaches initiated partly by senior company executives, partly by the heads of major business divisions, partly by functional-area managers, and partly by operating managers on the frontlines. A single business enterprise has three levels of strategy—business strategy for the company as a whole, functional-area strategies for each main area within the business, and operating strategies undertaken by lower-echelon managers. In diversified, multibusiness companies, the strategy-making task involves four distinct types or levels of strategy: corporate strategy for the company as a whole, business strategy (one for each business the company has diversified into), functional-area strategies within each business, and operating strategies. Typically, the strategy-making task is more top-down than bottom-up, with higher-level strategies serving as the guide for developing lower-level strategies.

4. *Implementing and executing the chosen strategy efficiently and effectively.* Managing the implementation and execution of strategy is an operations-oriented, make-things-happen activity aimed at shaping the performance of core business activities in a strategy supportive manner. Management's handling of the strategy implementation process can be considered successful if things go smoothly enough that the company meets or beats its strategic and financial performance targets and shows good progress in achieving management's strategic vision.

Key Points at the end of each chapter provide a handy summary of essential ideas and things to remember.

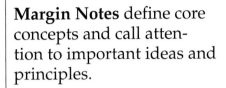

2. Based on the strategic group map in Concepts & Connections 3.1, who are Nordstrom's closest competitors? Between which two strategic groups is competition the strongest? Why do you think no retail chains are positioned in the upper-right corner of the map? Which company/strategic group faces the weakest competition from the members of other strategic groups?

LO1

connect
www.mcgrawhillconnect.com

3. The Snack Food Association publishes an annual state-of-the-industry report that can be found at www.sfa.org. Based on information in the latest report, does it appear that the economic characteristics of the industry will present industry participants with attractive opportunities for growth and profitability? Explain.

LO1, LO3

EXERCISES FOR SIMULATION PARTICIPANTS

1. Which of the five competitive forces is creating the strongest competitive pressures for your company?

LO1, LO2, LO3

2. What are the "weapons of competition" that rival companies in your industry can use to gain sales and market share? See Figure 3.7 to help you identify the various competitive factors.

3. What are the factors affecting the intensity of rivalry in the industry in which your company is competing? Use Figure 3.7 and the accompanying discussion to help you in pinpointing the specific factors most affecting competitive intensity. Would you characterize the rivalry and jockeying for better market position, increased sales, and market share among the companies in your industry as fierce, very strong, strong, moderate, or relatively weak? Why?

4. Are there any driving forces in the industry in which your company is competing? What impact will these driving forces have? Will they cause competition to be more or less intense? Will they act to boost or squeeze profit margins? List at least two actions your company should consider taking to combat any negative impacts of the driving forces.

5. Draw a strategic group map showing the market positions of the companies in your industry. Which companies do you believe are in the most attractive position on the map? Which companies are the most weakly positioned? Which companies do you believe are likely to try to move to a different position on the strategic group map?

6. What do you see as the key factors for being a successful competitor in your industry? List at least three.

7. Does your overall assessment of the industry suggest that industry rivals have sufficiently attractive opportunities for growth and profitability? Explain.

ENDNOTES

1. Michael E. Porter, *Competitive Strategy: Techniques for Analyzing Industries and Competitors* (New York: Free Press, 1980), chap. 1; Michael E. Porter, "The Five Competitive Forces That Shape Strategy," *Harvard Business Review* 86, no. 1 (January 2008).

2. J. S. Bain, *Barriers to New Competition* (Cambridge, MA: Harvard University Press, 1956); F. M. Scherer, *Industrial Market Structure and Economic Performance* (Chicago: Rand McNally & Co., 1971).

67

> **Exercises** at the end of each chapter, linked to learning objectives, provide a basis for class discussion, oral presentations, and written assignments. Two exercises in each chapter are linked to the Connect online assignment and assessment platform for the text.

Case 1

MYSTIC MONK COFFEE

David L. Turnipseed
University of South Alabama

As Father Daniel Mary, the prior of the Carmelite Order of monks in Clark, Wyoming, walked to chapel to preside over Mass, he noticed the sun glistening across the four-inch snowfall from the previous evening. Snow in June was not unheard of in Wyoming, but the late snowfall and the bright glow of the rising sun made him consider the opposing forces accompanying change and how he might best prepare his monastery to achieve his vision of creating a new Mount Carmel in the Rocky Mountains. His vision of transforming the small brotherhood of 13 monks living in a small home used as makeshift rectory into a 500-acre monastery that would include accommodations for 30 monks, a Gothic church, a convent for Carmelite nuns, a retreat center for lay visitors, and a hermitage presented a formidable challenge. However, as a former high school football player, boxer, bull rider, and man of great faith, Father Prior Daniel Mary was unaccustomed to shrinking from a challenge.

Father Prior had identified a nearby ranch for sale that met the requirements of his vision perfectly, but its current listing price of $8.9 million presented a financial obstacle to creating a place of prayer, worship, and solitude in the Rockies. The Carmelites had received a $250,000 donation that could be used toward the purchase, and the monastery had earned nearly $75,000 during the first year of its Mystic Monk coffee-roasting operations, but more money would be needed. The coffee roaster used to produce packaged coffee sold to Catholic consumers at the Mystic Monk Coffee website was reaching its capacity, but a larger roaster could be purchased for $35,000. Also, local Cody, Wyoming, business owners had begun a foundation for those wishing to donate to the monks' cause. Father Prior Daniel Mary did not have a great deal of experience in business matters but considered to what extent the monastery could rely on its Mystic Monk Coffee operations to fund the purchase of the ranch. If Mystic Monk Coffee was capable of making the vision a reality, what were the next steps in turning the coffee into land?

THE CARMELITE MONKS OF WYOMING

Carmelites are a religious order of the Catholic Church that was formed by men who traveled to the Holy Land as pilgrims and crusaders and had chosen to remain near Jerusalem to seek God. The men established their hermitage at Mount Carmel because of its beauty, seclusion, and biblical importance as the site where Elijah stood against King Ahab and the false prophets of Jezebel to prove Jehovah to be the one true God. The Carmelites led a life of solitude, silence, and prayer at Mount Carmel before eventually returning to Europe and becoming a recognized order of the Catholic Church. The size of the Carmelite Order varied widely

---

> **Sixteen cases** detail the strategic circumstances of actual companies and provide practice in applying the concepts and tools of strategic analysis.

FOR STUDENTS: AN ASSORTMENT OF SUPPORT MATERIALS

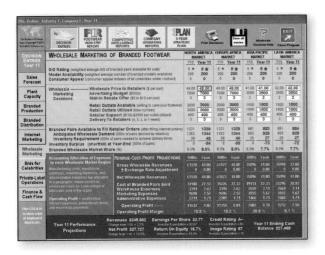

The Business Strategy Game or GLO-BUS **Simulation Exercises** Either one of these text supplements involves teams of students managing companies in a head-to-head contest for global market leadership. Company co-managers have to make decisions relating to product quality, production, workforce compensation and training, pricing and marketing, and financing of company operations. The challenge is to craft and execute a strategy that is powerful enough to deliver good financial performance despite the competitive efforts of rival companies. Each company competes in America, Latin America, Europe-Africa, and Asia-Pacific.

Less Managing. More Teaching. Greater Learning.

McGraw-Hill *Connect Management* is an online assignment and assessment solution that connects students with the tools and resources they'll need to achieve success.

McGraw-Hill *Connect Management* helps prepare students for their future by enabling faster learning, more efficient studying, and higher retention of knowledge.

McGraw-Hill *Connect Management* features

Connect Management offers a number of powerful tools and features to make managing assignments easier, so faculty can spend more time teaching. With Connect Management, students can engage with their coursework anytime and anywhere, making the learning process more accessible and efficient. *Connect Management* offers you the features described below.

Simple assignment management

With *Connect Management*, creating assignments is easier than ever, so you can spend more time teaching and less time managing. The assignment management function enables you to:

- Create and deliver assignments easily with selectable end-of-chapter questions and test bank items.
- Streamline lesson planning, student progress reporting, and assignment grading to make classroom management more efficient than ever.
- Go paperless with the e-book and online submission and grading of student assignments.

Smart grading

When it comes to studying, time is precious. *Connect Management* helps students learn more efficiently by providing feedback and practice material when they need it, where they need it. When it comes to teaching, your time also is precious. The grading function enables you to:

- Have assignments scored automatically, giving students immediate feedback on their work and side-by-side comparisons with correct answers.
- Access and review each response; manually change grades or leave comments for students to review.
- Reinforce classroom concepts with practice tests and instant quizzes.

Instructor library

The *Connect Management* Instructor Library is your repository for additional resources to improve student engagement in and out of class. You can select and use any asset that enhances your lecture. The *Connect Management* Instructor Library includes:

- e-book
- Instructors Manual
- PowerPoint files
- Videos and Instructional Notes

Student study center

The *Connect Management* Student Study Center is the place for students to access additional resources. The Student Study Center:

- Offers students quick access to lectures, practice materials, e-books, and more.
- Provides instant practice material and study questions, easily accessible on the go.
- Gives students access to the Personalized Learning Plan described below.

Student progress tracking

Connect Management keeps instructors informed about how each student, section, and class is performing, allowing for more productive use of lecture and office hours. The progress-tracking function enables you to:

- View scored work immediately and track individual or group performance with assignment and grade reports.
- Access an instant view of student or class performance relative to learning objectives.
- Collect data and generate reports required by many accreditation organizations, such as AACSB.

Lecture capture

Increase the attention paid to lecture discussion by decreasing the attention paid to note taking. For an additional charge Lecture Capture offers new ways for students to focus on the in-class discussion, knowing they can revisit important topics later. Lecture Capture enables you to:

- Record and distribute your lecture with a click of button.
- Record and index PowerPoint presentations and anything shown on your computer so it is easily searchable, frame by frame.
- Offer access to lectures anytime and anywhere by computer, iPod, or mobile device.
- Increase intent listening and class participation by easing students' concerns about note-taking. Lecture Capture will make it more likely you will see students' faces, not the tops of their heads.

McGraw-Hill *Connect Plus Management*

McGraw-Hill reinvents the textbook learning experience for the modern student with *Connect Plus Management*. A seamless integration of an e-book and *Connect Management, Connect Plus Management* provides all of the *Connect Management* features plus the following:

- An integrated e-book, allowing for anytime, anywhere access to the textbook.
- Dynamic links between the problems or questions you assign to your students and the location in the e-book where that problem or question is covered.
- A powerful search function to pinpoint and connect key concepts in a snap.

In short, *Connect Management* offers you and your students powerful tools and features that optimize your time and energies, enabling you to focus on course content, teaching, and student learning. *Connect Management* also offers a wealth of content resources for both instructors and students. This state-of-the-art, thoroughly tested system supports you in preparing students for the world that awaits.

For more information about Connect, go to **www.mcgrawhillconnect.com,** or contact your local McGraw-Hill sales representative.

TEGRITY CAMPUS: LECTURES 24/7

Tegrity Campus is a service that makes class time available 24/7 by automatically capturing every lecture in a searchable format for students to review when they study and complete assignments. With a simple one-click start-and-stop process, you capture all computer screens and corresponding audio. Students can replay any part of any class with easy-to-use browser-based viewing on a PC or Mac.

Educators know that the more students can see, hear, and experience class resources, the better they learn. In fact, studies prove it. With Tegrity Campus, students quickly recall key moments by using Tegrity Campus's unique search feature. This search helps students efficiently find what they need, when they need it, across an entire semester of class recordings. Help turn all your students' study time into learning moments immediately supported by your lecture.

To learn more about Tegrity watch a two-minute Flash demo at **http://tegritycampus.mhhe.com.**

ASSURANCE OF LEARNING READY

Many educational institutions today are focused on the notion of *assurance of learning,* an important element of some accreditation standards. *Essentials of Strategic Management* is designed specifically to support your assurance of learning initiatives with a simple, yet powerful solution.

Each test bank question for *Essentials of Strategic Management* maps to a specific chapter learning outcome/objective listed in the text. You can use our test bank software, EZ Test and EZ Test Online, or *Connect Management* to easily query for learning outcomes/objectives that directly relate to the learning objectives for your course. You can then use the reporting features of EZ Test to aggregate student results in similar fashion, making the collection and presentation of assurance of learning data simple and easy.

MCGRAW-HILL AND BLACKBOARD

McGraw-Hill Higher Education and Blackboard have teamed up. What does this mean for you?

1. **Your life, simplified.** Now you and your students can access McGraw-Hill's Connect™ and Create™ right from within your Blackboard course—all with one single sign-on. Say goodbye to the days of logging in to multiple applications.

2. **Deep integration of content and tools.** Not only do you get single sign-on with Connect™ and Create™, you also get deep integration of McGraw-Hill content and content engines right in Blackboard. Whether you're choosing a book for your course or building Connect™ assignments, all the tools you need are right where you want them—inside of Blackboard.

The **Best** of **Both Worlds**

Do More

3. **Seamless Gradebooks.** Are you tired of keeping multiple gradebooks and manually synchronizing grades into Blackboard? We thought so. When a student completes an integrated Connect™ assignment, the grade for that assignment automatically (and instantly) feeds your Blackboard grade center.

4. **A solution for everyone.** Whether your institution is already using Blackboard or you just want to try Blackboard on your own, we have a solution for you. McGraw-Hill and Blackboard can now offer you easy access to industry leading technology and content, whether your campus hosts it, or we do. Be sure to ask your local McGraw-Hill representative for details.

AACSB STATEMENT

The McGraw-Hill Companies is a proud corporate member of AACSB International. Understanding the importance and value of AACSB accreditation, *Essentials of Strategic Management,* Third Edition, recognizes the curricula guidelines detailed in the AACSB standards for business accreditation by connecting selected questions in the test bank to the six general knowledge and skill guidelines in the AACSB standards.

The statements contained in *Essentials of Strategic Management,* Third Edition, are provided only as a guide for the users of this textbook. The AACSB leaves content coverage and assessment within the purview of individual schools, the mission of the school, and the faculty. While *Essentials of Strategic Management*, Third Edition, and the teaching package make no claim of any specific AACSB qualification or evaluation, we have within *Essentials of Strategic Management*, Third Edition, labeled selected questions according to the six general knowledge and skills areas.

MCGRAW-HILL CUSTOMER CARE CONTACT INFORMATION

At McGraw-Hill, we understand that getting the most from new technology can be challenging. That's why our services don't stop after you purchase our products. You can e-mail our Product Specialists 24 hours a day to get product-training online. Or you can search our knowledge bank of Frequently Asked Questions on our support website. For Customer Support, call **800-331-5094**, e-mail **hmsupport@mcgraw-hill.com**, or visit **www.mhhe.com/support**. One of our Technical Support Analysts will be able to assist you in a timely fashion.

e-BOOK OPTIONS

e-books are an innovative way for students to save money and to "go green." McGraw-Hill's e-books are typically 40% off the bookstore price. Students have the choice between an online and a downloadable CourseSmart e-book.

Through CourseSmart, students have the flexibility to access an exact replica of their textbook from any computer that has Internet service without plug-ins or special software via the online version, or to create a library of books on their hard drive via the downloadable version. Access to the CourseSmart e-books lasts for one year.

Features CourseSmart e-books allow students to highlight, take notes, organize notes, and share the notes with other CourseSmart users. Students can also search for terms across all e-books in their purchased CourseSmart library. CourseSmart e-books can be printed (five pages at a time).

More info and purchase Please visit **www.coursesmart.com** for more information and to purchase access to our e-books. CourseSmart allows students to try one chapter of the e-book, free of charge, before purchase.

chapter 1

WHAT IS STRATEGY AND WHY IS IT IMPORTANT?

LEARNING OBJECTIVES

LO1 Understand why every company needs a sound strategy to compete successfully, manage its business operations, and strengthen its prospects for long-term success.

LO2 Develop an awareness of the five most dependable strategic approaches for setting a company apart from rivals and winning a sustainable competitive advantage.

LO3 Understand that a company's strategy tends to evolve over time because of changing circumstances and ongoing management efforts to improve the strategy.

LO4 Learn why it is important for a company to have a viable business model that outlines the company's customer value proposition and its profit formula.

LO5 Learn the three tests of a winning strategy.

Managers in all types of businesses face three central questions. *Where are we now? Where do we want to go from here? How are we going to get there?* Arriving at a thoughtful and probing answer to the question, *"Where are we now?"* prompts managers to examine the company's current financial performance and market standing, its competitively valuable resources and capabilities, its competitive weaknesses, and changing industry conditions that might affect the company. The question *"Where do we want to go from here?"* pushes managers to consider what emerging buyer needs to try to satisfy, which growth opportunities to emphasize, and how the company should change its business makeup. The question *"How are we going to get there?"* challenges managers to craft a series of competitive moves and business approaches—what henceforth will be referred to as the company's **strategy**—for moving the company in the intended direction, staking out a market position, attracting customers, and achieving targeted financial and market performance.

The role of this chapter is to define the concepts of strategy and competitive advantage, the relationship between a company's strategy and its business model, why strategies are partly proactive and partly reactive, and why company strategies evolve over time. Particular attention will be paid to what sets a winning strategy apart from a ho-hum or flawed strategy and why the caliber of a company's strategy determines whether it will enjoy a competitive advantage or be burdened by competitive disadvantage. By the end of this chapter, you will have a clear idea of why the tasks of crafting and executing strategy are core management functions and why excellent execution of an excellent strategy is the most reliable recipe for turning a company into a standout performer.

WHAT DO WE MEAN BY *STRATEGY?*

LO1

Understand why every company needs a sound strategy to compete successfully, manage its business operations, and strengthen its prospects for long-term success.

Developing clear answers to the question *"How are we going to get there?"* is the essence of managing strategically. Rather than rely on the status quo as a road map and dealing with new opportunities and threats as they emerge, managing strategically involves developing a full-blown game plan that spells out the particular competitive moves and operating approaches that will be employed to move the company in the intended direction, strengthen its market position and competitiveness, and meet or beat performance objectives. Thus, a company's strategy is all about *how*:

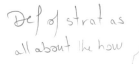

Def of strat as all about the how

- *How* to attract and please customers.
- *How* to compete against rivals.
- *How* to position the company in the marketplace and capitalize on attractive opportunities to grow the business.
- *How* best to respond to changing economic and market conditions.
- *How* to manage each functional piece of the business (e.g., R&D, supply chain activities, production, sales and marketing, distribution, finance, and human resources).
- *How* to achieve the company's performance targets.

Of course, a company's strategy includes planning for topics not included in the list above. The important thing to recognize is that every activity involved in

▶FIGURE 1.1 **Elements of a Company's Strategy**

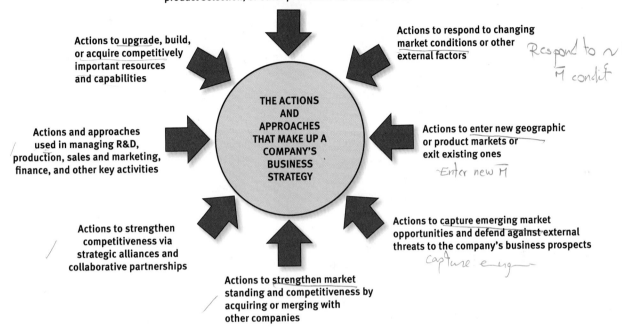

Actions to gain sales and market share by adjusting pricing, product features, product styling, quality, customer service, product selection, or other product or service attributes

Actions to upgrade, build, or acquire competitively important resources and capabilities

Actions to respond to changing market conditions or other external factors   Respond to ~ in M condit

Actions and approaches used in managing R&D, production, sales and marketing, finance, and other key activities

THE ACTIONS AND APPROACHES THAT MAKE UP A COMPANY'S BUSINESS STRATEGY

Actions to enter new geographic or product markets or exit existing ones   Enter new M

Actions to strengthen competitiveness via strategic alliances and collaborative partnerships

Actions to capture emerging market opportunities and defend against external threats to the company's business prospects   Capture emrg—

Actions to strengthen market standing and competitiveness by acquiring or merging with other companies

delivering a business's product or service should be guided by strategic thinking. There's really no single activity, process, department, or functional area that should be left to chance. Figure 1.1 presents a diagram showing actions and approaches that make up a company's strategy. Concepts & Connections 1.1 describes the various elements of McDonald's strategy in the quick-service restaurant industry. The capsule makes it clear how the strategy includes actions related to such wide-ranging issues as menu selection, supplier relationships, advertising expenditures, expansion into foreign markets, restaurant operating policies and practices, and responses to changing economic and market conditions.

> **CORE CONCEPT**
>
> A company's **strategy** consists of the competitive moves and business approaches management has developed to attract and please customers, compete successfully, capitalize on opportunities to grow the business, respond to changing market conditions, conduct operations, and achieve performance objectives.

STRATEGY AND THE QUEST FOR COMPETITIVE ADVANTAGE

The heart and soul of any strategy is the actions and moves in the marketplace that managers are taking to gain a competitive edge over rivals.[1] In Concepts & Connections 1.1, it's evident that McDonald's has gained a competitive advantage over rivals through its efforts to minimize costs, ensure a high level

▶**LO2**

Develop an awareness of the five most dependable strategic approaches for setting a company apart from rivals and winning a sustainable competitive advantage.

CONCEPTS & CONNECTIONS 1.1

MCDONALD'S STRATEGY IN THE QUICK-SERVICE RESTAURANT INDUSTRY

In 2011, McDonald's was setting new sales records despite a widespread economic slowdown and declining consumer confidence in the United States. More than 60 million customers visited one of McDonald's 32,000 restaurants in 117 countries each day, which allowed the company to record 2010 revenues and earnings of more than $24.1 billion and $4.9 billion, respectively. McDonald's performance in the marketplace allowed its share price to increase by more than 150 percent between 2005 and early 2011. The company's sales were holding up well amid the ongoing economic uncertainty in early 2011, with global sales as measured in constant currencies increasing by more than 4 percent in the first quarter. Its earnings per share had risen to nearly 30 percent. The company's success was a result of its well-conceived and executed Plan-to-Win strategy that focused on "being better, not just bigger." Key initiatives of the Plan-to-Win strategy included:

- **Improved restaurant operations.** McDonald's global restaurant operations improvement process involved employee training programs ranging from on-the-job training for new crew members to college-level management courses offered at the company's Hamburger University. The company also sent nearly 200 high-potential employees annually to its McDonald's Leadership Institute to build the leadership skills needed by its next generation of senior managers. McDonald's commitment to employee development earned the company a place on *Fortune's* list of Top 25 Global Companies for Leaders in 2010. The company also trained its store managers to closely monitor labor, food, and utility costs.

- **Affordable pricing.** In addition to tackling operating costs in each of its restaurants, McDonald's kept its prices low by scrutinizing administrative costs and other corporate expenses. McDonald's saw the poor economy in the United States as opportunity to renegotiate its advertising contracts with newspapers and television networks. The company also began to replace its company-owned vehicles with more fuel-efficient models when gasoline prices escalated dramatically in the United States. However, McDonald's did not choose to sacrifice product quality in order to offer lower prices. The company implemented extensive supplier monitoring programs to ensure that its suppliers did not change product specifications to lower costs. For example, the company's chicken breasts were routinely checked for weight when arriving from suppliers' production facilities. The company's broad approach to minimizing non-value-adding expenses allowed it to offer more items on its Dollar Menu in the United States, its Ein Mal Eins menu in Germany, and its 100 Yen menu in Japan.

- **Wide menu variety and beverage choices.** McDonald's has expanded its menu beyond the popular-selling Big Mac and Quarter Pounder to include such new healthy quick-service items as grilled chicken salads, chicken snack wraps, and premium chicken sandwiches in the United States, Lemon Shrimp Burgers in Germany, and Ebi shrimp wraps in Japan. The company has also added an extensive line of premium coffees that included espressos, cappuccinos, and lattes sold in its McCafe restaurant locations in the United States, Europe, and Asia/Pacific. McDonald's latte was judged "as good or better" than lattes sold by Starbucks or Dunkin' Donuts in a review by the *Chicago Tribune*.

- **Convenience and expansion of dining opportunities.** The addition of McCafes helped McDonald's increase same-store sales by extending traditional dining hours. Customers wanting a mid-morning coffee or an afternoon snack helped keep store traffic high after McDonald's had sold it last Egg McMuffin, McGriddle, or chicken biscuit and before the lunch crowd arrived to order Big Macs, Quarter Pounders, chicken sandwiches, or salads. The company also extended its drive-thru hours to 24 hours in more than 25,000 locations in cities around the world where consumers tended to eat at all hours of the day. At many high-traffic locations in the United States, double drive-thru lanes were added to get customers served more quickly.

- **Ongoing restaurant reinvestment and international expansion.** With more than 14,000 restaurants in the United States, the focus of McDonald's expansion of units was in rapidly growing emerging markets such as China. McDonald's planned to have nearly 2,000 restaurants in China by 2013. The company also intended to refurbish 90 percent of the interiors and 50 percent of the exteriors of its restaurants by the end of 2012 to make its restaurants a pleasant place for both customers to dine and employees to work.

Sources: Janet Adamy, "McDonald's Seeks Way to Keep Sizzling," *The Wall Street Journal Online,* March 10, 2009; various annual reports; various company press releases.

of food quality, add innovative new menu items, and keep its prices low. A creative, distinctive strategy such as that used by McDonald's is a company's most reliable ticket for developing a sustainable competitive advantage and earning above-average profits. A **sustainable competitive advantage** allows a company to attract sufficiently large numbers of buyers who have a lasting preference for its products or services over those offered by rivals, despite the efforts of competitors to offset that appeal and overcome the company's advantage. The bigger and more durable the competitive advantage, the better a company's prospects for winning in the marketplace and earning superior long-term profits relative to rivals.

[handwritten: Def]

> **CORE CONCEPT**
> A company achieves **sustainable competitive advantage** when an attractively large number of buyers develop a durable preference for its products or services over the offerings of competitors, despite the efforts of competitors to overcome or erode its advantage.

In most industries companies have considerable freedom in choosing among marketplace moves and business approaches designed to produce a competitive edge over rivals. For example, a company can compete against rivals by striving to keep costs low and selling its products at attractively low prices. Or it can aim at offering buyers more features or better performance or more personalized customer service. But whatever the strategic approach taken, it stands a better chance of succeeding when aimed at (1) appealing to buyers in ways that *set a company apart from its rivals* and (2) staking out a market position that is not crowded with strong competitors. Indeed, the essence of good strategy making is about choosing to compete differently—doing what rivals don't do or can't do—and thereby delivering value to buyers that proves to be superior and unique to what is offered by rivals.

[handwritten margin notes: Appeal to buyers in ways that set a co apart from rivals / Stake out π posit not crowded with compls]

> Mimicking the strategies of successful industry rivals—with either copycat product offerings or efforts to stake out the same market position—rarely works. A creative, distinctive strategy that sets a company apart from rivals and yields a competitive advantage is a company's most reliable ticket for earning above-average profits.

Five of the most frequently used and dependable strategic approaches to setting a company apart from rivals and winning a sustainable competitive advantage are:

[handwritten: 5 strat]

1. *A low-cost provider strategy*—achieving a cost-based advantage over rivals. Walmart and Southwest Airlines have earned strong market positions because of the low-cost advantages they have achieved over their rivals and their consequent ability to underprice competitors. Low-cost provider strategies can produce a durable competitive edge when rivals find it hard to match the low-cost leader's approach to driving costs out of the business.

[handwritten: • Low-cost provider strat: Walmart / • A broad diff strat: Apple / • A focused low cost strat: ? / • A focused diff strat: Rolex, / • A best cost provider strat: hybrid strat]

2. *A broad differentiation strategy*—seeking to differentiate the company's product or service from rivals' in ways that will appeal to a broad spectrum of buyers. Successful adopters of broad differentiation strategies include Johnson & Johnson in baby products (product reliability) and Apple (innovative products). Differentiation strategies can be powerful so long as a company is sufficiently innovative to thwart rivals' attempts to copy or closely imitate its product offering.

3. *A focused low-cost strategy*—concentrating on a narrow buyer segment (or market niche) and outcompeting rivals by having lower costs than rivals and thus being able to serve niche members at a lower price. Private-label manufacturers of food, health and beauty products, and nutritional supplements use their low-cost advantage to offer supermarket buyers lower prices than those demanded by producers of branded products.

4. *A focused differentiation strategy*—concentrating on a narrow buyer segment (or market niche) and outcompeting rivals by offering niche members customized attributes that meet their tastes and requirements better than rivals' products. Chanel and Rolex have sustained their advantage in the luxury goods industry through a focus on affluent consumers demanding luxury and prestige.

5. *A best-cost provider strategy*—giving customers more value for the money by satisfying buyers' expectations on key quality/features/performance/service attributes, while beating their price expectations. This approach is a hybrid strategy that blends elements of low-cost provider and differentiation strategies; the aim is to have the lowest (best) costs and prices among sellers offering products with comparable differentiating attributes. Target's best-cost advantage allows it to give discount store shoppers more value for the money by offering an attractive product lineup and an appealing shopping ambience at low prices.

WHY A COMPANY'S STRATEGY EVOLVES OVER TIME

The appeal of a strategy that yields a sustainable competitive advantage is that it offers the potential for an enduring edge over rivals. However, managers of every company must be willing and ready to modify the strategy in response to the unexpected moves of competitors, shifting buyer needs and preferences, emerging market opportunities, new ideas for improving the strategy, and mounting evidence that the strategy is not working well. Most of the time, a company's strategy evolves incrementally as management fine-tunes various pieces of the strategy and adjusts the strategy to respond to unfolding events. However, on occasion, major strategy shifts are called for, such as when the strategy is clearly failing or when industry conditions change in dramatic ways.

Regardless of whether a company's strategy changes gradually or swiftly, the important point is that the task of crafting strategy is not a onetime event, but is always a work in progress.[2] The evolving nature of a company's strategy means the typical company strategy is a blend of (1) *proactive* moves to improve the company's financial performance and secure a competitive edge and (2) *adaptive* reactions to unanticipated developments and fresh market conditions—see Figure 1.2.[3] The biggest portion of a company's current strategy flows from ongoing actions that have proven themselves in the marketplace and newly launched initiatives aimed at building a larger lead over rivals

> Changing circumstances and ongoing management efforts to improve the strategy cause a company's strategy to evolve over time—a condition that makes the task of crafting a strategy a work in progress, not a onetime event.

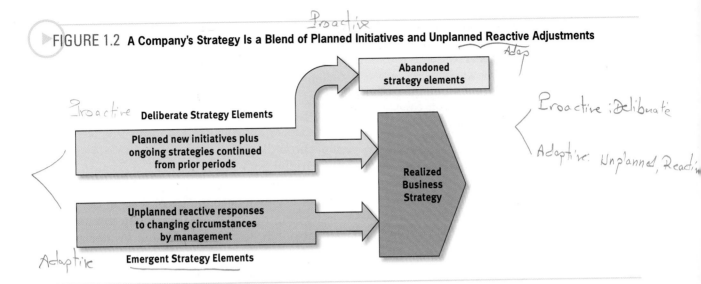

▶FIGURE 1.2 **A Company's Strategy Is a Blend of Planned Initiatives and Unplanned Reactive Adjustments**

[Handwritten annotations: Proactive; Adap; Proactive; Deliberate Strategy Elements; Proactive: Deliberate; Adaptive: Unplanned, Reacti...; Adaptive]

and further boosting financial performance. This part of management's action plan for running the company is its proactive, **deliberate strategy.**

At times, certain components of a company's deliberate strategy will fail in the marketplace and become **abandoned strategy elements.** Also, managers must always be willing to supplement or modify planned, deliberate strategy elements with as-needed reactions to unanticipated developments. Inevitably, there will be occasions when market and competitive conditions take unexpected turns that call for some kind of strategic reaction. Novel strategic moves on the part of rival firms, unexpected shifts in customer preferences, fast-changing technological developments, and new market opportunities call for unplanned, reactive adjustments that form the company's **emergent strategy.** As shown in Figure 1.2, a company's **realized strategy** tends to be a *combination* of deliberate planned elements and unplanned, emergent elements.

THE RELATIONSHIP BETWEEN A COMPANY'S STRATEGY AND ITS BUSINESS MODEL

Closely related to the concept of strategy is the concept of a company's **business model.** A company's business model is management's blueprint for delivering a valuable product or service to customers in a manner that will generate revenues sufficient to cover costs and yield an attractive profit.[4] The two elements of a company's business model are (1) its *customer value proposition* and (2) its *profit formula.* The customer value proposition lays out the company's approach to satisfying buyer wants and needs at a price customers will consider a good value. The greater the value provided and the lower the price, the more attractive the value proposition is to customers. The profit formula describes the company's approach to determining a cost structure that will allow for acceptable profits given the pricing tied to its customer value proposition. The lower the costs given the customer value proposition, the greater the ability of the business model to be a moneymaker. The nitty-gritty issue surrounding a company's business model is whether it can execute its customer value proposition profitably. Just because company managers have crafted a strategy

▶**LO4**

Learn why it is important for a company to have a viable business model that outlines the company's customer value proposition and its profit formula.

[Handwritten annotations: Business Model; Profit form...; Cmer value pro...]

for competing and running the business does not automatically mean that the strategy will lead to profitability—it may or it may not.[5]

Mobile phone providers, satellite radio companies, and broadband providers employ a subscription-based business model. The business model of network TV and radio broadcasters entails providing free programming to audiences but charging advertising fees based on audience size. Gillette's business model in razor blades involves achieving economies of scale in the production of its shaving products, selling razors at an attractively low price, and then making money on repeat purchases of razor blades. Printer manufacturers such as Hewlett-Packard, Lexmark, and Epson pursue much the same business model as Gillette—achieving economies of scale in production and selling printers at a low (virtually break-even) price and making large profit margins on the repeat purchases of printer supplies, especially ink cartridges. Concepts & Connections 1.2 discusses the contrasting business models of Netflix and Redbox in the movie rental industry.

THE THREE TESTS OF A WINNING STRATEGY

LO5

Learn the three tests of a winning strategy.

Three questions can be used to distinguish a winning strategy from a so-so or flawed strategy:

1. *How well does the strategy fit the company's situation?* To qualify as a winner, a strategy has to be well matched to the company's external and internal situations. The strategy must fit competitive conditions in the industry and other aspects of the enterprise's external environment. At the same time, it should be tailored to the company's collection of competitively important resources and capabilities. It's unwise to build a strategy upon the company's weaknesses or pursue a strategic approach that requires resources that are deficient in the company. Unless a strategy exhibits tight fit with both the external and internal aspects of a company's overall situation, it is unlikely to produce respectable first-rate business results.

   A winning strategy must fit the company's external and internal situation, build sustainable competitive advantage, and improve company performance.

2. *Is the strategy helping the company achieve a sustainable competitive advantage?* Strategies that fail to achieve a durable competitive advantage over rivals are unlikely to produce superior performance for more than a brief period of time. Winning strategies enable a company to achieve a competitive advantage over key rivals that is long lasting. The bigger and more durable the competitive edge that the strategy helps build, the more powerful it is.

3. *Is the strategy producing good company performance?* The mark of a winning strategy is strong company performance. Two kinds of performance improvements tell the most about the caliber of a company's strategy: (1) gains in profitability and financial strength and (2) advances in the company's competitive strength and market standing.

CONCEPTS & CONNECTIONS 1.2

NETFLIX AND REDBOX: TWO CONTRASTING BUSINESS MODELS

The strategies of rival companies are often predicated on strikingly different business models. Consider, for example, the business models of Redbox and Netflix in the movie rental industry.

The business models of movie rental companies Netflix and Redbox have both proven to be moneymakers even though they differ significantly. Netflix's subscription-based business model allows subscribers paying a flat monthly fee to receive movies delivered to their homes by mail and stream movies and TV episodes over the Internet. In 2011, Netflix had more than 23 million subscribers in the United States and Canada and had generated revenues of more than $2.1 billion in fiscal 2010. The company's net income in 2010 exceeded $160 million. The business model employed by

Redbox entailed the deployment of more 30,000 DVD rental vending machines in high-traffic retail locations such as discount stores, drugstores, convenience stores, and quick-service restaurants. Redbox charged customers $1 per day to rent movies from its vending machine kiosks and allowed customers to return the movie to the same location or any other Redbox kiosk location. Customers were able to browse each machine's inventory of available movies while using the machine's touch screen or could reserve a movie online or from a smartphone. Customers could also purchase movies from a Redbox kiosk for $7. Redbox's annual revenues and operating income in 2010 were approximately $1.2 billion and $193 million, respectively.

	NETFLIX	REDBOX
Customer Value Proposition	Convenient delivery of movies to customers' mailboxes or streamed to their PCs, Macs, or TVs. Eight subscription plans ranging from $4.99 to $47.99 allowed customers to choose from limited or unlimited video streaming and receive limited or unlimited DVDs. Netflix's subscription plan pricing allowed customers to have as few as one DVD out at a time and as many as 8 movies out at a given time.	Economical 24-hour movie rentals and purchases that could be picked up at conveniently located DVD kiosks. DVDs could be returned to any kiosk location. DVDs could also be reserved online or from a smartphone.
Profit Formula	*Revenue Generation:* Monthly subscription fees started at $4.99 for up to two hours of video streaming to a PC or Mac and two DVDs per month. The company's $8.99 plan allowed unlimited DVDs per month with one title out at a time, plus unlimited video streaming to a PC, Mac, or to a TV via a Netflix-ready device. The company's $47.99 plan allowed eight titles out at a time and unlimited streaming. Netflix had more than 23 million subscribers to the various plans in 2011.	*Revenue Generation:* Customers could rent DVDs for $1 per day and purchase DVDs for $7 from any of Redbox's 30,000 + DVD vending machine kiosks.
	Cost Structure: Fixed and variable costs associated with DVD acquisitions, licensing fees and revenue sharing agreements, development of movie selection software, website operation and maintenance, Internet streaming capabilities, distribution center operations, and administrative activities.	*Cost Structure:* Fixed and variable costs associated with the kiosk purchases and deployment, DVD acquisitions, licensing fees and revenue sharing agreements, website operation and maintenance, kiosk stocking, and administrative activities.
	Profit Margin: Netflix's profitability was dependent on attracting a sufficiently large number of subscribers to cover its costs and provide for attractive profits.	*Profit Margin:* Redbox's profitability was dependent on generating sufficient revenues from DVD rentals and sales to cover costs and provide for a healthy bottom line.

Source: Company documents, 10-Ks, and information posted on their websites.

Strategies that come up short on one or more of the above tests are plainly less appealing than strategies passing all three tests with flying colors. Managers should use the same questions when evaluating either proposed or existing strategies. New initiatives that don't seem to match the company's internal and external situation should be scrapped before they come to fruition, while existing strategies must be scrutinized on a regular basis to ensure they have good fit, offer a competitive advantage, and have contributed to above-average performance or performance improvements.

THE ROAD AHEAD

Throughout the chapters to come and the accompanying case collection, the spotlight is trained on the foremost question in running a business enterprise: *What must managers do, and do well, to make a company a winner in the marketplace?* The answer that emerges is that doing a good job of managing inherently requires good strategic thinking and good management of the strategy-making, strategy-executing process.

The mission of this book is to provide a solid overview of what every business student and aspiring manager needs to know about crafting and executing strategy. We will explore what good strategic thinking entails, describe the core concepts and tools of strategic analysis, and examine the ins and outs of crafting and executing strategy. The accompanying cases will help build your skills in both diagnosing how well the strategy-making, strategy-executing task is being performed and prescribing actions for how the strategy in question or its execution can be improved. The strategic management course that you are enrolled in may also include a strategy simulation exercise where you will run a company in head-to-head competition with companies run by your classmates. Your mastery of the strategic management concepts presented in the following chapters will put you in a strong position to craft a winning strategy for your company and figure out how to execute it in a cost-effective and profitable manner. As you progress through the chapters of the text and the activities assigned during the term, we hope to convince you that first-rate capabilities in crafting and executing strategy are essential to good management.

 KEY POINTS

1. A company's strategy is management's game plan to grow the business, attract and please customers, compete successfully, conduct operations, and achieve targeted levels of performance.

2. The central thrust of a company's strategy is undertaking moves to build and strengthen the company's long-term competitive position and financial performance. Ideally, this results in a competitive advantage over rivals that then becomes the company's ticket to above-average profitability.

3. A company's strategy typically evolves over time, arising from a blend of (1) proactive and deliberate actions on the part of company managers and (2) adaptive emergent responses to unanticipated developments and fresh market conditions.

4. Closely related to the concept of strategy is the concept of a company's business model. A company's business model is management's blueprint for delivering a valuable product or service to customers in a manner that will generate revenues sufficient to cover costs and yield an attractive profit. The two elements of a company's business model are its (1) customer value proposition and (2) its profit formula.

5. A winning strategy fits the circumstances of a company's external and internal situations, builds competitive advantage, and boosts company performance.

→ → ASSURANCE OF LEARNING EXERCISES

1. Based on what you know about the quick-service restaurant industry, does McDonald's strategy as described in Concepts & Connections 1.1 seem to be well matched to industry and competitive conditions? Does the strategy seem to be keyed to a cost-based advantage, differentiating features, serving the unique needs of a niche, or some combination of these? What is there about McDonald's strategy that can lead to sustainable competitive advantage?

    LO1, LO2

    www.mcgrawhillconnect.com

2. Elements of Walmart's strategy have evolved in meaningful ways since the company's founding in 1962. Prepare a one- to two-page report that discusses how its strategy has evolved after reviewing all of the links at Walmart's About Us page, which can be found at walmartstores.com/AboutUs/. Your report should also assess how well Walmart's strategy passes the three tests of a winning strategy.

    LO3, LO5

    www.mcgrawhillconnect.com

3. Go to www.nytco.com/investors and check whether *The New York Times'* recent financial reports indicate that its business model is working. Does the company's business model remain sound as more consumers go to the Internet to find general information and stay abreast of current events and news stories? Is its revenue stream from advertisements growing or declining? Are its subscription fees and circulation increasing or declining?

    LO4

→ → EXERCISES FOR SIMULATION PARTICIPANTS

This chapter discusses three questions that must be answered by managers of organizations of all sizes:

*   Where are we now?
*   Where do we want to go from here?
*   How are we going to get there?

After you have read the Participant's Guide or Player's Manual for the strategy simulation exercise that you will participate in this academic term, you and your co-managers should come up with brief one- or two-paragraph answers to these three questions *before* entering your first set of decisions. While your answers to the first of the three questions can be developed from your reading of the manual, the second and third questions will require a collaborative discussion among the members of your company's management team about how you intend to manage the company you have been assigned to run.

LO1, LO2

1. What is our company's current situation? A substantive answer to this question should cover the following issues:
   - Is your company in a good, average, or weak competitive position vis-à-vis rival companies?
   - Does your company appear to be in sound financial condition?
   - What problems does your company have that need to be addressed?

LO3, LO5

2. Where do we want to take the company during the time we are in charge? A complete answer to this question should say something about each of the following:
   - What goals or aspirations do you have for your company?
   - What do you want the company to be known for?
   - What market share would you like your company to have after the first five decision rounds?
   - By what amount or percentage would you like to increase total profits of the company by the end of the final decision round?
   - What kinds of performance outcomes will signal that you and your co-managers are managing the company in a successful manner?

LO3, LO4

3. How are we going to get there? Your answer should cover these issues:
   - Which of the basic strategic and competitive approaches discussed in this chapter do you think makes the most sense to pursue?
   - What kind of competitive advantage over rivals will you try to achieve?
   - How would you describe the company's business model?
   - What kind of actions will support these objectives?

ENDNOTES

1. Michael E. Porter, "What Is Strategy?" *Harvard Business Review* 74, no. 6 (November–December 1996).

2. Cynthia A. Montgomery, "Putting Leadership Back Into Strategy," *Harvard Business Review* 86, no. 1 (January 2008).

3. Henry Mintzberg and Joseph Lampel, "Reflecting on the Strategy Process, *Sloan Management Review* 40, no. 3 (Spring 1999); Henry Mintzberg and J. A. Waters, "Of Strategies, Deliberate and Emergent," *Strategic Management Journal* 6 (1985); Costas Markides, "Strategy as Balance: From 'Either-Or' to 'And,'" *Business Strategy Review* 12, no. 3 (September 2001); Henry Mintzberg, Bruce Ahlstrand, and Joseph Lampel, *Strategy Safari: A Guided Tour through the Wilds of Strategic Management* (New York: Free Press, 1998); and C. K. Prahalad and Gary Hamel, "The Core Competence of the Corporation," *Harvard Business Review* 70, no. 3 (May–June 1990).

4. Mark W. Johnson, Clayton M. Christensen, and Henning Kagermann, "Reinventing Your Business Model," *Harvard Business Review* 86, no. 12 (December 2008); and Joan Magretta, "Why Business Models Matter," *Harvard Business Review* 80, no. 5 (May 2002).

5. W. Chan Kim and Renée Mauborgne, "How Strategy Shapes Structure," *Harvard Business Review* 87, no. 9 (September 2009).

chapter 2

CHARTING A COMPANY'S DIRECTION: VISION AND MISSION, OBJECTIVES, AND STRATEGY

LEARNING OBJECTIVES

LO1 Grasp why it is critical for company managers to have a clear strategic vision of where a company needs to head and why.

LO2 Understand the importance of setting both strategic and financial objectives.

LO3 Understand why the strategic initiatives taken at various organizational levels must be tightly coordinated to achieve companywide performance targets.

LO4 Become aware of what a company must do to achieve operating excellence and to execute its strategy proficiently.

LO5 Become aware of the role and responsibility of a company's board of directors in overseeing the strategic management process.

Crafting and executing strategy are the heart and soul of managing a business enterprise. But exactly what is involved in developing a strategy and executing it proficiently? What are the various components of the strategy-making, strategy-executing process and to what extent are company personnel—aside from senior management—involved in the process? This chapter presents an overview of the ins and outs of crafting and executing company strategies. Special attention will be given to management's direction-setting responsibilities—charting a strategic course, setting performance targets, and choosing a strategy capable of producing the desired outcomes. We will also explain why strategy making is a task for a company's entire management team and discuss which kinds of strategic decisions tend to be made at which levels of management. The chapter concludes with a look at the roles and responsibilities of a company's board of directors and how good corporate governance protects shareholder interests and promotes good management.

WHAT DOES THE STRATEGY-MAKING, STRATEGY-EXECUTING PROCESS ENTAIL?

The managerial process of crafting and executing a company's strategy consists of five integrated stages:

1. *Developing a strategic vision* that charts the company's long-term direction, a *mission statement* that describes the company's business, and a set of *core values* to guide the pursuit of the strategic vision and mission.

2. *Setting objectives* for measuring the company's performance and tracking its progress in moving in the intended long-term direction.

3. *Crafting a strategy* for advancing the company along the path to management's envisioned future and achieving its performance objectives.

4. *Implementing and executing the chosen strategy* efficiently and effectively.

5. Monitoring dev, evaluating performance & initiating corrective adjust—

▶FIGURE 2.1 **The Strategy-Making, Strategy-Executing Process**

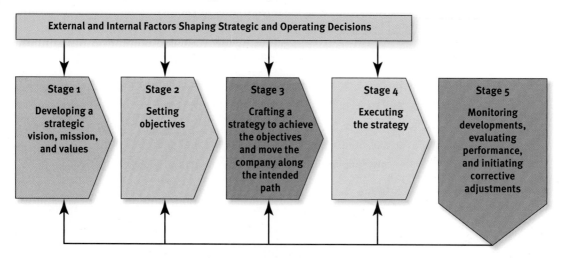

5. *Monitoring developments, evaluating performance, and initiating corrective adjustments* that are needed in the company's long-term direction, objectives, strategy, or approach to strategy execution.

Figure 2.1 displays this five-stage process. The model illustrates the need for management to evaluate a number of external and internal factors in deciding upon a strategic direction, appropriate objectives, and approaches to crafting and executing strategy (see Table 2.1). Management's decisions that are made in the strategic management process must be shaped by the prevailing economic conditions and competitive environment and the company's own internal resources and competitive capabilities. These strategy-shaping conditions will be the focus of Chapters 3 and 4.

The model shown in Figure 2.1 also illustrates the need for management to evaluate the company's performance on an ongoing basis. Any indication that the company is failing to achieve its objectives calls for corrective adjustments in one of the first four stages of the process. The company's implementation efforts might have fallen short and new tactics must be devised to fully exploit the potential of the company's strategy. If management determines that the company's execution efforts are sufficient, it should challenge the assumptions underlying the company's business strategy and alter the strategy to better fit competitive conditions and the company's internal capabilities. If the company's strategic approach to competition is rated as sound, then perhaps management set overly ambitious targets for the company's performance.

▶ TABLE 2.1

Factors Shaping Decisions in the Strategy-Making, Strategy-Executing Process

External Considerations

- Does sticking with the company's present strategic course present attractive opportunities for growth and profitability?
- What kind of competitive forces are industry members facing and are they acting to enhance or weaken the company's prospects for growth and profitability?
- What factors are driving industry change and what impact on the company's prospects will they have?
- How are industry rivals positioned and what strategic moves are they likely to make next?
- What are the key factors of future competitive success and does the industry offer good prospects for attractive profits for companies possessing those capabilities?

Internal Considerations

- Does the company have an appealing customer value proposition?
- What are the company's competitively important resources and capabilities and are they potent enough to produce a sustainable competitive advantage?
- Does the company have sufficient business and competitive strength to seize market opportunities and nullify external threats?
- Are the company's prices and costs competitive with those of key rivals?
- Is the company competitively stronger or weaker than key rivals?

The evaluation stage of the strategic management process shown in Figure 2.1 also allows for a change in the company's vision, but this should be necessary only when it becomes evident to management that the industry has changed in a significant way that renders its vision obsolete. Such occasions can be referred to as **strategic inflection points.** When a company reaches a strategic inflection point, management has tough decisions to make about the company's direction because abandoning an established course carries considerable risk. However, responding to unfolding changes in the marketplace in a timely fashion lessens a company's chances of becoming trapped in a stagnant or declining business or letting attractive new growth opportunities slip away.

> A company's **strategic plan** lays out its future direction, performance targets, and strategy.

The first three stages of the strategic management process make up a strategic plan. A **strategic plan** maps out where a company is headed, establishes strategic and financial targets, and outlines the competitive moves and approaches to be used in achieving the desired business results.[1]

STAGE 1: DEVELOPING A STRATEGIC VISION, A MISSION, AND CORE VALUES

> **LO1**
>
> Grasp why it is critical for company managers to have a clear strategic vision of where a company needs to head and why.

At the outset of the strategy-making process, a company's senior managers must wrestle with the issue of what directional path the company should take and whether its market positioning and future performance prospects could be improved by changing the company's product offerings and/or the markets in which it participates and/or the customers it caters to and/or the technologies it employs. Top management's views about the company's direction and future product-customer-market-technology focus constitute a **strategic vision** for the company. A clearly articulated strategic vision communicates management's aspirations to stakeholders about "where we are going" and helps steer the energies of company personnel in a common direction. For instance, Henry Ford's vision of a car in every garage had power because it captured the imagination of others, aided internal efforts to mobilize the Ford Motor Company's resources, and served as a reference point for gauging the merits of the company's strategic actions.

> **CORE CONCEPT**
>
> A **strategic vision** describes "where we are going"—the course and direction management has charted and the company's future product-customer-market-technology focus.

Well-conceived visions are *distinctive* and *specific* to a particular organization; they avoid generic, feel-good statements like "We will become a global leader and the first choice of customers in every market we choose to serve"—which could apply to any of hundreds of organizations.[2] And they are not the product of a committee charged with coming up with an innocuous but well-meaning one-sentence vision that wins consensus approval from various stakeholders. Nicely worded vision statements with no specifics about the company's product-market-customer-technology focus fall well short of what it takes for a vision to measure up.

For a strategic vision to function as a valuable managerial tool, it must provide understanding of what management wants its business to look like and provide managers with a reference point in making strategic decisions. It must say something definitive about how the company's leaders intend to position the company beyond where it is today. Table 2.2 lists some characteristics of effective vision statements.

A surprising number of the vision statements found on company websites and in annual reports are vague and unrevealing, saying very little about the company's future product-market-customer-technology focus. Some could apply to most any company in any industry. Many read like a public relations statement—lofty words that someone came up with because it is fashionable for companies to have an official vision statement.[3] Table 2.3 provides a list of

▶ TABLE 2.2

Characteristics of Effectively Worded Vision Statements

Graphic—Paints a picture of the kind of company that management is trying to create and the market position(s) the company is striving to stake out.

Directional—Is forward looking; describes the strategic course that management has charted and the kinds of product-market-customer-technology changes that will help the company prepare for the future.

Focused—Is specific enough to provide managers with guidance in making decisions and allocating resources.

Flexible—Is not so focused that it makes it difficult for management to adjust to changing circumstances in markets, customer preferences, or technology.

Feasible—Is within the realm of what the company can reasonably expect to achieve.

Desirable—Indicates why the directional path makes good business sense.

Easy to communicate—Is explainable in 5 to 10 minutes and, ideally, can be reduced to a simple, memorable "slogan" (like Henry Ford's famous vision of "a car in every garage").

Source: Based partly on John P. Kotter, *Leading Change* (Boston: Harvard Business School Press, 1996), p. 72.

▶ TABLE 2.3

Common Shortcomings in Company Vision Statements

Vague or incomplete—Short on specifics about where the company is headed or what the company is doing to prepare for the future.

Not forward looking—Doesn't indicate whether or how management intends to alter the company's current product-market-customer-technology focus.

Too broad—So all-inclusive that the company could head in most any direction, pursue most any opportunity, or enter most any business.

Bland or uninspiring—Lacks the power to motivate company personnel or inspire shareholder confidence about the company's direction.

Not distinctive—Provides no unique company identity; could apply to companies in any of several industries (including rivals operating in the same market arena).

Too reliant on superlatives—Doesn't say anything specific about the company's strategic course beyond the pursuit of such distinctions as being a recognized leader, a global or worldwide leader, or the first choice of customers.

Sources: Based on information in Hugh Davidson, *The Committed Enterprise* (Oxford: Butterworth Heinemann, 2002), chap. 2; and Michel Robert, *Strategy Pure and Simple II* (New York: McGraw-Hill, 1998), chaps. 2, 3, and 6.

CONCEPTS & CONNECTIONS 2.1

EXAMPLES OF STRATEGIC VISIONS—HOW WELL DO THEY MEASURE UP?

VISION STATEMENT	EFFECTIVE ELEMENTS	SHORTCOMINGS
Coca-Cola Our vision serves as the framework for our roadmap and guides every aspect of our business by describing what we need to accomplish in order to continue achieving sustainable, quality growth. • People: Be a great place to work where people are inspired to be the best they can be. • Portfolio: Bring to the world a portfolio of quality beverage brands that anticipate and satisfy people's desires and needs. • Partners: Nurture a winning network of customers and suppliers, together we create mutual, enduring value. • Planet: Be a responsible citizen that makes a difference by helping build and support sustainable communities. • Profit: Maximize long-term return to shareowners while being mindful of our overall responsibilities. • Productivity: Be a highly effective, lean and fast-moving organization.	• Focused • Flexible • Feasible • Desirable	• Long • Not forward-looking
UBS We are determined to be the best global financial services company. We focus on wealth and asset management, and on investment banking and securities businesses. We continually earn recognition and trust from clients, shareholders, and staff through our ability to anticipate, learn and shape our future. We share a common ambition to succeed by delivering quality in what we do. Our purpose is to help our clients make financial decisions with confidence. We use our resources to develop effective solutions and services for our clients. We foster a distinctive, meritocratic culture of ambition, performance and learning as this attracts, retains and develops the best talent for our company. By growing both our client and our talent franchises, we add sustainable value for our shareholders.	• Focused • Feasible • Desirable	• Not forward-looking • Bland or uninspiring
Walmart Saving People Money So They Can Live Better	• Focused • Easy to communicate • Feasible • Flexible • Desirable	• Not forward-looking

Sources: Company documents and websites.

the most common shortcomings in company vision statements. Like any tool, vision statements can be used properly or improperly, either clearly conveying a company's strategic course or not. Concepts & Connections 2.1 provides a critique of the strategic visions of several prominent companies.

The Importance of Communicating the Strategic Vision

A strategic vision has little value to the organization unless it's effectively communicated down the line to lower-level managers and employees. It would be difficult for a vision statement to provide direction to decision makers and energize employees toward achieving long-term strategic intent unless they know of the vision and observe management's commitment to that vision. Communicating the vision to organization members nearly always means putting "where we are going and why" in writing, distributing the statement organizationwide, and having executives personally explain the vision and its rationale to as many people as feasible. Ideally, executives should present their vision for the company in a manner that reaches out and grabs people's attention. An engaging and convincing strategic vision has enormous motivational value—for the same reason that a stonemason is inspired by building a great cathedral for the ages. Therefore, an executive's ability to paint a convincing and inspiring picture of a company's journey to a future destination is an important element of effective strategic leadership.[4]

Expressing the Essence of the Vision in a Slogan   The task of effectively conveying the vision to company personnel is assisted when management can capture the vision of where to head in a catchy or easily remembered slogan. A number of organizations have summed up their vision in a brief phrase. Nike's vision slogan is "To bring innovation and inspiration to every athlete in the world." The Mayo Clinic's vision is to provide "The best care to every patient every day," while Greenpeace's envisioned future is "To halt environmental abuse and promote environmental solutions." Creating a short slogan to illuminate an organization's direction and then using it repeatedly as a reminder of "where we are headed and why" helps rally organization members to hurdle whatever obstacles lie in the company's path and maintain their focus.

> An effectively communicated vision is a valuable management tool for enlisting the commitment of company personnel to engage in actions that move the company in the intended direction.

Why a Sound, Well-Communicated Strategic Vision Matters   A well-thought-out, forcefully communicated strategic vision pays off in several respects: (1) it crystallizes senior executives' own views about the firm's long-term direction; (2) it reduces the risk of rudderless decision making by management at all levels; (3) it is a tool for winning the support of employees to help make the vision a reality; (4) it provides a beacon for lower-level managers in forming departmental missions; and (5) it helps an organization prepare for the future.

Developing a Company Mission Statement

The defining characteristic of a well-conceived **strategic vision** is what it says about the company's *future strategic course*—*"where we are headed and what our future product-customer-market-technology focus will be."* The **mission statements** of most companies say much more about the enterprise's *present* business scope and purpose—"who we are, what we do, and why we are here." Very few mission statements are forward looking in content or emphasis. Consider, for example, the mission statement of Trader Joe's (a specialty grocery chain):

> The distinction between a **strategic vision** and a mission statement is fairly clear-cut: A strategic vision portrays a company's *future business scope* ("where we are going") whereas a company's **mission** typically describes its *present business and purpose* ("who we are, what we do, and why we are here").

> The mission of Trader Joe's is to give our customers the best food and beverage values that they can find anywhere and to provide them with the information required for informed buying decisions. We provide these with a dedication to the highest quality of customer satisfaction delivered with a sense of warmth, friendliness, fun, individual pride, and company spirit.

Note that Trader Joe's mission statement does a good job of conveying "who we are, what we do, and why we are here," but it provides no sense of "where we are headed."

An example of a well-stated mission statement with ample specifics about what the organization does is that of the Occupational Safety and Health Administration (OSHA): "to assure the safety and health of America's workers by setting and enforcing standards; providing training, outreach, and education; establishing partnerships; and encouraging continual improvement in workplace safety and health." Google's mission statement, while short, still captures the essence of what the company is about: "to organize the world's information and make it universally accessible and useful." An example of a not-so-revealing mission statement is that of Microsoft. "To help people and businesses throughout the world realize their full potential" says nothing about its products or business makeup and could apply to many companies in many different industries. A well-conceived mission statement should employ language specific enough to give the company its own identity. A mission statement that provides scant indication of "who we are and what we do" has no apparent value.

> **CORE CONCEPT**
> A well-conceived **mission statement** conveys a company's purpose in language specific enough to give the company its own identity.

Ideally, a company mission statement is sufficiently descriptive to:

Mission
Statement

- Identify the company's products or services.
- Specify the buyer needs it seeks to satisfy.
- Specify the customer groups or markets it is endeavoring to serve.
- Specify its approach to pleasing customers.
- Give the company its own identity.

Occasionally, companies state that their mission is to simply earn a profit. This is misguided. Profit is more correctly an *objective* and a *result* of what a company does. Moreover, earning a profit is the obvious intent of every commercial enterprise. Such companies as BMW, Netflix, Shell Oil, Procter & Gamble, Google, and McDonald's are each striving to earn a profit for shareholders, but the fundamentals of their businesses are substantially different when it comes to "who we are and what we do."

Linking the Strategic Vision and Mission with Company Values

Many companies have developed a statement of **values** (sometimes called *core values*) to guide the actions and behavior of company personnel in conducting the company's business and pursuing its strategic vision and mission. These values are the designated beliefs and desired ways of doing things at the company and frequently relate to such things as fair treatment, honor and integrity, ethical behavior, innovativeness, teamwork, a passion for excellence, social responsibility, and community citizenship.

> **CORE CONCEPT**
>
> A company's **values** are the beliefs, traits, and behavioral norms that company personnel are expected to display in conducting the company's business and pursuing its strategic vision and mission.

Most companies normally have four to eight core values. At Kodak, the core values are respect for the dignity of the individual, uncompromising integrity, unquestioned trust, constant credibility, continual improvement and personal renewal, and open celebration of individual and team achievements. Home Depot embraces eight values—entrepreneurial spirit, excellent customer service, giving back to the community, respect for all people, doing the right thing, taking care of people, building strong relationships, and creating shareholder value—in its quest to be the world's leading home improvement retailer.[5]

Do companies practice what they preach when it comes to their professed values? Sometimes no, sometimes yes—it runs the gamut. At one extreme are companies with window-dressing values; the professed values are given lip service by top executives but have little discernible impact on either how company personnel behave or how the company operates. At the other extreme are companies whose executives are committed to grounding company operations on sound values and principled ways of doing business. Executives at these companies deliberately seek to ingrain the designated core values into the corporate culture—the core values thus become an integral part of the company's DNA and what makes it tick. At such values-driven companies, executives "walk the talk" and company personnel are held accountable for displaying the stated values. Concepts & Connections 2.2 describes how core values drive the company's mission at Zappos, a widely known and quite successful online shoe and apparel retailer.

STAGE 2: SETTING OBJECTIVES

The managerial purpose of setting **objectives** is to convert the strategic vision into specific performance targets. Objectives reflect management's aspirations for company performance in light of the industry's prevailing economic and competitive conditions and the company's internal capabilities. Well-stated objectives are *quantifiable*, or *measurable*, and contain a *deadline for achievement*. Concrete, measurable objectives are managerially valuable

▶ **LO2**

Understand the importance of setting both strategic and financial objectives.

CONCEPTS & CONNECTIONS 2.2

ZAPPOS MISSION AND CORE VALUES

We've been asked by a lot of people how we've grown so quickly, and the answer is actually really simple. . . . We've aligned the entire organization around one mission: *to provide the best customer service possible.* Internally, we call this our **WOW** philosophy.

These are the 10 core values that we live by:

Deliver Wow through Service. At Zappos, anything worth doing is worth doing with WOW. WOW is such a short, simple word, but it really encompasses a lot of things. To WOW, you must differentiate yourself, which means doing something a little unconventional and innovative. You must do something that's above and beyond what's expected. And whatever you do must have an emotional impact on the receiver. We are not an average company, our service is not average, and we don't want our people to be average. We expect every employee to deliver WOW.

Embrace and Drive Change. Part of being in a growing company is that change is constant. For some people, especially those who come from bigger companies, the constant change can be somewhat unsettling at first. If you are not prepared to deal with constant change, then you probably are not a good fit for the company.

Create Fun and a Little Weirdness. At Zappos, We're Always Creating Fun and A Little Weirdness! One of the things that makes Zappos different from a lot of other companies is that we value being fun and being a little weird. We don't want to become one of those big companies that feels corporate and boring. We want to be able to laugh at ourselves. We look for both fun and humor in our daily work.

Be Adventurous, Creative, and Open Minded. At Zappos, we think it's important for people and the company as a whole to be bold and daring (but not reckless). We do not want people to be afraid to take risks and make mistakes. We believe if people aren't making mistakes, then that means they're not taking enough risks. Over time, we want everyone to develop his/her gut about business decisions. We want people to develop and improve their decision-making skills. We encourage people to make mistakes as long as they learn from them.

Pursue Growth and Learning. At Zappos, we think it's important for employees to grow both personally and professionally. It's important to constantly challenge and stretch yourself and not be stuck in a job where you don't feel like you are growing or learning.

Build Open and Honest Relationships with Communication. Fundamentally, we believe that openness and honesty make for the best relationships because that leads to trust and faith. We value strong relationships in all areas: with managers, direct reports, customers (internal and external), vendors, business partners, team members, and co-workers.

Build a Positive Team and Family Spirit. At Zappos, we place a lot of emphasis on our culture because we are both a team and a family. We want to create an environment that is friendly, warm, and exciting. We encourage diversity in ideas, opinions, and points of view.

Do More with Less. Zappos has always been about being able to do more with less. While we may be casual in our interactions with each other, we are focused and serious about the operations of our business. We believe in working hard and putting in the extra effort to get things done.

Be Passionate and Determined. Passion is the fuel that drives us and our company forward. We value passion, determination, perseverance, and the sense of urgency. We are inspired because we believe in what we are doing and where we are going. We don't take "no" or "that'll never work" for an answer because if we had, then Zappos would have never started in the first place.

Be Humble. While we have grown quickly in the past, we recognize that there are always challenges ahead to tackle. We believe that no matter what happens we should always be respectful of everyone.

Source: Information posted at www.zappos.com, accessed June 6, 2010.

because they serve as yardsticks for tracking a company's performance and progress toward its vision. Vague targets such as "maximize profits," "reduce costs," "become more efficient," or "increase sales," which specify neither how much nor when, offer little value as a management tool to improve company performance. Ideally, managers should develop *challenging*, yet *achievable* objectives that *stretch an organization to perform at its full potential.* As Mitchell Leibovitz, former CEO of the auto parts and service retailer Pep Boys, once said, "If you want to have ho-hum results, have ho-hum objectives."

> **CORE CONCEPT**
>
> **Objectives** are an organization's performance targets—the results management wants to achieve.
>
> ⟹ Track Cny's performance & progress toward its vision

What Kinds of Objectives to Set

Two very distinct types of performance yardsticks are required: those relating to financial performance and those relating to strategic performance. **Financial objectives** communicate management's targets for financial performance. Common financial objectives relate to revenue growth, profitability, and return on investment. **Strategic objectives** are related to a company's marketing standing and competitive vitality. The importance of attaining financial objectives is intuitive. Without adequate profitability and financial strength, a company's long-term health and ultimate survival is jeopardized. Furthermore, subpar earnings and a weak balance sheet alarm shareholders and creditors and put the jobs of senior executives at risk. However, good financial performance, by itself, is not enough.

+to do — Revenue growth, ROI, profitability

> **CORE CONCEPT**
>
> **Financial objectives** relate to the financial performance targets management has established for the organization to achieve.
>
> **Strategic objectives** relate to target outcomes that indicate a company is strengthening its market standing, competitive vitality, and future business prospects.
>
> *Lagging indic (past)*
>
> *Marketing standing & competitive vitality*

A company's financial objectives are really *lagging indicators* that reflect the results of past decisions and organizational activities.[6] The results of past decisions and organizational activities are not reliable indicators of a company's future prospects. Companies that have been poor financial performers are sometimes able to turn things around, and good financial performers on occasion fall upon hard times. Hence, the best and most reliable predictors of a company's success in the marketplace and future financial performance are strategic objectives. Strategic outcomes are *leading indicators* of a company's future financial performance and business prospects. The accomplishment of strategic objectives signals the company is well positioned to sustain or improve its performance. For instance, if a company is achieving ambitious strategic objectives, then there's reason to expect that its *future* financial performance will be better than its current or past performance. If a company begins to lose competitive strength and fails to achieve important strategic objectives, then its ability to maintain its present profitability is highly suspect.

Consequently, utilizing a performance measurement system that strikes a *balance* between financial objectives and strategic objectives is optimal.[7] Just tracking a company's financial performance overlooks the fact that what ultimately enables a company to deliver better financial results is the achievement of strategic objectives that improve its competitiveness and market *strength*

▶ TABLE 2.4

The Balanced Scorecard Approach to Performance Measurement

FINANCIAL OBJECTIVES		STRATEGIC OBJECTIVES
• An x percent increase in annual revenues • Annual increases in earnings per share of x percent • An x percent return on capital employed (ROCE) or shareholder investment (ROE) • Bond and credit ratings of x • Internal cash flows of x to fund new capital investment	• Win an x percent market share • Achieve customer satisfaction rates of x percent • Achieve a customer retention rate of x percent • Acquire x number of new customers • Introduce x number of new products in the next three years • Reduce product development times to x months	• Increase percentage of sales coming from new products to x percent • Improve information systems capabilities to give frontline managers defect information in x minutes • Improve teamwork by increasing the number of projects involving more than one business unit to x

strength. Representative examples of financial and strategic objectives that companies often include in a **balanced scorecard** approach to measuring their performance are displayed in Table 2.4.[8]

In 2010, nearly 50 percent of global companies used a balanced scorecard approach to measuring strategic and financial performance.[9] Examples of organizations that have adopted a balanced scorecard approach to setting objectives and measuring performance include SAS Institute, UPS, Ann Taylor Stores, Fort Bragg Army Garrison, Caterpillar, Daimler AG, Hilton Hotels, Susan G. Komen for the Cure, and Siemens AG.[10] Concepts & Connections 2.3 provides selected strategic and financial objectives of three prominent companies.

CORE CONCEPT

The **balanced scorecard** is a widely used method for combining the use of both strategic and financial objectives, tracking their achievement, and giving management a more complete and balanced view of how well an organization is performing.

Short-Term and Long-Term Objectives A company's set of financial and strategic objectives should include both near-term and long-term performance targets. Short-term objectives focus attention on delivering performance improvements in the current period, while long-term targets force the organization to consider how actions currently under way will affect the company at a later date. Specifically, long-term objectives stand as a barrier to an undue focus on short-term results by nearsighted management. When trade-offs have to be made between achieving long-run and short-run objectives, long-run objectives should take precedence (unless the achievement of one or more short-run performance targets has unique importance).

The Need for Objectives at All Organizational Levels Objective setting should not stop with the establishment of companywide performance targets. Company objectives need to be broken into performance targets for each of the organization's separate businesses, product lines, functional

CONCEPTS & CONNECTIONS 2.3

EXAMPLES OF COMPANY OBJECTIVES

PEPSICO

Accelerate top-line growth; build and expand our better-for-your snacks and beverages and nutrition businesses; improve our water use efficiency by 20 percent per unit of production by 2015; reduce packaging weight by 350 million pounds by 2012; improve our electricity use efficiency by 20 percent per unit of production by 2015; maintain appropriate financial flexibility with ready access to global capital and credit markets at favorable interest rates.

GOODYEAR

Increase operating income from $917 million in 2010 to $1.6 billion in 2013; increase operating income from international tire division from $899 million in 2010 to $1,150 million in 2013; increase operating income from North American division from $18 million in 2010 to $450 million in 2013; reduce the percentage of non-branded replacement tires sold from 16 percent in 2010 to 9 percent in 2013; improve brand awareness in Mexico; increase number of retail outlets in China from 735 in 2010 to 1,555 in 2015; increase fuel efficiency of automobile and truck tires; improve braking distance on new tire designs;

improve tread-life on new tire designs; collaborate with regulatory agencies in the U.S. and Europe to develop tire labeling standards by 2013.

YUM! BRANDS (KFC, PIZZA HUT, TACO BELL, LONG JOHN SILVER'S)

Increase operating profit derived from international operations from 65 percent in 2010 to 75 percent in 2010; increase operating profit derived from operations in emerging markets from 48 percent in 2010 to 60 percent in 2015; increase number of KFC units in Africa from 655 in 2010 to 2,100 in 2020; increase KFC revenues in Africa from $865 million in 2010 to $1.94 billion in 2014; increase number of KFC units in India from 101 in 2010 to 1,250 in 2020; increase number of KFC units in Vietnam from 87 in 2010 to 500 in 2020; increase number of KFC units in Russia from 150 in 2010 to 500 in 2020; open 100+ new Taco Bell units in international markets in 2015; increase annual cash flows from operations from $1.5 billion in 2010 to $2 + billion in 2015.

Source: Information posted on company websites, accessed May 27, 2011.

---

departments, and individual work units. Employees within various functional areas and operating levels will be guided much better by narrow objectives relating directly to their departmental activities than broad organizational level goals. Objective setting is thus a top-down process that must extend to the lowest organizational levels. And it means that each organizational unit must take care to set performance targets that support—rather than conflict with or negate—the achievement of companywide strategic and financial objectives.

Narrow objectives

STAGE 3: CRAFTING A STRATEGY

As indicated earlier, the task of stitching a strategy together entails addressing a series of *hows: how* to attract and please customers, *how* to compete against rivals, *how* to position the company in the marketplace and capitalize on attractive opportunities to grow the business, *how* best to respond to changing economic and market conditions, *how* to manage each functional piece of the business, and *how* to achieve the company's performance targets. It also means choosing among the various strategic alternatives and proactively searching for opportunities to do new things or to do existing things in new or better ways.[11]

All about how

▶ **LO3**

Understand why the strategic initiatives taken at various organizational levels must be tightly coordinated to achieve companywide performance targets.

Strategy Making Involves Managers at All Organizational Levels

In some enterprises, the CEO or owner functions as strategic visionary and chief architect of the strategy, personally deciding what the key elements of the company's strategy will be, although the CEO may seek the advice of key subordinates in fashioning an overall strategy and deciding on important strategic moves. However, it is a mistake to view strategy making as a *top* management function—the exclusive province of owner-entrepreneurs, CEOs, high-ranking executives, and board members. The more a company's operations cut across different products, industries, and geographical areas, the more that headquarters executives have little option but to delegate considerable strategy-making authority to down-the-line managers. On-the-scene managers who oversee specific operating units are likely to have a more detailed command of the strategic issues and choices for the particular operating unit under their supervision—knowing the prevailing market and competitive conditions, customer requirements and expectations, and all the other relevant aspects affecting the several strategic options available.

> In most companies, crafting strategy is a *collaborative team effort* that includes managers in various positions and at various organizational levels. Crafting strategy is rarely something only high-level executives do.

A Company's Strategy-Making Hierarchy

Diverse & large => better => relevant strat making

The larger and more diverse the operations of an enterprise, the more points of strategic initiative it will have and the more managers at different organizational levels will have a relevant strategy-making role. In diversified companies, where multiple and sometimes strikingly different businesses have to be managed, crafting a full-fledged strategy involves four distinct types of strategic actions and initiatives, each undertaken at different levels of the organization and partially or wholly crafted by managers at different organizational levels, as shown in Figure 2.2. A company's overall strategy is therefore *a collection of strategic initiatives and actions* devised by managers up and down the whole organizational hierarchy. Ideally, the pieces of a company's strategy up and down the strategy hierarchy should be cohesive and mutually reinforcing, fitting together like a jigsaw puzzle.

> **Corporate strategy** establishes an overall game plan for managing a *set of businesses* in a diversified, multibusiness company.
> **Business strategy** is primarily concerned with strengthening the company's market position and building competitive advantage in a single business company or a single business unit of a diversified multibusiness corporation.

As shown in Figure 2.2, **corporate strategy** is orchestrated by the CEO and other senior executives and establishes an overall game plan for managing a *set of businesses* in a diversified, multibusiness company. Corporate strategy addresses the questions of how to capture cross-business synergies, what businesses to hold or divest, which new markets to enter, and how to best enter new markets—by acquisition, creation of a strategic alliance, or through internal development. Corporate strategy and business diversification are the subject of Chapter 8, where they are discussed in detail.

Business strategy is primarily concerned with building competitive advantage in a single business unit of a diversified company or strengthening the

▶ FIGURE 2.2 **A Company's Strategy-Making Hierarchy**

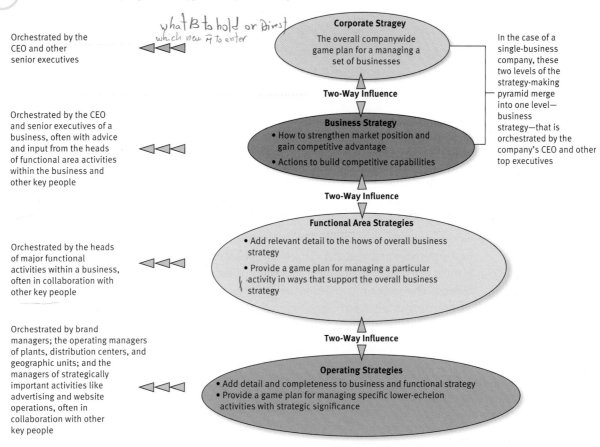

(handwritten annotation) what B to hold or Divest / which new A to enter

Orchestrated by the CEO and other senior executives

Corporate Stragey
The overall companywide game plan for a managing a set of businesses

In the case of a single-business company, these two levels of the strategy-making pyramid merge into one level—business strategy—that is orchestrated by the company's CEO and other top executives

Two-Way Influence

Orchestrated by the CEO and senior executives of a business, often with advice and input from the heads of functional area activities within the business and other key people

Business Strategy
• How to strengthen market position and gain competitive advantage
• Actions to build competitive capabilities

Two-Way Influence

Orchestrated by the heads of major functional activities within a business, often in collaboration with other key people

Functional Area Strategies
• Add relevant detail to the hows of overall business strategy
• Provide a game plan for managing a particular activity in ways that support the overall business strategy

Two-Way Influence

Orchestrated by brand managers; the operating managers of plants, distribution centers, and geographic units; and the managers of strategically important activities like advertising and website operations, often in collaboration with other key people

Operating Strategies
• Add detail and completeness to business and functional strategy
• Provide a game plan for managing specific lower-echelon activities with strategic significance

market position of a nondiversified single business company. Business strategy is also the responsibility of the CEO and other senior executives, but key business-unit heads may also be influential, especially in strategic decisions affecting the businesses they lead. *In single-business companies, the corporate and business levels of the strategy-making hierarchy merge into a single level—business strategy—*because the strategy for the entire enterprise involves only one distinct business. So, a single-business company has three levels of strategy: business strategy, functional-area strategies, and operating strategies.

Functional-area strategies concern the actions related to particular functions or processes within a business. A company's product development strategy, for example, represents the managerial game plan for creating new products that are in tune with what buyers are looking for. Lead responsibility for functional strategies within a business is normally delegated to the heads of the respective functions, with the general manager of the business having final approval over functional strategies. For the overall business strategy to have maximum impact, a company's marketing strategy, production strategy, finance strategy, customer service strategy, product development strategy, and human resources strategy should be compatible and mutually reinforcing rather than each serving its own narrower purpose.

(handwritten margin notes) Single Business Cp has 3 level of Strat { Bu Funq Op

Operating strategies concern the relatively narrow strategic initiatives and approaches for managing key operating units (plants, distribution centers, geographic units) and specific operating activities such as materials purchasing or Internet sales. Operating strategies are limited in scope, but add further detail to functional-area strategies and the overall business strategy. Lead responsibility for operating strategies is usually delegated to frontline managers, subject to review and approval by higher-ranking managers.

STAGE 4: IMPLEMENTING AND EXECUTING THE CHOSEN STRATEGY

LO4

Become aware of what a company must do to achieve operating excellence and to execute its strategy proficiently.

Managing the implementation and execution of strategy is easily the most demanding and time-consuming part of the strategic management process. Good strategy execution entails that managers pay careful attention to how key internal business processes are performed and see to it that employees' efforts are directed toward the accomplishment of desired operational outcomes. The task of implementing and executing the strategy also necessitates an ongoing analysis of the efficiency and effectiveness of a company's internal activities and a managerial awareness of new technological developments that might improve business processes. In most situations, managing the strategy execution process includes the following principal aspects:

- Staffing the organization to provide needed skills and expertise.
- Allocating ample resources to activities critical to good strategy execution.
- Ensuring that policies and procedures facilitate rather than impede effective execution.
- Installing information and operating systems that enable company personnel to perform essential activities.
- Pushing for continuous improvement in how value chain activities are performed.
- Tying rewards and incentives directly to the achievement of performance objectives.
- Creating a company culture and work climate conducive to successful strategy execution.
- Exerting the internal leadership needed to propel implementation forward.

STAGE 5: EVALUATING PERFORMANCE AND INITIATING CORRECTIVE ADJUSTMENTS

The fifth stage of the strategy management process—monitoring new external developments, evaluating the company's progress, and making corrective adjustments—is the trigger point for deciding whether to continue or change the company's vision, objectives, strategy, and/or strategy execution methods.

So long as the company's direction and strategy seem well matched to indus-try and competitive conditions and performance targets are being met, com-pany executives may well decide to stay the course. Simply fine-tuning the strategic plan and continuing with efforts to improve strategy execution are sufficient.

But whenever a company encounters disruptive changes in its environ-ment, questions need to be raised about the appropriateness of its direction and strategy. If a company experiences a downturn in its market position or persistent shortfalls in performance, then com-pany managers are obligated to ferret out the causes—do they relate to poor strategy, poor strat-egy execution, or both?—and take timely correc-tive action. A company's direction, objectives, and strategy have to be revisited any time external or internal conditions warrant.

> A company's vision, objectives, strategy, and approach to strategy execution are never final; managing strategy is an ongoing pro-cess, not an every-now-and-then task.

Also, it is not unusual for a company to find that one or more aspects of its strategy implementation and execution are not going as well as intended. Proficient strategy execution is always the product of much organizational learning. It is achieved unevenly—coming quickly in some areas and proving nettlesome in others. Successful strategy execution entails vigilantly searching for ways to improve and then making corrective adjustments whenever and wherever it is useful to do so.

CORPORATE GOVERNANCE: THE ROLE OF THE BOARD OF DIRECTORS IN THE STRATEGY-MAKING, STRATEGY-EXECUTING PROCESS

Although senior managers have *lead responsibility* for crafting and executing a company's strategy, it is the duty of the board of directors to exercise strong oversight and see that the five tasks of strategic management are done in a manner that benefits shareholders (in the case of investor-owned enterprises) or stakeholders (in the case of not-for-profit organizations). In watching over management's strategy-making, strategy-executing actions, a company's board of directors has four important corporate governance obligations to fulfill:

▶ **LO5**

Become aware of the role and responsibility of a company's board of directors in overseeing the strategic management process.

1. *Oversee the company's financial accounting and financial reporting practices.* While top management, particularly the company's CEO and CFO (chief financial officer), is primarily responsible for seeing that the company's financial statements accurately report the results of the company's opera-tions, board members have a fiduciary duty to protect shareholders by exercising oversight of the company's financial practices. In addition, cor-porate boards must ensure that generally acceptable accounting principles (GAAP) are properly used in preparing the company's financial state-ments and determine whether proper financial controls are in place to prevent fraud and misuse of funds. Virtually all boards of directors moni-tor the financial reporting activities by appointing an audit committee, always composed entirely of *outside directors* (*inside directors* hold manage-ment positions in the company and either directly or indirectly report to

the CEO). The members of the audit committee have lead responsibility for overseeing the decisions of the company's financial officers and consulting with both internal and external auditors to ensure that financial reports are accurate and adequate financial controls are in place. Faulty oversight of corporate accounting and financial reporting practices by audit committees and corporate boards during the early 2000s resulted in the federal investigation of more than 20 major corporations between 2000 and 2002. The investigations of such well-known companies as AOL Time Warner, Global Crossing, Enron, Qwest Communications, and WorldCom found that upper management had employed fraudulent or unsound accounting practices to artificially inflate revenues, overstate assets, and reduce expenses. The scandals resulted in the conviction of a number of corporate executives and the passage of the Sarbanes-Oxley Act of 2002, which tightened financial reporting standards and created additional compliance requirements for public boards.

2. *Diligently critique and oversee the company's direction, strategy, and business approaches.* Even though board members have a legal obligation to warrant the accuracy of the company's financial reports, directors must set aside time to guide management in choosing a strategic direction and to make independent judgments about the validity and wisdom of management's proposed strategic actions. Many boards have found that meeting agendas become consumed by compliance matters and little time is left to discuss matters of strategic importance. The board of directors and management at Philips Electronics hold annual two- to three-day retreats devoted to evaluating the company's long-term direction and various strategic proposals. The company's exit from the semiconductor business and its increased focus on medical technology and home health care resulted from management–board discussions during such retreats.[12]

3. *Evaluate the caliber of senior executives' strategy-making and strategy-executing skills.* The board is always responsible for determining whether the current CEO is doing a good job of strategic leadership and whether senior management is actively creating a pool of potential successors to the CEO and other top executives.[13] Evaluation of senior executives' strategy-making and strategy-executing skills is enhanced when outside directors go into the field to personally evaluate how well the strategy is being executed. Independent board members at GE visit operating executives at each major business unit once per year to assess the company's talent pool and stay abreast of emerging strategic and operating issues affecting the company's divisions. Home Depot board members visit a store once per quarter to determine the health of the company's operations.[14]

4. *Institute a compensation plan for top executives that rewards them for actions and results that serve shareholder interests.* A basic principle of corporate governance is that the owners of a corporation delegate operating authority and managerial control to top management in return for compensation. In their role as an *agent* of shareholders, top executives have a clear

CONCEPTS & CONNECTIONS 2.4

CORPORATE GOVERNANCE FAILURES AT FANNIE MAE AND FREDDIE MAC

Executive compensation in the financial services industry during the mid-2000s ranks high among examples of failed corporate governance. Corporate governance at the government-sponsored mortgage giants Fannie Mae and Freddie Mac was particularly weak. The politically appointed boards at both enterprises failed to understand the risks of the subprime loan strategies being employed, did not adequately monitor the decisions of the CEO, did not exercise effective oversight of the accounting principles being employed (which led to inflated earnings), and approved executive compensation systems that allowed management to manipulate earnings to receive lucrative performance bonuses. The audit and compensation committees at Fannie Mae were particularly ineffective in protecting shareholder interests, with the audit committee allowing the government-sponsored enterprise's financial officers to audit reports prepared under their direction and used to determine performance bonuses. Fannie Mae's audit committee also was aware of management's use of questionable accounting practices that reduced losses and recorded one-time gains to achieve EPS targets linked to bonuses. In addition, the audit committee failed to investigate formal charges of accounting improprieties filed by a manager in the Office of the Controller.

Fannie Mae's compensation committee was equally ineffective. The committee allowed the company's CEO, Franklin Raines, to select the consultant employed to design the mortgage firm's executive compensation plan and agreed to a tiered bonus plan that would permit Raines and other senior managers to receive maximum bonuses without great difficulty. The compensation plan allowed Raines to earn performance-based bonuses of $52 million and total compensation of $90 million between 1999 and 2004. Raines was forced to resign in December 2004 when the Office of Federal Housing Enterprise Oversight found that Fannie Mae executives had fraudulently inflated earnings to receive bonuses linked to financial performance. Securities and Exchange Commission investigators also found evidence of improper accounting at Fannie Mae and required it to restate its earnings between 2002 and 2004 by $6.3 billion.

Poor governance at Freddie Mac allowed its CEO and senior management to manipulate financial data to receive performance-based compensation as well. Freddie Mac CEO Richard Syron received 2007 compensation of $19.8 million while the mortgage company's share price declined from a high of $70 in 2005 to $25 at year-end 2007. During Syron's tenure as CEO the company become embroiled in a multibillion-dollar accounting scandal, and Syron personally disregarded internal reports dating to 2004 that warned of an impending financial crisis at the company. Forewarnings within Freddie Mac and by federal regulators and outside industry observers proved to be correct, with loan underwriting policies at Freddie Mac and Fannie Mae leading to combined losses at the two firms in 2008 of more than $100 billion. The price of Freddie Mac's shares had fallen to below $1 by Syron's resignation in September 2008.

Both organizations were placed into a conservatorship under the direction of the U.S. government in September 2008 and were provided bailout funds of more than $150 billion by early 2011. The U.S. Federal Housing Finance Agency estimated the bailout of Fannie Mae and Freddie Mac would potentially reach $200 billion to $300 billion by 2013.

Sources: Chris Isidore, "Fannie, Freddie Bailout: $153 Billion . . . and Counting," *CNNMoney,* February 11, 2011; "Adding Up the Government's Total Bailout Tab," *The New York Times Online,* February 4, 2009; Eric Dash, "Fannie Mae to Restate Results by $6.3 Billion Because of Accounting," *The New York Times Online,* www.nytimes.com, December 7, 2006; Annys Shin, "Fannie Mae Sets Executive Salaries," *The Washington Post,* February 9, 2006, p. D4; and Scott DeCarlo, Eric Weiss, Mark Jickling, and James R. Cristie, *Fannie Mae and Freddie Mac: Scandal in U.S. Housing* (Nova Publishers, 2006), pp. 266–286.

and unequivocal duty to make decisions and operate the company in accord with shareholder interests (but this does not mean disregarding the interests of other stakeholders, particularly those of employees, with whom they also have an agency relationship). Most boards of directors have a compensation committee, composed entirely of directors from

Reward for boosting
cry that

outside the company, to develop a salary and incentive compensation plan that rewards senior executives for boosting the company's long-term performance and growing the economic value of the enterprise on behalf of shareholders; the compensation committee's recommendations are presented to the full board for approval. But during the past 10 to 15 years, many boards of directors have done a poor job of ensuring that executive salary increases, bonuses, and stock option awards are tied tightly to performance measures that are truly in the long-term interests of shareholders. Rather, compensation packages at many companies have increasingly rewarded executives for short-term performance improvements—most notably, achieving quarterly and annual earnings targets and boosting the stock price by specified percentages. This has had the perverse effect of causing company managers to become preoccupied with actions to improve a company's near-term performance, often motivating them to take unwise business risks to boost short-term earnings by amounts sufficient to qualify for multimillion-dollar bonuses and stock option awards (that, in the view of many people, were obscenely large). The greater weight being placed on short-term performance improvements has worked against shareholders since, in many cases, the excessive risk-taking has proved damaging to long-term company performance—witness the huge loss of shareholder wealth that occurred at many financial institutions in 2008–2009 because of executive risk-taking in subprime loans, credit default swaps, and collateralized mortgage securities in 2006–2007. As a consequence, the need to overhaul and reform executive compensation has become a hot topic in both public circles and corporate boardrooms. Concepts & Connections 2.4 discusses how weak governance at Fannie Mae and Freddie Mac allowed opportunistic senior managers to secure exorbitant bonuses, while making decisions that imperiled the futures of the companies they managed.

Every corporation should have a strong, independent board of directors that (1) is well informed about the company's performance, (2) guides and judges the CEO and other top executives, (3) has the courage to curb management actions it believes are inappropriate or unduly risky, (4) certifies to shareholders that the CEO is doing what the board expects, (5) provides insight and advice to management, and (6) is intensely involved in debating the pros and cons of key decisions and actions.[15] Boards of directors that lack the backbone to challenge a strong-willed or "imperial" CEO or that rubber-stamp most anything the CEO recommends without probing inquiry and debate abandon their duty to represent and protect shareholder interests.

KEY POINTS

The strategic management process consists of five interrelated and integrated stages:

1. *Developing a strategic vision* of where the company needs to head and what its future product-customer-market-technology focus should be. This managerial step provides long-term direction, infuses the organization with a sense of purposeful action, and communicates to stakeholders management's aspirations for the company.

2. *Setting objectives* and using the targeted results as yardsticks for measuring the company's performance. Objectives need to spell out *how much* of *what kind* of performance *by when*. A *balanced scorecard* approach for measuring company performance entails setting both *financial objectives and strategic objectives*.

3. *Crafting a strategy to achieve the objectives* and move the company along the strategic course that management has charted. The total strategy that emerges is really a collection of strategic actions and business approaches initiated partly by senior company executives, partly by the heads of major business divisions, partly by functional-area managers, and partly by operating managers on the frontlines. A single business enterprise has three levels of strategy—business strategy for the company as a whole, functional-area strategies for each main area within the business, and operating strategies undertaken by lower-echelon managers. In diversified, multibusiness companies, the strategy-making task involves four distinct types or levels of strategy: corporate strategy for the company as a whole, business strategy (one for each business the company has diversified into), functional-area strategies within each business, and operating strategies. Typically, the strategy-making task is more top-down than bottom-up, with higher-level strategies serving as the guide for developing lower-level strategies.

4. *Implementing and executing the chosen strategy efficiently and effectively.* Managing the implementation and execution of strategy is an operations-oriented, make-things-happen activity aimed at shaping the performance of core business activities in a strategy supportive manner. Management's handling of the strategy implementation process can be considered successful if things go smoothly enough that the company meets or beats its strategic and financial performance targets and shows good progress in achieving management's strategic vision.

5. *Evaluating performance and initiating corrective adjustments* in vision, long-term direction, objectives, strategy, or execution in light of actual experience, changing conditions, new ideas, and new opportunities. This stage of the strategy management process is the trigger point for deciding whether to continue or change the company's vision, objectives, strategy, and/or strategy execution methods.

The sum of a company's strategic vision, objectives, and strategy constitutes a *strategic plan*.

Boards of directors have a duty to shareholders to play a vigilant role in overseeing management's handling of a company's strategy-making, strategy-executing process. A company's board is obligated to (1) ensure that the company issues accurate financial reports and has adequate financial controls, (2) critically appraise and ultimately approve strategic action plans, (3) evaluate the strategic leadership skills of the CEO, and (4) institute a compensation plan for top executives that rewards them for actions and results that serve stakeholder interests, most especially those of shareholders.

33

ASSURANCE OF LEARNING EXERCISES

LO1

1. Using the information in Tables 2.2 and 2.3, critique the adequacy and merit of the following vision statements, listing effective elements and shortcomings. Rank the vision statements from best to worst once you complete your evaluation.

VISION STATEMENT	EFFECTIVE ELEMENTS	SHORTCOMINGS

www.mcgrawhillconnect.com

Wells Fargo

We want to satisfy all of our customers' financial needs, help them succeed financially, be the premier provider of financial services in every one of our markets, and be known as one of America's great companies.

Hilton Hotels Corporation

Our vision is to be the first choice of the world's travelers. Hilton intends to build on the rich heritage and strength of our brands by:

• Consistently delighting our customers
• Investing in our team members
• Delivering innovative products and services
• Continuously improving performance
• Increasing shareholder value
• Creating a culture of pride
• Strengthening the loyalty of our constituents

H. J. Heinz Company

Be the world's premier food company, offering nutritious, superior tasting foods to people everywhere. Being the premier food company does not mean being the biggest but it does mean being the best in terms of consumer value, customer service, employee talent, and consistent and predictable growth.

BASF

We are "The Chemical Company" successfully operating in all major markets.

• Our customers view BASF as their partner of choice.
• Our innovative products, intelligent solutions and services make us the most competent worldwide supplier in the chemical industry.
• We generate a high return on assets.
• We strive for sustainable development.
• We welcome change as an opportunity.
• We, the employees of BASF, together ensure our success.

Source: Company websites and annual reports.

LO2

2. Go to the company investor relations websites for Home Depot (http://corporate.homedepot.com/wps/portal), Avon (www.avoncompany.com/), and Intel (www.intc.com) to find examples of strategic and financial objectives. List four objectives for each company and indicate which of these are strategic and which are financial.

LO3

3. The primary strategic initiatives of Ford Motor Company's restructuring plan executed between 2005 and 2010 involved accelerating the development of new cars that customers would value, improving its balance sheet, working with its union employees to improve manufacturing competitiveness, reducing product engineering costs, reducing production capacity by approximately 40 percent,

34

and reducing hourly head count by 40 to 50 percent. At the conclusion of the restructuring plan in 2010, Ford was ranked first among U.S. automobile manufacturers by J.D. Power in initial quality and had earned more than $5.4 billion in pre-tax profit on net revenues of $64.4 billion. Explain why its strategic initiatives taken at various organizational levels and functions were necessarily tightly coordinated to achieve its commendable results.

4. Go to the investor relations website for Walmart (http://investors.walmartstores .com) and review past presentations it has made during various investor conferences by clicking on the Events option in the navigation bar. Prepare a one- to two-page report that outlines what Walmart has said to investors about its approach to strategy execution. Specifically, what has management discussed concerning staffing, resource allocation, policies and procedures, information and operating systems, continuous improvement, rewards and incentives, corporate culture, and internal leadership at the company?

LO4

5. Based on the information provided in Concepts & Connections 2.4 on page 31, explain how corporate governance at Freddie Mac failed the enterprise's shareholders and other stakeholders. Which important obligations to shareholders were fulfilled by Fannie Mae's board of directors? What is your assessment of how well Fannie Mae's compensation committee handled executive compensation at the government-sponsored mortgage giant?

LO5

www.mcgrawhillconnect.com

EXERCISES FOR SIMULATION PARTICIPANTS

1. Meet with your co-managers and prepare a strategic vision statement for your company. It should be at least one sentence long and no longer than a brief paragraph. When you are finished, check to see if your vision statement meets the conditions for an effectively worded strategic vision set forth in Table 2.2 and avoids the shortcomings set forth in Table 2.3. If not, then revise it accordingly. What would be a good slogan that captures the essence of your strategic vision and that could be used to help communicate the vision to company personnel, shareholders, and other stakeholders?

LO1

2. What are your company's financial objectives? What are your company's strategic objectives?

LO2

3. What are the three or four key elements of your company's strategy?

LO3

ENDNOTES

1. Gordon Shaw, Robert Brown, and Philip Bromiley, "Strategic Stories: How 3M Is Rewriting Business Planning," *Harvard Business Review* 76, no. 3 (May–June 1998); and David J. Collins and Michael G. Rukstad, "Can You Say What Your Strategy Is?" *Harvard Business Review* 86, no. 4 (April 2008).

2. Hugh Davidson, *The Committed Enterprise: How to Make Vision and Values Work* (Oxford: Butterworth Heinemann, 2002); W. Chan Kim and Renée Mauborgne, "Charting Your Company's Future," *Harvard Business Review* 80, no. 6 (June 2002); James C. Collins and Jerry I. Porras, "Building Your Company's Vision," *Harvard Business Review* 74, no. 5 (September–October 1996); Jim Collins and Jerry Porras, *Built to Last: Successful Habits of Visionary Companies* (New York: HarperCollins, 1994); Michel Robert, *Strategy Pure and Simple II: How Winning Companies Dominate Their Competitors* (New York: McGraw-Hill, 1998).

3. Hugh Davidson, *The Committed Enterprise* (Oxford: Butterworth Heinemann, 2002).

4. Ibid.

5. Jeffrey K. Liker, *The Toyota Way* (New York: McGraw-Hill, 2004); and Steve Hamm, "Taking a Page from Toyota's Playbook," *BusinessWeek,* August 22/29, 2005, p. 72.

6. Robert S. Kaplan and David P. Norton, *The Strategy-Focused Organization* (Boston: Harvard Business School Press, 2001).

7. Ibid. Also, see Robert S. Kaplan and David P. Norton, *The Balanced Scorecard: Translating Strategy into Action* (Boston: Harvard Business School Press, 1996); Kevin B. Hendricks, Larry Menor, and Christine Wiedman, "The Balanced Scorecard: To Adopt or Not to Adopt," *Ivey Business Journal* 69, no. 2 (November–December 2004); and Sandy Richardson, "The Key Elements of Balanced Scorecard Success," *Ivey Business Journal* 69, no. 2 (November–December 2004).

8. Kaplan and Norton, *The Balanced Scorecard: Translating Strategy into Action*, pp. 25–29. Kaplan and Norton classify strategic objectives under the categories of customer-related, business processes, and learning and growth. In practice, companies using the balanced scorecard may choose categories of strategic objectives that best reflect the organization's value-creating activities and processes.

9. Information posted on the website of Bain and Company, www.bain.com, accessed May 27, 2011.

10. Information posted on the website of Balanced Scorecard Institute, accessed May 27, 2011.

11. Henry Mintzberg, Bruce Ahlstrand, and Joseph Lampel, *Strategy Safari: A Guided Tour through the Wilds of Strategic Management* (New York: Free Press, 1998); Bruce Barringer and Allen C. Bluedorn, "The Relationship between Corporate Entrepreneurship and Strategic Management," *Strategic Management Journal* 20 (1999); Jeffrey G. Covin and Morgan P. Miles, "Corporate Entrepreneurship and the Pursuit of Competitive Advantage," *Entrepreneurship: Theory and Practice* 23, no. 3 (Spring 1999); and David A. Garvin and Lynned C. Levesque, "Meeting the Challenge of Corporate Entrepreneurship," *Harvard Business Review* 84, no. 10 (October 2006).

12. Jay W. Lorsch and Robert C. Clark, "Leading from the Boardroom," *Harvard Business Review* 86, no. 4 (April 2008).

13. Ibid., p. 110.

14. Stephen P. Kaufman, "Evaluating the CEO," *Harvard Business Review* 86, no. 10 (October 2008).

15. David A. Nadler, "Building Better Boards," *Harvard Business Review* 82, no. 5 (May 2004); Cynthia A. Montgomery and Rhonda Kaufman, "The Board's Missing Link," *Harvard Business Review* 81, no. 3 (March 2003); John Carver, "What Continues to Be Wrong with Corporate Governance and How to Fix It," *Ivey Business Journal* 68, no. 1 (September/October 2003); and Gordon Donaldson, "A New Tool for Boards: The Strategic Audit," *Harvard Business Review* 73, no. 4 (July–August 1995).

chapter 3

EVALUATING A COMPANY'S EXTERNAL ENVIRONMENT

LEARNING OBJECTIVES

LO1 Gain command of the basic concepts and analytical tools widely used to diagnose a company's industry and competitive conditions.

LO2 Become adept at recognizing the factors that cause competition in an industry to be fierce, more or less normal, or relatively weak.

LO3 Learn how to determine whether an industry's outlook presents a company with sufficiently attractive opportunities for growth and profitability.

In Chapter 1, we learned that one of the three central questions that managers must address in evaluating their company's business prospects is *"Where are we now?"* Two facets of the company's situation are especially pertinent: (1) the industry and competitive environments in which the company operates—its external environment; and (2) the company's resources and organizational capabilities—its internal environment. Developing answers to the questions *"Where do we want to go from here?"* and *"How are we going to get there?"* without first gaining an understanding of the company's external and internal environments hamstrings attempts to build competitive advantage and boost company performance. Indeed, the first test of a winning strategy inquires, *"How well does the strategy fit the company's situation?"*

This chapter presents the concepts and analytical tools for zeroing in on a single-business company's external environment. Attention centers on the competitive arena in which the company operates, the drivers of market change, the market positions of rival companies, and the factors that determine competitive success. Chapter 4 explores the methods of evaluating a company's internal circumstances and competitiveness.

THE STRATEGICALLY RELEVANT COMPONENTS OF A COMPANY'S MACRO-ENVIRONMENT

LO1

Gain command of the basic concepts and analytical tools widely used to diagnose a company's industry and competitive conditions.

The performance of all companies is affected by such external characteristics as general economic conditions and global factors; population demographics; societal values and lifestyles; political, regulatory, and legal factors; the natural environment; and technological factors. Strictly speaking, a company's "macro-environment" includes *all relevant factors and influences* outside the company's boundaries; by *relevant*, we mean these factors are important enough that they should shape management's decisions regarding the company's long-term direction, objectives, strategy, and business model. Figure 3.1 presents a depiction of macro-environmental factors with a high potential to affect a company's business situation. The impact of outer-ring factors on a company's choice of strategy can range from big to small. But even if the factors in the outer ring of the macro-environment change slowly or are likely to have a low impact on the company's business situation, they still merit a watchful eye. Motor vehicle companies must adapt their strategies to current customer concerns about carbon emissions and high gasoline prices. The demographics of an aging population and longer life expectancies will have a dramatic impact on the health care and prescription drug industries in the next few decades. As company managers scan the external environment, they must be alert for potentially important outer-ring developments, assess their impact and influence, and adapt the company's direction and strategy as needed.

However, the factors and forces in a company's macro-environment that have the *biggest* strategy-shaping impact typically pertain to the company's immediate industry and competitive environment—competitive pressures, the actions of rivals firms, buyer behavior, supplier-related considerations, and so on. Consequently, this chapter concentrates on a company's industry and competitive environment.

▶FIGURE 3.1 **The Components of a Company's Macro-Environment**

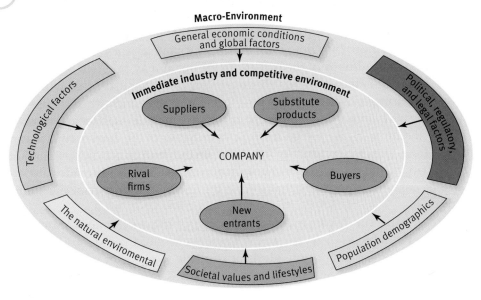

ASSESSING THE COMPANY'S INDUSTRY AND COMPETITIVE ENVIRONMENT

Thinking strategically about a company's industry and competitive environment entails using some well-validated concepts and analytical tools to get clear answers to seven questions:

1. Do the dominant economic characteristics of the industry offer sellers opportunities for growth and attractive profits?
2. What kinds of competitive forces are industry members facing, and how strong is each force?
3. What forces are driving industry change, and what impact will these changes have on competitive intensity and industry profitability?
4. What market positions do industry rivals occupy—who is strongly positioned and who is not?
5. What strategic moves are rivals likely to make next?
6. What are the key factors of competitive success?
7. Does the industry outlook offer good prospects for profitability?

Analysis-based answers to these questions are prerequisites for a strategy offering good fit with the external situation. The remainder of this chapter is devoted to describing the methods of obtaining solid answers to the seven questions above.

QUESTION 1: WHAT ARE THE INDUSTRY'S DOMINANT ECONOMIC CHARACTERISTICS?

Analyzing a company's industry and competitive environment begins with identifying the industry's dominant economic characteristics. While the general economic conditions of the macro-environment may prove to be strategically relevant, it is the economic characteristics of the industry that will have a greater bearing on the industry's prospects for growth and attractive profits. An industry's dominant economic characteristics include such factors as market size and growth rate, the geographic boundaries of the market (which can extend from local to worldwide), market demand-supply conditions, market segmentation, and the pace of technological change. Table 3.1 provides a summary of analytical questions that define the industry's dominant economic features.

Getting a handle on an industry's distinguishing economic features not only provides a broad overview of the attractiveness of the industry, but also promotes understanding of the kinds of strategic moves that industry members are likely to employ. For example, industries that are characterized by rapid technological change may require substantial investments in R&D and the development of strong product innovation capabilities—continuous

▶ TABLE 3.1

What to Consider in Identifying an Industry's Dominant Economic Features

ECONOMIC CHARACTERISTIC	QUESTIONS TO ANSWER
Market size and growth rate	• How big is the industry and how fast is it growing? • What does the industry's position in the life cycle (early development, rapid growth and takeoff, early maturity and slowing growth, saturation and stagnation, decline) reveal about the industry's growth prospects?
Scope of competitive rivalry	• Is the geographic area over which most companies compete local, regional, national, multinational, or global?
Demand-supply conditions *Geographic boundaries*	• Is a surplus of capacity pushing prices and profit margins down? • Is the industry overcrowded with too many competitors?
Market segmentation	• Is the industry characterized by various product characteristics or customer wants, needs, or preferences that divide the market into distinct segments?
Pace of technological change	• What role does advancing technology play in this industry? • Do most industry members have or need strong technological capabilities? Why?

product innovation is primarily a survival strategy in such industries as video games, computers, and pharmaceuticals.

QUESTION 2: HOW STRONG ARE THE INDUSTRY'S COMPETITIVE FORCES?

▶**LO2**

Become adept at recognizing the factors that cause competition in an industry to be fierce, more or less normal, or relatively weak.

After gaining an understanding of the industry's general economic characteristics, industry and competitive analysis should focus on the competitive dynamics of the industry. The nature and subtleties of competitive forces are never the same from one industry to another and must be wholly understood to accurately form answers to the question *"Where are we now?"* Far and away the most powerful and widely used tool for assessing the strength of the industry's competitive forces is the *five-forces model of competition*.[1] This model, as depicted in Figure 3.2, holds that competitive forces affecting industry

▶FIGURE 3.2 **The Five-Forces Model of Competition** → Assess the strength of the industry

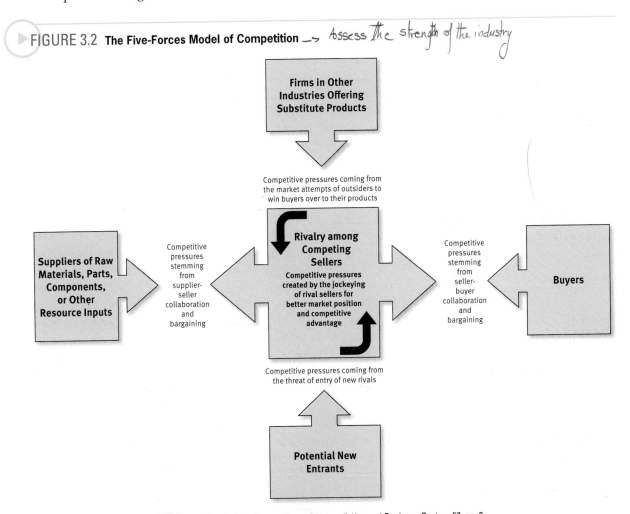

Sources: Based on Michael E. Porter, "How Competitive Forces Shape Strategy," *Harvard Business Review* 57, no. 2 (March–April 1979), pp. 137–45; and Michael E. Porter, "The Five Competitive Forces That Shape Strategy," *Harvard Business Review* 86, no. 1 (January 2008), pp. 80–86.

attractiveness go beyond rivalry among competing sellers and include pressures stemming from four coexisting sources. The five competitive forces affecting industry attractiveness are listed below.

1. Competitive pressures stemming from *buyer* bargaining power.
2. Competitive pressures coming from companies in other industries to win buyers over to *substitute products*.
3. Competitive pressures stemming from *supplier* bargaining power.
4. Competitive pressures associated with the threat of *new entrants* into the market.
5. Competitive pressures associated with *rivalry among competing sellers* to attract customers. This is usually the strongest of the five competitive forces.

strongest

The Competitive Force of Buyer Bargaining Power

Depends on:

Whether seller-buyer relationships represent a minor or significant competitive force depends on (1) whether some or many buyers have sufficient bargaining leverage to obtain price concessions and other favorable terms, and (2) the extent to which buyers are price sensitive. Buyers with strong bargaining power can limit industry profitability by demanding price concessions, better payment terms, or additional features and services that increase industry members' costs. Buyer price sensitivity limits the profit potential of industry members by restricting the ability of sellers to raise prices without losing volume or unit sales.

The leverage that buyers have in negotiating favorable terms of the sale can range from weak to strong. Individual consumers, for example, rarely have much bargaining power in negotiating price concessions or other favorable terms with sellers. The primary exceptions involve situations in which price haggling is customary, such as the purchase of new and used motor vehicles, homes, and other big-ticket items such as jewelry and pleasure boats. For most consumer goods and services, individual buyers have no bargaining leverage—their option is to pay the seller's posted price, delay their purchase until prices and terms improve, or take their business elsewhere.

In contrast, large retail chains such as Walmart, Best Buy, Staples, and Home Depot typically have considerable negotiating leverage in purchasing products from manufacturers because retailers usually stock just two or three competing brands of a product and rarely carry all competing brands. In addition, the strong bargaining power of major supermarket chains such as Kroger, Safeway, and Albertsons allows them to demand promotional allowances and lump-sum payments (called slotting fees) from food products manufacturers in return for stocking certain brands or putting them in the best shelf locations. Motor vehicle manufacturers have strong bargaining power in negotiating to buy original equipment tires from Goodyear, Michelin, Bridgestone/Firestone, Continental, and Pirelli not only because they buy in large quantities, but also because tire makers have judged original equipment tires to be important contributors to brand awareness and brand loyalty.

Even if buyers do not purchase in large quantities or offer a seller important market exposure or prestige, they gain a degree of bargaining leverage in the following circumstances:

- *If buyers' costs of switching to competing brands or substitutes are relatively low.* Buyers who can readily switch between several sellers have more negotiating leverage than buyers who have high switching costs. When the products of rival sellers are virtually identical, it is relatively easy for buyers to switch from seller to seller at little or no cost. For example, the screws, rivets, steel, and capacitors used in the production of large home appliances such as washers and dryers are all commodity-like and available from many sellers. The potential for buyers to easily switch from one seller to another encourages sellers to make concessions to win or retain a buyer's business.

- *If the number of buyers is small or if a customer is particularly important to a seller.* The smaller the number of buyers, the less easy it is for sellers to find alternative buyers when a customer is lost to a competitor. The prospect of losing a customer who is not easily replaced often makes a seller more willing to grant concessions of one kind or another. Because of the relatively small number of digital camera brands, the sellers of lenses and other components used in the manufacture of digital cameras are in a weak bargaining position in their negotiations with buyers of their components.

- *If buyer demand is weak.* Weak or declining demand creates a "buyers' market"; conversely, strong or rapidly growing demand creates a "sellers' market" and shifts bargaining power to sellers.

- *If buyers are well informed about sellers' products, prices, and costs.* The more information buyers have, the better bargaining position they are in. The mushrooming availability of product information on the Internet is giving added bargaining power to individuals. It has become common for automobile shoppers to arrive at dealerships armed with invoice prices, dealer holdback information, a summary of incentives, and manufacturers' financing terms.

- *If buyers pose a credible threat of integrating backward into the business of sellers.* Companies such as Anheuser-Busch, Coors, and Heinz have integrated backward into metal can manufacturing to gain bargaining power in obtaining the balance of their can requirements from otherwise powerful metal can manufacturers.

Figure 3.3 summarizes factors causing buyer bargaining power to be strong or weak.

Not all buyers of an industry's product have equal degrees of bargaining power with sellers, and some may be less sensitive than others to price, quality, or service differences. For example, apparel manufacturers confront significant bargaining power when selling to big retailers such as Macy's, T. J. Maxx, or Target, but they can command much better prices selling to small owner-managed apparel boutiques.

▶FIGURE 3.3 **Factors Affecting the Strength of Buyer Bargaining Power**

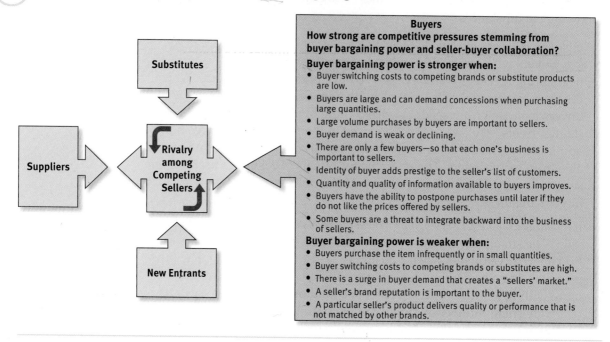

Buyers

How strong are competitive pressures stemming from buyer bargaining power and seller-buyer collaboration?

Buyer bargaining power is stronger when:
- Buyer switching costs to competing brands or substitute products are low.
- Buyers are large and can demand concessions when purchasing large quantities.
- Large volume purchases by buyers are important to sellers.
- Buyer demand is weak or declining.
- There are only a few buyers—so that each one's business is important to sellers.
- Identity of buyer adds prestige to the seller's list of customers.
- Quantity and quality of information available to buyers improves.
- Buyers have the ability to postpone purchases until later if they do not like the prices offered by sellers.
- Some buyers are a threat to integrate backward into the business of sellers.

Buyer bargaining power is weaker when:
- Buyers purchase the item infrequently or in small quantities.
- Buyer switching costs to competing brands or substitutes are high.
- There is a surge in buyer demand that creates a "sellers' market."
- A seller's brand reputation is important to the buyer.
- A particular seller's product delivers quality or performance that is not matched by other brands.

The Competitive Force of Substitute Products

Companies in one industry are vulnerable to competitive pressure from the actions of companies in another industry whenever buyers view the products of the two industries as good substitutes. For instance, the producers of sugar experience competitive pressures from the sales and marketing efforts of the makers of Equal, Splenda, and Sweet'N Low. Similarly, the producers of eyeglasses and contact lenses face competitive pressures from doctors who do corrective laser surgery. First-run movie theater chains are feeling competitive heat as more and more consumers are attracted to simply watch video on demand or movie DVDs at home in media rooms equipped with big-screen, high-definition TVs and surround sound. The producers of metal cans are becoming increasingly engaged in a battle with the makers of retort pouches for the business of companies producing packaged fruits, vegetables, meats, and pet foods. Retort pouches, which are multilayer packages made from polypropylene, aluminum foil, and polyester, are more attractively priced than metal cans because they are less expensive to produce and ship than cans.

Just how strong the competitive pressures are from the sellers of substitute products depends on three factors:

1. *Whether substitutes are readily available and attractively priced.* The presence of readily available and attractively priced substitutes creates competitive pressure by placing a ceiling on the prices industry members can charge. When substitutes are cheaper than an industry's product, industry members come under heavy competitive pressure to reduce their prices and find ways to absorb the price cuts with cost reductions.

2. *Whether buyers view the substitutes as comparable or better in terms of quality, performance, and other relevant attributes.* Customers are prone to compare performance and other attributes as well as price. For example, consumers have found digital cameras to be a superior substitute to film cameras because of the superior ease of use, the ability to download images to a home computer, and the ability to delete bad shots without paying for film developing.

3. *Whether the costs that buyers incur in switching to the substitutes are high or low.* High switching costs deter switching to substitutes while low switching costs make it easier for the sellers of attractive substitutes to lure buyers to their products. Typical switching costs include the inconvenience of switching to a substitute, the costs of additional equipment, the psychological costs of severing old supplier relationships, and employee retraining costs.

Figure 3.4 summarizes the conditions that determine whether the competitive pressures from substitute products are strong, moderate, or weak.

▶ FIGURE 3.4 **Factors Affecting Competition from Substitute Products**

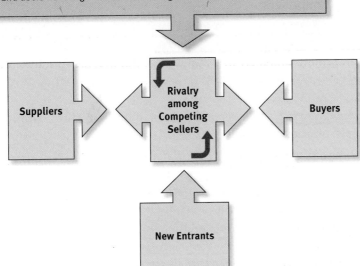

Firms in Other Industries Offering Substitute Products

How strong are competitive pressures coming from substitute products from outside the industry?

Competitive pressures from substitutes are stronger when:
- Good substitutes are readily available or new ones are emerging.
- Substitutes are attractively priced.
- Substitutes have comparable or better performance features.
- End users have low costs in switching to substitutes.
- End users grow more comfortable with using substitutes.

Competitive pressures from substitutes are weaker when:
- Good substitutes are not readily available or don't exist.
- Substitutes are higher priced relative to the performance they deliver.
- End users have high costs in switching to substitutes.

Signs that Competition from Substitutes Is Strong
- Sales of substitutes are growing faster than sales of the industry being analyzed (an indication that the sellers of substitutes are drawing customers away from the industry in question).
- Producers of substitutes are moving to add new capacity.
- Profits of the producers of substitutes are on the rise.

Suppliers → Rivalry among Competing Sellers ← Buyers

New Entrants

Lower P → (Qu) → lower
switch cost => more intense
competit.

As a rule, the lower the price of substitutes, the higher their quality and performance, and the lower the user's switching costs, the more intense the competitive pressures posed by substitute products.

The Competitive Force of Supplier Bargaining Power

Whether the suppliers of industry members represent a weak or strong competitive force depends on the degree to which suppliers have sufficient *bargaining power* to influence the terms and conditions of supply in their favor. Suppliers with strong bargaining power can erode industry profitability by charging industry members higher prices, passing costs on to them, and limiting their opportunities to find better deals. For instance, Microsoft and Intel, both of which supply PC makers with essential components, have been known to use their dominant market status not only to charge PC makers premium prices but also to leverage PC makers in other ways. The bargaining power possessed by Microsoft and Intel when negotiating with customers is so great that both companies have faced antitrust charges on numerous occasions. Before a legal agreement ending the practice, Microsoft pressured PC makers to load only Microsoft products on the PCs they shipped. Intel has also defended against antitrust charges resulting from its bargaining strength, but continues to give PC makers that use the biggest percentages of Intel chips in their PC models top priority in filling orders for newly introduced Intel chips. Being on Intel's list of preferred customers helps a PC maker get an early allocation of Intel's latest chips and thus allows a PC maker to get new models to market ahead of rivals.

The factors that determine whether any of the industry suppliers are in a position to exert substantial bargaining power or leverage are fairly clear-cut:

- *If the item being supplied is a commodity that is readily available from many suppliers.* Suppliers have little or no bargaining power or leverage whenever industry members have the ability to source from any of several alternative and eager suppliers.

- *The ability of industry members to switch their purchases from one supplier to another or to switch to attractive substitutes.* High switching costs increase supplier bargaining power, whereas low switching costs and the ready availability of good substitute inputs weaken supplier bargaining power.

- *If certain inputs are in short supply.* Suppliers of items in short supply have some degree of pricing power.

- *If certain suppliers provide a differentiated input that enhances the performance, quality, or image of the industry's product.* The greater the ability of a particular input to enhance a product's performance, quality, or image, the more bargaining leverage its suppliers are likely to possess.

- *Whether certain suppliers provide equipment or services that deliver cost savings to industry members in conducting their operations.* Suppliers who provide cost-saving equipment or services are likely to possess some degree of bargaining leverage.

- *The fraction of the costs of the industry's product accounted for by the cost of a particular input.* The bigger the cost of a specific part or component, the more opportunity for competition in the marketplace to be affected by the actions of suppliers to raise or lower their prices.

- *If industry members are major customers of suppliers.* As a rule, suppliers have less bargaining leverage when their sales to members of this one industry constitute a big percentage of their total sales. In such cases, the well-being of suppliers is closely tied to the well-being of their major customers.

- *Whether it makes good economic sense for industry members to vertically integrate backward.* The make-or-buy decision generally boils down to whether suppliers are able to supply a particular component at a lower cost than industry members could achieve if they were to integrate backward.

Figure 3.5 summarizes the conditions that tend to make supplier bargaining power strong or weak.

The Competitive Force of Potential New Entrants

Several factors determine whether the threat of new companies entering the marketplace presents a significant competitive pressure. One factor relates to the size of the pool of likely entry candidates and the resources at their command. As a rule, the bigger the pool of entry candidates, the stronger the *threat of potential entry*

▷ FIGURE 3.5 **Factors Affecting the Strength of Supplier Bargaining Power**

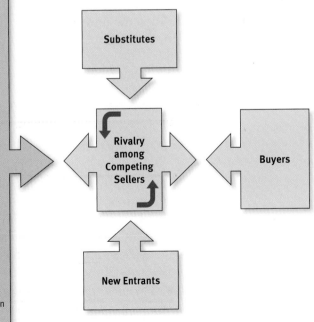

threat of potential entry. This is especially true when some of the likely entry candidates have ample resources to support entry into a new line of business. Frequently, the strongest competitive pressures associated with potential entry come not from outsiders but from current industry participants looking for growth opportunities. *Existing industry members are often strong candidates to enter market segments or geographic areas where they currently do not have a market presence.*

A second factor concerns whether the likely entry candidates face high or low entry barriers. High barriers reduce the competitive threat of potential entry, while low barriers make entry more likely, especially if the industry is growing and offers attractive profit opportunities. The most widely encountered barriers that entry candidates must hurdle include:[2]

- *The presence of sizable economies of scale in production or other areas of operation.* When incumbent companies enjoy cost advantages associated with large-scale operations, outsiders must either enter on a large scale (a costly and perhaps risky move) or accept a cost disadvantage and consequently lower profitability.

- *Cost and resource disadvantages not related to scale of operation.* Aside from enjoying economies of scale, industry incumbents can have cost advantages that stem from the possession of proprietary technology, partnerships with the best and cheapest suppliers, low fixed costs (because they have older facilities that have been mostly depreciated), and experience/learning curve effects. The microprocessor industry is an excellent example of how learning/experience curves put new entrants at a substantial cost disadvantage. Manufacturing unit costs for microprocessors tend to decline about 20 percent each time *cumulative* production volume doubles. With a 20 percent experience curve effect, if the first 1 million chips cost $100 each, once production volume reaches 2 million the unit cost would fall to $80 (80 percent of $100), and by a production volume of 4 million the unit cost would be $64 (80 percent of $80).[3] The bigger the learning or experience curve effect, the bigger the cost advantage of the company with the largest *cumulative* production volume.

- *Strong brand preferences and high degrees of customer loyalty.* The stronger the attachment of buyers to established brands, the harder it is for a newcomer to break into the marketplace.

- *High capital requirements.* The larger the total dollar investment needed to enter the market successfully, the more limited the pool of potential entrants. The most obvious capital requirements for new entrants relate to manufacturing facilities and equipment, introductory advertising and sales promotion campaigns, working capital to finance inventories and customer credit, and sufficient cash to cover start-up costs.

- *The difficulties of building a network of distributors-retailers and securing adequate space on retailers' shelves.* A potential entrant can face numerous distribution channel challenges. Wholesale distributors may be reluctant to take on a product that lacks buyer recognition. Retailers have to be recruited and convinced to give a new brand ample display space and an adequate trial period. Potential entrants sometimes have to "buy" their way into wholesale or retail channels by cutting their prices to provide dealers and distributors with higher markups and profit margins or by giving them big advertising and promotional allowances.

- *Restrictive regulatory policies.* Government agencies can limit or even bar entry by requiring licenses and permits. Regulated industries such as cable TV, telecommunications, electric and gas utilities, and radio and television broadcasting entail government-controlled entry.

- *Tariffs and international trade restrictions.* National governments commonly use tariffs and trade restrictions (antidumping rules, local content requirements, local ownership requirements, quotas, etc.) to raise entry barriers for foreign firms and protect domestic producers from outside competition.

- *The ability and willingness of industry incumbents to launch vigorous initiatives to block a newcomer's successful entry.* Even if a potential entrant has or can acquire the needed competencies and resources to attempt entry, it must still worry about the reaction of existing firms.[4] Sometimes, there's little that incumbents can do to throw obstacles in an entrant's path. But there are times when incumbents use price cuts, increase advertising, introduce product improvements, and launch legal attacks to prevent the entrant from building a clientele. Cable TV companies have vigorously fought the entry of satellite TV into the industry by seeking government intervention to delay satellite providers in offering local stations, offering satellite customers discounts to switch back to cable, and charging satellite customers high monthly rates for cable Internet access.

Figure 3.6 summarizes conditions making the threat of entry strong or weak.

The Competitive Force of Rivalry among Competing Sellers

The strongest of the five competitive forces is nearly always the rivalry among competing sellers of a product or service. In effect, *a market is a competitive battlefield* where there's no end to the campaign for buyer patronage. Rival sellers are prone to employ whatever weapons they have in their business arsenal to improve their market positions, strengthen their market position with buyers, and earn good profits. The strategy-making challenge is to craft a competitive strategy that, at the very least, allows a company to hold its own against rivals and that, ideally, *produces a competitive edge over rivals.* But competitive contests are ongoing and dynamic. When one firm makes a strategic move that produces good results, its rivals typically respond with offensive or defensive countermoves of their own. This pattern of action and reaction produces a continually evolving competitive landscape where the market battle ebbs and flows and produces winners and losers. But the current market leaders have no guarantees of continued leadership. In every industry, the ongoing jockeying of rivals leads to one or more companies

▶FIGURE 3.6 **Factors Affecting the Threat of Entry**

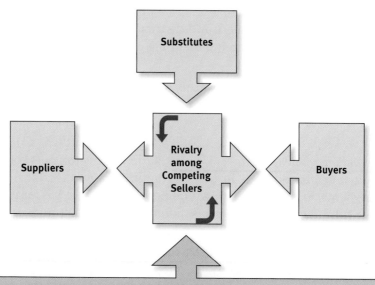

Potential New Entrants

How strong are the competitive pressures associated with the entry threat from new rivals?

Entry threats are stronger when:

- The pool of entry candidates is large and some have resources that would make them formidable market contenders.
- Entry barriers are low or can be readily hurdled by the likely entry candidates.
- Existing industry members are looking to expand their market reach by entering product segments or geographic areas where they currently do not have a presence.
- Newcomers can expect to earn attractive profits.
- Buyer demand is growing rapidly.
- Industry members are unable (or unwilling) to strongly contest the entry of newcomers.

Entry threats are weaker when:

- The pool of entry candidates is small.
- Entry barriers are high.
- Existing competitors are struggling to earn good profits.
- The industry's outlook is risky or uncertain.
- Buyer demand is growing slowly or is stagnant.
- Industry members will strongly contest the efforts of new entrants to gain a market foothold.

gaining or losing momentum in the marketplace according to whether their latest strategic maneuvers succeed or fail.[5]

Figure 3.7 shows a sampling of competitive weapons that firms can deploy in battling rivals and indicates the factors that influence the intensity of their rivalry. Some of the factors that influence the tempo of rivalry among industry competitors include:

- *Rivalry intensifies when competing sellers regularly launch fresh actions to boost their market standing and business performance.* Normally, competitive jockeying among rival sellers is fairly intense. Indicators of strong competitive rivalry include lively price competition, the rapid introduction of next-generation products, and moves to differentiate products by offering better performance features, higher quality, improved customer service, or a wider product selection. Other common tactics used to temporarily boost

▶FIGURE 3.7 **Factors Affecting the Strength of Competitive Rivalry**

Substitutes

Rivalry among Competing Sellers

How strong is seller-related competition?

Rivalry is generally stronger when:

- Competing sellers are active in making fresh moves to improve their market standing and business performance.
- Buyer demand is growing slowly.
- Buyer demand falls off and sellers find themselves with excess capacity and/or inventory.
- The number of rivals increases and rivals are of roughly equal size and competitive capability.
- The products of rival sellers are commodities or else weakly differentiated.
- Buyer costs to switch brands are low.
- Outsiders have recently acquired weak competitors and are trying to turn them into major contenders.

Rivalry is generally weaker when:

- Industry members aren't aggressive in drawing sales and market share away from rivals.
- Buyer demand is growing rapidly.
- The products of rival sellers are strongly differentiated and customer loyalty is high.
- Buyer costs to switch brands are high.
- There are fewer than 5 sellers or else so many rivals that any one company's actions have little direct impact on rivals' business.

Suppliers

Buyers

Typical "Weapons" for Battling Rivals and Attracting Buyers

- Lower prices
- More or different features
- Better product performance
- Higher quality
- Stronger brand image
- Wider selection of models
- Bigger/better dealer network
- Low interest rate financing
- Higher levels of advertising
- Better customer service
- Product customization

New Entrants

sales include special sales promotions, heavy advertising, rebates, or low-interest-rate financing.

- *Rivalry is stronger in industries where competitors are equal in size and capability.* Competitive rivalry in the quick-service restaurant industry is particularly strong where there are numerous relatively equal-sized hamburger, deli sandwich, chicken, and taco chains. For the most part, McDonald's, Burger King, Taco Bell, KFC, Arby's, and other national fast-food chains have comparable capabilities and are required to compete aggressively to hold their own in the industry.

- *Rivalry is usually stronger in slow-growing markets and weaker in fast-growing markets.* Rapidly expanding buyer demand produces enough new business for all industry members to grow. But in markets where growth is sluggish or where buyer demand drops off unexpectedly, it is not uncommon for competitive rivalry to intensify significantly as rivals battle for market share and volume gains.

- *Rivalry is usually weaker in industries comprised of vast numbers of small rivals; likewise, it is often weak when there are fewer than five competitors.* Head-to-head rivalry tends to be weak once an industry becomes populated with so many rivals that the strategic moves of any one competitor have little discernible impact on the success of rivals. Rivalry also *tends* to be weak if an industry consists of just two to four sellers. In a market with few rivals, each competitor soon learns that aggressive moves to grow its sales and market share can have an immediate adverse impact on rivals' businesses, almost certainly provoking vigorous retaliation. However, some caution must be exercised in concluding that rivalry is weak just because there are only a few competitors. The fierceness of the current battle between Google and Microsoft and the decades-long war between Coca-Cola and Pepsi are prime examples.

- *Rivalry increases when buyer demand falls off and sellers find themselves with excess capacity and/or inventory.* Excess supply conditions create a "buyers' market," putting added competitive pressure on industry rivals to scramble for profitable sales levels (often by price discounting).

- *Rivalry increases as it becomes less costly for buyers to switch brands.* The less expensive it is for buyers to switch their purchases from the seller of one brand to the seller of another brand, the easier it is for sellers to steal customers away from rivals.

- *Rivalry increases as the products of rival sellers become more standardized and diminishes as the products of industry rivals become more differentiated.* When the offerings of rivals are identical or weakly differentiated, buyers have less reason to be brand loyal—a condition that makes it easier for rivals to persuade buyers to switch to their offering. On the other hand, strongly differentiated product offerings among rivals breed high brand loyalty on the part of buyers.

- *Rivalry is more intense when industry conditions tempt competitors to use price cuts or other competitive weapons to boost unit volume.* When a product is perishable, seasonal, or costly to hold in inventory, competitive pressures build quickly any time one or more firms decide to cut prices and dump supplies on the market. Likewise, whenever fixed costs account for a large fraction of total cost, so that unit costs tend to be lowest at or near full capacity, firms come under significant pressure to cut prices or otherwise try to boost sales whenever they are operating below full capacity.

- *Rivalry increases when one or more competitors become dissatisfied with their market position.* Firms that are losing ground or are in financial trouble often pursue aggressive (or perhaps desperate) turnaround strategies that can involve price discounts, greater advertising, or merger with other rivals. Such strategies can turn competitive pressures up a notch.

- *Rivalry increases when strong companies outside the industry acquire weak firms in the industry and launch aggressive, well-funded moves to build market share.* A concerted effort to turn a weak rival into a market leader nearly always entails launching well-financed strategic initiatives to dramatically improve the competitor's product offering, excite buyer interest, and win a much bigger market share—actions that, if successful, put added pressure on rivals to counter with fresh strategic moves of their own.

Rivalry can be characterized as *cutthroat* or *brutal* when competitors engage in protracted price wars or habitually employ other aggressive tactics that are mutually destructive to profitability. Rivalry can be considered *fierce* to *strong* when the battle for market share is so vigorous that the profit margins of most industry members are squeezed to bare-bones levels. Rivalry can be characterized as *moderate* or *normal* when the maneuvering among industry members, while lively and healthy, still allows most industry members to earn acceptable profits. Rivalry is *weak* when most companies in the industry are relatively well satisfied with their sales growth and market share and rarely undertake offensives to steal customers away from one another.

The Collective Strengths of the Five Competitive Forces and Industry Profitability

Scrutinizing each of the five competitive forces one by one provides a powerful diagnosis of what competition is like in a given market. Once the strategist has gained an understanding of the competitive pressures associated with each of the five forces, the next step is to evaluate the collective strength of the five forces and determine if companies in this industry should reasonably expect to earn decent profits.

As a rule, the stronger the collective impact of the five competitive forces, the lower the combined profitability of industry participants. The most extreme case of a "competitively unattractive" industry is when all five forces are producing strong competitive pressures: Rivalry among sellers is vigorous, low entry barriers allow new rivals to gain a market foothold, competition from substitutes is intense, and both suppliers and customers are able to exercise considerable bargaining leverage. Fierce to strong competitive pressures coming from all five directions nearly always drive industry profitability to unacceptably low levels, frequently producing losses for many industry members and forcing some out of business. But an industry can be competitively unattractive without all five competitive forces being strong. Fierce competitive pressures from just one of the five forces, such as brutal price competition among rival sellers, may suffice to destroy the conditions for good profitability.

> The stronger the forces of competition, the harder it becomes for industry members to attractive profits.

In contrast, when the collective impact of the five competitive forces is moderate to weak, an industry is competitively attractive in the sense that industry members can reasonably expect to earn good profits and a nice return on investment. The ideal competitive environment for earning superior profits is one in which both suppliers and customers are in weak bargaining positions, there are no good substitutes, high barriers block further entry, and rivalry among present sellers generates only moderate competitive pressures. Weak competition is the best of all possible worlds for companies with mediocre strategies and second-rate implementation because even they can expect a decent profit.

QUESTION 3: WHAT ARE THE INDUSTRY'S DRIVING FORCES OF CHANGE AND WHAT IMPACT WILL THEY HAVE?

The intensity of competitive forces and the level of industry attractiveness are almost always fluid and subject to change. It is essential for strategy makers to understand the current competitive dynamics of the industry, but it is equally important for strategy makers to consider how the industry is changing and the effect of industry changes that are under way. Any strategies devised by management will play out in a dynamic industry environment, so it's imperative that such plans consider what the industry environment might look like during the near term.

The Concept of Industry Driving Forces

Industry and competitive conditions change because forces are enticing or pressuring certain industry participants (competitors, customers, suppliers) to alter their actions in important ways. The most powerful of the change agents are called **driving forces** because they have the biggest influences in reshaping the industry landscape and altering competitive conditions. Some driving forces originate in the outer ring of the company's macro-environment (see Figure 3.1) but most originate in the company's more immediate industry and competitive environment.

> **CORE CONCEPT**
>
> **Driving forces** are the major underlying causes of change in industry and competitive conditions.

Driving forces analysis has three steps: (1) identifying what the driving forces are, (2) assessing whether the drivers of change are, individually or collectively, acting to make the industry more or less attractive, and (3) determining what strategy changes are needed to prepare for the impact of the driving forces.

[Handwritten margin notes:]

Analyss
✓ Identify the DF
✓ Assess whether the DF are indiv or collect acting
✓ Determin what strat chges are needed

Identifying an Industry's Driving Forces

Many developments can affect an industry powerfully enough to qualify as driving forces, but most drivers of industry and competitive change fall into one of the following categories:

- *Changes in an industry's long-term growth rate.* Shifts in industry growth have the potential to affect the balance between industry supply and buyer demand, entry and exit, and the character and strength of competition. An upsurge in buyer demand triggers a race among established firms and newcomers to capture the new sales opportunities. A slowdown in the growth of demand nearly always brings an increase in rivalry and increased efforts by some firms to maintain their high rates of growth by taking sales and market share away from rivals.

- *Increasing globalization.* Competition begins to shift from primarily a regional or national focus to an international or global focus when industry members begin seeking out customers in foreign markets or when production activities begin to migrate to countries where costs are lowest. The forces of globalization are sometimes such a strong driver that companies find it highly advantageous, if not necessary, to spread their operating reach into more and more country markets. Globalization is very much a driver of industry change in such industries as credit cards, mobile phones, digital cameras, motor vehicles, steel, petroleum, personal computers, and video games.

- *Emerging new Internet capabilities and applications.* Mushrooming Internet use and an ever-growing series of Internet applications and capabilities have been major drivers of change in industry after industry. The ability of companies to reach consumers via the Internet increases the number of rivals a company faces and often escalates rivalry by pitting pure online sellers against local brick-and-mortar sellers. The Internet gives buyers unprecedented ability to research the product offerings of competitors and shop the market for the best value. Widespread use of e-mail has forever eroded the business of providing fax services and the first-class mail delivery revenues of governmental postal services worldwide. Videoconferencing via the Internet erodes the demand for business travel. Online course offerings are profoundly affecting higher education. The Internet of the future will feature faster speeds, dazzling applications, and over a billion connected gadgets performing an array of functions, thus driving further industry and competitive changes. But Internet-related impacts vary from industry to industry. The challenges here are to assess precisely how emerging Internet developments are altering a particular industry's landscape and to factor these impacts into the strategy-making equation.

- *Changes in who buys the product and how they use it.* Shifts in buyer demographics and the ways products are used can alter competition by affecting how customers perceive value, how customers make purchasing decisions, and where customers purchase the product. The burgeoning popularity of downloading and streaming music from the Internet has significantly changed the recording industry. According to IFPI, digital music accounted for more than 25 percent of industry sales in 2009. However, the ability of consumers to purchase individual tracks rather than albums and share files among other users caused industry sales to decline by 30 percent between 2004 and 2009.

- *Product innovation.* An ongoing stream of product innovations tends to alter the pattern of competition in an industry by attracting more first-time buyers, rejuvenating industry growth, and/or creating wider or narrower product differentiation among rival sellers. Product innovation has been a key driving force in such industries as computers, digital cameras, televisions, video games, and prescription drugs.

- *Technological change and manufacturing process innovation.* Advances in technology can dramatically alter an industry's landscape, making it possible to produce new and better products at lower cost and opening new industry frontiers. For instance, Voice over Internet Protocol technology (VoIP) has spawned low-cost, Internet-based phone networks that have begun competing with traditional telephone companies worldwide (whose higher-cost technology depends on hard-wire connections via overhead and underground telephone lines).

- *Marketing innovation.* When firms are successful in introducing *new ways* to market their products, they can spark a burst of buyer interest, widen industry demand, increase product differentiation, and lower unit costs—any or all of which can alter the competitive positions of rival firms and force strategy revisions.

- *Entry or exit of major firms.* The entry of one or more foreign companies into a geographic market once dominated by domestic firms nearly always shakes up competitive conditions. Likewise, when an established domestic firm from another industry attempts entry either by acquisition or by launching its own start-up venture, it usually pushes competition in new directions.

- *Diffusion of technical know-how across more companies and more countries.* As knowledge about how to perform a particular activity or execute a particular manufacturing technology spreads, the competitive advantage held by firms originally possessing this know-how erodes. Knowledge diffusion can occur through scientific journals, trade publications, on-site plant tours, word of mouth among suppliers and customers, employee migration, and Internet sources.

- *Changes in cost and efficiency.* Widening or shrinking differences in the costs among key competitors tend to dramatically alter the state of competition. Declining costs to produce PCs have enabled price cuts and spurred PC sales (especially lower-priced models) by making them more affordable to lower-income households worldwide.

- *Growing buyer preferences for differentiated products instead of a commodity product (or for a more standardized product instead of strongly differentiated products).* When a shift from standardized to differentiated products occurs, rivals must adopt strategies to outdifferentiate one another. However, buyers sometimes decide that a standardized, budget-priced product suits their requirements as well as a premium-priced product with lots of snappy features and personalized services.

- *Regulatory influences and government policy changes.* Government regulatory actions can often force significant changes in industry practices and strategic approaches. Net neutrality rules established by the Federal Communications Commission (FCC) in 2010 had the potential to alter the cost structure, capital budgets, and pricing policies of Internet service providers such as Comcast and AT&T. The FCC net neutrality policy was implemented to prevent Internet service providers from limiting the download speed of bandwidth-consuming content such as video. The requirement to treat all content equally would require greater investments in infrastructure and generate additional costs for such providers. However, the addition of broadband capacity would allow content providers to potentially boost site traffic by making more content requiring a large amount of bandwidth to consumers. In 2011, most content providers were pushing for full implementation of the FCC's net neutrality policies because such policies created new revenue opportunities, while Internet service providers were lobbying Congress to pass legislation restricting the FCC's authority over Internet service to avoid additional capital expenditures, higher operating costs, and price increases to customers.

- *Changing societal concerns, attitudes, and lifestyles.* Emerging social issues and changing attitudes and lifestyles can be powerful instigators of industry change. Consumer concerns about salt, sugar, chemical additives, saturated fat, cholesterol, carbohydrates, and nutritional value have forced food producers to revamp food-processing techniques, redirect R&D efforts into the use of healthier ingredients, and compete in developing nutritious, good-tasting products.

While many forces of change may be at work in a given industry, *no more than three or four* are likely to be true driving forces powerful enough to qualify as the *major determinants* of why and how the industry is changing. Thus, company strategists must resist the temptation to label every change they see as a driving force. Table 3.2 lists the most common driving forces.

Assessing the Impact of the Industry Driving Forces

The second step in driving forces analysis is to determine whether the prevailing driving forces are acting to make the industry environment more or less attractive. Getting a handle on the collective impact of the driving forces usually requires looking at the likely effects of each force separately, because the driving forces may not all be pushing change in the same direction. For example, two driving forces may be acting to spur demand for the industry's product while one driving force may be working to curtail demand. Whether the net effect on industry demand is up or down hinges on which driving forces are the more powerful.

> An important part of driving forces analysis is to determine whether the individual or collective impact of the driving forces will be to increase or decrease market demand, make competition more or less intense, and lead to higher or lower industry profitability.

► TABLE 3.2

Common Driving Forces

1. Changes in the long-term industry growth rate.
2. Increasing globalization.
3. Emerging new Internet capabilities and applications.
4. Changes in who buys the product and how they use it.
5. Product innovation.
6. Technological change and manufacturing process innovation.
7. Marketing innovation.
8. Entry or exit of major firms.
9. Diffusion of technical know-how across more companies and more countries.
10. Changes in cost and efficiency.
11. Growing buyer preferences for differentiated products instead of a standardized commodity product (or for a more standardized product instead of strongly differentiated products).
12. Regulatory influences and government policy changes.
13. Changing societal concerns, attitudes, and lifestyles.

Determining Strategy Changes Needed to Prepare for the Impact of Driving Forces

The third step of driving forces analysis—where the real payoff for strategy making comes—is for managers to draw some conclusions about what strategy adjustments will be needed to deal with the impact of the driving forces. Without understanding the forces driving industry change and the impacts these forces will have on the industry environment over the next one to three years, managers are ill prepared to craft a strategy tightly matched to emerging conditions. Similarly, if managers are uncertain about the implications of one or more driving forces, or if their views are off-base, it will be difficult for them to craft a strategy that is responsive to the consequences of driving forces. So driving forces analysis is not something to take lightly; it has practical value and is basic to the task of thinking strategically about where the industry is headed and how to prepare for the changes ahead.

> The real payoff of driving forces analysis is to help managers understand what strategy changes are needed to prepare for the impacts of the driving forces.

QUESTION 4: HOW ARE INDUSTRY RIVALS POSITIONED?

The nature of competitive strategy inherently positions companies competing in an industry into strategic groups with diverse price/quality ranges, different distribution channels, varying product features, and different geographic coverages. The best technique for revealing the market positions of industry competitors is **strategic group mapping**. This analytical tool is useful for comparing the market positions of industry competitors or for grouping industry combatants into like positions.

> **CORE CONCEPT**
> **Strategic group mapping** is a technique for displaying the different market or competitive positions that rival firms occupy in the industry.

Using Strategic Group Maps to Assess the Positioning of Key Competitors

A **strategic group** consists of those industry members with similar competitive approaches and positions in the market. Companies in the same strategic group can resemble one another in any of several ways—they may have comparable product-line breadth, sell in the same price/quality range, emphasize the same distribution channels, use essentially the same product attributes to appeal to similar types of buyers, depend on identical technological approaches, or offer buyers similar services and technical assistance.[6] An industry with a commodity-like product may contain only one strategic group whereby all sellers pursue essentially identical strategies and have comparable market positions. But even with commodity products, there is

> **CORE CONCEPT**
> A **strategic group** is a cluster of industry rivals that have similar competitive approaches and market positions.

likely some attempt at differentiation occurring in the form of varying delivery times, financing terms, or levels of customer service. Most industries offer a host of competitive approaches that allow companies to find unique industry positioning and avoid fierce competition in a crowded strategic group. Evaluating strategy options entails examining what strategic groups exist, identifying which companies exist within each group, and determining if a competitive "white space" exists where industry competitors are able to create and capture altogether new demand.

The procedure for constructing a *strategic group map* is straightforward:

- Identify the competitive characteristics that delineate strategic approaches used in the industry. Typical variables used in creating strategic group maps are the price/quality range (high, medium, low), geographic coverage (local, regional, national, global), degree of vertical integration (none, partial, full), product-line breadth (wide, narrow), choice of distribution channels (retail, wholesale, Internet, multiple channels), and degree of service offered (no-frills, limited, full).

- Plot firms on a two-variable map based upon their strategic approaches.

- Assign firms occupying the same map location to a common strategic group.

- Draw circles around each strategic group, making the circles proportional to the size of the group's share of total industry sales revenues.

This produces a two-dimensional diagram like the one for the retail chain store industry in Concepts & Connections 3.1.

Several guidelines need to be observed in creating strategic group maps. First, the two variables selected as axes for the map should not be highly correlated; if they are, the circles on the map will fall along a diagonal and strategy makers will learn nothing more about the relative positions of competitors than they would by considering just one of the variables. For instance, if companies with broad product lines use multiple distribution channels while companies with narrow lines use a single distribution channel, then looking at product line breadth reveals just as much about industry positioning as looking at the two competitive variables. Second, the variables chosen as axes for the map should reflect key approaches to offering value to customers and expose big differences in how rivals position themselves in the marketplace. Third, the variables used as axes don't have to be either quantitative or continuous; rather, they can be discrete variables or defined in terms of distinct classes and combinations. Fourth, drawing the sizes of the circles on the map proportional to the combined sales of the firms in each strategic group allows the map to reflect the relative sizes of each strategic group. Fifth, if more than two good competitive variables can be used as axes for the map, multiple maps can be drawn to give different exposures to the competitive positioning in the industry. Because there is not necessarily one best map for portraying how competing firms are positioned in the market, it is advisable to experiment with different pairs of competitive variables.

CONCEPTS & CONNECTIONS 3.1

COMPARATIVE MARKET POSITIONS OF SELECTED RETAIL CHAINS: A STRATEGIC GROUP MAP APPLICATION

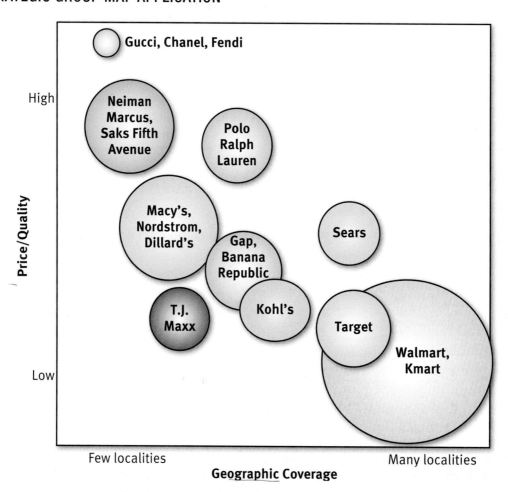

Note: Circles are drawn roughly proportional to the total revenues of the retail chains included in each strategic group.

The Value of Strategic Group Maps

Strategic group maps are revealing in several respects. The *most important* has to do with identifying which rivals are similarly positioned and are thus close rivals and which are distant rivals. Generally, *the closer strategic groups are to each other on the map, the stronger the cross-group competitive rivalry tends to be.* Although firms in the same strategic group are the closest rivals, the next closest rivals are in the immediately adjacent groups.[7] Often, firms in strategic groups that are far apart on the map hardly compete at all. For instance,

Walmart's clientele, merchandise selection, and pricing points are much too different to justify calling them close competitors of Neiman Marcus or Saks Fifth Avenue in retailing. For the same reason, Timex is not a meaningful competitive rival of Rolex, and Kia is not a close competitor of Porsche or Lexus.

> Some strategic groups are more favorably positioned than others because they confront weaker competitive forces and/or because they are more favorably impacted by industry driving forces.

The second thing to be gleaned from strategic group mapping is that *not all positions on the map are equally attractive.* Two reasons account for why some positions can be more attractive than others:

1. *Industry driving forces may favor some strategic groups and hurt others.* Driving forces in an industry may be acting to grow the demand for the products of firms in some strategic groups and shrink the demand for the products of firms in other strategic groups—as is the case in the news industry where Internet news services and cable news networks are gaining ground at the expense of newspapers and network television. The industry driving forces of emerging Internet capabilities and applications, changes in who buys the product and how they use it, and changing societal concerns, attitudes, and lifestyles are making it increasingly difficult for traditional media to increase audiences and attract new advertisers.

2. *Competitive pressures may cause the profit potential of different strategic groups to vary.* The profit prospects of firms in different strategic groups can vary from good to poor because of differing degrees of competitive rivalry within strategic groups, differing degrees of exposure to competition from substitute products outside the industry, and differing degrees of supplier or customer bargaining power from group to group. For instance, the competitive battle between Walmart and Target is more intense (with consequently smaller profit margins) than the rivalry among Versace, Chanel, Fendi, and other high-end fashion retailers.

Thus, part of strategic group analysis always entails drawing conclusions about where on the map is the "best" place to be and why. Which companies or strategic groups are in the best positions to prosper and which might be expected to struggle? And equally important, how might firms in poorly positioned strategic groups reposition themselves to improve their prospects for good financial performance?

QUESTION 5: WHAT STRATEGIC MOVES ARE RIVALS LIKELY TO MAKE NEXT?

As in sports, scouting the business opposition is an essential part of game plan development. **Competitive intelligence** about rivals' strategies, their latest actions and announcements, their resources and organizational capabilities, and the thinking and leadership styles of their executives is valuable for predicting the strategic moves competitors are likely to make next. Having good information to predict the likely moves of key competitors allows a company to prepare defensive countermoves and to exploit any openings that arise from competitors' missteps.

CONCEPTS & CONNECTIONS 3.2

BUSINESS ETHICS AND COMPETITIVE INTELLIGENCE

Those who gather competitive intelligence on rivals can sometimes cross the fine line between honest inquiry and unethical or even illegal behavior. For example, calling rivals to get information about prices, the dates of new-product introductions, or wage and salary levels is legal, but misrepresenting one's company affiliation during such calls is unethical. Pumping rivals' representatives at trade shows is ethical only if one wears a name tag with accurate company affiliation indicated. Avon Products at one point secured information about its biggest rival, Mary Kay Cosmetics (MKC), by having its personnel search through the garbage bins outside MKC's headquarters.[8] When MKC officials learned of the action and sued, Avon claimed it did nothing illegal because a 1988 Supreme Court ruling declared that trash left on public property (in this case, a sidewalk) was anyone's for the taking. Avon even produced a videotape of its removal of the trash at the MKC site. Avon won the lawsuit—but Avon's action, while legal, scarcely qualifies as ethical.

Considerations in trying to predict what strategic moves rivals are likely to make next include the following:

- What executives are saying about where the industry is headed, the firm's situation, and their past actions and leadership styles.

- Identifying trends in the timing of product launches or new marketing promotions.

- Determining which rivals badly need to increase unit sales and market share.

- Considering which rivals have a strong incentive, along with the resources, to make major strategic changes.

- Knowing which rivals are likely to enter new geographic markets.

- Deciding which rivals are strong candidates to expand their product offerings and enter new product segments.

To succeed in predicting a competitor's next moves, company strategists need to have a good understanding of each rival's situation, its pattern of behavior and preferences in responding to prior strategic attacks, what its best strategic options are, and how rival management measures success. Doing the necessary detective work can be tedious and time-consuming, but scouting competitors well enough to anticipate their next moves allows managers to prepare effective countermoves and to take rivals' probable actions into account in crafting their own offensive strategies.[9] Concepts & Connections 3.2 discusses the ethical limits to gathering competitive intelligence.

> Studying competitors' past behavior and preferences provides a valuable assist in anticipating what moves rivals are likely to make next and outmaneuvering them in the marketplace.

QUESTION 6: WHAT ARE THE INDUSTRY KEY SUCCESS FACTORS?

An industry's **key success factors (KSFs)** are those competitive factors that most affect industry members' ability to prosper in the marketplace. Key success factors may include particular strategy elements, product attributes, resources, competitive capabilities, or intangible assets. KSFs by their very nature are so important to future competitive success that *all firms* in the industry must pay close attention to them or risk an eventual exit from the industry.

> ### CORE CONCEPT
> **Key success factors** are the strategy elements, product attributes, competitive capabilities, or intangible assets with the greatest impact on future success in the marketplace.

In the ready-to-wear apparel industry, the KSFs are appealing designs and color combinations, low-cost manufacturing, a strong network of retailers or company-owned stores, distribution capabilities that allow stores to keep the best-selling items in stock, and advertisements that effectively convey the brand's image. These attributes and capabilities apply to all brands of apparel ranging from private-label brands sold by discounters to premium-priced ready-to-wear brands sold by upscale department stores. Table 3.3 on the next page lists the most common types of industry key success factors.

An industry's key success factors can usually be deduced through identifying the industry's dominant characteristics, assessing the five competitive forces, considering the impacts of the driving forces, comparing the market positions of industry members, and forecasting the likely next moves of key rivals. In addition, the answers to the following three questions help identify an industry's key success factors:

1. On what basis do buyers of the industry's product choose between the competing brands of sellers? That is, what product attributes are crucial?
2. Given the nature of the competitive forces prevailing in the marketplace, what resources and competitive capabilities does a company need to have to be competitively successful?
3. What shortcomings are almost certain to put a company at a significant competitive disadvantage?

Only rarely are there more than five or six key factors for future competitive success. Managers should therefore resist the temptation to label a factor that has only minor importance a KSF. To compile a list of every factor that matters even a little bit defeats the purpose of concentrating management attention on the factors truly critical to long-term competitive success.

QUESTION 7: DOES THE INDUSTRY OFFER GOOD PROSPECTS FOR ATTRACTIVE PROFITS?

The final step in evaluating the industry and competitive environment is boiling down the results of the analyses performed in Questions 1–6 to determine if the industry offers a company strong prospects for attractive profits.

▶**LO3**

Learn how to determine whether an industry's outlook presents a company with sufficiently attractive opportunities for growth and profitability.

▶ TABLE 3.3

Common Types of Industry Key Success Factors

Technology-related KSFs	• Expertise in a particular technology or in scientific research (important in pharmaceuticals, Internet applications, mobile communications, and most high-tech industries) • Proven ability to improve production processes (important in industries where advancing technology opens the way for higher manufacturing efficiency and lower production costs)
Manufacturing-related KSFs	• Ability to achieve scale economies and/or capture experience curve effects (important to achieving low production costs) • Quality control know-how (important in industries where customers insist on product reliability) • High utilization of fixed assets (important in capital-intensive/high-fixed-cost industries) • Access to attractive supplies of skilled labor • High labor productivity (important for items with high labor content) • Low-cost product design and engineering (reduces manufacturing costs) • Ability to manufacture or assemble products that are customized to buyer specifications
Distribution-related KSFs	• A strong network of wholesale distributors/dealers • Strong direct sales capabilities via the Internet and/or having company-owned retail outlets • Ability to secure favorable display space on retailer shelves
Marketing-related KSFs	• Breadth of product line and product selection • A well-known and well-respected brand name • Fast, accurate technical assistance • Courteous, personalized customer service • Accurate filling of buyer orders (few back orders or mistakes) • Customer guarantees and warranties (important in mail-order and online retailing, big-ticket purchases, and new-product introductions) • Clever advertising
Skills- and capability-related KSFs	• A talented workforce (superior talent is important in professional services such as accounting and investment banking) • National or global distribution capabilities • Product innovation capabilities (important in industries where rivals are racing to be first to market with new product attributes or performance features) • Design expertise (important in fashion and apparel industries) • Short delivery time capability • Supply chain management capabilities • Strong e-commerce capabilities—a user-friendly website and/or skills in using Internet technology applications to streamline internal operations
Other types of KSFs	• Overall low costs (not just in manufacturing) to be able to meet low-price expectations of customers • Convenient locations (important in many retailing businesses) • Ability to provide fast, convenient, after-the-sale repairs and service • A strong balance sheet and access to financial capital (important in newly emerging industries with high degrees of business risk and in capital-intensive industries) • Patent protection

The important factors on which to base such a conclusion include:

- The industry's growth potential.
- Whether powerful competitive forces are squeezing industry profitability to subpar levels and whether competition appears destined to grow stronger or weaker.
- Whether industry profitability will be favorably or unfavorably affected by the prevailing driving forces.
- The company's competitive position in the industry vis-à-vis rivals. (Well-entrenched leaders or strongly positioned contenders have a much better chance of earning attractive margins than those fighting a steep uphill battle.)
- How competently the company performs industry key success factors.

It is a mistake to think of a particular industry as being equally attractive or unattractive to all industry participants and all potential entrants. Conclusions have to be drawn from the perspective of a particular company. Industries attractive to insiders may be unattractive to outsiders. Industry environments unattractive to weak competitors may be attractive to strong competitors. A favorably positioned company may survey a business environment and see a host of opportunities that weak competitors cannot capture.

> The degree to which an industry is attractive or unattractive is not the same for all industry participants and potential new entrants. The attractiveness of an industry depends on the degree of fit between a company's competitive capabilities and industry key success factors.

When a company decides an industry is fundamentally attractive, a strong case can be made that it should invest aggressively to capture the opportunities it sees. When a strong competitor concludes an industry is relatively unattractive, it may elect to simply protect its present position, investing cautiously if at all, and begin looking for opportunities in other industries. A competitively weak company in an unattractive industry may see its best option as finding a buyer, perhaps a rival, to acquire its business.

⇒ ⇒ KEY POINTS

Thinking strategically about a company's external situation involves probing for answers to the following seven questions:

1. *What are the industry's dominant economic features?* Industries differ significantly on such factors as market size and growth rate, the number and relative sizes of both buyers and sellers, the geographic scope of competitive rivalry, the degree of product differentiation, the speed of product innovation, demand-supply conditions, the extent of vertical integration, and the extent of scale economies and learning curve effects.

2. *What kinds of competitive forces are industry members facing, and how strong is each force?* The strength of competition is a composite of five forces: (1) competitive pressures stemming from buyer bargaining power and seller-buyer collaboration, (2) competitive pressures associated with the sellers of substitutes, (3) competitive pressures stemming from supplier bargaining power and supplier-seller collaboration,

(4) competitive pressures associated with the threat of new entrants into the market, and (5) competitive pressures stemming from the competitive jockeying among industry rivals.

3. *What forces are driving changes in the industry, and what impact will these changes have on competitive intensity and industry profitability?* Industry and competitive conditions change because forces are in motion that create incentives or pressures for change. The first phase is to identify the forces that are driving industry change. The second phase of driving forces analysis is to determine whether the driving forces, taken together, are acting to make the industry environment more or less attractive.

4. *What market positions do industry rivals occupy—who is strongly positioned and who is not?* Strategic group mapping is a valuable tool for understanding the similarities and differences inherent in the market positions of rival companies. Rivals in the same or nearby strategic groups are close competitors, whereas companies in distant strategic groups usually pose little or no immediate threat. Some strategic groups are more favorable than others. The profit potential of different strategic groups may not be the same because industry driving forces and competitive forces likely have varying effects on the industry's distinct strategic groups.

5. *What strategic moves are rivals likely to make next?* Scouting competitors well enough to anticipate their actions can help a company prepare effective countermoves (perhaps even beating a rival to the punch) and allows managers to take rivals' probable actions into account in designing their own company's best course of action.

6. *What are the key factors for competitive success?* An industry's key success factors (KSFs) are the particular product attributes, competitive capabilities, and intangible assets that spell the difference between being a strong competitor and a weak competitor—and sometimes between profit and loss. KSFs by their very nature are so important to competitive success that *all firms* in the industry must pay close attention to them or risk being driven out of the industry.

7. *Does the outlook for the industry present the company with sufficiently attractive prospects for profitability?* Conclusions regarding industry attractiveness are a major driver of company strategy. When a company decides an industry is fundamentally attractive and presents good opportunities, a strong case can be made that it should invest aggressively to capture the opportunities it sees. When a strong competitor concludes an industry is relatively unattractive and lacking in opportunity, it may elect to simply protect its present position, investing cautiously if at all and looking for opportunities in other industries. A competitively weak company in an unattractive industry may see its best option as finding a buyer, perhaps a rival, to acquire its business. On occasion, an industry that is unattractive overall is still very attractive to a favorably situated company with the skills and resources to take business away from weaker rivals.

ASSURANCE OF LEARNING EXERCISES

LO1, LO2

1. Prepare a brief analysis of the coffee industry using the information provided on industry trade association websites. Based upon information provided on the websites of these associations, draw a five-forces diagram for the coffee industry and briefly discuss the nature and strength of each of the five competitive forces.

2. Based on the strategic group map in Concepts & Connections 3.1, who are Nordstrom's closest competitors? Between which two strategic groups is competition the strongest? Why do you think no retail chains are positioned in the upper-right corner of the map? Which company/strategic group faces the weakest competition from the members of other strategic groups?

LO1

≣ connect
www.mcgrawhillconnect.com

3. The Snack Food Association publishes an annual state-of-the-industry report that can be found at www.sfa.org. Based on information in the latest report, does it appear that the economic characteristics of the industry will present industry participants with attractive opportunities for growth and profitability? Explain.

LO1, LO3

→ → EXERCISES FOR SIMULATION PARTICIPANTS

1. Which of the five competitive forces is creating the strongest competitive pressures for your company?

LO1, LO2, LO3

2. What are the "weapons of competition" that rival companies in your industry can use to gain sales and market share? See Figure 3.7 to help you identify the various competitive factors.

3. What are the factors affecting the intensity of rivalry in the industry in which your company is competing? Use Figure 3.7 and the accompanying discussion to help you in pinpointing the specific factors most affecting competitive intensity. Would you characterize the rivalry and jockeying for better market position, increased sales, and market share among the companies in your industry as fierce, very strong, strong, moderate, or relatively weak? Why?

4. Are there any driving forces in the industry in which your company is competing? What impact will these driving forces have? Will they cause competition to be more or less intense? Will they act to boost or squeeze profit margins? List at least two actions your company should consider taking to combat any negative impacts of the driving forces.

5. Draw a strategic group map showing the market positions of the companies in your industry. Which companies do you believe are in the most attractive position on the map? Which companies are the most weakly positioned? Which companies do you believe are likely to try to move to a different position on the strategic group map?

6. What do you see as the key factors for being a successful competitor in your industry? List at least three.

7. Does your overall assessment of the industry suggest that industry rivals have sufficiently attractive opportunities for growth and profitability? Explain.

ENDNOTES

1. Michael E. Porter, *Competitive Strategy: Techniques for Analyzing Industries and Competitors* (New York: Free Press, 1980), chap. 1; Michael E. Porter, "The Five Competitive Forces That Shape Strategy," *Harvard Business Review* 86, no. 1 (January 2008).

2. J. S. Bain, *Barriers to New Competition* (Cambridge, MA: Harvard University Press, 1956); F. M. Scherer, *Industrial Market Structure and Economic Performance* (Chicago: Rand McNally & Co., 1971).

3. Pankaj Ghemawat, "Building Strategy on the Experience Curve," *Harvard Business Review* 64, no. 2 (March–April 1985).

4. Michael E. Porter, "How Competitive Forces Shape Strategy," *Harvard Business Review* 57, no. 2 (March–April 1979)

5. Pamela J. Derfus, Patrick G. Maggitti, Curtis M. Grimm, and Ken G. Smith, "The Red Queen Effect: Competitive Actions and Firm Performance," *Academy of Management Journal* 51, no. 1 (February 2008).

6. Mary Ellen Gordon and George R. Milne, "Selecting the Dimensions That Define Strategic Groups: A Novel Market-Driven Approach," *Journal of Managerial Issues* 11, no. 2 (Summer 1999).

7. Avi Fiegenbaum and Howard Thomas, "Strategic Groups as Reference Groups: Theory, Modeling and Empirical Examination of Industry and Competitive Strategy," *Strategic Management Journal* 16 (1995); and S. Ade Olusoga, Michael P. Mokwa, and Charles H. Noble, "Strategic Groups, Mobility Barriers, and Competitive Advantage," *Journal of Business Research* 33 (1995).

8. Larry Kahaner, *Competitive Intelligence* (New York: Simon and Schuster, 1996).

9. Kevin P. Coyne and John Horn, "Predicting Your Competitor's Reaction," *Harvard Business Review* 87, no. 4 (April 2009).

chapter 4

EVALUATING A COMPANY'S RESOURCES, COST POSITION, AND COMPETITIVENESS

LEARNING OBJECTIVES

LO1 Learn how to assess how well a company's current strategy is working.

LO2 Understand why a company's resources and capabilities are central to its strategic approach and how to evaluate their potential for giving the company a competitive edge over rivals.

LO3 Grasp how and why activities performed internally by a company and those performed externally by its suppliers and forward channel allies determine a company's cost structure and the value it provides to customers.

LO4 Learn how to evaluate a company's competitive strength relative to key rivals.

LO5 Understand how a comprehensive evaluation of a company's external and internal situations can assist managers in making critical decisions about their next strategic moves.

Chapter 3 described how to use the tools of industry and competitive analysis to assess a company's external environment and lay the groundwork for matching a company's strategy to its external situation. This chapter discusses the techniques of evaluating a company's internal situation, including its collection of resources and capabilities, its relative cost position, and its competitive strength versus its rivals. The analytical spotlight will be trained on five questions:

1. How well is the company's strategy working?
2. What are the company's competitively important resources and capabilities?
3. Are the company's cost structure and customer value proposition competitive?
4. Is the company competitively stronger or weaker than key rivals?
5. What strategic issues and problems merit front-burner managerial attention?

The answers to these five questions complete management's understanding of *"Where are we now?"* and position the company for a good strategy-situation fit required by the *"Three Tests of a Winning Strategy"* (see Chapter 1, page 8).

QUESTION 1: HOW WELL IS THE COMPANY'S STRATEGY WORKING?

▶ LO1

Learn how to assess how well a company's current strategy is working.

The two best indicators of how well a company's strategy is working are (1) whether the company is recording gains in financial strength and profitability and (2) whether the company's competitive strength and market standing is improving. Persistent shortfalls in meeting company financial performance targets and weak performance relative to rivals are reliable warning signs that the company suffers from poor strategy making, less-than-competent strategy execution, or both. Other indicators of how well a company's strategy is working include:

- Trends in the company's sales and earnings growth.
- Trends in the company's stock price.
- The company's overall financial strength.
- The company's customer retention rate.
- The rate at which new customers are acquired.
- Changes in the company's image and reputation with customers.
- Evidence of improvement in internal processes such as defect rate, order fulfillment, delivery times, days of inventory, and employee productivity.

The stronger a company's current overall performance, the less likely the need for radical changes in strategy. The weaker a company's financial performance and market standing, the more its current strategy must be questioned. (A compilation of financial ratios most commonly used to evaluate a company's financial performance and balance sheet strength is presented in the Appendix on pages 234–235).

QUESTION 2: WHAT ARE THE COMPANY'S COMPETITIVELY IMPORTANT RESOURCES AND CAPABILITIES?

▶**LO2**

Understand why a company's resources and capabilities are central to its strategic approach and how to evaluate their potential for giving the company a competitive edge over rivals.

As discussed in Chapter 1, a company's business model and strategy must be well-matched to its collection of resources and capabilities. An attempt to create and deliver customer value in a manner that depends on resources or capabilities that are deficient and cannot be readily acquired or developed is unwise and positions the company for failure. A company's competitive approach requires a tight fit with a company's internal situation and is strengthened when it exploits resources that are competitively valuable, rare, hard to copy, and not easily trumped by rivals' substitute resources. In addition, long-term competitive advantage requires the ongoing development and expansion of resources and capabilities to pursue emerging market opportunities and defend against future threats to its market standing and profitability.[1]

For example, Dell has put considerable time and money into developing and enhancing its supply chain capabilities to keep its costs low and to allow for the rapid introduction of new models when more powerful PC components become available. Competitively valuable resources and capabilities have also aided cable news channels in strengthening their competitive positions in the media industry. Because Fox News and CNN have the capability to devote more airtime to breaking news stories and get reporters on the scene very quickly compared to the major over-the-air networks ABC, NBC, and CBS, many viewers turn to the cable networks when a major news event occurs.

Identifying Competitively Important Resources and Capabilities

A company's **resources** are competitive assets that are owned or controlled by the company and may either be *tangible resources* such as plants, distribution centers, manufacturing equipment, patents, information systems, and capital reserves or creditworthiness or *intangible assets* such as a well-known brand or a results-oriented organizational culture. Table 4.1 lists the common types of tangible and intangible resources that a company may possess.

A **capability** is the capacity of a firm to competently perform some internal activity. A capability may also be referred to as a **competence**. Capabilities or competences also vary in form, quality, and competitive importance, with some being more competitively valuable than others. *Organizational capabilities are developed and enabled through the deployment of a company's resources or some combination of its resources.*[2] Some capabilities rely heavily on a company's intangible resources, such as human assets and

> **CORE CONCEPT**
>
> A **resource** is a competitive asset that is owned or controlled by a company; a **capability** is the capacity of a company to competently perform some internal activity. Capabilities are developed and enabled through the deployment of a company's resources. *competence*

TABLE 4.1

Common Types of Tangible and Intangible Resources

Tangible Resources

- *Physical resources*—state-of-the-art manufacturing plants and equipment, efficient distribution facilities, attractive real estate locations, or ownership of valuable natural resource deposits.
- *Financial resources*—cash and cash equivalents, marketable securities, and other financial assets such as a company's credit rating and borrowing capacity.
- *Technological assets*—patents, copyrights, superior production technology, and technologies that enable activities.
- *Organizational resources*—information and communication systems (servers, workstations, etc.), proven quality control systems, and strong network of distributors or retail dealers.

Intangible Resources

- *Human assets and intellectual capital*—an experienced and capable workforce, talented employees in key areas, collective learning embedded in the organization, or proven managerial know-how.
- *Brand, image, and reputational assets*—brand names, trademarks, product or company image, buyer loyalty, and reputation for quality, superior service.
- *Relationships*—alliances or joint ventures that provide access to technologies, specialized know-how, or geographic markets, and trust established with various partners.
- *Company culture*—the norms of behavior, business principles, and ingrained beliefs within the company.

intellectual capital. For example, General Mills' brand management capabilities draw upon the knowledge of the company's brand managers, the expertise of its marketing department, and the company's relationships with retailers. Electronic Arts' video game design capabilities result from the creative talents and technological expertise of its game developers and the company's culture that encourages creative thinking.

Determining the Competitive Power of a Company's Resources and Capabilities

What is most telling about a company's aggregation of resources and capabilities is how powerful they are in the marketplace. The competitive power of a resource or capability is measured by how many of the following four tests it can pass:[3]

1. *Is the resource or capability really competitively valuable?* All companies possess a collection of resources and capabilities—some have the potential to contribute to a competitive advantage while others may not. Apple's operating system for its personal computers by some accounts is superior to Windows 7, but Apple has failed miserably in converting its resources devoted to operating system design into competitive success in the global PC market.

A capability that passes the "competitively valuable" test and is *central* to a company's strategy and competitiveness is frequently referred to as a **core competence**. A competitively valuable capability that is performed with a very high level of proficiency is sometimes known as a **distinctive competence**. Most often, *a core competence or distinctive competence is knowledge-based, residing in people and in a company's intellectual capital and not in its assets on the balance sheet.*

> **CORE CONCEPT**
>
> A **core competence** is a proficiently performed internal activity that is *central* to a company's strategy and competitiveness. A core competence that is performed with a very high level of proficiency is referred to as a **distinctive competence.**

2. *Is the resource or capability rare—is it something rivals lack?* Companies have to guard against pridefully believing that their collection of resources and competitive capabilities is more powerful than that of their rivals. Who can really say whether Coca-Cola's consumer marketing prowess is better than PepsiCo's or whether the Mercedes-Benz brand name is more powerful than that of BMW or Lexus? Although many retailers claim to be quite proficient in product selection and in-store merchandising, a number run into trouble in the marketplace because they encounter rivals whose capabilities in product selection and in-store merchandising are equal to or better than theirs.

3. *Is the resource or capability hard to copy or imitate?* The more difficult and more expensive it is to imitate a company's resource or capability, the greater its potential competitive value. Resources tend to be difficult to copy when they are unique (a fantastic real estate location, patent protection), when they must be built over time (a brand name, a strategy-supportive organizational culture), and when they carry big capital requirements (a cost-effective plant to manufacture cutting-edge microprocessors). Walmart's competitors have failed miserably in their attempts over the past two decades to match its state-of-the-art distribution capabilities.

4. *Can the resource or capability be trumped by substitute resources and competitive capabilities?* Resources that are competitively valuable, rare, and costly to imitate lose their ability to offer competitive advantage if rivals possess equivalent substitute resources. For example, manufacturers relying on automation to gain a cost-based advantage in production activities may find their technology-based advantage nullified by rivals' use of low-wage offshore manufacturing. Resources can contribute to a competitive advantage only when resource substitutes don't exist.

Understanding the nature of competitively important resources allows managers to identify resources or capabilities that should be further developed to play an important role in the company's future strategies. In addition, management may determine that it doesn't possess a resource that independently passes all four tests listed here with high marks, but that it does have a *bundle of resources* that can pass the tests. Although Nike's resources dedicated to research and development, marketing research, and product design are matched relatively well by rival Adidas, its cross-functional design process allows it to set the pace for innovation in athletic apparel and footwear and consistently outperform Adidas and other rivals in the marketplace. Nike's footwear designers get ideas for new performance features from the professional athletes who endorse its products and then work alongside footwear materials researchers, consumer trend analysts, color designers, and market-

> **CORE CONCEPT**
> Companies that lack a stand-alone resource that is competitively powerful may nonetheless develop a competitive advantage through **resource bundles** that enable the superior performance of important cross-functional capabilities.

ers to design new models that are presented to a review committee. Nike's review committee is made up of hundreds of individuals who evaluate prototype details such as shoe proportions and color designs, the size of the swoosh, stitching patterns, sole color and tread pattern, and insole design. About 400 models are approved by the committee each year, which are sourced from contract manufacturers and marketed in more than 180 countries. The bundling of Nike's professional endorsements, R&D activities, marketing research efforts, styling expertise, and managerial know-how has become an important source of the company's competitive advantage and has allowed it to remain number one in the athletic footwear and apparel industry for more than 20 years.

Companies lacking certain resources needed for competitive success in an industry may be able to adopt strategies directed at eroding or at least neutralizing the competitive potency of a particular rival's resources and capabilities by identifying and developing **substitute resources** to accomplish the same

> Rather than try to match the resources possessed by a rival company, a company may develop entirely different resources that substitute for the strengths of the rival.

purpose. For example, Amazon.com lacks a big network of retail stores to compete with those operated by rival Barnes & Noble, but Amazon's much larger, readily accessible, and searchable book inventory—coupled with its short delivery times and free shipping on orders over $25—are more attractive to many busy consumers than visiting a big-box bookstore. In other words, Amazon has carefully and consciously developed a set of competitively valuable resources that are proving to be effective substitutes for competing head-to-head against Barnes & Noble without having to invest in hundreds of brick-and-mortar retail stores.[4]

A Company's Resources and Capabilities Must Be Managed Dynamically

Resources and capabilities must be continually strengthened and nurtured to sustain their competitive power and, at times, may need to be broadened and deepened to allow the company to position itself to pursue emerging market opportunities.[5] Organizational resources and capabilities that grow stale can impair competitiveness unless they are refreshed, modified, or even phased out and replaced in response to ongoing market changes and shifts in company strategy. In addition, disruptive environmental change may destroy the value of key strategic assets, turning resources and capabilities "from diamonds to rust."[6] Management's organization-building challenge has two elements: (1) attending to ongoing recalibration of existing capabilities and resources, and (2) casting a watchful eye for opportunities to develop totally new capabilities for delivering better customer value and/or outcompeting rivals. Such expertise, in itself, qualifies as a unique and valuable organizational capability. A company possessing a **dynamic capability** is adept in modifying, upgrading, or deepening existing resources and capabilities to solidify its standing in the marketplace and prepare it to seize market opportunities and defend against external threats to its vitality.[7]

Management at Toyota has aggressively upgraded the company's capabilities in fuel-efficient hybrid engine technology and constantly fine-tuned the famed Toyota Production System to enhance the company's already proficient capabilities in manufacturing top-quality vehicles at relatively low costs. Likewise, management at Honda has recently accelerated the company's efforts to broaden its expertise and capabilities in hybrid engines to stay close to Toyota. Microsoft retooled the manner in which its programmers attacked the task of writing code for its Windows 7 operating systems for PCs and servers.

> **CORE CONCEPT**
>
> A **dynamic capability** is developed when a company has become proficient in modifying, upgrading, or deepening its resources and capabilities to sustain its competitiveness and prepare it to seize future market opportunities and nullify external threats to its well-being.

> A company requires a dynamically evolving portfolio of resources and capabilities in order to sustain its competitiveness and position itself to pursue future market opportunities.

Are Company Resources and Capabilities Sufficient to Allow It to Seize Market Opportunities and Nullify External Threats?

An essential element in evaluating a company's overall situation entails examining the company's resources and competitive capabilities in terms of the degree to which they enable it to pursue its best market opportunities and defend against the external threats to its future well-being. The simplest and most easily applied tool for conducting this examination is widely known as *SWOT analysis,* so named because it zeros in on a company's internal **S**trengths and **W**eaknesses, market **O**pportunities, and external **T**hreats. A first-rate SWOT analysis provides the basis for crafting a strategy that capitalizes on the company's strengths, aims squarely at capturing the company's best opportunities, and defends against the threats to its well-being.

> **CORE CONCEPT**
>
> **SWOT analysis** is a simple but powerful tool for sizing up a company's internal strengths and competitive deficiencies, its market opportunities, and the external threats to its future well-being.

Identifying a Company's Internal Strengths A company's strengths determine whether its competitive power in the marketplace will be impressively strong or disappointingly weak. A company that is well endowed with strengths stemming from potent resources and core competencies normally has considerable competitive power—especially when its management team skillfully utilizes the company's resources in ways that build sustainable competitive advantage. Companies with modest or

> Basing a company's strategy on its strengths resulting from most competitively valuable resources and capabilities gives the company its best chance for market success.

weak competitive assets nearly always are relegated to a trailing position in the industry. Table 4.2 lists the kinds of factors to consider in compiling a company's resource strengths and weaknesses.

▶ TABLE 4.2

Factors to Consider When Identifying a Company's Strengths, Weaknesses, Opportunities, and Threats

Potential Internal Strengths and Competitive Capabilities

- Core competencies in _____.
- A strong financial condition; ample financial resources to grow the business.
- Strong brand name image/company reputation.
- Economies of scale and/or learning and experience curve advantages over rivals.
- Proprietary technology/superior technological skills/important patents.
- Cost advantages over rivals.
- Product innovation capabilities.
- Proven capabilities in improving production processes.
- Good supply chain management capabilities.
- Good customer service capabilities.
- Better product quality relative to rivals.
- Wide geographic coverage and/or strong global distribution capability.
- Alliances/joint ventures with other firms that provide access to valuable technology, competencies, and/or attractive geographic markets.

Potential Market Opportunities

- Serving additional customer groups or market segments.
- Expanding into new geographic markets.
- Expanding the company's product line to meet a broader range of customer needs.
- Utilizing existing company skills or technological know-how to enter new product lines or new businesses.
- Falling trade barriers in attractive foreign markets.
- Acquiring rival firms or companies with attractive technological expertise or capabilities.

Potential Internal Weaknesses and Competitive Deficiencies

- No clear strategic direction.
- No well-developed or proven core competencies.
- A weak balance sheet; burdened with too much debt.
- Higher overall unit costs relative to key competitors.
- A product/service with features and attributes that are inferior to those of rivals.
- Too narrow a product line relative to rivals.
- Weak brand image or reputation.
- Weaker dealer network than key rivals.
- Behind on product quality, R&D, and/or technological know-how.
- Lack of management depth.
- Short on financial resources to grow the business and pursue promising initiatives.

Potential External Threats to a Company's Future Prospects

- Increasing intensity of competition among industry rivals—may squeeze profit margins.
- Slowdowns in market growth.
- Likely entry of potent new competitors.
- Growing bargaining power of customers or suppliers.
- A shift in buyer needs and tastes away from the industry's product.
- Adverse demographic changes that threaten to curtail demand for the industry's product.
- Vulnerability to unfavorable industry driving forces.
- Restrictive trade policies on the part of foreign governments.
- Costly new regulatory requirements.

STRENGTH

OPP

WEAKNESSES

THREATS

Identifying Company Resource Weaknesses and Competitive Deficiencies A *weakness* or *competitive deficiency* is something a company lacks or does poorly or a condition that puts it at a disadvantage in the marketplace. As a rule, strategies that place heavy demands on areas where the company is weakest or has unproven ability are suspect and should be avoided. A company's weaknesses can relate to:

- Deficiencies in competitively important tangible or intangible resources.
- Missing or competitively inferior capabilities in key areas.

Nearly all companies have competitive deficiencies of one kind or another. Whether a company's weaknesses make it competitively vulnerable depends on how much they matter in the marketplace and whether they are offset by the company's strengths. Sizing up a company's complement of strengths and deficiencies is akin to constructing a *strategic balance sheet*, where strengths represent *competitive assets* and weaknesses represent *competitive liabilities*.

Identifying a Company's Market Opportunities Market opportunity is a big factor in shaping a company's strategy. Indeed, managers can't properly tailor strategy to the company's situation without first identifying its market opportunities and appraising the growth and profit potential each one holds. (See Table 4.2, under "Potential Market Opportunities.") Depending on the prevailing circumstances, a company's opportunities can be plentiful or scarce and can range from wildly attractive to unsuitable.

In evaluating the attractiveness of a company's market opportunities, managers have to guard against viewing every *industry* opportunity as a suitable opportunity. Not every company is equipped with the resources to successfully pursue each opportunity that exists in its industry. Some companies are more capable of going after particular opportunities than others. *The market opportunities most relevant to a company are those that match up well with the company's financial and organizational resources and capabilities, offer the best growth and profitability, and present the most potential for competitive advantage.*

Identifying Threats to a Company's Future Profitability Often, certain factors in a company's external environment pose *threats* to its profitability and competitive well-being. Threats can stem from the emergence of cheaper or better technologies, rivals' introduction of new or improved products, the entry of lower-cost foreign competitors into a company's market stronghold, new regulations that are more burdensome to a company than to its competitors, vulnerability to a rise in interest rates, the potential of a hostile takeover, unfavorable demographic shifts, or adverse changes in foreign exchange rates. (See Table 4.2, under "Potential External Threats to a Company's Future Prospects.")

External threats may pose no more than a moderate degree of adversity or they may be so imposing as to make a company's situation and outlook quite tenuous. On rare occasions, market shocks can throw a company into an immediate crisis and battle to survive. Many of the world's major airlines have been plunged into unprecedented financial crisis because of a combination of factors: rising prices for jet fuel, a global economic slowdown that has affected business and leisure travel, mounting competition from low-fare carriers, shifting traveler preferences for low fares as opposed to lots of in-flight amenities, and "out-of-control" labor costs. It is management's job to identify the threats to the company's future prospects and to evaluate what strategic actions can be taken to neutralize or lessen their impact.

The Value of a SWOT Analysis　A SWOT analysis involves more than making four lists. The most important parts of SWOT analysis are:

> Simply listing a company's strengths, weaknesses, opportunities, and threats is not enough; the payoff from SWOT analysis comes from the conclusions about a company's situation and the implications for strategy improvement that flow from the four lists.

1. Drawing conclusions from the SWOT listings about the company's overall situation.

2. Translating these conclusions into strategic actions to better match the company's strategy to its strengths and market opportunities, correcting problematic weaknesses, and defending against worrisome external threats.

QUESTION 3: ARE THE COMPANY'S COST STRUCTURE AND CUSTOMER VALUE PROPOSITION COMPETITIVE?

LO3

Grasp how and why activities performed internally by a company and those performed externally by its suppliers and forward channel allies determine a company's cost structure and the value it provides to customers.

Company managers are often stunned when a competitor cuts its prices to "unbelievably low" levels or when a new market entrant comes on strong with a great new product offered at a surprisingly low price. Such competitors may not, however, be buying market positions with prices that are below costs. They may simply have substantially lower costs and therefore are able to offer prices that result in more appealing customer value propositions. One of the most telling signs of whether a company's business position is strong or precarious is whether its cost structure and customer value proposition are competitive with industry rivals.

Cost comparisons are especially critical in industries where price competition is typically the ruling market force. But even in industries where products are differentiated, rival companies have to keep their costs in line with rivals offering value propositions based upon a similar mix of differentiating features. Two analytical tools are particularly useful in determining whether a company's value proposition and costs are competitive: value chain analysis and benchmarking.

Company Value Chains

Every company's business consists of a collection of activities undertaken in the course of designing, producing, marketing, delivering, and supporting its product or service. All of the various activities that a company performs internally combine to form a **value chain**, so-called because the underlying intent of a company's activities is to do things that ultimately *create value for buyers.* The value chain includes a profit margin component since delivering customer value profitably (with a sufficient return on invested capital) is the essence of a sound business model.

> **CORE CONCEPT**
>
> A company's **value chain** identifies the primary activities that create customer value and related support activities.

▶ FIGURE 4.1 **A Representative Company Value Chain**

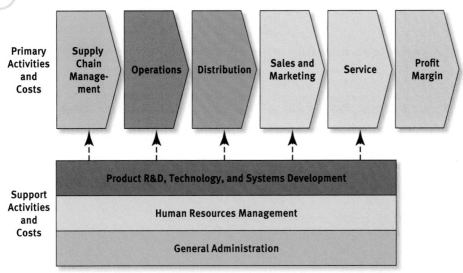

PRIMARY ACTIVITIES

- **Supply Chain Management**—Activities, costs, and assets associated with purchasing fuel, energy, raw materials, parts and components, merchandise, and consumable items from vendors; receiving, storing, and disseminating inputs from suppliers; inspection; and inventory management.

- **Operations**—Activities, costs, and assets associated with converting inputs into final product form (production, assembly, packaging, equipment maintenance, facilities, operations, quality assurance, environmental protection).

- **Distribution**—Activities, costs, and assets dealing with physically distributing the product to buyers (finished goods warehousing, order processing, order picking and packing, shipping, delivery vehicle operations, establishing and maintaining a network of dealers and distributors).

- **Sales and Marketing**—Activities, costs, and assets related to sales force efforts, advertising and promotion, market research and planning, and dealer/distributor support.

- **Service**—Activities, costs, and assets associated with providing assistance to buyers, such as installation, spare parts delivery, maintenance and repair, technical assistance, buyer inquiries, and complaints.

SUPPORT ACTIVITIES

- **Product R&D, Technology, and Systems Development**—Activities, costs, and assets relating to product R&D, process R&D, process design improvement, equipment design, computer software development, telecommunications systems, computer-assisted design and engineering, database capabilities, and development of computerized support systems.

- **Human Resources Management**—Activities, costs, and assets associated with the recruitment, hiring, training, development, and compensation of all types of personnel; labor relations activities; and development of knowledge-based skills and core competencies.

- **General Administration**—Activities, costs, and assets relating to general management, accounting and finance, legal and regulatory affairs, safety and security, management information systems, forming strategic alliances and collaborating with strategic partners, and other "overhead" functions.

Source: Based on the discussion in Michael E. Porter, *Competitive Advantage* (New York: Free Press, 1985), pp. 37–43.

As shown in Figure 4.1, a company's value chain consists of two broad categories of activities that drive costs and create customer value: the *primary activities* that are foremost in creating value for customers and the requisite *support activities* that facilitate and enhance the performance of the primary

CONCEPTS & CONNECTIONS 4.1

VALUE CHAIN ACTIVITIES AND COSTS FOR JUST COFFEE, A PRODUCER OF FAIR TRADE ORGANIC COFFEE

Value Chain Activities and Costs in Producing, Roasting, and Selling a Pound of Fair Trade Organic Coffee	
1. Average cost of procuring the coffee from coffee grower cooperatives	$2.30
2. Import fees, storage costs, and freight charges	.73
3. Labor cost of roasting and bagging	.89
4. Cost of labels and bag	.45
5. Average overhead costs	$3.03
6. Total company costs	7.40
7. Average retail markup over company costs (company operating profit)	$2.59
8. Average price to consumer at retail	$9.99

Source: Developed by the authors from information on Just Coffee's website, www.justcoffee.coop/the_coffee_dollar_breakdown; accessed June 16, 2010.

activities.[8] For example, the primary activities and cost drivers for a big-box retailer such as Target include merchandise selection and buying, store layout and product display, advertising, and customer service; its support activities that affect customer value and costs include site selection, hiring and training, store maintenance, plus the usual assortment of administrative activities. A hotel chain's primary activities and costs are mainly comprised of reservations and hotel operations (check-in and check-out, maintenance and housekeeping, dining and room service, and conventions and meetings); principal support activities that drive costs and impact customer value include accounting, hiring and training hotel staff, and general administration. Supply chain management is a crucial activity for Nissan or Amazon.com but is not a value chain component at Google or CBS. Sales and marketing are dominant activities at Procter & Gamble and Sony but have minor roles at oil-drilling companies and natural gas pipeline companies. Whether an activity is classified as primary or supporting varies with each company's business model and strategy, so it is important to view the listing of the primary and support activities in Figure 4.1 as illustrative rather than definitive. Concepts & Connections 4.1 shows representative costs for various activities performed by Just Coffee, a cooperative producer and roaster of fair trade organic coffee.

Benchmarking: A Tool for Assessing Whether a Company's Value Chain Activities Are Competitive

Benchmarking entails comparing how different companies perform various value chain activities—how materials are purchased, how inventories are managed, how products are assembled, how customer orders are filled and shipped, and how maintenance is performed—and then making cross-company comparisons of the costs and effectiveness of these activities.[9] The objectives of benchmarking are to identify the best practices in performing an activity and to emulate those best practices when they are possessed by others.

Xerox became one of the first companies to use benchmarking in 1979 when Japanese manufacturers began selling midsize copiers in the United States for $9,600 each—less than Xerox's production costs.[10] Xerox management sent a team of line managers and its head of manufacturing to Japan to study competitors' business processes

> **CORE CONCEPT**
>
> **Benchmarking** is a potent tool for learning which companies are best at performing particular activities and then using their techniques (or "best practices") to improve the cost and effectiveness of a company's own internal activities.

and costs. With the aid of Xerox's joint-venture partner in Japan (Fuji-Xerox), who knew the competitors well, the team found that Xerox's costs were excessive due to gross inefficiencies in the company's manufacturing processes and business practices. The findings triggered a major internal effort at Xerox to become cost-competitive and prompted Xerox to begin benchmarking 67 of its key work processes. Xerox quickly decided not to restrict its benchmarking efforts to its office equipment rivals but to extend them to any company regarded as "world class" in performing *any activity* relevant to Xerox's business. Other companies quickly picked up on Xerox's approach. Toyota managers got their idea for just-in-time inventory deliveries by studying how U.S. supermarkets replenished their shelves. Southwest Airlines reduced the turnaround time of its aircraft at each scheduled stop by studying pit crews on the auto racing circuit. Over 80 percent of Fortune 500 companies reportedly use benchmarking for comparing themselves against rivals on cost and other competitively important measures.

The tough part of benchmarking is not whether to do it, but rather how to gain access to information about other companies' practices and costs. Sometimes benchmarking can be accomplished by collecting information from published reports, trade groups, and industry research firms and by talking to knowledgeable industry analysts, customers, and suppliers. Sometimes field trips to the facilities of competing or noncompeting companies can be arranged to observe how things are done, compare practices and processes, and perhaps exchange data on productivity and other cost components. However, such companies, even if they agree to host facilities tours and answer questions, are unlikely to share competitively sensitive cost information. Furthermore, comparing two companies' costs may not involve comparing apples to apples if the two companies employ different cost accounting principles to calculate the costs of particular activities.

However, a fairly reliable source of benchmarking information has emerged. The explosive interest of companies in benchmarking costs and identifying best practices has prompted consulting organizations (e.g., Accenture, A. T. Kearney, Benchnet—The Benchmarking Exchange, Towers Watson, and Best Practices, LLC) and several councils and associations (e.g., the APQC, the Qualserve Benchmarking Clearinghouse, and the Strategic Planning Institute's Council on Benchmarking) to gather benchmarking data, distribute information about best practices, and provide comparative cost data without identifying the names of particular companies. Having an independent group gather the information and report it in a manner that disguises the names of individual companies avoids the disclosure of competitively sensitive data and lessens the potential for unethical behavior on the part of company personnel in gathering their own data about competitors.

⌗ The Value Chain System for an Entire Industry

A company's value chain is embedded in a larger system of activities that includes the value chains of its suppliers and the value chains of whatever distribution channel allies it utilizes in getting its product or service to end users. The value chains of forward channel partners are relevant because (1) the costs and margins of a company's distributors and retail dealers are part of the price the consumer ultimately pays, and (2) the activities that distribution allies perform affect customer value. For these reasons, companies normally work closely with their suppliers and forward channel allies to perform value chain activities in mutually beneficial ways. For instance, motor vehicle manufacturers work closely with their forward channel allies (local automobile dealers) to ensure that owners are satisfied with dealers' repair and maintenance services.[11] Also, many automotive parts suppliers have built plants near the auto assembly plants they supply to facilitate just-in-time deliveries, reduce warehousing and shipping costs, and promote close collaboration on parts design and production scheduling. Irrigation equipment companies, suppliers of grape-harvesting and winemaking equipment, and firms making barrels, wine bottles, caps, corks, and labels all have facilities in the California wine country to be close to the nearly 700 winemakers they supply.[12] The lesson here is that a company's value chain activities are often closely linked to the value chains of their suppliers and the forward allies.

> A company's customer value proposition and cost competitiveness depend not only on internally performed activities (its own company value chain), but also on the value chain activities of its suppliers and forward channel allies.

As a consequence, _accurately assessing the competitiveness of a company's cost structure and value proposition requires that company managers understand an industry's entire value chain system for delivering a product or service to customers, not just the company's own value chain._ A typical industry value chain that incorporates the value-creating activities, costs, and margins of suppliers and forward channel allies (if any) is shown in Figure 4.2. However, industry value chains vary significantly by industry. For example, the primary value chain activities in the bottled water industry (spring operation or water purification, processing of basic ingredients used in flavored or vitamin-enhanced water, bottling, wholesale distribution, advertising, and retail merchandising) differ from those for the computer software industry (programming, disk loading, marketing, distribution). Producers of bathroom and kitchen faucets depend heavily on the activities of wholesale distributors and building supply retailers in winning sales to home builders and do-it-yourselfers but producers of papermaking machines internalize their distribution activities by selling directly to the operators of paper plants.

▶ FIGURE 4.2 **Representative Value Chain for an Entire Industry**

Supplier-Related Value Chains	A Company's Own Value Chain	Forward Channel Value Chains	
Activities, costs, and margins of suppliers	Internally performed activities, costs, and margins	Activities, costs, and margins of forward channel allies and strategic partners	Buyer or End-user value chains

Source: Based in part on the single-industry value chain displayed in Michael E. Porter, *Competitive Advantage* (New York: Free Press, 1985), p. 35.

Strategic Options for Remedying a Cost or Value Disadvantage

The results of value chain analysis and benchmarking may disclose cost or value disadvantages relative to key rivals. These competitive disadvantages are likely to lower a company's relative profit margin or weaken its customer value proposition. In such instances, actions to improve a company's cost structure are called for to boost profitability or to allow for the addition of new features that drive customer value. There are three main areas in a company's overall value chain where important differences between firms in costs and value can occur: a company's own internal activities, the suppliers' part of the industry value chain, and the forward channel portion of the industry chain.

Remedying an Internal Cost or Value Disadvantage   Managers can pursue any of several strategic approaches to restore cost parity or rectify a deficiency in customer value when the disadvantage stems from the performance of internal value chain activities:

1. *Implement the use of best practices* throughout the company, particularly for high-cost activities.

2. *Try to eliminate some cost-producing activities* by revamping the value chain. Many retailers have found that donating returned items to charitable organizations and taking the appropriate tax deduction results in a smaller loss than incurring the costs of the value chain activities involved in reverse logistics.

3. *Relocate high-cost activities* (such as manufacturing) to geographic areas such as China, Latin America, or Eastern Europe where they can be performed more cheaply.

4. *See if certain internally performed activities can be outsourced* from vendors or performed by contractors more cheaply than they can be done in-house.

5. *Invest in productivity-enhancing, cost-saving technological improvements* (robotics, flexible manufacturing techniques, state-of-the-art electronic networking).

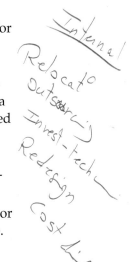

6. *Find ways to detour around the activities or items where costs are high*— computer chip makers regularly design around the patents held by others to avoid paying royalties; automakers have substituted lower-cost plastic for metal at many exterior body locations.

7. *Redesign the product* and/or some of its components to facilitate speedier and more economical manufacture or assembly.

8. *Try to make up the internal cost disadvantage* by reducing costs in the supplier or forward channel portions of the industry value chain—usually a last resort.

Remedying a Supplier-Related Cost Disadvantage   Supplier-related cost disadvantages can be attacked by pressuring suppliers for lower prices, switching to lower-priced substitute inputs, and collaborating closely with suppliers to identify mutual cost-saving opportunities.[13] For example, just-in-time deliveries from suppliers can lower a company's inventory and internal logistics costs, eliminate capital expenditures for additional warehouse space, and improve cash flow and financial ratios by reducing accounts payable. In a few instances, companies may find that it is cheaper to integrate backward into the business of high-cost suppliers and make the item in-house instead of buying it from outsiders.

Remedying a Cost Disadvantage Associated with Activities Performed by Forward Channel Allies   There are three main ways to combat a cost disadvantage in the forward portion of the industry value chain: (1) Pressure dealer-distributors and other forward channel allies to reduce their costs and markups; (2) work closely with forward channel allies to identify win-win opportunities to reduce costs—for example, a chocolate manufacturer learned that by shipping its bulk chocolate in liquid form in tank cars instead of 10-pound molded bars, it could not only save its candy bar manufacturing customers the costs associated with unpacking and melting but also eliminate its own costs of molding bars and packing them; and (3) change to a more economical distribution strategy or perhaps integrate forward into company-owned retail outlets. Dell has eliminated all activities, costs, and margins of forward channel allies by adopting a direct sales business model that allows buyers to purchase customized PCs directly from the manufacturer. The direct sales model allows Dell to easily match competitors' prices, while earning larger profit margins.

QUESTION 4: WHAT IS THE COMPANY'S COMPETITIVE STRENGTH RELATIVE TO KEY RIVALS?

LO4

Learn how to evaluate a company's competitive strength relative to key rivals.

An additional component of evaluating a company's situation is developing a comprehensive assessment of the company's overall competitive strength. Making this determination requires answers to two questions:

1. How does the company rank relative to competitors on each of the important factors that determine market success?

2. All things considered, does the company have a net competitive advantage or disadvantage versus major competitors?   *Assign wt.*

Step 1 in doing a competitive strength assessment is to list the industry's key success factors and other telling measures of competitive strength or weakness (6 to 10 measures usually suffice). Step 2 is to assign a weight to each measure of competitive strength based on its perceived importance in shaping competitive success. (The sum of the weights for each measure must add up to 1.0.) Step 3 is to calculate weighted strength ratings by scoring each competitor on each strength measure (using a 1 to 10 rating scale where 1 is very weak and 10 is very strong) and multiplying the assigned rating by the assigned weight. Step 4 is to sum the weighted strength ratings on each factor to get an overall measure of competitive strength for each company being rated. Step 5 is to use the overall strength ratings to draw conclusions about the size and extent of the company's net competitive advantage or disadvantage and to take specific note of areas of strength and weakness. Table 4.3 provides an example of a competitive strength assessment, using the hypothetical ABC Company against four rivals. ABC's total score of 5.95 signals a net competitive advantage over Rival 3 (with a score of 2.10) and Rival 4 (with a score of 3.70), but indicates a net competitive disadvantage against Rival 1 (with a score of 7. 70) and Rival 2 (with an overall score of 6.85).

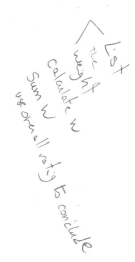

Interpreting the Competitive Strength Assessments

Competitive strength assessments provide useful conclusions about a company's competitive situation. The ratings show how a company compares against rivals, factor by factor or capability by capability, thus revealing where it is strongest and weakest. Moreover, the overall competitive strength scores indicate whether the company is at a net competitive advantage or disadvantage against each rival.

> A company's competitive strength scores pinpoint its strengths and weaknesses against rivals and point to offensive and defensive strategies capable of producing first-rate results.

In addition, the strength ratings provide guidelines for designing wise offensive and defensive strategies. For example, consider the ratings and weighted scores in Table 4.3. If ABC Co. wants to go on the offensive to win additional sales and market share, such an offensive probably needs to be aimed directly at winning customers away from Rivals 3 and 4 (which have lower overall strength scores) rather than Rivals 1 and 2 (which have higher overall strength scores). ABC's advantages over Rival 4 tend to be in areas that are moderately important to competitive success in the industry, but ABC outclasses Rival 3 on the two most heavily weighted strength factors—relative cost position and customer service capabilities. Therefore, Rival 3 should be viewed as the primary target of ABC's offensive strategies, with Rival 4 being a secondary target.

A competitively astute company should utilize the strength scores in deciding what strategic moves to make. When a company has important competitive strengths in areas where one or more rivals are weak, it makes sense to

▲ TABLE 4.3

Illustration of a Competitive Strength Assessment

Key Success Factor/Strength Measure	Importance Weight	ABC CO. Strength Rating	Score	RIVAL 1 Strength Rating	Score	RIVAL 2 Strength Rating	Score	RIVAL 3 Strength Rating	Score	RIVAL 4 Strength Rating	Score
Quality/product performance	0.10	8	0.80	5	0.50	10	1.00	1	0.10	6	0.60
Reputation/image	0.10	8	0.80	7	0.70	10	1.00	1	0.10	6	0.60
Manufacturing capability	0.10	2	0.20	10	1.00	4	0.40	5	0.50	1	0.10
Technological skills	0.05	10	0.50	1	0.05	7	0.35	3	0.15	8	0.40
Dealer network/distribution capability	0.05	9	0.45	4	0.20	10	0.50	5	0.25	1	0.05
New-product innovation capability	0.05	9	0.45	4	0.20	10	0.50	5	0.25	1	0.05
Financial resources	0.10	5	0.50	10	1.00	7	0.70	3	0.30	1	0.10
Relative cost position	0.30	5	1.50	10	3.00	3	0.95	1	0.30	4	1.20
Customer service capabilities	0.15	5	0.75	7	1.05	10	1.50	1	0.15	4	0.60
Sum of importance weights	1.00										
Weighted overall strength rating			**5.95**		**7.70**		**6.85**		**2.10**		**3.70**

(Rating scale: 1 = very weak; 10 = very strong)

consider offensive moves to exploit rivals' competitive weaknesses. When a company has competitive weaknesses in important areas where one or more rivals are strong, it makes sense to consider defensive moves to curtail its vulnerability.

QUESTION 5: WHAT STRATEGIC ISSUES AND PROBLEMS MUST BE ADDRESSED BY MANAGEMENT?

The final and most important analytical step is to zero in on exactly what strategic issues company managers need to address. This step involves drawing on the results of both industry and competitive analysis and the evaluations of the company's internal situation. The task here is to get a clear fix on exactly what industry and competitive challenges confront the company, which of the company's internal weaknesses need fixing, and what specific problems merit front-burner attention by company managers. *Pinpointing the precise things that management needs to worry about sets the agenda for deciding what actions to take next to improve the company's performance and business outlook.*

> **▶LO5**
>
> Understand how a comprehensive evaluation of a company's external and internal situations can assist managers in making critical decisions about their next strategic moves.

If the items on management's "worry list" are relatively minor, which suggests the company's strategy is mostly on track and reasonably well matched to the company's overall situation, company managers seldom need to go much beyond fine-tuning the present strategy. If, however, the issues and problems confronting the company are serious and indicate the present strategy is not well suited for the road ahead, the task of crafting a better strategy has got to go to the top of management's action agenda.

> Compiling a "worry list" of problems and issues creates an agenda for managerial strategy making.

KEY POINTS

In analyzing a company's own particular competitive circumstances and its competitive position vis-à-vis key rivals consider five key questions:

1. *How well is the present strategy working?* This involves evaluating the strategy from a qualitative standpoint (completeness, internal consistency, rationale, and suitability to the situation) and also from a quantitative standpoint (the strategic and financial results the strategy is producing). The stronger a company's current overall performance, the less likely the need for radical strategy changes. The weaker a company's performance and/or the faster the changes in its external situation (which can be gleaned from industry and competitive analysis), the more its current strategy must be questioned.

2. *What are the company's competitively important resources and capabilities?* A company's resources, competitive capabilities, and core competencies are strategically relevant because they are the most logical and appealing building blocks for strategy. The most potent resources are *competitively valuable, rare, hard to copy or imitate, and are not easily trumped by substitute resources.* Organizational resources

and capabilities must be continually strengthened and nurtured to sustain their competitive power. In addition, resources and capabilities may need to be broadened and deepened to position the company to seize market opportunities and defend against emerging threats to its well-being. A *SWOT analysis* is a simple but powerful tool for sizing up a company's resource strengths and competitive deficiencies, its market opportunities, and the external threats to its future well-being. Resource weaknesses are important because they may represent vulnerabilities that need correction. External opportunities and threats come into play because a good strategy necessarily aims at capturing a company's most attractive opportunities and at defending against threats to its well-being.

3. *Are the company's prices and costs competitive?* One telling sign of whether a company's situation is strong or precarious is whether its prices and costs are competitive with those of industry rivals. Value chain analysis and benchmarking are essential tools in determining whether the company is performing particular functions and activities cost-effectively, learning whether its costs are in line with competitors, and deciding which internal activities and business processes need to be scrutinized for improvement. Value chain analysis teaches that how competently a company manages its value chain activities relative to rivals is a key to building a competitive advantage based on either better competencies and competitive capabilities or lower costs than rivals.

4. *Is the company competitively stronger or weaker than key rivals?* The key appraisals here involve how the company matches up against key rivals on industry key success factors and other chief determinants of competitive success and whether and why the company has a competitive advantage or disadvantage. Quantitative competitive strength assessments, using the method presented in Table 4.3, indicate where a company is competitively strong and weak and provide insight into the company's ability to defend or enhance its market position. As a rule a company's competitive strategy should be built around its competitive strengths and should aim at shoring up areas where it is competitively vulnerable. When a company has important competitive strengths in areas where one or more rivals are weak, it makes sense to consider offensive moves to exploit rivals' competitive weaknesses. When a company has important competitive weaknesses in areas where one or more rivals are strong, it makes sense to consider defensive moves to curtail its vulnerability.

5. *What strategic issues and problems merit front-burner managerial attention?* This analytical step zeros in on the strategic issues and problems that stand in the way of the company's success. It involves using the results of both industry and competitive analysis and company situation analysis to identify a "worry list" of issues to be resolved for the company to be financially and competitively successful in the years ahead. Actually deciding upon a strategy and what specific actions to take comes after the list of strategic issues and problems that merit front-burner management attention has been developed.

Good company situation analysis, like good industry and competitive analysis, is a valuable precondition for good strategy making.

ASSURANCE OF LEARNING EXERCISES

1. Using the financial ratios provided in the Appendix and the financial statement information for Avon Products, Inc., below, calculate the following ratios for Avon for both 2009 and 2010:

   LO1

   a. Gross profit margin.

   b. Operating profit margin.

   c. Net profit margin.

   d. Times interest earned coverage.

   e. Return on shareholders' equity.

   f. Return on assets.

   g. Debt-to-equity ratio.

   h. Days of inventory.

   i. Inventory turnover ratio.

   j. Average collection period.

   Based on these ratios, did Avon's financial performance improve, weaken, or remain about the same from 2009 to 2010?

Consolidated Statements of Income for Avon Products, Inc., 2009–2010 (in millions, except per share data)

YEARS ENDED DECEMBER 31	2010	2009
Net sales	$10,731.3	$10,084.8
Other revenue	131.5	120.4
Total revenue	10,862.8	10,205.2
Costs, expenses and other:		
Cost of sales	4,041.3	3,825.5
Selling, general, and administrative expenses	5,748.4	5,374.1
Operating profit	1,073.1	1,005.6
Interest expense	87.1	104.8
Interest income	(14.0)	(20.2)
Other expense, net	54.6	7.3
Total other expenses	127.7	91.9
Income from continuing operations, before taxes	945.4	913.7
Income taxes	350.2	294.5
Income from continuing operations, net of tax	595.2	619.2
Discontinued operations, net of tax	14.1	9.0
Net income	$ 609.3	$ 628.2
Earnings per share:		
Basic from continuing operations	$ 1.37	$ 1.43
Diluted from continuing operations	$ 1.36	$ 1.43
Weighted-average shares outstanding:		
Basic	428.75	426.90
Diluted	431.35	428.54

Consolidated Balance Sheets for Avon Products, Inc., 2009–2010 (in millions, except per share data)

DECEMBER 31	2010	2009
Assets		
Current assets		
Cash, including cash equivalents of $572.0 and $670.5	$1,179.9	$ 963.4
Accounts receivable (less allowances of $232.0 and $165.1)	826.3	765.7
Inventories	1,152.9	1,049.8
Prepaid expenses and other	1,025.2	1,042.3
Current assets of discontinued operations	--	50.3
Total current assets	4,184.3	4,206.2
Property, plant and equipment, at cost Land	69.2	115.9
Buildings and improvements	1,140.2	954.2
Equipment	1,541.5	1,435.8
	2,750.9	2,505.9
Less accumulated depreciation	(1,123.5)	(1,036.9)
	1,627.4	1,469.0
Other assets	1,018.6	846.1
Total assets	$7,873.7	$6,823.4
Liabilities and Shareholders' Equity Current liabilities		
Debt maturing within one year	$ 727.6	$ 137.8
Accounts payable	809.8	739.0
Accrued compensation	293.2	282.6
Other accrued liabilities	771.6	706.3
Sales and taxes other than income	207.6	254.1
Income taxes	146.5	134.5
Total current liabilities	2,956.3	2,291.7
Long-term debt	2,408.6	2,307.2
Employee benefit plans	561.3	577.8
Long-term income taxes	128.9	147.6
Other liabilities	146.0	186.5
Total liabilities	$6,201.1	$5,510.8
Commitments and contingencies		
Shareholders' equity		
Common stock, par value $.25–authorized 1,500 shares; issued 743.3 and 740.9 shares	$ 186.6	$ 186.1
Additional paid-in capital	2,024.2	1,941.0
Retained earnings	4,610.8	4,383.9
Accumulated other comprehensive loss	(605.8)	(692.6)
Treasury stock, at cost –313.8 and 313.4 shares	(4,559.3)	(4,545.8)
Noncontrolling interest	16.1	40.0
Total shareholders' equity	$1,672.6	$1,312.6
Total liabilities and shareholders' equity	$7,873.7	$6,823.4

Source: Avon Products, Inc., 2010, 10-K.

LO2 2. Starbucks operates more than 17,000 stores in more than 50 countries. How many of the four tests of the competitive power of a resource does the store network pass? Explain your answer.

3. Review the information in Concepts & Connections 4.1 concerning producing and selling fair trade coffee. Then answer the following questions:

LO3

■ connect
www.mcgrawhillconnect.com

   a. Companies that do not sell fair trade coffee can buy coffee direct from small farmers for as little as $0.75 per pound. By paying substandard wages, they can also reduce their labor costs of roasting and bagging coffee to $0.70 per pound and reduce their overhead by 20 percent. If they sell their coffee at the same average price as Just Coffee, what would their profit margin be and how would this compare to Just Coffee's?

   b. How can Just Coffee respond to this type of competitive threat? Does it have any valuable competitive assets that can help it respond or will it need to acquire new ones. Would your answer change the company's value chain in any way?

4. Using the methodology illustrated in Table 4.3 and your knowledge as an automobile owner, prepare a competitive strength assessment for General Motors and its rivals Ford, Chrysler, Toyota, and Honda. Each of the five automobile manufacturers should be evaluated on the key success factors/strength measures of: cost competitiveness, product line breadth, product quality and reliability, financial resources and profitability, and customer service. What does your competitive strength assessment disclose about the overall competitiveness of each automobile manufacturer? What factors account most for Toyota's competitive success? Does Toyota have competitive weaknesses that were disclosed by your analysis? Explain.

LO4

EXERCISES FOR SIMULATION PARTICIPANTS

1. Using the formulas in the Appendix and the data in your company's latest financial statements, calculate the following measures of financial performance for your company:

   a. Operating profit margin

   b. Return on total assets

   c. Current ratio

   d. Working capital

   e. Long-term debt-to-capital ratio

   f. Price-earnings ratio

LO1

LO1

2. Based on your company's latest financial statements and all of the other available data regarding your company's performance that appear in the Industry Report, list the three measures of financial performance on which your company did "best" and the three measures on which your company's financial performance was "worst."

3. What hard evidence can you cite that indicates your company's strategy is working fairly well (or perhaps not working so well, if your company's performance is lagging that of rival companies)?

LO1

4. What internal strengths and weaknesses does your company have? What external market opportunities for growth and increased profitability exist for your company? What external threats to your company's future well-being and

LO2

profitability do you and your co-managers see? What does the preceding SWOT analysis indicate about your company's present situation and future prospects—where on the scale from "exceptionally strong" to "alarmingly weak" does the attractiveness of your company's situation rank?

LO2   5. Does your company have any core competencies? If so, what are they?

LO3   6. What are the key elements of your company's value chain? Refer to Figure 4.1 in developing your answer.

LO4   7. Using the methodology illustrated in Table 4.3, do a weighted competitive strength assessment for your company and two other companies that you and your co-managers consider to be very close competitors.

ENDNOTES

1. Birger Wernerfelt, "A Resource-Based View of the Firm," *Strategic Management Journal* 5, no. 5 (September–October 1984); Jay Barney, "Firm Resources and Sustained Competitive Advantage," *Journal of Management* 17, no. 1 (1991); Margaret A. Peteraf, "The Cornerstones of Competitive Advantage: A Resource-Based View," *Strategic Management Journal* 14, no. 3 (March 1993).

2. R. Amit and P. Schoemaker, "Strategic Assets and Organizational Rent," *Strategic Management Journal* 14, no. 1 (1993).

3 David J. Collis and Cynthia A. Montgomery, "Competing on Resources: Strategy in the 1990s," *Harvard Business Review* 73, no. 4 (July–August 1995).

4. George Stalk, Philip Evans, and Lawrence E. Schulman, "Competing on Capabilities: The New Rules of Corporate Strategy," *Harvard Business Review* 70, no. 2 (March–April 1992).

5. David J. Teece, Gary Pisano, and Amy Shuen, "Dynamic Capabilities and Strategic Management," *Strategic Management Journal* 18, no.

7 (1997); and Constance E. Helfat and Margaret A. Peteraf, "The Dynamic Resource-Based View: Capability Lifecycles," *Strategic Management Journal* 24, no. 10 (2003).

6. C. Montgomery, "Of Diamonds and Rust: A New Look at Resources" in *Resource-Based and Evolutionary Theories of the Firm*, ed. C. Montgomery (Boston: Kluwer Academic Publishers, 1995), pp. 251–68.

7. K. Eisenhardt and J. Martin, "Dynamic Capabilities: What are They?" *Strategic Management Journal*, 21, nos. 10–11 (2000); and M. Zollo and S. Winter, "Deliberate Learning and the Evolution of Dynamic Capabilities," *Organization Science* 13 (2002).

8. Michael E. Porter, *Competitive Advantage* (New York: Free Press, 1985).

9. Gregory H. Watson, *Strategic Benchmarking: How to Rate Your Company's Performance Against the World's Best* (New York: John Wiley & Sons, 1993); Robert C. Camp, *Benchmarking: The Search for Industry Best Practices That Lead to Superior Performance* (Milwaukee:

ASQC Quality Press, 1989); Christopher E. Bogan and Michael J. English, *Benchmarking for Best Practices: Winning through Innovative Adaptation* (New York: McGraw-Hill, 1994); and Dawn Iacobucci and Christie Nordhielm, "Creative Benchmarking," *Harvard Business Review* 78, no. 6 (November–December 2000).

10. Jeremy Main, "How to Steal the Best Ideas Around," *Fortune*, October 19, 1992, pp. 102–3.

11. M. Hegert and D. Morris, "Accounting Data for Value Chain Analysis," *Strategic Management Journal* 10 (1989); Robin Cooper and Robert S. Kaplan, "Measure Costs Right: Make the Right Decisions," *Harvard Business Review* 66, no. 5 (September–October 1988); and John K. Shank and Vijay Govindarajan, *Strategic Cost Management* (New York: Free Press, 1993).

12. Michael E. Porter, "Clusters and the New Economics of Competition," *Harvard Business Review* 76, no. 6 (November–December 1998).

13. Reuben E. Stone, "Leading a Supply Chain Turnaround," *Harvard Business Review* 82, no. 10 (October 2004).

chapter 5

THE FIVE GENERIC COMPETITIVE STRATEGIES

LEARNING OBJECTIVES

LO1 Gain an understanding of how each of the five generic competitive strategies goes about building competitive advantage and delivering superior value to customers.

LO2 Learn the major avenues for achieving a competitive advantage based on lower costs.

LO3 Recognize why some generic strategies work better in certain kinds of industry and competitive conditions than others.

LO4 Gain command of the major avenues for developing a competitive advantage based on differentiating a company's product or service offering from the offerings of rivals.

LO5 Recognize the required conditions for delivering superior value to customers through the use of a hybrid of low-cost provider and differentiation strategies.

There are several basic approaches to competing successfully and gaining a competitive advantage, but they all involve giving buyers what they perceive as superior value compared to the offerings of rival sellers. Superior value can mean offering a good product at a lower price, a superior product that is worth paying more for, or a best-value offering that represents an attractive combination of price, features, quality, service, and other appealing attributes.

This chapter describes the five *generic competitive strategy options* for building competitive advantage and delivering superior value to customers. Which of the five to employ is a company's first and foremost choice in crafting an overall strategy and beginning its quest for competitive advantage.

COMPETITIVE STRATEGIES AND MARKET POSITIONING

▶ LO1

Gain an understanding of how each of the five generic competitive strategies goes about building competitive advantage and delivering superior value to customers.

A company's **competitive strategy** deals exclusively with the specifics of management's game plan for competing successfully—its specific efforts to please customers, its offensive and defensive moves to counter the maneuvers of rivals, its responses to whatever market conditions prevail at the moment, and its approach to securing a competitive advantage vis-à-vis rivals. There are countless variations in the competitive strategies that companies employ, mainly because each company's strategic approach entails custom-designed actions to fit its own circumstances and industry environment. The custom-tailored nature of each company's strategy is also the result of management's efforts to uniquely position the company in its market. Companies are much more likely to achieve competitive advantage and earn above-average profits if they find a unique way of delivering superior value to customers. For example, the iPod's attractive styling, easy-to-use controls, attention-grabbing ads, and extensive collection of music available at Apple's iTunes Store have given Apple a competitive advantage in the digital media player industry. Microsoft has attempted to imitate Apple's competitive strategy with introduction of its Zune music player and store, but Microsoft has fared no better in its attack on the iPod than any of the other makers of digital media players. By choosing a unique approach to providing value to customers, Apple has achieved an enduring brand loyalty that makes it difficult for others to triumph by merely copying its strategic approach. "Me too" strategies can rarely be expected to deliver competitive advantage and stellar performance unless the imitator possesses resources or competencies that allow it to provide greater value to customers than that offered by firms with similar strategic approaches.

> **CORE CONCEPT**
>
> A **competitive strategy** concerns the specifics of management's game plan for competing successfully and securing a competitive advantage over rivals in the marketplace.

Competitive strategies that provide distinctive industry positioning and competitive advantage in the marketplace involve choosing between (1) a market target that is either broad or narrow, and (2) whether the company should pursue a competitive advantage linked to low costs or product

▶FIGURE 5.1 **The Five Generic Competitive Strategies**

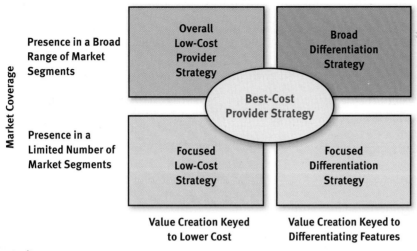

Source: This is an author-expanded version of a three-strategy classification discussed in Michael E. Porter, *Competitive Strategy* (New York: Free Press, 1980), pp. 35–40.

differentiation. These two factors give rise to the five competitive strategy options shown in Figure 5.1 and listed below.[1]

1. *A low-cost provider strategy*—striving to achieve lower overall costs than rivals and appealing to a broad spectrum of customers, usually by under-pricing rivals.

2. *A broad differentiation strategy*—seeking to differentiate the company's product or service from rivals' in ways that will appeal to a broad spectrum of buyers.

3. *A focused low-cost strategy*—concentrating on a narrow buyer segment (or market niche) and outcompeting rivals by having lower costs than rivals and thus being able to serve niche members at a lower price.

4. *A focused differentiation strategy*—concentrating on a narrow buyer segment (or market niche) and outcompeting rivals by offering niche members customized attributes that meet their tastes and requirements better than rivals' products.

5. *A best-cost provider strategy*—giving customers more value for the money by satisfying buyers' expectations on key quality/features/ performance/service attributes while beating their price expectations. This option is a *hybrid* strategy that blends elements of low-cost provider and differentiation strategies; the aim is to have the lowest (best) costs and prices among sellers offering products with comparable differentiating attributes.

The remainder of this chapter explores the ins and outs of the five generic competitive strategies and how they differ.

LOW-COST PROVIDER STRATEGIES

Striving to be the industry's overall low-cost provider is a powerful competitive approach in markets with many price-sensitive buyers. A company achieves low-cost leadership when it becomes the industry's lowest-cost provider rather than just being one of perhaps several competitors with low costs. Successful low-cost providers boast meaningfully lower costs than rivals, but not necessarily the absolutely lowest possible cost. In striving for a cost advantage over rivals, managers must include features and services that buyers consider essential. A product offering that is too frills-free can be viewed by consumers as offering little value, regardless of its pricing.

> **CORE CONCEPT**
>
> A **low-cost leader**'s basis for competitive advantage is lower overall costs than competitors. Success in achieving a low-cost edge over rivals comes from eliminating and/or curbing "nonessential" activities and/or outmanaging rivals in performing essential activities.

A company has two options for translating a low-cost advantage over rivals into attractive profit performance. Option 1 is to use the lower-cost edge to underprice competitors and attract price-sensitive buyers in great enough numbers to increase total profits. Option 2 is to maintain the present price, be content with the present market share, and use the lower-cost edge to earn a higher profit margin on each unit sold, thereby raising the firm's total profits and overall return on investment.

The Two Major Avenues for Achieving Low-Cost Leadership

LO2

Learn the major avenues for achieving a competitive advantage based on lower costs.

To achieve a low-cost edge over rivals, a firm's cumulative costs across its overall value chain must be lower than competitors' cumulative costs. There are two major avenues for accomplishing this:[2]

1. Performing essential value chain activities more cost-effectively than rivals.
2. Revamping the firm's overall value chain to eliminate or bypass some cost-producing activities.

Cost-Efficient Management of Value Chain Activities For a company to do a more cost-efficient job of managing its value chain than rivals, managers must launch a concerted, ongoing effort to ferret out cost-saving opportunities in every part of the value chain. No activity can escape cost-saving scrutiny, and all company personnel must be expected to use their talents and ingenuity to come up with innovative and effective ways to keep costs down. All avenues for performing value chain activities at a lower cost than rivals must be explored. These can include:

- *Striving to capture all available economies of scale.* Economies of scale stem from an ability to lower unit costs by increasing the scale of operation. For example, occasions may arise when a large plant is more economical to operate than a small or medium-sized plant or when a large distribution center is more cost efficient than a small one.

- *Taking full advantage of experience and learning curve effects.* The cost of performing an activity can decline over time as the learning and experience of company personnel build.

- *Trying to operate facilities at full capacity.* Whether a company is able to operate at or near full capacity has a big impact on unit costs when its value chain contains activities associated with substantial fixed costs. Higher rates of capacity utilization allow depreciation and other fixed costs to be spread over a larger unit volume, thereby lowering fixed costs per unit.

*fixed cost per unit ↓
if units ↑*

- *Pursuing efforts to boost sales volumes and thus spread outlays for R&D, advertising, and general administration over more units.* The more units a company sells, the more it lowers cost per unit for expenses such as new-product development, sales promotion campaigns, and administrative support activities.

- *Substituting lower cost inputs whenever there's little or no sacrifice in product quality or product performance.* If the costs of certain raw materials and parts are "too high," a company can switch to using lower-cost alternatives when they exist.

- *Employing advanced production technology and process design to improve overall efficiency.* Often production costs can be cut by utilizing design for manufacture (DFM) procedures and computer-assisted design (CAD) techniques that enable more integrated and efficient production methods, investing in highly automated robotic production technology, and shifting to production processes that enable manufacturing multiple versions of a product as cost efficiently as mass producing a single version. A number of companies are ardent users of total quality management systems, business process reengineering, Six Sigma methodology, and other business process management techniques that aim at boosting efficiency and reducing costs.

- *Using communication systems and information technology to achieve operating efficiencies.* For example sharing data and production schedules with suppliers, coupled with the use of enterprise resource planning (ERP) and manufacturing execution system (MES) software, can reduce parts inventories, trim production times, and lower labor requirements.

- *Pursuing ways to reduce workforce size and lower overall compensation costs.* A company can economize on labor costs by installing labor-saving technology, shifting production from geographic areas where pay scales are high to geographic areas where pay scales are low, using incentive compensation systems that promote high labor productivity, and avoiding the use of union labor where possible (because costly work rules can stifle productivity and because of "unreasonable" union demands for above-market pay scales and costly fringe benefits).

- *Using the company's bargaining power vis-à-vis suppliers to gain concessions.* A company may have sufficient bargaining clout with suppliers to win price discounts on large-volume purchases or realize other cost-savings.

- *Being alert to the cost advantages of outsourcing and vertical integration.* Outsourcing the performance of certain value chain activities can be more economical than performing them in-house if outside specialists, by virtue of their expertise and volume, can perform the activities at lower cost.

Revamping the Value Chain Dramatic cost advantages can often emerge from reengineering the company's value chain in ways that eliminate costly work steps and bypass certain cost-producing value chain activities. Such value chain revamping can include:

- *Selling directly to consumers and cutting out the activities and costs of distributors and dealers.* To circumvent the need for distributors–dealers, a company can (1) create its own direct sales force (which adds the costs of maintaining and supporting a sales force but may be cheaper than utilizing independent distributors and dealers to access buyers), and/or (2) conduct sales operations at the company's website (costs for website operations and shipping may be a substantially cheaper way to make sales to customers than going through distributor–dealer channels). Costs in the wholesale/retail portions of the value chain frequently represent 35 to 50 percent of the price final consumers pay, so establishing a direct sales force or selling online may offer big cost savings.

- *Streamlining operations by eliminating low value-added or unnecessary work steps and activities.* At Walmart, some items supplied by manufacturers are delivered directly to retail stores rather than being routed through Walmart's distribution centers and delivered by Walmart trucks. In other instances, Walmart unloads incoming shipments from manufacturers' trucks arriving at its distribution centers directly onto outgoing Walmart trucks headed to particular stores without ever moving the goods into the distribution center.

- *Reducing materials handling and shipping costs by having suppliers locate their plants or warehouses close to a company's own facilities.* Having suppliers locate their plants or warehouses very close to a company's own plant not only lowers inbound shipping costs, but also facilitates just-in-time deliveries of parts and components.

Concepts & Connections 5.1 describes Walmart's broad approach to managing its value chain in the retail grocery portion of its business to achieve a dramatic cost advantage over rival supermarket chains and become the world's biggest grocery retailer.

When a Low-Cost Provider Strategy Works Best

▶**LO3**

Recognize why some generic strategies work better in certain kinds of industry and competitive conditions than others.

A competitive strategy predicated on low-cost leadership is particularly powerful when:

1. *Price competition among rival sellers is especially vigorous.* Low-cost providers are in the best position to compete offensively on the basis of price and to survive price wars.

2. *The products of rival sellers are essentially identical and are readily available from several sellers.* Commodity-like products and/or ample supplies set the stage for lively price competition; in such markets, it is the less efficient, higher-cost companies that are most vulnerable.

3. *There are few ways to achieve product differentiation that have value to buyers.* When the product or service differences between brands do not matter much to buyers, buyers nearly always shop the market for the best price.

CONCEPTS & CONNECTIONS 5.1

HOW WALMART MANAGED ITS VALUE CHAIN TO ACHIEVE A LOW-COST ADVANTAGE OVER RIVAL SUPERMARKET CHAINS

Walmart has achieved a very substantial cost and pricing advantage over rival supermarket chains by both revamping portions of the grocery retailing value chain and outmanaging its rivals in efficiently performing various value chain activities. Its cost advantage stems from a series of initiatives and practices:

- Instituting extensive information sharing with vendors via online systems that relay sales at its checkout counters directly to suppliers of the items, thereby providing suppliers with real-time information on customer demand and preferences (creating an estimated 6 percent cost advantage).

- Pursuing global procurement of some items and centralizing most purchasing activities so as to leverage the company's buying power (creating an estimated 2.5 percent cost advantage).

- Investing in state-of-the-art automation at its distribution centers, efficiently operating a truck fleet that makes daily deliveries to Walmart's stores, and putting assorted other cost-saving practices into place at its headquarters, distribution centers, and stores (resulting in an estimated 4 percent cost advantage).

- Striving to optimize the product mix and achieve greater sales turnover (resulting in about a 2 percent cost advantage).

- Installing security systems and store operating procedures that lower shrinkage rates (producing a cost advantage of about 0.5 percent).

- Negotiating preferred real estate rental and leasing rates with real estate developers and owners of its store sites (yielding a cost advantage of 2 percent).

- Managing and compensating its workforce in a manner that produces lower labor costs (yielding an estimated 5 percent cost advantage).

Altogether, these value chain initiatives give Walmart an approximately 22 percent cost advantage over Kroger, Safeway, and other leading supermarket chains. With such a sizable cost advantage, Walmart has been able to underprice its rivals and become the world's leading supermarket retailer.

Source: www.walmart.com; and Marco Iansiti and Roy Levien, "Strategy as Ecology," *Harvard Business Review* 82, no. 3 (March 2004), p. 70.

4. *Buyers incur low costs in switching their purchases from one seller to another.* Low switching costs give buyers the flexibility to shift purchases to lower-priced sellers having equally good products. A low-cost leader is well positioned to use low price to induce its customers not to switch to rival brands.

5. *The majority of industry sales are made to a few, large-volume buyers.* Low-cost providers are in the best position among sellers in bargaining with high-volume buyers because they are able to beat rivals' pricing to land a high-volume sale while maintaining an acceptable profit margin.

6. *Industry newcomers use introductory low prices to attract buyers and build a customer base.* The low-cost leader can use price cuts of its own to make it harder for a new rival to win customers.

As a rule, the more price-sensitive buyers are, the more appealing a low-cost strategy becomes. A low-cost company's ability to set the industry's price floor and still earn a profit erects protective barriers around its market position.

Pitfalls to Avoid in Pursuing a Low-Cost Provider Strategy

Perhaps the biggest pitfall of a low-cost provider strategy is getting carried away with *overly aggressive price cutting* and ending up with lower, rather than higher, profitability. A low-cost/low-price advantage results in superior profitability only if (1) prices are cut by less than the size of the cost advantage or (2) the added volume is large enough to bring in a bigger total profit despite lower margins per unit sold. Thus, a company with a 5 percent cost advantage cannot cut prices 20 percent, end up with a volume gain of only 10 percent, and still expect to earn higher profits!

A second big pitfall is *relying on an approach to reduce costs that can be easily copied by rivals.* The value of a cost advantage depends on its sustainability. Sustainability, in turn, hinges on whether the company achieves its cost advantage in ways difficult for rivals to replicate or match. If rivals find it relatively easy or inexpensive to imitate the leader's low-cost methods, then the leader's advantage will be too short-lived to yield a valuable edge in the marketplace.

A third pitfall is becoming *too fixated on cost reduction.* Low costs cannot be pursued so zealously that a firm's offering ends up being too features-poor to gain the interest of buyers. Furthermore, a company driving hard to push its costs down has to guard against misreading or ignoring increased buyer preferences for added features or declining buyer price sensitivity. Even if these mistakes are avoided, a low-cost competitive approach still carries risk. Cost-saving technological breakthroughs or process improvements by rival firms can nullify a low-cost leader's hard-won position.

BROAD DIFFERENTIATION STRATEGIES

Differentiation strategies are attractive whenever buyers' needs and preferences are too diverse to be fully satisfied by a standardized product or service. A company attempting to succeed through differentiation must study buyers' needs and behavior carefully to learn what buyers think has value and what they are willing to pay for. Then the company must include these desirable features to clearly set itself apart from rivals lacking such product or service attributes.

CORE CONCEPT

The essence of a **broad differentiation strategy** is to offer unique product or service attributes that a wide range of buyers find appealing and worth paying for.

Successful differentiation allows a firm to:

- Command a premium price, and/or
- Increase unit sales (because additional buyers are won over by the differentiating features), and/or
- Gain buyer loyalty to its brand (because some buyers are strongly attracted to the differentiating features and bond with the company and its products).

Differentiation enhances profitability whenever the extra price the product commands outweighs the added costs of achieving the differentiation.

Company differentiation strategies fail when buyers don't value the brand's uniqueness and/or when a company's approach to differentiation is easily copied or matched by its rivals.

Approaches to Differentiation

Companies can pursue differentiation from many angles: a unique taste (Red Bull, Listerine), multiple features (Microsoft Office, Apple iPhone), wide selection and one-stop shopping (Home Depot, Amazon.com), superior service (Ritz-Carlton, Nordstrom), spare parts availability (Caterpillar guarantees 48-hour spare parts delivery to any customer anywhere in the world or else the part is furnished free), engineering design and performance (Mercedes-Benz, BMW), luxury and prestige (Rolex, Gucci, Chanel), product reliability (Whirlpool and Bosch in large home appliances), quality manufacturing (Michelin in tires, Toyota and Honda in automobiles), technological leadership (3M Corporation in bonding and coating products), a full range of services (Charles Schwab in stock brokerage), and a complete line of products (Campbell soups, Frito-Lay snack foods).

▶ **LO4**

Gain command of the major avenues for developing a competitive advantage based on differentiating a company's product or service offering from the offerings of rivals.

The most appealing approaches to differentiation are those that are hard or expensive for rivals to duplicate. Resourceful competitors can, in time, clone almost any product or feature or attribute. If Coca-Cola introduces a vitamin-enhanced bottled water, so can Pepsi; if Firestone offers customers attractive financing terms, so can Goodyear. As a rule, differentiation yields a longer-lasting and more profitable competitive edge when it is based on product innovation, technical superiority, product quality and reliability, comprehensive customer service, and unique competitive capabilities. Such differentiating attributes tend to be tough for rivals to copy or offset profitably and buyers widely perceive them as having value.

> Easy-to-copy differentiating features cannot produce sustainable competitive advantage; differentiation based on hard-to-copy competencies and capabilities tends to be more sustainable.

Delivering Superior Value via a Differentiation Strategy

While it is easy enough to grasp that a successful differentiation strategy must offer value in ways unmatched by rivals, a big issue in crafting a differentiation strategy is deciding what is valuable to customers. Typically, value can be delivered to customers in three basic ways.

1. *Include product attributes and user features that lower the buyer's costs.* Commercial buyers value products that can reduce their cost of doing business. For example, making a company's product more economical for a buyer to use can be done by reducing the buyer's raw materials waste (providing cut-to-size components), reducing a buyer's inventory requirements (providing just-in-time deliveries), increasing product reliability to lower a buyer's repair and maintenance costs, and providing free technical support. Similarly, consumers find value in differentiating features that will reduce their expenses. Rising costs for gasoline prices have spurred the efforts of motor vehicle manufacturers worldwide to introduce models with better fuel economy.

2. *Incorporate tangible features that improve product performance.* Commercial buyers and consumers alike value higher levels of performance in many types of products. Product reliability, output, durability, convenience, and ease of use are aspects of product performance that differentiate products offered to buyers. Mobile phone manufacturers are currently in a race to improve the performance of their products through the introduction of next-generation phones with a more appealing, trend-setting array of user features and options.

3. *Incorporate intangible features that enhance buyer satisfaction in noneconomic ways.* Toyota's Prius appeals to environmentally conscious motorists who wish to help reduce global carbon dioxide emissions. Bentley, Ralph Lauren, Louis Vuitton, Tiffany, Cartier, and Rolex have differentiation-based competitive advantages linked to buyer desires for status, image, prestige, upscale fashion, superior craftsmanship, and the finer things in life. L.L. Bean makes its mail-order customers feel secure in their purchases by providing an unconditional guarantee with no time limit.

> Differentiation can be based on *tangible* or *intangible* features and attributes.

Managing the Value Chain in Ways That Enhance Differentiation

Differentiation is not necessarily something hatched in marketing and advertising departments, nor is it limited to quality and service. Differentiation opportunities can exist in activities all along the value chain. Value chain activities that affect the value of a product or service include the following:

- *Supplier and purchasing activities* that ultimately spill over to affect the performance or quality of the company's end product. Starbucks gets high ratings on its coffees partly because it has very strict specifications on the coffee beans purchased from suppliers.

- *Product R&D activities* that aim at improved product designs and performance, expanded end uses and applications, more frequent first-to-market victories, added user safety, greater recycling capability, or enhanced environmental protection.

- *Production R&D and technology-related activities* that permit the manufacture of customized products at an efficient cost; make production methods safer for the environment; or improve product quality, reliability, and appearance. Many manufacturers have developed flexible manufacturing systems that allow different models and product versions to be made on the same assembly line. Being able to provide buyers with made-to-order products can be a potent differentiating capability.

- *Manufacturing activities* that reduce product defects, extend product life, allow better warranty coverages, or enhance product appearance. The quality edge enjoyed by Japanese automakers stems partly from their distinctive competence in performing assembly line activities.

- *Distribution and shipping activities* that allow for fewer warehouse and on-the-shelf stockouts, quicker delivery to customers, more accurate order filling, and/or lower shipping costs.

- *Marketing, sales, and customer service activities* that result in superior technical assistance to buyers, faster maintenance and repair services, better credit terms, quicker order processing, or greater customer convenience.

Perceived Value and the Importance of Signaling Value

The price premium commanded by a differentiation strategy reflects *the value actually delivered* to the buyer and *the value perceived* by the buyer. The value of certain differentiating features is rather easy for buyers to detect, but in some instances buyers may have trouble assessing what their experience with the product will be. Successful differentiators go to great lengths to make buyers knowledgeable about a product's value and incorporate signals of value such as attractive packaging; extensive ad campaigns; the quality of brochures and sales presentations; the seller's list of customers; the length of time the firm has been in business; and the professionalism, appearance, and personality of the seller's employees. Such signals of value may be as important as actual value (1) when the nature of differentiation is subjective or hard to quantify, (2) when buyers are making a first-time purchase, (3) when repurchase is infrequent, and (4) when buyers are unsophisticated.

When a Differentiation Strategy Works Best

Differentiation strategies tend to work best in market circumstances where:

► **LO3**

Recognize why some generic strategies work better in certain kinds of industry and competitive conditions than others.

1. *Buyer needs and uses of the product are diverse.* Diverse buyer preferences allow industry rivals to set themselves apart with product attributes that appeal to particular buyers. For instance, the diversity of consumer preferences for menu selection, ambience, pricing, and customer service gives restaurants exceptionally wide latitude in creating differentiated concepts. Other industries offering opportunities for differentiation based upon diverse buyer needs and uses include magazine publishing, automobile manufacturing, footwear, kitchen appliances, and computers.

2. *There are many ways to differentiate the product or service that have value to buyers.* Industries that allow competitors to add features to product attributes are well suited to differentiation strategies. For example, hotel chains can differentiate on such features as location, size of room, range of guest services, in-hotel dining, and the quality and luxuriousness of bedding and furnishings. Similarly, cosmetics producers are able to differentiate based upon prestige and image, formulations that fight the signs of aging, UV light protection, exclusivity of retail locations, the inclusion of antioxidants and natural ingredients, or prohibitions against animal testing.

3. *Few rival firms are following a similar differentiation approach.* The best differentiation approaches involve trying to appeal to buyers on the basis of attributes that rivals are not emphasizing. A differentiator encounters less head-to-head rivalry when it goes its own separate way to create uniqueness and does not try to outdifferentiate rivals on the very same attributes. When many rivals are all claiming "ours tastes better than theirs" or "ours gets your clothes cleaner than theirs," competitors tend to end up chasing the same buyers with very similar product offerings.

4. *Technological change is fast-paced and competition revolves around rapidly evolving product features.* Rapid product innovation and frequent introductions of next-version products heighten buyer interest and provide space for companies to pursue distinct differentiating paths. In video game hardware and video games, golf equipment, PCs, mobile phones, and automobile navigation systems, competitors are locked into an ongoing battle to set themselves apart by introducing the best next-generation products; companies that fail to come up with new and improved products and distinctive performance features quickly lose out in the marketplace.

Pitfalls to Avoid in Pursuing a Differentiation Strategy

Differentiation strategies can fail for any of several reasons. *A differentiation strategy keyed to product or service attributes that are easily and quickly copied is always suspect.* Rapid imitation means that no rival achieves meaningful differentiation, because whatever new feature one firm introduces that strikes the fancy of buyers is almost immediately added by rivals. This is why a firm must search out sources of uniqueness that are time-consuming or burdensome for rivals to match if it hopes to use differentiation to win a sustainable competitive edge over rivals.

Differentiation strategies can also falter when buyers see little value in the unique attributes of a company's product. Thus even if a company sets the attributes of its brand apart from its rivals' brands, its strategy can fail because of trying to differentiate on the basis of something that does not deliver adequate value to buyers. Any time many potential buyers look at a company's differentiated product offering and conclude "so what," the company's differentiation strategy is in deep trouble; buyers will likely decide the product is not worth the extra price and sales will be disappointingly low.

Overspending on efforts to differentiate is a strategy flaw that can erode profitability. Company efforts to achieve differentiation nearly always raise costs. The trick to profitable differentiation is either to keep the costs of achieving differentiation below the price premium the differentiating attributes can command in the marketplace or to offset thinner profit margins by selling enough additional units to increase total profits. If a company goes overboard in pursuing costly differentiation, it could be saddled with unacceptably thin profit margins or even losses. The need to contain differentiation costs is why many companies add little touches of differentiation that add to buyer satisfaction but are inexpensive to institute.

Other common pitfalls and mistakes in crafting a differentiation strategy include:

- *Overdifferentiating so that product quality or service levels exceed buyers' needs.* Buyers are unlikely to pay extra for features and attributes that will go unused. For example, consumers are unlikely to purchase programmable large appliances such as washers, dryers, and ovens if they are satisfied with manually controlled appliances.

- *Trying to charge too high a price premium.* Even if buyers view certain extras or deluxe features as "nice to have," they may still conclude that the added benefit or luxury is not worth the price differential over that of lesser differentiated products.

- *Being timid and not striving to open up meaningful gaps in quality or service or performance features vis-à-vis the products of rivals.* Tiny differences between rivals' product offerings may not be visible or important to buyers.

A low-cost provider strategy can always defeat a differentiation strategy when buyers are satisfied with a basic product and don't think "extra" attributes are worth a higher price.

FOCUSED (OR MARKET NICHE) STRATEGIES

What sets focused strategies apart from low-cost leadership or broad differentiation strategies is a concentration on a narrow piece of the total market. The targeted segment, or niche, can be defined by geographic uniqueness or by special product attributes that appeal only to niche members. The advantages of focusing a company's entire competitive effort on a single market niche are considerable, especially for smaller and medium-sized companies that may lack the breadth and depth of resources to tackle going after a national customer base with a "something for everyone" lineup of models, styles, and product selection. Community Coffee, the largest family-owned specialty coffee retailer in the United States, has a geographic focus on the state of Louisiana and communities across the Gulf of Mexico. Community holds only a 1.1 percent share of the national coffee market, but has recorded sales in excess of $100 million and has won a 50 percent share of the coffee business in the 11-state region where it is distributed. Examples of firms that concentrate on a well-defined market niche keyed to a particular product or buyer segment include Discovery Channel and Comedy Central (in cable TV), Google (in Internet search engines), Porsche (in sports cars), and CGA, Inc. (a specialist in providing insurance to cover the cost of lucrative hole-in-one prizes at golf tournaments). Microbreweries, local bakeries, bed-and-breakfast inns, and local owner-managed retail boutiques are all good examples of enterprises that have scaled their operations to serve narrow or local customer segments.

A Focused Low-Cost Strategy

A focused strategy based on low cost aims at securing a competitive advantage by serving buyers in the target market niche at a lower cost and a lower price than rival competitors. This strategy has considerable attraction when a firm can lower costs significantly by limiting its customer base to a well-defined buyer segment. The avenues to achieving a cost advantage over rivals also serving the target market niche are the same as for low-cost leadership—outmanage rivals in keeping the costs to a bare minimum and searching for innovative ways to bypass or reduce nonessential activities. The only real difference between a low-cost provider strategy and a focused low-cost strategy is the size of the buyer group to which a company is appealing.

Focused low-cost strategies are fairly common. Producers of private-label goods are able to achieve low costs in product development, marketing, distribution, and advertising by concentrating on making generic items similar to name-brand merchandise and selling directly to retail chains wanting a low-priced store brand. The Perrigo Company has become a leading

CONCEPTS & CONNECTIONS 5.2

VIZIO'S FOCUSED LOW-COST STRATEGY

California-based Vizio, Inc., designs flat-panel LCD and plasma TVs, which are sold only by big box discount retailers such as Walmart, Sam's Club, Costco Wholesale, and Best Buy. If you've shopped for a flat-panel TV recently, you've probably noticed that Vizio is among the lowest-priced brands and that its picture quality is surprisingly good considering the price. The company keeps its cost low by designing TVs and then sourcing production to a limited number of contract manufacturers in Taiwan. In fact, 80 percent of its production is handled by AmTran Technology. Such a dependence on a supplier can place a buyer in a precarious situation by making it vulnerable to price increases or product shortages, but Vizio has countered this possible threat by making AmTran a major stockholder. AmTran Technology owns a 23 percent stake in Vizio and earns about 80 percent of its revenues from its sales of televisions to Vizio. This close relationship with its major supplier and its focus on a single product category sold through limited distribution channels allow Vizio to offer its customers deep price discounts.

Vizio's first major account was landed in 2003 when it approached Costco buyers with a 46-inch plasma TV with a wholesale price that was half the price of the next-lowest-price competitor. Within two months, Costco was carrying Vizio flat-screen TVs in 320 of its warehouse stores in the United States. In October 2007, Vizio approached buyers for Sam's Club with a 20-inch LCD TV that could be sold at retail for less than $350. The price and quality of the 20-inch TV led Sam's Club buyers to place an order for 20,000 TVs for a March 2008 delivery. Vizio has since expanded its product line to include HDTVs as large as 65 inches and planned a 2011 launch of a 3DTV line that would sell for less than $500. In 2010, Vizio was the largest seller of flat-panel HDTVs in the United States with a market share of 28 percent.

Source: Vizio's rapid success was highlighted in "Picture Shift: U.S. Upstart Takes On TV Giants in Price War," *The Wall Street Journal,* April 15, 2008, p. A1; and "Vizio Takes Top Spot for 2010 LCD TV Sales," Vizio press release, February 25, 2011.

manufacturer of over-the-counter health care products with 2010 sales of more than $2.2 billion by focusing on producing private-label brands for retailers such as Walmart, CVS, Walgreens, Rite Aid, and Safeway. Even though Perrigo doesn't make branded products, a focused low-cost strategy is appropriate for the makers of branded products as well. Concepts & Connections 5.2 describes how Vizio's low costs and focus on big box retailers have allowed it to become the largest seller of flat-panel HDTVs in the United States.

A Focused Differentiation Strategy

Focused differentiation strategies are keyed to offering carefully designed products or services to appeal to the unique preferences and needs of a narrow, well-defined group of buyers (as opposed to a broad differentiation strategy aimed at many buyer groups and market segments). Companies such as Four Seasons Hotels and Resorts, Chanel, Gucci, and Louis Vuitton employ successful differentiation-based focused strategies targeted at affluent buyers wanting products and services with world-class attributes. Indeed, most markets contain a buyer segment willing to pay a price premium for the very finest items available, thus opening the strategic window for some competitors to pursue differentiation-based focused strategies aimed at the very top of the market pyramid. Ferrari markets its 1,500 cars sold in North America each year to a list of just 20,000 highly affluent car enthusiasts.

CONCEPTS & CONNECTIONS 5.3

NESTLÉ NESPRESSO'S FOCUSED DIFFERENTIATION STRATEGY IN THE COFFEE INDUSTRY

Nestlé's strategy in the gourmet coffee industry has allowed its Nespresso brand of espresso coffee to become the fastest-growing billion-dollar brand in its broad lineup of chocolates and confectionery, bottled waters, coffee, ready-to-eat cereals, frozen food, dairy products, ice cream, and baby foods. The Nespresso concept was developed in 1986 to allow consumers to create a perfect cup of espresso coffee, equal to that of a skilled barista, with the use of a proprietary line of coffeemakers designed to accommodate Nespresso's single-serving coffee capsules. Nespresso capsules were available in 16 different roasts and aromatic profiles and could be purchased online at Nestlé's Nespresso Club website, in any of Nestlé's 200 lavish Nespresso boutiques located in the world's most exclusive shopping districts, and in select upscale retailers across the globe. Nespresso coffee machines were designed for ease-of-use while having advanced technological features that maximized the aroma of the coffee and automated the entire process even down to creating a thick and creamy froth from cold milk for cappuccinos. Nespresso coffeemakers also set standards for aesthetics with classic, sleek models, avant-garde models, and retro-modern models.

The ease-of-use of the stylish Nespresso coffeemakers and the high-quality coffee selected by Nestlé for its single-serving coffee pods allowed coffee drinkers with little experience in preparing gourmet coffees to master great-tasting lattes, cappuccinos, and espresso drinks. Nespresso was sold in more than 50 countries in 2011 and had averaged annual growth in revenues of 30 percent since 2000 to reach sales of more than $3 billion Swiss francs in 2010.

Nestlé's focus differentiation strategy for Nespresso includes the following primary elements:

- **Unsurpassed product quality and proven coffee expertise.** Through its unique business model, Nespresso has the ability to guarantee highest quality at every stage of the coffee value chain. Nespresso's team of passionate green coffee experts, agronomists, and supply partners regularly crisscross the globe in search of the highest-quality beans from specialty farms in the finest countries of origin. They work with a variety of other Nespresso coffee experts including coffee sensory, aroma, and flavor experts who create the Nespresso Grand Crus at state-of-the-art coffee production facilities in Orbe and Avenches, Switzerland.

- **Unstoppable drive for innovation and distinctive design.** Obsessed about innovation, compulsive about the fine details, and passionate about the fusion between technology and design, the Nespresso in-house research and development team has pioneered many award-winning machine innovations and cutting-edge designs, in collaboration with external design and machine experts. These breakthroughs have resulted in more than 1,700 patents.

- **Inspirational, iconic global reputation of the brand.** Nespresso is continually infusing itself with original ideas, flavors, and innovations from around the world to define its own unique lifestyle. Its journey toward becoming an iconic brand has made it a well-recognized and respected reference for highest quality around the world. Through Nespresso's network of more than 200 exclusive boutiques in key cities around the world, coffee lovers can come together to experience the brand with all senses, such as tasting Nespresso's luxurious coffees or learning more about the coffee countries of origin. These stylish sanctuaries are the perfect destinations for people who love the very best coffee.

- **Global brand community thanks to direct customer relationships.** Much of the success Nespresso has enjoyed in recent years can be attributed to the privileged relationships the brand has developed with its consumers and the reciprocal enthusiasm consumers have consistently shown for the brand. More than 50 percent of all new Nespresso Club Members first experience the brand through existing members. Between 2001 and 2009, the number of Nespresso Club Members worldwide jumped from 600,000 to more than 6 million.

- **Exclusive routes to market.** The Nespresso business model enables the company to maintain direct relationships with its customers through three channels. A global Internet boutique is available at www.nespresso.com; a global retail boutique network gives consumers the opportunity to experience the brand with all senses; and Customer Relationship Centers help consumers connect with friendly coffee specialists by phone.

- **Expertise in sustainable quality development.** Nespresso and its key suppliers work closely with more than 30,000 farmers who are part of the AAA Sustainable Quality Program to ensure they are implementing farming practices that lead to the highest-quality beans and economic viability, while respecting the environment. Coffee farmers who are part of the program are rewarded not only with higher compensation but also with a long-term partnership with Nespresso. Approximately 50 percent of the coffee Nespresso buys is AAA Sustainable Quality.

Source: Nestlé press releases, June 9, 2009, September 21, 2009, and August 11, 2010.

Another successful focused differentiator is "fashion food retailer" Trader Joe's, a 300-store, 25-state chain that is a combination gourmet deli and food warehouse. Customers shop Trader Joe's as much for entertainment as for conventional grocery items; the store stocks out-of-the-ordinary culinary treats such as raspberry salsa, salmon burgers, and jasmine fried rice, as well as the standard goods normally found in supermarkets. What sets Trader Joe's apart is not just its unique combination of food novelties and competitively priced grocery items but also its capability to turn an otherwise mundane grocery excursion into a whimsical treasure hunt that is just plain fun. Concepts & Connections 5.3 describes Nestlé's focused differentiation strategy for Nespresso.

When a Focused Low-Cost or Focused Differentiation Strategy Is Viable

LO3

Recognize why some generic strategies work better in certain kinds of industry and competitive conditions than others.

A focused strategy aimed at securing a competitive edge based either on low cost or differentiation becomes increasingly attractive as more of the following conditions are met:

- The target market niche is big enough to be profitable and offers good growth potential.
- Industry leaders have chosen not to compete in the niche—focusers can avoid battling head-to-head against the industry's biggest and strongest competitors.
- It is costly or difficult for multisegment competitors to meet the specialized needs of niche buyers and at the same time satisfy the expectations of mainstream customers.
- The industry has many different niches and segments, thereby allowing a focuser to pick a niche suited to its resource strengths and capabilities.
- Few, if any, rivals are attempting to specialize in the same target segment.

The Risks of a Focused Low-Cost or Focused Differentiation Strategy

Focusing carries several risks. The *first major risk* is the chance that competitors will find effective ways to match the focused firm's capabilities in serving the target niche. In the lodging business, large chains such as Marriott and Hilton have launched multibrand strategies that allow them to compete effectively in several lodging segments simultaneously. Marriott has flagship hotels with a full complement of services and amenities that allow it to attract travelers and vacationers going to major resorts; it has J.W. Marriott and Ritz-Carlton hotels that provide deluxe comfort and service to business and leisure travelers; it has Courtyard by Marriott and SpringHill Suites brands for business travelers looking for moderately priced lodging; it has Marriott Residence Inns and TownePlace Suites designed as a "home away from home" for travelers staying five or more nights; and it has more than 650 Fairfield Inn locations that cater to travelers looking for quality lodging at an "affordable" price.

Similarly, Hilton has a lineup of brands (Waldorf Astoria, Conrad Hotels, Doubletree Hotels, Embassy Suites Hotels, Hampton Inns, Hilton Hotels, Hilton Garden Inns, and Homewood Suites) that enable it to compete in multiple segments and compete head-to-head against lodging chains that operate only in a single segment. Multibrand strategies are attractive to large companies such as Marriott and Hilton precisely because they enable a company to enter a market niche and siphon business away from companies that employ a focus strategy.

A *second risk* of employing a focus strategy is the potential for the preferences and needs of niche members to shift over time toward the product attributes desired by the majority of buyers. An erosion of the differences across buyer segments lowers entry barriers into a focuser's market niche and provides an open invitation for rivals in adjacent segments to begin competing for the focuser's customers. A *third risk* is that the segment may become so attractive it is soon inundated with competitors, intensifying rivalry and splintering segment profits.

BEST-COST PROVIDER STRATEGIES

▶**LO5**
Recognize the required conditions for delivering superior value to customers through the use of a hybrid of low-cost provider and differentiation strategies.

As Figure 5.1 indicates, **best-cost provider strategies** are a *hybrid* of low-cost provider and differentiation strategies that aim at satisfying buyer expectations on key quality/features/performance/service attributes and beating customer expectations on price. Companies pursuing best-cost strategies aim squarely at the sometimes great mass of value-conscious buyers looking for a good-to-very-good product or service at an economical price. The essence of a best-cost provider strategy is giving customers *more value for the money* by satisfying buyer desires for appealing features/ performance/quality/service and charging a lower price for these attributes compared to rivals with similar caliber product offerings.[3]

> **CORE CONCEPT**
> **Best-cost provider strategies** are a *hybrid* of low-cost provider and differentiation strategies that aim at satisfying buyer expectations on key quality/features/performance/service attributes and beating customer expectations on price.

To profitably employ a best-cost provider strategy, a company *must have the capability to incorporate attractive or upscale attributes at a lower cost than rivals.* This capability is contingent on (1) a superior value chain configuration that eliminates or minimizes activities that do not add value, (2) unmatched efficiency in managing essential value chain activities, and (3) core competencies that allow differentiating attributes to be incorporated at a low cost. When a company can incorporate appealing features, good-to-excellent product performance or quality, or more satisfying customer service into its product offering *at a lower cost than rivals,* then it enjoys "best-cost" status—it is the low-cost provider of a product or service with *upscale attributes.* A best-cost provider can use its low-cost advantage to underprice rivals whose products or services have similar upscale attributes and still earn attractive profits.

Concepts & Connections 5.4 describes how Toyota has applied the principles of a best-cost provider strategy in producing and marketing its Lexus brand.

CONCEPTS & CONNECTIONS 5.4

TOYOTA'S BEST-COST PRODUCER STRATEGY FOR ITS LEXUS LINE

Toyota Motor Company is widely regarded as a low-cost producer among the world's motor vehicle manufacturers. Despite its emphasis on product quality, Toyota has achieved low-cost leadership because it has developed considerable skills in efficient supply chain management and low-cost assembly capabilities, and because its models are positioned in the low-to-medium end of the price spectrum, where high production volumes are conducive to low unit costs. But when Toyota decided to introduce its new Lexus models to compete in the luxury-car market, it employed a classic best-cost provider strategy. Toyota took the following four steps in crafting and implementing its Lexus strategy:

- Designing an array of high-performance characteristics and upscale features into the Lexus models so as to make them comparable in performance and luxury to other high-end models and attractive to Mercedes-Benz, BMW, Audi, Jaguar, Cadillac, and Lincoln buyers.

- Transferring its capabilities in making high-quality Toyota models at low cost to making premium-quality Lexus models at costs below other luxury-car makers. Toyota's supply chain capabilities and low-cost assembly know-how allowed it to incorporate high-tech performance features

and upscale quality into Lexus models at substantially less cost than comparable Mercedes and BMW models.

- Using its relatively lower manufacturing costs to under-price comparable Mercedes and BMW models. Toyota believed that with its cost advantage it could price attractively equipped Lexus cars low enough to draw price-conscious buyers away from Mercedes and BMW. Toyota's pricing policy also allowed it to induce Toyota, Honda, Ford, or GM owners desiring more luxury to switch to a Lexus. Lexus's pricing advantage over Mercedes and BMW was sometimes quite significant. For example, in 2011 the Lexus RX 350, a midsize SUV, carried a sticker price in the $39,000–$52,000 range (depending on how it was equipped), whereas variously equipped Mercedes ML 350 SUVs had price tags in the $46,000–$92,000 range, and a BMW X5 SUV could range anywhere from $47,000 to $86,000, depending on the optional equipment chosen.

- Establishing a new network of Lexus dealers, separate from Toyota dealers, dedicated to providing a level of personalized, attentive customer service unmatched in the industry.

Lexus's best-cost strategy allowed it to become the number-one-selling luxury car brand worldwide in 2000—a distinction it has held through 2010.

When a Best-Cost Provider Strategy Works Best

LO3

Recognize why some generic strategies work better in certain kinds of industry and competitive conditions than others.

2 cases

A best-cost provider strategy works best in markets where product differentiation is the norm and attractively large numbers of value-conscious buyers can be induced to purchase midrange products rather than the basic products of low-cost producers or the expensive products of top-of-the-line differentiators. A best-cost provider usually needs to position itself near the middle of the market with either a medium-quality product at a below-average price or a high-quality product at an average or slightly higher-than-average price. Best-cost provider strategies also work well in recessionary times when great masses of buyers become value-conscious and are attracted to economically priced products and services with especially appealing attributes.

The Danger of an Unsound Best-Cost Provider Strategy

A company's biggest vulnerability in employing a best-cost provider strategy is not having the requisite core competencies and efficiencies in managing value chain activities to support the addition of differentiating features without significantly increasing costs. A company with a modest degree of differentiation and no real cost advantage will most likely find itself squeezed between the firms using low-cost strategies and those using differentiation strategies. Low-cost providers may be able to siphon customers away with the appeal of a lower price (despite having marginally less appealing product attributes). High-end differentiators may be able to steal customers away with the appeal of appreciably better product attributes (even though their products carry a somewhat higher price tag). Thus, a successful best-cost provider must offer buyers *significantly* better product attributes to justify a price above what low-cost leaders are charging. Likewise, it has to achieve significantly lower costs in providing upscale features so that it can outcompete high-end differentiators on the basis of a *significantly* lower price.

SUCCESSFUL COMPETITIVE STRATEGIES ARE RESOURCE BASED

For a company's competitive strategy to succeed in delivering good performance and the intended competitive edge over rivals, it has to be well-matched to a company's internal situation and underpinned by an appropriate set of resources, know-how, and competitive capabilities. To succeed in employing a low-cost provider strategy, a company has to have the resources and capabilities to keep its costs below those of its competitors; this means having the expertise to cost-effectively manage value chain activities better than rivals and/or the innovative capability to bypass certain value chain activities being performed by rivals. To succeed in strongly differentiating its product in ways that are appealing to buyers, a company must have the resources and capabilities (such as better technology, strong skills in product innovation, expertise in customer service) to incorporate unique attributes into its product offering that a broad range of buyers will find appealing and worth paying for. Strategies focusing on a narrow segment of the market require the capability to do an outstanding job of satisfying the needs and expectations of niche buyers. Success in employing a strategy keyed to a best value offering requires the resources and capabilities to incorporate upscale product or service attributes at a lower cost than rivals.

> A company's competitive strategy should be well matched to its internal situation and predicated on leveraging its collection of competitively valuable resources and competencies.

KEY POINTS

1. Early in the process of crafting a strategy, company managers have to decide which of the five basic competitive strategies to employ—overall low-cost, broad differentiation, focused low-cost, focused differentiation, or best-cost provider.

2. In employing a low-cost provider strategy, a company must do a better job than rivals of cost-effectively managing internal activities and/or it must find innovative ways to eliminate or bypass cost-producing activities. Low-cost provider strategies work particularly well when price competition is strong and the products of rival sellers are very weakly differentiated. Other conditions favoring a low-cost provider strategy are when supplies are readily available from eager

sellers, when there are not many ways to differentiate that have value to buyers, when the majority of industry sales are made to a few large buyers, when buyer switching costs are low, and when industry newcomers are likely to use a low introductory price to build market share.

3. Broad differentiation strategies seek to produce a competitive edge by incorporating attributes and features that set a company's product/service offering apart from rivals in ways that buyers consider valuable and worth paying for. Successful differentiation allows a firm to (1) command a premium price for its product, (2) increase unit sales (because additional buyers are won over by the differentiating features), and/or (3) gain buyer loyalty to its brand (because some buyers are strongly attracted to the differentiating features and bond with the company and its products). Differentiation strategies work best in markets with diverse buyer preferences where there are big windows of opportunity to strongly differentiate a company's product offering from those of rival brands, in situations where few other rivals are pursuing a similar differentiation approach, and in circumstances where technological change is fast-paced and competition centers on rapidly evolving product features. A differentiation strategy is doomed when competitors are able to quickly copy most or all of the appealing product attributes a company comes up with, when a company's differentiation efforts meet with a ho-hum or so-what market reception, or when a company erodes profitability by overspending on efforts to differentiate its product offering.

4. A focus strategy delivers competitive advantage either by achieving lower costs than rivals in serving buyers comprising the target market niche or by offering niche buyers an appealingly differentiated product or service that meets their needs better than rival brands. A focused strategy becomes increasingly attractive when the target market niche is big enough to be profitable and offers good growth potential, when it is costly or difficult for multisegment competitors to put capabilities in place to meet the specialized needs of the target market niche and at the same time satisfy the expectations of their mainstream customers, when there are one or more niches that present a good match with a focuser's resource strengths and capabilities, and when few other rivals are attempting to specialize in the same target segment.

5. Best-cost provider strategies stake out a middle ground between pursuing a low-cost advantage and a differentiation-based advantage and between appealing to the broad market as a whole and a narrow market niche. The aim is to create competitive advantage by giving buyers more value for the money—satisfying buyer expectations on key quality/features/performance/service attributes while beating customer expectations on price. To profitably employ a best-cost provider strategy, a company *must have the capability to incorporate attractive or upscale attributes at a lower cost than rivals.* This capability is contingent on (1) a superior value chain configuration, (2) unmatched efficiency in managing essential value chain activities, and (3) resource strengths and core competencies that allow differentiating attributes to be incorporated at a low cost. A best-cost provider strategy works best in markets where opportunities to differentiate exist and where many buyers are sensitive to price and value.

6. Deciding which generic strategy to employ is perhaps the most important strategic commitment a company makes—it tends to drive the rest of the strategic actions a company decides to undertake and it sets the whole tone for the pursuit of a competitive advantage over rivals.

ASSURANCE OF LEARNING EXERCISES

1. Best Buy is the largest consumer electronics retailer in the United States with 2011 sales of more than $50 billion. The company competes aggressively on price with rivals such as Costco Wholesale, Sam's Club, Walmart, and Target, but is also known by consumers for its first-rate customer service. Best Buy customers have commented that the retailer's sales staff is exceptionally knowledgeable about products and can direct them to the exact location of difficult to find items. Best Buy customers also appreciate that demonstration models of PC monitors, digital media players, and other electronics are fully powered and ready for in-store use. Best Buy's Geek Squad tech support and installation services are additional customer service features valued by many customers.

   How would you characterize Best Buy's competitive strategy? Should it be classified as a low-cost provider strategy? a differentiation strategy? a best-cost strategy? Explain your answer.

   LO1, LO2, LO3, LO4, LO5

2. Concepts & Connections 5.1 discusses Walmart's low-cost advantage in the supermarket industry. Based on information provided in the illustration, explain how Walmart has built its low-cost advantage in the supermarket industry and why a low-cost provider strategy is well-suited to the industry.

   LO2, LO3

   www.mcgrawhillconnect.com

3. Stihl is the world's leading manufacturer and marketer of chain saws with annual sales exceeding $2 billion. With innovations dating to its 1929 invention of the gasoline-powered chain saw, the company holds more than 1,000 patents related to chain saws and outdoor power tools. The company's chain saws, leaf blowers, and hedge trimmers sell at price points well above competing brands and are sold only by its network of some 8,000 independent dealers.

   How would you characterize Stihl's competitive strategy? Should it be classified as a low-cost provider strategy? a differentiation strategy? a best-cost strategy? Also, has the company chosen to focus on a narrow piece of the market or does it appear to pursue a broad market approach? Explain your answer.

   LO1, LO2, LO3, LO4, LO5

4. Explore BMW's website at www.bmwgroup.com and see if you can identify at least three ways in which the company seeks to differentiate itself from rival automakers. Is there reason to believe that BMW's differentiation strategy has been successful in producing a competitive advantage? Why or why not?

   LO3, LO4

   connect
   www.mcgrawhillconnect.com

EXERCISES FOR SIMULATION PARTICIPANTS

1. Which one of the five generic competitive strategies best characterizes your company's strategic approach to competing successfully?

2. Which rival companies appear to be employing a low-cost provider strategy?

3. Which rival companies appear to be employing a broad differentiation strategy?

4. Which rival companies appear to be employing a best-cost provider strategy?

LO1, LO2, LO3, LO4, LO5

5. Which rival companies appear to be employing some type of focus strategy?

6. What is your company's action plan to achieve a sustainable competitive advantage over rival companies? List at least three (preferably more than three) specific kinds of decision entries on specific decision screens that your company has made or intends to make to win this kind of competitive edge over rivals.

ENDNOTES

1. Michael E. Porter, *Competitive Strategy: Techniques for Analyzing Industries and Competitors* (New York: Free Press, 1980), chap. 2; and Michael E. Porter, "What Is Strategy?" *Harvard Business Review* 74, no. 6 (November–December 1996).

2. Michael E. Porter, *Competitive Advantage* (New York: Free Press, 1985).

3. Peter J. Williamson and Ming Zeng, "Value-for-Money Strategies for Recessionary Times," *Harvard Business Review* 87, no. 3 (March 2009).

chapter 6

SUPPLEMENTING THE CHOSEN COMPETITIVE STRATEGY—OTHER IMPORTANT STRATEGY CHOICES

LEARNING OBJECTIVES

LO1   Learn whether and when to pursue offensive strategic moves to improve a company's market position.

LO2   Learn whether and when to employ defensive strategies to protect the company's market position.

LO3   Recognize when being a first mover or a fast follower or a late mover can lead to competitive advantage.

LO4   Learn the advantages and disadvantages of extending a company's scope of operations via vertical integration.

LO5   Understand the conditions that favor farming out certain value chain activities to outside parties.

LO6   Gain an understanding of how strategic alliances and collaborative partnerships can bolster a company's collection of resources and capabilities.

LO7   Become aware of the strategic benefits and risks of mergers and acquisitions.

Once a company has settled on which of the five generic competitive strategies to employ, attention turns to what *other strategic actions* it can take to complement its competitive approach and maximize the power of its overall strategy. Several decisions regarding the company's operating scope and how to best strengthen its market standing must be made:

- Whether and when to go on the offensive and initiate aggressive strategic moves to improve the company's market position.
- Whether and when to employ defensive strategies to protect the company's market position.
- When to undertake strategic moves based upon whether it is advantageous to be a first mover or a fast follower or a late mover.
- Whether to integrate backward or forward into more stages of the industry value chain.
- Which value chain activities, if any, should be outsourced.
- Whether to enter into strategic alliances or partnership arrangements with other enterprises.
- Whether to bolster the company's market position by merging with or acquiring another company in the same industry.

This chapter presents the pros and cons of each of these measures that round out a company's overall strategy.

LAUNCHING STRATEGIC OFFENSIVES TO IMPROVE A COMPANY'S MARKET POSITION

LO1

Learn whether and when to pursue offensive strategic moves to improve a company's market position.

No matter which of the five generic competitive strategies a company employs, there are times when a company *should be aggressive and go on the offensive.* Strategic offensives are called for when a company spots opportunities to gain profitable market share at the expense of rivals or when a company has no choice but to try to whittle away at a strong rival's competitive advantage. Companies such as Walmart, Apple, Southwest Airlines, and Google play hardball, aggressively pursuing competitive advantage and trying to reap the benefits a competitive edge offers—a leading market share, excellent profit margins, and rapid growth.[1]

Choosing the Basis for Competitive Attack

Generally, strategic offensives should be grounded in a company's competitive assets and strong points and should be aimed at exploiting competitor weaknesses.[2] Ignoring the need to tie a strategic offensive to a company's competitive strengths is like going to war with a popgun—the prospects for success are dim. For instance, it is foolish for a company with relatively high costs to employ a price-cutting offensive. Likewise, it is ill advised to pursue a product innovation offensive without having proven expertise in R&D, new-product development, and speeding new or improved products to market.

> The best offensives use a company's most competitively potent resources to attack rivals in those competitive areas where they are weakest.

The principal offensive strategy options include the following:

1. *Attacking the competitive weaknesses of rivals.* For example, a company with especially good customer service capabilities can make special sales pitches to the customers of those rivals who provide subpar customer service. Aggressors with a recognized brand name and strong marketing skills can launch efforts to win customers away from rivals with weak brand recognition.

2. *Offering an equally good or better product at a lower price.* Lower prices can produce market share gains if competitors offering similarly performing products don't respond with price cuts of their own. Price-cutting offensives are best initiated by companies that have *first achieved a cost advantage.*[3]

3. *Pursuing continuous product innovation to draw sales and market share away from less innovative rivals.* Ongoing introductions of new/improved products can put rivals under tremendous competitive pressure, especially when rivals' new-product development capabilities are weak.

4. *Leapfrogging competitors by being the first to market with next-generation technology or products.* Microsoft got its next-generation Xbox 360 to market 12 months ahead of Sony's PlayStation 3 and Nintendo's Wii, helping it build a sizable market share and develop a reputation for cutting-edge innovation in the video game industry.

5. *Adopting and improving on the good ideas of other companies (rivals or otherwise).* The idea of warehouse-type home improvement centers did not originate with Home Depot co-founders Arthur Blank and Bernie Marcus; they got the "big box" concept from their former employer, Handy Dan Home Improvement. But they were quick to improve on Handy Dan's business model and strategy and take Home Depot to a higher plateau in terms of product-line breadth and customer service.

6. *Deliberately attacking those market segments where a key rival makes big profits.* Toyota has launched a hardball attack on General Motors, Ford, and Chrysler in the U.S. market for light trucks and SUVs, the very market arena where the Detroit automakers typically earn their big profits (roughly $10,000 to $15,000 per vehicle). Toyota's pickup trucks and SUVs have weakened the Big 3 U.S. automakers by taking away sales and market share that they desperately need.

7. *Maneuvering around competitors to capture unoccupied or less contested market territory.* Examples include launching initiatives to build strong positions in geographic areas or product categories where close rivals have little or no market presence.

8. *Using hit-and-run or guerrilla warfare tactics to grab sales and market share from complacent or distracted rivals.* Options for "guerrilla offensives" include occasional lowballing on price (to win a big order or steal a key account from a rival) or surprising key rivals with sporadic but intense bursts of promotional activity (offering a 20 percent discount for one week to draw customers away from rival brands).[4] Guerrilla offensives

are particularly well suited to small challengers who have neither the resources nor the market visibility to mount a full-fledged attack on industry leaders.

9. *Launching a preemptive strike to capture a rare opportunity or secure an industry's limited resources.*[5] What makes a move preemptive is its one-of-a-kind nature—whoever strikes first stands to acquire competitive assets that rivals can't readily match. Examples of preemptive moves include (1) securing the best distributors in a particular geographic region or country; (2) moving to obtain the most favorable site at a new interchange or intersection, in a new shopping mall, and so on; and (3) tying up the most reliable, high-quality suppliers via exclusive partnerships, long-term contracts, or even acquisition. To be successful, a preemptive move doesn't have to totally block rivals from following or copying; it merely needs to give a firm a prime position that is not easily circumvented.

Choosing Which Rivals to Attack

Offensive-minded firms need to analyze which of their rivals to challenge as well as how to mount that challenge. The following are the best targets for offensive attacks:

- *Market leaders that are vulnerable.* Offensive attacks make good sense when a company that leads in terms of size and market share is not a true leader in terms of serving the market well. Signs of leader vulnerability include unhappy buyers, an inferior product line, a weak competitive strategy with regard to low-cost leadership or differentiation, a preoccupation with diversification into other industries, and mediocre or declining profitability.

- *Runner-up firms with weaknesses in areas where the challenger is strong.* Runner-up firms are an especially attractive target when a challenger's resource strengths and competitive capabilities are well suited to exploiting their weaknesses.

- *Struggling enterprises that are on the verge of going under.* Challenging a hard-pressed rival in ways that further sap its financial strength and competitive position can hasten its exit from the market.

- *Small local and regional firms with limited capabilities.* Because small firms typically have limited expertise and resources, a challenger with broader capabilities is well positioned to raid their biggest and best customers.

Blue Ocean Strategy—A Special Kind of Offensive

A **blue ocean strategy** seeks to gain a dramatic and durable competitive advantage *by abandoning efforts to beat out competitors in existing markets and, instead, inventing a new industry or distinctive market segment that renders existing competitors largely irrelevant and allows a company to create and capture altogether new demand.*[6] This strategy views the business universe as consisting of two distinct types of market space. One is where industry boundaries are defined and accepted, the competitive rules of the game are well understood by all industry members, and companies try to outperform rivals by capturing a bigger share of existing demand; in such markets, lively competition constrains a company's prospects for rapid growth and superior profitability since rivals move quickly to either imitate or counter the successes of competitors. The second type of market space is a "blue ocean" where the industry does not really exist yet, is untainted by competition, and offers wide open opportunity for profitable and rapid growth if a company can come up with a product offering and strategy that allows it to create new demand rather than fight over existing demand. A terrific example of such wide open or blue ocean market space is the online auction industry that eBay created and now dominates.

> **CORE CONCEPT**
>
> **Blue ocean strategies** offer growth in revenues and profits by discovering or inventing new industry segments that create altogether new demand.

Other examples of companies that have achieved competitive advantages by creating blue ocean market spaces include Starbucks in the coffee shop industry, Dollar General in extreme discount retailing, FedEx in overnight package delivery, and Cirque du Soleil in live entertainment. Cirque du Soleil "reinvented the circus" by creating a distinctively different market space for its performances (Las Vegas nightclubs and theater-type settings) and pulling in a whole new group of customers—adults and corporate clients—who were willing to pay several times more than the price of a conventional circus ticket to have an "entertainment experience" featuring sophisticated clowns and star-quality acrobatic acts in a comfortable atmosphere. Companies that create blue ocean market spaces can usually sustain their initially won competitive advantage without encountering major competitive challenges for 10 to 15 years because of high barriers to imitation and the strong brand name awareness that a blue ocean strategy can produce.

USING DEFENSIVE STRATEGIES TO PROTECT A COMPANY'S MARKET POSITION AND COMPETITIVE ADVANTAGE

▶ **LO2**

Learn whether and when to employ defensive strategies to protect the company's market position.

In a competitive market, all firms are subject to offensive challenges from rivals. The purposes of defensive strategies are to lower the risk of being attacked, weaken the impact of any attack that occurs, and influence challengers to aim their efforts at other rivals. While defensive strategies usually don't enhance a firm's competitive advantage, they can definitely help fortify its competitive position. Defensive strategies can take either of two forms: actions to block challengers and actions signaling the likelihood of strong retaliation.

> Good defensive strategies can help protect competitive advantage but rarely are the basis for creating it.

Blocking the Avenues Open to Challengers

The most frequently employed approach to defending a company's present position involves actions to restrict a competitive attack by a challenger. A number of obstacles can be put in the path of would-be challengers.[7] A defender can introduce new features, add new models, or broaden its product

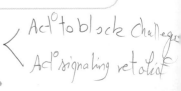

Ways for Def

line to close off vacant niches to opportunity-seeking challengers. It can thwart the efforts of rivals to attack with a lower price by maintaining economy-priced options of its own. It can try to discourage buyers from trying competitors' brands by making early announcements about upcoming new products or planned price changes. Finally, a defender can grant volume discounts or better financing terms to dealers and distributors to discourage them from experimenting with other suppliers.

Signaling Challengers that Retaliation Is Likely

The goal of signaling challengers that strong retaliation is likely in the event of an attack is either to dissuade challengers from attacking or to divert them to less threatening options. Either goal can be achieved by letting challengers know the battle will cost more than it is worth. Would-be challengers can be signaled by:

- Publicly announcing management's commitment to maintain the firm's present market share.
- Publicly committing the company to a policy of matching competitors' terms or prices.
- Maintaining a war chest of cash and marketable securities.
- Making an occasional strong counter response to the moves of weak competitors to enhance the firm's image as a tough defender.

TIMING A COMPANY'S OFFENSIVE AND DEFENSIVE STRATEGIC MOVES

 LO3

Recognize when being a first mover or a fast follower or a late mover can lead to competitive advantage.

When to make a strategic move is often as crucial as *what* move to make. Timing is especially important when *first-mover advantages* or *disadvantages* exist. Being first to initiate a strategic move can have a high payoff when (1) pioneering helps build a firm's image and reputation with buyers; (2) early commitments to new technologies, new-style components, new or emerging distribution channels, and so on, can produce an absolute cost advantage over rivals; (3) first-time customers remain strongly loyal to pioneering firms in making repeat purchases; and (4) moving first constitutes a preemptive strike, making imitation extra hard or unlikely. The bigger the first-mover advantages, the more attractive making the first move becomes.[8]

> **CORE CONCEPT**
>
> Because of **first-mover advantages and disadvantages,** competitive advantage can spring from *when* a move is made as well as from *what* move is made.

Sometimes, though, markets are slow to accept the innovative product offering of a first mover, in which case a fast follower with substantial resources and marketing muscle can overtake a first mover (as Fox News has done in competing against CNN to become the leading cable news network). Sometimes furious technological change or product innovation makes a first mover vulnerable to quickly appearing next-generation technology or products. For instance, former market leaders in mobile phones Nokia and Research in Motion (Blackberry) have been victimized by Apple's far more innovative iPhone models and new smartphones based on Google's Android operating system. Hence, there are no guarantees that a first mover will win sustainable competitive advantage.[9]

To sustain any advantage that may initially accrue to a pioneer, a first mover needs to be a fast learner and continue to move aggressively to capitalize on any initial pioneering advantage. If a first mover's skills, know-how, and actions are easily copied or even surpassed, then followers and even late movers can catch or overtake the first mover in a relatively short period. What makes being a first mover strategically important is not being the first company to do something but rather being the first competitor to put together the precise combination of features, customer value, and sound revenue/cost/profit economics that gives it an edge over rivals in the battle for market leadership.[10] If the marketplace quickly takes to a first mover's innovative product offering, a first mover must have large-scale production, marketing, and distribution capabilities if it is to stave off fast followers that possess similar resources capabilities. If technology is advancing at a torrid pace, a first mover cannot hope to sustain its lead without having strong capabilities in R&D, design, and new-product development, along with the financial strength to fund these activities. Concepts & Connections 6.1 describes how Amazon.com achieved a first-mover advantage in online retailing.

[margin note: Sustain the advantage of being a first mover.]

The Potential for Late-Mover Advantages or First-Mover Disadvantages

There are instances when there are actually *advantages* to being an adept follower rather than a first mover. Late-mover advantages (or *first-mover disadvantages*) arise in four instances:

- When pioneering leadership is more costly than followership and only negligible experience or learning curve benefits accrue to the leader—a condition that allows a follower to end up with lower costs than the first mover.

  [margin note: Leadership costly & provide negligible benefit]

- When the products of an innovator are somewhat primitive and do not live up to buyer expectations, thus allowing a clever follower to win disenchanted buyers away from the leader with better-performing products.

  [margin note: pdts primitive & buyers expect]

- When potential buyers are skeptical about the benefits of a new technology or product being pioneered by a first mover.

  [margin note: buyers are skeptical about b--]

- When rapid market evolution (due to fast-paced changes in either technology or buyer needs and expectations) gives fast followers and maybe even cautious late movers the opening to leapfrog a first mover's products with more attractive next-version products.

  [margin note: Rapid M evolut, provide more attractive version]

Deciding Whether to Be an Early Mover or Late Mover

In weighing the pros and cons of being a first mover versus a fast follower versus a slow mover, it matters whether the race to market leadership in a particular industry is a marathon or a sprint. In marathons, a slow mover is not unduly penalized—first-mover advantages can be fleeting, and there's

[margin note: excessively]

CONCEPTS & CONNECTIONS 6.1

AMAZON.COM'S FIRST-MOVER ADVANTAGE IN ONLINE RETAILING

Amazon.com's path to world's largest online retailer began in 1994 when Jeff Bezos, a Manhattan hedge fund analyst at the time, noticed the number of Internet users was increasing by 2,300 percent annually. Bezos saw the tremendous growth as an opportunity to sell products online that would be demanded by a large number of Internet users and could be easily shipped. Bezos launched the online bookseller, Amazon.com, in 1995. The start-up's revenues soared to $148 million in 1997, $610 million in 1998, and $1.6 billion in 1999. Bezo's business plan, hatched while on a cross-country trip with his wife in 1994, made him *Time*'s Person of the Year in 1999.

Amazon.com's early entry into online retailing had delivered a first-mover advantage, but between 2000 and 2011, Bezos undertook a series of additional strategic initiatives to solidify the company's number-one ranking in the industry. Bezos undertook a massive $300 million building program in the late 1990s that added five new warehouses and fulfillment centers. The additional warehouse space was added years before it was needed, but Bezos wanted to ensure that, as demand continued to grow, the company could continue to offer its customers the best selection, the lowest prices, and the cheapest and most convenient delivery. The company also expanded its product line to include Kindle readers, sporting goods, tools, toys, automotive parts, appliances, electronics, and digital music downloads. Amazon.com's 2010 revenues of $34.2 billion made it the world's largest Internet retailer, and Jeff Bezos' shares in Amazon.com made him the 12th wealthiest person in the United States with an estimated net worth of $12.6 billion.

Not all of Bezos' efforts to maintain a first-mover advantage in online retailing were a success. Bezos commented in a 2008 *Fortune* article profiling the company, "We were investors in every bankrupt, 1999-vintage e-commerce start-up. Pets.com, living.com, kozmo.com. We invested in a lot of high-profile flameouts." He went on to specify that although the ventures were a "waste of money," they "didn't take us off our own mission." Bezos also suggested that gaining advantage as a first mover is "taking a million tiny steps—and learning quickly from your missteps."

Sources: Mark Brohan, "The Top 500 Guide," *Internet Retailer,* June 2009, accessed at www.internetretailer.com on June 17, 2009; and Josh Quittner, "How Jeff Bezos Rules the Retail Space," *Fortune,* May 5, 2008, pp. 126–34.

ample time for fast followers and sometimes even late movers to catch up.[11] Thus the speed at which the pioneering innovation is likely to catch on matters considerably as companies struggle with whether to pursue a particular emerging market opportunity aggressively or cautiously. For instance, it took 5.5 years for worldwide mobile phone use to grow from 10 million to 100 million worldwide and close to 10 years for the number of at-home broadband subscribers to grow to 100 million worldwide. The lesson here is that there is a market-penetration curve for every emerging opportunity; typically, the curve has an inflection point at which all the pieces of the business model fall into place, buyer demand explodes, and the market takes off. The inflection point can come early on a fast-rising curve (like use of e-mail) or farther on up a slow-rising curve (such as use of broadband). Any company that seeks competitive advantage by being a first mover thus needs to ask some hard questions:

- Does market takeoff depend on the development of complementary products or services that currently are not available?

- Is new infrastructure required before buyer demand can surge?

- Will buyers need to learn new skills or adopt new behaviors? Will buyers encounter high switching costs?
- Are there influential competitors in a position to delay or derail the efforts of a first mover?

When the answers to any of these questions are yes, then a company must be careful not to pour too many resources into getting ahead of the market opportunity—the race is likely going to be more of a 10-year marathon than a 2-year sprint.

VERTICAL INTEGRATION: OPERATING ACROSS MORE INDUSTRY VALUE CHAIN SEGMENTS

Vertical integration extends a firm's competitive and operating scope within the same industry. It involves expanding the firm's range of value chain activities backward into sources of supply and/or forward toward end users. Thus, if a manufacturer invests in facilities to produce certain component parts that it formerly purchased from outside suppliers or if it opens its own chain of retail stores to market its products to consumers, it remains in essentially the same industry as before. The only change is that it has operations in two stages of the industry value chain. For example, paint manufacturer Sherwin-Williams remains in the paint business even though it has integrated forward into retailing by operating nearly 4,000 retail stores that market its paint products directly to consumers.

LO4

Learn the advantages and disadvantages of extending a company's scope of operations via vertical integration.

> **CORE CONCEPT**
>
> A **vertically integrated** firm is one that performs value chain activities along more than one stage of an industry's overall value chain.

A firm can pursue vertical integration by starting its own operations in other stages of the vertical activity chain, by acquiring a company already performing the activities it wants to bring in-house, or by means of a strategic alliance or joint venture. Vertical integration strategies can aim at *full integration* (participating in all stages of the vertical chain) or *partial integration* (building positions in selected stages of the vertical chain). Companies may choose to pursue *tapered integration*, a strategy that involves both outsourcing and performing the activity internally. Oil companies' practice of supplying their refineries with both crude oil produced from their own wells and crude oil supplied by third-party operators and well owners is an example of tapered backward integration. Boston Beer Company, the maker of Samuel Adams, engages in tapered forward integration since it operates brew pubs, but sells the majority of its products through third-party distributors.

> **CORE CONCEPT**
>
> **Backward integration** involves performing industry value chain activities previously performed by suppliers or other enterprises engaged in earlier stages of the industry value chain; **forward integration** involves performing industry value chain activities closer to the end user.

The Advantages of a Vertical Integration Strategy

The two best reasons for investing company resources in vertical integration are to strengthen the firm's competitive position and/or to boost its profitability.[12] Vertical integration has no real payoff unless it produces sufficient cost savings to justify the extra investment, adds materially to a company's technological and competitive strengths, and/or helps differentiate the company's product offering.

Integrating Backward to Achieve Greater Competitiveness   It is harder than one might think to generate cost savings or boost profitability by integrating backward into activities such as parts and components manufacture. For backward integration to be a viable and profitable strategy, a company must be able to (1) achieve the same scale economies as outside suppliers and (2) match or beat suppliers' production efficiency with no decline in quality. Neither outcome is easily achieved. To begin with, a company's in-house requirements are often too small to reach the optimum size for low-cost operation—for instance, if it takes a minimum production volume of 1 million units to achieve scale economies and a company's in-house requirements are just 250,000 units, then it falls way short of being able to match the costs of outside suppliers (who may readily find buyers for 1 million or more units).

But that said, there are still occasions when a company can improve its cost position and competitiveness by performing a broader range of value chain activities in-house rather than having these activities performed by outside suppliers. The best potential for being able to reduce costs via a backward integration strategy exists in situations where suppliers have very large profit margins, where the item being supplied is a major cost component, and where the requisite technological skills are easily mastered or acquired. Backward vertical integration can produce a differentiation-based competitive advantage when performing activities internally contributes to a better-quality product/service offering, improves the caliber of customer service, or in other ways enhances the performance of a final product. Other potential advantages of backward integration include sparing a company the uncertainty of being dependent on suppliers for crucial components or support services and lessening a company's vulnerability to powerful suppliers inclined to raise prices at every opportunity. Apple recently decided to integrate backward into producing its own chips for iPhones, chiefly because chips are a major cost component, have big profit margins, and in-house production would help protect Apple's proprietary iPhone technology.

Integrating Forward to Enhance Competitiveness   Vertical integration into forward stages of the industry value chain allows manufacturers to gain better access to end users, improve market visibility, and include the end user's purchasing experience as a differentiating feature. In many industries, independent sales agents, wholesalers, and retailers handle competing brands of the same product and have no allegiance to any one company's brand—they tend to push whatever offers the biggest profits. An independent insurance agency, for example, represents a number of different insurance companies and tries to find the best match between a customer's insurance requirements and the policies of alternative insurance companies. Under this arrangement, it is possible an agent will develop a preference for one company's policies or underwriting practices and neglect other represented insurance companies. An insurance company may conclude, therefore, that it is better off integrating forward and setting up its own local sales offices. The insurance company also has the ability to make consumers' interactions with local agents and office personnel a differentiating feature. Likewise, apparel manufacturers as varied as Polo Ralph Lauren, Ann Taylor, and Nike have integrated forward into retailing by operating full-price stores, factory outlet stores, and Internet retailing websites.

Forward Vertical Integration and Internet Retailing   Bypassing regular wholesale/retail channels in favor of direct sales and Internet retailing can have appeal if it lowers distribution costs, produces a relative cost advantage over certain rivals, offers higher margins, or results in lower selling prices to end users. In addition, sellers are compelled to include the Internet as a retail channel when a sufficiently large number of buyers in an industry prefer to make purchases online. However, a company that is vigorously pursuing online sales to consumers at the same time that it is also heavily promoting sales to consumers through its network of wholesalers and retailers *is competing directly against its distribution allies*. Such actions constitute *channel conflict* and create a tricky route to negotiate. A company that is actively trying to grow online sales to consumers is signaling *a weak strategic commitment to its dealers* and *a willingness to cannibalize dealers' sales and growth potential*. The likely result is angry dealers and loss of dealer goodwill. Quite possibly, a company may stand to lose more sales by offending its dealers than it gains from its own online sales effort. Consequently, in industries where the strong support and goodwill of dealer networks is essential, companies may conclude that it is important to avoid channel conflict and that *their website should be designed to partner with dealers rather than compete with them*.

The Disadvantages of a Vertical Integration Strategy

Vertical integration has some substantial drawbacks beyond the potential for channel conflict.[13] The most serious drawbacks to vertical integration include:

- Vertical integration *increases a firm's capital investment* in the industry.
- Integrating into more industry value chain segments *increases business risk* if industry growth and profitability sour.
- Vertically integrated companies are often *slow to embrace technological advances* or more efficient production methods when they are saddled with older technology or facilities.
- Integrating backward potentially results in less flexibility in accommodating shifting buyer preferences when a new product design doesn't include parts and components that the company makes in-house.

CONCEPTS & CONNECTIONS 6.2

AMERICAN APPAREL'S VERTICAL INTEGRATION STRATEGY

American Apparel—known for its hip line of basic garments and its provocative advertisements—is no stranger to the concept of "doing it all." The Los Angeles-based casual wear company has made both forward and backward vertical integration a central part of its strategy, making it a rarity in the fashion industry. Not only does it do all its own fabric cutting and sewing, but it also owns several knitting and dyeing facilities in Southern California, as well as a distribution warehouse, a wholesale operation, and more than 270 retail stores in 20 countries. American Apparel even does its own clothing design, marketing, and advertising, often using its employees as photographers and clothing models.

Founder and CEO Dov Charney claims the company's vertical integration strategy lets American Apparel respond more quickly to rapid market changes, allowing the company to bring an item from design to its stores worldwide in the span of a week. End-to-end coordination also improves inventory control, helping prevent common problems in the fashion business such as stock-outs and steep markdowns. The company capitalizes on its California-based vertically integrated operations by using taglines such as "Sweatshop Free. Made in the USA" to bolster its "authentic" image.

However, this strategy is not without risks and costs. In an industry where 97 percent of goods are imported,

American Apparel pays its workers wages and benefits above the relatively high mandated American minimum. Furthermore, operating in so many key vertical chain activities makes it impossible to be expert in all of them, and creates optimal scale and capacity mismatches—problems with which the firm has partly dealt by tapering its backward integration into knitting and dyeing. Lastly, while the company can respond quickly to new fashion trends, its vertical integration strategy may make it more difficult for the company to scale back in an economic downturn or respond to radical change in the industry environment. Ultimately, only time will tell whether American Apparel will dilute or capitalize on its vertical integration strategy in its pursuit of profitable growth.

Developed with John R. Moran.

Sources: American Apparel website, www.americanapparel.net, accessed June 16, 2010; American Apparel investor presentation, June 2009, http://files.shareholder.com/downloads/APP/938846703x0x300331/3dd0b7ca-e458-45b8-8516-e25ca272016d/NYC%20JUNE%202009.pdf; YouTube, "American Apparel—Dov Charney Interview," CBS News, http://youtube.com/watch?v=hYqR8UIl8A4; and Christopher Palmeri, "Living on the Edge at American Apparel," *BusinessWeek*, June 27, 2005.

- Vertical integration poses all kinds of *capacity matching problems*. In motor vehicle manufacturing, for example, the most efficient scale of operation for making axles is different from the most economic volume for radiators, and different yet again for both engines and transmissions. Consequently, integrating across several production stages in ways that achieve the lowest feasible costs can be a monumental challenge.

- Integration forward or backward often requires the *development of new skills and business capabilities*. Parts and components manufacturing, assembly operations, wholesale distribution and retailing, and direct sales via the Internet are different businesses with different key success factors.

> A vertical integration strategy has appeal *only* if it significantly strengthens a firm's competitive position and/or boosts its profitability.

American Apparel, the largest U.S. clothing manufacturer, has made vertical integration a central part of its strategy, as described in Concepts & Connections 6.2.

OUTSOURCING STRATEGIES: NARROWING THE SCOPE OF OPERATIONS

▶**LO5**

Understand the conditions that favor farming out certain value chain activities to outside parties.

Outsourcing forgoes attempts to perform certain value chain activities internally and instead farms them out to outside specialists and strategic allies. Outsourcing makes strategic sense whenever:

- *An activity can be performed better or more cheaply by outside specialists.* A company should generally *not* perform any value chain activity internally that can be performed more efficiently or effectively by outsiders. The chief exception is when a particular activity is strategically crucial and internal control over that activity is deemed essential.

> **CORE CONCEPT**
>
> **Outsourcing** involves contracting out certain value chain activities to outside specialists and strategic allies.

- *The activity is not crucial to the firm's ability to achieve sustainable competitive advantage and won't hollow out its capabilities, core competencies, or technical know-how.* Outsourcing of support activities such as maintenance services, data processing and data storage, fringe benefit management, and website operations has become common. Colgate-Palmolive, for instance, has been able to reduce its information technology operational costs by more than 10 percent per year through an outsourcing agreement with IBM.

- *It improves organizational flexibility and speeds time to market.* Outsourcing gives a company the flexibility to switch suppliers in the event that its present supplier falls behind competing suppliers. Also, to the extent that its suppliers can speedily get next-generation parts and components into production, a company can get its own next-generation product offerings into the marketplace quicker.

- *It reduces the company's risk exposure to changing technology and/or buyer preferences.* When a company outsources certain parts, components, and services, its suppliers must bear the burden of incorporating state-of-the-art technologies and/or undertaking redesigns and upgrades to accommodate a company's plans to introduce next-generation products.

- *It allows a company to concentrate on its core business, leverage its key resources and core competencies, and do even better what it already does best.* A company is better able to build and develop its own competitively valuable competencies and capabilities when it concentrates its full resources and energies on performing those activities. Nike, for example, devotes its energy to designing, marketing, and distributing athletic footwear, sports apparel, and sports equipment, while outsourcing the manufacture of all its products to some 600 contract factories in 46 countries. Apple also outsources production of its iPod, iPhone, and iPad models to Chinese contract manufacturer Foxconn. Hewlett-Packard and others have sold some of their manufacturing plants to outsiders and contracted to repurchase the output from the new owners.

> A company should guard against outsourcing activities that hollow out the resources and capabilities that it needs to be a master of its own destiny.

The Big Risk of an Outsourcing Strategy　　The biggest danger of outsourcing is that a company will farm out the wrong types of activities and thereby hollow out its own capabilities.[14] In such cases, a company loses touch with the very activities and expertise that over the long run determine its success. But most companies are alert to this danger and take actions to protect against being held hostage by outside suppliers. Cisco Systems guards against loss of control and protects its manufacturing expertise by designing the production methods that its contract manufacturers must use. Cisco keeps the source code for its designs proprietary, thereby controlling the initiation of all improvements and safeguarding its innovations from imitation. Further, Cisco uses the Internet to monitor the factory operations of contract manufacturers around the clock and can know immediately when problems arise and decide whether to get involved.

STRATEGIC ALLIANCES AND PARTNERSHIPS

LO6

Gain an understanding of how strategic alliances and collaborative partnerships can bolster a company's collection of resources and capabilities.

Companies in all types of industries have elected to form strategic alliances and partnerships to complement their accumulation of resources and capabilities and strengthen their competitiveness in domestic and international markets. A **strategic alliance** is a formal agreement between two or more separate companies in which there is strategically relevant collaboration of some sort, joint contribution of resources, shared risk, shared control, and mutual dependence. Collaborative relationships between partners may entail a contractual agreement but they commonly stop short of formal ownership ties between the partners (although there are a few strategic alliances where one or more allies have minority ownership in certain of the other alliance members). Collaborative arrangements involving shared ownership are called joint ventures. A **joint venture** is a partnership involving the establishment of an independent corporate entity that is jointly owned and controlled by two or more companies. Since joint ventures involve setting up a mutually owned business, they tend to be more durable but also riskier than other arrangements.

> **CORE CONCEPT**
>
> A **strategic alliance** is a formal agreement between two or more companies to work cooperatively toward some common objective.

The most common reasons companies enter into strategic alliances are to expedite the development of promising new technologies or products, to overcome deficits in their own technical and manufacturing expertise, to bring together the personnel and expertise needed to create desirable new skill sets and capabilities, to improve supply chain efficiency, to gain economies of scale in production and/or marketing, and to acquire or improve market access through joint marketing agreements.[15] Because of the varied benefits of strategic alliances, many large corporations have become involved in 30 to 50 alliances, and a number have formed hundreds of alliances. Most automakers have forged long-term strategic partnerships with suppliers of automotive parts and components, both to achieve lower costs and to improve the quality and reliability of their vehicles. Microsoft collaborates very closely with independent software developers to ensure their programs will run on the next-generation versions of Windows. Over the past 10 years, South Korean giant

Samsung Electronics has entered into more than 30 strategic alliances with such companies as Sony, Yahoo, Hewlett-Packard, Nokia, Motorola, Intel, Microsoft, Dell, Mitsubishi, Disney, IBM, Maytag, Cisco, Rockwell Automation, and Giorgio Armani. Samsung's alliances have involved joint investments, technology transfer arrangements, joint R&D projects, and agreements to supply parts and components, with most having the objective of facilitating the company's strategic efforts to establish itself as a leader in the worldwide electronics industry.

> **CORE CONCEPT**
> A **joint venture** is a type of strategic alliance that involves the establishment of an independent corporate entity that is jointly owned and controlled by the two partners.

Failed Strategic Alliances and Cooperative Partnerships

Most alliances with an objective of technology sharing or providing market access turn out to be temporary, fulfilling their purpose after a few years because the benefits of mutual learning have occurred. Although long-term alliances sometimes prove mutually beneficial, most partners don't hesitate to terminate the alliance and go it alone when the payoffs run out. Alliances are more likely to be long lasting when (1) they involve collaboration with suppliers or distribution allies, or (2) both parties conclude that continued collaboration is in their mutual interest, perhaps because new opportunities for learning are emerging.

A surprisingly large number of alliances never live up to expectations. A 1999 study by Accenture, a global business consulting organization, revealed that 61 percent of alliances were either outright failures or "limping along." In 2004, McKinsey & Co. estimated the overall success rate of alliances was about 50 percent, based on whether the alliance achieved the stated objectives. Another study, published in 2007, found that while the number of strategic alliances was increasing about 25 percent annually, some 60 to 70 percent of alliances failed each year. The high "divorce rate" among strategic allies has several causes, the most common of which are:[16]

- Diverging objectives and priorities.
- An inability to work well together.
- Changing conditions that make the purpose of the alliance obsolete.
- The emergence of more attractive technological paths.
- Marketplace rivalry between one or more allies.

Experience indicates that *alliances stand a reasonable chance of helping a company reduce competitive disadvantage but very rarely have they proved a strategic option for gaining a durable competitive edge over rivals.*

The Strategic Dangers of Relying on Alliances for Essential Resources and Capabilities

The Achilles' heel of alliances and cooperative strategies is becoming dependent on other companies for *essential* expertise and capabilities. To be a market leader (and perhaps even a serious market contender), a company must ultimately develop its own resources and capabilities in areas where internal strategic

some alliance hold limited potent or guards valuable skills

control is pivotal to protecting its competitiveness and building competitive advantage. Moreover, some alliances hold only limited potential because the partner guards its most valuable skills and expertise; in such instances, acquiring or merging with a company possessing the desired know-how and resources is a better solution.

MERGER AND ACQUISITION STRATEGIES

LO7

Become aware of the strategic benefits and risks of mergers and acquisitions.

Mergers and acquisitions are well suited for situations in which strategic alliances or joint ventures do not go far enough in providing a company with access to needed resources and capabilities. Resources that are deemed to be essential to a company's competitive capabilities and its strength in the marketplace are more dependably and permanently deployed when owned and autonomously controlled. A **merger** is the combining of two or more companies into a single corporate entity, with the newly created company often taking on a new name. An **acquisition** is a combination in which one company, the acquirer, purchases and absorbs the operations of another, the acquired. The difference between a merger and an acquisition relates more to the details of ownership, management control, and financial arrangements than to strategy and competitive advantage.

> Combining the operations of two companies, via merger or acquisition, is an attractive strategic option for achieving operating economies, strengthening the resulting company's competencies and competitiveness, and opening avenues of new market opportunity.

The resources and competitive capabilities of the newly created enterprise end up much the same whether the combination is the result of acquisition or merger.

Merger and acquisition strategies typically set sights on achieving any of five objectives:[17]

1. *To create a more cost-efficient operation out of the combined companies.* When a company acquires another company in the same industry, there's usually enough overlap in operations that certain inefficient plants can be closed or distribution and sales activities can be partly combined and downsized. The combined companies may also be able to reduce supply chain costs because of buying in greater volume from common suppliers. Likewise, it is usually feasible to squeeze out cost savings in administrative activities, again by combining and downsizing such activities as finance and accounting, information technology, human resources, and so on.

2. *To expand a company's geographic coverage.* One of the best and quickest ways to expand a company's geographic coverage is to acquire rivals with operations in the desired locations. Food products companies such as Nestlé, Kraft, Unilever, and Procter & Gamble have made acquisitions an integral part of their strategies to expand internationally.

3. *To extend the company's business into new product categories.* Many times a company has gaps in its product line that need to be filled. Acquisition can be a quicker and more potent way to broaden a company's product line than going through the exercise of introducing a company's own new product to fill the gap. PepsiCo acquired Quaker Oats chiefly to bring Gatorade into the Pepsi family of beverages. While Coca-Cola has expanded its beverage lineup by introducing its own new products

(such as Powerade and Dasani), it has also expanded its offerings by acquiring Minute Maid, Glacéau VitaminWater, and Hi-C.

4. *To gain quick access to new technologies or other resources and competitive capabilities.* Making acquisitions to bolster a company's technological know-how or to expand its skills and capabilities allows a company to bypass a time-consuming and perhaps expensive *internal effort* to build desirable new resource strengths. From 2000 through April 2011, Cisco Systems purchased 97 companies to give it more technological reach and product breadth, thereby enhancing its standing as the world's biggest provider of hardware, software, and services for building and operating Internet networks.

5. *To lead the convergence of industries whose boundaries are being blurred by changing technologies and new market opportunities.* Such acquisitions are the result of a company's management betting that two or more distinct industries are converging into one and deciding to establish a strong position in the consolidating markets by bringing together the resources and products of several different companies. News Corporation has prepared for the convergence of media services with the purchase of satellite TV companies to complement its media holdings in TV broadcasting (the Fox network and TV stations in various countries), cable TV (Fox News, Fox Sports, and FX), filmed entertainment (Twentieth Century Fox and Fox Studios), newspapers, magazines, and book publishing.

Why Mergers and Acquisitions Sometimes Fail to Produce Anticipated Results

Companies such as Wells Fargo and Clear Channel Communications have used mergers and acquisitions to catapult themselves into positions of market leadership. But mergers and acquisitions do not always produce the hoped-for outcomes. The managers appointed to oversee the integration of a newly acquired company can make mistakes in deciding what activities to leave alone and what activities to meld into the acquired company's operations. Cost savings may prove smaller than expected. Gains in competitive capabilities may take substantially longer to realize or may never materialize. Efforts to mesh the corporate cultures can stall due to formidable resistance from organization members. Managers and employees at the acquired company may argue forcefully for continuing to do certain things the way they were done before the acquisition. And key employees at the acquired company can quickly become disenchanted and leave.

A number of mergers/acquisitions have been notably unsuccessful. eBay's $2.6 billion acquisition of Skype in 2005 proved to be a mistake—eBay wrote off $900 million of its Skype investment in 2007 and sold 70 percent of its ownership in Skype in September 2009 to a group of investors. The merger of Daimler-Benz (Mercedes) and Chrysler was a failure, as was Ford's $2.5 billion acquisition of Jaguar and its $2.5 billion acquisition of Land Rover (both were sold to India's Tata Motors in 2008 for $2.3 billion). Several recent mergers/acquisitions have yet to live up to expectations—prominent examples include Oracle's acquisition of Sun Microsystems, the Fiat-Chrysler deal, and Bank of America's acquisition of Countrywide Financial.

KEY POINTS

Once a company has selected which of the five basic competitive strategies to employ in its quest for competitive advantage, then it must decide whether and how to supplement its choice of a basic competitive strategy approach.

1. Companies have a number of offensive strategy options for improving their market positions and trying to secure a competitive advantage: (1) attacking competitors' weaknesses, (2) offering an equal or better product at a lower price, (3) pursuing sustained product innovation, (4) leapfrogging competitors by being first to adopt next-generation technologies or the first to introduce next-generation products, (5) adopting and improving on the good ideas of other companies, (6) deliberately attacking those market segments where key rivals make big profits, (7) going after less contested or unoccupied market territory, (8) using hit-and-run tactics to steal sales away from unsuspecting rivals, and (9) launching preemptive strikes. A blue ocean offensive strategy seeks to gain a dramatic and durable competitive advantage by abandoning efforts to beat out competitors in existing markets and, instead, inventing a new industry or distinctive market segment that renders existing competitors largely irrelevant and allows a company to create and capture altogether new demand.

2. Defensive strategies to protect a company's position usually take the form of making moves that put obstacles in the path of would-be challengers and fortify the company's present position while undertaking actions to dissuade rivals from even trying to attack (by signaling that the resulting battle will be more costly to the challenger than it is worth).

3. The timing of strategic moves also has relevance in the quest for competitive advantage. Company managers are obligated to carefully consider the advantages or disadvantages that attach to being a first mover versus a fast follower versus a wait-and-see late mover.

4. Vertically integrating forward or backward makes strategic sense only if it strengthens a company's position via either cost reduction or creation of a differentiation-based advantage. Otherwise, the drawbacks of vertical integration (increased investment, greater business risk, increased vulnerability to technological changes, and less flexibility in making product changes) are likely to outweigh any advantages.

5. Outsourcing pieces of the value chain formerly performed in-house can enhance a company's competitiveness whenever (1) an activity can be performed better or more cheaply by outside specialists; (2) the activity is not crucial to the firm's ability to achieve sustainable competitive advantage and won't hollow out its core competencies, capabilities, or technical know-how; (3) it improves a company's ability to innovate; and/or (4) it allows a company to concentrate on its core business and do what it does best.

6. Many companies are using strategic alliances and collaborative partnerships to help them in the race to build a global market presence or be a leader in the industries of the future. Strategic alliances are an attractive, flexible, and often cost-effective means by which companies can gain access to missing technology, expertise, and business capabilities.

7. Mergers and acquisitions are another attractive strategic option for strengthening a firm's competitiveness. When the operations of two companies are combined via merger or acquisition, the new company's competitiveness can be enhanced

in any of several ways—lower costs; stronger technological skills; more or better competitive capabilities; a more attractive lineup of products and services; wider geographic coverage; and/or greater financial resources with which to invest in R&D, add capacity, or expand into new areas.

ASSURANCE OF LEARNING EXERCISES

1. Does it appear that Nintendo relies more heavily on offensive or defensive strategies as it competes in the video game industry? Has Nintendo's timing of strategic moves made it an early mover or a fast follower? Could Nintendo's introduction of the Wii be characterized as a blue ocean strategy? You may rely on your knowledge of the video game industry and information provided at Nintendo's investor relations website (www.nintendo.com) to provide justification for your answers to these questions.

   LO1, LO2, LO3

   www.mcgrawhillconnect.com

2. American Apparel, known for its hip line of basic garments and its provocative advertisements, is no stranger to the concept of "doing it all." Concepts & Connections 6.2 on page 126 describes how American Apparel has made vertical integration a central part of its strategy. What value chain segments has American Apparel chosen to enter and perform internally? How has vertical integration aided the company in building competitive advantage? Has vertical integration strengthened its market position? Explain why or why not.

   LO4

   www.mcgrawhillconnect.com

3. Perform an Internet search to identify at least two companies in different industries that have entered into outsourcing agreements with firms with specialized services. In addition, describe what value chain activities the companies have chosen to outsource. Do any of these outsourcing agreements seem likely to threaten any of the companies' competitive capabilities?

   LO5

4. Using your university library's subscription to Lexis-Nexis, EBSCO, or a similar database, find two examples of how companies have relied on strategic alliances or joint ventures to substitute for horizontal or vertical integration.

   LO6

5. Using your university library's subscription to Lexis-Nexis, EBSCO, or a similar database, identify at least two companies in different industries that are using mergers and acquisitions to strengthen their market positions. How have these mergers and acquisitions enhanced the acquiring companies' resources and competitive capabilities?

   LO7

EXERCISES FOR SIMULATION PARTICIPANTS

1. Has your company relied more on offensive or defensive strategies to achieve your rank in the industry? What options for being a first mover does your company have? Do any of these first-mover options hold competitive advantage potential?

   LO1, LO2, LO3

2. Is your company vertically integrated? Explain.

   LO4

3. Is your company able to engage in outsourcing? If so, what do you see as the pros and cons of outsourcing?

   LO5

4. Does your company have the option to merge with or acquire other companies? If so, which rival companies would you like to acquire or merge with?

   LO7

ENDNOTES

1. George Stalk, Jr., and Rob Lachenauer, "Hardball: Five Killer Strategies for Trouncing the Competition," *Harvard Business Review* 82, no. 4 (April 2004); Richard D'Aveni, "The Empire Strikes Back: Counterrevolutionary Strategies for Industry Leaders," *Harvard Business Review* 80, no. 11 (November 2002); and David J. Bryce and Jeffrey H. Dyer, "Strategies to Crack Well-Guarded Markets," *Harvard Business Review* 85, no. 5 (May 2007).

2. David B. Yoffie and Mary Kwak, "Mastering Balance: How to Meet and Beat a Stronger Opponent," *California Management Review* 44, no. 2 (Winter 2002).

3. Ian C. MacMillan, Alexander B. van Putten, and Rita Gunther McGrath, "Global Gamesmanship," *Harvard Business Review* 81, no. 5 (May 2003); and Askay R. Rao, Mark E. Bergen, and Scott Davis, "How to Fight a Price War," *Harvard Business Review* 78, no. 2 (March–April 2000).

4. Ming-Jer Chen and Donald C. Hambrick, "Speed, Stealth, and Selective Attack: How Small Firms Differ from Large Firms in Competitive Behavior," *Academy of Management Journal* 38, no. 2 (April 1995); Ian MacMillan, "How Business Strategists Can Use Guerrilla Warfare Tactics," *Journal of Business Strategy* 1, no. 2 (Fall 1980); William E. Rothschild, "Surprise and the Competitive Advantage," *Journal of Business Strategy* 4, no. 3 (Winter 1984); Kathryn R. Harrigan, *Strategic Flexibility* (Lexington, MA: Lexington Books, 1985); and Liam Fahey, "Guerrilla Strategy: The Hit-and-Run Attack," in *The Strategic Management Planning Reader*, ed. Liam Fahey (Englewood Cliffs, NJ: Prentice Hall, 1989).

5. Ian MacMillan, "Preemptive Strategies," *Journal of Business Strategy* 14, no. 2 (Fall 1983).

6. W. Chan Kim and Renée Mauborgne, "Blue Ocean Strategy," *Harvard Business Review* 82, no. 10 (October 2004).

7. Michael E. Porter, *Competitive Advantage* (New York: Free Press, 1985).

8. Jeffrey G. Covin, Dennis P. Slevin, and Michael B. Heeley, "Pioneers and Followers: Competitive Tactics, Environment, and Growth," *Journal of Business Venturing* 15, no. 2 (March 1999); and Christopher A. Bartlett and Sumantra Ghoshal, "Going Global: Lessons from Late-Movers," *Harvard Business Review* 78, no. 2 (March–April 2000).

9. Fernando Suarez and Gianvito Lanzolla, "The Half-Truth of First-Mover Advantage," *Harvard Business Review* 83 no. 4 (April 2005).

10. Gary Hamel, "Smart Mover, Dumb Mover," *Fortune*, September 3, 2001.

11. Costas Markides and Paul A. Geroski, "Racing to Be 2nd: Conquering the Industries of the Future," *Business Strategy Review* 15, no. 4 (Winter 2004).

12. Kathryn R. Harrigan, "Matching Vertical Integration Strategies to Competitive Conditions," *Strategic Management Journal* 7, no. 6 (November–December 1986); and John Stuckey and David White, "When and When Not to Vertically Integrate," *Sloan Management Review*, Spring 1993.

13. Thomas Osegowitsch and Anoop Madhok, "Vertical Integration Is Dead, or Is It?" *Business Horizons* 46, no. 2 (March–April 2003).

14. Jérôme Barthélemy, "The Seven Deadly Sins of Outsourcing," *Academy of Management Executive* 17, no. 2 (May 2003); Gary P. Pisano and Willy C. Shih, "Restoring American Competitiveness," *Harvard Business Review* 87, no. 7/8 (July–August 2009); and Ronan McIvor, "What Is the Right Outsourcing Strategy for Your Process?" *European Management Journal* 26, no. 1 (February 2008).

15. Michael E. Porter, *The Competitive Advantage of Nations* (New York: Free Press, 1990); K. M. Eisenhardt and C. B. Schoonhoven, "Resource-Based View of Strategic Alliance Formation: Strategic and Social Effects in Entrepreneurial Firms," *Organization Science* 7, no. 2 (March–April 1996); Nancy J. Kaplan and Jonathan Hurd, "Realizing the Promise of Partnerships," *Journal of Business Strategy* 23, no. 3 (May–June 2002); Salvatore Parise and Lisa Sasson, "Leveraging Knowledge Management across Strategic Alliances," *Ivey Business Journal* 66, no. 4 (March–April 2002); and David Ernst and James Bamford, "Your Alliances Are Too Stable," *Harvard Business Review* 83, no. 6 (June 2005).

16. Yves L. Doz and Gary Hamel, *Alliance Advantage; The Art of Creating Value through Partnering* (Boston: Harvard Business School Press, 1998).

17. Joseph L. Bower, "Not All M&As Are Alike—And That Matters," *Harvard Business Review* 79, no. 3 (March 2001); and O. Chatain and P. Zemsky, "The Horizontal Scope of the Firm: Organizational Trade-offs vs. Buyer-Supplier Relationships," *Management Science* 53, no. 4 (April 2007).

chapter 7

STRATEGIES FOR COMPETING IN INTERNATIONAL MARKETS

LEARNING OBJECTIVES

LO1 Develop an understanding of the primary reasons companies choose to compete in international markets.

LO2 Learn why and how differing market conditions across countries influence a company's strategy choices in international markets.

LO3 Gain familiarity with the five general modes of entry into foreign markets.

LO4 Learn the three main options for tailoring a company's international strategy to cross-country differences in market conditions and buyer preferences.

LO5 Understand how multinational companies are able to use international operations to improve overall competitiveness.

LO6 Gain an understanding of the unique characteristics of competing in developing-country markets.

Any company that aspires to industry leadership in the twenty-first century must think in terms of global, not domestic, market leadership. The world economy is globalizing at an accelerating pace as countries previously closed to foreign companies open their markets, as countries with previously planned economies embrace market or mixed economies, as information technology shrinks the importance of geographic distance, and as ambitious, growth-minded companies race to build stronger competitive positions in the markets of more and more countries. The forces of globalization are changing the competitive landscape in many industries, offering companies attractive new opportunities while at the same time introducing new competitive threats. Companies in industries where these forces are greatest are under considerable pressure to develop strategies for competing successfully in international markets.

This chapter focuses on strategy options for expanding beyond domestic boundaries and competing in the markets of either a few or many countries. We will discuss the factors that shape the choice of strategy in international markets and the specific market circumstances that support the adoption of multidomestic, transnational, and global strategies. The chapter also includes sections on strategy options for entering foreign markets; how international operations may be used to improve overall competitiveness; and the special circumstances of competing in such emerging markets as China, India, Brazil, Russia, and Eastern Europe.

WHY COMPANIES EXPAND INTO INTERNATIONAL MARKETS

▶ **LO1**

Develop an understanding of the primary reasons companies choose to compete in international markets.

A company may opt to expand outside its domestic market for any of five major reasons:

1. *To gain access to new customers.* Expanding into foreign markets offers potential for increased revenues, profits, and long-term growth and becomes an especially attractive option when a company's home markets are mature.

2. *To achieve lower costs and enhance the firm's competitiveness.* Many companies are driven to sell in more than one country because domestic sales volume alone is not large enough to fully capture manufacturing economies of scale or learning curve effects. The relatively small size of country markets in Europe explains why companies such as Michelin, BMW, and Nestlé long ago began selling their products all across Europe and then moved into markets in North America and Latin America.

3. *To further exploit its core competencies.* A company may be able to leverage its competencies and capabilities into a position of competitive advantage in foreign markets as well as domestic markets. Walmart is capitalizing on its considerable expertise in discount retailing to expand into the United Kingdom, Japan, China, and Latin America. Walmart executives are particularly excited about the company's growth opportunities in China.

4. *To gain access to resources and capabilities located in foreign markets.* An increasingly important motive for entering foreign markets is to acquire

resources and capabilities that cannot be accessed as readily in a company's home market. Companies often enter into cross-border alliances, make acquisitions abroad, or establish operations in foreign countries to access local resources such as distribution networks, low-cost labor, natural resources, or specialized technical knowledge.[1]

5. *To spread its business risk across a wider market base.* A company spreads business risk by operating in a number of different foreign countries rather than depending entirely on operations in its domestic market. Thus, if the economies of North American countries turn down for a period of time, a company with operations across much of the world may be sustained by buoyant sales in Latin America, Asia, or Europe.

FACTORS THAT SHAPE STRATEGY CHOICES IN INTERNATIONAL MARKETS

Four important factors shape a company's strategic approach to competing in foreign markets: (1) the degree to which there are important cross-country differences in buyer tastes, market sizes, and growth potential; (2) whether opportunities exist to gain a location-based advantage based on wage rates, worker productivity, inflation rates, energy costs, tax rates, and other factors that impact cost structure; (3) the risks of adverse shifts in currency exchange rates; and (4) the extent to which governmental policies affect the business environment.

▶ **LO2**

Learn why and how differing market conditions across countries influence a company's strategy choices in international markets.

Cross-Country Differences in Buyer Tastes, Market Sizes, and Growth Potential

Buyer tastes for a particular product or service sometimes differ substantially from country to country. For example, Italian coffee drinkers prefer espressos, but in North America the preference is for milder-roasted coffees. In parts of Asia, refrigerators are a status symbol and may be placed in the living room, leading to preferences for stylish designs and colors; bright blue and red are popular colors in India. People in Hong Kong and Japan prefer compact appliances, but in Taiwan large appliances are more popular. Consequently, companies operating in a global marketplace must wrestle with *whether and how much to customize their offerings in each different country market to match the tastes and preferences of local buyers or whether to pursue a strategy of offering a mostly standardized product worldwide.* While making products that are closely matched to local tastes makes them more appealing to local buyers, customizing a company's products country by country may raise production and distribution costs. Greater standardization of a global company's product offering, on the other hand, can lead to scale economies and learning curve effects, thus contributing to the achievement of a low-cost advantage. *The tension between the market pressures to localize a company's product offerings country by country and the competitive pressures to lower costs is one of the big strategic issues that participants in foreign markets have to resolve.*

Understandably, differing population sizes, income levels, and other demographic factors give rise to considerable differences in market size and growth rates from country to country. In emerging markets such as India, China, Brazil, and Malaysia, market growth potential is far higher for such products as PCs, mobile phones, steel, credit cards, and electric energy than in the more mature economies of Britain, Canada, and Japan. The potential for market growth in motor vehicles in China, which has a population of 1.3 billion people, is explosive; already the world's largest market, vehicle sales in China were up 45 percent in 2009 and 32 percent in 2010. Owing to widely differing population demographics and income levels, there is a far bigger market for luxury automobiles in the United States and Germany than in Argentina, India, Mexico, and Thailand. Cultural influences can also affect consumer demand for a product. For instance, in China, many parents are reluctant to purchase PCs even when they can afford them because of concerns that their children will be distracted from their schoolwork by surfing the Web, playing PC-based video games, and downloading and listening to pop music.

Market growth can be limited by the lack of infrastructure or established distribution and retail networks in emerging markets. India has well-developed national channels for distribution of goods to the nation's 3 million retailers, whereas in China distribution is primarily local. Also, the competitive rivalry in some country marketplaces is only moderate, while others are characterized by strong or fierce competition. The managerial challenge at companies with international or global operations is how best to tailor a company's strategy to take all these cross-country differences into account.

Opportunities for Location-Based Cost Advantages

Differences from country to country in wage rates, worker productivity, energy costs, environmental regulations, tax rates, inflation rates, and the like are often so big that *a company's operating costs and profitability are significantly impacted by where its production, distribution, and customer service activities are located.* Wage rates, in particular, vary enormously from country to country. For example, in 2009, hourly compensation for manufacturing workers averaged about $1.36 in China, $1.50 in the Philippines, $5.38 in Mexico, $5.96 in Brazil, $7.76 in Taiwan, $8.62 in Hungary, $11.95 in Portugal, $14.20 in South Korea, $30.36 in Japan, $33.53 in the United States, $29.60 in Canada, $46.52 in Germany, and $53.89 in Norway.[2] Not surprisingly, the big cross-country difference in wages rates have turned low-wage countries such as China, India, Pakistan, Cambodia, Vietnam, Mexico, Brazil, Guatemala, Honduras, the Philippines, and several countries in Africa and Eastern Europe into production havens for goods that can be manufactured or assembled by a relatively unskilled labor force. China has emerged as the manufacturing capital of the world; virtually all of the world's major manufacturing companies now have facilities in China. A manufacturer can also gain cost advantages by locating its manufacturing and assembly plants in countries with less costly government regulations, low taxes, low energy costs, and cheaper access to essential natural resources.

The Risks of Adverse Exchange Rate Shifts

When companies produce and market their products and services in many different countries, they are subject to the impacts of sometimes favorable and sometimes unfavorable changes in currency exchange rates. The rates of exchange between different currencies can vary by as much as 20 to 40 percent annually, with the changes occurring sometimes gradually and sometimes swiftly. Sizable shifts in exchange rates, which tend to be hard to predict because of the variety of factors involved and the uncertainties surrounding when and by how much these factors will change, *shuffle the global cards of which countries represent the low-cost manufacturing location* and *which rivals have the upper hand in the marketplace.*

To illustrate the competitive risks associated with fluctuating exchange rates, consider the case of a U.S. company that has located manufacturing facilities in Brazil (where the currency is reals—pronounced *ray-alls*) and that exports most of its Brazilian-made goods to markets in the European Union (where the currency is euros). To keep the numbers simple, assume the exchange rate is 4 Brazilian reals for 1 euro and that the product being made in Brazil has a manufacturing cost of 4 Brazilian reals (or 1 euro). Now suppose that for some reason the exchange rate shifts from 4 reals per euro to 5 reals per euro (meaning the real has declined in value and the euro is stronger). Making the product in Brazil is now more cost-competitive because a Brazilian good costing 4 reals to produce has fallen to only 0.8 euros at the new exchange rate (4 reals divided by 5 reals per euro = 0.8 euros). On the other hand, should the value of the Brazilian real grow stronger in relation to the euro—resulting in an exchange rate of 3 reals to 1 euro— the same Brazilian-made good formerly costing 4 reals to produce now has a cost of 1.33 euros (4 reals divided by 3 reals per euro = 1.33). This increase in the value of the real has eroded the cost advantage of the Brazilian manufacturing facility for goods shipped to Europe and affects the ability of the U.S. company to underprice European producers of similar goods. Thus, *the lesson of fluctuating exchange rates is that companies that export goods to foreign countries always gain in competitiveness when the currency of the country in which the goods are manufactured is weak. Exporters are disadvantaged when the currency of the country where goods are being manufactured grows stronger.*

The Impact of Host Government Policies on the Local Business Climate

National governments enact all kinds of measures affecting business conditions and the operation of foreign companies in their markets. It matters whether these measures create a favorable or unfavorable business climate. Governments of countries eager to spur economic growth, create more jobs, and raise living standards for their citizens usually make a special effort to create a business climate that outsiders will view favorably. They may provide such incentives as reduced taxes, low-cost loans, and site-development assistance to companies agreeing to construct or expand production and distribution facilities in the host country.

On the other hand, governments sometimes enact policies that, from a business perspective, make locating facilities within a country's borders less attractive. For example, the nature of a company's operations may make it particularly costly to achieve compliance with environmental regulations in certain countries. Some governments, wishing to discourage foreign imports, may enact deliberately burdensome customs procedures and requirements or impose tariffs or quotas on imported goods. Host-country governments may also specify that products contain a certain percentage of locally produced parts and components, require prior approval of capital spending projects, limit withdrawal of funds from the country, and require local ownership stakes in foreign-company operations in the host country. Such governmental actions make a country's business climate unattractive, and in some cases may be sufficiently onerous as to discourage a company from locating facilities in that country or sell its products there.

A country's business climate is also a function of the political and economic risks associated with operating within its borders. **Political risks** have to do with the instability of weak governments or the potential for future elections to produce government leaders hostile to foreign-owned businesses. **Economic risks** have to do with the threat of piracy and lack of protection for the company's intellectual property and the stability of a country's economy—whether inflation rates might skyrocket or whether uncontrolled deficit spending on the part of government could lead to a breakdown of the country's monetary system and prolonged economic distress.

> **CORE CONCEPT**
>
> **Political risks** stem from instability or weakness in national governments and hostility to foreign business; **economic risks** stem from the stability of a country's monetary system, economic and regulatory policies, and the lack of property rights protections.

STRATEGY OPTIONS FOR ENTERING FOREIGN MARKETS

LO3

Gain familiarity with the five general modes of entry into foreign markets.

A company choosing to expand outside its domestic market may elect one of the following five general modes of entry into a foreign market:

1. *Maintain a national (one-country) production base and export goods to foreign markets.*
2. *License foreign firms to produce and distribute the company's products.*
3. *Employ a franchising strategy.*
4. *Establish a subsidiary in a foreign market.*
5. *Rely on strategic alliances or joint ventures with foreign partners to enter new country markets.*

The following sections discuss the five general options in more detail.

Export Strategies

Using domestic plants as a production base for exporting goods to foreign markets is an excellent initial strategy for pursuing international sales. It is a conservative way to test the international waters. The amount of capital needed to begin exporting is often quite minimal and existing production capacity may be sufficient to make goods for export. With an export-based entry strategy, a manufacturer can limit its involvement in foreign markets by contracting with foreign wholesalers experienced in importing to handle the entire distribution and marketing function in their countries or regions of the world. If it is more advantageous to maintain control over these functions, however, a manufacturer can establish its own distribution and sales organizations in some or all of the target foreign markets. Either way, a home-based production and export strategy helps the firm minimize its direct investments in foreign countries.

An export strategy is vulnerable when (1) manufacturing costs in the home country are substantially higher than in foreign countries where rivals have plants, (2) the costs of shipping the product to distant foreign markets are relatively high, or (3) adverse shifts occur in currency exchange rates. Unless an exporter can both keep its production and shipping costs competitive with rivals and successfully hedge against unfavorable changes in currency exchange rates, its success will be limited.

Vulnerability

Licensing Strategies

Licensing as an entry strategy makes sense when a firm with valuable technical know-how or a unique patented product has neither the internal organizational capability nor the resources to enter foreign markets. Licensing also has the advantage of avoiding the risks of committing resources to country markets that are unfamiliar, politically volatile, economically unstable, or otherwise risky. By licensing the technology or the production rights to foreign-based firms, the firm does not have to bear the costs and risks of entering foreign markets on its own, yet it is able to generate income from royalties. The big disadvantage of licensing is the risk of providing valuable technological know-how to foreign companies and thereby losing some degree of control over its use. Also, monitoring licensees and safeguarding the company's proprietary know-how can prove quite difficult in some circumstances. But if the royalty potential is considerable and the companies to whom the licenses are being granted are both trustworthy and reputable, then licensing can be a very attractive option. Many software and pharmaceutical companies use licensing strategies.

Franchising Strategies

While licensing works well for manufacturers and owners of proprietary technology, franchising is often better suited to the global expansion efforts of service and retailing enterprises. McDonald's, Yum! Brands (the parent of A&W, Pizza Hut, KFC, Long John Silver's, and Taco Bell), the UPS Store, 7-Eleven, and Hilton Hotels have all used franchising to build a presence in international markets. Franchising has much the same advantages as licensing. The franchisee bears most of the costs and risks of establishing foreign locations, so a franchisor has to expend only the resources to recruit, train, support, and monitor franchisees. The big problem a franchisor faces is maintaining quality control. In many cases, foreign franchisees do not always exhibit strong commitment to consistency and standardization, especially when the local culture does not stress the same kinds of quality concerns. Another problem that can arise is whether to allow foreign franchisees to modify the franchisor's product *offering*

offering to better satisfy the tastes and expectations of local buyers. Should McDonald's allow its franchised units in Japan to modify Big Macs slightly to suit Japanese tastes? Should the franchised KFC units in China be permitted to substitute spices that appeal to Chinese consumers? Or should the same menu offerings be rigorously and unvaryingly required of all franchisees worldwide?

Establishing a Subsidiary in a Foreign Market

While exporting, licensing, and franchising rely upon the resources and capabilities of allies in international markets to deliver goods or services to buyers, companies pursuing international expansion may elect to take responsibility for the performance of all essential value chain activities in foreign markets. Companies that prefer direct control over all aspects of operating in a foreign market can establish a wholly owned subsidiary, either by acquiring a foreign company or by establishing operations from the ground up via internal development.

Acquisition is the quicker of the two options, and it may be the least risky and cost-efficient means of hurdling such entry barriers as gaining access to local distribution channels, building supplier relationships, and establishing working relationships with key government officials and other constituencies. Buying an ongoing operation allows the acquirer to move directly to the task of transferring resources and personnel to the newly acquired business, integrating and redirecting the activities of the acquired business into its own operation, putting in its own strategy into place, and accelerating efforts to build a strong market position.[3]

The big issue an acquisition-minded firm must consider is whether to pay a premium price for a successful local company or to buy a struggling competitor at a bargain price. If the buying firm has little knowledge of the local market but ample capital, it is often better off purchasing a capable, strongly positioned firm—unless the acquisition price is prohibitive. However, when the acquirer sees promising ways to transform a weak firm into a strong one and has the resources and managerial know-how to do it, a struggling company can be the better long-term investment.

Entering a new foreign country via internal development and building a foreign subsidiary from scratch makes sense when a company already operates in a number of countries, has experience in getting new subsidiaries up and running and overseeing their operations, and has a sufficiently large pool of resources and competencies to rapidly equip a new subsidiary with the personnel and capabilities it needs to compete successfully and profitably. Four other conditions make an internal start-up strategy appealing:

- When creating an internal start-up is cheaper than making an acquisition.
- When adding new production capacity will not adversely impact the supply–demand balance in the local market.
- When a start-up subsidiary has the ability to gain good distribution access (perhaps because of the company's recognized brand name).
- When a start-up subsidiary will have the size, cost structure, and resources to compete head-to-head against local rivals.

Using International Strategic Alliances and Joint Ventures to Build Competitive Strength in Foreign Markets

Strategic alliances, joint ventures, and other cooperative agreements with foreign companies are a favorite and potentially fruitful means for entering a foreign market or strengthening a firm's competitiveness in world markets.[4] Historically, export-minded firms in industrialized nations sought alliances with firms in less-developed countries to import and market their products locally—such arrangements were often necessary to win approval for entry from the host country's government. Both Japanese and American companies are actively forming alliances with European companies to strengthen their ability to compete in the 27-nation European Union (and the three countries that are candidates to become EU members) and to capitalize on the opening of Eastern European markets. Many U.S. and European companies are allying with Asian companies in their efforts to enter markets in China, India, Malaysia, Thailand, and other Asian countries. Many foreign companies, of course, are particularly interested in strategic partnerships that will strengthen their ability to gain a foothold in the U.S. market.

However, cooperative arrangements between domestic and foreign companies have strategic appeal for reasons besides gaining better access to attractive country markets.[5] A second big appeal of cross-border alliances is to capture economies of scale in production and/or marketing. By joining forces in producing components, assembling models, and marketing their products, companies can realize cost savings not achievable with their own small volumes. A third motivation for entering into a cross-border alliance is to fill gaps in technical expertise and/or knowledge of local markets (buying habits and product preferences of consumers, local customs, and so on). A fourth motivation for cross-border alliances is to share distribution facilities and dealer networks, and to mutually strengthen each partner's access to buyers.

A fifth benefit is that cross-border allies can direct their competitive energies more toward mutual rivals and less toward one another; teaming up may help them close the gap on leading companies. A sixth driver of cross-border alliances comes into play when companies wanting to enter a new foreign market conclude that alliances with local companies are an effective way to establish working relationships with key officials in the host-country government.[6] And, finally, alliances can be a particularly useful way for companies across the world to gain agreement on important technical standards—they have been used to arrive at standards for assorted PC devices, Internet-related technologies, high-definition televisions, and mobile phones.

What makes cross-border alliances an attractive strategic means of gaining the aforementioned types of benefits (as compared to acquiring or merging with foreign-based companies) is that entering into alliances and strategic partnerships allows a company to preserve its independence and avoid using perhaps scarce financial resources to fund acquisitions. Furthermore, an alliance offers the flexibility to readily disengage once its purpose has been served or if the benefits prove elusive, whereas an acquisition is a more permanent sort of arrangement.[7] Concepts & Connections 7.1 provides examples of cross-border strategic alliances.

CONCEPTS & CONNECTIONS 7.1

EXAMPLES OF CROSS-BORDER STRATEGIC ALLIANCES

1. Verio, a subsidiary of Japan-based NTT Communications and one of the leading global providers of Web hosting services and IP data transport, has developed an alliance-oriented business model that combines the company's core competencies with the skills and products of best-of-breed technology partners. Verio's strategic partners include Arsenal Digital Solutions (a provider of worry-free tape backup, data restore, and data storage services), Internet Security Systems (a provider of firewall and intrusion detection systems), and Mercantec (which develops storefront and shopping cart software). Verio management believes that its portfolio of strategic alliances allows it to use innovative, best-of-class technologies in providing its customers with fast, efficient, accurate data transport and a complete set of Web hosting services. An independent panel of 12 judges recently selected Verio as the winner of the Best Technology Foresight Award for its efforts in pioneering new technologies.

2. The engine of General Motors' growth strategy in Asia is its three-way joint venture with Wulung, a Chinese producer of mini commercial vehicles, and SAIC (Shanghai Automotive Industrial Corporation), China's largest automaker. The success of the SAIC-GM-Wulung Automotive Company is also GM's best hope for financial recovery since it emerged from bankruptcy July 10, 2009. While GM lost $4.8 billion overall before interest and taxes during the last six months of 2009, its international operations (everything except North America and Europe) earned $1.2 billion. Its Chinese joint ventures accounted for approximately one-third of that profit, due in part to the roaring success of the no-frills Wulung Sunshine, a lightweight minivan that has become China's best-selling vehicle.

In 2010, General Motors' sales in China topped its U.S. sales—the first time that sales in a foreign market have done so in the 102-year history of the company. GM is now positioning its Chinese joint venture to serve as a springboard for the company's expansion in India.

3. Cisco, the worldwide leader in networking components, entered into a strategic alliance with Finnish telecommunications firm Nokia Siemens Networks to develop communications networks capable of transmitting data across either the Internet or by mobile technologies. Nokia Siemens Networks was created through a 2006 international joint venture between German-based Siemens AG and the Finnish communications giant Nokia. The Cisco-Nokia Siemens alliance was created to better position both companies for convergence among Internet technologies and wireless communication devices that was expected to dramatically change how both computer networks and wireless telephones would be used.

4. European Aeronautic Defence and Space Company (EADS) was formed by an alliance of aerospace companies from Britain, Spain, Germany, and France that included British Aerospace, Daimler-Benz Aerospace, and Aerospatiale. The objective of the alliance was to create a European aircraft company capable of competing with U.S.-based Boeing Corp. The alliance has proved highly successful, infusing its commercial airline division, Airbus, with the know-how and resources to compete head-to-head with Boeing for world leadership in large commercial aircraft (over 100 passengers).

Developed with Mukund Kulashekeran.

Sources: Company websites and press releases.

The Risks of Strategic Alliances with Foreign Partners Alliances and joint ventures with foreign partners have their pitfalls, however. Cross-border allies typically have to overcome language and cultural barriers and figure out how to deal with diverse (or perhaps conflicting) operating practices. The communication, trust-building, and coordination costs are high in terms of management time.[8] It is not unusual for partners to discover they have conflicting objectives and strategies, deep differences of opinion about how to proceed, or important differences in corporate values and ethical standards. Tensions build, working relationships cool, and the hoped-for benefits never materialize. The recipe for successful alliances requires many meetings of many people working in good faith over a period of time to iron out what is to be shared, what is to remain proprietary, and how the cooperative arrangements will work.[9]

Even if the alliance becomes a win-win proposition for both parties, there is the danger of becoming overly dependent on foreign partners for essential expertise and competitive capabilities. If a company is aiming for global market leadership and needs to develop capabilities of its own, then at some juncture cross-border merger or acquisition may have to be substituted for cross-border alliances and joint ventures. One of the lessons about cross-border alliances is that they are more effective in helping a company establish a beachhead of new opportunity in world markets than they are in enabling a company to achieve and sustain global market leadership.

TAILORING A COMPANY'S INTERNATIONAL STRATEGY TO COUNTRY DIFFERENCES IN MARKET CONDITIONS AND BUYER PREFERENCES

▶**LO4**

Learn the three main options for tailoring a company's international strategy to cross-country differences in market conditions and buyer preferences.

Broadly speaking, a company's **international strategy** is simply its strategy for competing in two or more countries simultaneously. Typically, a company will start to compete internationally by entering just one or perhaps a select few foreign markets, selling its products or services in countries where there is a ready market for them. But as it expands further internationally, it will have to confront head-on the conflicting pressures of local responsiveness versus efficiency gains from standardizing its product offering globally. As discussed earlier in the chapter, deciding upon the degree to vary its competitive approach to fit the specific market conditions and buyer preferences in each host country is perhaps the foremost strategic issue that must be addressed when operating in two or more foreign markets.[10] Figure 7.1 shows a company's three strategic approaches for competing internationally and resolving this issue.

> **CORE CONCEPT**
>
> A company's **international strategy** is its strategy for competing in two or more countries simultaneously.

Multidomestic Strategy—A Think Local, Act Local Approach to Strategy Making

A **multidomestic strategy** or **think local, act local** approach to strategy making is essential when there are significant country-to-country differences in customer preferences and buying habits, when there are significant cross-country differences in distribution channels and marketing methods, when host governments enact regulations requiring that

> **CORE CONCEPT**
>
> A **multidomestic strategy** calls for varying a company's product offering and competitive approach from country to country in an effort to be responsive to significant cross-country differences in customer preferences, buyer purchasing habits, distribution channels, or marketing methods. **Think local, act local** strategy-making approaches are also essential when host-government regulations or trade policies preclude a uniform, coordinated worldwide market approach.

▶ FIGURE 7.1   **A Company's Three Fundamental Strategic Options for Competing Internationally**

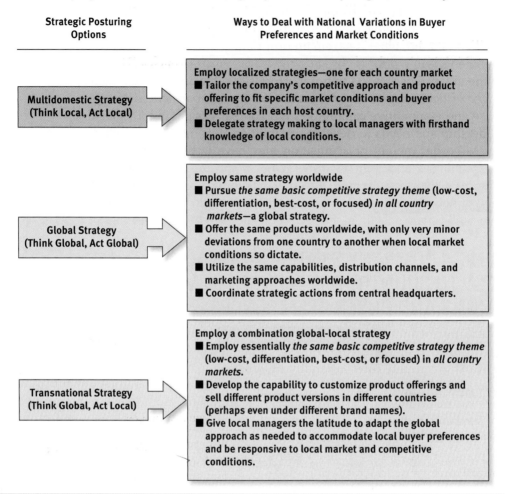

products sold locally meet strict manufacturing specifications or performance standards, and when the trade restrictions of host governments are so diverse and complicated that they preclude a uniform, coordinated worldwide market approach. With localized strategies, a company often has different product versions for different countries and sometimes sells the products under different brand names. Government requirements for gasoline additives that help reduce carbon monoxide, smog, and other emissions are almost never the same from country to country. BP utilizes localized strategies in its gasoline and service station business segment because of these cross-country formulation differences and because of customer familiarity with local brand names. For example, the company markets gasoline in the United States under its BP and Arco brands, but markets gasoline in Germany, Belgium, Poland, Hungary, and the Czech Republic under the Aral brand. Companies in the food products industry often vary the ingredients in their products and sell the localized versions under local brand names to cater to country-specific tastes and eating preferences. The strength of employing a set of localized or multidomestic strategies is that the company's actions and business approaches are deliberately crafted to appeal to the tastes and expectations of buyers in each country and to stake out the most attractive market positions vis-à-vis local competitors.[11]

However, think local, act local strategies have two big drawbacks: (1) They hinder transfer of a company's competencies and resources across country boundaries because the strategies in different host countries can be grounded in varying competencies and capabilities; and (2) they do not promote building a single, unified competitive advantage, especially one based on low cost. Companies employing highly localized or multidomestic strategies face big hurdles in achieving low-cost leadership *unless* they find ways to customize their products and *still* be in a position to capture scale economies and learning curve effects. Toyota's unique mass customization production capability has been key to its ability to effectively adapt product offerings to local buyer tastes, while maintaining low-cost leadership.

Global Strategy—A Think Global, Act Global Approach to Strategy Making

While multidomestic strategies are best suited for industries where a fairly high degree of local responsiveness is important, global strategies are best suited for globally standardized industries. A **global strategy** is one in which the company's approach is predominantly the same in all countries—it sells the same products under the same brand names everywhere, utilizes much the same distribution channels in all countries, and competes on the basis of the same capabilities and marketing approaches worldwide. Although the company's strategy or product offering may be adapted in very minor ways to accommodate specific situations in a few host countries, the company's fundamental competitive approach (low-cost, differentiation, or focused) remains very much intact worldwide and local managers stick close to the global strategy. A **think global, act global** strategic theme prompts company managers to integrate and coordinate the company's strategic moves worldwide and to expand into most if not all nations where there is significant buyer demand. It puts considerable strategic emphasis on building a *global* brand name and aggressively pursuing opportunities to transfer ideas, new products, and capabilities from one country to another.

> **CORE CONCEPT**
>
> **Global strategies** employ the same basic competitive approach in all countries where a company operates and are best suited to industries that are globally standardized in terms of customer preferences, buyer purchasing habits, distribution channels, or marketing methods. This is the **think global, act global** strategic theme.

Ford's global design strategy is a move toward a think global, act global strategy by the company and involves the development and production of standardized models with country-specific modifications limited primarily to what is required to meet local country emission and safety standards. The 2010 Ford Fiesta and 2011 Ford Focus were the company's first global design models to be marketed in Europe, North America, Asia, and Australia.

Whenever country-to-country differences are small enough to be accommodated within the framework of a global strategy, a global strategy is preferable to localized strategies because a company can more readily unify its operations and focus on establishing a brand image and reputation that is uniform from country to country. Moreover, with a global strategy a company is better able to focus its full resources on securing a sustainable low-cost or differentiation-based competitive advantage over both domestic rivals and global rivals.

Transnational Strategy—A Think Global, Act Local Approach to Strategy Making

A **transnational strategy** is a **think global, act local** approach to developing strategy that accommodates cross-country variations in buyer tastes, local customs, and market conditions while also striving for the benefits of standardization. This middle-ground approach entails utilizing the same basic competitive theme (low-cost, differentiation, or focused) in each country but allows local managers the latitude to (1) incorporate whatever country-specific variations in product attributes are needed to best satisfy local buyers and (2) make whatever adjustments in production, distribution, and marketing are needed to respond to local market conditions and compete successfully against local rivals. Slightly different product versions sold under the same brand name may suffice to satisfy local tastes, and it may be feasible to accommodate these versions rather economically in the course of designing and manufacturing the company's product offerings. Philip Morris International markets brands such as Marlboro, Chesterfield, Parliament, and Virginia Slims worldwide. However, the company also makes different versions of Marlboro cigarettes available in different parts of the world to better meet the somewhat different preferences and habits of smokers in each market. The company's Marlboro Mix 9 is a high-nicotine, clove-infused cigarette sold in Indonesia where smokers prefer powerful, sweet-smelling cigarettes. Its Marlboro Intense was formulated for the Turkish market, while its smooth-tasting Marlboro Filter Plus caters to the tastes of smokers in South Korea, Russia, Kazakhstan, and the Ukraine.

> **CORE CONCEPT**
>
> A **transnational strategy** is a **think global, act local** approach to strategy making that involves employing essentially the same strategic theme (low-cost, differentiation, focused, best-cost) in all country markets, while allowing some country-to-country customization to fit local market conditions.

As a rule, most companies that operate multinationally endeavor to employ as global a strategy as customer needs and market conditions permit. Electronic Arts has two major design studios—one in Vancouver, British Columbia, and one in Los Angeles—and smaller design studios in San Francisco, Orlando, London, and Tokyo. This dispersion of design studios helps EA to design games that are specific to different cultures—for example, the London studio took the lead in designing the popular FIFA Soccer game to suit European tastes and to replicate the stadiums, signage, and team rosters; the U.S. studio took the lead in designing games involving NFL football, NBA basketball, and NASCAR racing.

USING INTERNATIONAL OPERATIONS TO IMPROVE OVERALL COMPETITIVENESS

A firm can gain competitive advantage by expanding outside its domestic market in two important ways. One, it can use location to lower costs or help achieve greater product differentiation. And two, it can use cross-border coordination in ways that a domestic-only competitor cannot.

▶ **LO5**

Understand how multinational companies are able to use international operations to improve overall competitiveness.

[handwritten margin note: use locat° to lower cost or better p↓+ ≠that coordinate]

Using Location to Build Competitive Advantage

To use location to build competitive advantage, a company must consider two issues: (1) whether to concentrate each internal process in a few countries or to disperse performance of each process to many nations, and (2) in which countries to locate particular activities.

When to Concentrate Internal Processes in a Few Locations   Companies tend to concentrate their activities in a limited number of locations in the following circumstances:

- *When the costs of manufacturing or other activities are significantly lower in some geographic locations than in others.* For example, much of the world's athletic footwear is manufactured in Asia (China and Korea) because of low labor costs; much of the production of circuit boards for PCs is located in Taiwan because of both low costs and the high-caliber technical skills of the Taiwanese labor force.

- *When there are significant scale economies.* The presence of significant economies of scale in components production or final assembly means a company can gain major cost savings from operating a few super efficient plants as opposed to a host of small plants scattered across the world. Makers of digital cameras and LCD TVs located in Japan, South Korea, and Taiwan have used their scale economies to establish a low-cost advantage.

- *When there is a steep learning curve associated with performing an activity.* In some industries learning curve effects in parts manufacture or assembly are so great that a company establishes one or two large plants from which it serves the world market. The key to riding down the learning curve is to concentrate production in a few locations to increase the accumulated volume at a plant (and thus the experience of the plant's workforce) as rapidly as possible.

- *When certain locations have superior resources, allow better coordination of related activities, or offer other valuable advantages.* A research unit or a sophisticated production facility may be situated in a particular nation because of its pool of technically trained personnel. Samsung became a leader in memory chip technology by establishing a major R&D facility in Silicon Valley and transferring the know-how it gained back to headquarters and its plants in South Korea.

> Companies that compete multinationally can pursue competitive advantage in world markets by locating their value chain activities in whichever nations prove most advantageous.

When to Disperse Internal Processes Across Many Locations   There are several instances when dispersing a process is more advantageous than concentrating it in a single location. Buyer-related activities, such as distribution to dealers, sales and advertising, and after-sale service, usually must take place close to buyers. This makes it necessary to physically locate the capability to perform such activities in every country market where a global firm has major customers. For example, the four biggest public accounting firms have numerous international offices to service the foreign operations of their multinational corporate clients. Dispersing activities to many locations is also competitively important when high transportation costs, diseconomies of large size, and trade barriers make it too expensive to operate from a central location. In addition, it is strategically advantageous to disperse activities to hedge against the risks of fluctuating exchange rates and adverse political developments.

Using Cross-Border Coordination to Build Competitive Advantage

Multinational and global competitors are able to coordinate activities across different countries to build competitive advantage.[12] If a firm learns how to assemble its product more efficiently at, say, its Brazilian plant, the accumulated expertise and knowledge can be shared with assembly plants in other world locations. Also, knowledge gained in marketing a company's product in Great Britain, for instance, can readily be exchanged with company personnel in New Zealand or Australia. Other examples of cross-border coordination include shifting production from a plant in one country to a plant in another to take advantage of exchange rate fluctuations and to respond to changing wage rates, energy costs, or changes in tariffs and quotas.

Efficiencies can also be achieved by shifting workloads from where they are unusually heavy to locations where personnel are underutilized. Whirlpool's efforts to link its product R&D and manufacturing operations in North America, Latin America, Europe, and Asia allowed it to accelerate the discovery of innovative appliance features, coordinate the introduction of these features in the appliance products marketed in different countries, and create a cost-efficient worldwide supply chain. Whirlpool's conscious efforts to integrate and coordinate its various operations around the world have helped it become a low-cost producer and also speed product innovations to market, thereby giving Whirlpool an edge over rivals worldwide.

STRATEGIES FOR COMPETING IN THE MARKETS OF DEVELOPING COUNTRIES

▶ **LO6**

Gain an understanding of the unique characteristics of competing in developing-country markets.

Companies racing for global leadership have to consider competing in developing-economy markets such as China, India, Brazil, Indonesia, Thailand, Poland, Russia, and Mexico—countries where the business risks are considerable but where the opportunities for growth are huge, especially as their economies develop and living standards climb toward levels in the industrialized world.[13] For example, in 2010 China was the world's second-largest economy (behind the United States) based upon purchasing power and its population

CONCEPTS & CONNECTIONS 7.2

YUM! BRANDS' STRATEGY FOR BECOMING THE LEADING FOOD SERVICE BRAND IN CHINA

In 2011, Yum! Brands operated more than 38,000 restaurants in more than 110 countries. Its best-known brands were KFC, Taco Bell, Pizza Hut, and Long John Silver's. Its fastest revenue growth and 36 percent of its operating profit in 2010 came from its 3,700 restaurants in China. KFC was the largest quick-service chain in China with 3,200 units in 2010, while Pizza Hut was the largest casual dining chain with more than 500 units. Yum! planned to open at least 475 new restaurant locations annually in China, including new Pizza Hut Home delivery units and East Dawning units, which had a menu offering traditional Chinese food. All of Yum! Brands' menu items for China were developed in its R&D facility in Shanghai.

In addition to adapting its menu to local tastes and adding new units at a rapid pace, Yum! Brands also adapted the restaurant ambience and décor to appeal to local consumer preferences and behavior. The company changed its KFC store formats to provide educational displays that supported parents' priorities for their children and to make KFC a fun place for children to visit. The typical KFC outlet in China averaged two birthday parties per day.

In 2010, Yum! Brands operated 60 KFC, Taco Bell, Pizza Hut, A&W, and Long John Silver's restaurants for every 1 million Americans. The company's 3,200 units in China represented only three restaurants per 1 million people in China. Yum! Brands management believed that its strategy keyed to continued expansion in the number of units in China and additional menu refinements would allow its operating profits from restaurants located in China to account for more than 50 percent of systemwide operating profits by 2015.

Sources: Yum! Brands 2010 10-K; information posted at www.yum.com.

of 1.3 billion people made it the world's largest market for many commodities and types of consumer goods. China's growth in demand for consumer goods put it on track to become the world's largest market for luxury goods by 2014.[14] Thus, no company pursuing global market leadership can afford to ignore the strategic importance of establishing competitive market positions in China, India, other parts of the Asian-Pacific region, Latin America, and Eastern Europe. Concepts & Connections 7.2 describes Yum! Brands' strategy to boost its sales and market share in China.

Tailoring products to fit conditions in an emerging country market such as China, however, often involves more than making minor product changes and becoming more familiar with local cultures. McDonald's has had to offer vegetable burgers in parts of Asia and to rethink its prices, which are often high by local standards and affordable only by the well-to-do. Kellogg has struggled to introduce its cereals successfully because consumers in many less-developed countries do not eat cereal for breakfast—changing habits is difficult and expensive. Single-serving packages of detergents, shampoos, pickles, cough syrup, and cooking oils are very popular in India because they allow buyers to conserve cash by purchasing only what they need immediately. Thus, many companies find that trying to employ a strategy akin to that used in the markets of developed countries is hazardous.[15] Experimenting with some, perhaps many, local twists is usually necessary to find a strategy combination that works.

Strategy Options for Competing in Developing-Country Markets

Several strategy options for tailoring a company's strategy to fit the sometimes unusual or challenging circumstances presented in developing-country markets are the following:

- *Prepare to compete on the basis of low price.* Consumers in emerging markets are often highly focused on price, which can give low-cost local competitors the edge unless a company can find ways to attract buyers with bargain prices as well as better products. For example, when Unilever entered the market for laundry detergents in India, it developed a low-cost detergent (named Wheel) that was not harsh to the skin, constructed new super efficient production facilities, distributed the product to local merchants by hand carts, and crafted an economical marketing campaign that included painted signs on buildings and demonstrations near stores—the new brand quickly captured $100 million in sales and was the top detergent brand in India in 2010 based on dollar sales. Unilever later replicated the strategy with low-price shampoos and deodorants in India and in South America with a detergent brand named Ala.

- *Be prepared to modify aspects of the company's business model or strategy to accommodate local circumstances (but not so much that the company loses the advantage of global scale and global branding).* For instance when Dell entered China, it discovered that individuals and businesses were not accustomed to placing orders via the Internet. To adapt, Dell modified its direct sales model to rely more heavily on phone and fax orders and decided to be patient in getting Chinese customers to place Internet orders. Further, because numerous Chinese government departments and state-owned enterprises insisted that hardware vendors make their bids through distributors and systems integrators (as opposed to dealing directly with Dell salespeople as did large enterprises in other countries), Dell opted to use third parties in marketing its products to this buyer segment (although it did sell through its own sales force where it could). But Dell was careful not to abandon those parts of its business model that gave it a competitive edge over rivals.

- *Try to change the local market to better match the way the company does business elsewhere.* A multinational company often has enough market clout to drive major changes in the way a local country market operates. When Japan's Suzuki entered India in 1981, it triggered a quality revolution among Indian auto parts manufacturers. Local parts and components suppliers teamed up with Suzuki's vendors in Japan and worked with Japanese experts to produce higher-quality products. Over the next two decades, Indian companies became very proficient in making top-notch parts and components for vehicles, won more prizes for quality than companies in any country other than Japan, and broke into the global market as suppliers to many automakers in Asia and other parts of the world. Mahindra and Mahindra, one of India's premier automobile manufacturers, has been recognized by a number of organizations for its product quality. Among its most noteworthy awards was its number-one ranking by J.D. Power Asia Pacific for new vehicle overall quality.

- *Stay away from those emerging markets where it is impractical or uneconomical to modify the company's business model to accommodate local circumstances.* Home Depot expanded into Mexico in 2001 and China in 2006, but has avoided entry into other emerging countries because its value proposition of good quality, low prices, and attentive customer service relies on (1) good highways and logistical systems to minimize store inventory costs, (2) employee stock ownership to help motivate store personnel to provide good customer service, and (3) high labor costs for housing construction and home repairs to encourage homeowners to engage in do-it-yourself projects. Relying on these factors in the U.S. and Canadian markets has worked spectacularly for Home Depot, but Home Depot has found that it cannot count on these factors in nearby Latin America.

Company experiences in entering developing markets such as China, India, Russia, and Brazil indicate that profitability seldom comes quickly or easily. Building a market for the company's products can often turn into a long-term process that involves reeducation of consumers, sizable investments in advertising and promotion to alter tastes and buying habits, and upgrades of the local infrastructure (the supplier base, transportation systems, distribution channels, labor markets, and capital markets). In such cases, a company must be patient, work within the system to improve the infrastructure, and lay the foundation for generating sizable revenues and profits once conditions are ripe for market take-off.

> Profitability in emerging markets rarely comes quickly or easily—new entrants have to adapt their business models and strategies to local conditions and be patient in earning a profit.

KEY POINTS

1. Competing in international markets allows multinational companies to (1) gain access to new customers, (2) achieve lower costs and enhance the firm's competitiveness by more easily capturing scale economies or learning curve effects, (3) leverage core competencies refined domestically in additional country markets, (4) gain access to resources and capabilities located in foreign markets, and (5) spread business risk across a wider market base.

2. Companies electing to expand into international markets must consider cross-country differences in buyer tastes, market sizes, and growth potential; location-based cost drivers; adverse exchange rates; and host government policies when evaluating strategy options.

3. Options for entering foreign markets include maintaining a national (one-country) production base and exporting goods to foreign markets, licensing foreign firms to use the company's technology or produce and distribute the company's products, employing a franchising strategy, establishing a foreign subsidiary, and using strategic alliances or other collaborative partnerships.

4. In posturing to compete in foreign markets, a company has three basic options: (1) a multidomestic or think local, act local approach to crafting a strategy,

(2) a global or think global, act global approach to crafting a strategy, and (3) a transnational strategy or combination think global, act local approach. A "think local, act local" or multicountry strategy is appropriate for industries or companies that must vary their product offerings and competitive approaches from country to country to accommodate differing buyer preferences and market conditions. A "think global, act global" approach (or global strategy) works best in markets that support employing the same basic competitive approach (low-cost, differentiation, focused) in all country markets and marketing essentially the same products under the same brand names in all countries where the company operates. A "think global, act local" approach can be used when it is feasible for a company to employ essentially the same basic competitive strategy in all markets, but still customize its product offering and some aspect of its operations to fit local market circumstances.

5. There are two general ways in which a firm can gain competitive advantage (or offset domestic disadvantages) in global markets. One way involves locating various value chain activities among nations in a manner that lowers costs or achieves greater product differentiation. A second way draws on a multinational or global competitor's ability to deepen or broaden its resources and capabilities and to coordinate its dispersed activities in ways that a domestic-only competitor cannot.

6. Companies racing for global leadership have to consider competing in emerging markets such as China, India, Brazil, Indonesia, and Mexico—countries where the business risks are considerable but the opportunities for growth are huge. To succeed in these markets, companies often have to (1) compete on the basis of low price, (2) be prepared to modify aspects of the company's business model or strategy to accommodate local circumstances (but not so much that the company loses the advantage of global scale and global branding), and/or (3) try to change the local market to better match the way the company does business elsewhere. Profitability is unlikely to come quickly or easily in emerging markets, typically because of the investments needed to alter buying habits and tastes and/or the need for infrastructure upgrades. And there may be times when a company should simply stay away from certain emerging markets until conditions for entry are better suited to its business model and strategy.

ASSURANCE OF LEARNING EXERCISES

LO1, LO3

1. Chile's largest producer of wine, Concha y Toro, chooses to compete in Europe, North America, the Caribbean, and Asia using an export strategy. Go to the investor relations section of the company's website (www.conchaytoro.com/the-company/investor-relations/) to review the company's press releases, annual reports, and presentations. Why does it seem that the company has avoided developing vineyards and wineries in wine growing regions outside of South America? For what reasons does Concha y Toro likely have to pursue exporting rather than stick to a domestic-only sales and distribution strategy?

LO1, LO3

2. Collaborative agreements with foreign companies in the form of strategic alliances or joint ventures are widely used as a means of entering foreign markets. Concepts & Connections 7.1, page 144, provides four examples of cross-border strategic alliances, General Motors and SAIC, EADS, Cisco and Nokia Siemens

Networks, and NTT Communications. How has GM's three-way joint venture with Wulung and Shanghai Automotive Industrial Corporation contributed to its success in China? How has the strategic alliance between Cisco and Nokia Siemens allowed both companies to improve their ability to develop new Internet capabilities? Why has Verio's cross-border strategic alliances with best-in-class partners been proven to be more successful than acquiring firms providing the technology it needs in its Web hosting business? What complementary resources needed to compete in the industry were provided through the alliance of aerospace companies from Britain, Spain, Germany, and France that made EADS (Airbus) a viable competitor?

3. Assume you are in charge of developing the strategy for a multinational company selling products in some 50 countries around the world. One of the issues you face is whether to employ a multidomestic, a transnational, or a global strategy.

    a. If your company's product is mobile phones, do you think it would make better strategic sense to employ a multidomestic strategy, a transnational strategy, or a global strategy? Why?

    b. If your company's product is dry soup mixes and canned soups, would a multidomestic strategy seem to be more advisable than a transnational or global strategy? Why?

    c. If your company's product is large home appliances such as washing machines, ranges, ovens, and refrigerators, would it seem to make more sense to pursue a multidomestic strategy or a transnational strategy or a global strategy? Why?

LO2, LO4

connect
www.mcgrawhillconnect.com

4. Using your university library's subscription to Lexis-Nexis, EBSCO, or a similar database, identify and discuss three key strategies that Volkswagen is using to compete in China.

LO5, LO6

EXERCISES FOR SIMULATION PARTICIPANTS

The questions below are for simulation participants whose companies operate in an international market arena. If your company competes only in a single country, then skip the questions in this section.

1. To what extent, if any, have you and your co-managers adapted your company's strategy to take shifting exchange rates into account? In other words, have you undertaken any actions to try to minimize the impact of adverse shifts in exchange rates?

LO2

2. To what extent, if any, have you and your co-managers adapted your company's strategy to consider geographic differences in import tariffs or import duties?

LO2

3. Which one of the following best describes the strategic approach your company is taking to try to compete successfully on an international basis?

LO4

- Multidomestic or think local, act local approach.
- Global or think global, act global approach.
- Transnational or think global, act local approach.

Explain your answer and indicate two or three chief elements of your company's strategy for competing in two or more different geographic regions.

ENDNOTES

1. A. C. Inkpen and A. Dinur, "Knowledge Management Processes and International Joint Ventures," *Organization Science* 9, no. 4 (July–August 1998); P. Dussauge, B. Garrette, and W. Mitchell, "Learning from Competing Partners: Outcomes and Durations of Scale and Link Alliances in Europe, North America and Asia," *Strategic Management Journal* 21, no. 2 (February 2000); C. Dhanaraj, M. A. Lyles, H. K. Steensma, et al., "Managing Tacit and Explicit Knowledge Transfer in IJVS: The Role of Relational Embeddedness and the Impact on Performance," *Journal of International Business Studies* 35, no. 5 (September 2004); K. W. Glaister and P. J. Buckley, "Strategic Motives for International Alliance Formation," *Journal of Management Studies* 33, no. 3 (May 1996); J. Anand and B. Kogut, "Technological Capabilities of Countries, Firm Rivalry and Foreign Direct Investment," *Journal of International Business Studies* 28, no. 3 (1997); J. Anand and A. Delios, "Absolute and Relative Resources as Determinants of International Acquisitions," *Strategic Management Journal* 23, no. 2 (February 2002); A. Seth, K. Song, and A. Pettit, "Value Creation and Destruction in Cross-Border Acquisitions: An Empirical Analysis of Foreign Acquisitions of U.S. Firms," *Strategic Management Journal* 23, no. 10 (October 2002); J. Anand, L. Capron, and W. Mitchell, "Using Acquisitions to Access Multinational Diversity: Thinking Beyond the Domestic Versus Cross-Border M&A Comparison," *Industrial & Corporate Change* 14, no. 2 (April 2005).

2. U.S. Department of Labor, Bureau of Labor Statistics, "International Comparisons of Hourly Compensation Costs in Manufacturing, 2009," March 8, 2011, pp. 3, 6.

3. E. Pablo, "Determinants of Cross-Border M&As in Latin America," *Journal of Business Research* 62, no. 9 (2009); R. Olie, "Shades of Culture and Institutions in International Mergers," *Organization Studies* 15, no. 3 (1994); and K. E. Meyer, M. Wright, and S. Pruthi, "Institutions, Resources, and Entry Strategies in Emerging Economies," *Strategic Management Journal* 30, no. 5 (2009).

4. Joel Bleeke and David Ernst, "The Way to Win in Cross-Border Alliances," *Harvard Business Review* 69, no. 6 (November–December 1991); and Gary Hamel, Yves L. Doz, and C. K. Prahalad, "Collaborate with Your Competitors—and Win," *Harvard Business Review* 67, no. 1 (January–February 1989).

5. Yves L. Doz and Gary Hamel, *Alliance Advantage* (Boston: Harvard Business School Press, 1998); Bleeke and Ernst, "The Way to Win in Cross-Border Alliances"; Hamel, Doz, and Prahalad, "Collaborate with Your Competitors—and Win"; and Michael Porter, *The Competitive Advantage of Nations* (New York: Free Press, 1990).

6. H. Kurt Christensen, "Corporate Strategy: Managing a Set of Businesses," in *The Portable MBA in Strategy*, ed. Liam Fahey and Robert M. Randall (New York: John Wiley & Sons, 2001).

7. Jeffrey H. Dyer, Prashant Kale, and Harbir Singh, "When to Ally and When to Acquire," *Harvard Business Review* 82, no. 7/8 (July–August 2004).

8. Rosabeth Moss Kanter, "Collaborative Advantage: The Art of the Alliance," *Harvard Business Review* 72, no. 4 (July–August 1994).

9. Jeremy Main, "Making Global Alliances Work," *Fortune,* December 19, 1990, p. 125.

10. Pankaj Ghemawat, "Managing Differences: The Central Challenge of Global Strategy," *Harvard Business Review* 85, no. 3 (March 2007).

11. C. A. Bartlett and S. Ghoshal, *Managing Across Borders: The Transnational Solution*, 2nd ed. (Boston: Harvard Business School Press, 1998).

12. C. K. Prahalad and Yves L. Doz, *The Multinational Mission* (New York: Free Press, 1987), pp. 58–60.

13. David J. Arnold and John A. Quelch, "New Strategies in Emerging Markets," *Sloan Management Review* 40, no. 1 (Fall 1998); and C. K. Prahalad, *The Fortune at the Bottom of the Pyramid: Eradicating Poverty through Profits* (Upper Saddle River, NJ: Wharton, 2005).

14. Brenda Cherry, "What China Eats (and Drinks and . . .)," *Fortune,* October 4, 2004, pp. 152–153; "A Ravenous Dragon," *The Economist* 386, no. 8571 (March 15, 2008), online edition; and "China: Just the Facts," *Journal of Commerce,* June 2, 2008, p. 24.

15. Tarun Khanna, Krishna G. Palepu, and Jayant Sinha, "Strategies That Fit Emerging Markets," *Harvard Business Review* 83, no. 6 (June 2005); and Arindam K. Bhattacharya and David C. Michael, "How Local Companies Keep Multinationals at Bay," *Harvard Business Review* 86, no. 3 (March 2008).

chapter 8

CORPORATE STRATEGY: DIVERSIFICATION AND THE MULTIBUSINESS COMPANY

LEARNING OBJECTIVES

LO1 Understand when and how diversifying into multiple businesses can enhance shareholder value.

LO2 Gain an understanding of how related diversification strategies can produce cross-business strategic fit capable of delivering competitive advantage.

LO3 Become aware of the merits and risks of corporate strategies keyed to unrelated diversification.

LO4 Gain command of the analytical tools for evaluating a company's diversification strategy.

LO5 Understand a diversified company's four main corporate strategy options for solidifying its diversification strategy and improving company performance.

This chapter moves up one level in the strategy-making hierarchy, from strategy making in a single-business enterprise to strategy making in a diversified enterprise. Because a diversified company is a collection of individual businesses, the strategy-making task is more complicated. In a one-business company, managers have to come up with a plan for competing successfully in only a single industry environment—the result is what Chapter 2 labeled as *business strategy* (or *business-level strategy*). But in a diversified company, the strategy-making challenge involves assessing multiple industry environments and developing a *set* of business strategies, one for each industry arena in which the diversified company operates. And top executives at a diversified company must still go one step further and devise a companywide or *corporate strategy* for improving the attractiveness and performance of the company's overall business lineup and for making a rational whole out of its diversified collection of individual businesses.

In most diversified companies, corporate-level executives delegate considerable strategy-making authority to the heads of each business, usually giving them the latitude to craft a business strategy suited to their particular industry and competitive circumstances and holding them accountable for producing good results. But the task of crafting a diversified company's overall corporate strategy falls squarely in the lap of top-level executives and involves four distinct facets:

1. *Picking new industries to enter and deciding on the means of entry.* The decision to pursue business diversification requires that management decide what new industries offer the best growth prospects and whether to enter by starting a new business from the ground up, acquiring a company already in the target industry, or forming a joint venture or strategic alliance with another company.

2. *Pursuing opportunities to leverage cross-business value chain relationships into competitive advantage.* Companies that diversify into businesses with strategic fit across the value chains of their business units have a much better chance of gaining a $1 + 1 = 3$ effect than multibusiness companies lacking strategic fit.

3. *Establishing investment priorities and steering corporate resources into the most attractive business units.* A diversified company's business units are usually not equally attractive, and it is incumbent on corporate management to channel resources into areas where earnings potentials are higher.

4. *Initiating actions to boost the combined performance of the corporation's collection of businesses.* Corporate strategists must craft moves to improve the overall performance of the corporation's business lineup and sustain increases in shareholder value. Strategic options for diversified corporations include *(a)* sticking closely with the existing business lineup and pursuing opportunities presented by these businesses, *(b)* broadening the scope of diversification by entering additional industries, *(c)* retrenching to a narrower scope of diversification by divesting poorly performing businesses, and *(d)* broadly restructuring the business lineup with multiple divestitures and/or acquisitions.

The first portion of this chapter describes the various means a company can use to diversify and explores the pros and cons of related versus unrelated diversification strategies. The second part of the chapter looks at how to evaluate the attractiveness of a diversified company's business lineup, decide whether it has a good diversification strategy, and identify ways to improve its future performance.

WHEN BUSINESS DIVERSIFICATION BECOMES A CONSIDERATION

As long as a single-business company can achieve profitable growth opportunities in its present industry, there is no urgency to pursue diversification. However, a company's opportunities for growth can become limited if the industry becomes competitively unattractive. Consider, for example, what the growing use of debit cards and online bill payment have done to the check printing business and what mobile phone companies and marketers of Voice over Internet Protocol (VoIP) have done to the revenues of long-distance providers such as AT&T, British Telecommunications, and NTT in Japan. Thus, *diversifying into new industries always merits strong consideration whenever a single-business company encounters diminishing market opportunities and stagnating sales in its principal business.*[1]

▶**LO1**

Understand when and how diversifying into multiple businesses can enhance shareholder value.

BUILDING SHAREHOLDER VALUE: THE ULTIMATE JUSTIFICATION FOR BUSINESS DIVERSIFICATION

Diversification must do more for a company than simply spread its business risk across various industries. In principle, diversification cannot be considered a success unless it results in *added shareholder value*—value that shareholders cannot capture on their own by spreading their investments across the stocks of companies in different industries.

Business diversification stands little chance of building shareholder value without passing the following three tests:[2]

1. *The industry attractiveness test.* The industry to be entered through diversification must offer an opportunity for profits and return on investment that is equal to or better than that of the company's present business(es).

2. *The cost-of-entry test.* The cost to enter the target industry must not be so high as to erode the potential for good profitability. A Catch-22 can prevail here, however. The more attractive an industry's prospects are for growth and good long-term profitability, the more expensive it can be to enter. It's easy for acquisitions of companies in highly attractive industries to fail the cost-of-entry test.

3. *The better-off test.* Diversifying into a new business must offer potential for the company's existing businesses and the new business to perform better together under a single corporate umbrella than they would perform operating as independent, stand-alone businesses. For example, let's say company A diversifies by purchasing company B in another industry. If A and B's consolidated profits in the years to come prove no greater than

what each could have earned on its own, then A's diversification won't provide its shareholders with added value. Company A's shareholders could have achieved the same $1 + 1 = 2$ result by merely purchasing stock in company B. Shareholder value is not created by diversification unless it produces a $1 + 1 = 3$ effect.

> Creating added value for shareholders via diversification requires building a multibusiness company where the whole is greater than the sum of its parts.

Diversification moves that satisfy all three tests have the greatest potential to grow shareholder value over the long term. Diversification moves that can pass only one or two tests are suspect.

APPROACHES TO DIVERSIFYING THE BUSINESS LINEUP

The means of entering new industries and lines of business can take any of three forms: acquisition, internal development, or joint ventures with other companies.

Diversification by Acquisition of an Existing Business

Acquisition is a popular means of diversifying into another industry. Not only is it quicker than trying to launch a new operation, but it also offers an effective way to hurdle such entry barriers as acquiring technological know-how, establishing supplier relationships, achieving scale economies, building brand awareness, and securing adequate distribution. Buying an ongoing operation allows the acquirer to move directly to the task of building a strong market position in the target industry, rather than getting bogged down in the fine points of launching a start-up.

The big dilemma an acquisition-minded firm faces is whether to pay a premium price for a successful company or to buy a struggling company at a bargain price.[3] If the buying firm has little knowledge of the industry but has ample capital, it is often better off purchasing a capable, strongly positioned firm—unless the price of such an acquisition is prohibitive and flunks the cost-of-entry test. However, when the acquirer sees promising ways to transform a weak firm into a strong one, a struggling company can be the better long-term investment.

Entering a New Line of Business through Internal Development

Achieving diversification through *internal development* involves starting a new business subsidiary from scratch. Generally, forming a start-up subsidiary to enter a new business has appeal only when (1) the parent company already has in-house most or all of the skills and resources needed to compete effectively; (2) there is ample time to launch the business; (3) internal entry has lower costs than entry via acquisition; (4) the targeted industry is populated with many relatively small firms such that the new start-up does not have to compete against large, powerful rivals; (5) adding new production capacity will not adversely impact the supply–demand balance in the industry; and (6) incumbent firms are likely to be slow or ineffective in responding to a new entrant's efforts to crack the market.

Using Joint Ventures to Achieve Diversification

A joint venture to enter a new business can be useful in at least two types of situations.[4] First, a joint venture is a good vehicle for pursuing an opportunity that is too complex, uneconomical, or risky for one company to pursue alone. Second, joint ventures make sense when the opportunities in a new industry require a broader range of competencies and know-how than an expansion-minded company can marshal. Many of the opportunities in biotechnology call for the coordinated development of complementary innovations and tackling an intricate web of technical, political, and regulatory factors simultaneously. In such cases, pooling the resources and competencies of two or more companies is a wiser and less risky way to proceed.

However, as discussed in Chapters 6 and 7, partnering with another company—either in the form of a joint venture or collaborative alliance—has significant drawbacks due to the potential for conflicting objectives, disagreements over how to best operate the venture, culture clashes, and so on. Joint ventures are generally the least durable of the entry options, usually lasting only until the partners decide to go their own ways.

CHOOSING THE DIVERSIFICATION PATH: RELATED VERSUS UNRELATED BUSINESSES

> **CORE CONCEPT**
>
> **Related businesses** possess competitively valuable cross-business value chain and resource matchups; **unrelated businesses** have dissimilar value chains and resources requirements, with no competitively important cross-business value chain relationships.

Once a company decides to diversify, its first big corporate strategy decision is whether to diversify into **related businesses, unrelated businesses,** or some mix of both (see Figure 8.1). *Businesses are said to be related when their value chains possess competitively valuable cross-business relationships.* These value chain matchups present opportunities for the businesses to perform better under the same corporate umbrella than they could by operating as stand-alone entities. *Businesses are said to be unrelated when the activities comprising their respective value chains and resource requirements are so dissimilar that no competitively valuable cross-business relationships are present.*

The next two sections explore the ins and outs of related and unrelated diversification.

▶ **LO2**

Gain an understanding of how related diversification strategies can produce cross-business strategic fit capable of delivering competitive advantage.

THE CASE FOR RELATED DIVERSIFICATION

A related diversification strategy involves building the company around businesses whose value chains possess competitively valuable strategic fit, as shown in Figure 8.2. **Strategic fit** exists whenever one or more activities comprising the value chains of different businesses are sufficiently similar to present opportunities for:[5]

> **CORE CONCEPT**
>
> **Strategic fit** exists when the value chains of different businesses present opportunities for cross-business skills transfer, cost sharing, or brand sharing.

- *Transferring competitively valuable resources, expertise, technological know-how, or other* capabilities

from one B to another

▶FIGURE 8.1 **Strategic Themes of Multibusiness Corporations**

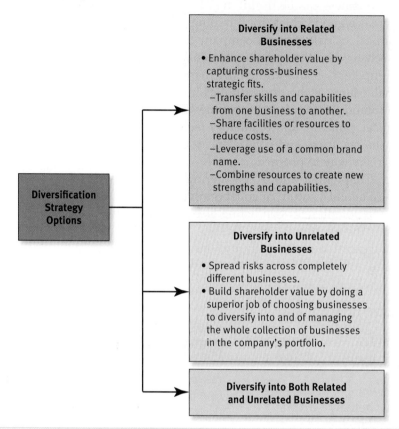

capabilities from one business to another. Google's technological know-how and innovation capabilities refined in its Internet search business have aided considerably in the development of its Android mobile operating system and Chrome operating system for computers. After acquiring Marvel Comics in 2009, Walt Disney Company shared Marvel's iconic characters such as Spider-Man, Iron Man, and the Black Widow with many of the other Disney businesses, including its theme parks, retail stores, motion picture division, and video game business.

- *Cost sharing between separate businesses where value chain activities can be combine*d. For instance, it is often feasible to manufacture the products of different businesses in a single plant or have a single sales force for the products of different businesses if they are marketed to the same types of customers.

- *Brand sharing between business units that have common customers or that draw upon common core competencies.* For example, Yamaha's name in motorcycles gave it instant credibility and recognition in entering the personal watercraft business, allowing it to achieve a significant market share without spending large sums on advertising to establish a brand identity for the WaveRunner. Likewise, Apple's reputation for producing easy-to-operate computers was a competitive asset that facilitated the company's diversification into digital music players and smartphones.

▶FIGURE 8.2 Related Diversification Is Built upon Competitively Valuable Strategic Fit in Value Chain Activities

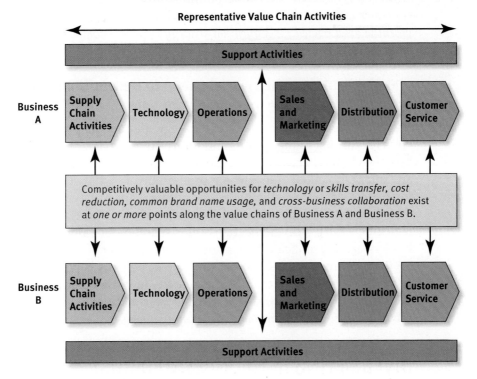

Cross-business strategic fit can exist anywhere along the value chain—in R&D and technology activities, in supply chain activities, in manufacturing, in sales and marketing, or in distribution activities. Likewise, different businesses can often use the same administrative and customer service infrastructure. For instance, a cable operator that diversifies as a broadband provider can use the same customer data network, the same customer call centers and local offices, the same billing and customer accounting systems, and the same customer service infrastructure to support all its products and services.[6]

Strategic Fit and Economies of Scope

Strategic fit in the value chain activities of a diversified corporation's different businesses opens up opportunities for economies of scope—a concept distinct from *economies of scale*. Economies of *scale* are cost savings that accrue directly from a larger operation; for example, unit costs may be lower in a large plant than in a small plant. **Economies of scope,** however, stem directly from cost-saving strategic fit along the value chains of related businesses. Such economies are open only to a multibusiness enterprise and are the result of a related diversification strategy that allows sibling businesses to share technology, perform R&D together, use common manufacturing ⌐ Dist facilities

> ### CORE CONCEPT
> **Economies of scope** are cost reductions stemming from strategic fit along the value chains of related businesses (thereby, a larger scope of operations), whereas *economies of scale* accrue from a larger operation.

or distribution facilities, share a common sales force or distributor/dealer network, and/or share the same administrative infrastructure. *The greater the cross-business economies associated with cost-saving strategic fit, the greater the potential for a related diversification strategy to yield a competitive advantage based on lower costs than rivals.*

The Ability of Related Diversification to Deliver Competitive Advantage and Gains in Shareholder Value

Economies of scope and the other strategic-fit benefits provide a dependable basis for earning higher profits and returns than what a diversified company's businesses could earn as stand-alone enterprises. Converting the competitive advantage potential into greater profitability is what fuels $1 + 1 = 3$ gains in shareholder value—the necessary outcome for satisfying the *better-off test.* There are three things to bear in mind here: (1) Capturing cross-business strategic fit via related diversification builds shareholder value in ways that shareholders cannot replicate by simply owning a diversified portfolio of stocks; (2) the capture of cross-business strategic-fit benefits is possible only through related diversification; and (3) the benefits of cross-business strategic fit are not automatically realized—*the benefits materialize only after management has successfully pursued internal actions to capture them.*[7]

DIVERSIFYING INTO UNRELATED BUSINESSES

LO3

Become aware of the merits and risks of corporate strategies keyed to unrelated diversification.

An unrelated diversification strategy discounts the importance of pursuing cross-business strategic fit and, instead, focuses squarely on entering and operating businesses in industries that allow the company as a whole to increase its earnings. Companies that pursue a strategy of unrelated diversification generally exhibit a willingness to diversify into *any industry* where senior managers see opportunity to realize improved financial results. Such companies are frequently labeled *conglomerates* because their business interests range broadly across diverse industries.

Companies that pursue unrelated diversification nearly always enter new businesses by acquiring an established company rather than by internal development. The premise of acquisition-minded corporations is that growth by acquisition can deliver enhanced shareholder value through upward-trending corporate revenues and earnings and a stock price that *on average* rises enough year after year to amply reward and please shareholders. Three types of acquisition candidates are usually of particular interest: (1) businesses that have bright growth prospects but are short on investment capital, (2) undervalued companies that can be acquired at a bargain price, and (3) struggling companies whose operations can be turned around with the aid of the parent company's financial resources and managerial know-how.

Building Shareholder Value Through Unrelated Diversification

Given the absence of cross-business strategic fit with which to capture added competitive advantage, the task of building shareholder value via unrelated diversification ultimately hinges on the ability of the parent company to improve its businesses via other means. To succeed with a corporate strategy keyed to unrelated diversification, corporate executives must:

- Do a superior job of identifying and acquiring new businesses that can produce consistently good earnings and returns on investment.
- Do an excellent job of negotiating favorable acquisition prices.
- Do such a good job *overseeing* and *parenting* the firm's businesses that they perform at a higher level than they would otherwise be able to do through their own efforts alone. The parenting activities of corporate executives can take the form of providing expert problem-solving skills, creative strategy suggestions, and first-rate advice and guidance on how to improve competitiveness and financial performance to the heads of the various business subsidiaries.[8]

The Pitfalls of Unrelated Diversification

Unrelated diversification strategies have two important negatives that undercut the pluses: very demanding managerial requirements and limited competitive advantage potential.

Demanding Managerial Requirements   Successfully managing a set of fundamentally different businesses operating in fundamentally different industry and competitive environments is an exceptionally difficult proposition for corporate-level managers. The greater the number of businesses a company is in and the more diverse they are, the more difficult it is for corporate managers to:

1. Stay abreast of what's happening in each industry and each subsidiary.
2. Pick business-unit heads having the requisite combination of managerial skills and know-how to drive gains in performance.
3. Tell the difference between those strategic proposals of business-unit managers that are prudent and those that are risky or unlikely to succeed.
4. Know what to do if a business unit stumbles and its results suddenly head downhill.[9]

As a rule, the more unrelated businesses that a company has diversified into, the more corporate executives are forced to "manage by the numbers"— that is, keep a close track on the financial and operating results of each subsidiary and assume that the heads of the various subsidiaries have most everything under control so long as the latest key financial and operating measures look good. Managing by the numbers works if the heads of the various business units are quite capable and consistently meet their numbers. But problems arise when things start to go awry and corporate management has to get deeply involved in turning around a business it does not know much about.

> Unrelated diversification requires that corporate executives rely on the skills and expertise of business-level managers to build competitive advantage and boost the performance of individual businesses.

Limited Competitive Advantage Potential   The second big negative associated with unrelated diversification is that such a strategy *offers limited potential for competitive advantage beyond what each individual business can generate on its own.* Unlike a related diversification strategy, there is no cross-business strategic fit to draw on for reducing costs; transferring capabilities, skills, and technology; or leveraging use of a powerful brand name and thereby adding to the competitive advantage possessed by individual businesses. *Without the competitive advantage potential of strategic fit, consolidated performance of an unrelated group of businesses is unlikely to be better than the sum of what the individual business units could achieve independently in most instances.*

Misguided Reasons for Pursuing Unrelated Diversification

Competently overseeing a set of widely diverse businesses can turn out to be much harder than it sounds. In practice, comparatively few companies have proved that they have top management capabilities that are up to the task. Far more corporate executives have failed than been successful at delivering consistently good financial results with an unrelated diversification strategy.[10] Odds are that the result of unrelated diversification will be 1 + 1 = 2 or less. In addition, management sometimes undertakes a strategy of unrelated diversification for the wrong reasons.

- *Risk reduction.* Managers sometimes pursue unrelated diversification to reduce risk by spreading the company's investments over a set of diverse industries. But this cannot create long-term shareholder value alone since the company's shareholders can more efficiently reduce their exposure to risk by investing in a diversified portfolio of stocks and bonds.
- *Growth.* While unrelated diversification may enable a company to achieve rapid or continuous growth in revenues, only profitable growth can bring about increases in shareholder value and justify a strategy of unrelated diversification.
- *Earnings stabilization.* In a broadly diversified company, there's a chance that market downtrends in some of the company's businesses will be partially offset by cyclical upswings in its other businesses, thus producing somewhat less earnings volatility. In actual practice, however, there's no convincing evidence that the consolidated profits of firms with unrelated diversification strategies are more stable than the profits of firms with related diversification strategies.
- *Managerial motives.* Unrelated diversification can provide benefits to managers such as higher compensation, which tends to increase with firm size and degree of diversification. Diversification for this reason alone is far more likely to reduce shareholder value than to increase it.

CORPORATE STRATEGIES COMBINING RELATED AND UNRELATED DIVERSIFICATION

There's nothing to preclude a company from diversifying into both related and unrelated businesses. Indeed, the business makeup of diversified companies varies considerably. Some diversified companies are really *dominant-business enterprises*—one major "core" business accounts for 50 to 80 percent of total revenues and a collection of small related or unrelated businesses accounts for the remainder. Some diversified companies are *narrowly diversified* around a few (two to five) related or unrelated businesses. Others are *broadly diversified* around a wide-ranging collection of related businesses, unrelated businesses, or a mixture of both. And a number of multibusiness enterprises have diversified into *several unrelated groups of related businesses.* There's ample room for companies to customize their diversification strategies to incorporate elements of both related and unrelated diversification.

EVALUATING THE STRATEGY OF A DIVERSIFIED COMPANY

Strategic analysis of diversified companies builds on the methodology used for single-business companies discussed in Chapters 3 and 4 but utilizes tools that streamline the overall process. The procedure for evaluating the pluses and minuses of a diversified company's strategy and deciding what actions to take to improve the company's performance involves six steps:

▶ **LO4**

Gain command of the analytical tools for evaluating a company's diversification strategy.

1. Assessing the attractiveness of the industries the company has diversified into.
2. Assessing the competitive strength of the company's business units.
3. Evaluating the extent of cross-business strategic fit along the value chains of the company's various business units.
4. Checking whether the firm's resources fit the requirements of its present business lineup.
5. Ranking the performance prospects of the businesses from best to worst and determining a priority for allocating resources.
6. Crafting new strategic moves to improve overall corporate performance.

The core concepts and analytical techniques underlying each of these steps are discussed further in this section of the chapter.

Step 1: Evaluating Industry Attractiveness

A principal consideration in evaluating the caliber of a diversified company's strategy is the attractiveness of the industries in which it has business operations. The more attractive the industries (both individually and as a group) a diversified company is in, the better its prospects for good long-term performance. A simple and reliable analytical tool for gauging industry attractiveness involves calculating quantitative industry attractiveness scores based upon the following measures.

- *Market size and projected growth rate.* Big industries are more attractive than small industries, and fast-growing industries tend to be more attractive than slow-growing industries, other things being equal.
- *The intensity of competition.* Industries where competitive pressures are relatively weak are more attractive than industries with strong competitive pressures.

- *Emerging opportunities and threats.* Industries with promising opportunities and minimal threats on the near horizon are more attractive than industries with modest opportunities and imposing threats.

- *The presence of cross-industry strategic fit.* The more the industry's value chain and resource requirements match up well with the value chain activities of other industries in which the company has operations, the more attractive the industry is to a firm pursuing related diversification. However, cross-industry strategic fit may be of no consequence to a company committed to a strategy of unrelated diversification.

- *Resource requirements.* Industries having resource requirements within the company's reach are more attractive than industries where capital and other resource requirements could strain corporate financial resources and organizational capabilities.

- *Seasonal and cyclical factors.* Industries where buyer demand is relatively steady year-round and not unduly vulnerable to economic ups and downs tend to be more attractive than industries with wide seasonal or cyclical swings in buyer demand.

- *Social, political, regulatory, and environmental factors.* Industries with significant problems in such areas as consumer health, safety, or environmental pollution or that are subject to intense regulation are less attractive than industries where such problems are not burning issues.

- *Industry profitability.* Industries with healthy profit margins are generally more attractive than industries where profits have historically been low or unstable.

- *Industry uncertainty and business risk.* Industries with less uncertainty on the horizon and lower overall business risk are more attractive than industries whose prospects for one reason or another are quite uncertain.

Each attractiveness measure should be assigned a weight reflecting its relative importance in determining an industry's attractiveness; it is weak methodology to assume that the various attractiveness measures are equally important. The intensity of competition in an industry should nearly always carry a high weight (say, 0.20 to 0.30). Strategic-fit considerations should be assigned a high weight in the case of companies with related diversification strategies; but for companies with an unrelated diversification strategy, strategic fit with other industries may be given a low weight or even dropped from the list of attractiveness measures. Seasonal and cyclical factors generally are assigned a low weight (or maybe even eliminated from the analysis) unless a company has diversified into industries strongly characterized by seasonal demand and/or heavy vulnerability to cyclical upswings and downswings. The importance weights must add up to 1.0.

Next, each industry is rated on each of the chosen industry attractiveness measures, using a rating scale of 1 to 10 (where 10 signifies *high* attractiveness and 1 signifies *low* attractiveness). Weighted attractiveness scores are then calculated by multiplying the industry's rating on each measure by the corresponding weight. For example, a rating of 8 times a weight of 0.25 gives a weighted attractiveness score of 2.00. The sum of the weighted scores for all

TABLE 8.1

Calculating Weighted Industry Attractiveness Scores

Rating scale: 1 = Very unattractive to company; 10 = Very attractive to company

Industry Attractiveness Measure	Importance Weight	Industry A Rating/Score	Industry B Rating/Score	Industry C Rating/Score	Industry D Rating/Score
Market size and projected growth rate	0.10	8/0.80	5/0.50	2/0.20	3/0.30
Intensity of competition	0.25	8/2.00	7/1.75	3/0.75	2/0.50
Emerging opportunities and threats	0.10	2/0.20	9/0.90	4/0.40	5/0.50
Cross-industry strategic fit	0.20	8/1.60	4/0.80	8/1.60	2/0.40
Resource requirements	0.10	9/0.90	7/0.70	5/0.50	5/0.50
Seasonal and cyclical influences	0.05	9/0.45	8/0.40	10/0.50	5/0.25
Societal, political, regulatory, and environmental factors	0.05	10/0.50	7/0.35	7/0.35	3/0.15
Industry profitability	0.10	5/0.50	10/1.00	3/0.30	3/0.30
Industry uncertainty and business risk	0.05	5/0.25	7/0.35	10/0.50	1/0.05
Sum of the assigned weights	1.00				
Overall weighted industry attractiveness scores		**7.20**	**6.75**	**5.10**	**2.95**

the attractiveness measures provides an overall industry attractiveness score. This procedure is illustrated in Table 8.1.

Calculating Industry Attractiveness Scores There are two necessary conditions for producing valid industry attractiveness scores using this method. One is deciding on appropriate weights for the industry attractiveness measures. This is not always easy because different analysts have different views about which weights are most appropriate. Also, different weightings may be appropriate for different companies—based on their strategies, performance targets, and financial circumstances. For instance, placing a low weight on financial resource requirements may be justifiable for a cash-rich company, whereas a high weight may be more appropriate for a financially strapped company. The second requirement for creating accurate attractiveness scores is to have sufficient knowledge to rate the industry on each attractiveness measure. It's usually rather easy to locate statistical data needed to compare industries on market size, growth rate, seasonal and cyclical influences, and industry profitability. Cross-industry fit and resource requirements are also fairly easy to judge. But the attractiveness measure that is toughest to rate is that of intensity of competition. It is not always easy to conclude whether competition in one industry is stronger or weaker than in another industry. In the event that the available information is too skimpy to confidently assign a rating value to an industry on a particular attractiveness measure, then it is usually best to use a score of 5, which avoids biasing the overall attractiveness score either up or down.

Despite the hurdles, calculating industry attractiveness scores is a systematic and reasonably reliable method for ranking a diversified company's industries from most to least attractive.

Step 2: Evaluating Business-Unit Competitive Strength

The second step in evaluating a diversified company is to determine how strongly positioned its business units are in their respective industries. Doing an appraisal of each business unit's strength and competitive position in its industry not only reveals its chances for industry success but also provides a basis for ranking the units from competitively strongest to weakest. Quantitative measures of each business unit's competitive strength can be calculated using a procedure similar to that for measuring industry attractiveness. The following factors may be used in quantifying the competitive strengths of a diversified company's business subsidiaries:

- *Relative market share.* A business unit's *relative market share* is defined as the ratio of its market share to the market share held by the largest rival firm in the industry, with market share measured in unit volume, not dollars. For instance, if business A has a market-leading share of 40 percent and its largest rival has 30 percent, A's relative market share is 1.33. If business B has a 15 percent market share and B's largest rival has 30 percent, B's relative market share is 0.5.

- *Costs relative to competitors' costs.* There's reason to expect that business units with higher relative market shares have lower unit costs than competitors with lower relative market shares because of the possibility of scale economies and experience or learning curve effects. Another indicator of low cost can be a business unit's supply chain management capabilities.

- *Products or services that satisfy buyer expectations.* A company's competitiveness depends in part on being able to offer buyers appealing features, performance, reliability, and service attributes.

- *Ability to benefit from strategic fit with sibling businesses.* Strategic fit with other businesses within the company enhance a business unit's competitive strength and may provide a competitive edge.

- *Number and caliber of strategic alliances and collaborative partnerships.* Well-functioning alliances and partnerships may be a source of potential competitive advantage and thus add to a business's competitive strength.

- *Brand image and reputation.* A strong brand name is a valuable competitive asset in most industries.

- *Competitively valuable capabilities.* All industries contain a variety of important competitive capabilities related to product innovation, production capabilities, distribution capabilities, or marketing prowess.

- *Profitability relative to competitors.* Above-average returns on investment and large profit margins relative to rivals are usually accurate indicators of competitive advantage.

After settling on a set of competitive strength measures that are well matched to the circumstances of the various business units, weights indicating each measure's importance need to be assigned. As in the assignment of weights to industry attractiveness measures, the importance weights must add up to 1.0. Each business unit is then rated on each of the chosen strength measures, using a rating scale of 1 to 10 (where 10 signifies competitive *strength* and a rating of 1 signifies competitive *weakness*). If the available information is too skimpy to confidently assign a rating value to a business unit on a particular strength measure, then it is usually best to use a score of 5. Weighted strength ratings are calculated by multiplying the business unit's rating on each strength measure by the assigned weight. For example, a strength score of 6 times a weight of 0.15 gives a weighted strength rating of 0.90. The sum of weighted ratings across all the strength measures provides a quantitative measure of a business unit's overall market strength and competitive standing. Table 8.2 provides sample calculations of competitive strength ratings for four businesses.

Using a Nine-Cell Matrix to Evaluate the Strength of a Diversified Company's Business Lineup The industry attractiveness and business strength scores can be used to portray the strategic positions of each business in a diversified company. Industry attractiveness is plotted on the vertical axis and competitive strength on the horizontal axis. A nine-cell grid

▶ TABLE 8.2

Calculating Weighted Competitive Strength Scores for a Diversified Company's Business Units

Rating scale: 1 = Very weak; 10 = Very strong

Competitive Strength Measure	Importance Weight	Business A In Industry A Rating/Score	Business B In Industry B Rating/Score	Business C In Industry C Rating/Score	Business D In Industry D Rating/Score
Relative market share	0.15	10/1.50	1/0.15	6/0.90	2/0.30
Costs relative to competitors' costs	0.20	7/1.40	2/0.40	5/1.00	3/0.60
Ability to match or beat rivals on key product attributes	0.05	9/0.45	4/0.20	8/0.40	4/0.20
Ability to benefit from strategic fit with sister businesses	0.20	8/1.60	4/0.80	4/0.80	2/0.60
Bargaining leverage with suppliers/ buyers; caliber of alliances	0.05	9/0.45	3/0.15	6/0.30	2/0.10
Brand image and reputation	0.10	9/0.90	2/0.20	7/0.70	5/0.50
Competitively valuable capabilities	0.15	7/1.05	2/0.30	5/0.75	3/0.45
Profitability relative to competitors	0.10	5/0.50	1/0.10	4/0.40	4/0.40
Sum of the assigned weights	1.00				
Overall weighted competitive strength scores		**7.85**	**2.30**	**5.25**	**3.15**

A 9 cell grid

emerges from dividing the vertical axis into three regions (high, medium, and low attractiveness) and the horizontal axis into three regions (strong, average, and weak competitive strength). As shown in Figure 8.3, high attractiveness is associated with scores of 6.7 or greater on a rating scale of 1 to 10, medium attractiveness to scores of 3.3 to 6.7, and low attractiveness to scores below 3.3. Likewise, high competitive strength is defined as a score greater than 6.7, average strength as scores of 3.3 to 6.7, and low strength as scores below 3.3. *Each business unit is plotted on the nine-cell matrix according to its overall attractiveness and strength scores, and then shown as a "bubble." The size of each bubble is*

▶ FIGURE 8.3 **A Nine-Cell Industry Attractiveness–Competitive Strength Matrix**

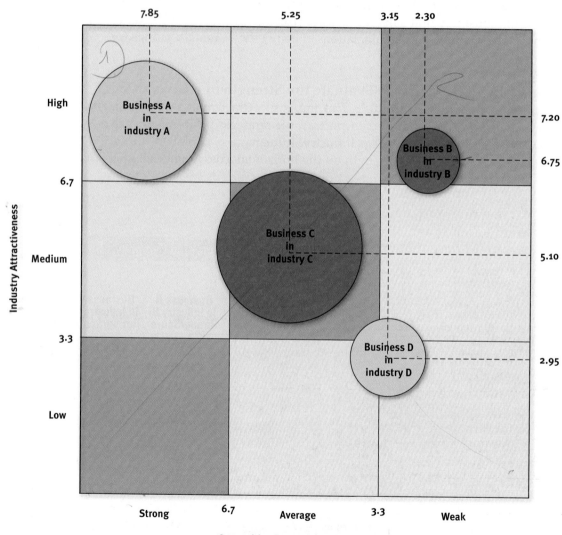

High priority for resource allocation
Medium priority for resource allocation
Low priority for resource allocation

Note: Circle sizes are scaled to reflect the percentage of companywide revenues generated by the business unit.

scaled to what percentage of revenues the business generates relative to total corporate revenues. The bubbles in Figure 8.3 were located on the grid using the four industry attractiveness scores from Table 8.1 and the strength scores for the four business units in Table 8.2.

The locations of the business units on the attractiveness–strength matrix provide valuable guidance in deploying corporate resources. In general, *a diversified company's best prospects for good overall performance involve concentrating corporate resources on business units having the greatest competitive strength and industry attractiveness.* Businesses plotted in the three cells in the upper left portion of the attractiveness–strength matrix have both favorable industry attractiveness and competitive strength and should receive a high investment priority. Business units plotted in these three cells (such as business A in Figure 8.3) are referred to as "grow and build" businesses because of their capability to drive future increases in shareholder value.

Next in priority come businesses positioned in the three diagonal cells stretching from the lower left to the upper right (businesses B and C in Figure 8.3). Such businesses usually merit medium or intermediate priority in the parent's resource allocation ranking. However, some businesses in the medium-priority diagonal cells may have brighter or dimmer prospects than others. For example, a small business in the upper right cell of the matrix (like business B), despite being in a highly attractive industry, may occupy too weak a competitive position in its industry to justify the investment and resources needed to turn it into a strong market contender. If, however, a business in the upper right cell has attractive opportunities for rapid growth and a good potential for winning a much stronger market position over time, management may designate it as a grow and build business—the strategic objective here would be to move the business leftward in the attractiveness–strength matrix over time.

Businesses in the three cells in the lower right corner of the matrix (business D in Figure 8.3) typically are weak performers and have the lowest claim on corporate resources. Such businesses are typically good candidates for being divested or else managed in a manner calculated to squeeze out the maximum cash flows from operations. The cash flows from low-performing/low-potential businesses can then be diverted to financing expansion of business units with greater market opportunities. In exceptional cases where a business located in the three lower right cells is nonetheless fairly profitable or has the potential for good earnings and return on investment, the business merits retention and the allocation of sufficient resources to achieve better performance.

The nine-cell attractiveness–strength matrix provides clear, strong logic for why a diversified company needs to consider both industry attractiveness and business strength in allocating resources and investment capital to its different businesses. A good case can be made for concentrating resources in those businesses that enjoy higher degrees of attractiveness and competitive strength, being very selective in making investments in businesses with intermediate positions on the grid, and withdrawing resources from businesses that are lower in attractiveness and strength unless they offer exceptional profit or cash flow potential.

Step 3: Determining the Competitive Value of Strategic Fit in Multibusiness Companies

The potential for competitively important strategic fit is central to making conclusions about the effectiveness of a company's related diversification strategy. This step can be bypassed for diversified companies whose businesses are all unrelated (because, by design, no cross-business strategic fit is present). Checking the competitive advantage potential of cross-business strategic fit involves evaluating how much benefit a diversified company can gain from value chain matchups that present:

> The greater the value of cross-business strategic fit in enhancing a company's performance in the marketplace or the bottom line, the more powerful is its strategy of related diversification.

1. Opportunities to combine the performance of certain activities, thereby reducing costs and capturing economies of scope.

2. Opportunities to transfer skills, technology, or intellectual capital from one business to another.

3. Opportunities to share use of a well-respected brand name across multiple product and/or service categories.

But more than just strategic fit identification is needed. The real test is what competitive value can be generated from this fit. To what extent can cost savings be realized? How much competitive value will come from cross-business transfer of skills, technology, or intellectual capital? Will transferring a potent brand name to the products of sibling businesses grow sales significantly? Absent significant strategic fit and dedicated company efforts to capture the benefits, one has to be skeptical about the potential for a diversified company's businesses to perform better together than apart.

Step 4: Evaluating Resource Fit

The businesses in a diversified company's lineup need to exhibit good resource fit. **Resource fit** exists when (1) businesses, individually, strengthen a company's overall mix of resources and capabilities and (2) a company has sufficient resources that add customer value to support its entire group of businesses without spreading itself too thin.

> **CORE CONCEPT**
>
> A diversified company exhibits **resource fit** when its businesses add to a company's overall mix of resources and capabilities and when the parent company has sufficient resources to support its entire group of businesses without spreading itself too thin.

> **CORE CONCEPT**
>
> A strong **internal capital market** allows a diversified company to add value by shifting capital from business units generating *free cash flow* to those needing additional capital to expand and realize their growth potential.

Financial Resource Fit One important dimension of resource fit concerns whether a diversified company can generate the internal cash flows sufficient to fund the capital requirements of its businesses, pay its dividends, meet its debt obligations, and otherwise remain financially healthy. While additional capital can usually be raised in financial markets, it is also important for a diversified firm to have a healthy **internal capital market** that can support the financial requirements of its business lineup. The greater the extent to which a diversified company is able to fund investment in its businesses through internally generated free cash flows rather than from equity issues or borrowing, the more powerful its financial resource fit and the less dependent the firm is on external financial resources.

A *portfolio approach* to ensuring financial fit among the firm's businesses is based on the fact that different businesses have different cash flow and investment characteristics. For example, business units in rapidly growing industries are often **cash hogs**—so labeled because the cash flows they generate from internal operations aren't big enough to fund their expansion. To keep pace with rising buyer demand, rapid-growth businesses frequently need sizable annual capital infusions—for new facilities and equipment, for technology improvements, and for additional working capital to support inventory expansion. Because a cash hog's financial resources must be provided by the corporate parent, corporate managers have to decide whether it makes good financial and strategic sense to keep pouring new money into a cash hog business.

> **CORE CONCEPT**
>
> A **cash hog** generates operating cash flows that are too small to fully fund its operations and growth; a cash hog must receive cash infusions from outside sources to cover its working capital and investment requirements.

In contrast, business units with leading market positions in mature industries may be **cash cows**—businesses that generate substantial cash surpluses over what is needed to adequately fund their operations. Market leaders in slow-growth industries often generate sizable positive cash flows *over and above what is needed for growth and reinvestment* because the slow-growth nature of their industry often entails relatively modest annual investment requirements. Cash cows, though not always attractive from a growth standpoint, are valuable businesses from a financial resource perspective. The surplus cash flows they generate can be used to pay corporate dividends, finance acquisitions, and provide funds for investing in the company's promising cash hogs. It makes good financial and strategic sense for diversified companies to keep cash cows in healthy condition, fortifying and defending their market position to preserve their cash-generating capability over the long term and thereby have an ongoing source of financial resources to deploy elsewhere.

> **CORE CONCEPT**
>
> A **cash cow** generates operating cash flows over and above its internal requirements, thereby providing financial resources that may be used to invest in cash hogs, finance new acquisitions, fund share buyback programs, or pay dividends.

A diversified company has good financial resource fit when the excess cash generated by its cash cow businesses is sufficient to fund the investment requirements of promising cash hog businesses. Ideally, investing in promising cash hog businesses over time results in growing the hogs into self-supporting *star businesses* that have strong or market-leading competitive positions in attractive, high-growth markets and high levels of profitability. Star businesses are often the cash cows of the future—when the markets of star businesses begin to mature and their growth slows, their competitive strength should produce self-generated cash flows more than sufficient to cover their investment needs. The "success sequence" is thus cash hog to young star (but perhaps still a cash hog) to self-supporting star to cash cow.

Star B → grown hogs

Cash hog ——→ young star —→ self-supporting star —→ cash cow

If, however, a cash hog has questionable promise (either because of low industry attractiveness or a weak competitive position), then it becomes a logical candidate for divestiture. Aggressively investing in a cash hog with an uncertain future seldom makes sense because it requires the corporate parent to keep pumping more capital into the business with only a dim hope of turning the cash hog into a future star. Such businesses are a financial drain and fail the resource fit test because they strain the corporate parent's ability to adequately fund its other businesses. Divesting a less attractive cash hog business is usually the best alternative unless (1) it has highly valuable strategic fit with other business units or (2) the capital infusions needed from the corporate parent are modest relative to the funds available, and (3) there's a decent chance of growing the business into a solid bottom-line contributor.

Aside from cash flow considerations, two other factors to consider in assessing the financial resource fit for businesses in a diversified firm's portfolio are:

- *Do individual businesses adequately contribute to achieving companywide performance targets?* A business exhibits poor financial fit if it soaks up a disproportionate share of the company's financial resources, while making subpar or insignificant contributions to the bottom line. Too many under-performing businesses reduce the company's overall performance and ultimately limit growth in shareholder value.

- *Does the corporation have adequate financial strength to fund its different businesses and maintain a healthy credit rating?* A diversified company's strategy fails the resource fit test when the resource needs of its portfolio unduly stretch the company's financial health and threaten to impair its credit rating. General Motors, Time Warner, and Royal Ahold, for example, found themselves so financially overextended that they had to sell some of their business units to raise the money to pay down burdensome debt obligations and continue to fund essential capital expenditures for the remaining businesses.

Examining a Diversified Company's Nonfinancial Resource Fit Diversified companies must also ensure that the nonfinancial resource needs of its portfolio of businesses are met by its corporate capabilities. Just as a diversified company must avoid allowing an excessive number of cash hungry businesses to jeopardize its financial stability, it should also avoid adding to the business lineup in ways that overly stretch such nonfinancial resources as managerial talent, technology and information systems, and marketing support.

- *Does the company have or can it develop the specific resources and competitive capabilities needed to be successful in each of its businesses?*[11] Sometimes the resources a company has accumulated in its core business prove to be a poor match with the competitive capabilities needed to succeed in businesses into which it has diversified. For instance, BTR, a multibusiness company in Great Britain, discovered that the company's resources and managerial skills were quite well suited for parenting industrial manufacturing businesses but not for parenting its

> Resource fit extends beyond financial resources to include a good fit between the company's resources and core competencies and the key success factors of each industry it has diversified into.

distribution businesses (National Tyre Services and Texas-based Summers Group). As a result, BTR decided to divest its distribution businesses and focus exclusively on diversifying around small industrial manufacturing.

- *Are the company's resources being stretched too thinly by the resource requirements of one or more of its businesses?* A diversified company has to guard against overtaxing its resources, a condition that can arise when (1) it goes on an acquisition spree and management is called upon to assimilate and oversee many new businesses very quickly or (2) when it lacks sufficient resource depth to do a creditable job of transferring skills and competencies from one of its businesses to another.

Step 5: Ranking Business Units and Setting a Priority for Resource Allocation

Once a diversified company's businesses have been evaluated from the standpoints of industry attractiveness, competitive strength, strategic fit, and resource fit, the next step is to use this information to rank the performance prospects of the businesses from best to worst. Such rankings help top-level executives assign each business a priority for corporate resource support and new capital investment.

The locations of the different businesses in the nine-cell industry attractiveness/competitive strength matrix provide a solid basis for identifying high-opportunity businesses and low-opportunity businesses. Normally, competitively strong businesses in attractive industries have significantly better performance prospects than competitively weak businesses in unattractive industries. Also, normally, the revenue and earnings outlook for businesses in fast-growing businesses is better than for businesses in slow-growing businesses. As a rule, *business subsidiaries with the brightest profit and growth prospects, attractive positions in the nine-cell matrix, and solid strategic and resource fit should receive top priority for allocation of corporate resources.* However, in ranking the prospects of the different businesses from best to worst, it is usually wise to also consider each business's past performance as concerns sales growth, profit growth, contribution to company earnings, return on capital invested in the business, and cash flow from operations. While past performance is not always a reliable predictor of future performance, it does signal whether a business already has good to excellent performance or has problems to overcome.

Allocating Financial Resources   Figure 8.4 shows the chief strategic and financial options for allocating a diversified company's financial resources. Divesting businesses with the weakest future prospects and businesses that lack adequate strategic fit and/or resource fit is one of the best ways of generating additional funds for redeployment to businesses with better opportunities and better strategic and resource fit. Free cash flows from cash cow businesses also add to the pool of funds that can be usefully redeployed. *Ideally,* a diversified company will have sufficient financial resources to strengthen or grow its existing businesses, make any new acquisitions that are desirable, fund other promising business opportunities, pay off existing

▶FIGURE 8.4 **The Chief Strategic and Financial Options for Allocating a Diversified Company's Financial Resources**

Strategic Options for Allocation Company Financial Resources	Financial Options for Allocating Company Financial Resources
Invest in ways to strengthen or grow existing business	Pay off existing long-term or short-term debt
Make acquisitions to establish positions in new industries or to complement existing businesses	Increase dividend payments to shareholders
Fund long-range R&D ventures aimed at opening market opportunities in new or exsisting businesses	Repurchase shares of the company's common stock
	Build cash reserves; invest in short-term securities

debt, and periodically increase dividend payments to shareholders and/or repurchase shares of stock. But, as a practical matter, a company's financial resources are limited. Thus, for top executives to make the best use of the available funds, they must steer resources to those businesses with the best opportunities and performance prospects and allocate little if any resources to businesses with marginal or dim prospects—this is why ranking the performance prospects of the various businesses from best to worst is so crucial. Strategic uses of corporate financial resources (see Figure 8.4) should usually take precedence unless there is a compelling reason to strengthen the firm's balance sheet or better reward shareholders.

Step 6: Crafting New Strategic Moves to Improve the Overall Corporate Performance

LO5

Understand a diversified company's four main corporate strategy options for solidifying its diversification strategy and improving company performance.

The conclusions flowing from the five preceding analytical steps set the agenda for crafting strategic moves to improve a diversified company's overall performance. The strategic options boil down to four broad categories of actions:

1. Sticking closely with the existing business lineup and pursuing the opportunities these businesses present.
2. Broadening the company's business scope by making new acquisitions in new industries.
3. Divesting some businesses and retrenching to a narrower base of business operations.
4. Restructuring the company's business lineup and putting a whole new face on the company's business makeup.

Sticking Closely with the Existing Business Lineup The option of sticking with the current business lineup makes sense when the company's present businesses offer attractive growth opportunities and can be counted on to generate good earnings and cash flows. As long as the company's set of existing businesses puts it in a good position for the future and these businesses have good strategic and/or resource fit, then rocking the boat with major changes in the company's business mix is usually unnecessary. Corporate executives can concentrate their attention on getting the best performance from each of the businesses, steering corporate resources into those areas of greatest potential and profitability. However, in the event that corporate executives are not entirely satisfied with the opportunities they see in the company's present set of businesses, they can opt for any of the three strategic alternatives listed in the following sections.

Broadening the Diversification Base   Diversified companies sometimes find it desirable to add to the diversification base for any one of the same reasons a single business company might pursue initial diversification. Sluggish growth in revenues or profits, vulnerability to seasonality or recessionary influences, potential for transferring resources and capabilities to other related businesses, or unfavorable driving forces facing core businesses are all reasons management of a diversified company might choose to broaden diversification. An additional, and often very important, motivating factor for adding new businesses is to complement and strengthen the market position and competitive capabilities of one or more of its present businesses. Procter & Gamble's acquisition of Gillette strengthened and extended P&G's reach into personal care and household products—Gillette's businesses included Oral-B toothbrushes, Gillette razors and razor blades, Duracell batteries, Braun shavers and small appliances (coffeemakers, mixers, hair dryers, and electric toothbrushes), and toiletries (Right Guard, Foamy, Soft & Dry, White Rain, and Dry Idea).

Reasons to broaden Div [handwritten annotation]

Diversting Some Businesses and Retrenching to a Narrower Diversification Base   A number of diversified firms have had difficulty managing a diverse group of businesses and have elected to get out of some of them. Retrenching to a narrower diversification base is usually undertaken when top management concludes that its diversification strategy has ranged too far afield and that the company can improve long-term performance by concentrating on building stronger positions in a smaller number of core businesses

> Focusing corporate resources on a few core and mostly related businesses avoids the mistake of diversifying so broadly that resources and management attention are stretched too thin.

and industries. Hewlett-Packard spun off its testing and measurement businesses into a stand-alone company called Agilent Technologies so that it could better concentrate on its PC, workstation, server, printer and peripherals, and electronics businesses.

But there are other important reasons for divesting one or more of a company's present businesses. Sometimes divesting a business has to be considered because market conditions in a once-attractive industry have badly deteriorated. A business can become a prime candidate for divestiture because it lacks adequate strategic or resource fit, because it is a cash hog with questionable long-term potential, or because it is weakly positioned in its industry with little prospect of earning a decent return on investment. Sometimes a company acquires businesses that, down the road, just do not work out as expected even though management has tried all it can think of to make them profitable. Other business units, despite adequate financial performance, may not mesh as well with the rest of the firm as was originally thought. For instance, PepsiCo divested its group of fast-food restaurant businesses to focus its resources on its core soft drink and snack foods businesses, where their resources and capabilities could add more value.

Evidence indicates that pruning businesses and narrowing a firm's diversification base improves corporate performance.[12] Corporate parents often end up selling businesses too late and at too low a price, sacrificing shareholder value.[13] A useful guide to determine whether or when to divest a business subsidiary is to ask, "If we were not in this business today, would we want to get into it now?"[14] When the answer is no or probably not, divestiture should be considered. Another signal that a business should become a divestiture candidate is whether it is worth more to another company than to the present parent; in such cases, shareholders would be well served if the company were to sell the business and collect a premium price from the buyer for whom the business is a valuable fit.[15]

Selling a business outright to another company is far and away the most frequently used option for divesting a business. But sometimes a business selected for divestiture has ample resources to compete successfully on its own. In such cases, a corporate parent may elect to spin the unwanted business off as a financially and managerially independent company, either by selling shares to the investing public via an initial public offering or by distributing shares in the new company to existing shareholders of the corporate parent.

Broadly Restructuring the Business Lineup Through a Mix of Divestitures and New Acquisitions

Corporate restructuring strategies involve divesting some businesses and acquiring others so as to put a new face on the company's business lineup. Performing radical surgery on a company's group of businesses is an appealing corporate strategy when its financial performance is squeezed or eroded by:

- Too many businesses in slow-growth, declining, low-margin, or otherwise unattractive industries.

- Too many competitively weak businesses.

- An excessive debt burden with interest costs that eat deeply into profitability.

- Ill-chosen acquisitions that haven't lived up to expectations.

CORE CONCEPT

Corporate restructuring involves radically altering the business lineup by divesting businesses that lack strategic fit or are poor performers and acquiring new businesses that offer better promise for enhancing shareholder value.

Candidates for divestiture in a corporate restructuring effort typically include not only weak or up-and-down performers or those in unattractive industries but also business units that lack strategic fit with the businesses to be retained, businesses that are cash hogs or that lack other types of resource fit, and businesses incompatible with the company's revised diversification

CONCEPTS & CONNECTIONS 8.1

VF'S CORPORATE RESTRUCTURING STRATEGY THAT MADE IT THE STAR OF THE APPAREL INDUSTRY

VF Corporation's corporate restructuring that included a mix of divestitures and acquisitions has provided its shareholders with returns that are more than five times greater than shareholder returns provided by competing apparel manufacturers. In fact, VF delivered a total shareholder return of 21 percent between 2000 and 2010, and its 2010 revenues of $7.7 billion made it number 310 on *Fortune*'s list of the 500 largest U.S. companies. The company's corporate restructuring began in 2000 when it divested its slow-growing businesses including its namesake Vanity Fair brand of lingerie and sleepwear. The company's $136 million acquisition of North Face in 2000 was the first in a series of many acquisitions of "lifestyle brands" that connected with the way people lived, worked, and played. Since the acquisition and turnaround of North Face, VF has spent nearly $5 billion to acquire 19 additional businesses, including about $2 billion in 2011 to acquire Timberland. New apparel brands acquired by VF Corporation include Timberland, Vans skateboard shoes, Nautica, John Varvatos, and 7 For All Mankind sportswear, Reef surf wear, and Lucy athletic wear. The company also acquired a variety of apparel companies specializing in apparel segments such as uniforms for professional baseball and football teams and law enforcement.

VF Corporation's acquisitions came after years of researching each company and developing a relationship with an acquisition candidate's chief managers before closing the deal. The company made a practice of leaving management of acquired companies in place, while bringing in new managers only when necessary talent and skills were lacking. In addition, companies acquired by VF were allowed to keep long-standing traditions that shaped culture and spurred creativity. For example, the Vans headquarters in Cypress, California, retained its half-pipe and concrete floor so that its employees could skateboard to and from meetings.

In 2010, VF Corporation was among the most profitable apparel firms in the industry with net earnings of $571 million. The company expected new acquisitions that would push the company's revenues to $8.5 billion in 2011.

Sources: Suzanne Kapner, "How a 100-Year-Old Apparel Firm Changed Course," *Fortune,* April 9, 2008, online edition; and www.vf.com, accessed July 26, 2011.

strategy (even though they may be profitable or in an attractive industry). As businesses are divested, corporate restructuring generally involves aligning the remaining business units into groups with the best strategic fit and then redeploying the cash flows from the divested business to either pay down debt or make new acquisitions.

Over the past decade, corporate restructuring has become a popular strategy at many diversified companies, especially those that had diversified broadly into many different industries and lines of business. In 2004, GE's CEO Jeffrey Immelt led GE's withdrawal from the insurance business by divesting several companies and spinning off others. He further restructured GE's business lineup with other major initiatives including (1) spending $10 billion to acquire British-based Amersham and extend GE's Medical Systems business into diagnostic pharmaceuticals and biosciences, thereby creating a $15 billion business designated as GE Healthcare and (2) acquiring the entertainment assets of debt-ridden French media conglomerate Vivendi Universal Entertainment and integrating its operations into GE's NBC division, thereby creating a broad-based $13 billion media business positioned to compete against Walt Disney, Time Warner, Fox, and Viacom. In 2009, GE agreed to sell a 51 percent stake in NBC Universal to Comcast for about $30 billion. Immelt suggested that the divestiture of its media business unit would allow the company to redeploy resources into its energy business. In 2011, the company spent approximately $8 billion to acquire Converteam, a French company that specialized in wind turbines and two oil-industry companies, John Wood Group and Dresser. Concepts & Connections 8.1 discusses how VF Corporation shareholders have benefited through the company's large-scale restructuring program.

→→→→ KEY POINTS

1. The purpose of diversification is to build shareholder value. Diversification builds shareholder value when a diversified group of businesses can perform better under the auspices of a single corporate parent than they would as independent, stand-alone businesses—the goal is to achieve not just a $1 + 1 = 2$ result but rather to realize important $1 + 1 = 3$ performance benefits. Whether getting into a new business has potential to enhance shareholder value hinges on whether a company's entry into that business can pass the attractiveness test, the cost-of-entry test, and the better-off test.

2. Entry into new businesses can take any of three forms: acquisition, internal development, or joint venture/strategic partnership. Each has its pros and cons, but acquisition usually provides quickest entry into a new entry; internal development takes the longest to produce home-run results; and joint venture/strategic partnership tends to be the least durable.

3. There are two fundamental approaches to diversification—into related businesses and into unrelated businesses. The rationale for *related* diversification is based on cross-business *strategic fit:* Diversify into businesses with strategic fit along their respective value chains, capitalize on strategic fit relationships to gain competitive advantage, and then use competitive advantage to achieve the desired $1 + 1 = 3$ impact on shareholder value.

4. *Unrelated diversification* strategies surrender the competitive advantage potential of strategic fit. Given the absence of cross-business strategic fit, the task of building shareholder value through a strategy of unrelated diversification hinges on the ability of the parent company to: (1) do a superior job of identifying and acquiring new businesses that can produce consistently good earnings and returns on investment; (2) do an excellent job of negotiating favorable acquisition prices; and (3) do such a good job of overseeing and parenting the collection of businesses that they perform at a higher level than they would on their own efforts. The greater the number of businesses a company has diversified into and the more diverse these businesses are, the harder it is for corporate executives to select capable managers to run each business, know when the major strategic proposals of business units are sound, or decide on a wise course of recovery when a business unit stumbles.

5. Evaluating a company's diversification strategy is a six-step process:

   • Step 1: *Evaluate the long-term attractiveness of the industries into which the firm has diversified.* Determining industry attractiveness involves developing a list of industry attractiveness measures, each of which might have a different importance weight.

- Step 2: *Evaluate the relative competitive strength of each of the company's business units.* The purpose of rating each business's competitive strength is to gain clear understanding of which businesses are strong contenders in their industries, which are weak contenders, and the underlying reasons for their strength or weakness. The conclusions about industry attractiveness can be joined with the conclusions about competitive strength by drawing an industry attractiveness–competitive strength matrix that helps identify the prospects of each business and what priority each business should be given in allocating corporate resources and investment capital.

- Step 3: *Check for cross-business strategic fit.* A business is more attractive strategically when it has value chain relationships with sibling business units that offer the potential to (1) realize economies of scope or cost-saving efficiencies; (2) transfer technology, skills, know-how, or other resources and capabilities from one business to another; and/or (3) leverage use of a well-known and trusted brand name. Cross-business strategic fit represents a significant avenue for producing competitive advantage beyond what any one business can achieve on its own.

- Step 4: *Check whether the firm's resources fit the requirements of its present business lineup.* Resource fit exists when (1) businesses, individually, strengthen a company's overall mix of resources and capabilities and (2) a company has sufficient resources to support its entire group of businesses without spreading itself too thin. One important test of financial resource fit involves determining whether a company has ample cash cows and not too many cash hogs.

- Step 5: *Rank the performance prospects of the businesses from best to worst and determine what the corporate parent's priority should be in allocating resources to its various businesses.* The most important considerations in judging business-unit performance are sales growth, profit growth, contribution to company earnings, cash flow characteristics, and the return on capital invested in the business. Normally, strong business units in attractive industries should head the list for corporate resource support.

- Step 6: *Crafting new strategic moves to improve overall corporate performance.* This step entails using the results of the preceding analysis as the basis for selecting one of four different strategic paths for improving a diversified company's performance: (*a*) Stick closely with the existing business lineup and pursue opportunities presented by these businesses, (*b*) broaden the scope of diversification by entering additional industries, (*c*) retrench to a narrower scope of diversification by divesting poorly performing businesses, and (*d*) broadly restructure the business lineup with multiple divestitures and/or acquisitions.

ASSURANCE OF LEARNING EXERCISES

1. See if you can identify the value chain relationships that make the businesses of the following companies related in competitively relevant ways. In particular, you should consider whether there are cross-business opportunities for (*a*) transferring competitively valuable resources, expertise, technological know-how and other capabilities, (*b*) cost sharing where value chain activities can be combined, and/or (*c*) leveraging use of a well-respected brand name.

LO1, LO2, LO3

www.mcgrawhillconnect.com

OSI Restaurant Partners

- Outback Steakhouse.
- Carrabba's Italian Grill.
- Roy's Restaurant (Hawaiian fusion cuisine).
- Bonefish Grill (Market-fresh fine seafood).
- Fleming's Prime Steakhouse & Wine Bar.
- Lee Roy Selmon's (Southern comfort food).
- Cheeseburger in Paradise.
- Blue Coral Seafood & Spirits (fine seafood).

L'Oréal

- Maybelline, Lancôme, Helena Rubenstein, Kiehl's, Garner, and Shu Uemura cosmetics.
- L'Oréal and Soft Sheen/Carson hair care products.
- Redken, Matrix, L'Oréal Professional, and Kerastase Paris professional hair care and skin care products.
- Ralph Lauren and Giorgio Armani fragrances.
- Biotherm skin care products.
- La Roche–Posay and Vichy Laboratories dermocosmetics.

Johnson & Johnson

- Baby products (powder, shampoo, oil, lotion).
- Band-Aids and other first-aid products.
- Women's health and personal care products (Stayfree, Carefree, Sure & Natural).
- Neutrogena and Aveeno skin care products.
- Nonprescription drugs (Tylenol, Motrin, Pepcid AC, Mylanta, Monistat).
- Prescription drugs.
- Prosthetic and other medical devices.
- Surgical and hospital products.
- Accuvue contact lenses.

LO1, LO2, LO3, LO4, LO5

2. Peruse the business group listings for United Technologies shown below and listed at its website (www.utc.com). How would you characterize the company's corporate strategy? Related diversification, unrelated diversification, or a combination related-unrelated diversification strategy? Explain your answer.

Carrier—the world's largest provider of air-conditioning, heating, and refrigeration solutions.

Hamilton Sundstrand—technologically advanced aerospace and industrial products.

Otis—the world's leading manufacturer, installer and maintainer of elevators, escalators and moving walkways.

Pratt & Whitney—designs, manufactures, services and supports aircraft engines, industrial gas turbines and space propulsion systems.

Sikorsky—a world leader in helicopter design, manufacture and service.

UTC Fire & Security—fire and security systems developed for commercial, industrial, and residential customers.

UTC Power—a full-service provider of environmentally advanced power solutions.

3. The Walt Disney Company is in the following businesses:

LO1, LO2, LO3, LO4, LO5

www.mcgrawhillconnect.com

- Theme parks.
- Disney Cruise Line.
- Resort properties.
- Movie, video, and theatrical productions (for both children and adults).
- Television broadcasting (ABC, Disney Channel, Toon Disney, Classic Sports Network, ESPN and ESPN2, E!, Lifetime, and A&E networks).
- Radio broadcasting (Disney Radio).
- Musical recordings and sales of animation art.
- Anaheim Mighty Ducks NHL franchise.
- Anaheim Angels Major League Baseball franchise (25 percent ownership).
- Books and magazine publishing.
- Interactive software and Internet sites.
- The Disney Store retail shops.

Based on the above listing, would you say that Walt Disney's business lineup reflects a strategy of related diversification, unrelated diversification, or a combination of related and unrelated diversification? What benefits are generated from any strategic fit existing between Disney's businesses? Also, what types of companies should Walt Disney Company consider acquiring that might improve shareholder value? Justify your answer.

→ → EXERCISES FOR SIMULATION PARTICIPANTS

1. In the event that your company had the opportunity to diversify into other products or businesses of your choosing, would you opt to pursue related diversification, unrelated diversification, or a combination of both? Explain why.

LO1, LO2, LO3

2. What specific resources and capabilities does your company possess that would make it attractive to diversify into related businesses? Indicate what kinds of strategic fit benefits could be captured by transferring these resources and competitive capabilities to newly acquired related businesses.

LO1, LO2

3. If your company opted to pursue a strategy of related diversification, what industries or product categories could your company diversify into that would allow it to achieve economies of scope? Name at least two or three such industries/product categories and indicate the specific kinds of cost savings that might accrue from entry into each of these businesses/product categories.

LO1, LO2

4. If your company opted to pursue a strategy of related diversification, what industries or product categories could your company diversify into that would allow your company to capitalize on using your company's present brand name and corporate image to good advantage in these newly entered businesses or

LO1, LO2

product categories? Name at least two or three such industries or product categories and indicate *the specific benefits* that might be captured by transferring your company's brand name to each of these other businesses/product categories.

Would you prefer to pursue a strategy of related or unrelated diversification? Why?

ENDNOTES

1. Constantinos C. Markides, "To Diversify or Not to Diversify," *Harvard Business Review* 75, no. 6 (November–December 1997).

2. Michael E. Porter, "From Competitive Advantage to Corporate Strategy," *Harvard Business Review* 45, no. 3 (May–June 1987).

3. Michael E. Porter, *Competitive Strategy: Techniques for Analyzing Industries and Competitors* (New York: Free Press, 1980).

4. Yves L. Doz and Gary Hamel, *Alliance Advantage: The Art of Creating Value through Partnering* (Boston: Harvard Business School Press, 1998).

5. Michael E. Porter, *Competitive Advantage* (New York: Free Press, 1985); and Constantinos C. Markides and Peter J. Williamson, "Corporate Diversification and Organization Structure: A Resource-Based View," *Academy of Management Journal* 39, no. 2 (April 1996).

6. Jeanne M. Liedtka, "Collaboration across Lines of Business for Competitive Advantage," *Academy of Management Executive* 10, no. 2 (May 1996).

7. Kathleen M. Eisenhardt and D. Charles Galunic, "Coevolving: At Last, a Way to Make Synergies Work," *Harvard Business Review* 78, no. 1 (January–February 2000); and Constantinos C. Markides and Peter J. Williamson, "Related Diversification, Core Competencies and Corporate Performance," *Strategic Management Journal* 15 (Summer 1994).

8. A. Campbell, M. Goold, and M. Alexander, "Corporate Strategy: The Quest for Parenting Advantage," *Harvard Business Review* 73, no. 2 (March/April 1995); and Cynthia A. Montgomery and Birger Wernerfelt, "Diversification, Ricardian Rents, and Tobin-Q," *RAND Journal of Economics* 19, no. 4 (1988).

9. Patricia L. Anslinger and Thomas E. Copeland, "Growth through Acquisitions: A Fresh Look," *Harvard Business Review* 74, no. 1 (January–February 1996).

10. Lawrence G. Franko, "The Death of Diversification? The Focusing of the World's Industrial Firms, 1980–2000," *Business Horizons* 47, no. 4 (July–August 2004).

11. Andrew Campbell, Michael Gould, and Marcus Alexander, "Corporate Strategy: The Quest for Parenting Advantage," *Harvard Business Review* 73, no. 2 (March–April 1995).

12. Constantinos C. Markides, "Diversification, Restructuring, and Economic Performance," *Strategic Management Journal* 16 (February 1995).

13. Lee Dranikoff, Tim Koller, and Antoon Schneider, "Divestiture: Strategy's Missing Link," *Harvard Business Review* 80, no. 5 (May 2002).

14. Peter F. Drucker, *Management: Tasks, Responsibilities, Practices* (New York: Harper & Row, 1974).

15. David J. Collis and Cynthia A. Montgomery, "Creating Corporate Advantage," *Harvard Business Review* 76, no. 3 (May–June 1998).

chapter 9

STRATEGY, ETHICS, AND CORPORATE SOCIAL RESPONSIBILITY

LEARNING OBJECTIVES

LO1   Understand why the standards of ethical behavior in business are no different from ethical standards in general.

LO2   Recognize conditions that give rise to unethical business strategies and behavior.

LO3   Gain an understanding of the costs of business ethics failures.

LO4   Learn the concepts of corporate social responsibility and environmental sustainability and how companies balance these duties with economic responsibilities to shareholders.

Clearly, a company has a responsibility to make a profit and grow the business, but just as clearly, a company and its personnel also have a duty to obey the law and play by the rules of fair competition. But does a company have a duty to go beyond legal requirements and operate according to the ethical norms of the societies in which it operates? And does it have a duty or obligation to contribute to the betterment of society independent of the needs and preferences of the customers it serves? Should a company display a social conscience and devote a portion of its resources to bettering society? Should its strategic initiatives be screened for possible negative effects on future generations of the world's population?

This chapter focuses on whether a company, in the course of trying to craft and execute a strategy that delivers value to both customers and shareholders, also has a duty to (1) act in an ethical manner, (2) demonstrate socially responsible behavior by being a committed corporate citizen, and (3) adopt business practices that conserve natural resources and protect the interest of future generations.

WHAT DO WE MEAN BY *BUSINESS ETHICS?*

LO1

Understand why the standards of ethical behavior in business are no different from ethical standards in general.

Business ethics is the application of ethical principles and standards to the actions and decisions of business organizations and the conduct of their personnel.[1] Ethical principles in business are not materially different from ethical principles in general because business actions have to be judged in the context of society's standards of right and wrong. There is not a special set of rules that businesspeople decide to apply to their own conduct. If dishonesty is considered unethical and immoral, then dishonest behavior in business—whether it relates to customers, suppliers, employees, or shareholders—qualifies as equally unethical and immoral. If being ethical entails adhering to generally accepted norms about conduct that is right and wrong, then managers must consider such norms when crafting and executing strategy.

> **CORE CONCEPT**
>
> **Business ethics** involves the application of general ethical principles to the actions and decisions of businesses and the conduct of their personnel.

While most company managers are careful to ensure that a company's strategy is within the bounds of what is legal, evidence indicates they are not always so careful to ensure that their strategies are within the bounds of what is considered ethical. In recent years, managers at Enron, Tyco International, HealthSouth, Adelphia, Royal Dutch/Shell, Parmalat (an Italy-based food products company), Rite Aid, Mexican oil giant Pemex, AIG, Citigroup, several leading brokerage houses, mutual fund companies and investment banking firms, and a host of mortgage lenders have deliberately ignored society's ethical norms. Much of the crisis in residential real estate that emerged in the United States in 2007–2008 stemmed from consciously unethical strategies at certain banks and mortgage companies to boost the fees they earned on home mortgages by deliberately lowering lending standards to grant home loans to people whose incomes were insufficient to make their monthly mortgage payments. Once these banks and mortgage companies earned the fees on the so-called subprime loans they made to unqualified borrowers, they secured the assistance of investment banking firms to bundle these and other home mortgages into collateralized debt obligations and mortgage-backed securities, found means of having these high-risk securities assigned triple-A bond ratings, and auctioned them to unsuspecting investors, who later suffered huge losses when the borrowers began to default on their loan payments. The consequences of crafting strategies that cannot pass the test of moral scrutiny are manifested in sharp drops in stock price that cost shareholders billions of dollars, devastating public relations hits, sizable fines, and criminal indictments and convictions of company executives.

DRIVERS OF UNETHICAL STRATEGIES AND BUSINESS BEHAVIOR

Apart from "the business of business is business, not ethics" kind of thinking apparent in recent high-profile business scandals, three other main drivers of unethical business behavior also stand out:[2]

▶ **LO2**

Recognize conditions that give rise to unethical business strategies and behavior.

- *Overzealous pursuit of wealth and other selfish interests.* People who are obsessed with wealth accumulation, greed, power, status, and other selfish interests often push ethical principles aside in their quest for self-gain. Driven by their ambitions, they exhibit few qualms in skirting the rules or doing whatever is necessary to achieve their goals. The first and only priority of such corporate "bad apples" is to look out for their own best interests, and if climbing the ladder of success means having few scruples and ignoring the welfare of others, so be it. Bernard Madoff's $50 billion Ponzi scheme illustrates such behavior.

- *Heavy pressures on company managers to meet or beat performance targets.* When key personnel find themselves scrambling to meet the quarterly and annual sales and profit expectations of investors and financial analysts or to hit other ambitious performance targets, they often feel enormous pressure to *do whatever it takes* to protect their reputation for delivering good results. As the pressure builds, they start stretching the rules further and further, until the limits of ethical conduct are overlooked.[3] Once people cross ethical boundaries to "meet or beat their numbers," the threshold for making more extreme ethical compromises becomes lower.

- *A company culture that puts profitability and good business performance ahead of ethical behavior.* When a company's culture spawns an ethically corrupt or amoral work climate, people have a company-approved license to ignore "what's right" and engage in most any behavior or employ most any strategy they think they can get away with. Such cultural norms as "everyone else does it" and "it is OK to bend the rules to get the job done" permeate the work environment. At such companies, ethically immoral or amoral people are certain to play down observance of ethical strategic actions and business conduct. Moreover, cultural pressures to utilize unethical means if circumstances become challenging can prompt otherwise honorable people to behave unethically.

LO3

Gain an understanding
of the costs of
business ethics
failures.

THE BUSINESS CASE FOR ETHICAL STRATEGIES

While it is undoubtedly true that unethical business behavior may sometimes contribute to higher company profits (*so long as such behavior escapes public scrutiny*), deliberate pursuit of unethical strategies and tolerance of unethical conduct is a risky practice from both a shareholder perspective and a reputational standpoint. Figure 9.1 shows the wide-ranging costs a company can incur when unethical behavior is discovered and it is forced to make amends for its behavior. The more egregious a company's ethical violations, the higher are the costs and the bigger the damage to its reputation (and to the reputations of the company personnel involved). In high-profile instances, the costs of ethical misconduct can easily run into the hundreds of millions and even billions of dollars, especially if they provoke widespread public outrage and many people were harmed.

The fallout of ethical misconduct on the part of a company goes well beyond just the costs of making amends for the misdeeds. Buyers shun companies known for their shady behavior. Companies known to have engaged in unethical conduct have difficulty recruiting and retaining talented employees.[4] Most ethically upstanding people don't want to get entrapped in a compromising situation, nor do they want their personal reputations tarnished by the actions of an unsavory employer. A company's unethical behavior risks considerable damage to shareholders in the form of lost revenues, higher costs, lower profits, lower stock prices, and a diminished business reputation. To a significant degree, therefore, ethical strategies and ethical conduct are *good business.*

> Shareholders suffer major damage when a company's unethical behavior is discovered and punished. Making amends for unethical business conduct is costly, and it takes years to rehabilitate a tarnished company reputation.

▶FIGURE 9.1 **The Costs Companies Incur When Ethical Wrongdoing Is Discovered and Punished**

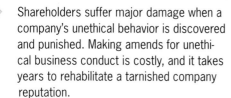

Visible Costs	Internal Administrative Costs	Intangible or Less Visible Costs
• Government fines and penalties • Civil penalties arising from class-action lawsuits and other litigation aimed at punishing the company for its offense and the harm done to others • The costs to shareholders in the form of a lower stock price (and possibly lower dividends)	• Legal and investigative costs incurred by the company • The costs of providing remedial education and ethics training to company personnel • Costs of taking corrective actions • Administration costs associated with ensuring future compliance	• Customer defections • Loss of reputation • Lost employee morale and higher degrees of employee cynicism • Higher employee turnover • Higher recruiting costs and difficulty in attracting employees • Adverse effects on employee productivity • The costs of complying with often harsher government regulation

Source: Adapted from Terry Thomas, John R. Schermerhorn, and John W. Dienhart, "Strategic Leadership of Ethical Behavior," *Academy of Management Executive* 18, no. 2 (May 2004), p. 58.

CONCEPTS & CONNECTIONS 9.1

APPLE'S CHALLENGES IN ENFORCING ITS SUPPLIER CODE OF CONDUCT

Apple requires its suppliers to comply with the company's Supplier Code of Conduct as a condition of being awarded contracts. To ensure compliance, Apple's supplier monitoring program includes audits of supplier factories, corrective action plans, and verification measures. In the company's 24-page 2010 Progress Report on Supplier Responsibility, Apple reported that in 2009 it conducted 102 audits of supplier facilities in such countries as China, the Czech Republic, Malaysia, the Philippines, Singapore, South Korea, Taiwan, Thailand, and the United States; 80 of these audits were first-time audits and 22 were repeat audits.

Apple distinguishes among the seriousness of infractions, designating "core violations" as those that go directly against the core principles of its Supplier Code of Conduct and must be remedied immediately. Seventeen such violations were discovered as part of the 2009 audit, including three cases of underage labor, eight cases involving excessive recruitment fees, three cases of improper hazardous waste disposal, and three cases of deliberately falsified audit records. Apple responded by ensuring that immediate corrective actions were taken, placing violators on probation, and planning to audit them again in a year's time.

While all six of Apple's final assembly manufacturers had high compliance scores—on average, registering well above 90 percent compliance on all issues—other suppliers did not fare so well on the 2009 audit. At 60 of the audited facilities, workers were required to work more than 60 hours per week more than 50 percent of the time—Apple sets a maximum of 60 hours per week (except in unusual or emergency circumstances). In 65 of the audited facilities, workers were found to have been required to work more than six consecutive days a week at least once per month—Apple requires at least one day of rest per seven days of work (except in unusual or emergency circumstances).

At 48 facilities, Apple found that overtime wages had been calculated improperly, resulting in underpayment of overtime compensation. Apple auditors discovered that at 24 facilities workers were being paid less than the specified minimum wage and that at 45 facilities wage deductions were used to discipline employees. At 57 of the audited facilities, worker benefits (for such things as retirement, sick leave, or maternity leave) were below the legally required amounts.

Apple requires suppliers to provide a safe working environment and to eliminate physical hazards to employees where possible. But the 2009 audits revealed that workers were not wearing appropriate protective personal equipment at 49 facilities. Violations were found at 70 facilities where workers were improperly trained, where unlicensed workers were operating equipment, and where required inspections of equipment were not being conducted. Apple auditors found 44 facilities that had failed to conduct environmental impact assessments; 11 facilities did not have permits for air emissions, and 4 facilities did not meet the conditions specified in their emission permits. Moreover, the audits revealed 55 supplier facilities that did not have any personnel assigned to ensuring compliance with Apple's Supplier Code of Conduct.

For Apple, the audits represent a starting point for bringing its suppliers into compliance, through greater scrutiny, education and training of suppliers' personnel, and incentives. Apple collects quarterly data to hold its suppliers accountable for their actions and makes procurement decisions based, in part, on these numbers. Suppliers that are unable to meet Apple's high standards of conduct ultimately end up losing Apple's business.

Sources: Apple's 2010 Progress Report on Supplier Responsibility; Dan Moren, "Apple Releases 2010 Report on Supplier Responsibility," *Macworld.com,* February 23, 2010; www.macworld.com/article/146653/2010/02/suppliers_2010.htm, accessed July 1, 2010; Andrew Morse and Nick Wingfield, "Apple Audits Labor Practices: Company Says Suppliers Hired Underage Workers, Violated Other Core Policies," *Wall Street Journal Online,* March 1, 2010, http://online.wsj.com/article/SB1000142405274870423130457509 1920704104154.html, accessed July1, 2010; Nicholas Kolakowski, "Apple Finds Violations During 2009 Supplier and Manufacturer Audit," *eWeek. com,* March 1, 2010, www.eweek.com/c/a/Mobile-and-Wireless/Apple-Finds-Violations-During-2009-Supplier-and-Manufacturer-Audit-522622/, accessed July 1, 2010.

Many companies have a code of ethics governing how they will conduct business—in the United States, the Sarbanes-Oxley Act, enacted in 2002, requires that companies whose stock is publicly traded have a code of ethics or else explain in writing to the Securities and Exchange Commission why they do not.

ENSURING A STRONG COMMITMENT TO BUSINESS ETHICS IN COMPANIES WITH INTERNATIONAL OPERATIONS

Notions of right and wrong, fair and unfair, moral and immoral, ethical and unethical are present in all societies, organizations, and individuals. But there are three schools of thought about the extent to which the ethical standards travel across cultures and whether multinational companies can apply the same set of ethical standards in all of the locations where they operate. Concepts & Connections 9.1 describes the difficulties Apple has faced in trying to enforce a common set of ethical standards across its vast global supplier network.

The School of Ethical Universalism

According to the school of **ethical universalism,** some concepts of what is right and what is wrong are *universal* and transcend most all cultures, societies, and religions.[5] For instance, being truthful strikes a chord of what's right in the peoples of all nations. Ethical norms considered universal by many ethicists include honesty, trustworthiness, respecting the rights of others, practicing the Golden Rule, and avoiding unnecessary harm to workers or to the users of the company's product or service.[6] *To the extent there is common moral agreement about right and wrong actions and behaviors across multiple cultures and countries, there exists a set of universal ethical standards to which all societies, companies, and individuals can be held accountable.* The strength of ethical universalism is that it draws upon the collective views of multiple societies and cultures to put some clear boundaries on what constitutes ethical business behavior no matter what country market its personnel are operating in. This means that in those instances where basic moral standards really do not vary significantly according to local cultural beliefs, traditions, or religious convictions, a multinational company can develop a code of ethics that it applies more or less evenly across its worldwide operations.

> **CORE CONCEPT**
>
> According to the school of **ethical universalism,** the same standards of what's ethical and what's unethical resonate with peoples of most societies regardless of local traditions and cultural norms; hence, common ethical standards can be used to judge employee conduct in a variety of country markets and cultural circumstances.

The School of Ethical Relativism

Beyond widely accepted ethical norms, many ethical standards likely vary from one country to another because of divergent religious beliefs, social customs, and prevailing political and economic doctrines (whether a country leans more toward a capitalistic market economy or one heavily dominated by socialistic or communistic principles). The school of **ethical relativism** holds that when there are national or cross-cultural differences in what is deemed an ethical or unethical business situation, it is appropriate for local moral standards to take precedence

> **CORE CONCEPT**
>
> According to the school of **ethical relativism,** different societal cultures and customs create divergent standards of right and wrong—thus, what is ethical or unethical must be judged in the light of local customs and social mores and can vary from one culture or nation to another.

over what the ethical standards may be in a company's home market. The thesis is that whatever a culture thinks is right or wrong really is right or wrong for that culture.[7]

A company that adopts the principle of ethical relativism and holds company personnel to local ethical standards necessarily assumes that what prevails as local morality is an adequate guide to ethical behavior. This can be ethically dangerous; it leads to the conclusion that if a country's culture generally accepts bribery or environmental degradation or exposing workers to dangerous conditions, then managers working in that country are free to engage in such activities. Adopting such a position places a company in a perilous position if it is required to defend these activities to its stakeholders in countries with higher ethical expectations. Moreover, from a global markets perspective, ethical relativism results in a maze of conflicting ethical standards for multinational companies. Imagine, for example, that a multinational company in the name of ethical relativism takes the position that it is acceptable for company personnel to pay bribes and kickbacks in countries where such payments are customary but forbids company personnel from making such payments in those countries where bribes and kickbacks are considered unethical or illegal. Having thus adopted conflicting ethical standards for operating in different countries, company managers have little moral basis for enforcing ethical standards companywide—rather, the clear message to employees would be that the company has no ethical standards or principles of its own, preferring to let its practices be governed by the countries in which it operates.

> Codes of conduct based upon ethical relativism can be *ethically dangerous* by creating a maze of conflicting ethical standards for multinational companies.

Integrative Social Contracts Theory

Integrative social contracts theory provides yet a middle position between the opposing views of universalism and relativism.[8] According to **integrative social contracts theory,** the ethical standards a company should try to uphold are governed both by (1) a limited number of universal ethical principles that are widely recognized as putting legitimate ethical boundaries on actions and behavior in *all* situations and (2) the circumstances of local cultures, traditions, and shared values that further prescribe what constitutes ethically permissible behavior and what does not. This "social contract" by which managers in all situations have a duty to serve provides that *"first-order" universal ethical norms always take precedence over "second-order" local ethical norms in circumstances where local ethical norms are more permissive.* Integrative social contracts theory offers managers in multinational companies clear guidance in resolving cross-country

> **CORE CONCEPT**
> According to **integrative social contracts theory,** universal ethical principles based on collective views of multiple cultures combine to form a "social contract" that all employees in all country markets have a duty to observe. Within the boundaries of this social contract, there is room for host country cultures to exert *some* influence in setting their own moral and ethical standards. However, *"first-order"* universal ethical norms always take precedence over *"second-order"* local ethical norms in circumstances where local ethical norms are more permissive.

ethical differences: Those parts of the company's code of ethics that involve universal ethical norms must be enforced worldwide, but within these boundaries there is room for ethical diversity and opportunity for host-country cultures to exert *some* influence in setting their own moral and ethical standards.

A good example of the application of integrative social contracts theory involves the payment of bribes and kickbacks. Bribes and kickbacks seem to be common in some countries, but does this justify paying them? Just because bribery flourishes in a country does not mean that it is an authentic or legitimate ethical norm. Virtually all of the world's major religions (Buddhism, Christianity, Confucianism, Hinduism, Islam, Judaism, Sikhism, and Taoism) and all moral schools of thought condemn bribery and corruption.[9] Therefore, a multinational company might reasonably conclude that the right ethical standard is one of refusing to condone bribery and kickbacks on the part of company personnel no matter what the second-order local norm is and no matter what the sales consequences are. An example of the application of integrative social contracts theory that allows second-order local customs to set ethical boundaries involves employee recruiting and selection practices. A company that has adopted a first-order universal norm of equal opportunity in the workplace might allow applicants to include photographs with résumés in countries where such is the norm. Managers in the United States are prohibited by law from accepting employment applications including a photograph, but managers in Europe would find it very unusual for an application to not be accompanied by a photograph of the applicant. A policy that prohibited managers from accepting applications containing a photo of the applicant would result in almost all applications being rejected. But even with the guidance provided by integrative social contracts theory, there are many instances where cross-country differences in ethical norms create "gray areas" where it is tough to draw a line in the sand between right and wrong decisions, actions, and business practices.

CORPORATE SOCIAL RESPONSIBILITY AND ENVIRONMENTAL SUSTAINABILITY

LO4

Learn the concepts of corporate social responsibility and environmental sustainability and how companies balance these duties with economic responsibilities to shareholders.

The idea that businesses have an obligation to foster social betterment, a much-debated topic in the past 50 years, took root in the nineteenth century when progressive companies in the aftermath of the industrial revolution began to provide workers with housing and other amenities. The notion that corporate executives should balance the interests of all stakeholders—shareholders, employees, customers, suppliers, the communities in which they operated, and society at large—began to blossom in the 1960s. The essence of socially responsible business behavior is that a company should balance strategic actions to benefit shareholders against the *duty* to be a good corporate citizen. The underlying thesis is that company managers should display a *social conscience* in operating the business and specifically consider how management decisions and company actions affect the well-being of employees, local communities, the environment, and society at large.[10] Acting in a socially responsible manner thus encompasses more than just participating in community service projects and donating monies to charities and other worthy social causes. Demonstrating **corporate social responsibility (CSR)** also entails undertaking actions that earn trust and respect from all stakeholders—operating in an honorable and ethical manner, striving to make the company a great place to work, demonstrating genuine respect for the environment, and trying to make a difference in bettering society. Corporate social responsibility programs commonly involve:

> **CORE CONCEPT**
>
> **Corporate social responsibility (CSR)** refers to a company's *duty* to operate in an honorable manner, provide good working conditions for employees, encourage workforce diversity, be a good steward of the environment, and actively work to better the quality of life in the local communities where it operates and in society at large.

- *Efforts to employ an ethical strategy and observe ethical principles in operating the business.* A sincere commitment to observing ethical principles is a necessary component of a CSR strategy simply because unethical conduct is incompatible with the concept of good corporate citizenship and socially responsible business behavior.

- *Making charitable contributions, supporting community service endeavors, engaging in broader philanthropic initiatives, and reaching out to make a difference in the lives of the disadvantaged.* Some companies fulfill their philanthropic obligations by spreading their efforts over a multitude of charitable and community activities—for instance, Microsoft and Johnson & Johnson support a broad variety of community, art, and social welfare programs. Others prefer to focus their energies more narrowly. McDonald's, for example, concentrates on sponsoring the Ronald McDonald House program (which provides a home away from home for the families of seriously ill children receiving treatment at nearby hospitals). British Telecom gives 1 percent of its profits directly to communities, largely for education—teacher training, in-school workshops, and digital technology. Leading prescription drug maker GlaxoSmithKline and other pharmaceutical companies either donate or heavily discount medicines for distribution in the least-developed nations. Companies frequently reinforce their philanthropic efforts by encouraging employees to support charitable causes and participate in community affairs, often through programs that match employee contributions.

- *Actions to protect the environment and, in particular, to minimize or eliminate any adverse impact on the environment stemming from the company's own business activities.* Corporate social responsibility as it applies to environmental protection entails actively striving to be good stewards of the environment. This means using the best available science and technology to reduce environmentally harmful aspects of its operations *below the levels required by prevailing environmental regulations.* It also means putting time and money into improving the environment in ways that extend past a company's own industry boundaries—such as participating in recycling projects, adopting energy conservation practices, and supporting efforts to clean up local water supplies.

- *Actions to create a work environment that enhances the quality of life for employees.* Numerous companies exert extra effort to enhance the quality of life for their employees, both at work and at home. This can include on-site day care, flexible work schedules, workplace exercise facilities, special leaves to care for sick family members, work-at-home opportunities, career development programs and education opportunities, special safety programs, and the like.

- *Actions to build a workforce that is diverse with respect to gender, race, national origin, and other aspects that different people bring to the workplace.* Most large companies in the United States have established workforce diversity programs, and some go the extra mile to ensure that their workplaces are attractive to ethnic minorities and inclusive of all groups and perspectives.

The particular combination of socially responsible endeavors a company elects to pursue defines its **corporate social responsibility strategy**. Concepts & Connections 9.2 describes John Deere's approach to corporate social responsibility. But the specific components emphasized in a CSR strategy vary from company to company and are typically linked to a company's core values. General Mills, for example, builds its CSR strategy around the theme of "nourishing lives" to emphasize its commitment to good nutrition as well as philanthropy, community building, and environmental protection.[11] Starbucks's CSR strategy includes four main elements (ethical sourcing, community service, environmental stewardship, and farmer support), all of which have touch points with the way that the company's procures its coffee—a key aspect of its product differentiation strategy.[12]

CORE CONCEPT

A company's **corporate social responsibility strategy** is defined by the specific combination of socially beneficial activities it opts to support with its contributions of time, money, and other resources.

Environmental Sustainability Strategies: A New Priority

A rapidly growing number of companies are now expanding their exercise of corporate social responsibility to include efforts to operate in a more environmentally sustainable fashion. **Environmental sustainability** strategies entail deliberate and concerted actions to operate businesses in a manner that protects and maybe even enhances natural resources and ecological support systems, guards against outcomes that will ultimately endanger the planet, and is therefore sustainable for centuries.[13] Sustainability initiatives undertaken by companies are directed at improving the company's triple bottom line—its performance on economic, environment, and social metrics.[14] Unilever, a diversified producer of processed foods, personal care, and home cleaning products, is among the most committed corporations pursuing environmentally sustainable business practices. The company tracks 11 sustainable agricultural indicators in its processed-foods business and has launched a variety of programs to improve the environmental performance of its suppliers. Examples of such programs include special low-rate financing for tomato suppliers choosing to switch to water-conserving irrigation systems and training programs in India that have allowed contract

CORE CONCEPT

Environmental sustainability involves deliberate actions to protect the environment, provide for the longevity of natural resources, maintain ecological support systems for future generations, and guard against the ultimate endangerment of the planet.

CONCEPTS & CONNECTIONS 9.2

JOHN DEERE'S APPROACH TO CORPORATE SOCIAL RESPONSIBILITY

Principal Components of John Deere's Corporate Social Responsibility Strategy	Specific Actions to Execute the Strategy
Adhering to the Core Values of Integrity, Quality Commitment, and Innovation *Integrity* means telling the truth, keeping our word, and treating others with fairness and respect. *Quality* means delivering the value customers, employees, shareholders, and other business partners expect every day. *Commitment* means doing our best to meet expectations over the long run. *Innovation* means inventing, designing, and developing breakthrough products and services that customers want to buy from John Deere.	• Committing to ethical behavior and fair dealing in all relationships • Providing Business Conduct Guidelines to show employees how they are expected to carry out company business • Creating an Office of Corporate Compliance to ensure ethical and fair business practices are maintained throughout global operations • Instituting a 24-hour hotline for confidential anonymous reporting of ethical violations • Offering employees professional guidance when they feel they are operating in complicated or ambiguous business and cultural situations
Engaging in Philanthropy and Community Betterment	• Supporting agricultural development in resource-poor countries • Providing increased access to financing for the rural poor in Africa (in partnership with Opportunity International) • Helping start *BackPack* programs in the United States to supply supplemental food for school-age children • Supporting a variety of higher educational programs and such programs as Junior Achievement, FFA, and the National 4-H Council • Instituting an employee matching gift program
Conserving Resources and Sustaining the Environment	• Establishing ambitious greenhouse-gas reduction goals to be achieved over the next 5 to 10 years • Mandating the use of recycling and waste reduction practices across all company operations • Implementing a worldwide Environmental Management System geared to ISO14001 standards • Helping to develop long-term comprehensive climate change strategies through EPA's Climate Leaders program • Designing products to conserve water, encourage biofuel development, and support sustainable agriculture

continued

▶ **CONCEPTS & CONNECTIONS 9.2** *continued*

Principal Components of John Deere's Corporate Social Responsibility Strategy	Specific Actions to Execute the Strategy
Supporting and Enhancing the Workforce	• Maintaining effective workplace safety programs; more than 1,000 awards from the U.S. National Safety Council • Providing programs to promote employee health and wellness and work-life balance • Establishing global occupational health programs keyed to local health issues and infrastructure • Helping employees with career development through mentoring, coaching, and a programmatic approach • Creating a continuous learning environment with extensive training opportunities and a tuition reimbursement program
Promoting Diversity and Inclusiveness	• Creating an inclusive culture in which employees of all backgrounds can develop their leadership potential • Providing training and tools designed to make work teams more diverse, productive, and effective • Sponsoring employee networks that bring together people from around the world with shared interests, gender, ethnicity, or skills • Encouraging diversity within the company's dealer and supplier base • Supporting minority education programs and collegiate diversity initiatives

Source: Information posted at www.deere.com, accessed July 8, 2010.

cucumber growers to reduce pesticide use by 90 percent, while improving yields by 78 percent.

Unilever has also reengineered many internal processes to improve the company's overall performance on sustainability measures. For example, the company's factories have reduced water usage by 50 percent and manufacturing waste by 14 percent through the implementation of sustainability initiatives. Unilever has also redesigned packaging for many of its products to conserve natural resources and reduce the volume of consumer waste. The company's Suave shampoo bottles in the United States were reshaped to save almost 150 tons of plastic resin per year, which is the equivalent of 15 million fewer empty bottles making it to landfills annually. Also, the width of Unilever's Lipton soup cartons was reduced to save 154 tons of cardboard per year. Because 40 percent of Unilever's sales are made to consumers in developing countries, the company also is committed to addressing societal needs of consumers in those countries. Examples of the company's social performance include free laundries in poor neighborhoods in developing countries, start-up assistance for women-owned micro businesses in India, and free drinking water provided to villages in Ghana.

Sometimes cost savings and improved profitability are drivers of corporate sustainability strategies. DuPont's sustainability initiatives regarding energy usage have resulted in energy conservation savings of more than $2 billion between 1990 and 2005. Procter & Gamble's Swiffer cleaning system, one of the company's best-selling new products, was developed as a sustainable product; not only does the Swiffer system have an earth-friendly design, but it also outperforms less ecologically friendly alternatives. Although most consumers probably aren't aware that the Swiffer mop reduces demands on municipal water sources, saves electricity that would be needed to heat water, and doesn't add to the amount of detergent making its way into waterways and waste treatment facilities, they are attracted to purchasing Swiffer mops because they prefer Swiffer's disposable cleaning sheets to filling and refilling a mop bucket and wringing out a wet mop until the floor is clean.

Crafting Social Responsibility and Sustainability Strategies   While striving to be socially responsible and to engage in environmentally sustainable business practices, there's plenty of room for every company to make its own statement about what charitable contributions to make, what kinds of community service projects to emphasize, what environmental actions to support, how to make the company a good place to work, where and how workforce diversity fits into the picture, and what else it will do to support worthy causes and projects that benefit society. A company may choose to focus its social responsibility strategy on generic social issues, but social responsibility strategies linked to its customer value proposition or key value chain activities may also help build competitive advantage.[15] For example, while carbon emissions may be a generic social issue for a financial institution such as Wells Fargo, Toyota's social responsibility strategy aimed at reducing carbon emissions has produced both competitive advantage and environmental benefits. Its Prius hybrid electric/gasoline-powered automobile not only is among the least polluting automobiles, but also is the best-selling hybrid vehicle in the United States and has earned the company the loyalty of fuel-conscious buyers and given Toyota a green image.

> CSR strategies that have the effect of both providing valuable social benefits and fulfilling customer needs in a superior fashion can lead to competitive advantage. Corporate social agendas that address generic social issues may help boost a company's reputation, but are unlikely to improve its competitive strength in the marketplace.

THE BUSINESS CASE FOR SOCIALLY RESPONSIBLE BEHAVIOR

It has long been recognized that it is in the enlightened self-interest of companies to be good citizens and devote some of their energies and resources to the betterment of employees, the communities in which they operate, and society in general. In short, there are several reasons why the exercise of corporate social responsibility is good business:

- *Such actions can lead to increased buyer patronage.* A strong visible social responsibility strategy gives a company an edge in differentiating itself from rivals and in appealing to those consumers who prefer to do business with companies that are good corporate citizens. Ben & Jerry's, Whole Foods Market, Stonyfield Farm, and the Body Shop have definitely expanded their customer bases because of their visible and well-publicized activities as socially conscious companies.

- *A strong commitment to socially responsible behavior reduces the risk of reputation-damaging incidents.* Companies that place little importance on operating in a socially responsible manner are more prone to scandal and embarrassment. Consumer, environmental, and human rights activist groups are quick to criticize businesses whose behavior they consider to be out of line, and they are adept at getting their message into the media and onto the Internet. For many years, Nike received stinging criticism for not policing sweatshop conditions in the Asian factories that produced Nike footwear, causing Nike co-founder and former CEO Phil Knight to observe, "Nike has become synonymous with slave wages, forced overtime, and arbitrary abuse."[16] In 1997, Nike began an extensive effort to monitor conditions in the 800 factories of the contract manufacturers that produced Nike shoes. As Knight said, "Good shoes come from good factories and good factories have good labor relations." Nonetheless, Nike has continually been plagued by complaints from human rights activists that its monitoring procedures are flawed and that it is not doing enough to correct the plight of factory workers.

- *Socially responsible actions yield internal benefits (particularly for employee recruiting, workforce retention, and training costs) and can improve operational efficiency.* Companies with deservedly good reputations for contributing time and money to the betterment of society are better able to attract and retain employees compared to companies with tarnished reputations. Some employees just feel better about working for a company committed to improving society.[17] This can contribute to lower turnover and better worker productivity. Other direct and indirect economic benefits include lower costs for staff recruitment and training. For example, Starbucks is said to enjoy much lower rates of employee turnover because of its full benefits package for both full-time and part-time employees, management efforts to make Starbucks a great place to work, and the company's socially responsible practices. When a U.S. manufacturer of recycled paper, taking eco-efficiency to heart, discovered how to increase its fiber recovery rate, it saved the equivalent of 20,000 tons of waste paper—a factor that helped the company become the industry's lowest-cost producer. By helping two-thirds of its employees stop smoking and investing in a number of wellness programs for employees, Johnson & Johnson has saved $250 million on its health care costs over the past decade.[18]

- *Well-conceived social responsibility strategies work to the advantage of shareholders.* A two-year study of leading companies found that improving environmental compliance and developing environmentally friendly products can enhance earnings per share, profitability, and the likelihood of winning contracts. The stock prices of companies that rate high on social and environmental performance criteria have been found to perform 35 to 45 percent better than the average of the 2,500 companies comprising the Dow Jones Global Index.[19] A review of some 135 studies indicated there is a positive, but small, correlation between good corporate behavior and good financial performance; only 2 percent of the studies showed that dedicating corporate resources to social responsibility harmed the interests of shareholders.[20]

In sum, companies that take social responsibility seriously can improve their business reputations and operational efficiency while also reducing their risk exposure and encouraging loyalty and innovation. Overall, companies that take special pains to protect the environment (beyond what is required by law), are active in community affairs, and are generous supporters of charitable causes and projects that benefit society are more likely to be seen as good investments and as good companies to work for or do business with. Shareholders are likely to view the business case for social responsibility as a strong one, even though they certainly have a right to be concerned about whether the time and money their company spends to carry out its social responsibility strategy outweigh the benefits and reduce the bottom line by an unjustified amount.

KEY POINTS

Business ethics concerns the application of ethical principles and standards to the actions and decisions of business organizations and the conduct of their personnel. Ethical principles in business are not materially different from ethical principles in general.

1. The three main drivers of unethical business behavior stand out:
    - Overzealous or obsessive pursuit of personal gain, wealth, and other selfish interests.
    - Heavy pressures on company managers to meet or beat earnings targets.
    - A company culture that puts profitability and good business performance ahead of ethical behavior.

2. Business ethics failures can result in visible costs (fines, penalties, civil penalties arising from lawsuits, stock price declines), the internal administrative or "cleanup" costs, and intangible or less visible costs (customer defections, loss of reputation, higher turnover, harsher government regulations).

3. There are three schools of thought about ethical standards for companies with international operations:
    - According to the *school of ethical universalism*, the same standards of what's ethical and unethical resonate with peoples of most societies regardless of local traditions and cultural norms; hence, common ethical standards can be used to judge the conduct of personnel at companies operating in a variety of international markets and cultural circumstances.

- According to the *school of ethical relativism,* different societal cultures and customs have divergent values and standards of right and wrong—thus, what is ethical or unethical must be judged in the light of local customs and social mores and can vary from one culture or nation to another.

- According to *integrative social contracts theory,* universal ethical principles or norms based on the collective views of multiple cultures and societies combine to form a "social contract" that all individuals in all situations have a duty to observe. Within the boundaries of this social contract, local cultures can specify other impermissible actions; however, universal ethical norms always take precedence over local ethical norms.

4. The term *corporate social responsibility* concerns a company's *duty* to operate in an honorable manner, provide good working conditions for employees, encourage workforce diversity, be a good steward of the environment, and support philanthropic endeavors in local communities where it operates and in society at large. The particular combination of socially responsible endeavors a company elects to pursue defines its corporate social responsibility (CSR) strategy.

5. The triple bottom line refers to company performance in three realms: economic, social, environmental. Increasingly, companies are reporting their performance with respect to all three performance dimensions.

6. Sustainability is a term that is used variously, but most often it concerns a firm's relationship to the environment and its use of natural resources. Environmentally sustainable business practices are those capable of meeting the needs of the present without compromising the world's ability to meet future needs. A company's environmental sustainability strategy consists of its deliberate actions to protect the environment, provide for the longevity of natural resources, maintain ecological support systems for future generations, and guard against ultimate endangerment of the planet.

7. There are also solid reasons CSR and environmental sustainability strategies may be good business—they can be conducive to greater buyer patronage, reduce the risk of reputation-damaging incidents, provide opportunities for revenue enhancement, and lower costs. Well-crafted CSR and environmental sustainability strategies are in the best long-term interest of shareholders, for the reasons above and because they can avoid or preempt costly legal or regulatory actions.

→→→→ ASSURANCE OF LEARNING EXERCISES

LO1, LO4

1. Ikea is widely known for its commitment to business ethics and environmental sustainability. After reviewing the About Ikea section of its website (www.ikea.com/ms/en_US/about_ikea/index.html), prepare a list of 10 specific policies and programs that help the company achieve its vision of creating a better everyday life for people around the world.

LO2, LO3

2. Prepare a one- to two-page analysis of a recent ethics scandal using your university library's access to Lexis-Nexis or other Internet resources. Your report should (a) discuss the conditions that gave rise to unethical business strategies and behavior and (b) provide an overview of the costs resulting from the company's business ethics failure.

3. Based on the information provided in Concepts & Connections 9.2 on pages 197 and 198, explain how John Deere ensures that the company employs an ethical strategy and that its employees observe ethical principles in operating the business. Describe how John Deere's philanthropy and support for community service bolsters its corporate social responsibility strategy. Does John Deere engage in sustainable business practices? Explain your answer.

LO4

connect
www.mcgrawhillconnect.com

4. Go to www.nestle.com and read the company's latest sustainability report. What are Nestlé's key environmental sustainability policies? How do these initiatives relate to the company's principles, values, and culture? How do these initiatives help build competitive advantage in the food industry?

LO4

connect
www.mcgrawhillconnect.com

→ → EXERCISES FOR SIMULATION PARTICIPANTS

1. Is your company's strategy ethical? Why or why not? Is there anything that your company has done or is now doing that could legitimately be considered as "shady" by your competitiors?

LO1

2. In what ways, if any, is your company exercising corporate social responsibility? What are the elements of your company's CSR strategy? What changes to this strategy would you suggest?

LO4

3. If some shareholders complained that you and your co-managers have been spending too little or too much on corporate social responsibility, what would you tell them?

LO3, LO4

4. Is your company striving to conduct its business in an environmentally sustainable manner? What specific *additional* actions could your company take that would make an even greater contribution to environmental sustainability?

LO4

5. In what ways is your company's environmental sustainability strategy in the best long-term interest of shareholders? Does it contribute to your company's competitive advantage or profitability?

LO4

ENDNOTES

1. James E. Post, Anne T. Lawrence, and James Weber, *Business and Society: Corporate Strategy, Public Policy, Ethics*, 10th ed. (New York: McGraw-Hill Irwin, 2002).

2. John F. Veiga, Timothy D. Golden, and Kathleen Dechant, "Why Managers Bend Company Rules," *Academy of Management Executive* 18, no. 2 (May 2004).

3. Ronald R. Sims and Johannes Brinkmann, "Enron Ethics (Or: Culture Matters More than Codes)," *Journal of Business Ethics* 45, no. 3 (July 2003).

4. Archie B. Carroll, "The Four Faces of Corporate Citizenship," *Business and Society Review* 100/101 (September 1998).

5. Mark S. Schwartz, "Universal Moral Values for Corporate Codes of Ethics," *Journal of Business Ethics* 59, no. 1 (June 2005).

6. Mark. S. Schwartz, "A Code of Ethics for Corporate Codes of Ethics," *Journal of Business Ethics* 41, nos. 1–2 (November–December 2002).

7. T. L. Beauchamp and N. E. Bowie, *Ethical Theory and Business* (Upper Saddle River, NJ: Prentice Hall, 2001).

8. Thomas Donaldson and Thomas W. Dunfee, "Towards a Unified Conception of Business Ethics: Integrative Social Contracts Theory," *Academy of Management Review* 19, no. 2 (April 1994);

Thomas Donaldson and Thomas W. Dunfee, *Ties That Bind: A Social Contracts Approach to Business Ethics* (Boston: Harvard Business School Press, 1999); and Andrew Spicer, Thomas W. Dunfee, and Wendy J. Bailey, "Does National Context Matter in Ethical Decision Making? An Empirical Test of Integrative Social Contracts Theory," *Academy of Management Journal* 47, no. 4 (August 2004).

9. P. M. Nichols, "Outlawing Transnational Bribery through the World Trade Organization," *Law and Policy in International Business* 28, no. 2 (1997).

10. Timothy M. Devinney, "Is the Socially Responsible Corporation a Myth? The Good, the Bad, and the Ugly of Corporate Social Responsibility," *Academy of Management Perspectives* 23, no. 2 (May 2009).

11. "General Mills' 2010 Corporate Social Responsibility Report Highlights New and Longstanding Achievements in the Areas of Health, Community, and Environment," *CSRwire*, April 15, 2010, www.csrwire.com/press_releases/29347-General-Mills-2010-Corporate-Social-Responsibility-report-now-available.html.

12. Arthur A. Thompson and Amit J. Shah, "Starbucks' Strategy and Internal Initiatives to Return to Profitable Growth," 2010.

13. Robert Goodland, "The Concept of Environmental Sustainability," *Annual Review of Ecology and Systematics* 26 (1995); and J. G. Speth, *The Bridge at the End of the World: Capitalism, the Environment, and Crossing from Crisis to Sustainability* (New Haven, CT: Yale University Press, 2008).

14. Gerald I. J. M. Zwetsloot and Marcel N. A. van Marrewijk, "From Quality to Sustainability," *Journal of Business Ethics* 55, (December 2004); and John B. Elkington, *Cannibals with Forks: The Triple Bottom Line of 21st Century Business* (Oxford: Capstone Publishing, 1997).

15. Michael E. Porter and Mark R. Kramer, "Strategy & Society: The Link between Competitive Advantage and Corporate Social Responsibility," *Harvard Business Review* 84, no. 12 (December 2006).

16. Tom McCawley, "Racing to Improve Its Reputation: Nike Has Fought to Shed Its Image as an Exploiter of Third-World Labor Yet It Is Still a Target of Activists," *Financial Times*, December 2000.

17. N. Craig Smith, "Corporate Responsibility: Whether and How," *California Management Review* 45, no. 4 (Summer 2003), p. 63; see also, World Economic Forum, "Findings of a Survey on Global Corporate Leadership," accessed at www.weforum.org/corporatecitizenship, October 11, 2003.

18. Michael E. Porter and Mark Kramer, "Creating Shared Value," *Harvard Business Review* 89, no. 1/2 (January–February 2011).

19. James C. Collins and Jerry I. Porras, *Built to Last: Successful Habits of Visionary Companies,* 3rd ed. (London: HarperBusiness, 2002).

20. Joshua D. Margolis and Hillary A. Elfenbein, "Doing Well by Doing Good: Don't Count on It," *Harvard Business Review* 86, no. 1 (January 2008); Lee E. Preston and Douglas P. O'Bannon, "The Corporate Social-Financial Performance Relationship," *Business and Society* 36, no. 4 (December 1997); Ronald M. Roman, Sefa Hayibor, and Bradley R. Agle, "The Relationship between Social and Financial Performance: Repainting a Portrait," *Business and Society* 38, no. 1 (March 1999); and Joshua D. Margolis and James P. Walsh, *People and Profits* (Mahwah, NJ: Lawrence Erlbaum, 2001).

chapter 10

SUPERIOR STRATEGY EXECUTION—ANOTHER PATH TO COMPETITIVE ADVANTAGE

LEARNING OBJECTIVES

LO1 Gain command of what managers must do to build an organization capable of good strategy execution.

LO2 Learn why resource allocation should always be based on strategic priorities.

LO3 Understand why policies and procedures should be designed to facilitate good strategy execution.

LO4 Understand how process management programs that drive continuous improvement help an organization achieve operating excellence.

LO5 Recognize the role of information and operating systems in enabling company personnel to carry out their strategic roles proficiently.

LO6 Learn how and why the use of well-designed incentives and rewards can be management's single most powerful tool for promoting operating excellence.

LO7 Gain an understanding of how and why a company's culture can aid the drive for proficient strategy execution.

LO8 Understand what constitutes effective managerial leadership in achieving superior strategy execution.

Once managers have decided on a strategy, the emphasis turns to converting it into actions and good results. Putting the strategy into place and getting the organization to execute it well call for different sets of managerial skills. Whereas crafting strategy is largely a market-driven and resource-driven activity, strategy implementation is an operations-driven activity primarily involving the management of people and business processes. Successful strategy execution depends on management's ability to direct organizational change and do a good job of allocating resources, building and strengthening competitive capabilities, instituting strategy-supportive policies, improving processes and systems, motivating and rewarding people, creating and nurturing a strategy-supportive culture, and consistently meeting or beating performance targets. While an organization's chief executive officer and other senior managers are ultimately responsible for ensuring that the strategy is executed successfully, it is middle and lower-level managers who must see to it that frontline employees and work groups competently perform the strategy-critical activities that allow companywide performance targets to be met. *Hence, strategy execution requires every manager to think through the answer to the question: "What does my area have to do to implement its part of the strategic plan, and what should I do to get these things accomplished effectively and efficiently?"*

> **CORE CONCEPT**
>
> Good strategy execution requires a *team effort*. All managers have strategy executing responsibility in their areas of authority, and all employees are active participants in the strategy execution process.

THE PRINCIPAL MANAGERIAL COMPONENTS OF THE STRATEGY EXECUTION PROCESS

Executing strategy entails figuring out the specific techniques, actions, and behaviors that are needed to get things done and deliver results. The exact items that need to be placed on management's action agenda always have to be customized to fit the particulars of a company's situation. The hot buttons for successfully executing a low-cost provider strategy are different from those in executing a differentiation strategy. Implementing a new strategy for a struggling company in the midst of a financial crisis is different from improving strategy execution in a company where the execution is already pretty good. While there's no definitive managerial recipe for successful strategy execution that cuts across all company situations and all types of strategies, certain managerial bases have to be covered no matter what the circumstances. Eight managerial tasks crop up repeatedly in company efforts to execute strategy (see Figure 10.1).

1. Building an organization with the capabilities, people, and structure needed to execute the strategy successfully.

2. Allocating ample resources to strategy-critical activities.

3. Ensuring that policies and procedures facilitate rather than impede effective strategy execution.

4. Adopting process management programs that drive continuous improvement in how strategy execution activities are performed.

▶FIGURE 10.1   **The Eight Components of Strategy Execution**

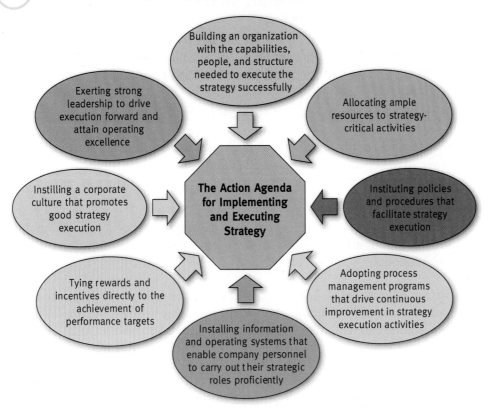

5. Installing information and operating systems that enable company personnel to perform essential activities.

6. Tying rewards directly to the achievement of performance objectives.

7. Fostering a corporate culture that promotes good strategy execution.

8. Exerting the internal leadership needed to propel implementation forward.

How well managers perform these eight tasks has a decisive impact on whether the outcome is a spectacular success, a colossal failure, or something in between. In the remainder of this chapter, we will discuss what is involved in performing the eight key managerial tasks that shape the process of implementing and executing strategy.

BUILDING AN ORGANIZATION WITH THE CAPABILITIES, PEOPLE, AND STRUCTURE NEEDED FOR GOOD STRATEGY EXECUTION

▶**LO1**

Gain command of what managers must do to build an organization capable of good strategy execution.

Proficient strategy execution depends heavily on competent personnel, better-than-adequate competitive capabilities, and an effective internal organization. Building a capable organization is thus always a top priority in strategy execution. Three types of organization building actions are paramount.

1. *Staffing the organization*—putting together a strong management team and recruiting and retaining employees with the needed experience, technical skills, and intellectual capital.

2. *Building and strengthening capabilities and core competencies*—developing proficiencies in performing strategy-critical value chain activities and updating them to match changing market conditions and customer expectations.

3. *Structuring the organization and work effort*—organizing value chain activities and business processes, establishing lines of authority and reporting relationships, and deciding how much decision-making authority to push down to lower-level managers and frontline employees.

Staffing the Organization

No company can hope to perform the activities required for successful strategy execution without attracting and retaining talented managers and employees with suitable skills and intellectual capital.

Building Managerial Talent Assembling a capable management team is a cornerstone of the organization-building task.[1] While company circumstances sometimes call for different mixes of backgrounds, experiences, management styles, and know-how, *the most important consideration is to fill key managerial slots with people who are good at figuring out what needs to be done and skilled in "making it happen" and delivering good results.*[2] Without a capable, results-oriented management team, the implementation–execution process ends up being hampered by missed deadlines, misdirected or wasteful efforts, and/or managerial ineptness.[3] Weak executives are serious impediments to getting optimal results because they are unable to differentiate between ideas that have merit and those that are misguided. In contrast, managers with strong strategy implementing capabilities have a talent for asking tough, incisive questions. They know enough about the details of the business to be able to challenge and ensure the soundness of the approaches of the people around them, and they can discern whether the resources people are asking for make sense strategically. They are good at getting things done through others, typically by making sure they have the right people under them and that these people are put in the right jobs. They consistently follow through on issues and do not let important details slip through the cracks.

Sometimes a company's existing management team is suitable; at other times it may need to be strengthened or expanded by promoting qualified people from within or by bringing in outsiders. The overriding aim in building a management team should be to assemble a *critical mass* of talented managers who can function as agents of change and further the cause of first-rate strategy execution. When a first-rate manager enjoys the help and support of other first-rate managers, it's possible to create a managerial whole that is greater than the sum of individual efforts—talented managers who work well together as a team can produce organizational results that are dramatically better than what one or two star managers acting individually can achieve.[4]

Recruiting and Retaining a Capable Workforce   Assembling a capable management team is not enough. Staffing the organization with the right kinds of people must go much deeper than managerial jobs in order for value chain activities to be performed competently. *The quality of an organization's people is always an essential ingredient of successful strategy execution—knowledgeable, engaged employees are a company's best source of creative ideas for the nuts-and-bolts operating improvements that lead to operating excellence.* Companies such as Procter & Gamble, Southwest Airlines, and Intel make a concerted effort to recruit the best and brightest people they can find and then retain them with excellent compensation packages, opportunities for rapid advancement and professional growth, and challenging and interesting assignments. Having a pool of "A players" with strong skill sets and lots of brainpower is essential to their business. Microsoft makes a point of hiring the very brightest and most talented programmers it can find and motivating them with both good monetary incentives and the challenge of working on cutting-edge software design projects. The leading global accounting firms screen candidates not only on the basis of their accounting expertise but also on whether they possess the people skills needed to relate well with clients and colleagues. Southwest Airlines goes to considerable lengths to hire people who can have fun and be fun on the job; it uses special interviewing and screening methods to gauge whether applicants for customer-contact jobs have outgoing personality traits that match its strategy of creating a high-spirited, fun-loving, in-flight atmosphere for passengers. Southwest Airlines is so selective that only about 3 percent of the people who apply are offered jobs.

The tactics listed below are common among companies dedicated to staffing jobs with the best people they can find:

1. Putting forth considerable effort in screening and evaluating job applicants—selecting only those with suitable skill sets, energy, initiative, judgment, aptitudes for learning, and adaptability to the company's culture.

2. Investing in training programs that continue throughout employees' careers.

3. Providing promising employees with challenging, interesting, and skill-stretching assignments.

4. Rotating people through jobs that span functional and geographic boundaries.

5. Striving to retain talented, high-performing employees via promotions, salary increases, performance bonuses, stock options and equity ownership, fringe benefit packages, and other perks.

6. Coaching average performers to improve their skills and capabilities, while weeding out underperformers and benchwarmers.

Building and Strengthening Core Competencies and Competitive Capabilities

High among the organization-building priorities in the strategy implementing/executing process is the need to build and strengthen competitively valuable capabilities and core competencies. Whereas managers identify the desired capabilities and competencies in the course of crafting strategy, good strategy execution requires putting the desired capabilities and competencies in place, upgrading them as needed, and then modifying them as market conditions evolve.[5] Sometimes a company already has some semblance of the needed competencies and capabilities, in which case managers can concentrate on strengthening and nurturing them to promote better strategy execution. More often, however, company managers have to significantly broaden or deepen certain capabilities or even add entirely new competencies to put strategic initiatives in place and execute them proficiently. Management's organization-building challenge is one of deciding when and how to recalibrate existing competencies and capabilities, and when and how to develop new ones. Concepts & Connections 10.1 discusses how Toyota has aggressively upgraded its capabilities in fuel-efficient hybrid engine technology and constantly fine-tuned its famed Toyota Production System to enhance its already proficient capabilities in manufacturing top-quality vehicles at relatively low costs.

Matching Organizational Structure to the Strategy

Building an organization capable of good strategy execution also relies on an organizational structure that lays out lines of authority and reporting relationships in a manner that supports the company's key strategic initiatives. The best approach to settling on an organizational structure is to first consider the key value chain activities that deliver value to the customer. In any business, some activities in the value chain are always more critical than others. For instance, hotel/motel enterprises have to be good at fast check-in/check-out, housekeeping, food service, and creating a pleasant ambience. In specialty chemicals, the strategy-critical activities include R&D, product innovation, getting new products onto the market quickly, effective marketing, and expertise in assisting customers. It is important for management to build its organization structure around proficient performance of these activities, making them the centerpieces or main building blocks on the organization chart.

The rationale for making strategy-critical activities the main building blocks in structuring a business is compelling: If activities crucial to strategic success are to have the resources, decision-making influence, and organizational impact they need, they have to be centerpieces in the organizational scheme. In addition, a new or changed strategy is likely to entail new or different key activities or capabilities and therefore to require a new or different organizational structure.[6] Attempting to carry out a new strategy with an old organizational structure is usually unwise.

Types of Organizational Structures It is common for companies engaged in a single line of business to utilize a **functional (or departmental) organizational structure** that organizes strategy-critical activities into distinct *functional, product, geographic, process,* or *customer* groups. For instance, a technical instruments manufacturer may be organized around research and development, engineering, supply chain management, assembly, quality control, marketing technical services, and corporate adminis-

CONCEPTS & CONNECTIONS 10.1

TOYOTA'S LEGENDARY PRODUCTION SYSTEM—A CAPABILITY THAT TRANSLATES INTO COMPETITIVE ADVANTAGE

The heart of Toyota's strategy in motor vehicles is to outcompete rivals by manufacturing world-class, quality vehicles at lower costs and selling them at competitive price levels. Executing this strategy requires top-notch manufacturing capability and super-efficient management of people, equipment, and materials. Toyota began conscious efforts to improve its manufacturing competence more than 50 years ago. Through tireless trial and error, the company gradually took what started as a loose collection of techniques and practices and integrated them into a full-fledged process that has come to be known as the Toyota Production System (TPS). The TPS drives all plant operations and the company's supply chain management practices. TPS is grounded in the following principles, practices, and techniques:

- *Use just-in-time delivery of parts and components to the point of vehicle assembly.* The idea here is to cut out all the bits and pieces of transferring materials from place to place and to discontinue all activities on the part of workers that don't add value (particularly activities where nothing ends up being made or assembled).

- *Develop people who can come up with unique ideas for production improvements.* Toyota encourages employees at all levels to question existing ways of doing things—even if it means challenging a boss on the soundness of a directive. Former Toyota President Katsuaki Watanabe encouraged the company's employees to "pick a friendly fight." Also, Toyota doesn't fire its employees who, at first, have little judgment for improving work flows; instead, the company gives them extensive training to become better problem solvers.

- *Emphasize continuous improvement.* Workers are expected to use their heads and develop better ways of doing things, rather than mechanically follow instructions. Toyota mangers tout messages such as "Never be satisfied" and "There's got to be a better way." Another mantra at Toyota is that the *T* in TPS also stands for "Thinking." The thesis is that a work environment where people have to think generates the wisdom to spot opportunities for making tasks simpler and easier to perform, increasing the speed and efficiency with which activities are performed, and constantly improving product quality.

- *Empower workers to stop the assembly line when there's a problem or a defect is spotted.* Toyota views worker efforts to purge defects and sort out the problem immediately as critical to the whole concept of building quality into the production process. According to TPS, "If the line doesn't stop, useless defective items will move on to the next stage. If you don't know where the problem occurred, you can't do anything to fix it."

- *Deal with defects only when they occur.* TPS philosophy holds that when things are running smoothly, they should not be subject to control; if attention is directed to fixing problems that are found, quality control along the assembly line can be handled with fewer personnel.

- *Ask yourself "Why?" five times.* While errors need to be fixed whenever they occur, the value of asking "Why?" five times enables identifying the root cause of the error and correcting it so that the error won't recur.

- *Organize all jobs around human motion to create a production/assembly system with no wasted effort.* Work organized in this fashion is called "standardized work," and people are trained to observe standardized work procedures (which include supplying parts to each process on the assembly line at the proper time, sequencing the work in an optimal manner, and allowing workers to do their jobs continuously in a set sequence of sub-processes).

- *Find where a part is made cheaply and use that price as a benchmark.*

The TPS utilizes a unique vocabulary of terms (such as *kanban, takt-time, jikoda, kaizen, heijunka, monozukuri, poka yoke,* and *muda*) that facilitates precise discussion of specific TPS elements. In 2003, Toyota established a Global Production Center to efficiently train large numbers of shop-floor experts in the latest TPS methods and better operate an increasing number of production sites worldwide. Since then, additional upgrades and refinements have been introduced, some in response to the large number of defects in Toyota vehicles that surfaced in 2009–2010.

There's widespread agreement that Toyota's ongoing effort to refine and improve on its renowned TPS gives it important manufacturing capabilities that are the envy of other motor vehicle manufacturers. Not only have such auto manufacturers as Ford, Daimler, Volkswagen, and General Motors attempted to emulate key elements of TPS, but elements of Toyota's production philosophy have been adopted by hospitals and postal services.

Sources: Information posted at www.toyotageorgetown.com; Hirotaka Takeuchi, Emi Osono, and Norihiko Shimizu, "The Contradictions that Drive Toyota's Success," *Harvard Business Review* 86, no. 6 (June 2008), pp. 96–104; and Taiichi Ohno, *Toyota Production System: Beyond Large-Scale Production* (New York: Sheridan Books, 1988).

tration. A company with operations scattered across a large geographic area or many countries may organize activities and reporting relationships by geography. Many diversified companies utilize a **multidivisional (or divisional) organizational structure**. A multidivisional structure is appropriate for a diversified building materials company that designs, produces, and markets cabinets, plumbing fixtures, windows, and paints and stains. The divisional structure organizes all of the value chain activities involved with making each type of home construction product available to home builders and do-it-yourselfers into a common division and makes each division an independent profit center. **Matrix organizational structures** allow companies to specify dual reporting relationships for various value-creating building blocks. For example, in the diversified building materials company just mentioned, a matrix structure could require the marketing department for the plumbing fixtures division to report to both the corporate marketing department and the chief manager of the plumbing equipment division.

Organizational Structure and Authority in Decision Making

Responsibility for results of decisions made throughout the organization ultimately lies with managers at the top of the organizational structure, but in practice, lower-level managers might possess a great deal of authority in decision making. Companies vary in the degree of authority delegated to managers of each organization unit and how much decision-making latitude is given to individual employees in performing their jobs. The two extremes are to *centralize decision making* at the top (the CEO and a few close lieutenants) or to *decentralize decision making* by giving managers and employees considerable decision-making latitude in their areas of responsibility. The two approaches are based on sharply different underlying principles and beliefs, with each having its pros and cons. *In a highly decentralized organization, decision-making authority is pushed down to the lowest organizational level capable of making timely, informed, competent decisions.* The objective is to put adequate decision-making authority in the hands of the people closest to and most familiar with the situation and train them to weigh all the factors and exercise good judgment. Decentralized decision making means that the managers of each organizational unit are delegated lead responsibility for deciding how best to execute strategy.

The case for empowering down-the-line managers and employees to make decisions related to daily operations and executing the strategy is based on the belief that a company that draws on the combined intellectual capital of all its employees can outperform a command-and-control company.[7] Decentralized decision making means, for example, employees with customer contact may be empowered to do what it takes to please customers. At Starbucks, for example, employees are encouraged to exercise initiative in promoting customer satisfaction—there's the story of a store employee who, when the computerized cash register system went offline, enthusiastically offered free coffee to waiting customers.

> The ultimate goal of decentralized decision making is to put decision-making authority in the hands of those persons or teams closest to and most knowledgeable about the situation.

Pushing decision-making authority deep down into the organization structure and empowering employees presents its own organizing challenge: *how to exercise adequate control over the actions of empowered employees so that the business is not put at risk at the same time that the benefits of empowerment are realized.* Maintaining adequate organizational control over empowered employees is generally accomplished by placing limits on the authority that empowered personnel can exercise, holding people accountable for their decisions, instituting compensation incentives that reward people for doing their jobs in a manner that contributes to good company performance, and creating a corporate culture where there's strong peer pressure on individuals to act responsibly.

In a highly centralized organization structure, top executives retain authority for most strategic and operating decisions and keep a tight rein on business-unit heads, department heads, and the managers of key operating units; comparatively little discretionary authority is granted to frontline supervisors and rank-and-file employees. The command-and-control paradigm of centralized structures is based on the underlying assumption that frontline personnel have neither the time nor the inclination to direct and properly control the work they are performing, and that they lack the knowledge and judgment to make wise decisions about how best to do it.

The big advantage of an authoritarian structure is that it is easy to know who is accountable when things do not go well. But there are some serious disadvantages. Hierarchical command-and-control structures make an organization sluggish in responding to changing conditions because of the time it takes for the review/approval process to run up all the layers of the management bureaucracy. Also, centralized decision making is often impractical—the larger the company and the more scattered its operations, the more that decision-making authority has to be delegated to managers closer to the scene of the action.

ALLOCATING RESOURCES TO STRATEGY-CRITICAL ACTIVITIES

▶ **LO2**

Learn why resource allocation should always be based on strategic priorities.

Early in the process of implementing and executing a new or different strategy, top management must determine what funding is needed to execute new strategic initiatives, to bolster value-creating processes, and to strengthen the company's capabilities and competencies. This includes careful screening of requests for more people and new facilities and equipment, approving those that hold promise for making a contribution to strategy execution, and turning down those that don't. Should internal cash flows prove insufficient to fund the planned strategic initiatives, then management must raise additional funds through borrowing or selling additional shares of stock to willing investors.

A company's ability to marshal the resources needed to support new strategic initiatives has a major impact on the strategy execution process. Too little funding slows progress and impedes the efforts of organizational units to execute their pieces of the strategic plan proficiently. Too much funding wastes organizational resources and reduces financial performance. Both outcomes argue for managers to be deeply involved in reviewing budget proposals and directing the proper amounts of resources to strategy-critical organization units.

A change in strategy nearly always calls for budget reallocations and resource shifting. Previously important units having a lesser role in the new strategy may need downsizing. Units that now have a bigger strategic role may need more people, new equipment, additional facilities, and above-average increases in their operating budgets. Strategy implementers have to exercise their power to put enough resources behind new strategic initiatives to make things happen, and they have to make the tough decisions to kill projects and activities that are no longer justified. Honda's strong support of R&D activities allowed it to develop the first low-polluting four-stroke outboard marine engine, a wide range of ultra-low-emission cars, the first hybrid car (Honda Insight) in the U.S. market, and the first hydrogen fuel cell car

> A company's strategic priorities must drive how capital allocations are made and the size of each unit's operating budgets.

(Honda Clarity). However, Honda managers had no trouble stopping production of the Insight in 2006 when its sales failed to take off and then shifting resources to the development and manufacture of other promising hybrid models, including a redesigned Insight that was launched in the United States in 2009.

LO3

Understand why policies and procedures should be designed to facilitate good strategy execution.

INSTITUTING STRATEGY-SUPPORTIVE POLICIES AND PROCEDURES

A company's policies and procedures can either assist or become a barrier to good strategy execution. Anytime a company makes changes to its business strategy, managers are well advised to carefully review existing policies and procedures and revise or discard those that are out of sync. Well-conceived policies and operating procedures act to facilitate organizational change and good strategy execution in three ways:

> Well-conceived policies and procedures aid strategy execution; out-of-sync ones are barriers to effective implementation.

1. *Policies and procedures help enforce needed consistency in how particular strategy critical activities are performed.* Standardization and strict conformity are sometimes desirable components of good strategy execution. Eliminating significant differences in the operating practices of different plants, sales regions, or customer service centers helps a company deliver consistent product quality and service to customers.

2. *Policies and procedures support change programs by providing top-down guidance regarding how certain things now need to be done.* Asking people to alter established habits and procedures always upsets the internal order of things. It is normal for pockets of resistance to develop and for people to exhibit some degree of stress and anxiety about how the changes will affect them. Policies are a particularly useful way to counteract tendencies for some people to resist change—most people refrain from violating company policy or going against recommended practices and procedures without first gaining clearance or having strong justification.

3. *Well-conceived policies and procedures promote a work climate that facilitates good strategy execution.* Managers can use the policy-changing process as a

powerful lever for changing the corporate culture in ways that produce a stronger fit with the new strategy.

McDonald's policy manual spells out detailed procedures that personnel in each McDonald's unit are expected to observe to ensure consistent quality across its 31,000 units. For example, "Cooks must turn, never flip, hamburgers. If they haven't been purchased, Big Macs must be discarded in 10 minutes after being cooked and French fries in 7 minutes." To get store personnel to dedicate themselves to outstanding customer service, Nordstrom has a policy of promoting only those people whose personnel records contain evidence of "heroic acts" to please customers, especially customers who may have made "unreasonable requests" that require special efforts.

One of the big policy-making issues concerns what activities need to be rigidly prescribed and what activities allow room for independent action on the part of empowered personnel. Few companies need thick policy manuals to prescribe exactly how daily operations are to be conducted. Too much policy can be confusing and erect obstacles to good strategy implementation. There is wisdom in a middle approach: *Prescribe enough policies to place boundaries on employees' actions; then empower them to act within these boundaries in whatever way they think makes sense.* Allowing company personnel to act anywhere between the "white lines" is especially appropriate when individual creativity and initiative are more essential to good strategy execution than standardization and strict conformity.

STRIVING FOR CONTINUOUS IMPROVEMENT IN PROCESSES AND ACTIVITIES

Company managers can significantly advance the cause of superior strategy execution by pushing organization units and company personnel to strive for continuous improvement in how value chain activities are performed. In aiming for operating excellence, many companies have come to rely on three potent management tools: business process reengineering, total quality management (TQM) programs, and Six Sigma quality control techniques. *Business process reengineering* involves pulling the pieces of strategy-critical activities out of different departments and unifying their performance in a single department or cross-functional work group.[8] When done properly, business process reengineering can produce dramatic operating benefits. In the order-processing section of General Electric's circuit breaker division, elapsed time from order receipt to delivery was cut from three weeks to three days by consolidating six production units into one, reducing a variety of former inventory and handling steps, automating the design system to replace a human custom-design process, and cutting the organizational layers between managers and workers from three to one. Productivity rose 20 percent in one year, and unit manufacturing costs dropped 30 percent.[9]

Total quality management (TQM) is a philosophy of managing a set of business practices that emphasizes continuous improvement in all phases of operations, 100 percent accuracy in performing tasks, involvement and empowerment of employees at all levels, team-based work design, benchmarking,

> **▶ LO4**
>
> Understand how process management programs that drive continuous improvement help an organization achieve operating excellence.

and total customer satisfaction.[10] While TQM concentrates on the production of quality goods and fully satisfying customer expectations, it achieves its biggest successes when it is extended to employee efforts in *all departments*—human resources, billing, R&D, engineering, accounting and records, and information systems. It involves reforming the corporate culture and shifting to a total quality/continuous improvement business philosophy that permeates every facet of the organization.[11] TQM doctrine preaches that there's no such thing as "good enough" and that everyone has a responsibility to participate in continuous improvement. TQM is thus a race without a finish. Success comes from making little steps forward each day, a process that the Japanese call *kaizen.*

Six Sigma quality control consists of a disciplined, statistics-based system aimed at producing not more than 3.4 defects per million iterations for any business process—from manufacturing to customer transactions.[12] The Six Sigma process of define, measure, analyze, improve, and control (DMAIC, pronounced *Dee-may-ic*) is an improvement system for existing processes falling below specification. The Six Sigma DMADV (define, measure, analyze, design, and verify) methodology is used to develop *new* processes or products at Six Sigma quality levels.[13] DMADV is sometimes referred to as Design for Six Sigma (DFSS). The statistical thinking underlying Six Sigma is based on the following three principles: All work is a process, all processes have variability, and all processes create data that explain variability.[14] To illustrate how these three principles work, consider the case of a Milwaukee hospital that used Six Sigma to map the prescription-filling process. Prescriptions written in the hospital originated with a doctor's write-up, were filled by the hospital pharmacy, and then administered by nurses. DMAIC analysis revealed that most mistakes came from misreading the doctor's handwriting.[15] The hospital implemented a program requiring doctors to type the prescription into a computer, which slashed the number of errors dramatically.

While Six Sigma programs often improve the efficiency of many operating activities and processes, evidence shows that Six Sigma programs can stifle innovation. The essence of Six Sigma is to reduce variability in processes, but creative processes, by nature, include quite a bit of variability. In many instances, breakthrough innovations occur only after thousands of ideas have been abandoned and promising ideas have gone through multiple iterations and extensive prototyping. Google CEO Eric Schmidt has commented that the innovation process is "anti–Six Sigma" and applying Six Sigma principles to those performing creative work at Google would choke off innovation at the company.[16]

James McNerney, a GE executive and proponent of Six Sigma, became CEO at 3M Corporation and was unable to establish a long-term track record for innovation following his institution of Six Sigma-based principles at 3M. The company's researchers complained that the innovation process did not lend itself well to the extensive data collection and analysis required under Six Sigma and that too much time was spent completing reports that outlined the market potential and possible manufacturing concerns for projects in all stages of the R&D pipeline. Six Sigma rigidity and a freeze on 3M's R&D

budget from McNerney's first year as CEO through 2005 was blamed for the company's drop from number one to number seven on the Boston Consulting Group's list of Most Innovative Companies.[17]

A blended approach to Six Sigma implementation that is gaining in popularity pursues incremental improvements in operating efficiency, while R&D and other processes that allow the company to develop new ways of offering value to customers are given more free rein. Managers of these *ambidextrous organizations* are adept at employing continuous improvement in operating processes but allowing R&D to operate under a set of rules that allows for the development of breakthrough innovations. Ciba Vision, a global leader in contact lenses, dramatically reduced operating expenses through the use of continuous improvement programs, while simultaneously and harmoniously developing new series of contact lens products that grew its revenues by 300 percent over a 10-year period.[18]

The Difference between Business Process Reengineering and Continuous Improvement Programs

Business process reengineering and continuous improvement efforts such as TQM and Six Sigma both aim at improved efficiency, better product quality, and greater customer satisfaction. The essential difference between business process reengineering and continuous improvement programs is that reengineering aims at *quantum gains* on the order of 30 to 50 percent or more whereas total quality programs stress *incremental progress*—striving for inch-by-inch gains again and again in a never-ending stream. The two approaches to improved performance of value chain activities and operating excellence are not mutually exclusive; it makes sense to use them in tandem. Reengineering can be used first to produce a good basic design that

> The purpose of using benchmarking, best practices, business process reengineering, TQM, Six Sigma, or other operational improvement programs is to improve the performance of strategy-critical activities and promote superior strategy execution.

yields quick, dramatic improvements in performing a business process. Total quality programs can then be used as a follow-up to deliver continuing improvements.

INSTALLING INFORMATION AND OPERATING SYSTEMS

Company strategies and value-creating internal processes can't be executed well without a number of internal operating systems. Amazon.com ships books, CDs, toys, and a myriad of other items from fully computerized warehouses with a capacity of over 17½ million square feet. The warehouses are so technologically sophisticated that they require about as many lines of code to run as Amazon's website does. Using complex picking algorithms, computers initiate the order-picking process by sending signals to workers' wireless receivers, telling them which items to pick off the shelves in which order. Computers also generate data on misboxed items, chute backup times, line speed, worker productivity, and shipping weights on orders. Systems

▶LO5

Recognize the role of information and operating systems in enabling company personnel to carry out their strategic roles proficiently.

are upgraded regularly, and productivity improvements are aggressively pursued. In 2003 Amazon's systems allowed it to achieve an inventory turnover of 20, compared to an industry average inventory turnover of 15. Amazon's warehouse efficiency and cost per order filled was so low that one of the fastest-growing and most profitable parts of Amazon's business was using its warehouses to run the e-commerce operations of large retail chains such as Target.

Telephone companies have elaborate information systems to measure signal quality, connection times, interrupts, wrong connections, billing errors, and other measures of reliability that affect customer service and satisfaction. British Petroleum (BP) has outfitted railcars carrying hazardous materials with sensors and global-positioning systems so that it can track the status, location, and other information about these shipments via satellite and relay the data to its corporate intranet.

> Having state-of-the-art operating systems, information systems, and real-time data is integral to competent strategy execution and operating excellence.

At eBay, there are systems for real-time monitoring of new listings, bidding activity, website traffic, and page views.

Information systems need to cover five broad areas: (1) customer data, (2) operations data, (3) employee data, (4) supplier/partner/collaborative ally data, and (5) financial performance data. All key strategic performance indicators have to be tracked and reported as often as practical. Long the norm, monthly profit-and-loss statements and monthly statistical summaries are fast being replaced with daily statistical updates and even up-to-the-minute performance monitoring. Many retail companies have automated online systems that generate daily sales reports for each store and maintain up-to-the-minute inventory and sales records on each item. Manufacturing plants typically generate daily production reports and track labor productivity on every shift. Many retailers and manufacturers have online data systems connecting them with their suppliers that monitor the status of inventories, track shipments and deliveries, and measure defect rates. Regardless of the industry, real-time information systems permit company managers to stay on top of implementation initiatives and daily operations, and to intervene if things seem to be drifting off course.

USING REWARDS AND INCENTIVES TO PROMOTE BETTER STRATEGY EXECUTION

LO6

Learn how and why the use of well-designed incentives and rewards can be management's single most powerful tool for promoting operating excellence.

To create a strategy-supportive system of rewards and incentives, a company must emphasize rewarding people for accomplishing results related to creating value for customers, not for just dutifully performing assigned tasks. Focusing jobholders' attention and energy on what to *achieve* as opposed to what to *do* makes the work environment results-oriented. It is flawed management to tie incentives and rewards to satisfactory performance of duties and activities instead of desired business outcomes and company achievements.[19] In any job, performing assigned tasks is not equivalent to achieving intended outcomes. Diligently showing up for work and attending to job assignment does not, by itself, guarantee results. As any student knows, the fact that an instructor teaches and students go to class doesn't necessarily mean that the students are learning.

> A properly designed reward structure is management's most powerful tool for gaining employee commitment to superior strategy execution and excellent operating results.

Motivation and Reward Systems

It is important for both organization units and individuals to be properly aligned with strategic priorities and enthusiastically committed to executing strategy. *To get employees' sustained, energetic commitment, management has to be resourceful in designing and using motivational incentives—both monetary and nonmonetary.* The more a manager understands what motivates subordinates and is able to use appropriate motivational incentives, the greater will be employees' commitment to good day-in, day-out strategy execution and achievement of performance targets.

Guidelines for Designing Monetary Incentive Systems

Guidelines for creating incentive compensation systems that link employee behavior to organizational objectives include:

1. *Make the performance payoff a major, not minor, piece of the total compensation package.* The payoff for high-performing individuals and teams must be meaningfully greater than the payoff for average performers, and the payoff for average performers meaningfully bigger than for below-average performers.

2. *Have incentives that extend to all managers and all workers, not just top management.* Lower-level managers and employees are just as likely as senior executives to be motivated by the possibility of lucrative rewards.

3. *Administer the reward system with scrupulous objectivity and fairness.* If performance standards are set unrealistically high or if individual/group performance evaluations are not accurate and well documented, dissatisfaction with the system will overcome any positive benefits.

4. *Tie incentives to performance outcomes directly linked to good strategy execution and financial performance.* Incentives should never be paid just because people are thought to be "doing a good job" or because they "work hard." An argument can be presented that exceptions should be made in giving rewards to people who've come up short because of circumstances beyond their control. The problem with making exceptions for unknowable, uncontrollable, or unforeseeable circumstances is that once good excuses start to creep into justifying rewards for subpar results, the door is open for all kinds of reasons why actual performance has failed to match targeted performance.

5. *Make sure the performance targets that each individual or team is expected to achieve involve outcomes that the individual or team can personally affect.* The role of incentives is to enhance individual commitment and channel behavior in beneficial directions.

6. *Keep the time between achieving the target performance outcome and the payment of the reward as short as possible.* Weekly or monthly payments for good performance work much better than annual payments for employees in most job categories. Annual bonus payouts work best for higher-level managers and for situations where target outcome relates to overall company profitability or stock price performance.

Once the incentives are designed, they have to be communicated and explained. Everybody needs to understand how their incentive compensation is calculated and how individual/group performance targets contribute to organizational performance targets.

Nonmonetary Rewards

Financial incentives generally head the list of motivating tools for trying to gain wholehearted employee commitment to good strategy execution and operating excellence. But most successful companies also make extensive use of nonmonetary incentives. Some of the most important nonmonetary approaches used to enhance motivation are listed below:[20]

- *Provide attractive perks and fringe benefits.* The various options include full coverage of health insurance premiums; college tuition reimbursement; paid vacation time; on-site child care; on-site fitness centers; telecommuting; and compressed workweeks (four 10-hour days instead of five 8-hour days).

- *Adopt promotion from within policies.* This practice helps bind workers to their employers and employers to their workers, plus it is an incentive for good performance.

- *Act on suggestions from employees.* Research indicates that the moves of many companies to push decision making down the line and empower employees increases employee motivation and satisfaction, as well as boosting productivity.

- *Create a work atmosphere in which there is genuine sincerity, caring, and mutual respect among workers and between management and employees.* A "family" work environment where people are on a first-name basis and there is strong camaraderie promotes teamwork and cross-unit collaboration.

- *Share information with employees about financial performance, strategy, operational measures, market conditions, and competitors' actions.* Broad disclosure and prompt communication send the message that managers trust their workers.

- *Have attractive office spaces and facilities.* A workplace environment with appealing features and amenities usually has decidedly positive effects on employee morale and productivity.

Concepts & Connections 10.2 presents specific examples of the motivational tactics employed by several prominent companies that have appeared on *Fortune*'s list of "The 100 Best Companies to Work for in America."

CONCEPTS & CONNECTIONS 10.2

WHAT COMPANIES DO TO MOTIVATE AND REWARD EMPLOYEES

Companies have come up with an impressive variety of motivational and reward practices to help create a work environment that energizes employees and promotes better strategy execution. Here's a sampling of what companies are doing:

- Google has a sprawling 20-building headquarters complex known as the Googleplex where its several thousand employees have access to 19 cafes and 60 snack centers, unlimited ice cream, four gyms, heated swimming pools, ping-pong and pool tables, and community bicycles to go from building to building. Management built the Googleplex to be "a dream workplace" and a showcase for environmentally correct building design and construction.

- Lincoln Electric, widely known for its piecework pay scheme and incentive bonus plan, rewards individual productivity by paying workers for each nondefective piece produced. Workers have to correct quality problems on their own time; defects in products used by customers can be traced back to the worker who caused them. Lincoln's piecework plan motivates workers to pay attention to both quality and volume produced. In addition, the company sets aside a substantial portion of its profits above a specified base for worker bonuses. To determine bonus size, Lincoln Electric rates each worker on four equally important performance measures: (1) dependability, (2) quality, (3) output, and (4) ideas and cooperation. The higher a worker's merit rating, the higher the incentive bonus earned; the highest rated

workers in good profit years receive bonuses of as much as 110 percent of their piecework compensation.

- Nordstrom, widely regarded for its superior in-house customer service experience, typically pays its retail salespeople an hourly wage higher than the prevailing rates paid by other department store chains plus a commission on each sale. Spurred by a culture that encourages salespeople to go all out to satisfy customers and to seek out and promote new fashion ideas, Nordstrom salespeople often earn twice the average incomes of sales employees at competing stores. The typical Nordstrom salesperson earns nearly $38,000 per year, and sales department managers earn, on average, $49,500 per year. Nordstrom's rules for employees are simple: "Rule #1: Use your good judgment in all situations. There will be no additional rules."

- At W. L. Gore (the maker of Gore-Tex), employees get to choose what project/team they work on and each team member's compensation is based on other team members' rankings of his or her contribution to the enterprise.

- At biotech leader Amgen, employees get 16 paid holidays, generous vacation time, tuition reimbursements up to $10,000, on-site massages, discounted car-wash services, and the convenience of shopping at on-site farmers' markets.

Sources: *Fortune*'s lists of the 100 best companies to work for in America, 2002, 2004, 2005, 2008, 2009, and 2010; Jefferson Graham, "The Search Engine That Could," *USA Today*, August 26, 2003, p. B3; and company websites, accessed June 2010.

INSTILLING A CORPORATE CULTURE THAT PROMOTES GOOD STRATEGY EXECUTION

LO7

Gain an understanding of how and why a company's culture can aid the drive for proficient strategy execution.

Every company has its own unique culture. The character of a company's culture or work climate defines "how we do things around here," its approach to people management, and the "chemistry" that permeates its work environment. The meshing of shared core values, beliefs, ingrained behaviors and attitudes, and business principles constitutes a company's **corporate culture**. A company's culture is important because it influences the organization's actions and approaches to conducting business—in a very real sense, the culture is the company's organizational DNA.[21]

> **CORE CONCEPT**
>
> **Corporate culture** is a company's internal work climate and is shaped by its core values, beliefs, and business principles. A company's culture is important because it influences its traditions, work practices, and style of operating.

The psyche of corporate cultures varies widely. For instance, the bedrock of Walmart's culture is dedication to customer satisfaction, zealous pursuit of low costs and frugal operating practices, a strong work ethic, ritualistic Saturday-morning headquarters meetings to exchange ideas and review problems, and company executives' commitment to visiting stores, listening to customers, and soliciting suggestions from employees. General Electric's culture is founded on a hard-driving, results-oriented atmosphere (where all of the company's business divisions are held to a standard of being number one or two in their industries as well as achieving good business results); extensive cross-business sharing of ideas, best practices, and learning; the reliance on "workout sessions" to identify, debate, and resolve burning issues; a commitment to Six Sigma quality; and globalization of the company.

High-Performance Cultures

Some companies have so-called "high-performance" cultures where the stand-out cultural traits are a "can-do" spirit, pride in doing things right, no-excuses accountability, and a pervasive results-oriented work climate where people go the extra mile to meet or beat stretch objectives. In high-performance cultures, there's a strong sense of involvement on the part of company personnel and emphasis on individual initiative and creativity. Performance expectations are clearly stated for the company as a whole, for each organizational unit, and for each individual. Issues and problems are promptly addressed—there's a razor-sharp focus on what needs to be done. A high-performance culture where there's constructive pressure to achieve good results is a valuable contributor to good strategy execution and operating excellence. Results-oriented cultures are permeated with a spirit of achievement and have a good track record in meeting or beating performance targets.[22]

The challenge in creating a high-performance culture is to inspire high loyalty and dedication on the part of employees, such that they are energized to put forth their very best efforts to do things right. Managers have to take pains to reinforce constructive behavior, reward top performers, and purge habits and behaviors that stand in the way of good results. They must work at knowing the strengths and weaknesses of their subordinates, so as to better match talent with task. In sum, there has to be an overall disciplined, performance-focused approach to managing the organization.

Adaptive Cultures

The hallmark of adaptive corporate cultures is willingness on the part of organizational members to accept change and take on the challenge of introducing and executing new strategies. In direct contrast to change-resistant cultures, **adaptive cultures** are very supportive of managers and employees at all ranks who propose or help initiate useful change. Internal entrepreneurship on the part of individuals and groups is encouraged and rewarded. Senior executives seek out, support, and promote individuals who exercise initiative, spot opportunities for improvement, and display the skills to take advantage of them.

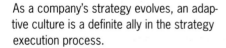
As a company's strategy evolves, an adaptive culture is a definite ally in the strategy execution process.

As in high-performance cultures, the company exhibits a proactive approach to identifying issues, evaluating the implications and options, and quickly moving ahead with workable solutions.

Technology companies, software companies, and Internet-based companies are good illustrations of organizations with adaptive cultures. Such companies thrive on change—driving it, leading it, and capitalizing on it (but sometimes also succumbing to change when they make the wrong move or are swamped by better technologies or the superior business models of rivals). Companies such as Google, Cisco Systems, eBay, Apple, Amazon.com, and Dell cultivate the capability to act and react rapidly. They are avid practitioners of entrepreneurship and innovation, with a demonstrated willingness to take bold risks to create new products, new businesses, and new industries. To create and nurture a culture that can adapt rapidly to changing or shifting business conditions, they staff their organizations with people who are proactive, who rise to the challenge of change, and who have an aptitude for adapting.

In fast-changing business environments, a corporate culture that is receptive to altering organizational practices and behaviors is a virtual necessity. However, adaptive cultures work to the advantage of all companies, not just those in rapid-change environments. Every company operates in a market and business climate that is changing to one degree or another. *As a company's strategy evolves, an adaptive culture is a definite ally in the strategy-implementing, strategy-executing process as compared to cultures that have to be coaxed and cajoled to change.*

Unhealthy Corporate Cultures

The distinctive characteristic of an unhealthy corporate culture is the presence of counterproductive cultural traits that adversely impact the work climate and company performance.[23] Five particularly unhealthy cultural traits are a heavily politicized internal environment, hostility to change, an insular "not invented here" mind-set, a disregard for high ethical standards, and the presence of incompatible, clashing subcultures.

Politicized Cultures   A politicized internal environment is unhealthy because political infighting consumes a great deal of organizational energy and often results in the company's strategic agenda taking a backseat to political maneuvering. In companies where internal politics pervades the work climate, empire-building managers pursue their own agendas, and the positions they take on issues are usually aimed at protecting or expanding their turf. The support or opposition of politically influential executives and/or coalitions among departments with vested interests in a particular outcome typically weighs heavily in deciding what actions the company takes. All this maneuvering detracts from efforts to execute strategy with real proficiency and frustrates company personnel who are less political and more inclined to do what is in the company's best interests.

Change-Resistant Cultures   Change-resistant cultures encourage a number of undesirable or unhealthy behaviors—avoiding risks, hesitation in pursuing emerging opportunities, and widespread aversion to continuous improvement in performing value chain activities. Change-resistant companies have little appetite for being first movers or fast followers, believing that being in the forefront of change is too risky and that acting too quickly increases vulnerability to costly mistakes. They are more inclined to adopt a wait-and-see posture, learn from the missteps of early movers, and then move forward cautiously with initiatives that are deemed safe. Hostility to change is most often found in companies with multilayered management bureaucracies that have enjoyed considerable market success in years past and that are wedded to the "We have done it this way for years" syndrome.

General Motors, IBM, Sears, and Eastman Kodak are classic examples of companies whose change-resistant bureaucracies have damaged their market standings and financial performance; clinging to what made them successful, they were reluctant to alter operating practices and modify their business approaches when signals of market change first sounded. As strategies of gradual change won out over bold innovation, all four lost market share to rivals that quickly moved to institute changes more in tune with evolving market conditions and buyer preferences. While IBM has made strides in building a culture needed for market success, Sears, GM, and Kodak are still struggling to recoup lost ground.

Insular, Inwardly Focused Cultures   Sometimes a company reigns as an industry leader or enjoys great market success for so long that its personnel start to believe they have all the answers or can develop them on their own. Such confidence breeds arrogance—company personnel discount the merits of what outsiders are doing and what can be learned by studying best-in-class performers. Benchmarking and a search for the best practices of outsiders are seen as offering little payoff. The big risk of a must-be-invented-here mind-set and insular cultural thinking is that the company can underestimate the competencies and accomplishments of rival companies and overestimate its own progress—with a resulting loss of competitive advantage over time.

Unethical and Greed-Driven Cultures   Companies that have little regard for ethical standards or that are run by executives driven by greed and ego gratification are scandals waiting to happen. Enron's collapse in 2001 was largely the product of an ethically dysfunctional corporate culture—while Enron's culture embraced the positives of product innovation, aggressive risk taking, and a driving ambition to lead global change in the energy business, its executives exuded the negatives of arrogance, ego, greed, and an "ends-justify-the-means" mentality in pursuing stretch revenue and profitability targets.[24] A number of Enron's senior managers were all too willing to wink at unethical behavior, to cross over the line to unethical (and sometimes criminal) behavior themselves, and to deliberately stretch generally accepted accounting principles to make Enron's financial performance look far better than it really was.

Incompatible Subcultures   It is not unusual for companies to have multiple subcultures with values, beliefs, and ingrained behaviors and attitudes varying to some extent by department, geographic location, division, or business unit. These subcultures within a company don't pose a problem as long as the subcultures don't conflict with the overarching corporate work climate and are supportive of the strategy execution effort. Multiple subcultures become unhealthy when they are incompatible with each other or the overall corporate culture. The existence of conflicting business philosophies and values eventually leads to inconsistent strategy execution. Incompatible subcultures arise most commonly because of important cultural differences between a company's culture and those of a recently acquired company or because of a merger between companies with cultural differences. Cultural due diligence is often as important as financial due diligence in deciding whether to go forward on an acquisition or merger. On a number of occasions, companies have decided to pass on acquiring particular companies because of culture conflicts they believed would be hard to resolve.

Changing a Problem Culture

Changing a company culture that impedes proficient strategy execution is among the toughest management tasks. It is natural for company personnel to cling to familiar practices and to be wary, if not hostile, to new approaches toward how things are to be done. Consequently, it takes concerted management action over a period of time to root out certain unwanted behaviors and replace an out-of-sync culture with more effective ways of doing things. *The single most visible factor that distinguishes successful culture-change efforts from failed attempts is competent leadership at the top.* Great power is needed to force major cultural change and overcome the unremitting resistance of entrenched cultures—and great power is possessed only by the most senior executives, especially the CEO. However, while top management must lead the culture change effort, instilling new cultural behaviors is a job for the whole management team. Middle managers and frontline supervisors play a key role in implementing the new work practices and operating approaches, helping win rank-and-file acceptance of and support for the changes, and instilling the desired behavioral norms.

As shown in Figure 10.2, the first step in fixing a problem culture is for top management to identify those facets of the present culture that pose obstacles to executing new strategic initiatives. Second, managers have to clearly define the desired new behaviors and features of the culture they want to create. Third, managers have to convince company personnel why the present culture poses problems and why and how new behaviors and operating approaches will improve company performance. Finally, all the talk about remodeling the present culture has to be followed swiftly by visible, forceful actions on the part of management to promote the desired new behaviors and work practices.

Making a Compelling Case for a Culture Change The place for management to begin a major remodeling of the corporate culture is by selling company personnel on the need for new-style behaviors and work practices. This means making a compelling case for why the company's new strategic direction and culture-remodeling efforts are in the organization's best interests and why company personnel should wholeheartedly join the effort to do things somewhat differently. This can be done by:

▶FIGURE 10.2 **Steps in Changing a Problem Culture**

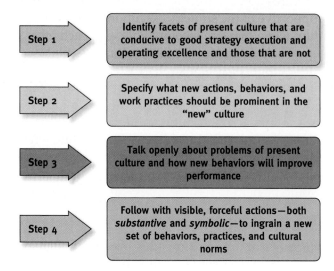

- Step 1 → Identify facets of present culture that are conducive to good strategy execution and operating excellence and those that are not
- Step 2 → Specify what new actions, behaviors, and work practices should be prominent in the "new" culture
- Step 3 → Talk openly about problems of present culture and how new behaviors will improve performance
- Step 4 → Follow with visible, forceful actions—both *substantive* and *symbolic*—to ingrain a new set of behaviors, practices, and cultural norms

- Citing reasons the current strategy has to be modified and why new strategic initiatives are being undertaken. The case for altering the old strategy usually needs to be predicated on its shortcomings—why sales are growing slowly, why too many customers are opting to go with the products of rivals, why costs are too high, and so on. There may be merit in holding events where managers and other key personnel are forced to listen to dissatisfied customers or the complaints of strategic allies.
- Citing why and how certain behavioral norms and work practices in the current culture pose obstacles to good execution of new strategic initiatives.
- Explaining why new behaviors and work practices have important roles in the new culture and will produce better results.

Management's efforts to make a persuasive case for changing what is deemed to be a problem culture must be *quickly followed* by forceful, high-profile actions across several fronts. The actions to implant the new culture must be both substantive and symbolic.

Substantive Culture-Changing Actions   No culture change effort can get very far when leaders merely talk about the need for different actions, behaviors, and work practices. Company executives have to give the culture-change effort some teeth by initiating *a series of actions* that company personnel will see as *unmistakable support* for the change program. The strongest signs that management is truly committed to instilling a new culture include:

1. Replacing key executives who stonewall needed organizational and cultural changes.
2. Promoting individuals who have stepped forward to advocate the shift to a different culture and who can serve as role models for the desired cultural behavior.

3. Appointing outsiders with the desired cultural attributes to high-profile positions—bringing in new-breed managers sends an unambiguous message that a new era is dawning.

4. Screening all candidates for new positions carefully, hiring only those who appear to fit in with the new culture.

5. Mandating that all company personnel attend culture-training programs to better understand the culture-related actions and behaviors that are expected.

6. Designing compensation incentives that boost the pay of teams and individuals who display the desired cultural behaviors, while hitting change-resisters in the pocketbook.

7. Revising policies and procedures in ways that will help drive cultural change.

Symbolic Culture-Changing Actions   There's also an important place for symbolic managerial actions to alter a problem culture and tighten the strategy–culture fit. The most important symbolic actions are those that top executives take to *lead by example.* For instance, if the organization's strategy involves a drive to become the industry's low-cost producer, senior managers must display frugality in their own actions and decisions: inexpensive decorations in the executive suite, conservative expense accounts and entertainment allowances, a lean staff in the corporate office, few executive perks, and so on. At Walmart, all the executive offices are simply decorated; executives are habitually frugal in their own actions, and they are zealous in their own efforts to control costs and promote greater efficiency. At Nucor, one of the world's low-cost producers of steel products, executives fly coach class and use taxis at airports rather than limousines. Top executives must be alert to the fact that company personnel will be watching their actions and decisions to see if they are walking the talk.[25]

Another category of symbolic actions includes holding ceremonial events to single out and honor people whose actions and performance exemplify what is called for in the new culture. A point is made of holding events to celebrate each culture-change success. Executives sensitive to their role in promoting the strategy–culture fit make a habit of appearing at ceremonial functions to praise individuals and groups that get with the program. They show up at employee training programs to stress strategic priorities, values, ethical principles, and cultural norms. Every group gathering is seen as an opportunity to repeat and ingrain values, praise good deeds, and cite instances of how the new work practices and operating approaches have led to improved results.

LEADING THE STRATEGY EXECUTION PROCESS

For an enterprise to execute its strategy in truly proficient fashion and approach operating excellence, top executives have to take the lead in the implementation/execution process and personally drive the pace of progress. They have to be out in the field, seeing for themselves how well operations are going, gathering information firsthand, and gauging the progress being

▶**LO8**

Understand what constitutes effective managerial leadership in achieving superior strategy execution.

made. Proficient strategy execution requires company managers to be diligent and adept in spotting problems, learning what obstacles lie in the path of good execution, and then clearing the way for progress—the goal must be to produce better results speedily and productively.[26] In general, leading the drive for good strategy execution and operating excellence calls for three actions on the part of the manager:

- Staying on top of what is happening and closely monitoring progress.
- Putting constructive pressure on the organization to execute the strategy well and achieve operating excellence.
- Initiating corrective actions to improve strategy execution and achieve the targeted performance results.

Staying on Top of How Well Things Are Going

One of the best ways for executives to stay on top of the strategy execution process is by regularly visiting the field and talking with many different people at many different levels—a technique often labeled *managing by walking around* (MBWA). Walmart executives have had a long-standing practice of spending two to three days every week visiting stores and talking with store managers and employees. Jeff Bezos, Amazon.com's CEO, is noted for his frequent facilities visits and his insistence that other Amazon managers spend time in the trenches with their people to prevent overly abstract thinking and getting disconnected from the reality of what's happening.[27]

Most managers practice MBWA, attaching great importance to gathering information from people at different organizational levels about how well various aspects of the strategy execution are going. They believe facilities visits and face-to-face contacts give them a good feel for what progress is being made, what problems are being encountered, and whether additional resources or different approaches may be needed. Just as important, MBWA provides opportunities to give encouragement, lift spirits, shift attention from old to new priorities, and create excitement—all of which help mobilize organizational efforts behind strategy execution.

Putting Constructive Pressure on Organizational Units to Achieve Good Results and Operating Excellence

Managers have to be out front in mobilizing the effort for good strategy execution and operating excellence. Part of the leadership requirement here entails fostering a results-oriented work climate, where performance standards are high and a spirit of achievement is pervasive. Successfully leading the effort to foster a results-oriented, high-performance culture generally entails such leadership actions and managerial practices as:

- *Treating employees with dignity and respect.*
- *Encouraging employees to use initiative and creativity in performing their work.*
- *Setting stretch objectives* and clearly communicating an expectation that company personnel are to give their best in achieving performance targets.
- *Focusing attention on continuous improvement.*

- *Using the full range of motivational techniques and compensation incentives to reward high performance.*

- *Celebrating individual, group, and company successes.* Top management should miss no opportunity to express respect for individual employees and show appreciation of extraordinary individual and group effort.[28]

While leadership efforts to instill a spirit of high achievement into the culture usually accentuate the positive, there are negative reinforcers too. Low-performing workers and people who reject the results-oriented cultural emphasis have to be weeded out or at least moved to out-of-the-way positions. Average performers have to be candidly counseled that they have limited career potential unless they show more progress in the form of additional effort, better skills, and improved ability to deliver good results. In addition, managers whose units consistently perform poorly have to be replaced.

Pushing Corrective Actions to Improve Both the Company's Strategy and Its Execution

The leadership challenge of making corrective adjustments is twofold: deciding when adjustments are needed and deciding what adjustments to make. Both decisions are a normal and necessary part of managing the strategic management process, since no scheme for implementing and executing strategy can foresee all the events and problems that will arise.[29] There comes a time at every company when managers have to fine-tune or overhaul the company's strategy or its approaches to strategy execution and push for better results. Clearly, when a company's strategy or its execution efforts are not delivering good results, it is the leader's responsibility to step forward and push corrective actions.

→ → KEY POINTS

Implementing and executing strategy is an operations-driven activity revolving around the management of people and business processes. The managerial emphasis is on converting strategic plans into actions and good results. *Management's handling of the process of implementing and executing the chosen strategy can be considered successful if and when the company achieves the targeted strategic and financial performance and shows good progress in making its strategic vision a reality.*

Like crafting strategy, executing strategy is a job for a company's whole management team, not just a few senior managers. Top-level managers have to rely on the active support and cooperation of middle and lower-level managers to push strategy changes into functional areas and operating units and to see that the organization actually operates in accordance with the strategy on a daily basis.

Eight managerial tasks crop up repeatedly in company efforts to execute strategy:

1. *Building an organization capable of executing the strategy successfully.* Building an organization capable of good strategy execution entails three types of organization-building actions: (a) *staffing the organization*—assembling a talented,

can-do management team, and recruiting and retaining employees with the needed experience, technical skills, and intellectual capital, *(b) building and strengthening capabilities and core competencies* that will enable good strategy execution and updating them as strategy and external conditions change, and *(c) structuring the organization and work effort*—organizing value chain activities and business processes and deciding how much decision-making authority to push down to lower-level managers and frontline employees.

2. *Allocating ample resources to strategy-critical activities.* Managers implementing and executing a new or different strategy must identify the resource requirements of each new strategic initiative and then consider whether the current pattern of resource allocation and the budgets of the various subunits are suitable.

3. *Ensuring that policies and procedures facilitate rather than impede effective strategy execution.* Any time a company alters its strategy, managers should review existing policies and operating procedures, proactively revise or discard those that are out of sync, and formulate new ones to facilitate execution of new strategic initiatives.

4. *Adopting business processes that drive continuous improvement in how strategy execution activities are performed.* Reengineering core business processes and continuous improvement initiatives such as total quality management (TQM) or Six Sigma programs all aim at improved efficiency, lower costs, better product quality, and greater customer satisfaction.

5. *Installing information and operating systems that enable company personnel to perform essential activities.* Well-conceived state-of-the-art support systems not only facilitate better strategy execution but also strengthen organizational capabilities enough to provide a competitive edge over rivals.

6. *Tying rewards directly to the achievement of performance objectives.* For an incentive compensation system to work well *(a)* the monetary payoff should be a major piece of the compensation package, *(b)* the use of incentives should extend to all managers and workers, *(c)* the system should be administered with care and fairness, *(d)* the incentives should be linked to performance targets spelled out in the strategic plan, *(e)* each individual's performance targets should involve outcomes the person can personally affect, *(f)* rewards should promptly follow the determination of good performance, and *(g)* monetary rewards should be supplemented with liberal use of nonmonetary rewards.

7. *Fostering a corporate culture that promotes good strategy execution.* The psyche of corporate cultures varies widely. There are five types of unhealthy cultures: *(a)* those that are highly political and characterized by empire-building, *(b)* those that are change resistant, *(c)* those that are insular and inwardly focused, *(d)* those that are ethically unprincipled and are driven by greed, and *(e)* those that possess clashing subcultures that prevent a company from coordinating its strategy execution efforts. High-performance cultures and adaptive cultures both have positive features that are conducive to good strategy execution.

8. *Exerting the internal leadership needed to propel implementation forward.* Leading the drive for good strategy execution and operating excellence calls for three actions on the part of the manager: *(a)* staying on top of what is happening, closely monitoring progress, and learning what obstacles lie in the path of good execution; *(b)* putting constructive pressure on the organization to achieve good results and operating excellence; and *(c)* pushing corrective actions to improve strategy execution and achieve the targeted results.

ASSURANCE OF LEARNING EXERCISES

1. The heart of Toyota's strategy in motor vehicles is to outcompete rivals by manufacturing world-class, quality vehicles at lower costs and selling them at competitive price levels. Executing this strategy requires top-notch manufacturing capability and super-efficient management of people, equipment, and materials. Concepts & Connections 10.1, on page 211, discusses the principles, practices, and techniques grounded in Toyota's famed Toyota Production System. How does Toyota's philosophy of dealing with defects, empowering employees, and developing capabilities impact strategy execution? Why are its slogans such as "Never be satisfied" and "Ask yourself 'Why?' five times" important?

LO1

connect

www.mcgrawhillconnect.com

2. Implementing and executing a new or different strategy call for new resource allocations. Using your university's access to Lexis-Nexis or EBSCO, search for recent articles that discuss how a company has revised its pattern of resource allocation and divisional budgets to support new strategic initiatives.

LO2

3. Policies and procedures facilitate strategy execution when they are designed to fit the company's strategy and objectives. Using your university's access to Lexis-Nexis or EBSCO, search for recent articles that discuss how a company has revised its policies and procedures to provide better top-down guidance to company personnel about how certain things should be done.

LO3

4. Read some of the recent Six Sigma articles posted at www.isixsigma.com. Prepare a one-page report to your instructor detailing how Six Sigma is being used in various companies and what benefits these companies are reaping from Six Sigma implementation.

LO4

5. Company strategies can't be implemented or executed well without a number of support systems to carry on business operations. Using your university's access to Lexis-Nexis or EBSCO, search for recent articles that discuss how a company has used real-time information systems and control systems to aid the cause of good strategy execution.

LO5

6. Concepts & Connections 10.2, on page 221, provides a sampling of motivational tactics employed by several prominent companies (many of which appear on *Fortune*'s list of the 100 best companies to work for in America). Discuss how rewards at Google, Lincoln Electric, Nordstrom, W. L. Gore, and Amgen aid in the strategy execution efforts of each company.

LO6

connect

www.mcgrawhillconnect.com

7. Go to the Jobs section at www.intel.com and see what Intel has to say about its culture under the links for Careers, Diversity, and The Workplace. Does what's on this website appear to be just recruiting propaganda, or does it convey the type of work climate that management is actually trying to create? Explain your answer.

LO7

8. In the past couple of years, Liz Claiborne, Inc., has been trying to turn around its faltering Mexx chain. Use your favorite browser to search for information on the turnaround plan at Mexx and read at least two articles or reports on this subject. Describe in one to two pages the approach being taken. In your opinion, have the managers involved been demonstrating the kind of internal leadership needed for superior strategy execution at Mexx? Explain your answer.

LO8

LO1

1. How would you describe the organization of your company's top management team? Is some decision making decentralized and delegated to individual managers? If so, explain how the decentralization works. Or are decisions made more by consensus, with all co-managers having input? What do you see as the advantages and disadvantages of the decision-making approach your company is employing?

LO2

2. Have you and your co-managers allocated ample resources to strategy-critical areas? If so, explain how these investments have contributed to good strategy execution and improved company performance.

LO6

3. Does your company have opportunities to use incentive compensation techniques? If so, explain your company's approach to incentive compensation. Is there any hard evidence you can cite that indicates your company's use of incentive compensation techniques has worked? For example, have your company's compensation incentives actually boosted productivity? Can you cite evidence indicating the productivity gains have resulted in lower labor costs? If the productivity gains have *not* translated into lower labor costs, then is it fair to say that your company's use of incentive compensation is a failure?

LO7

4. If you were making a speech to company personnel, what would you tell them about the kind of corporate culture you would like to have at your company? What specific cultural traits would you like your company to exhibit? Explain.

LO8

5. Following each decision round, do you and your co-managers make corrective adjustments in either your company's strategy or how well the strategy is being executed? List at least three such adjustments you made in the most recent decision round. What hard evidence (in the form of results relating to your company's performance in the most recent year) can you cite that indicates the various corrective adjustments you made either succeeded or failed to improve your company's performance?

ENDNOTES

1. Christopher A. Bartlett and Sumantra Ghoshal, "Building Competitive Advantage through People," *MIT Sloan Management Review* 43, no. 2 (Winter 2002).

2. Justin Menkes, "Hiring for Smarts," *Harvard Business Review* 83, no. 11 (November 2005); and Justin Menkes, *Executive Intelligence* (New York: HarperCollins, 2005).

3. Larry Bossidy and Ram Charan, *Execution: The Discipline of Getting Things Done* (New York: Crown Business, 2002).

4. Jim Collins, *Good to Great* (New York: HarperBusiness, 2001).

5. David J. Teece, Gary Pisano, and Amy Shuen, "Dynamic Capabilities and Strategic Management," *Strategic Management Journal* 18, no. 7 (1997); and Constance E. Helfat and Margaret A. Peteraf, "The Dynamic Resource-Based View: Capability Lifecycles," *Strategic Management Journal* 24, no. 10 (2003).

6. Alfred Chandler, *Strategy and Structure* (Cambridge, MA: MIT Press, 1962).

7. Stanley E. Fawcett, Gary K. Rhoads, and Phillip Burnah, "People as the Bridge to Competitiveness:

Benchmarking the 'ABCs' of an Empowered Workforce," *Benchmarking: An International Journal* 11, no. 4 (2004).

8. Michael Hammer and James Champy, *Reengineering the Corporation* (New York: HarperBusiness, 1993).

9. Gene Hall, Jim Rosenthal, and Judy Wade, "How to Make Reengineering Really Work," *Harvard Business Review* 71, no. 6 (November–December 1993).

10. M. Walton, *The Deming Management Method* (New York: Pedigree, 1986); J. Juran, *Juran on Quality*

by Design (New York: Free Press, 1992); Philip Crosby, *Quality Is Free: The Act of Making Quality Certain* (New York: McGraw-Hill, 1979); S. George, *The Baldrige Quality System* (New York: John Wiley & Sons, 1992); and Mark J. Zbaracki, "The Rhetoric and Reality of Total Quality Management," *Administrative Science Quarterly* 43, no. 3 (September 1998).

11. Robert T. Amsden, Thomas W. Ferratt, and Davida M. Amsden, "TQM: Core Paradigm Changes," *Business Horizons* 39, no. 6 (November–December 1996).

12. Peter S. Pande and Larry Holpp, *What Is Six Sigma?* (New York: McGraw-Hill, 2002); Jiju Antony, "Some Pros and Cons of Six Sigma: An Academic Perspective," *The TQM Magazine* 16, no. 4 (2004); Peter S. Pande, Robert P. Neuman, and Roland R. Cavanagh, *The Six Sigma Way: How GE, Motorola and Other Top Companies Are Honing Their Performance* (New York: McGraw-Hill, 2000); Joseph Gordon and M. Joseph Gordon, Jr., *Six Sigma Quality for Business and Manufacture* (New York: Elsevier, 2002); and Godecke Wessel and Peter Burcher, "Six Sigma for Small and Medium-sized Enterprises," *The TQM Magazine* 16, no. 4 (2004).

13. Based on information posted at www.sixsigma.com, November 4, 2002.

14. Kennedy Smith, "Six Sigma for the Service Sector," *Quality Digest Magazine*, May 2003, www.qualitydigest.com, accessed September 28, 2003.

15. Del Jones, "Taking the Six Sigma Approach," *USA Today*, October 31, 2002.

16. As quoted in "A Dark Art No More," *The Economist* 385, no. 8550 (October 13, 2007).

17. Brian Hindo, "At 3M, a Struggle between Efficiency and Creativity," *BusinessWeek*, June 11, 2007.

18. Charles A. O'Reilly and Michael L. Tushman, "The Ambidextrous Organization," *Harvard Business Review* 82, no. 4 (April 2004).

19. See Steven Kerr, "On the Folly of Rewarding A while Hoping for B," *Academy of Management Executive* 9, no. 1 (February 1995); Steven Kerr, "Risky Business: The New Pay Game," *Fortune*, July 22, 1996; and Doran Twer, "Linking Pay to Business Objectives," *Journal of Business Strategy* 15, no. 4 (July–August 1994).

20. Jeffrey Pfeffer and John F. Veiga, "Putting People First for Organizational Success," *Academy of Management Executive* 13, no. 2 (May 1999); Linda K. Stroh and Paula M. Caliguiri, "Increasing Global Competitiveness through Effective People Management," *Journal of World Business* 33, no. 1 (Spring 1998); and articles in *Fortune* on the 100 best companies to work for (various issues).

21. Joanne Reid and Victoria Hubbell, "Creating a Performance Culture," *Ivey Business Journal* 69, no. 4 (March/April 2005).

22. Jay B. Barney and Delwyn N. Clark, *Resource-Based Theory: Creating and Sustaining Competitive Advantage* (New York: Oxford University Press, 2007).

23. John P. Kotter and James L. Heskett, *Corporate Culture and Performance* (New York: Free Press, 1992).

24. Kurt Eichenwald, *Conspiracy of Fools: A True Story* (New York: Broadway Books, 2005).

25. Judy D. Olian and Sara L. Rynes, "Making Total Quality Work: Aligning Organizational Processes, Performance Measures, and Stakeholders," *Human Resource Management* 30, no. 3 (Fall 1991).

26. Larry Bossidy and Ram Charan, *Confronting Reality: Doing What Matters to Get Things Right* (New York: Crown Business, 2004); Larry Bossidy and Ram Charan, *Execution: The Discipline of Getting Things Done* (New York: Crown Business, 2002): John P. Kotter, "Leading Change: Why Transformation Efforts Fail," *Harvard Business Review* 73, no. 2 (March–April 1995); Thomas M. Hout and John C. Carter, "Getting It Done: New Roles for Senior Executives," *Harvard Business Review* 73, no. 6 (November–December 1995); and Sumantra Ghoshal and Christopher A. Bartlett, "Changing the Role of Top Management: Beyond Structure to Processes," *Harvard Business Review* 73, no. 1 (January–February 1995).

27. Fred Vogelstein, "Winning the Amazon Way," *Fortune*, May 26, 2003.

28. Jeffrey Pfeffer, "Producing Sustainable Competitive Advantage through the Effective Management of People," *Academy of Management Executive* 9, no. 1 (February 1995).

29. Cynthia A. Montgomery, "Putting Leadership Back into Strategy," *Harvard Business Review* 86, no. 1 (January 2008).

Appendix

Ratio	How Calculated	What It Shows
Profitability Ratios		
1. Gross profit margin	$$\frac{\text{Sales revenues} - \text{Cost of goods sold}}{\text{Sales revenues}}$$	Shows the percentage of revenues available to cover operating expenses and yield a profit. Higher is better and the trend should be upward.
2. Operating profit margin (or return on sales)	$$\frac{\text{Sales revenues} - \text{Operating expenses}}{\text{Sales revenues}}$$ or $$\frac{\text{Operating income}}{\text{Sales revenues}}$$	Shows the profitability of current operations without regard to interest charges and income taxes. Higher is better and the trend should be upward.
3. Net profit margin (or net return on sales)	$$\frac{\text{Profits after taxes}}{\text{Sales revenues}}$$	Shows after-tax profits per dollar of sales. Higher is better and the trend should be upward.
4. Total return on assets	$$\frac{\text{Profits after taxes} + \text{Interest}}{\text{Total assets}}$$	A measure of the return on total monetary investment in the enterprise. Interest is added to after-tax profits to form the numerator since total assets are financed by creditors as well as by stockholders. Higher is better and the trend should be upward.
5. Net return on total assets (ROA)	$$\frac{\text{Profits after taxes}}{\text{Total assets}}$$	A measure of the return earned by stockholders on the firm's total assets. Higher is better, and the trend should be upward.
6. Return on stockholder's equity	$$\frac{\text{Profits after taxes}}{\text{Total stockholders' equity}}$$	Shows the return stockholders are earning on their capital investment in the enterprise. A return in the 12–15% range is "average," and the trend should be upward.
7. Return on invested capital (ROIC) — sometimes referred to as return on capital (ROCE)	$$\frac{\text{Profits after taxes}}{\text{Long term debt} + \text{Total stockholders' equity}}$$	A measure of the return shareholders are earning on the long-term monetary capital invested in the enterprise. Higher is better and the trend should be upward.
8. Earnings per share (EPS)	$$\frac{\text{Profits after taxes}}{\text{Number of shares of common stock outstanding}}$$	Shows the earnings for each share of common stock outstanding. The trend should be upward, and the bigger the annual percentage gains, the better.
Liquidity Ratios		
1. Current ratio	$$\frac{\text{Current assets}}{\text{Current liabilities}}$$	Shows a firm's ability to pay current liabilities using assets that can be converted to cash in the near term. Ratio should definitely be higher than 1.0; ratios of 2 or higher are better still.
2. Working capital	$$\text{Current assets} - \text{Current liabilities}$$	Bigger amounts are better because the company has more internal funds available to (1) pay its current liabilities on a timely basis and (2) finance inventory expansion, additional accounts receivable, and a larger base of operations without resorting to borrowing or raising more equity capital.
Leverage Ratios		
1. Total debt-to-assets ratio	$$\frac{\text{Total debt}}{\text{Total assets}}$$	Measures the extent to which borrowed funds (both short-term loans and long-term debt) have been used to finance the firm's operations. A low fraction or ratio is better—a high fraction indicates overuse of debt and greater risk of bankruptcy.

Ratio	How Calculated	What It Shows
2. Long-term debt-to-capital ratio	$\dfrac{\text{Long-term debt}}{\text{Long-term debt + Total stockholders' equity}}$	An important measure of creditworthiness and balance sheet strength. It indicates the percentage of capital investment in the enterprise that has been financed by both long-term lenders and stockholders. A ratio below 0.25 is usually preferable since monies invested by stockholders account for 75% or more of the company's total capital. The lower the ratio, the greater the capacity to borrow additional funds. Debt-to-capital ratios above 0.50 and certainly above 0.75 indicate a heavy and perhaps excessive reliance on long-term borrowing, lower creditworthiness, and weak balance sheet strength.
3. Debt-to-equity ratio	$\dfrac{\text{Total debt}}{\text{Total stockholders' equity}}$	Shows the balance between debt (funds borrowed both short-term and long-term) and the amount that stockholders have invested in the enterprise. The further the ratio is below 1.0, the greater the firm's ability to borrow additional funds. Ratios above 1.0 and definitely above 2.0 put creditors at greater risk, signal weaker balance sheet strength, and often result in lower credit ratings.
4. Long-term debt-to-equity ratio	$\dfrac{\text{Long-term debt}}{\text{Total stockholders' equity}}$	Shows the balance between long-term debt and stockholders' equity in the firm's *long-term* capital structure. Low ratios indicate greater capacity to borrow additional funds if needed.
5. Times-interest-earned (or coverage) ratio	$\dfrac{\text{Operating income}}{\text{Interest expenses}}$	Measures the ability to pay annual interest charges. Lenders usually insist on a minimum ratio of 2.0, but ratios progressively above 3.0 signal progressively better creditworthiness.

Activity Ratios

1. Days of inventory	$\dfrac{\text{Inventory}}{\text{Cost of goods sold} \div 365}$	Measures inventory management efficiency. Fewer days of inventory are usually better.
2. Inventory turnover	$\dfrac{\text{Cost of goods sold}}{\text{Inventory}}$	Measures the number of inventory turns per year. Higher is better.
3. Average collection period	$\dfrac{\text{Accounts receivable}}{\text{Total sales} \div 365}$ or $\dfrac{\text{Accounts receivable}}{\text{Average daily sales}}$	Indicates the average length of time the firm must wait after making a sale to receive cash payment. A shorter collection time is better.

Other Important Measures of Financial Performance

1. Dividend yield on common stock	$\dfrac{\text{Annual dividends per share}}{\text{Current market price per share}}$	A measure of the return that shareholders receive in the form of dividends. A "typical" dividend yield is 2–3%. The dividend yield for fast-growth companies is often below 1% (maybe even 0); the dividend yield for slow-growth companies can run 4–5%.
2. Price-earnings ratio	$\dfrac{\text{Current market price per share}}{\text{Earnings per share}}$	P-e ratios above 20 indicate strong investor confidence in a firm's outlook and earnings growth; firms whose future earnings are at risk or likely to grow slowly typically have ratios below 12.
3. Dividend payout ratio	$\dfrac{\text{Annual dividends per share}}{\text{Earnings per share}}$	Indicates the percentage of after-tax profits paid out as dividends.
4. Internal cash flow	After tax profits + Depreciation	A quick and rough estimate of the cash a company's business is generating after payment of operating expenses, interest, and taxes. Such amounts can be used for dividend payments or funding capital expenditures.
5. Free cash flow	After tax profits + Depreciation − Capital expenditures − Dividends	A quick and rough estimate of the cash a company's business is generating after payment of operating expenses, interest, taxes, dividends, and desirable reinvestments in the business. The larger a company's free cash flow, the greater is its ability to internally fund new strategic initiatives, repay debt, make new acquisitions, repurchase shares of stock, or increase dividend payments.

MYSTIC MONK COFFEE

David L. Turnipseed
University of South Alabama

As Father Daniel Mary, the prior of the Carmelite Order of monks in Clark, Wyoming, walked to chapel to preside over Mass, he noticed the sun glistening across the four-inch snowfall from the previous evening. Snow in June was not unheard of in Wyoming, but the late snowfall and the bright glow of the rising sun made him consider the opposing forces accompanying change and how he might best prepare his monastery to achieve his vision of creating a new Mount Carmel in the Rocky Mountains. His vision of transforming the small brotherhood of 13 monks living in a small home used as makeshift rectory into a 500-acre monastery that would include accommodations for 30 monks, a Gothic church, a convent for Carmelite nuns, a retreat center for lay visitors, and a hermitage presented a formidable challenge. However, as a former high school football player, boxer, bull rider, and man of great faith, Father Prior Daniel Mary was unaccustomed to shrinking from a challenge.

Father Prior had identified a nearby ranch for sale that met the requirements of his vision perfectly, but its current listing price of $8.9 million presented a financial obstacle to creating a place of prayer, worship, and solitude in the Rockies. The Carmelites had received a $250,000 donation that could be used toward the purchase, and the monastery had earned nearly $75,000 during the first year of its Mystic Monk coffee-roasting operations, but more money would be needed. The coffee roaster used to produce packaged coffee sold to Catholic consumers at the Mystic Monk Coffee website was reaching its capacity, but a larger roaster could be purchased for $35,000. Also, local Cody, Wyoming, business owners had begun a foundation for those wishing to donate to the monks' cause. Father Prior Daniel Mary did not have a great deal of experience in business matters but considered to what extent the monastery could rely on its Mystic Monk Coffee operations to fund the purchase of the ranch. If Mystic Monk Coffee was capable of making the vision a reality, what were the next steps in turning the coffee into land?

THE CARMELITE MONKS OF WYOMING

Carmelites are a religious order of the Catholic Church that was formed by men who traveled to the Holy Land as pilgrims and crusaders and had chosen to remain near Jerusalem to seek God. The men established their hermitage at Mount Carmel because of its beauty, seclusion, and biblical importance as the site where Elijah stood against King Ahab and the false prophets of Jezebel to prove Jehovah to be the one true God. The Carmelites led a life of solitude, silence, and prayer at Mount Carmel before eventually returning to Europe and becoming a recognized order of the Catholic Church. The size of the Carmelite Order varied widely throughout the centuries with its peak in the 1600s and stood at approximately 2,200 friars living on all inhabited continents at the beginning of the 21st century.

The Wyoming Carmelite monastery was founded by Father Daniel Mary who lived as a Carmelite hermit in Minnesota before moving to Clark, Wyoming, to establish the new monastery. The Wyoming Carmelites were a cloistered order and were allowed to leave the monastery only by permission of the bishop for medical needs or the death of a family member. The Wyoming monastery's abbey bore little resemblance to the great stone cathedrals and monasteries of Europe and was confined to a rectory that had once been a four-bedroom ranch-style home and an adjoining 42 acres of land that had been donated to the monastery.

There were 13 monks dedicated to a life of prayer and worship in the Wyoming Carmelite monastery. Since the founding of the monastery six years ago, there had been more than 500 inquiries from young men considering becoming a Wyoming Carmelite. Father Prior Daniel Mary wished to eventually have 30 monks who would join the brotherhood at age 19 to 30 and live out their lives in the monastery. However, the selection criteria for acceptance into the monastery were rigorous, with the monks making certain that applicants understood the reality of the vows of obedience, chastity, and poverty and the sacrifices associated with living a cloistered religious life.

THE DAILY ACTIVITIES OF A CARMELITE MONK

The Carmelite monks' day began at 4:10 a.m., when they arose and went to chapel for worship wearing traditional brown habits and handmade sandals. At about 6:00 a.m., the monks rested and contemplated in silence for one hour before Father Prior began morning Mass. After Mass, the monks went about their manual labors. In performing their labors, each brother had a special set of skills that enabled the monastery to independently maintain its operations.

Brother Joseph Marie was an excellent mechanic, Brother Paul was a carpenter, Brother Peter Joseph (Brother Cook) worked in the kitchen, and five-foot, four-inch Brother Simon Mary (Little Monk) was the secretary to Father Daniel Mary. Brother Elias, affectionately known as Brother Java, was Mystic Monk Coffee's master roaster, although he was not a coffee drinker.

Each monk worked up to six hours per day; however, the monks' primary focus was spiritual, with eight hours of each day spent in prayer. At 11:40 a.m., the monks stopped work and went to Chapel. Afterward they had lunch, cleaned the dishes, and went back to work. At 3:00 p.m., the hour that Jesus was believed to have died on the cross, work stopped again for prayer and worship. The monks then returned to work until the bell was rung for Vespers (evening prayer). After Vespers, the monks had an hour of silent contemplation, an evening meal, and more prayers before bedtime.

THE NEW MOUNT CARMEL

Soon after arriving in Wyoming, Father Daniel Mary had formed the vision of acquiring a large parcel of land—a new Mount Carmel—and building a monastery with accommodations for 30 monks, a retreat center for lay visitors, a Gothic church, a convent for Carmelite nuns, and a hermitage. In a letter to supporters posted on the monastery's website, Father Daniel Mary succinctly stated his vision: "We beg your prayers, your friendship and your support that this vision, our vision may come to be that Mount Carmel may be refounded in Wyoming's Rockies for the glory of God."

The brothers located a 496-acre ranch for sale that would satisfy all of the requirements to create a new Mount Carmel. The Irma Lake Ranch was located about 21 miles outside Cody, Wyoming, and included a remodeled 17,800-square-foot residence, a 1,700-square-foot caretaker house, a 2,950-square-foot guesthouse, a hunting cabin, a dairy and horse barn, and forested land. The ranch was at the end of a seven-mile-long private gravel road and was bordered on one side by the private Hoodoo Ranch (100,000 acres) and on the other by the Shoshone National Park (2.4 million acres). Although the asking price was $8.9 million, the monks believed they would be able to acquire the property through donations and the profits generated by the monastery's Mystic Monk Coffee operations. The $250,000 donation they had received from an individual wishing to support the Carmelites could be applied toward whatever purpose the monks chose. Additionally, a group of Cody business owners had formed the New Mount Carmel Foundation to help the monks raise funds.

OVERVIEW OF THE COFFEE INDUSTRY

About 150 million consumers in the United States drank coffee, with 89 percent of U.S. coffee drinkers brewing their own coffee at home rather than purchasing ready-to-drink coffee at coffee shops and restaurants such as Starbucks, Dunkin' Donuts, or McDonald's. Packaged coffee for home brewing was easy to find in any grocery store and typically carried a retail price of $4 to $6 for a 12-ounce package. About 30 million coffee drinkers in the United States preferred premium-quality specialty coffees that sold for $7 to $10 per 12-ounce package. Specialty coffees are made from high-quality Arabica beans instead of the mix of low-quality Arabica beans and bitter, less flavorful Robusta beans that makers of value brands use. The wholesale price of Robusta coffee beans averaged $1.15 per pound, while mild Columbian Arabica wholesale prices averaged $1.43 per pound.

Prior to the 1990s, the market for premium-quality specialty coffees barely existed in the United States, but Howard Schultz's vision for Starbucks of bringing the Italian espresso bar experience to America helped specialty coffees become a large and thriving segment of the industry. The company's pursuit of its mission "To inspire and nurture the human spirit—one person, one cup, and one neighborhood at a time" had allowed Starbucks to become an iconic brand in most parts of the world. The company's success had given rise to a number of competing specialty coffee shops and premium brands of packaged specialty coffee, including Seattle's Best, Millstone, Green Mountain Coffee Roasters, and First Colony Coffee and Tea. Some producers such as First Colony had difficulty gaining shelf space in supermarkets and concentrated on private-label roasting and packaging for fine department stores and other retailers wishing to have a proprietary brand of coffee.

Specialty coffees sold under premium brands might be made from shade-grown or organically grown coffee beans, or have been purchased from a grower belonging to a World Fair Trade Organization (WFTO) cooperative. WFTO cooperative growers were paid above-market prices to better support the cost of operating their farms—for example, WFTO-certified organic wholesale prices averaged $1.55 per pound. Many consumers who purchased specialty coffees were willing to pay a higher price for organic, shade-grown, or fair trade coffee because of their personal health or social concerns—organic coffees are grown without the use of synthetic fertilizers or pesticides, shade-grown coffee plants are allowed to grow beneath the canopies of larger indigenous trees, and fair trade pricing makes it easier for farmers in developing countries to pay workers a living wage. The specialty coffee segment of the retail coffee industry had grown dramatically in the United States, with retail sales increasing from $8.3 billion to $13.5 billion during the last seven years. The retail sales of organic coffee accounted for about $1 billion of industry sales and had grown at an annual rate of 32 percent for each of the last seven years.

MYSTIC MONK COFFEE

Mystic Monk Coffee was produced using high-quality fair trade Arabica and fair trade/organic Arabica beans. The monks produced whole-bean and ground caffeinated and decaffeinated varieties in dark, medium, and light roasts and in different flavors. The most popular Mystic Monk flavors were Mystical

Chants of Carmel, Cowboy Blend, Royal Rum Pecan, and Mystic Monk Blend. With the exception of sample bags, which carried a retail price of $2.99, all varieties of Mystic Monk Coffee were sold via the monastery's website (www. mysticmonkcoffee.com) in 12-ounce bags at a price of $9.95. All purchases from the website were delivered by United Parcel Service (UPS) or the U.S. Postal Service. Frequent customers were given the option of joining a "coffee club," which offered monthly delivery of one to six bags of preselected coffee. Purchases of three or more bags qualified for free shipping. The Mystic Monk Coffee website also featured T-shirts, gift cards, CDs featuring the monastery's Gregorian chants, and coffee mugs.

Mystic Monk Coffee's target market was the segment of the U.S. Catholic population who drank coffee and wished to support the monastery's mission. More than 69 million Americans were members of the Catholic Church—making it four times larger than the second-largest Christian denomination in the United States. An appeal to Catholics to "use their Catholic coffee dollar for Christ and his Catholic church" was published on the Mystic Monk Coffee website.

MYSTIC MONK COFFEE-ROASTING OPERATIONS

After the morning religious services and breakfast, Brother Java roasted the green coffee beans delivered each week from a coffee broker in Seattle, Washington. The monks paid the Seattle broker the prevailing wholesale price per pound, which fluctuated daily with global supply and demand. The capacity of Mystic Monk Coffee's roaster limited production to 540 pounds per day; production was also limited by time devoted to prayer, silent meditation, and worship. Demand for Mystic Monk Coffee had not yet exceeded the roaster's capacity, but the monastery planned to purchase a larger, 130-pound-per-hour-roaster when demand further approached the current roaster's capacity. The monks had received a quote of $35,000 for the new larger roaster.

MARKETING AND WEBSITE OPERATIONS

Mystic Monk Coffee was promoted primarily by word of mouth among loyal customers in Catholic parishes across the United States. The majority of Mystic Monk's sales were made through its website, but on occasion telephone orders were placed with the monks' secretary, who worked outside the cloistered part of the monastery. Mystic Monk also offered secular website operators commissions on its sales through its Mystic Monk Coffee Affiliate Program, which placed banner ads and text ads on participating websites. Affiliate sites earned an 18 percent commission on sales made to customers who were directed to the Mystic Monk site from their site. The affiliate program's ShareASale participation level allowed affiliates to refer new affiliates to Mystic Monk and earn 56 percent of the new affiliate's commission. The monks had also just recently expanded Mystic Monk's business model to include wholesale sales to churches and local coffee shops.

MYSTIC MONK'S FINANCIAL PERFORMANCE

At the conclusion of Mystic Monk Coffee's first year in operation, its sales of coffee and coffee accessories averaged about $56,500 per month. Its cost of sales averaged about 30 percent of revenues, inbound shipping costs accounted for 19 percent of revenues, and broker fees were 3 percent of revenues—for a total cost of goods sold of 52 percent. Operating expenses such as utilities, supplies, telephone, and website maintenance averaged 37 percent of revenues. Thus, Mystic Monk's net profit margin averaged 11 percent of revenues.

REALIZING THE VISION

During a welcome period of solitude before his evening meal, Father Prior Daniel Mary again contemplated the purchase of the Irma Lake Ranch. He realized that his vision of purchasing the ranch would require careful planning and execution. For the Wyoming Carmelites, coffee sales were a means of support from the outside world that might provide the financial resources to purchase the land. Father Prior understood that the cloistered monastic environment offered unique challenges to operating a business enterprise, but it also provided opportunities that were not available to secular businesses. He resolved to develop an execution plan that would enable Mystic Monk Coffee to minimize the effect of its cloistered monastic constraints, maximize the potential of monastic opportunities, and realize his vision of buying the Irma Lake Ranch.

COMPETITION AMONG THE NORTH AMERICAN WAREHOUSE CLUBS: COSTCO WHOLESALE VERSUS SAM'S CLUB VERSUS BJ'S WHOLESALE

Arthur A. Thompson
The University of Alabama

In 2010, the nearly $125 billion discount warehouse and wholesale club segment of the North American retailing industry consisted of three principal competitors: Costco Wholesale, Sam's Club (a Walmart subsidiary), and BJ's Wholesale Club. Warehouse clubs operated no-frills, self-service big-box facilities where customers could choose from a relatively narrow assortment of discount-priced merchandise across a wide range of product categories, including food and household supplies, electronics, office supplies, selected appliances and furniture items, apparel, books and DVDs, home furnishings, and tires. Items were typically sold in case lots (cleaning supplies, paper products, office supplies, soft drinks, bottled waters); packaged in large containers (laundry detergents); shrink-wrapped in quantities of 6, 8, or 12 (canned goods); bundled in cartons of 100 or more (trash bags, paper plates, disposable cups), or giant-sized bags (potato chips, pretzels). In order to achieve high sales volumes and rapid inventory turnover, warehouse clubs generally limited merchandise selections to brand-name items that were leaders in their categories and an assortment of private-label items.

Warehouse clubs drew customers away from other wholesale and retail outlets such as supermarkets, department stores, drugstores, office supply stores, consumer electronics stores, and automotive stores chiefly because it was difficult for such sellers to match the low prices of a wholesale club. Costco, Sam's Club, and BJ's Wholesale had substantially lower operating costs than most retailers because they purchased full truckloads of merchandise directly from manufacturers, displayed items on pallets or inexpensive shelving, kept extra inventory on high shelving directly on the sales floor rather than in central warehouses, had very low costs for store decor and fixtures, had comparatively low labor costs (because warehouses were open fewer hours than conventional retailers and required comparatively fewer people to operate relative to the sales volumes that a store generated), and spent minimally on advertising and customer service. The low operating costs of warehouse clubs enabled them to charge significantly lower prices than traditional wholesalers, mass merchandisers, supermarkets, and other retailers. Moreover, because of high sales volumes at each store location and consequently rapid inventory turnover, warehouse clubs were able to receive cash for a large portion of their inventory before they had to pay many of their merchandise vendors (even in instances when a club elected to take advantage of early payment discounts offered by vendors rather than delay vendor payment until the standard 30 to 60 days after the merchandise was delivered). Thus, a warehouse club could finance a big percentage of its merchandise inventory through the payment terms provided by vendors rather than by having to maintain sizable working capital (defined as current assets minus current liabilities) to facilitate timely payment of suppliers.

The low prices and broad merchandise selection found at the three leading warehouse clubs were attractive to small-business owners, churches and nonprofit organizations, caterers, small restaurants, and individual households (particularly bargain hunters and those with large families). A significant number of business members shopped wholesale clubs for their personal needs as well as their business needs. Interested shoppers paid an annual membership fee to make purchases at a warehouse club.

There were more than 1,250 warehouse club locations in the United States, Canada, and Mexico; most every major metropolitan area had one, if not several, warehouse club operations. Costco had about a 56 percent share of warehouse club sales in North America (the United States, Canada, and Mexico); Sam's Club had roughly a 36 percent share; and BJ's Wholesale Club and several small warehouse club competitors had an 8 percent share. Competition was based on such factors as price, merchandise quality and selection, location, and member service. However, all three warehouse clubs also competed with a wide range of other types of retailers, including retail discounters like Walmart and Dollar General, general merchandise chains like Target and Kohl's, specialty chains like Office Depot and Staples in office supplies and Best Buy in electronics and DVDs, supermarkets, gasoline stations, and Internet retailers. Not only did Walmart, the world's largest retailer, compete directly with Costco and BJ Wholesale via its Sam's Club subsidiary, but its 3,000+ Walmart Supercenters in the United States, Canada, and Mexico sold many of the same types of merchandise at attractively low prices as well.

INDUSTRY BACKGROUND

The membership warehouse concept was pioneered by discount merchandising sage Sol Price, who opened the first Price Club in a converted airplane hangar on Morena Boulevard in San Diego in 1976. Price Club lost $750,000 in its first year of operation, but by 1979 it had two stores, 900 employees, 200,000 members, and a $1 million profit. Years earlier, Sol Price had experimented with discount retailing at a San Diego store called Fed-Mart. Jim Sinegal, the cofounder and current CEO of Costco Wholesale, got his start in retailing at the San Diego Fed-Mart at the age of 18, loading mattresses for $1.25 an hour while attending San Diego Community College. When Sol Price sold Fed-Mart, Sinegal left with Price to help him start the San Diego Price Club store; within a few years, Sol Price's Price Club emerged as the unchallenged leader in member warehouse retailing, with stores operating primarily on the West Coast. Although he originally conceived Price Club as a place where small local businesses could obtain needed merchandise at economical prices, Sol Price soon concluded that his fledgling operation could achieve far greater sales volumes and gain buying clout with suppliers by also granting membership to individuals—a conclusion that launched the deep-discount warehouse club industry on a steep growth curve.

When Sinegal was 26, Sol Price made him the manager of the original San Diego store, which had become unprofitable. Price saw that Jim Sinegal had a special knack for discount retailing and for spotting what a store was doing wrong (usually either not being in the right merchandise categories or not selling items at the right price points)—the very things that Sol Price was good at and that were at the root of the Price Club's growing success in the marketplace. Sinegal soon got the San Diego store back into the black. Over the next several years, Sinegal continued to build his prowess and talents for discount merchandising. He mirrored

Sol Price's attention to detail and absorbed all the nuances and subtleties of his mentor's style of operating—constantly improving store operations, keeping operating costs and overhead low, stocking items that moved quickly, and charging ultra-low prices that kept customers coming back to shop. Realizing that he had mastered the tricks of running a successful membership warehouse business from Sol Price, Sinegal decided to leave Price Club and form a new warehouse club operation, which he named Costco. His cofounder in the venture was Seattle entrepreneur Jeff Brotman (now chairman of Costco's board of directors).

The first Costco store began operations in Seattle in 1983, the same year that Walmart opened its first Sam's Club warehouses. By the end of 1984, there were nine Costco stores in five states, serving more than 200,000 members. In December 1985, Costco became a public company, selling shares to the public and raising additional capital for expansion. Costco became the first ever U.S. company to reach $1 billion in sales in less than six years. In October 1993, Costco merged with Price Club. Jim Sinegal became CEO of the merged company, presiding over 206 PriceCostco locations, which in total generated $16 billion in annual sales. Jeff Brotman, who had functioned as Costco's chairman since the company's founding, became vice chairman of PriceCostco in 1993 and was elevated to chairman in December 1994. In January 1997, after the spin-off of most of its nonwarehouse assets to Price Enterprises Inc., PriceCostco changed its name to Costco Companies Inc. When the company reincorporated from Delaware to Washington in August 1999, the name was changed to Costco Wholesale Corporation. The company's headquarters was in Issaquah, Washington, not far from Seattle.

Like Costco, Walmart proceeded to grow its Sam's Club operation at a rapid pace. In 1994, 11 years after opening its first three stores, Walmart had 419 Sam's Club operations open in 48 states, with total sales in fiscal 1993 exceeding $12.3 billion and average sales per store of just over $48 million. Expansion in the following years slowed somewhat. By 2000, Walmart

was operating 463 Sam's Clubs warehouses in the United States and 49 warehouses in five countries outside the United States; the domestic Sam's Clubs had total revenues of $24.8 billion (equal to average annual revenues of $53.6 million per store) and total operating income of $759 million (about $1.6 million per domestic store). But store growth and sales at Sam's Club had slowed since 2007, and Costco was extending its leadership position in the industry, especially in foreign markets, where it had more store locations than Sam's Club did (153 versus 121 in early 2010) and plans for additional stores.

BJ's Wholesale Club introduced the warehouse club concept to New England in 1984, one year after Costco and Sam's Club opened their first warehouses. BJ's grew modestly over the next 25 years, gradually expanding its operations to include 187 store locations in 15 states on the East Coast, from Maine to Florida. In 1997, BJ's became an independent, publicly owned Delaware corporation when Waban Inc., BJ's parent company at the time, distributed shares in BJ's Wholesale to all of Waban's stockholders; prior to then, BJ's operated as a division of Waban. BJ's was headquartered in Natick, Massachusetts, on the western outskirts of Boston.

Exhibit 1 presents comparative 2009 data for the three leading warehouse club competitors in North America.

COSTCO WHOLESALE

Costco was the third-largest retailer in the United States and the eighth-largest in the world. As of March 2010, Costco operated 567 warehouses, including 414 in the United States and Puerto Rico, 77 in Canada, 32 in Mexico (via a 50 percent–owned joint venture), 21 in the United Kingdom, 9 in Japan, 7 in Korea, 6 in Taiwan, and 1 in Australia. Plans called for opening four to six additional stores prior to the end of Costco's 2010 fiscal year in August. Costco warehouses averaged just over 1.4 million transactions per day. More than 50 of Costco's warehouses generated sales exceeding $200 million annually, and 2 had sales exceeding $300 million. The

▶ EXHIBIT 1

A Profile of the Leading Wholesale Clubs in North America in 2009

Company	2009 Revenues ($ millions)			2009 Operating Income ($ millions)	2009 Net Income ($ millions)
	Merchandise Sales	Membership Fees	Total		
Costco Wholesale	$69,889	$1,533	$71,422	$1,777	$1,086
Sam's Club	Not available	Not available	46,710[a]	1,512	n.a.[b]
BJ's Wholesale	9,954	182	10,187	224	132

		Number of Stores in 2010		
	Number of Members 2009	United States	Worldwide	Average Annual Net Sales per Store
Costco Wholesale	58.8 million[c]	413	566[d]	$132.6 million[e]
Sam's Club	47.0 million[f]	596	729[g]	76.3 million[h] (est., U.S. only)
BJ's Wholesale	9.4 million	187	187	53.2 million

[a]Includes U.S. revenues only; revenues for Sam's Club locations outside the United States are not separately available since they are reported as part of the Walmart International division, which includes all types of Walmart stores located outside the United States.

[b]Walmart does not report net income for subsidiary operations, only for the company as a whole.

[c]Includes 2,800,000 members of Costco Mexico, which was part of a 50% owned joint venture.

[d]Includes 36 warehouses operated in Mexico through a 50% owned joint venture.

[e]Does not include the 36 warehouses operated in Mexico through a 50% owned joint venture because sales for the joint venture were not publicly available.

[f]As of 2008; membership data for 2009 were not reported.

[g]Includes 23 Sam's Club locations in Brazil, 98 Sam's Club locations in Mexico, 9 Sam's Club locations in Puerto Rico, and 3 Sam's Club locations in China.

[h]Based on U.S. stores only and estimated membership fees of $1.2 billion (which are not a part of sales per store).

company's most profitable store was in Korea, and its second most profitable store was in Taiwan. Sales per store averaged $131 million annually. Some 5.7 million businesses and 31.1 million households had Costco memberships. The membership renewal rate in the United States and Canada was about 87 percent. Exhibit 2 shows Costco's key financial and operating statistics for fiscal years 2000–2009.

Costco's Strategy

Costco's strategy was aimed squarely at selling top-quality merchandise at prices consistently below what other wholesalers or retailers charged. The company stocked only those items that could be priced at bargain levels and thereby provide members with significant cost savings—Costco even refrained from stocking items frequently requested by customers unless it could price them low enough to remain true to its commitment of saving its members money. The philosophy was to keep members coming in to shop by wowing them with low prices and thereby generating big sales volumes. Examples of Costco's 2009 sales volumes in particular product categories included meat sales of $3.7 billion, seafood sales of $708 million, television sales of $2.2 billion, and fresh produce sales of $3.1 billion (sourced from 41 countries); amounts sold included 79,600 carats of diamonds, 47.7 million rotisserie chickens, 2.1 billion gallons of gasoline, 7.3 million tires, 30.4 million prescriptions, 3 million pairs of glasses, and 91 million $1.50 hot dog/soda combinations. Costco was the world's largest seller of fine wines ($597 million out of total 2009 wine sales of $1.1 billion).[1]

▶ EXHIBIT 2

Selected Financial and Operating Data for Costco Wholesale Corporation, Fiscal Years 2000–2009 ($ millions, except for per share data)

	Fiscal Years Ending on Sunday Closest to August 31					
	2009	**2008**	**2007**	**2006**	**2005**	**2000**
Income Statement Data						
Net sales	$69,889	$70,977	$63,088	$58,963	$51,862	$31,621
Membership fees	1,533	1,506	1,313	1,188	1,073	544
Total revenue	71,422	72,483	64,400	60,151	52,935	32,164
Operating expenses						
Merchandise costs	62,335	63,503	56,450	52,745	46,347	28,322
Selling, general, and administrative	7,252	6,954	6,273	5,732	5,044	2,755
Preopening expenses	41	57	55	43	53	42
Provision for impaired assets and store closing costs	17	0	14	5	16	7
Operating income	1,777	1,969	1,609	1,626	1,474	1,037
Other income (expense)						
Interest expense	(108)	(103)	(64)	(13)	(34)	(39)
Interest income and other	45	133	165	138	109	54
Income before income taxes	1,714	1,999	1,710	1,751	1,549	1,052
Provision for income taxes	628	716	627	648	486	421
Net income	$ 1,086	$ 1,283	$ 1,083	$ 1,103	$ 1,063	$ 631
Diluted net income per share	$2.47	$2.89	$2.37	$2.30	$2.18	$1.35
Dividends per share	$0.68	$0.61	$0.55	$0.49	$0.43	$0.00
Millions of shares used in per share calculations	440.5	444.2	457.6	480.3	492.0	475.7
Balance Sheet Data						
Cash and cash equivalents	$ 3,157	$ 2,619	$ 2,780	$ 1,511	$ 2,063	$ 525
Merchandise inventories	5,405	5,039	4,879	4,561	4,015	2,490
Current assets	10,337	9,462	9,324	8,232	8,238	3,470
Current liabilities	9,281	8,874	8,582	7,819	6,761	3,404
Net property and equipment	10,900	10,355	9,520	8,564	7,790	4,834
Total assets	21,979	20,682	19,607	17,495	16,514	8,634
Short-term borrowings	16	134	54	41	54	10
Long-term debt	2,206	2,206	2,108	215	711	790
Stockholders' equity	10,018	9,192	8,623	9,143	8,881	4,240
Cash Flow Data						
Net cash provided by operating activities	$ 2,092	$ 2,206	$ 2,076	$ 1,831	$ 1,773	$ 1,070

(continued)

▶**EXHIBIT 2** *(concluded)*

	Fiscal Years Ending on Sunday Closest to August 31					
	2009	**2008**	**2007**	**2006**	**2005**	**2000**
Warehouses in Operation						
Beginning of year	512	488	458	433	417	292
Opened	19	34	30	28	21	25
Closed	(4)	(10)	—	(3)	(5)	(4)
End of year	527	512	488	458	433	313
Members at year-end[a]						
Businesses (000s)	5,700	5,600	5,400	5,200	5,000	4,200
Gold Star members (000s)	21,500	20,200	18,600	17,300	16,200	10,500
Add-on cardholders (employees of business members, spouses of members)	28,800	27,700	26,400	25,000	n.a.	n.a.

[a]Membership numbers do not include cardholders of Costco Mexico.

Note: Some totals may not add due to rounding.

Sources: Costco, 10-K reports 2000, 2005, 2007, and 2009.

The key elements of Costco's strategy were ultra-low prices, a limited selection of nationally branded and private-label products, a "treasure hunt" shopping environment, strong emphasis on low operating costs, and a three-pronged growth initiative to boost sales and profits.

Pricing In keeping with Costco's mission, "To continually provide our members with quality goods and services at the lowest possible prices," Costco capped the margins on brand-name merchandise at 14 percent (whereas the markups over cost at other retailers often resulted in 20 to 50 percent margins for the very same items). The margins on Costco's private-label Kirkland Signature items—which included vitamins, juice, bottled water, coffee, spices, olive oil, canned salmon and tuna, nuts, laundry detergent, baby products, dog food, luggage, cookware, trash bags, batteries, wines and spirits, paper towels, toilet paper, and clothing—were a maximum of 15 percent, but the fractionally higher markups on Costco's private-label items still resulted in its private-label prices being about 20 percent below comparable name-brand items. As a result of these low markups, Costco's prices were just fractionally above break-even levels, producing net sales revenues (not counting membership fees) that barely covered all operating expenses and generated only a modest contribution to operating profits. As can be verified from Exhibit 2, every year during 2005–2009, over 70 percent of Costco's operating profits were attributable to membership fees and, in fact, membership fees were larger than Costco's net income in every year shown in Exhibit 2 but 2000. (To put it another way, without the revenues from membership fees, Costco's profits would be minuscule due to its strategy of capping the margins on branded goods at 14 percent and private-label goods at 15 percent.)

Costco CEO Jim Sinegal described the company's approach to pricing:

> We always look to see how much of a gulf we can create between ourselves and the competition. So that the competitors eventually say, "These guys are crazy. We'll compete somewhere else." Some years ago, we were selling a hot brand of jeans for $29.99. They were $50 in a department store. We got a great deal on them and could have

sold them for a higher price but we went down to $29.99. Why? We knew it would create a riot.[2]

At another time, he explained,

> We're very good merchants, and we offer value. The traditional retailer will say: "I'm selling this for $10. I wonder whether we can get $10.50 or $11." We say: "We're selling this for $9. How do we get it down to $8?" We understand that our members don't come and shop with us because of the window displays or the Santa Claus or the piano player. They come and shop with us because we offer great values.[3]

Indeed, Costco's markups and prices were so fractionally above the level needed to cover operating costs and interest expenses that Wall Street analysts had criticized Costco management for going all out to please customers at the expense of charging prices that would increase profits for shareholders. One retailing analyst said, "They could probably get more money for a lot of the items they sell."[4] Unimpressed with Wall Street's criticism, Sinegal commented, "Those people are in the business of making money between now and next Tuesday. We're trying to build an organization that's going to be here 50 years from now."[5] He went on to explain why Costco's approach to pricing fractionally above levels needed to cover operating expenses would remain unaltered during his tenure:

> When I started, Sears, Roebuck was the Costco of the country, but they allowed someone else to come in under them. We don't want to be one of the casualties. We don't want to turn around and say, "We got so fancy we've raised our prices," and all of a sudden a new competitor comes in and beats our prices.[6]

Product Quality and Selection   Most of the merchandise Costco sold was of good-to-excellent quality and was supplied by name-brand manufacturers. The specifications for Costco's private-label Kirkland Signature products were high, often resulting in their being of equal or better quality than those of highly regarded or better-known brands; but it was the company's strategy to purchase and stock only those private-label items that could be sold to members at prices significantly below comparable name-brand items. During the 2006–2009 period, Costco expanded its Kirkland Signature private-label line from some 400 items to nearly 600 items.

The selections of branded and private-label merchandise were deliberately limited in order to keep costs, and thereby prices, low. Whereas typical supermarkets stocked about 45,000 items and a Walmart Supercenter or SuperTarget could have 125,000 to 150,000 items for shoppers to choose from, Costco's merchandising strategy was to provide members with a selection of 3,800 to 4,000 items. Thus, while Costco's product range did cover a broad spectrum—fresh-baked breads and desserts, prime steaks, gourmet cheeses, flat-screen TVs, iPods, fresh flowers, electric toothbrushes, caskets, baby strollers, toys and games, musical instruments, basketballs, sheets and towels, vacuum cleaners, books, DVDs, stainless-steel cookware, seat-cover kits for autos, lightbulbs, washers and dryers, ballpoint pens, vitamins, office products, restaurant supplies, gasoline, one-hour photo finishing—the selection within each product category was restricted, in some cases to a single offering. The approximate percentage of Costco's net sales accounted for by each major category of items is shown in Exhibit 3.

The selections of appliances, equipment, and tools often included commercial and professional models because many of Costco's members were small businesses. Many consumable products like detergents, canned goods, office supplies, and soft drinks were sold only in case, carton, big-container, or multipack quantities. For example, Costco stocked only a 325-count bottle of Advil—a size many shoppers might find too large for their needs; Sinegal explained the reason behind the company's narrow selection strategy:

> If you had ten customers come in to buy Advil, how many are not going to buy any because you just have one size? Maybe one or two. We refer to that as the intelligent loss of sales. We are prepared to give up that one customer. But if we had four or five

▶ EXHIBIT 3

Costco's Sales by Major Product Category, 2003–2009					
	2009	**2008**	**2007**	**2005**	**2003**
Food (fresh produce, meats and fish, bakery and deli products, and dry and institutionally packaged foods)	33%	32%	31%	30%	30%
Sundries (candy, snack foods, tobacco, alcoholic and nonalcoholic beverages, and cleaning and institutional supplies)	23	22	23	25	26
Hardlines (major appliances, electronics, health and beauty aids, hardware, office supplies, garden and patio, sporting goods, furniture, cameras, and automotive supplies)	19	19	21	20	20
Softlines (including apparel, domestics, jewelry, housewares, books, movie DVDs, video games, music, home furnishings, and small appliances)	10	10	11	12	14
Ancillary and other (gasoline, pharmacy, food court, optical, one-hour photo, hearing aids, and travel)	15	17	14	13	10

Source: Costco, 10-K reports, 2005, 2007, and 2009.

sizes of Advil, as most grocery stores do, it would make our business more difficult to manage. Our business can only succeed if we are efficient. You can't go on selling at these margins if you are not.[7]

Management believed that its limited selection strategy contributed significantly to lower purchasing, shipping, and in-store handling and merchandising costs.

As a means of giving members reasons to shop at Costco more frequently and make Costco more of a one-stop shopping destination, the company had opened ancillary departments within or next to most Costco warehouses, as shown in the following table:

	2009	2008	2007
Total number of warehouses	527	512	488
Warehouses having stores with			
Food court and hot dog stands	521	506	482
One-hour photo centers	518	504	480
Optical dispensing centers	509	496	472
Pharmacies	464	451	429
Gas stations	323	307	279
Hearing aid centers	303	274	237
Print shops and copy centers	10	8	8

Treasure Hunt Merchandising Costco's merchandise buyers were constantly on the lookout to make one-time purchases of items that would appeal to the company's clientele and that would sell out quickly. A sizable number of these items were high-end or name-brand products that carried big price tags—like $800 espresso machines, expensive jewelry and diamond rings (priced from $50,000 to $250,000), Movado watches, exotic cheeses, Coach bags, $5,000 necklaces, cashmere sport coats, $1,500 digital pianos, and Dom Perignon champagne. Dozens of featured specials came and went quickly, sometimes in several days or a week—like Italian-made Hathaway shirts priced at $29.99 and $800 leather sectional sofas. The strategy was to entice shoppers to spend more than they might by offering irresistible deals on big-ticket items or name-brand specials and, further, to keep the mix of featured and treasure-hunt items constantly changing so that bargain-hunting shoppers would go to Costco more frequently than for periodic "stock-up" trips.

Costco members quickly learned that they needed to go ahead and buy treasure-hunt specials that interested them, because the items would very likely not be available on their next shopping trip. In many cases, Costco did not obtain its luxury offerings directly from high-end manufacturers like Calvin Klein or Waterford (which were unlikely to want their merchandise marketed at deep discounts at places like Costco). Rather, Costco's buyers searched for opportunities to source such items legally on the gray market from other wholesalers or distressed retailers looking to get rid of excess or slow-selling inventory.

Marketing and Advertising   Costco's low prices and its reputation for making shopping at Costco something of a treasure hunt made it unnecessary to engage in extensive advertising or sales campaigns. Marketing and promotional activities were generally limited to regular direct mail programs aimed at existing members, special campaigns for new warehouse openings, and occasional direct mail marketing to help recruit prospective new members. The company's primary direct mail program for members was the Costco Connection, a multipage mailout that contained a host of savings coupons for featured specials over upcoming weeks. For new warehouse openings, marketing teams personally contacted businesses in the area that were potential wholesale members; these contacts were supplemented with direct mailings during the period immediately prior to opening. In addition to using direct mail to recruit more individual members, the company also strove to attract members by working with local employee groups and businesses with large numbers of employees. After a membership base was established in an area, most new memberships came from word of mouth (existing members telling friends and acquaintances about their shopping experiences at Costco), follow-up messages distributed through regular payroll or other organizational communications to employee groups, and ongoing direct solicitations to prospective business and individual members. Management believed that its emphasis on direct mail advertising kept its marketing expenses low relative to those at typical retailers, discounters, and supermarkets.

Low-Cost Emphasis   Keeping operating costs to a bare minimum was a key element of Costco's strategy and a key to its low pricing; Jim Sinegal explained:

> Costco is able to offer lower prices and better values by eliminating virtually all the frills and costs historically associated with conventional wholesalers and retailers, including salespeople, fancy buildings, delivery, billing, and accounts receivable. We run a tight operation with extremely low overhead, which enables us to pass on dramatic savings to our members.[8]

While Costco management made a point of locating warehouses on high-traffic routes in or near upscale suburbs that were easily accessible by small businesses and residents with above-average incomes, it avoided prime real estate sites in order to contain land costs.

Because shoppers were attracted principally by Costco's low prices and merchandise selection, most warehouses were of a metal preengineered design, with concrete floors and minimal interior decor. Floor plans were designed for economy and efficiency in use of selling space, the handling of merchandise, and the control of inventory. Merchandise was generally stored on racks above the sales floor and displayed on pallets containing large quantities of each item, thereby reducing labor required for handling and stocking. In-store signage was done mostly on laser printers; there were no shopping bags at the checkout counter—merchandise was put directly into the shopping cart or sometimes loaded into empty boxes. Costco warehouses ranged in size from 70,000 to 205,000 square feet; the average size was 141,000 square feet. Newer units were usually in the range of 150,000 to 205,000 square feet. Scenes of Costco's warehouses are shown in Exhibit 4.

Warehouses generally operated on a seven-day, 69-hour week, typically being open between 10:00 a.m. and 8:30 p.m. weekdays, with earlier closing hours on the weekend; the gasoline operations outside many stores usually had extended hours. The shorter hours of operation—as compared with those of traditional retailers, discount retailers, and supermarkets—resulted in lower labor costs relative to the volume of sales.

▶EXHIBIT 4   Scenes from Costco's Warehouses

Growth Strategy Costco's strategy to grow sales and profits had three main elements: open more new warehouses; build an ever larger, fiercely loyal membership base; and employ well-executed merchandising techniques to induce members to shop at Costco more often and purchase more per shopping trip. Costco had opened 265 new warehouses since September 2000, a key reason why company revenues climbed from $31.6 billion in fiscal 2000 to $71.4 billion in fiscal 2009. Expansion efforts in the United States were focused on entering cities and states where Costco did not yet have a warehouse (10 states had no Costco stores in 2010) and opening additional warehouses in metropolitan areas big enough to support two or more Costco locations. Expansion was under way internationally as well, with further expansion being planned in all of the company's Asian markets. Costco planned to double its store count in Taiwan from 6 to 12 over the next five years and to open a new distribution center; the company's sales in Taiwan (where it was the only wholesale club) had nearly tripled between 2004 ($250 million) and 2009 ($747 million), a period in which retail sales in Taiwan had grown by only 8.3 percent.[9] Retailing in Taiwan was a $72 billion market. However, less than 10 percent of Costco's operating income came from warehouses located outside the United States and Canada. Exhibit 5 presents selected geographical operating data for Costco's 2005–2009 fiscal years.

Costco's strategy to attract more members and entice members to do a bigger percentage of their shopping at Costco had three components:

- Give members a place to buy supplies of practical, frequently used business and household items at money-saving prices.
- Make shopping at Costco interesting and rewarding because of opportunities to purchase an ever-changing array of big-ticket items and indulgences at rock-bottom prices—in this regard, it was important that members be able to spot appealing new items on the sales floor

each time they shopped at Costco. Costco buyers constantly scanned the manufacturing landscape, looking for one-time opportunities to buy items that would appeal to bargain-hunting members. And warehouse personnel strived to do an effective job of displaying and merchandising the special buys on the sales floor.

- Acclimate members to the merits of visiting Costco weekly or bimonthly so as not to miss out on the special one-time-only merchandise selections that typically sold out in a matter of days.

To further grow its business, Costco operated two websites—www.costco.com in the United States and www.costco.ca in Canada—as a means of expanding product offerings to include big-ticket items that could not be economically displayed on the warehouse sales floor (e.g., indoor and outdoor furniture, special buys on PCs or other electronic items), and as a convenience to members who were not always able to purchase certain items at the warehouse where they customarily shopped. At Costco's online photo center, members could upload images and pick up the prints at their local warehouse in little over an hour. Costco's e-commerce sales totaled $1.2 billion in fiscal 2007, up from $534 million in fiscal 2005 and $376 million in fiscal 2004 (more recent e-commerce sales data was not reported).

Jim Sinegal—Costco's Cofounder and CEO

Jim Sinegal was the driving force behind Costco's success. He was far from the stereotypical CEO. A grandfatherly 73-year-old, Sinegal dressed casually and unpretentiously, often going to the office or touring Costco stores wearing an open-collared cotton shirt that came from a Costco bargain rack and sporting a standard employee name tag that said, simply, "Jim." His informal dress, mustache, gray hair, and unimposing appearance made it easy for Costco shoppers to mistake him for a store clerk. He answered his own phone, once telling ABC News reporters, "If a customer's

▶ EXHIBIT 5

Selected Geographic Operating Data, Costco Wholesale Corporation, Fiscal Years 2005–2009 ($ millions)				
	U.S. Operations	Canadian Operations	Other International Operations	Total
Year Ended August 30, 2009				
Total revenue (including membership fees)	$56,548	$9,737	$5,137	$71,442
Operating income	1,273	354	150	1,777
Capital expenditures	904	135	211	1,250
Number of warehouses	406	77	44	527
Year Ended August 31, 2008				
Total revenue (including membership fees)	$56,903	$10,528	$5,052	$72,483
Operating income	1,393	420	156	1,969
Capital expenditures	1,190	246	163	1,599
Number of warehouses	398	75	39	512
Year Ended September 2, 2007				
Total revenue (including membership fees)	$51,532	$8,724	$4,144	$64,400
Operating income	1,217	287	105	1,609
Capital expenditures	1,104	207	74	1,386
Number of warehouses	383	71	34	488
Year Ended September 3, 2006				
Total revenue (including membership fees)	$48,466	$8,122	$3,564	$60,151
Operating income	1,246	293	87	1,626
Capital expenditures	934	188	90	1,213
Number of warehouses	358	68	32	458
Year Ended August 28, 2005				
Total revenue (including membership fees)	$43,064	$6,732	$3,155	$52,952
Operating income	1,168	242	65	1,474
Capital expenditures	734	140	122	995
Number of warehouses	338	65	30	433

Note: The dollar numbers shown for "Other" countries represent only Costco's ownership share, since all foreign operations were joint ventures (although Costco was the majority owner of these ventures); the 32 warehouses operated by Costco Mexico (33 warehouses as of 2009) in which Costco was only a 50% joint venture partner are not included in the data for the "Other" countries.

Source: Costco, 10-K reports, 2009 and 2007.

calling and they have a gripe, don't you think they kind of enjoy the fact that I picked up the phone and talked to them?"[10]

Sinegal spent much of his time touring Costco stores, using the company plane to fly from location to location and sometimes visiting 8 to 10 stores daily (the record for a single day was 12). Treated like a celebrity when he appeared at a store (the news "Jim's in the store" spread quickly), Sinegal made a point of greeting store employees. He observed, "The employees know that I want to say hello to them, because I like them. We have said from the very beginning: 'We're going to be a company that's on a first-name basis with everyone.'"[11] Employees genuinely seemed to like Sinegal. He talked quietly, in a commonsensical manner that suggested what he was saying was no big deal.[12] He came across as kind yet stern, but he was prone to display irritation when he disagreed sharply with what people were saying to him.

In touring a Costco store with the local store manager, Sinegal was very much the person in charge. He functioned as producer, director, and knowledgeable critic. He cut to the chase quickly, exhibiting intense attention to detail and pricing, wandering through store aisles firing a barrage of questions at store managers about sales volumes and stock levels of particular items, critiquing merchandising displays or the position of certain products in the stores, commenting on any aspect of store operations that caught his eye, and asking managers to do further research and get back to him with more information whenever he found their answers to his questions less than satisfying. It was readily apparent that Sinegal had tremendous merchandising savvy, that he demanded much of store managers and employees, and that his views about discount retailing set the tone for how the company operated. Knowledgeable observers regarded Jim Sinegal's merchandising expertise as being on a par with that of the legendary Sam Walton, the founder of Walmart.

Warehouse Operations

Costco bought the majority of its merchandise directly from manufacturers, routing it either directly to its warehouse stores or to one of nine cross-docking depots that served as distribution points for nearby stores. Depots received container-based shipments from manufacturers and reallocated these goods for combined shipment to individual warehouses, generally in less than 24 hours. This maximized freight volume and handling efficiencies. When merchandise arrived at a warehouse, it was moved directly onto the sales floor; very little was stored in locations off the sales floor, thereby lowering receiving costs by eliminating many of the costs associated with multiple-step handling of merchandise, such as purchasing from distributors as opposed to manufacturers, use of central receiving, operating regional distribution centers for inventory storage and distribution of merchandise to nearby stores, and having storage areas at retail sites where merchandise could be held in reserve off the sales floor.

Costco had direct buying relationships with many producers of national name-brand merchandise (e.g., Canon, Casio, Coca-Cola, Colgate-Palmolive, Dell, Fuji, Hewlett-Packard, Jones of New York, Kimberly-Clark, Kodak, Kitchen Aid, Levi Strauss, Michelin, Nestlé, Panasonic, Procter & Gamble, Samsung, and Sony) and with manufacturers that supplied its Kirkland Signature private-label products. No single manufacturer supplied a significant percentage of the merchandise that Costco stocked. Costco had not experienced any difficulty in obtaining sufficient quantities of merchandise, and management believed that if one or more of its current sources of supply became unavailable, the company could switch its purchases to alternative manufacturers without experiencing a substantial disruption of its business.

Costco warehouses accepted cash, checks, most debit cards, American Express, and a private-label Costco credit card. Costco accepted merchandise returns when members were dissatisfied with their purchases. Losses associated with dishonored checks were minimal because members who bounced checks were prevented from paying by check or cashing checks at the point of sale until restitution was made. The membership format facilitated strictly controlling the entrances and exits of warehouses, resulting in inventory losses of less than two-tenths of 1 percent of net sales—well below those of other retail discounters.

Warehouse Managers Costco's warehouse managers were delegated considerable authority over store operations and, in effect, functioned as entrepreneurs running their own retail operation. They were responsible for effectively merchandising the ever-changing lineup of treasure-hunt products, orchestrating in-store product locations and displays to maximize sales and quick turnover, and coming up with new ideas about what items would sell in their stores. In experimenting with what items to stock and what in-store merchandising techniques to employ, warehouse managers drew on their knowledge of the clientele that patronized their locations—for instance, big-ticket diamonds sold well at some warehouses but not at others. Costco's best managers kept their fingers on the pulse of the members who shopped their warehouse location to stay in sync with what would sell well, and they had a flair for creating a certain element of excitement, hum, and buzz in their warehouses that spurred above-average sales volumes (sales at Costco's top-volume warehouses often exceeded $5 million a week, with sales topping $1 million on many days). Successful managers also thrived on the rat race of running a high-traffic store and solving the inevitable crises of the moment.

Costco's Membership Base and Member Demographics

Costco had two primary types of memberships: Business and Gold Star. Gold Star memberships were for individuals who did not qualify for a Business membership. Businesses, including individuals with a business license, retail sales license, or other evidence of business existence, qualified as Business members. Business members generally paid an annual membership fee of $50 for the primary and spouse membership cards and could purchase add-on membership cards for an annual fee of $40 each for partners or employees (these add-ons also included a spouse card). A significant number of Business members also shopped at Costco for their personal needs.

Gold Star members generally paid an annual fee of $50, which included a spouse card. In addition, all members in the United States and Canada could upgrade to an Executive membership for an annual fee of $100; Executive members qualified for 2 percent additional savings on qualified purchases at Costco (redeemable at Costco warehouses), up to a maximum rebate of $500 per year. The Executive membership also offered savings and benefits on various business and consumer services offered by Costco, including merchant credit card processing, small-business loans, auto and home insurance, long-distance telephone service, check printing, and real estate and mortgage services; these services were mostly provided by third parties and varied by state. In 2009, Executive members represented 29 percent of Costco's primary membership base and generated more than 40 percent of consolidated net sales. Members could shop at any Costco warehouse; member renewal rates were about 87 percent.

Compensation and Workforce Practices

In September 2009, Costco had 79,000 full-time employees and 63,000 part-time employees worldwide, not including approximately 9,000 people employed by Costco Mexico, whose operations were not consolidated in Costco's financial and operating results. Approximately 13,500 hourly employees at locations in California, Maryland, New Jersey, and New York and one warehouse in Virginia were represented by the International Brotherhood of Teamsters. All remaining employees were non-union.

Starting wages for new Costco employees were in the $10.50–$11.00 per hour range in 2008. Depending on the job classification, the median pay scales for Costco employees with five or more years' experience were in the $17–$21 per hour range.[13] Warehouse employees received time-and-a-half pay for working on Sundays and were paid double time in the event they were called on to work more than 12 hours in a given shift. Median salaries for managerial positions at Costco warehouses in 2008 were in the $55,000–$75,000 range.[14]

Employees received biannual bonuses and a full spectrum of benefits that were regarded as being quite good in comparison to those of other retailers. Salaried employees were eligible for benefits on the first of the month after the date of hire. Full-time hourly employees were eligible for benefits on the first of the month after working a probationary 90 days; part-time hourly employees became benefit-eligible on the first of the month after working 180 days.

Although admitting that paying good wages and good benefits was contrary to conventional wisdom in discount retailing, Jim Sinegal was convinced that having a well-compensated workforce was very important to executing Costco's strategy successfully: "Paying good wages and keeping your people working with you is very good business."[15] When a reporter asked him about why Costco treated its workers so well compared with other retailers (particularly Walmart, which paid lower wages and had a skimpier benefits package), Sinegal replied: "Why shouldn't employees have the right to good wages and good careers? . . . It absolutely makes good business sense. Most people agree that we're the lowest-cost producer. Yet we pay the highest wages. So it must mean we get better productivity. It's axiomatic in our business—you get what you pay for."[16] In 2007, Sinegal announced his support for raising the minimum wage from $5.15 an hour to $7.25, saying "The more people make, the better lives they are going to have and the better consumers they're going to be."[17]

Selecting People for Open Positions
Costco's top management wanted employees to feel that they could have a long-term career at Costco. It was company policy to fill at least 86 percent of its higher-level opening by promotions from within; in actuality, the percentage ran close to 98 percent, which meant that the majority of Costco's management team (including warehouse, merchandise, administrative, membership, front-end, and receiving managers) were homegrown. Many of the company's vice presidents had started in entry-level jobs; according to Jim Sinegal, "We have guys who started pushing shopping carts out on the parking lot for us who are now vice presidents of our company."[18] However, Costco insisted that candidates for warehouse managers be top-flight merchandisers with a gift for the details of making items fly off the shelves; Sinegal said, "People who have a feel for it just start to get it. Others, you look at them and it's like staring at a blank canvas. I'm not trying to be unduly harsh, but that's the way it works."[19] Most newly appointed warehouse managers at Costco came from the ranks

of assistant warehouse managers who had a track record of being shrewd merchandisers tuned into what new or different products might sell well given the clientele that patronized their particular warehouse—just having skills in people management, crisis management, and cost-effective warehouse operations was not enough.

SAM'S CLUB

In early 2010, Sam's Club operated 596 U.S. warehouses in 48 states (the exceptions were Vermont and Oregon), 23 warehouses in Brazil, 98 warehouses in Mexico, 9 warehouses in Puerto Rico, and 3 warehouses in China. Six Sam's Club warehouses in Canada were closed in March 2009, and, in January 2010, Sam's Club CEO Brian Connell announced that 10 underperforming warehouses in the United States (including 4 in California) would be closed. Nonetheless, there were plans in place to open between 5 and 10 new Sam's Club warehouses (including relocations) in 2010. Recently, Sam's Club executives had launched a major warehouse remodeling program; some 52 remodels were completed during fiscal 2010, and another 60 to 80 clubs were targeted for remodeling during fiscal 2011 (February 2010 through January 2011). Selected financial and operating data for Sam's Club is shown in Exhibit 6.

The first Sam's Club opened in 1984, and management had pursued rapid expansion of the membership club format. Going into 2001, there were 475 warehouse locations in the United States and 53 international locations: Brazil, 8; China, 1; Mexico, 38; and Puerto Rico, 6. Over the next nine years, an additional 121 warehouses were opened in the United States and 80 internationally. Many Sam's Club locations were adjacent to Walmart Supercenters. The concept of the Sam's Club format was to sell merchandise at very low profit margins, resulting in low prices to members. The mission of Sam's Club was "to make savings simple for members by providing them with exciting, quality merchandise and a superior shopping experience, all at a great value."[20]

▶EXHIBIT 6

Selected Financial and Operating Data for Sam's Club, Fiscal Years 2000–2010

Sam's Club	Fiscal Years Ending January 31					
	2010	2009	2008	2007	2006	2001
U.S. sales[a] ($ millions)	$ 46,710	$ 46,899	$ 44,336	$ 41,582	$ 39,798	$ 26,798
Operating income ($ millions)	1,512	1,646	1,648	1,480	1,407	942
Assets ($ millions)	12,073	12,339	11,722	11,448	10,588	3,843
Number of locations at year-end	729	727	713	693	670	564
U.S.	596	602	591	579	567	475
International	133	125	122	114	103	64
Average sales per U.S. location ($ millions)	$78.4	$77.9	$75.1	$71.8	$70.2	$56.8
Sales growth at existing warehouses open more than 12 months:						
Including gasoline sales	−1.4%	4.9%	4.9%	2.5%	5.0%	n.a.
Not including gasoline sales	0.7%	3.7%	4.2%	2.9%	n.a.	n.a.
Average warehouse size (square feet)	133,000	133,000	132,000	132,000	129,400	122,100

[a]The sales figure includes membership fees and is for U.S. warehouses only. For financial reporting purposes, Walmart consolidates the operations of all foreign-based stores into a single "international" segment figure; thus, financial information for foreign-based Sam's Club locations is not separately available.

Source: Walmart,10-K reports and annual reports, fiscal years 2010, 2008, 2006, and 2001.

Facility sizes ranged between 71,000 and 190,000 square feet, with an average size of approximately 133,000 square feet. All warehouses had concrete floors; sparse decor; and goods displayed on pallets, simple wooden shelves, or racks (in the case of apparel).

Merchandise Offerings

Sam's Club stocked brand-name merchandise, including hardgoods, some softgoods, institutional-size grocery items, and selected private-label items sold under the brands Member's Mark, Bakers & Chefs, and Sam's Club. Generally, each Sam's Club warehouse also carried software, electronics, jewelry, sporting goods, toys, tires and batteries, books, DVDs, and office supplies; most had fresh-foods departments that included bakery, meat, produce, floral products, and a Sam's Cafe. A significant number of clubs had a one-hour photo processing department, a pharmacy that filled prescriptions, an optical department, and

self-service gasoline pumps. Members could shop for a broad assortment of merchandise and services online at www.samsclub.com.

Like Costco Wholesale, Sam's Club stocked about 4,000 items, a big fraction of which were standard and a small fraction of which represented special buys and one-time offerings. The treasure-hunt items at Sam's tended to be less upscale and carry lower price tags than those at Costco. The reported percentage composition of sales at Sam's Club is shown in the table on the next page.

Membership and Hours of Operation

The annual fee for Sam's Club business members was $35 for the primary membership card, with a spouse card available at no additional cost. Business members could add up to eight business associates for $35 each and could purchase memberships for employees at $30 per membership for 50 to 999 employees and $25 for 1,000 or more employees. The annual

	Fiscal year ending January 31	
	2010	**2009**
Food and beverages (dairy, meat, bakery, deli, produce, dry, chilled or frozen packaged foods, alcoholic and nonalcoholic beverages, floral and other grocery items)	39%	39%
Health and wellness (pharmacy and optical services, health and beauty aids, paper goods, laundry and home care, baby care, pet supplies and restaurant supplies)	19	18
Technology, office, and entertainment (electronics, wireless, software, video games, movies, books, music, toys, office supplies, office furniture and photo processing)	10	10
Home and apparel (home improvement Items, outdoor living, grills, gardening, furniture, apparel, jewelry, house wares, seasonal items, mattresses and small appliances)	8	9
Tobacco/candy and fuel/auto (tobacco, snack foods, tools and power equipment, sales of gasoline, and tire and battery centers)	24	24

membership fee for an Advantage (individual) member was $40, which included a spouse card. A Sam's Club Plus premium membership cost $100 and included an assortment of additional benefits and services, including health insurance; merchant credit card processing; website operation; personal and financial services; and an auto, boat, and recreational vehicle insurance program.

Operating hours for Sam's Clubs were Monday through Friday, 10:00 a.m. to 8:30 p.m.; Saturday, 9:00 a.m. to 8:30 p.m.; and Sunday, 10:00 a.m. to 6:00 p.m. All club locations offered a Gold Key program that permitted business members to shop before the regular operating hours Monday through Saturday, starting at 7:00 a.m. Members could use a variety of payment methods, including debit cards, certain types of credit cards, and a private-label co-branded Discover credit card issued by a third-party provider. The pharmacy and optical departments accepted payments for products and services through members' health insurance plans.

Distribution

Approximately 63 percent of the nonfuel merchandise at Sam's Club was shipped from the division's own distribution facilities and, in the case of perishable items, from some of Walmart's grocery distribution centers; the balance was shipped by suppliers direct to Sam's Club locations. Like Costco, Sam's Club distribution centers employed cross-docking techniques whereby incoming shipments were transferred immediately to outgoing trailers destined for Sam's Club locations; shipments typically spent less than 24 hours at a cross-docking facility and, in some instances less than an hour. The Sam's Club distribution center network consisted of 8 company-owned and operated distribution facilities and 18 third-party-owned and operated facilities. A combination of company-owned trucks and independent trucking companies was used to transport nonperishable merchandise from distribution centers to club locations; Sam's used independent trucking companies to transport perishable grocery items to distribution centers to its warehouses.

BJ'S WHOLESALE

Since the beginning of 2004, BJ's Wholesale had expanded from 150 warehouse club locations to 187 warehouse clubs; its operations were exclusively in the eastern United States, from Maine to Florida. BJ's planned to open seven to nine new warehouses in 2010 (including one relocation), all in existing geographic markets. BJ's had 167 "full-sized" warehouses, averaging 113,000 square feet, and 20 smaller format warehouses, averaging 72,000 square feet and located in markets too small to support a full-sized warehouse. Approximately 85 percent of BJ's full-sized warehouse clubs had at least one

Costco or Sam's Club warehouse operating in their trading areas (within 10 miles). Only one of the smaller BJ's clubs faced competition from a Costco or Sam's Club located within 10 miles. In early 2010, BJ's had approximately 23,500 full- and part-time employees; none of BJ's employees were represented by a union.

Exhibit 7 presents financial and operating data for BJ's Wholesale for 2006–2010.

BJ's Strategy

Like Costco and Sam's, BJ's Wholesale sold high-quality brand-name merchandise at prices that were significantly lower than those at supermarkets, discount retail chains, department stores, drugstores, and specialty retail stores like Best Buy. But BJ's had developed a strategy and operating model that management believed differentiated the company from its two primary competitors:

- It focused on its Inner Circle (individual) members through merchandising strategies that emphasized a customer-friendly shopping experience in several respects:
  - BJ's stocked a broader product assortment than Sam's Club and Costco, approximately 7,000 items.
  - To make shopping easier and more efficient for members, BJ's had aisle markers, express checkout lanes, self-checkout lanes, and low-cost video-based sales aids.
  - Stores were open more hours than both Costco and Sam's stores; typical hours of operation were 9:00 a.m. to 7:00 p.m. Monday through Friday and 9:00 a.m. to 6:00 p.m. Saturday and Sunday.
  - While many items were sold in bulk, BJ's offered some smaller package sizes that were easier to carry home and store, including sizes that were comparable to those offered in supermarkets. Smaller package sizes were typical in a number of fresh-food categories, including dairy, meat, bakery, fish, and produce. Management worked closely with manufacturers to develop packaging and sizes well suited for selling through the warehouse club format in order to economize on handling costs and help keep prices low.
- In some product assortments, BJ's had three price categories for members to choose from—good, deluxe, and luxury.
- BJ's was the only major warehouse club operator to accept manufacturers' coupons, which provided added value for members; it also accepted more credit and debit payment options than its warehouse club competitors.
- BJ's warehouses had a number of specialty services designed to enable members to complete more of their shopping at BJ's and to encourage more frequent trips to the clubs. These services included full-service optical centers, food courts, full-service Verizon Wireless centers, home improvement services, BJ's Vacations, garden and storage sheds, patios and sunrooms, installation of home security systems, a propane-tank-filling service, an automobile-buying service, a car rental service, muffler and brake services operated in conjunction with Monro Muffler Brake, television and home theater installation, and electronics and jewelry protection plans. Most of these services were provided by outside operators in space leased from BJ's. As of January 2010, there were gas station operations at 104 warehouse club locations; like Costco, BJ's sold gasoline at a discounted price as a means of displaying a favorable price image to prospective members and providing added value to existing members. In early 2007, BJ's abandoned prescription filling and closed all of its 46 in-club pharmacies.
- At the BJ's website (www.bjs.com), members could shop from thousands of additional products not found in the company's warehouse clubs. Items sold

▶EXHIBIT 7

Selected Financial and Operating Data, BJ's Wholesale Club, Fiscal Years 2006–2010

	Fiscal Year Ended				
	Jan. 30, 2010	Jan. 31, 2009	Feb. 2, 2008	Feb. 3, 2007 (53 weeks)	Jan. 28, 2006
Selected Income Statement Data ($ millions, except per share data)					
Net sales	$ 9,954	$ 9,802	$ 8,792	$ 8,280	$ 7,725
Membership fees	182	178	176	162	150
Other revenues	51	48	47	54	58
Total revenues	10,187	10,027	9,014	8,497	7,933
Cost of sales, including buying and occupancy costs	9,081	9,004	8,091	7,601	7,064
Selling, general and administrative expenses	875	799	724	740	643
Operating income	224	221	195	144	214
Interest income, net	(1)	1	4	3	3
Provision for income taxes	91	86	78	57	86
Net income	$ 132	$ 135	$ 123	$ 72	$ 129
Income per common share:					
Basic earnings per share:	$2.47	$2.32	$1.93	$1.10	$1.89
Diluted earnings per share:	2.42	2.28	1.90	1.08	1.87
Balance Sheet and Cash Flow Data ($ millions)					
Cash and cash equivalents	$ 59	$ 51	$ 97	$ 56	$ 162
Current assets	1,173	1,076	1,145	1,070	1,120
Current liabilities	1,006	909	946	867	862
Working capital	167	167	199	203	258
Merchandise inventories	930	860	877	851	813
Total assets	2,166	2,021	2,047	1,993	1,990
Long-term debt	1	1	2	2	3
Stockholders' equity	1,033	985	980	1,020	1,016
Cash flow from operations	298	224	305	173	192
Capital expenditures	176	138	90	191	123
Selected Operating Data					
Clubs open at end of year	187	180	177	172	163
Number of members (in thousands)	9,400	9,000	8,800	8,700	8,619
Average sales per club location ($ millions)	$53.2	$54.6	$49.7	$48.1	$47.4
Sales growth at existing clubs open more than 12 months	−1.9%	9.4%	3.7%	1.2%	3.6%

Source: BJ's Wholesale Club, 10-K reports for 2010, 2008, and 2007.

on the BJ's website included electronics, computers, video games, office equipment, products for the home, health and beauty aids, sporting goods, outdoor living products, baby products, toys and jewelry, and such services as auto and home insurance, home improvement, travel services, and television and home theater installation.

- Club locations were clustered in order to benefit from greater name recognition and maximize the efficiencies of management support, distribution, and marketing activities.

- BJ's strove to establish and maintain the first or second industry leading position in each major market area where it operated.

Food accounted for approximately 65 percent of BJ's merchandise sales in 2009. The remaining 35 percent consisted of a wide variety of general merchandise items. Food categories at BJ's included frozen foods, fresh meat and dairy products, beverages, dry grocery items, fresh produce and flowers, canned goods, and household paper products. General merchandise included consumer electronics, prerecorded media, small appliances, tires, jewelry, health and beauty aids, household needs, chemicals, computer software, books, greeting cards, apparel, furniture, toys and seasonal items. More than 70 percent of the products BJ's sold were items that could also be found in supermarkets.

BJ's private-label products were primarily of premium quality and were generally priced below the top-competing branded product. During the past two years, BJ's had pruned its private-label offerings by about 12 percent, opting to focus on those items having the highest margins and biggest sales volumes. Private-label goods accounted for approximately 10 percent of food and general merchandise sales in 2009, versus 11 percent in 2008 and 13 percent in 2007.

Warehouse Club Operations

BJ's warehouses were located in both freestanding locations and shopping centers. Construction and site development costs for a full-sized owned BJ's club were in the $6 to $10 million range; land acquisition costs ranged from $5 to $10 million but could be significantly higher in some locations. Each warehouse generally had an investment of $3.5 to $4.0 million for fixtures and equipment. Pre-opening expenses at a new club ran $1.0 to $1.5 million. Including space for parking, a typical full-sized BJ's club required 13 to 14 acres of land; smaller clubs typically required about 8 acres. During recent years, the company had financed all of its club expansions, as well as all other capital expenditures, with internally generated funds.

Merchandise purchased from manufacturers was routed either to a BJ's cross-docking facility or directly to clubs. Personnel at the cross-docking facilities broke down truckload quantity shipments from manufacturers and reallocated goods for shipment to individual clubs, generally within 24 hours. BJ's worked closely with manufacturers to minimize the amount of handling required once merchandise is received at a club. Merchandise was generally displayed on pallets containing large quantities of each item, thereby reducing labor required for handling, stocking, and restocking. Backup merchandise was generally stored in steel racks above the sales floor. Most merchandise was premarked by the manufacturer so that it did not require ticketing at the club. Full-sized clubs had approximately $2 million in inventory. Management had been able to limit inventory shrinkage to no more than 0.20 percent of net sales in each of the last three fiscal years (a percentage well below those of other types of retailers) by strictly controlling the exits of clubs, by generally limiting customers to members, and by using state-of-the-art electronic article surveillance technology. Exhibit 8 shows interior and exterior scenes at various BJ's locations.

Membership

Since 2006, the number of businesses and individuals with BJ's membership cards had climbed from 8.6 million to 9.4 million. The company charged $45 per year for a primary Inner Circle membership (for individuals and households),

► EXHIBIT 8 **Scenes of BJ's Wholesale Clubs**

which included one free supplemental membership; members in the same household could purchase additional supplemental memberships for $20. A business membership also cost $45 per year, which included one free supplemental membership and the ability to purchase additional supplemental memberships for $20. Since 2003, BJ's had offered a Rewards membership program geared to high-frequency, high-volume members that entailed a 2 percent rebate, capped at $500 per year, on most in-club purchases. In the fiscal year ending January 30, 2010, 5.5 percent of all BJ's members were Rewards members (which entailed an annual fee of $90); these members accounted for 13 percent of BJ's total merchandise and food sales.

BJ's was the only warehouse club that accepted MasterCard, Visa, Discover, and American Express cards at all locations; members could also pay for purchases by cash, check, and debit cards. BJ's accepted returns of most merchandise within 30 days of purchase. Losses associated with payments by check were insignificant; members who bounced checks were restricted to cash-only terms.

Information Systems

Starting in 2007, BJ's management began a large-scale technology initiative to upgrade or replace the company's sales reporting, financial, human resources, and membership systems; the effort was expected to take a minimum of five years to complete. A new warehouse management system, implemented in 2009, enabled the company to more efficiently manage its logistics, inventory, and warehouse replenishment activities. Sales data was analyzed daily for replenishment purposes. Detailed point-of-sale data enabled warehouse managers and buying staff to track changes in members' buying behavior. The company had recently improved the efficiency of its checkout process and implemented an online system to handle merchandise returns and refunds.

Advertising and Public Relations

BJ's Wholesale increased customer awareness of its clubs primarily through a variety of public relations and community involvement activities, marketing programs for newly opened clubs, social media outreach, and a publication called *BJ's Journal*, which was mailed to members throughout the year. During the holiday season, BJ's engaged in radio and TV advertising, a portion of which was funded by vendors. BJ's employed dedicated marketing personnel to solicit potential business members and to contact selected other organizations to attract new members. BJ's used one-day passes to introduce non-members to its club and, in the fall and spring, the company typically ran free trial membership promotions. Members could sign up for e-mail offers at the company's website.

In addition, BJ's had a co-branded Visa card that was underwritten by a major financial institution on a nonrecourse basis. Purchases made at BJ's with the co-branded Visa card earned a 2 percent rebate; all other purchases with the card earned a 1 percent rebate. Rebates were issued by the financial institution in the form of BJ's Bucks, which were certificates redeemable for merchandise at any BJ's club.

BJ's Charitable Foundation donated to dozens of nonprofit organizations providing basic-need services to children and families in communities where a BJ's Wholesale Club was located; in 2009, these donations amounted to more than $1.6 million.

ENDNOTES

[1] Costco management presentation, March 2010, www.costco.com, accessed April 7, 2010.

[2] As quoted in Matthew Boyle, "Why Costco Is So Damn Addictive," *Fortune,* October 30, 2006, pp. 128–29.

[3] Steven Greenhouse, "How Costco Became the Anti-Wal-Mart," *The New York Times,* July 17, 2005, www.wakeupwalmart.com/news, accessed November 28, 2006.

[4] Quoted in Greenhouse, "How Costco Became the Anti-Wal-Mart."

[5] Quoted in Nina Shapiro, "Company for the People," *Seattle Weekly,* December 15, 2004, www.seattleweekly.com, accessed November 14, 2006.

[6] Quoted in Greenhouse, "How Costco Became the Anti-Wal-Mart."

[7] Boyle, "Why Costco Is So Damn Addictive," p. 132.

[8] Costco, 2005 annual report.

[9] Andria Cheng, "Costco Cracks Taiwan Market," *The Wall Street Journal,* April 2, 2010, p. B5.

[10] As quoted in Alan B. Goldberg and Bill Ritter, "Costco CEO Finds Pro-Worker Means Profitability," *20/20,* August 2, 2006, http://abcnews.go.com/2020/Business/story?id=1362779, accessed November 15, 2006.

[11] Ibid.

[12] As described in Shapiro, "Company for the People," *Seattle Weekly,* December 15, 2004, www.seattleweekly.com, accessed November 14, 2006.

[13] Based on data for Costco posted at PayScale, www.payscale.com, accessed October 9, 2008.

[14] Ibid.

[15] Quoted in Goldberg and Ritter, "Costco CEO Finds Pro-Worker Means Profitability."

[16] Shapiro, "Company for the People."

[17] Quoted in Lori Montgomery, "Maverick Costco CEO Joins Push to Raise Minimum Wage," *The Washington Post,* January 30, 2007, p. D4.

[18] Quoted in Goldberg and Ritter, "Costco CEO Finds Pro-Worker Means Profitability."

[19] Ibid.

[20] Walmart, 2010 annual report, p. 8.

COMPETITION IN ENERGY DRINKS, SPORTS DRINKS, AND VITAMIN-ENHANCED BEVERAGES

John E. Gamble
University of South Alabama

Alternative beverages such as energy drinks, sports drinks, and vitamin-enhanced beverages were the stars of the beverage industry during the mid-2000s. Rapid growth in the category, coupled with premium prices and high profit margins made alternative beverages an important part of beverage companies' lineup of brands. Global beverage companies such as Coca-Cola and PepsiCo had relied on such beverages to sustain volume growth in mature markets where consumers were reducing their consumption of carbonated soft drinks. In addition, Coca-Cola, PepsiCo, and other beverage companies were intent on expanding the market for alternative beverages by introducing energy drinks, sports drinks, and vitamin drinks in more and more emerging international markets. Global beverage producers had not been the only ones to benefit from increasing consumer demand for alternative beverage choices. Entrepreneurs such as the founders of Red Bull GmbH, Rockstar, Inc., Hansen Natural Corporation (maker of Monster Energy), Living Essentials (maker of 5-Hour Energy), and Energy Brands (originator of glacéau vitaminwater) had become multimillionaires through their development and sale of alternative beverages.

However, the premium-priced alternative beverage market had been hit especially hard by the lingering economic downturn in the United States. Sales of sports drinks declined by 12.3 percent between 2008 and 2009, and sales of flavored and vitamin-enhanced waters had declined by 12.5 percent over the same period. The sales of energy drinks fared better, but 2009 segment sales exceeded sales in 2008 by only 0.2 percent. Industry analysts were undecided on what percentage of the poor 2009 performance for alternative beverages was related to the overall economy and how much could be attributed to market maturity. Beverage producers had made various attempts at increasing the size of the market for alternative beverages by extending existing product lines and developing altogether new products. For example, PepsiCo had expanded its lineup of Amp Energy drinks to 12 flavors, expanded SoBe vitamin-enhanced beverages to 28 flavors and variations, and increased the Gatorade lineup to include dozens of flavors and variations. Beverage producers were also seeking additional growth by quickly launching concentrated two-ounce energy shots to garner a share of the new beverage category that originated with the development of Living Essentials' 5-Hour Energy. Some beverage producers were also moving to capture demand for new relaxation drinks that were designed to have a calming effect or help those with insomnia.

While attempting to expand the market for alternative beverages and increase sales and market share, beverage producers also were forced to contend with criticism from some that energy drinks, energy shots, and relaxation drinks presented health risks for consumers and that some producers' strategies promoted reckless behavior. Excessive consumption of high-caffeine-content beverages could produce arrhythmias and insomnia, while mixing alcohol with energy drinks could mask the consumer's level of intoxication and lead to increased risk-taking and other serious alcohol-related problems. In addition, many physicians warned consumers against consuming relaxation drinks that contained the potentially harmful ingredients melatonin and kava. But as 2011 approached, the primary concern of most producers of energy drinks, sports drinks, and vitamin-enhanced beverages was how to best improve their competitive standing in the marketplace.

INDUSTRY CONDITIONS IN 2010

The global beverage industry was projected to grow from $1.58 trillion in 2009 to nearly $1.78 trillion in 2014 as beverage producers entered new geographic markets, developed new types of beverages, and continued to create demand for popular drinks. A great deal of industry growth was expected to result from steady growth in the purchasing power of consumers in developing countries, since the saturation rate for all types of beverages was high in developed countries. For example, market maturity and poor economic conditions caused the U.S. beverage industry to decline by 2.1 percent in 2008 and by 3.1 percent in 2009. The 2.3 percent decline in the volume sales of carbonated soft drinks marked the fifth consecutive year that U.S. consumers had purchased fewer carbonated soft drinks than the year before. Industry analysts believed that while carbonated soft drinks would remain the most-consumed beverage in the United States for some time, annual sales would continue to

decline as consumers developed preferences for bottled water, sports drinks, fruit juices, ready-to-drink tea, vitamin-enhanced beverages, energy drinks, ready-to-drink coffee, and other types of beverages.

As consumer preferences shifted during the 2000s, sports drinks, energy drinks, and vitamin-enhanced drinks had grown to become important segments within the industry in 2010. In addition, such alternative beverages tended to carry high price points, which made them attractive to both new entrants and established beverage companies such as the Coca-Cola Company and PepsiCo. Sports drinks and vitamin-enhanced beverages tended to carry retail prices that were 50 to 75 percent higher than similar-size carbonated soft drinks and bottled water, while energy drink pricing by volume might be as much as 400 percent higher than carbonated soft drinks. While the alternative beverage segment of the industry offered opportunities for bottlers, the poor economy had decreased demand for higher-priced beverages, with sales of sports drinks declining by 12.3 percent between 2008 and 2009 and the

▶ **EXHIBIT 1**

Dollar Value and Volume Sales of the Global Beverage Industry, 2005–2009, with Forecasts for 2010–2014

Year	Dollar Value ($ billions)	Volume Sales (billions of liters)
2005	$1,428.4	391.8
2006	1,469.3	409.1
2007	1,514.1	427.3
2008	1,548.3	442.6
2009	1,581.7	458.3
2010*	1,618.4	474.9
2011*	1,657.6	492.1
2012*	1,696.1	508.4
2013*	1,736.5	525.8
2014*	1,775.3	542.5

*Forecast.

Source: Global Beverages Industry Profile, Datamonitor, March 2010.

▶EXHIBIT 2

U.S. Beverage Industry Volume Sales by Segment, 2009

Category	Volume (millions of gallons)	Market Share	Growth	Share Point Change
Carbonated soft drinks	13,919.3	48.2%	−2.3%	+0.4
Bottled water	8,435.3	29.2	−2.7	+0.1
Fruit beverages	3,579.2	12.4	−3.7	−0.1
Sports drinks	1,157.8	4.0	−12.3	+0.4
Ready-to-drink tea	901.4	3.1	1.2	+0.1
Flavored or enhanced water	460.0	1.6	−12.5	−0.2
Energy drinks	354.5	1.2	0.2	0.0
Ready-to-drink coffee	51.5	0.3	−5.4	0.0
Total	28,859.0	100.0%	− 3.1%	0.0

Note: Totals may not match data reported by Datamonitor because of differences in research methods.

Source: Beverage Marketing Corporation, as reported in "A Market in Decline," *Beverage World,* April 2010, p. 52.

sales of flavored and vitamin-enhanced waters declining by 12.5 percent over the same period. The economy had also impacted the sales of energy drinks, but only by slowing the growth in volume sales to 0.2 percent between 2008 and 2009. Among all types of beverages, only energy drinks and ready-to-drink tea experienced volume growth between 2008 and 2009. Exhibits 1 and 2 present sales statistics for the global and U.S. beverage industry, respectively.

Worldwide dollar sales of alternative beverages (sports drinks, energy drinks, and vitamin-enhanced beverages) grew by more than 13 percent annually between 2005 and 2007 before slowing to about 6 percent annually between 2007 and 2009. Demand in the United States had contributed greatly to the worldwide growth in alternative beverage consumption, with the United States accounting for 42.3 percent of the industry's worldwide sales of $40.2 billion in 2009. In the United States, sports drinks accounted for nearly 60 percent of alternative beverage sales in 2009, while vitamin-enhanced drinks and energy drinks accounted for about 23 percent and 18 percent of 2009 alternative beverage sales, respectively. Exhibit 3 presents alternative beverage dollar value and volume sales for 2005 through 2009 and forecasts for alternative beverage sales for 2010 through 2014. Exhibits 4–7 present statis-

▶EXHIBIT 3

Dollar Value and Volume Sales of the Global Market for Alternative Beverages, 2005–2009, with Forecasts for 2010–2014

Year	Dollar Value ($ billions)	Volume (billions of liters)
2005	$27.7	9.4
2006	31.9	10.3
2007	35.5	11.1
2008	37.8	11.9
2009	40.2	12.7
2010*	42.8	13.5
2011*	45.5	14.4
2012*	48.0	15.1
2013*	50.8	16
2014*	53.5	16.8

*Forecast.

Source: Global Functional Drinks Industry Profile, Datamonitor, April 2010.

tics on the relative sizes of the regional markets for alternative beverages.

Even though energy drinks, sports drinks, and vitamin-enhanced drinks were all categorized as alternative beverages, the consumer profile varied substantially across the

▶EXHIBIT 4

Geographic Share of the Alternative Beverages Market, 2009

Country	Percentage
United States	42.3%
Asia-Pacific	31.5
Europe	22.2
Americas (excluding U.S.)	4.0
Total	100.0%

Source: Global Functional Drinks Industry Profile, Datamonitor, April 2010, and United States Functional Drinks Industry Profile, Datamonitor, April 2010.

three types of beverages. While the profile of an energy drink consumer was a teenage boy, sports drinks were most frequently purchased by those who engaged in sports, fitness, or other strenuous activities such as outdoor manual labor jobs. It was quite common for teens to consume sports drinks after practicing or

▶EXHIBIT 5

Dollar Value and Volume Sales of the U.S. Market for Alternative Beverages, 2005–2009, with Forecasts for 2010–2014

Year	Dollar Value ($ billions)	Volume (billions of liters)
2005	$ 9.2	2.8
2006	12.4	3.3
2007	14.8	3.7
2008	15.9	4.0
2009	17.0	4.2
2010*	18.2	4.5
2011*	19.5	4.7
2012*	20.8	5.0
2013*	22.2	5.3
2014*	23.6	5.5

*Forecast.

Source: United States Functional Drinks Industry Profile, Datamonitor, April 2010.

▶EXHIBIT 6

Volume Sales and Dollar Value of the Asia-Pacific Alternative Beverages Market, 2005–2009, Forecasts for 2010–2014

Year	Dollar Value ($ billions)	Volume (billions of liters)
2005	$10.2	4.80
2006	10.7	5.10
2007	11.2	5.44
2008	12.0	5.81
2009	12.7	6.20
2010*	13.5	6.63
2011*	14.3	7.09
2012*	14.9	7.41
2013*	15.7	7.82
2014*	16.5	8.23

*Forecast.

Source: Asia-Pacific Functional Drinks Industry Profile, Datamonitor, April 2010.

▶EXHIBIT 7

Volume Sales and Dollar Value of the European Alternative Beverages Market, 2005–2009, with Forecasts for 2010–2014

Year	Dollar Value ($ billions)	Volume (billions of liters)
2005	$ 7.4	1.27
2006	7.8	1.34
2007	8.2	1.43
2008	8.6	1.51
2009	9.1	1.60
2010*	9.5	1.69
2011*	9.9	1.78
2012*	10.4	1.88
2013*	10.8	1.98
2014*	11.3	2.08

*Forecast.

Source: Europe Functional Drinks Industry Profile, Datamonitor, April 2010.

participating in school sports events and for manual laborers to consume sports drinks on hot days. Vitamin-enhanced beverages could substitute for sports drinks but were frequently purchased by adult consumers interested in increasing their intakes of vitamins. Even though enhanced waters offered potential benefits, there were some features of enhanced waters that might cause consumers to limit their consumption of such products, including the need for sweeteners to disguise the taste of added vitamins and supplements. As a result, calorie counts for vitamin-enhanced beverages ranged from 20 calories per 16-ounce serving for Propel to 100 calories per 16-ounce serving for glacéau vitaminwater. In addition, some medical researchers had suggested that consumers would need to drink approximately 10 bottles of enhanced water each day to meet minimum dietary requirements for the vitamins promoted on the waters' labels.

Distribution and Sale of Alternative Beverages

Consumers could purchase most alternative beverages in supermarkets, supercenters, natural foods stores, wholesale clubs, and convenience stores. Convenience stores were a particularly important distribution channel for alternative beverages since sports drinks, vitamin-enriched drinks, and energy drinks were usually purchased for immediate consumption. In fact, convenience stores accounted for about 75 percent of energy drink sales in 2010. Although energy drinks were typically purchased in convenience stores, sports drinks and vitamin-enhanced beverages were also available in most delis and many restaurants, from vending machines, and sometimes at sporting events and other special events like concerts, outdoor festivals, and carnivals.

PepsiCo and Coca-Cola's soft drink businesses aided the two companies in making alternative beverages available in supermarkets, supercenters, wholesale clubs, and convenience stores. Soft drink sales were important to all types of food stores since soft drinks

made up a sizable percentage of the store's sales and since food retailers frequently relied on soft drink promotions to generate store traffic. Coca-Cola and PepsiCo were able to encourage their customers to purchase items across their product lines to ensure prompt and complete shipment of key soft drink products. Smaller producers typically used third parties like beer and wine distributors or food distributors to make sales and deliveries to supermarkets, convenience store buyers, and restaurants and delis. Most distributors made deliveries of alternative beverages to convenience stores and restaurants along with their regular scheduled deliveries of other foods and beverages.

Because of the difficulty for food service distributors to restock vending machines and provide alternative beverages to special events, Coca-Cola and Pepsi-Cola were able to dominate such channels since they could make deliveries of sports drinks and vitamin-enhanced drinks along with their deliveries of carbonated soft drinks. Coca-Cola and Pepsi-Cola's vast beverage distribution systems made it easy for the two companies to make Gatorade, SoBe, Powerade, and glacéau vitaminwater available anywhere Coke or Pepsi could be purchased.

Convenience stores were aggressive in pressing alternative beverage producers and food distributors for low prices and slotting fees. Most convenience stores carried only two to four brands of alternative beverages beyond what was distributed by Coca-Cola and PepsiCo, and required sellers to pay annual slotting fees in return for providing bottle facings on a cooler shelf. Food and beverage distributors usually allowed alternative beverage producers to negotiate slotting fees and any rebates directly with convenience store buyers.

There was not as much competition among producers of sports drinks and vitamin-enhanced drinks to gain shelf space in delis and restaurants, since volume was relatively low— making per unit distribution costs exceedingly high unless other beverages were delivered along with alternative beverages. PepsiCo

▶ EXHIBIT 8

Worldwide and Regional Market Shares for the Three Largest Producers of Alternative Beverages, 2009

Company	Worldwide	United States	Asia-Pacific	Europe
PepsiCo	26.5%	47.8%	12.4	12.9%
Coca-Cola	11.5	10.2	13.7	n.a.
Red Bull	7.0	10.6	n.a.	10.1
Others	55.0	31.4	73.9	77.0
Total	100.0%	100.1%	100.0%	100.0%

n.a. = Not available

Sources: Global Functional Drinks Industry Profile, Datamonitor, April 2010; United States Functional Drinks Industry Profile, Datamonitor, April 2010; Asia-Pacific Functional Drinks Industry Profile, Datamonitor, April 2010; and Europe Functional Drinks Industry Profile, Datamonitor, April 2010.

and Coca-Cola were among the better-suited alternative beverage producers to economically distribute sports drinks and vitamin-enhanced beverages to restaurants, since they likely provided fountain drinks to such establishments. Exhibit 8 presents worldwide and regional market shares for the three largest producers of alternative beverages in 2009. Distributors for the leading energy drink brands sold in the United States are listed in Exhibit 9.

Suppliers to the Industry

The suppliers to the alternative beverage industry included the makers of such nutritive and non-nutritive ingredients as sugar, aspartame, fructose, glucose, natural and artificial flavoring, artificial colors, caffeine, taurine, glucuronolactone, niacin, sodium, potassium, chloride, and other nutritional supplements. Suppliers to the industry also included the manufacturers of aluminum cans, plastic bot-

▶ EXHIBIT 9

Market Shares for the Leading Energy Drink Brands in the United States, 2006–2009

Brand	Distributor	2006 (% of dollar sales)	2007 (% of dollar sales)	2008 (% of dollar sales)	2009 (% of dollar sales)
Red Bull	Independent	43%	35%	40%	40%
Monster	Coca-Cola	15	27	23	27
Rockstar	PepsiCo	11	11	12	8
NOS	Coca-Cola	n.a.	2	2	4
Amp	PepsiCo	4	5	8	3
DoubleShot	PepsiCo	n.a.	n.a.	2	3
Full Throttle	Coca-Cola	7	7	4	2
Others		20	13	9	13
Total		100%	100%	100%	100%

n.a. = Not available.

Sources: "2010 State of the Industry Report," Beverage World, April 2010; BevNET.com.

tles and caps, label printers, and secondary packaging suppliers. While unique supplements like taurine might be available from only a few sources, most packaging supplies needed for the production of alternative beverages were readily available for a large number of suppliers. The numerous suppliers of secondary packaging materials (e.g., cardboard boxes, shrink-wrap, six-pack rings, printed film or paper labels) aggressively competed for the business of large alternative beverage producers. All but the largest sellers of alternative beverages contracted procurement and production activities to contract bottlers who produced energy drinks and other alternative beverages to the sellers' specifications.

Key Competitive Capabilities in the Alternative Beverages Market

Product innovation had been among the most important competitive features of the alternative beverage industry since the introduction of Gatorade in 1967. Alternative beverages competed on the basis of differentiation from traditional drinks such as carbonated soft drinks or fruit juices and were also positioned within their respective segments on the basis of differentiation. For example, all energy drink brands attempted to develop brand loyalty based on taste, the energy-boosting properties of their ingredients, and image. An energy drink's image was a factor of its brand name and packaging, clever ads, endorsements from celebrities and extreme sports athletes, and sponsorships of extreme sports events and music concerts. Differentiation among vitamin-enhanced beverages tended to center on brand name and packaging, advertising, unique flavors, and nutritional properties. Because of the importance of brand recognition, successful sellers of alternative beverages were required to possess well-developed brand-building skills. The industry's largest sellers were global food and beverage companies—having built respected brands in snack foods, soft drinks, and fruit juices prior to entering the alternative beverage industry.

Alternative beverage sellers also needed to have efficient distribution systems to supermarket and convenience store channels to be successful in the industry. It was imperative for alternative beverage distributors (whether direct store delivery by bottlers or delivery by third-parties) to maximize the number of deliveries per driver since distribution included high fixed costs for warehouses, trucks, hand-held inventory tracking devices, and labor. It was also critical for distributors and sellers to provide on-time deliveries and offer responsive customer service to large customers. Also, volume and market share were key factors in keeping marketing expenses at an acceptable per-unit level.

Recent Trends in the Alternative Beverage Market

Despite the impact of the ongoing U.S. recession on the entire beverage industry, alternative beverage producers were optimistic about prospects for the industry. Demand was expected to grow worldwide as consumer purchasing power increased, and even though volume was down in the United States for sports drinks and vitamin-enhanced drinks, alternative beverages offered profit margins much higher than those of other beverages. Innovation in brands, flavors, and formulations was expected to be necessary for supporting premium pricing and volume increases. Industry analysts believed that such exotic flavors as cardamom, hibiscus, and cupuacu might prove to be hits in 2011 and 2012.

The emergence of two-ounce energy shots sold on convenience store counters had proved to be an important growth category for the industry. The category was created with the introduction of Living Essentials' 5-Hour Energy in 2004. 5-Hour Energy contained amino acids and taurine plus 2,000 percent of the daily requirement for vitamin B_6, 8,333 percent of the daily requirement for B_{12}, and 100 milligrams of caffeine (the equivalent of a cup of coffee). By comparison, the caffeine content of energy drinks ranged from 160 milligrams

▶ **EXHIBIT 10**

Annual Revenues for the Top Five Energy Shot Brands in the United States, 2009

Brand	Revenues ($ millions)	Revenue Growth (2008–2009)
5-Hour Energy	$494.6	+58.6%
Stacker2 6-Hour Power	30.4	+32.9
Red Bull Energy Shot	22.1	n.a.
Monster Hitman	19.7	+611.7
NOS Energy Shot	11.8	−10.4

n.a. = Not available

Source: *Beverage World* 2010 State of the Industry Report, April 2010.

for Red Bull to 240 milligrams for Rockstar Punched. Unlike energy drinks that focused on teens, energy shots were targeted to office workers, parents, and other adults who might need a boost of energy during a demanding day. Red Bull, Coca-Cola's NOS, Hansen's Monster, PepsiCo's Amp, and Rockstar had all developed competing energy shots, but none were a serious threat to Living Essentials' 5-Hour Energy in 2010. 5-Hour Energy held an 85 percent market share in the category in 2009. Exhibit 10 presents annual revenues for the top five energy shot brands in the United States in 2009. Analysts believed that Europe, Australia, South America, and the Middle East were attractive markets for the expansion-minded makers of energy shots.

Unlike carbonated soft drinks, the caffeine content of energy shots and energy drinks was not regulated by the U.S. Food and Drug Administration and could contain as much caffeine as the producer thought appropriate. There was concern among some health professionals over the high caffeine content of energy drinks and the effects of large doses of caffeine on individuals, especially children. The most significant health problems related to high caffeine consumption were heart arrhythmia and insomnia. It was not unheard of for adults with

heart arrhythmias to be admitted to emergency rooms after consuming three or more energy drinks in one day. Also, physicians attributed a New Mexico man's appendicitis and gallstones to excessive consumption of energy drinks. Physicians also warned that the combination of energy drinks and over-the-counter drugs such as NoDoz could cause seizures. However, clinical studies had shown that, in moderate doses, caffeine contributed to healthy weight loss, was an effective treatment for asthma and headaches and reduced the risk of Parkinson's disease, depression, colon cancer, and type 2 diabetes. As a precaution, Monster Energy placed the following warning on its labels: "Limit 3 cans per day, not recommended for children, pregnant women or people sensitive to caffeine."[1]

There was also concern over the tendency of some individuals to mix alcohol with energy drinks. It was not uncommon at all for partiers to use energy drinks as a mixer to help off-set the depressive effects of alcohol and keep their energy levels high throughout the evening. It was estimated that more than 25 percent of college-age drinkers mixed alcohol with energy drinks. The frequency of the practice led MillerCoors to develop an alcohol energy drink that contained caffeine, taurine, guarana, and ginseng in addition to alcohol. Anheuser-Busch sold two similar drinks called Tilt and Bud Extra. Both companies removed the caffeine from the drinks after attorneys general in several states had written the U.S. Food and Drug Administration (FDA) to ask that the federal government force the removal of the products from the market. The attorneys general argued that the addition of caffeine to alcohol masked a drinker's level of intoxication and could lead to "increased risk-taking and other serious alcohol related problems such as traffic accidents, violence, sexual assault, and suicide."[2]

The relaxation drink niche within the alternative beverage industry also caused some concern among health professionals and members of law enforcement. Relaxation drinks such as Vacation in a Bottle (ViB) and Dream Water contained the hormone melatonin, which was produced by humans, plants, and animals and had many known and unknown effects on the human body. Melatonin had been associated with rapid-eye movement (REM) sleep and was used by some as a supplement to help treat insomnia. A Harvard Medical School sleep expert warned against the consumption of relaxation drinks by stating that hormones "should not be put in beverages, since the amount people drink often depends on thirst and taste rather than being taken only when needed like any other drug."[3] Kava and valerian root were two other common ingredients of relaxation drinks; the FDA warned against the use of kava and had not approved valerian root as a food additive.

Controversy also surrounded some relaxation drinks because of their association with the abuse of prescription cough syrup. The practice of mixing a prescription cough syrup whose ingredients included promethazine and codeine with Sprite or other carbonated soft drinks had become common in some inner-city areas, especially in southern U.S. states. The purple-colored cough syrup drink, which was commonly called "purple drank" or "sizzurp," was said to have been originated by Houston, Texas disc jockey and rapper DJ Screw, who died from an overdose of purple drank in 2000. Purple drank was frequently mentioned in hip-hop and rap songs such as those performed by Three 6 Mafia, Eminem, Lil'Wyte, Lil Boosie, Mike Jones, Lil' Wayne, Ludacris, T.I., and Kanye West. The use of sizzurp was also a problem in professional sports, and possession of the controlled substances used to make sizzurp had led to the arrests of a number of professional athletes, including Green Bay Packers defensive lineman Johnny Jolly and former Oakland Raiders quarterback JaMarcus Russell. Legal authorities believed that the purple-colored relaxation drinks Drank and Purple Stuff attempted to exploit the street use of purple drank. Innovative Beverage Group, the maker of Drank, had built its marketing plan on product placements in rap and hip-hop videos and launched a competition in summer

2010 that would award prizes to those who wrote the best new rap songs about the company's product. The market for relaxation drinks in the United States had increased from about 11 million cases in 2008 to 22.4 million cases in 2010. The U.S. market for relaxation drinks was projected to increase to nearly 50 million cases by 2014.

PROFILES OF THE LEADING ALTERNATIVE BEVERAGE PRODUCERS

PepsiCo

In 2010, PepsiCo was the world's fourth-largest food and beverage company, with 2009 sales of about $43 billion. The company's brands were sold in more than 200 countries and included such well-known names as Lay's, Tostitos, Cheetos, Mountain Dew, Pepsi, Doritos, Lipton Iced Tea, Tropicana, Aquafina, SoBe, Gatorade, Quaker, and Cracker Jack. The company held commanding market shares in many of the food and beverage categories where it competed. In 2009, it was the number one seller of beverages in the United States and its Frito-Lay division was four times as large as the next-largest seller of snacks in the United States. PepsiCo had upset Coca-Cola to become the largest seller of beverages in the United States, not by selling more carbonated soft drinks than Coke (Coca-Cola was the largest seller of carbonated soft drinks in 2009), but by leading in most other beverage categories. For example, Aquafina was the best-selling brand of water in the United States, Frappuccino was the number one brand of ready-to-drink coffee, Tropicana was ranked first in orange juice sales, and Gatorade held a commanding lead in sports drinks. The company's strength in non-carbonated beverages made it the world's largest seller of alternative beverages, with a global market share in 2009 of 26.5 percent. PepsiCo held more than a 2-to-1 worldwide market-share lead over industry runner-up, Coca-Cola, which had a global market share in alternative beverages of 11.5 percent in 2009. However,

PepsiCo's greatest strength was in the United States, where it held a 47.8 percent share of the total alternative beverage market in 2009.

PepsiCo's best-selling alternative beverages included Gatorade (which held a 75 percent share of the $1.57 billion U.S. sports drink market), Propel, SoBe Lifewater, and Amp Energy. PepsiCo produced 12 flavors of Amp Energy drinks and two flavors of No Fear energy drinks. Its SoBe brand included both energy drinks and vitamin-enhanced drinks. In 2010, PepsiCo bottled and marketed 2 varieties of SoBe Adrenaline Rush energy drinks and 28 varieties of SoBe vitamin-enhanced beverages. PepsiCo also marketed a line of DoubleShot Energy drinks that complemented its Starbucks Frappuccino drink line.

The company expanded its lineup of alternative drinks in 2009 with the launch of Charge, a lemon-flavored energy drink containing L-carnitine; Rebuild, a black tea drink fortified with amino acids and antioxidants; Defend, a drink fortified with antioxidants and beta-alanine; and Bloodshot, a juice drink containing 150 percent of the daily recommended dosage of vitamins B and C. The company also had a multiyear distribution agreement with Rockstar to distribute Rockstar energy drinks in the United States and Canada.

A summary of PepsiCo's financial performance between 2007 and 2009 is presented in Exhibit 11.

The Coca-Cola Company

The Coca-Cola Company was the world's leading manufacturer, marketer, and distributor of nonalcoholic beverage concentrates, with 2009 revenues of nearly $31 billion and sales in more than 200 countries. The company was best known for Coca-Cola, which had been called the world's most valuable brand. Along with the universal appeal of the Coca-Cola brand, Coca-Cola's vast global distribution system—which included independent bottlers, bottlers partially owned by Coca-Cola, and company-owned bottlers—made Coke an almost unstoppable international powerhouse.

▶EXHIBIT 11

Financial Summary for PepsiCo, 2007–2009 ($ millions, except per share information)

	2009	2008	2007
Net revenue	$43,232	$43,251	$39,474
Cost of sales	20,099	20,351	18,038
Selling, general and administrative expenses	15,026	15,877	14,196
Amortization of intangible assets	63	64	58
Operating profit	8,044	6,959	7,182
Bottling equity income	365	374	560
Interest expense	(397)	(329)	(224)
Interest income	67	41	125
Income before income taxes	8,079	7,045	7,643
Provision for income taxes	2,100	1,879	1,973
Net income	5,979	5,166	5,670
Less: Net income attributable to noncontrolling interests	33	24	12
Net income attributable to PepsiCo	$5,946	$5,142	$5,658
Net income attributable to PepsiCo per common share			
Basic	$3.81	$3.26	$3.48
Diluted	$3.77	$3.21	$3.41

Source: PepsiCo, 2009 10-K report.

Coca-Cola, Diet Coke, Fanta, and Sprite all ranked among the top five best-selling nonalcoholic beverages worldwide in 2009.

The strength of the Coca-Cola brand also aided the company in gaining distribution for new beverages. In the United States, Coca-Cola produced, marketed, and distributed Minute Maid orange juice products, Dasani purified water, Powerade sports drinks, an assortment of energy drink brands, Fuze vitamin-enhanced beverages, Nestea ready-to-drink teas, and glacéau vitaminwater. The company also produced and sold country- and region-specific beverages such as Bonaqua sparkling water in Europe, Georgia ready-to-drink coffee in Japan, and Hugo fruit and milk protein drinks in Latin America.

Even though Coca-Cola was the worldwide leader in carbonated soft drink sales, it had struggled to build market share in alternative beverages and trailed PepsiCo by a significant margin worldwide in energy drinks, sports drinks, and vitamin-enhanced beverages. Asia was the only geographic market where Coca-Cola's sales of alternative beverages exceeded the sales of PepsiCo's energy drinks, sports drinks, and vitamin-enhanced beverages. As of 2009, Coca-Cola had yet to gain strong demand for its alternative beverages in Europe and, as a result, was not listed among the leading sellers of alternative beverages in that market. In the United States, Coca-Cola was the third-largest seller of alternative beverages, with its combined sales of Powerade, Full Throttle, NOS, Rehab, TaB, and Vault energy drinks; glacéau vitaminwater; and Fuze vitamin-enhanced drinks, falling just short of the sales of Red Bull energy drinks.

Much of the company's efforts to build market share in 2009 and 2010 centered on new-product development and the introduction of existing brands into new country markets. In 2009, Coca-Cola introduced glacéau vitaminwater in South Africa, France, South Korea, Japan, Belgium, Portugal, Hong Kong, China, and Sweden; in that same year it also launched Cascal, a fermented fruit drink, in the United States and Burn energy drink in India. The company had introduced its newly developed Gladiator energy drink in Latin America in 2008. Among Coca-Cola's greatest resources in the energy drink category was its multiyear distribution agreement with Hansen Natural Corporation to distribute Hansen's Monster energy drink in parts of the United States, Canada, and six European countries.

A summary of the Coca-Cola Company's financial performance between 2007 and 2009 is presented in Exhibit 12.

Red Bull GmbH

Red Bull was the world's number one seller of energy drinks, which made it the third-largest producer of alternative beverages worldwide and the number two seller of alternative beverages in the United States and Europe. Red Bull's distinctive taste and formula of vitamins, taurine, and caffeine launched the energy drink market in the Western world in the late 1990s. Energy drinks similar to Red Bull had been produced and marketed in Asia since the 1970s. In fact, Red Bull's formula was modeled after Krating Daeng, a popular energy drink sold in Thailand that was recommended as a jet lag remedy to Austrian businessman Dietrich Mateschitz. Mateschitz had been in Thailand to call on T.C. Pharmaceutical, which was a client of his employer at the time and the manufacturer or Krating Daeng. Mateschitz was so impressed with the flavor and energy-boosting capabilities of Krating Daeng that he left his job and formed a partnership with T.C. Pharmaceutical's founder in 1984 to market the drink in Europe. The energy drink's formula was modified slightly to better appeal to Western palates and was renamed Red Bull, which was the English translation of Krating Daeng. Red Bull was launched in Austria in 1987 and sold more than 1 million cans during the year. The company expanded into Hungary and Slovenia in 1992, Germany and the United Kingdom in 1994, and the United States in 1997. In 2010, the company exported its energy drinks to more than 160 countries and delivered to retailers by independent distributors.

The company's slogan, "Red Bull gives you wings," signaled its energy-boosting properties,

▶EXHIBIT 12

Financial Summary for the Coca-Cola Company, 2007–2009 ($ millions)

	2009	2008	2007
Net operating revenues	$30,990	$31,944	$28,857
Cost of goods sold	11,088	11,374	10,406
Gross profit	19,902	20,570	18,451
Selling, general, and administrative expenses	11,358	11,774	10,945
Other operating charges	313	350	254
Operating income	8,231	8,446	7,252
Interest income	249	333	236
Interest expense	355	438	456
Equity income (loss)—net	781	(874)	668
Other income (loss)—net	40	39	219
Income before income taxes	8,946	7,506	7,919
Income taxes	2,040	1,632	1,892
Consolidated net income	6,906	5,874	6,027
Less: Net income attributable to noncontrolling interests	82	67	46
Net income	$ 6,824	$ 5,807	$ 5,981

Source: Coca-Cola Company, 2009 10-K report.

and the company's endorsements involved almost every high-energy sport worldwide. In 2010, Red Bull sponsored not only athletes and teams competing in sports ranging from auto racing to freestyle biking to wakeboarding to snowboarding to golf but also a number of music events around the world featuring hip-hop, rap, and hard rock groups. In addition, Red Bull fielded company-sponsored soccer teams in New York City; Salzburg, Austria; Leipzig, Germany; and São Paulo, Brazil. The company owned the Salzburg, Austria, hockey team that played under the Red Bull name.

Red Bull also promoted a series of Flugtag (flight day) events held around the world, during which participants were encouraged to fly their homemade human-powered flying machines—most of which seemed more comically designed than flightworthy. Teams of five designed and piloted their crafts to the end of a 30-foot-high ramp positioned over a body of water. Each team was scored for flight distance, creativity, and showmanship to determine a winner. The appeal of attending the events for spectators was to watch the vast majority of the flying machines merely crash off the end of the ramp.

In 2010, the company produced Red Bull Energy Drink, Red Bull Sugarfree, Red Bull Cola, Red Bull Energy Shots. The privately held company did not disclose financial information to the public, but it did announce shipments of 3.906 billion cans in 2009 and shipments of 3.921 billion cans in 2008.

Hansen Natural Corporation

Hansen Natural Corporation developed and marketed a variety of alternative beverages including natural sodas, blended fruit juices, energy drinks, sports drinks, fruit juice smoothies, ready-to-drink teas, and vitamin-enhanced drinks. The Corona, California, company was founded in 1935 by Hubert Hansen to produce a line of natural sodas and fruit juices and was acquired by South Africans Rodney Sacks and Hilton Schlosberg in 1992 for $14.5 million. Under the leadership of Sacks and Schlosberg, Hansen's sales steadily grew from about $17 million in 1992 to $80 million in 2001. However, the company's sales skyrocketed after its launch of Monster Energy drinks in 2002. By 2004, the company's revenues had increased to $180 million and its profits had grown from $3 million in 2001 to $20 million in 2004. In 2009, Monster was the second-best-selling energy drink brand in the United States and the company's annual revenues and net earnings had grown to more than $1.3 billion and $208 million, respectively. A summary of the company's financial performance between 2005 and 2009 is presented in Exhibit 13.

In 2010, Hansen's energy drink lineup included Monster Energy, X-Presso Monster Hammer, Nitrous Monster Energy, Monster Hitman Energy Shooter, Hansen Energy Pro, and Lost Energy. The company also produced and sold Hansen's natural juices and iced tea; Peace Tea, Rumba, Samba, and Tango energy juices; Blue Sky natural sodas; SELF Beauty Elixir; and Vidration enhanced alternative beverages. Sales of Monster energy drinks accounted for approximately 90 percent of Hansen Natural Corporation's total revenues in 2009.

Hansen Natural's rapid success in the energy drink market came about in large part because of its decision in 2002 to match Red Bull on price while packaging Monster drinks in 16-ounce containers (nearly double the size of Red Bull's 8.3-ounce container). The company also imitated Red Bull's image-building and marketing approaches through eye-catching in-store promotions and point-of-sale materials and extreme sports endorsements in snowboarding, BMX, mountain biking, skiing, snowmobiling, skateboarding, and automobile and motorcycle racing. In addition, Hansen and Vans co-sponsored music festivals featuring hard rock and alternative bands.

Hansen Natural outsourced 100 percent of its production of energy drinks and other beverages to contract bottlers throughout the United States. Distribution of the company's energy drinks and other beverages in the United States was split between Anheuser-Busch and Coca-Cola. Coca-Cola also distributed Monster energy drinks in Great Britain, France, Belgium, the Netherlands, Luxembourg, and Monaco. Hansen Natural had also entered into distribution agreements with beverage producers in

► EXHIBIT 13

Financial Summary for Hansen Natural Corporation, 2005–2009 ($ thousands, except per share information)

	2009	2008	2007	2006	2005
Gross sales	$1,309,335	$1,182,876	$1,025,795	$696,322	$415,417
Net sales	1,143,299	1,033,780	904,465	605,774	348,886
Gross profit	612,316	538,794	468,013	316,594	182,543
Gross profit as a percentage to net sales	53.6%	52.1%	51.7%	52.3%	52.3%
Operating income	337,309	163,591	230,986	158,579	103,443
Net income	$208,716	$108,032	$149,406	$97,949	$62,775
Net income per common share:					
Basic	$2.32	$1.17	$1.64	$1.09	$0.71
Diluted	$2.21	$1.11	$1.51	$0.99	$0.65
Cash, cash equivalents, and investments	$427,672	$375,513	$302,650	$136,796	$73,515
Total assets	800,070	761,837	544,603	308,372	163,890
Debt	206	959	663	303	525
Stockholders' equity	584,953	436,316	422,167	225,084	125,509

Source: Hansen Natural Corporation, 2009 10-K report.

Mexico and Australia to make Monster energy drinks available in those countries. While its energy drinks were sold in supermarkets, convenience stores, bars, nightclubs, and restaurants, Hansen's other beverage brands were typically found only in health food stores.

Other Sellers

In addition to the industry's leading sellers of alternative beverages, there were hundreds of regional and specialty brands of energy drinks, sports drinks, and enhanced beverages in the United States and internationally. Most of these companies were privately held bottlers with distribution limited to either small geographic regions or specialty grocers and health food stores. In some cases, regional brands were produced by divisions of large corporations and might have a commanding market share in one particular country but limited distribution outside that market. For example, global pharmaceutical giant GlaxoSmithKline did not sell alternative beverages in North America or Asia, but its sales of Lucozade Energy, Lucozade Sport, and Lucozade Alert energy shot made it the second-largest seller of alternative beverages in Europe, with a 2009 market share of 11.4 percent. GlaxoSmithKline's sales of alternative beverages accounted for $1.3 billion of its 2009 annual revenues of $44.2 billion. The majority of the company's revenues came from the sale of prescription drugs and over-the-counter medicines and oral care products such as Contact, Nicorette gum, Tums, and Aquafresh. Japanese pharmaceutical company Otsuka Pharmaceutical was the third-largest seller of energy drinks, sports drinks, and vitamin-enhanced beverages in the Asia-Pacific region, with a 9.4 percent market share in 2009.

Other than Red Bull, Rockstar was the most noteworthy privately held alternative beverage company. The Las Vegas, Nevada–based company entered the energy drink market in 2001 using a strategy that would be imitated by Hansen's Monster brand a year later. Rockstar was packaged in a 16-ounce can and priced comparably to Red Bull's pricing for its 8.3-ounce can. Rockstar's image, like that of Red Bull and Monster, was built on extreme sports endorsements and hard rock promotions. Among the company's annually sponsored music festivals was the Mayhem Festival, which in 2010 included such musical acts as Rob Zombie, Five Finger Death Punch, Korn, In This Moment, Chimaira, and 3 Inches of Blood. The company also sponsored other hard rock and metal tours such as Taste of Chaos, the Warped Tour, and the Uproar Festival. In 2010, Rockstar energy drinks were available in 11 flavors and Rockstar energy shots were available in two flavors. Rockstar beverages were distributed in the United States and Canada by PepsiCo and were distributed in Australia, New Zealand, Japan, Germany, Switzerland, Finland, Spain, the Netherlands, and the United Kingdom through agreements with beverage distributors in those countries.

The number of brands competing in the sports drinks, energy drinks, and vitamin-enhanced beverage segments of the alternative beverage industry continued to grow each year. In 2009, 231 new vitamin-enhanced beverages were introduced in the United States. The relative maturity of the sports drink segment and the dominant market position held by Gatorade limited the number of new sports drink introductions to 51 in 2009. Launches of new energy drink brands had grown steadily from 172 in 2005 to 380 in 2008, but energy drink introductions fell to 138 in 2009 as the segment matured and financially squeezed consumers became more price conscious. Overall, the relative strength of the energy drink, enhanced beverage, and sports drink beverage segments would likely attract additional entrants over the next several years.

ENDNOTES

[1] Quoted in "Energy Boost a Bummer? Hospital Study Raises Alarm about Drinks," *Chattanooga Times Free Press,* April 9, 2009, p. E6.

[2] Quoted in "FDA Questions Safety of Alcoholic Energy Drinks,"

Associated Press, November 13, 2009.

[3] Quoted in "These Drinks'll Knock You Out!" *Daily News (New York),* February 7, 2010, p. 6.

NETFLIX'S BUSINESS MODEL AND STRATEGY IN RENTING MOVIES AND TV EPISODES

Arthur A. Thompson
The University of Alabama

In May 2010, Netflix's strategy was producing impressive strategic and financial results. During the past five years, Netflix had emerged as the world's largest subscription service for sending DVDs by mail and streaming movies and TV episodes over the Internet. It had attracted 15 million subscribers as of July 2010, up from 4.2 million at year-end 2007 and 1.6 million at year-end 2004. Netflix was shipping about 2 million DVDs on average daily to subscribers, and some 61 percent of the company's subscribers were now watching movies and TV episodes streamed from Netflix over the Internet, up from 48 percent at year-end 2009 and 38 percent in the first quarter of 2009.

Netflix's revenues grew from $500 million in 2004 to $1.2 billion in 2007 to $1.7 billion in 2009 and were expected to surpass $2.1 billion in 2010. In the second quarter of 2010, revenues were $519.8 million, representing 27 percent year-over-year growth from $408.5 million in the second quarter of 2009 and 5 percent sequential growth from $493.7 million in the first quarter of 2010. The company's net income had increased from $21.6 million in 2004 to $115.8 million in 2009, equal to a compound annual growth rate of nearly 40 percent; top management expected net income for full-year 2010 to be in the range of $141 to $156 million. Netflix's stock price closed at an all-time high of $170.83 on September 29, 2010, up from closing prices of $55.09 on December 31, 2009, and $29.87 on January 2, 2009.

Meanwhile, Netflix's traditional video store competitors were experiencing sharp declines in sales and heavy losses. Blockbuster and Movie Gallery, both of which operated thousands of video stores where customers could rent DVDs, were facing financial disaster. During 2009, Blockbuster's worldwide revenues from rentals of movies and video games declined by nearly $530 million to $2.5 billion; many analysts believed that the downward trend in Blockbuster's rental revenues, which began in 2003 when its rental revenues were $4.5 billion, would be hard to reverse. In September 2010, Blockbuster filed for reorganization under Chapter 11 of the U.S. Bankruptcy Code, owing to declining revenues, net losses of $569 million in 2009 and $385 million in 2008, and the burden of its $963 million debt (including capital lease obligations). Since 2002, Blockbuster had only been profitable one year (earning $39 million) and had lost a total of $3.8 billion. Prior to its bankruptcy filing, Blockbuster was planning to close 500 to 545 of its 5,220 company-owned stores worldwide, after closing or selling 586 stores in 2009 and 1,459 stores in 2005–2008.

Movie Gallery filed for Chapter 11 bankruptcy in February 2010, less than two years after emerging from bankruptcy in the spring of 2008 under new owners. Movie Gallery's troubles began after the company took on too much debt to acquire Hollywood Entertainment Corporation in 2005 for more than $800 million. At the time of its second bankruptcy filing, Movie Gallery had $600 million in debt and was plagued with declining sales and losses. As part of its strategic moves to emerge from its February 2010 bankruptcy filing, Movie Gallery had begun closing 760 of its Movie Gallery, Hollywood Video, and Game Crazy rental locations across the United States. After these closings, company management was proposing to continue operations at 1,111 Movie Gallery, 545 Hollywood Video, and 250 Game Crazy locations that either generated or were expected to generate positive cash flows. However, in May 2010, Movie Gallery announced that it would begin closing all of its remaining stores and that its entire business would be liquidated.

INDUSTRY ENVIRONMENT

Since 2000, the introduction of new technologies and electronics products had rapidly multiplied consumer opportunities to view movies. It was commonplace in 2010 for people to view movies at theaters, on airline flights, in hotels, from the rear seats of motor vehicles equipped with video consoles, in homes, or most anywhere on a laptop PC or handheld device like an iPad or iPod Touch. Home viewing was possible on PCs, televisions, and video game consoles. The digital video disc (DVD) player was one of the most successful consumer electronic products of all time; as of 2010, more than 85 percent of U.S. households had one or more DVD players and increasing numbers of households had combination DVD players/recorders. Sales of combination DVD players-recorders surpassed sales of play-only DVD players in 2007–2008. Many households had big-screen high-definition televisions (HDTVs), and a much lesser number had upgraded to Blu-ray DVD players or players-recorders; both HDTVs and Blu-ray devices enabled more spectacular pictures and a significantly higher caliber in-home movie-viewing experience compared with standard televisions.

Consumers could obtain or view movie DVDs and TV episodes through a wide variety of distribution channels and providers. The options included:

- Purchasing movie DVDs and TV episodes from such retailers as Walmart, Target, Best Buy, Toys "R" Us, and Amazon.com.

- Renting movie DVDs from DVD outlets and vending machine kiosks such as Blockbuster, Movie Gallery/Hollywood Video, Redbox, and/or a host of locally owned providers.

- Renting movie DVDs online from Netflix, Blockbuster, or any of several other subscription services that either mailed DVDs directly to subscribers' homes or had the capability to stream content to subscribers via high-speed broadband connections to the Internet.

- Watching movies on assorted cable channels included in the TV and entertainment packages provided by traditional cable providers (such as Time Warner and Comcast), direct broadcast satellite providers (such as DirecTV and DISH Network), or telecommunication providers (e.g., AT&T and Verizon) that used fiber-optic technology to provide TV packages along with phone, Internet, and wireless services.

- Subscribing to any of several movie-only channels (such as HBO, Showtime, and Starz) through a cable, satellite, or telecommunications provider.

- Using a cable or satellite TV remote to order movies instantly streamed directly to their TVs on a pay-per-view basis—generally referred to as video on demand (VOD).

- Using the services of Internet movie and TV content providers, such as Apple's iTunes, Amazon.com, Hulu.com, and Google's YouTube.

- Pirating files of movies and other content from Internet sources via the use of illegal file-sharing software.

Exhibit 1 provides data showing the estimated sizes of selected segments of the market for renting movies, TV episodes, and video games in the United States during 2006–2009.

Traditionally, movie studios released filmed entertainment content for distribution to movie DVD retailers and rental companies three to six months after films were released for showing in theaters. Three to seven months after theatrical release, movie studios usually released their films to pay-per-view and VOD providers. Premium TV channels like HBO, Starz, Cinemax, and Showtime were next in the distribution window, getting access to filmed content one year after theatrical release. Movie studios released films

for viewing to basic cable and network TV two to three years after theatrical release. Recently, however, some movie studios had experimented with shortened release periods, including making new-release titles available to VOD providers or for online purchase on the same date as the DVD release. Other movie studios had implemented or announced their intention to implement policies preventing movie rental providers from renting movie DVDs until 30 to 45 days following release of a DVD title for sale by retailers. TV episodes were often made available for Internet viewing shortly after the original airing date. Movie studios and TV networks were expected to continue to experiment with the timing of the releases to various distribution channels and providers, in an ongoing effort to discover how best to maximize revenues.

▶ EXHIBIT 1

Estimated Sizes of Various Segments of the Markets for Rentals and Sales of Movies, TV Episodes, and Video Games in the United States, 2006–2009 ($ millions)

	2009	2008	2007	2006
In-store rentals of movies and TV episodes on DVDs	$ 5,118	$ 5,674	$ 6,215	$ 7,030
Vending machine rentals	917	486	198	79
By-mail rentals	2,114	1,949	1,797	1,291
Total physical DVD rentals	$ 8,149	$ 8,109	8,210	8,400
Cable video on demand (VOD)	$ 1,277	$ 1,094	$ 1,038	$ 977
Digital VOD	142	71	28	12
Subscription VOD	265	200	11	4
Total digital rentals of movies and TV episodes	$ 1,684	$ 1,365	$ 1,077	$ 993
Total rentals of films and TV episodes	$ 9,833	$ 9,474	$ 9,287	$ 9,393
Physical DVD sales of movies/TV episodes at retail	$13,008	$14,516	$15,932	$16,460
Digital download sales at retail	617	403	90	20
Total retail sales of movies and TV episodes	$13,625	$14,919	$16,022	$16,480
Video game software (rentals and sales at retail)	$ 9,916	$10,998	$ 6,016	$ 4,864
Total U.S. market for film rentals, film sales, and video game software	**$33,374**	**$35,391**	**$31,325**	**$30,737**

Source: Based on Blockbuster's compilations from reports and information published by Adams Media Research and NPD Group and included in Blockbuster's 2009 10-K report, p. 4, and 2008 10-K report, p. 5.

Market Trends in Home Viewing of Movies

The wave of the future in viewing movies at home was widely thought to be in streaming rented movies directly to big-screen HDTVs. Streaming had the advantage of allowing household members to order and instantly watch the movies they chose to rent. Renting a streamed movie could be done either by using the services of Netflix, Blockbuster Online, Amazon Video-on-Demand, Apple's iTunes, and other streaming video providers or by using a TV remote to place orders with a cable or satellite provider to instantly watch a movie from a list of several hundred selections that changed periodically. Providing VOD had been technically possible and available for many years prior to 2010, but it had not garnered substantial usage because movie studios were leery of the potential for movie-pirating and doubtful of whether they could earn acceptable profits from a VOD business model. However, streaming video was less subject to pirating than downloading movie rentals, and ongoing advances in streaming video technology had improved the likelihood that VOD would emerge as the dominant movie rental channel by 2015.

Several strategic initiatives to promote increased use of streaming video were under way in 2010. The owners of Hulu—NBC Universal; ABC's parent Walt Disney; and Fox Entertainment's parent, News Corp—had announced plans to begin offering a premium service for $10 per month that would provide a bigger library of TV shows to watch. Hulu (www.hulu.com) was a free online video service that offered a number of hit TV shows and movies from the libraries of its owners and several other cable networks and movie studios; Hulu derived its revenues from online advertisers, but it was striving to create a business model based on both advertising and subscriptions. Time Warner and Comcast were promoting a "TV Everywhere" concept whereby consumers could watch TV shows free at any time on any device (computers and such mobile devices as iPads and smartphones) so long as they were paying cable subscribers. Time Warner owned a number of cable channels (TNT, TBS, HBO, CNN, and Cartoon Network); CBS was the only major broadcast network currently participating in the trials, but Comcast was in the process of finalizing its acquisition of NBC Universal, which owned NBC, Universal Studios, and a share of Hulu.

In May 2010, Google announced the availability of beta versions of Google TV, based on Google's Android and Chrome software, that enabled households to combine their regular TV experience with the capability to access music, videos, and photos anywhere on the Internet. Google TV was a search-based feature that allowed users to easily and quickly navigate to television channels, apps, and Internet sites. Google's long-term strategy was to eliminate the need to download and install Google TV software by working with electronics manufacturers to equip their new models of televisions, Blu-ray players, and companion boxes with Google TV software. The first such models were expected to go on sale in the fall of 2010. In 2009, Apple had begun exploring the launch of a subscription television service that would offer a package of broadcast shows for $10 per month, but the effort fizzled when several of the biggest studios rejected Apple's proposed fee arrangement for their content and also its comeback proposal to charge 99 cents per TV episode.

In addition, several other developments were acting to reshape the movie rental marketplace:

- The 2009 requirement that all TV stations in the United States use digital technology and equipment to broadcast all their programs had resulted in far more programs being transmitted in high-definition format.

- Prices for wide-screen HDTVs had been dropping rapidly, and picture quality was exceptionally good, if not stunning, on most all models.

- Increasing numbers of devices were appearing in electronics stores that enabled TVs to be connected to the Internet and receive streamed movies from online providers with no hassle.

These devices made it simple for house-holds to order streamed movies with just a few clicks instead of traveling to a video rental store or waiting for a disk to be delivered through the mail.

- Sales of movie DVDs were declining; the chief reasons were said to be the flagging economy and the convenience of online rentals of movie DVDs and VOD. Hollywood movie producers had hoped that next-generation, high-definition optical disc format DVDs that incorporated Blu-ray technology would rejuvenate sales of movie DVDs. But movie rental outlets were renting Blu-ray movie DVDs and, so far, there was little evidence that growing numbers of households with Blu-ray players would spur movie DVD sales, given growing popularity of streaming rented movies directly to TVs, a desktop or laptop computer, or a small handheld device like an iPad or a netbook.

- Cable and satellite TV companies were promoting their VOD services and making more movie titles available to their customers. The Starz Entertainment Group claimed its research showed that Comcast customers who were using the Starz on Demand service tended to reduce their purchases and rentals of movie DVDs due to the ease of using the VOD service.

Competitive Intensity

The movie rental business was intensely competitive in 2010. Netflix was growing rapidly and gaining market share. One of the most attractive appeals of Internet movie providers like Netflix, Hulu, and iTunes was that they were a cheaper alternative to paying monthly cable fees for premium movie channels like HBO, Starz, Cinemax, and Showtime.

Local movie rental stores were rapidly losing market ground and were desperately looking for ways to stave off further declines in rental revenues. Movie Gallery, the second-largest movie rental chain, was in the process of liquidating its entire movie rental business and closing all of its store locations; Blockbuster was shutting stores by the hundreds and teetering on the edge of filing for bankruptcy. Redbox had recently entered the movie rental business with a vending-machine-based strategy whereby Redbox self-service DVD kiosks were placed in leading supermarkets, drugstores, mass merchants like Walmart, convenience stores, and fast-food restaurants like McDonald's; customers could rent new-release movie DVDs for $1 per day. Retailers with Redbox kiosks were paid a percentage of the rental revenues. In mid-2010, Redbox had deployed more than 22,000 of its vending kiosks in all states in the continental United States, Puerto Rico, and Great Britain and was aggressively pursuing efforts to put Redbox vending machines in 7,000 to 8,000 additional locations by year-end 2010.

VOD—streaming movies directly to in-home devices—seemed on the verge of becoming the fastest-growing movie rental segment. In February 2010, Walmart announced its intention to distribute movies over the Internet and had acquired Vudu, a leading provider of digital technologies that enabled the delivery of entertainment content directly to Internet-connected TVs and Blu-ray players. With Vudu technology, households with broadband Internet access and an Internet-ready TV or Blu-ray player could rent or purchase movies, typically in high definition, without needing a connected computer or cable/satellite service. Vudu had licensing agreements with almost every major movie studio and dozens of independent and international film distributors to offer approximately 16,000 movies, including the largest high-definition library of VOD movies available anywhere.

Cable companies were also going on the offensive to grow their VOD revenues. In March 2010, the Cable and Telecommunications Association for Marketing Co-op—a group that included Comcast, Time Warner, other cable providers, Sony Pictures, and Universal Pictures—announced plans to spend $30 million on an advertising campaign to expand consumer awareness of renting movies on demand

and illustrate how easy it was for digital cable customers to make a few clicks on their remotes and have movies instantly streamed to their homes. Both Time Warner and Comcast were in the process of creating an authentication system that enabled subscribers—and only subscribers—to access their TV shows and films online. As a defensive move, HBO (a subsidiary of Time Warner) had recently announced the launch of HBO Go, a video streaming service.

NETFLIX'S BUSINESS MODEL AND STRATEGY

Since launching the company's online movie rental service in 1999, Reed Hastings, founder and CEO of Netflix, had diligently striven to improve on the company's service offerings and better enable the company to outcompete its movie rental competitors. Hastings's goals for Netflix were simple: to build the world's best Internet movie service and to deliver a growing subscriber base and earnings per share every year. He had personally engineered the company's creative but simple subscription-based business model and strategy that had catapulted Netflix into becoming the world's largest online entertainment subscription service and revolutionized the way that many people rented movies.

Netflix's Subscription-Based Business Model

Netflix employed a subscription-based business model. Members could choose from eight "unlimited" subscription plans:

- An $8.99 per month plan that entailed unlimited DVDs each month, one title out at a time, plus unlimited streaming.
- A $13.99 per month plan that entailed unlimited DVDs each month, two titles out at a time, plus unlimited streaming.
- A $16.99 per month plan that entailed unlimited DVDs each month, three titles out at a time, plus unlimited streaming.
- A $23.99 per month plan that entailed unlimited DVDs each month, four titles out at a time, plus unlimited streaming.

- A $29.99 per month plan that entailed unlimited DVDs each month, five titles out at a time, plus unlimited streaming.
- A $35.99 per month plan that entailed unlimited DVDs each month, six titles out at a time, plus unlimited streaming.
- A $41.99 per month plan that entailed unlimited DVDs each month, seven titles out at a time, plus unlimited streaming.
- A $47.99 per month plan that entailed unlimited DVDs each month, eight titles out at a time, plus unlimited streaming.

The company also offered a "limited" plan for $4.99 that entailed a maximum of two DVDs per month with up to two hours of video streaming to a PC or Apple Mac (this plan did not allow members to stream movies to their TV via a Netflix-ready device—as was the case with the eight unlimited plans). All new subscribers were automatically enrolled for a free one-month trial that provided full access to Netflix's whole library of 120,000 movie titles and unlimited streaming to PCs, Apple Macs, or TVs via an Internet-connected Netflix-ready device. At the end of the free trial period, members were automatically enrolled as paying subscribers, unless they canceled their subscription. All paying subscribers were billed monthly in advance. Payments were made by credit card or debit card.

The most popular plans were the $8.99, $13.99, and $16.99 plans with unlimited streaming. Subscribers could cancel at any time. Average monthly revenue per paying subscriber was $14.95 in 2007, $13.75 in 2008, and $13.30 in 2009.

Streaming content was enabled by Netflix-controlled software that could run on a variety of Netflix-ready devices, including Netflix-capable Blu-ray players, increasing numbers of Internet-connected TV models and home theater systems that were Netflix-ready, TiVo DVRs, Nintendo's Wii, Microsoft's Xbox 360, Sony's PlayStation 3, and special Netflix players made by Roku and several other electronics manufacturers. However, Netflix subscribers could enjoy Netflix streaming without the need to buy additional hardware; they could use any Windows PC (XP/Vista/7) or Intel-based Apple Mac with decent video capabilities to access Netflix streaming directly through a Web browser and then connect a TV to the computer's video output. In mid-2010, Netflix had about 20,000 movie titles available for streaming. Streaming was highly attractive and economical because subscribers got unlimited access to thousands of hours of on-demand programming with no pay-per-view fees (beyond the chosen monthly subscription fee).

Subscribers who opted to receive movie and TV episode DVDs by mail went to Netflix's website, selected one or more movies from its DVD library, and received the movie DVDs by first-class mail generally within one business day—more than 97 percent of Netflix's subscribers lived within one-day delivery of the company's 50 distribution centers (plus 50 other shipping points) located throughout the United States. Subscribers could keep a DVD for as long as they wished, with no due dates, no late fees, no shipping fees, and no pay-per-view fees. Subscribers returned DVDs via the U.S. Postal Service in a prepaid return envelope that came with each movie order.

New subscribers were drawn to try Netflix's online movie rental service because of (1) the wide selection; (2) the extensive information

Netflix provided about each movie in its rental library (including critic reviews, member reviews, online trailers, and subscriber ratings); (3) the ease with which they could find and order movies; (4) Netflix's policies of no late fees and no due dates (which eliminated the hassle of getting DVDs back to local rental stores by the designated due date); (5) the convenience of being provided a postage-paid return envelope for mailing DVDs back to Netflix; and (6) the convenience of ordering and instantly watching movies streamed to their TVs or computers with no additional pay-per-view charge. Netflix had been highly rated in online retail customer satisfaction by Nielsen Online and ForeSee/FGI Research. Over 90 percent of surveyed subscribers said that they would recommend the Netflix service to a friend.

Management believed that Netflix's subscriber base consisted of three types of customers: those who liked the convenience of home delivery, bargain hunters who were enthused about being able to watch many movies for an economical monthly price, and movie buffs who wanted access to a very wide selection of films.

Exhibit 2 shows trends in Netflix's subscriber growth.

▶ EXHIBIT 2

Subscriber Data for Netflix, 2000–2009

	2000	2005	2006	2007	2008	2009
Total subscribers at beginning of period	107,000	2,610,000	4,179,000	6,316,000	7,479,000	9,390,000
Gross subscriber additions during period	515,000	3,729,000	5,250,000	5,340,000	6,859,000	9,322,000
Subscriber cancellations during the period	330,000	2,160,000	3,113,000	4,177,000	4,948,000	6,444,000
Total subscribers at end of period	292,000	4,179,000	6,316,000	7,479,000	9,390,000	12,268,000
Net subscriber additions during the period	185,000	1,569,000	2,137,000	1,163,000	1,911,000	2,878,000
Free trial subscribers at year-end	n.a.	153,000	162,000	153,000	226,000	376,000
Subscriber acquisition cost	$49.96	$38.78	$42.94	$40.86	$29.12	$25.48

n.a. = not available

Sources: Netflix, 2009 10-K report, pp. 26 and 32, and 2003 10-K report, p. 11.

Netflix's Strategy

Netflix had a multipronged strategy to build an ever-growing subscriber base that included:

- Providing subscribers with a comprehensive selection of DVD titles.
- Acquiring new content by building and maintaining mutually beneficial relationships with entertainment video providers.
- Making it easy for subscribers to identify movies they were likely to enjoy.
- Giving subscribers a choice of watching streaming content or receiving quickly delivered DVDs by mail.
- Spending aggressively on marketing to attract subscribers and build widespread awareness of the Netflix brand and service.
- Gradually transitioning subscribers to streaming delivery rather than mail delivery as the popularity of Internet-delivered content grew.

A Comprehensive Library of Movies and TV Episodes Since Netflix's early days, the company's strategy had been to offer subscribers a large and diverse selection of DVD titles. It was aggressive in seeking out attractive new titles to add to its offerings. Its library had grown from some 55,000 titles in 2005 to more than 100,000 titles in 2010. The lineup included the latest Hollywood releases, releases several decades old, movie classics, independent films, hard-to-locate documentaries, TV shows, and how-to videos; Netflix's DVD library far outdistanced the selection available in local brick-and-mortar movie rental stores.

In October 2008, Netflix and Starz Entertainment, a premium movie service provider operating in the United States, announced an agreement to make movies from Starz, through its Starz Play broadband subscription movie service, available to be streamed instantly at Netflix. Access to the Starz Play service at Netflix was included with Netflix members' current monthly subscription fee.

The agreement with Starz Play gave Netflix members access to an additional 2,500 movies that could be streamed directly to their TVs and boosted Netflix's library of instantly watchable movies from 12,000 to 14,500. In 2009, Netflix expanded the number of titles available for streaming by about 30 percent; management expected that the number of streaming content choices would continue to grow rapidly for the foreseeable future.

New Content Acquisition Netflix had invested substantial resources in establishing strong ties with various entertainment video providers and leveraging those ties to both expand its content library and gain access to new releases as early as possible. The company acquired new content from movie studios and distributors through direct purchases, revenue-sharing agreements, and licensing. During 2010, Netflix entered into agreements with such content providers as Universal Studios, Twentieth Century Fox, Warner Bros., Indie Films, Relativity Media, and Epix that expanded the number of movie and TV episodes in Netflix's library and, in particular, broadened the company's ability to stream movies and TV shows to subscribers. A free Netflix App for iPads became available at Apple's App Store at www.itunes.com in April 2010, allowing Netflix subscribers to instantly watch an unlimited number of TV episodes and movies streamed from Netflix to their iPads. Netflix management was firmly committed to continuing the company's long-standing strategy to expand the content options offered to subscribers; the emphasis in 2010 had been on acquiring the rights to stream greater numbers of movies and TV episodes and on expanding the number of devices to which content could be streamed. Analysts expected such emphasis would be ongoing.

Netflix acquired many of its new-release movie DVDs from studios for a low up-front fee in exchange for a commitment for a defined period either to share a percentage of its subscription revenues or to pay a fee based on content utilization. After the revenue-sharing period expired for a title, Netflix generally had the option of returning the title to the studio, purchasing the title, or destroying its copies of the title. On occasion, Netflix also purchased DVDs for a fixed fee per disc from various studios, distributors, and other suppliers. In the case of movie titles and TV episodes that were delivered to subscribers via the Internet for instant viewing, Netflix generally paid a fee to license the content for a defined period. Following expiration of the license term, Netflix either removed the content from its library of streamed offerings or negotiated extension or renewal of the license agreement.

The company's December 31, 2009, balance sheet indicated that its content had a net value of $108.8 million (after depreciation). New-release DVDs were amortized over one year; the useful life of back-library titles (some of which qualified as classics) was amortized over three years (since the personalized movie recommendation software generated significant rentals of older titles). Some directly purchased DVDs could be sold at the end of their useful lives, but most had a salvage value of zero; during 2005–2009, Netflix's losses on the disposal of used DVDs ranged between $2 and $7 million annually.

Netflix's Convenient, Easy-to-Use Movie Selection Software Netflix had developed proprietary software that enabled it to provide subscribers with detailed information about each title in the Netflix library as well as personalized movie recommendations every time they visited the Netflix website. The information for each title included length, rating, cast and crew, screen formats, movie trailers, plot synopses, and reviews written by Netflix editors, third parties, and subscribers. The personalized recommendations were based on a subscriber's individual likes and dislikes (determined by their rental or streaming history, their personal ratings of movies viewed, and movies on the subscriber's lists for future streamed viewing and/or mail delivery), the ratings of movie critics and other rating services, and the ratings submitted by other Netflix subscribers. Subscribers often began their search for movie titles by starting from a familiar title and then using the recommendations tool to find other titles they might enjoy.

The recommendation software had an Oracle database platform and used proprietary algorithms that organized Netflix's library of movies into clusters of similar movies and then sorted the movies in each cluster from most liked to least liked according to ratings provided by subscribers. In 2010, Netflix had more than 3 billion movie ratings from subscribers in its database and was adding new movie ratings from subscribers at the rate of about 20 million per week. Those subscribers who rated similar movies in similar clusters were categorized as like-minded viewers. When a subscriber was online and browsing through the movie selections, the software was programmed to check the clusters the subscriber had rented/viewed in the past, determine which movies the customer had yet to rent/view in that cluster, and recommend only those movies in the cluster that had been highly rated by viewers. Viewer ratings determined which available titles were displayed to a subscriber and in what order. The recommendations helped subscribers quickly create a list of DVD titles they wanted to receive by mail and/or a list indicating the titles they wished to have streamed; subscribers used these lists to specify the order in which movies would be mailed out or streamed and could alter the lists at any time. They could also reserve a copy of upcoming releases. Netflix management saw the movie recommendation tool as a quick and personalized means of helping subscribers identify titles they were likely to enjoy.

Netflix also used subscriber ratings to determine which titles to feature most prominently on the company's website, to generate lists of similar titles, and to select the promotional trailers that a subscriber would see when using the Previews feature. Netflix management believed that over 50 percent of the titles selected by subscribers came from the recommendations generated by its proprietary software. The software algorithms were thought to be particularly effective in promoting selections of lesser-known, high-quality films to subscribers who otherwise might not have discovered them in the company's massive and ever-changing collection. On average, about 85 percent of the titles in the Netflix library were rented each quarter, an indication of the effectiveness of the company's recommendation software in steering subscribers to movies of interest and achieving broader utilization of the company's entire library of titles. About 70 percent of the DVDs that Netflix shipped to subscribers during 2009 were titles that had been released to movie rental enterprises and available to subscribers for three months or longer.

A Choice of Mail Delivery versus Streaming
Until 2007–2008, when streaming technology had advanced to the point that made providing VOD a viable option, Netflix concentrated its efforts on speeding the time it took to deliver subscriber orders via mail delivery. The strategy was to establish a nationwide network of distribution centers and shipping points with the capability to deliver DVDs ordered by subscribers within one business day. To achieve quick delivery and return capability, Netflix created sophisticated software to track the location of each DVD title in inventory and determine the fastest way of getting the DVD orders to subscribers. When a subscriber placed an order for a specific DVD, the system first looked for that DVD at the shipping center closest to the customer. If that center didn't have the DVD in stock, the system then checked for availability at the next closest center. The search continued until the DVD was found, at which point the regional distribution center with the ordered DVD in inventory was provided with the information needed to initiate the order fulfillment and shipping process. If the DVD was unavailable anywhere in the system, it was wait-listed. The software system then moved to the customer's next choice and the process started over. And no matter where the DVD was sent from, the system knew to print the return label on the prepaid envelope to send the DVDs to the shipping center closest to the customer to reduce return mail times

and permit more efficient use of Netflix's DVD inventory. No subscriber orders were shipped on holidays or weekends.

By early 2007, Netflix had 50 regional distribution centers and another 50 shipping points scattered across the United States, giving it one-business-day delivery capability for 95 percent of its subscribers and, in most cases, also enabling one-day return times. As of 2010, additional improvements in Netflix's distribution and shipping network had resulted in one-business-day delivery capability for 98 percent of Netflix's subscribers.

In 2007, when entertainment studios became more willing to allow Internet delivery of their content (since recent technological advances prevented streamed movies from being pirated), Netflix moved quickly to better compete with the growing numbers of VOD providers by adding the feature of unlimited streaming to its regular monthly subscription plans. The market for Internet delivery of media content consisted of three segments: the rental of Internet-delivered content, the download-to-own segment, and the advertising-supported online delivery segment (mainly YouTube and Hulu). Netflix's objective was to be the clear leader in the rental segment via its Watch Instantly feature.

Giving subscribers the option of watching DVDs delivered by mail or instantly watching movies streamed to subscribers' computers or TVs had considerable strategic appeal to Netflix in two respects. First, giving subscribers the option to order and instantly watch streamed content put Netflix in position to compete head-to-head with the growing numbers of VOD providers. Second, providing streamed content to subscribers had the attraction of being cheaper than (1) paying the postage on DVD orders and returns, (2) having to obtain and manage an ever-larger inventory of DVDs, and (3) covering the labor costs of additional distribution center personnel to fill a growing volume of DVD orders and handle increased numbers of returned DVDs. But streaming content to subscribers was not cost-free; it required server capacity, software to authenticate orders from subscribers, and a system of computers containing copies of the content files placed at various points in a network so as to maximize bandwidth and allow subscribers to access a copy of the file on a server near the subscriber. Having subscribers accessing a central server ran the risk of an Internet transmission bottleneck. Netflix also used third-party content delivery networks to help it efficiently stream movies and TV episodes in high volume to Netflix subscribers over the Internet.

By combining streaming and DVDs-by-mail as part of the Netflix subscription, Netflix was able to offer members a uniquely compelling selection of movies for one low monthly price. Netflix executives believed this created a competitive advantage as compared to a postal-delivery-only or Internet-delivery-only subscription service. Furthermore, management believed that Netflix's combination postal-streaming subscription service delivered compelling customer value and customer satisfaction by eliminating the hassle involved in making trips to local movie rental stores to choose and return rented DVDs.

Marketing and Advertising   Netflix used multiple marketing channels to attract subscribers, including online advertising (paid search listings, banner ads, text on popular sites such as AOL and Yahoo, and permission-based e-mails), radio stations, regional and national television, direct mail, and print ads. It also participated in a variety of cooperative advertising programs with studios through which Netflix received cash consideration in return for featuring a studio's movies in its advertising. Most recently, Netflix had begun working closely with the makers of Netflix-ready electronics devices to help generate new subscribers for its service.

Advertising campaigns of one type or another were under way more or less continuously, with the lure of one-month free trials usually being the prominent ad feature. Advertising expenses totaled approximately $205.9 million in 2009, $181.4 million in 2008, and $207.9 million in 2007. Netflix management believed that its paid advertising efforts were significantly

enhanced by the benefits of word-of-mouth advertising, the referrals of satisfied subscribers, and its active public relations programs.

Management had boosted marketing expenditures of all kinds (including paid advertising) from $25.7 million in 2000 (16.8 percent of revenues) to $142.0 million in 2005 (20.8 percent of revenues) to $218.2 million in 2007 (18.1 percent of revenues). When the recession hit in late 2007 and 2008, management trimmed 2008 marketing expenditures to $199.7 million (14.6 percent of revenues) as a cost-containment measure, but in 2009 marketing expenditures resumed their upward trend, climbing to $237.7 million (14.2 percent of revenues).

Transitioning to Internet Delivery of Content
In early 2010, Netflix had two primary strategic objectives: (1) to continue to grow a large subscription business and (2) to gradually migrate subscribers from postal delivery of DVDs to Internet-based delivery of content as the popularity of Internet-delivery grew. Top executives at Netflix expected that Internet delivery of media content would surpass postal delivery within three to seven years and that eventually postal delivery would account for a relatively small fraction of Netflix's business.

NETFLIX'S PERFORMANCE AND PROSPECTS

Recent financial statement data for Netflix are shown in Exhibits 3 and 4. Management's latest forecast called for having between 15.5 million and 16.3 million subscribers by year-end 2010, full-year 2010 revenues of $2.11 billion to $2.16 billion, and diluted earnings per share of $2.41 to $2.63. The company announced a $100 million program to repurchase shares of its common stock in April 2007. A second stock repurchase program involving the expenditure of $100 million was announced in January 2008, and in March 2008 Netflix's board of directors authorized a third repurchase program to spend an additional $150 million to buy back shares during the remainder of 2008. A fourth program to repurchase shares

▶EXHIBIT 3

Netflix's Consolidated Statements of Operations, 2000–2009 ($ millions, except per share data)						
	2000	**2005**	**2006**	**2007**	**2008**	**2009**
Revenues	$ 35.9	$682.2	$996.7	$1,205.3	$1,364.7	$1,670.3
Cost of revenues:						
Subscription costs	24.9	393.8	532.6	664.4	761.1	909.5
Fulfillment expenses	10.2	72.0	94.4	121.3	149.1	169.8
Total cost of revenues	35.1	465.8	627.0	786.2	910.2	1,079.3
Gross profit	0.8	216.4	369.7	419.2	454.4	591.0
Operating expenses						
Technology and development	16.8	35.4	48.4	71.0	89.9	114.5
Marketing	25.7	144.6	225.5	218.2	199.7	237.7
General and administrative	7.0	35.5	36.2	52.4	49.7	51.3
Stock-based compensation*	9.7	—	—	—	—	—
Gain (loss) on disposal of DVDs	—	(2.0)	(4.8)	(7.2)	(6.3)	(4.6)
Gain on legal settlement	—	—	—	(7.0)	—	—
Total operating expenses	59.2	213.4	305.3	327.4	332.9	399.1
Operating income	(58.4)	3.0	64.4	91.8	121.5	191.9
Interest and other income (expense)	(0.2)	5.3	15.9	20.1	10.0	0.3
Income before income taxes	—	8.3	80.3	110.9	131.5	192.2
Provision for (benefit from) income taxes	—	(33.7)	31.2	44.3	48.5	76.3
Net income	$(58.5)	$42.0	$49.1	$66.7	$83.0	$115.9
Net income per share:						
Basic	$(20.61)	$0.79	$0.78	$0.99	$1.36	$2.05
Diluted	(20.61)	0.64	0.71	0.97	1.32	1.98
Weighted-average common shares outstanding:						
Basic	2.8	53.5	62.6	67.1	61.0	56.6
Diluted	2.8	65.5	69.1	68.9	62.8	58.4

Note: Totals may not add due to rounding.

*Stock-based compensation costs for 2005–2009 totaled $14.3 million in 2005, $12.7 million in 2006, $12.0 million in 2007, $12.3 million in 2008, and $12.6 million in 2009; these costs were allocated to fulfillment expenses, technology and development, marketing, and general and administrative based on the area of Netflix's business in which the personnel receiving the stock option awards were employed. Thus, the amounts shown in the line-item expenses for fulfillment, technology and development, marketing, and general and administrative for 2005–2009 include their respective allocation of stock-based compensation costs.

Source: Netflix, 10-K reports for 2003, 2006, and 2009.

was announced in January 2009; it resulted in expenditures of $175 million. In August 2009, the company's board of directors authorized expenditures of up to $300 million to repurchase shares of common stock through the end of 2010. As of early 2010, these programs had resulted in the repurchase of more than 20 million shares; the net reduction in shares outstanding was less than 20 million shares because of the issuance of new shares under the company's stock-based compensation program for executives and employees. In June 2010, Netflix's Board of Directors approved a stock repurchase program authorizing the repurchase of up to $300 million in common stock through the end of 2012.

▶EXHIBIT 4

Selected Balance Sheet and Cash Flow Data for Netflix, 2000–2009 (in millions of $)

	2000	2005	2006	2007	2008	2009
Selected Balance Sheet Data						
Cash and cash equivalents	$ 14.9	$212.3	$400.4	$177.4	$139.9	$134.2
Short-term investments	—	—	—	207.7	157.4	186.0
Current assets	n.a.	243.7	428.4	432.4	358.9	416.5
Net investment in DVD library	n.a.	57.0	104.9	112.1	98.5	108.8
Total assets	52.5	364.7	608.8	679.0	617.9	679.7
Current liabilities	n.a.	137.6	193.4	208.9	216.0	226.4
Working capital*	(1.7)	106.1	235.0	223.5	142.9	190.1
Stockholders' equity	(73.3)	226.3	414.2	429.8	347.2	199.1
Cash Flow Data						
Net cash provided by operating activities	$(22.7)	$ 157.5	$247.9	$277.4	$284.0	$325.1
Net cash used in investing activities	(25.0)	(133.2)	(185.9)	(436.0)	(145.0)	(246.1)
Net cash provided by financing activities	48.4	13.3	126.2	(64.4)	176.6	(84.6)

*Defined as current assets minus current liabilities.

Sources: Netflix, 10-K reports for 2003, 2005, 2007, 2008, and 2009.

BLOCKBUSTER'S SURVIVAL STRATEGY

Despite its troubles, Blockbuster remained the global leader in the movie rental industry in 2010, with nearly 47 million customers served daily in 18 countries. As of January 2010, it provided content to customers via rentals at some 6,500 store locations (1,300 of which were operated by franchisees), mail delivery, online delivery, digital download, and 2,225 vending machine kiosks. In 2009, it had an estimated 37 percent share of the roughly $8.1 billion U.S. market for renting movies for in-home viewing and a globally recognized brand in movie rentals.

Blockbuster recorded net losses of $2.8 billion during the 2003–2005 period; earned a modest $39.2 million after-tax profit in 2006; and lost $85.1 million in 2007, $385.4 million in 2008, and $569.3 million in 2009. Total revenues dropped from $5.1 billion in 2008 to $4.1 billion in 2009, a decline of 19.6 percent. In February 2010,

Standard & Poor's downgraded Blockbuster's corporate credit rating to CCC from B–, with a negative outlook; four weeks later, Standard & Poor's downgraded the company's credit rating again, this time to CC. In March 2010, Moody's downgraded both Blockbuster's probability of default rating and its corporate family rating to Caa3 from Caa1, with a negative outlook.

Blockbuster's financial troubles were in part attributable to the terms of its October 2004 split-off from media conglomerate Viacom (Viacom had acquired Blockbuster in 1994 for $8.4 billion), which entailed Blockbuster paying a special one-time $5 dividend (totaling $905 million) to all shareholders, including Viacom (which owned 81.5 percent of Blockbuster's shares prior to the divestiture deal). The $905 million cash dividend payment and other aspects of the spin-off forced Blockbuster to take on long-term debt of more than $1 billion, drove the company's annual interest expenses up to around $100 million annually, and severely limited the financial resources available for overcoming sluggish sales and eroding movie rentals that Blockbuster was already experiencing at its stores. In July 2007, James F. Keyes, former president and CEO of 7-Eleven, was appointed to replace John F. Antioco, who had served as Blockbuster's CEO since 1997. Keyes quickly initiated a series of efforts to recast Blockbuster's strategy and put the company in better position to improve its dismal bottom-line performance. But Keyes's initial strategy overhaul met with limited success and failed to turn the company's financial performance around.

In a second attempt to stem the bleeding, conserve cash, and get the company back on track, Blockbuster executives launched another round of strategic initiatives in 2009–2010:

- Selling the company's 184-store subsidiary in Ireland during the third quarter of 2009.

- Closing 470 underperforming Blockbuster stores in the first four months of 2010, on the heels of having closed 586 company-owned stores (and 299 franchised stores) in 2009.

- Going forward with plans to close an additional 81 stores by year-end 2010.

- Continuing to increase the size of its library of movie, TV episode, and video game titles. (The library included more than 125,000 titles as of May 2010.)

- Pursuing rapid expansion of the Blockbuster-branded vending machine kiosk network from 2,225 locations to 10,000 locations by the end of 2010. Seeking to expand its revenues from DVD rentals, Blockbuster entered into a strategic alliance with NCR in August 2008 to place vending machines containing a limited selection of movie DVDs in high-traffic locations; the kiosks were owned and operated by NCR, which also controlled the pricing and location of the kiosks. Blockbuster was responsible for providing the DVD titles that were older than 26 weeks past their

release dates on a consignment basis and received 50 percent of the rental revenue from these titles. NCR was responsible for providing the DVDs for newer titles and paid Blockbuster a license fee of 1 to 10 percent of net revenues, depending on the monthly revenues of each individual kiosk and the total number of kiosks deployed. Blockbuster's share of the revenues from the vending machine kiosk locations in place during the first three months of 2010 was less than $5 million. In May 2010, NCR had deployed over 4,000 Blockbuster Express kiosks and plans were proceeding to deploy an additional 6,000 kiosks by year-end.

- Instituting new in-store and online merchandising techniques and graphics packages to make it easier for prospective renters to make decisions on their entertainment selections and thereby reduce the store walkout rate and browse-but-don't-rent rate at the Blockbuster website.

- Giving Blockbuster Online subscribers the option of exchanging their DVDs through the mail or returning them to a nearby Blockbuster store in exchange for free in-store movie rentals.

- Instituting a Blockbuster Rewards program that offered in-store benefits to members and encouraged them to rent movies and games only from Blockbuster stores.

- Introducing Direct Access whereby in-store customers could access Blockbuster's by-mail inventory and have DVD titles shipped directly to their homes.

- Increasing store remodeling efforts in select locations. (The remodeling typically entailed brighter paint, lower shelves, and new merchandising displays.)

- Renegotiating the leases for 2,036 stores in the United States in 2009 and the first four months of 2010 to significantly reduce future store occupancy costs.

- Instituting a higher daily rental rate for each day a customer chose to keep a rental following the initial rental period.
- Selling the DVD inventories of titles that were rented infrequently.
- Curtailing non-essential or discretionary capital expenditures in 2010 and lengthening the payment cycle to certain vendors.
- Further reducing selling, general, and administrative expenses in 2010.
- Aggressively exploring options to sell, license, or divest some of the company's international operations.
- Suspending the payment of 7½ percent dividends on the company's Series A convertible preferred stock for five consecutive quarterly periods beginning February 15, 2009, and ending May 14, 2010. Suspension of the dividend payment for further quarters was expected because, under Delaware law

(the state where Blockbuster was incorporated), Blockbuster could only pay preferred stock dividends out of either net profits or a surplus of net assets over the aggregate par value of the outstanding shares of capital stock. As of April 2010, Blockbuster had no net profits and its capital surplus was negative.

So far, the results of these initiatives had done little to brighten Blockbuster's increasingly dismal outlook; however, management believed that the forthcoming Movie Gallery store closings would favorably affect rental revenues at hundreds of Blockbuster locations during the remainder of 2010. In the first quarter of 2010, Blockbuster's total revenues were 13.5 percent below the levels of a year earlier, and the company posted a quarterly net loss of $67.1 million (as compared to a net profit of $24.9 million in the first quarter of 2009)—see Exhibit 5. Blockbuster management attributed the revenue decline to increased competitive

▶ EXHIBIT 5

Blockbuster's Consolidated Statement of Operations, First Quarter 2010 versus First Quarter 2009 and Fiscal Years 2007–2009 ($ millions, except per share amounts)					
	Thirteen Weeks Ended		Fiscal Year Ended		
	April 4, 2010	April 5, 2009	January 3, 2010	January 3, 2009	January 3, 2008
Revenues					
Base rental revenues	$598.7	$704.9	$2,528.0	$3,166.5	$3,353.7
Previously rented product ("PRP") revenues	120.9	138.3	557.9	619.8	649.9
Merchandise sales	215.1	236.7	956.1	1,246.9	1,251.2
Other revenues	4.7	6.0	20.4	32.2	59.2
Total revenues	939.4	1,085.9	4,062.4	5,065.4	5,314.0
Cost of sales					
Cost of rental revenues	270.1	309.9	1,130.6	1,446.7	1,584.0
Cost of merchandise sold	167.1	202.7	753.6	988.4	956.3
Total cost of sales	437.2	512.6	1,884.2	2,435.1	2,540.3
Gross profit	502.2	573.3	2,178.2	2,630.3	2,773.7
Operating expenses					
General and administrative	484.4	477.9	1,928.7	2,235.3	2,454.9
Advertising	21.0	11.5	91.4	117.7	190.5

(continued)

▶EXHIBIT 5 *(concluded)*

	Thirteen Weeks Ended		Fiscal Year Ended		
	April 4, 2010	April 5, 2009	January 3, 2010	January 3, 2009	January 3, 2008
Depreciation and intangible amortization	26.2	33.7	144.1	146.6	180.3
Impairment of goodwill and other long-lived assets	—		369.2	435.0	2.2
Gain on sale of Gamestation	—		—	—	(81.5)
Total operating expenses	531.6	523.1	2,533.4	2,934.6	2,746.4
Operating income (loss)	(29.4)	50.2	(355.2)	(304.3)	27.3
Interest expense	(33.2)	(17.5)	(111.6)	(72.9)	(88.2)
Loss on extinguishment of debt			(29.9)	—	—
Interest income	—	0.2	1.3	2.4	6.4
Other items, net	(1.6)	(0.8)	(10.4)	16.3	(1.3)
Income (loss) from continuing operations before income taxes	(64.2)	32.1	(505.8)	(358.5)	(55.8)
Provision for income taxes	(1.1)	(5.5)	(11.8)	(24.4)	(28.4)
Income (loss) from continuing operations before income taxes	(65.3)	26.6	(517.6)	(382.9)	(84.2)
Income (loss) from discontinued operations, net of tax	(0.1)	1.1	(40.6)	8.8	10.4
Net income (loss)	(65.4)	27.7	(558.2)	(374.1)	(73.8)
Preferred stock dividends	(1.7)	(2.8)	(11.1)	(11.3)	(11.3)
Net income (loss) applicable to common stockholders	$(67.1)	$24.9	$(569.3)	$(385.4)	$(85.1)
Net income (loss) per common share:					
Basic	$(0.33)	$0.13	$(2.93)	$(2.01)	$(0.45)
Diluted	$(0.33)	$0.12	$(2.93)	$(2.01)	$(0.45)
Weighted-average common shares outstanding (in millions):					
Basic	202.9	192.7	194.1	191.8	190.3
Diluted	202.9	222.8	194.1	191.8	190.3

Source: Blockbuster's 10-Q report, May 14, 2010, and 2009 10-K report, p. 79.

pressures. Long-term debt (including the current portion) as of April 4, 2010, was $895.4 million, resulting in first-quarter 2010 interest expenses of $33.2 million. The company's cash and cash equivalents had dwindled to $109.9 million—see Exhibit 6.

In May 2010, Blockbuster's common stock was trading in the $0.35 to $0.45 range, down from a high of $10 in 2004 and a high of $6.87 in 2007. Because Blockbuster's stock price had remained below $1 per share for well over a month—a violation of New York Stock Exchange (NYSE) requirements for listing—the NYSE delisted Blockbuster's stock in June 2010.

As of October 2010, the company was continuing to operate its stores and kiosks in the United States as it reorganized under bankruptcy protection; Blockbuster's operations outside the United States and domestic and international franchisees were not part of the

▶EXHIBIT 6

Blockbuster's Consolidated Balance Sheets, April 4 and January 3, 2010, and January 4, 2009 ($ millions, except per share amounts)

	April 4, 2010	January 3, 2010	January 4, 2009
Assets			
Current assets:			
Cash and cash equivalents	$ 109.9	$ 188.7	$ 154.9
Receivables, less allowances of $5.1 and $6.0 for 2010 and 2009, respectively	55.6	79.4	117.1
Merchandise inventories	255.2	298.5	432.8
Rental library, net	319.3	340.7	355.8
Deferred income taxes	13.7	13.6	13.4
Prepaid and other current assets	126.9	139.1	184.6
Total current assets	880.6	1,060.0	1,258.6
Property and equipment, net	238.4	249.4	406.0
Deferred income taxes	110.0	114.6	124.3
Intangibles, net	7.5	7.7	11.5
Restricted cash	35.8	58.5	—
Other assets	46.5	48.1	16.0
Total assets	$1,318.8	$1,538.3	$2,154.5
Liabilities and Stockholders' Equity (Deficit)			
Current liabilities:			
Accounts payable	$ 206.6	$ 300.8	$ 427.3
Accrued expenses	390.8	407.7	493.8
Current portion of long-term debt	79.4	101.6	198.0
Current portion of capital lease obligations	5.7	6.1	8.5
Deferred income taxes	114.0	118.6	125.8
Total current liabilities	796.5	934.8	1,253.4
Long-term debt, less current portion	816.0	836.0	538.0
Capital lease obligations, less current portion	18.5	19.9	28.3
Other liabilities	62.0	61.9	75.5
Total liabilities	1,693.0	1,852.6	1,940.2
Stockholders' equity:			
Preferred stock, par value $0.01 per share; 100 shares authorized; .072 and 0.146 shares issued and outstanding for 2010 and 2009, respectively, with a liquidation preference of $1,000 per share	71.7	145.9	150.0
Class A common stock, par value $0.01 per share; 400 shares authorized; 137.7 and 122.4 shares issued and outstanding for 2010 and 2009	1.4	1.3	1.2
Class B common stock, par value $0.01 per share; 500 shares authorized; 72.0 shares issued and outstanding for 2010 and 2009	0.7	0.7	0.7
Additional paid-in capital	5,453.8	5,377.0	5,378.4
Accumulated deficit	(5,852.3)	(5,786.9)	(5,228.7)

(continued)

▶ **EXHIBIT 6** *(concluded)*

	April 4, 2010	January 3, 2010	January 4, 2009
Accumulated other comprehensive loss	(49.5)	(52.3)	(87.3)
Total stockholders' equity (deficit)	(374.2)	(314.3)	214.3
Total liabilities and stockholders' equity	$1,318.8	$1,538.3	$2,154.5

Source: Blockbuster's 10-Q report, May 14, 2010, and 2009 10-K report, p. 80

Chapter 11 reorganization. In its September 2010 bankruptcy filing, Blockbuster said that it had reached agreement with its bondholders on a recapitalization plan to reduce its debt from about $1 billion to about $100 million or less by swapping debt for shares of the company's common stock. Blockbuster's largest creditors included the Bank of New York Mellon, Twentieth Century Fox Home Entertainment, Warner Home Video, Sony Pictures Home Entertainment, The Walt Disney Co., Universal Studios Home Entertainment, and other movie studios. Analysts predicted that Blockbuster management would likely be forced to close additional Blockbuster stores beyond the 470 stores closed in early 2010 in order to restore company profitability.

REDBOX'S STRATEGY IN THE MOVIE RENTAL INDUSTRY

Arthur A. Thompson
The University of Alabama

Spotting what it believed was a promising opportunity in the self-service DVD rental business, Redbox in 2004 began deploying vending machine kiosks containing mostly new release movie DVDs in high-traffic shopping locations. The idea was that people could be easily enticed to rent movies at a place where they shopped regularly rather than making a special trip to a local movie rental store, especially if the rental fee was dirt cheap. Redbox charged a rental fee of $1 per day, and rented DVDs could be returned to Redbox kiosks at any location. Customers could also purchase new and used movie DVDs; Redbox's typical price for a previously rented DVD was $7. As of May 2010, Redbox had deployed 22,400 of its vending kiosks at locations in all states in the continental United States, Puerto Rico, and the United Kingdom. In the late-afternoon and early-evening hours of a typical Friday and Saturday in 2009, Redbox processed 70 to 80 rental transactions per second. It rented more than 365 million DVDs in 2009 and generated revenues of $773.5 million from rentals and sales of DVDs at its kiosks. On New Year's Eve 2009, Redbox rented a record-breaking 2 million DVDs. Redbox estimated that its share of the DVD rental market in the United States was 16.8 percent at the end of 2009, up from about 9 percent at the beginning of the year, with virtually all of the market share gains coming from rentals taken away from Blockbuster, Movie Gallery, and other local video rental outlets.

COMPANY BACKGROUND

Redbox was a wholly owned and operated subsidiary of Coinstar Inc., which, in addition to its Redbox movie rental business, was also a leading provider of money transfer services and self-service coin-counting kiosks where people could convert coins to cash, a gift-card, or e-certificates, among other options. In 2010, Coinstar products and services could be found at more than 80,000 points of presence, including supermarkets, drugstores, mass merchants, financial institutions, convenience stores, restaurants, and money transfer agent locations. Coinstar was incorporated in Delaware in 1993 and maintained its corporate headquarters in Bellevue, Washington; Redbox operated out of offices in Oakbrook Terrace, Illinois.

Redbox Automated Retail LLC began operations in 2004 with funding provided by McDonald's Ventures, a subsidiary of McDonald's Corporation. The initial Redbox vending machines were placed in a number of McDonald's fast-food restaurants. In 2005, Coinstar purchased a 47.3 percent ownership interest in Redbox. In January 2008, Coinstar exercised its option to acquire a majority ownership interest in the voting equity of Redbox Automated Retail, paying $5.1 million to boost its ownership share to 51.0 percent. Then in February 2009, Coinstar purchased the remaining ownership interests in Redbox for approximately $162.4 million.[1] At the time of the February 2009 acquisition, Redbox had some 12,000 kiosks in supermarkets, Walgreens and other drugstores, and select Walmart and McDonald's locations, with plans to add 6,000 to 8,000 kiosk locations during the remainder of 2009. Coinstar's own DVDXpress vending machine business (which was acquired in 2007) had an additional 1,700 kiosk installations. After acquiring full ownership of Redbox, Coinstar continued to operate DVDXpress and Redbox Automated Retail as separate subsidiaries.

Purchasing 100 percent ownership in Redbox, as opposed to remaining a minority owner, appealed to Coinstar executives for five reasons:

- Revenue growth at Redbox kiosks was attractive (reaching an average of $50,000 per kiosk after three years). Although many kiosks had been installed only a short while, sales growth at kiosks installed longer than one year averaged 52 percent in 2008 and 28 percent during 2009.
- The projected return on Coinstar's investment in Redbox was attractively high.
- Feedback from Redbox customers was quite positive.[2] Customers were attracted by the low price of $1 per day, ease of use, convenience, selection, the option of returning a rented DVD to any Redbox kiosk, and the online reservation feature guaranteeing in-stock status for a reserved DVD.
- In two of Redbox's oldest markets—Denver and Houston—there were indications that Redbox could capture as much as a 20 percent share of the DVD rental business in localities with good density of well-located Redbox kiosks.
- Survey data indicated that 80 percent of Redbox customers would recommend the service to a friend.

Coinstar reported 2009 consolidated revenues of $1.14 billion and net income of $53.6 million. Revenues from Redbox's operations accounted for 67.6 percent of Coinstar's 2009 revenues.

Interestingly, Greg Meyer, the cofounder and CEO of DVDXpress prior to its acquisition by Coinstar, had contacted Blockbuster in 2005, offering to partner with Blockbuster in setting up DVD rental machines outside Blockbuster stores. In his proposal, Meyer stated that by his calculations Blockbuster could save $140 million in store operating costs by shortening the number of hours Blockbuster stores were open and having customers get DVDs at vending machines located just outside its stores. Meyer never heard back on his offer. After selling DVDXpress to Coinstar in 2007, Meyer remained as Coinstar's managing director for the DVDXpress division until Coinstar acquired Redbox in 2009. Since leaving Coinstar, Meyer had purchased 645,000 shares of Blockbuster and in early 2010 submitted a proxy notice to Blockbuster shareholders seeking to replace board member James Crystal; Blockbuster's CEO, James Keyes, had expressed his opposition to Meyer's election, stating that stock ownership was insufficient grounds for board membership.

REDBOX'S STRATEGY

Redbox's strategy centered on (1) attracting customers with a combination of low price and convenience and (2) rapidly expanding the number of shopping locations with a Redbox kiosk. Its vending machines supplied the same functionality as a local video rental store, albeit with a smaller selection. But its $1 per day rental price was considerably cheaper than the $4.50 rental fee charged by many movie rental outlets. And the convenience of picking up a rental at a Redbox machine had considerable appeal—in mid-2009 Redbox's CEO, Mitch Lowe, estimated that every week 150 million people walked within 10 feet of one of Redbox's nearly 20,000 locations.[3] Lowe said, "The way we'll grow is by focusing on the customer experience. That's how we have come out of nowhere."[4] If a customer knew what movie title he or she wanted to rent, the rental process could be completed in less

► EXHIBIT 1   Renting a DVD at Redbox

than a minute. All a customer had to do was use a touch screen to select a DVD from as many as 200 different titles, swipe a valid credit or debit card, retrieve the DVD from the dispenser slot, and leave. Returns could be completed in 20 seconds or less at an unoccupied machine. The rental and return process was designed to be fast, efficient, and fully automated, with no membership fees. Exhibit 1 shows examples of Redbox kiosks and the features of the company's vending machine rental process.

Redbox machines read bar codes on each DVD to track when it went out on rental and when it was returned. Redbox maintained constant electronic contact with every Redbox machine (primarily via cell phone transmissions) to monitor how many copies of each title were in a given machine at any one time—machines could hold 630 discs representing up to 200 titles. The company's inventory monitoring system enabled it to give customers the option of going to Redbox's website to see what was in stock at nearby Redbox locations and reserve a DVD at a particular machine. In February 2010, Redbox executives said that the free Redbox iPhone app (which enabled customers to use an iPhone to reserve a DVD) had been downloaded more than 1 million times since its launch in November 2009. Renters could keep a DVD for as long as they wished at the $1 per day charge. After 25 days and a charge of $25, they could keep the DVD; in mid-2009, Redbox management indicated that about 10 percent did so.[5]

Since acquiring full ownership of Redbox in early 2009, Coinstar management had been aggressive in continuing to deploy additional vending machine kiosks—see Exhibit 2. The company planned to install 7,000 to 8,000 new kiosks in 2010, of which some 2,400 had been deployed by April 1, 2010. Plans called for capital expenditures of $115 million to $125 million for new kiosk locations.[6] Redbox kiosks were already in place at select store locations of such chains as Walgreens, Walmart, McDonald's, 7-Eleven, Kroger, and Albertson's. Redbox kiosks were also located

▶ **EXHIBIT 2**

Number of Redbox and DVDXpress Kiosk Locations, 2006–2010

Time Period	Total Number of Installed Redbox and DVDXpress Kiosks
Year-end 2006	2,200
Year-end 2007	7,000
Year-end 2008	13,700
Year-end 2009	22,400
March 31, 2010	24,800

Source: Coinstar's 10-Q and 10-K reports, various periods.

at select airports and libraries and within such landmark locations as the Pentagon, the Empire State Building in New York City, and the Willis Tower in Chicago. Most recently, Redbox had negotiated arrangements to locate 86 kiosks at Navy exchange stores on 48 or more of the naval bases in the continental United States and Hawaii, put kiosks in 100 Schnuck Markets stores in 7 states, and expand its presence to more than 281 of Kum & Go's 430+ convenience stores in 11 states.

Most Redbox kiosks were located in the area between a retail store's cash registers and front entrance. In many instances, retailers had historically generated little revenue from this space, which made it appealing to put a potentially high-traffic Redbox kiosk in that space (perhaps along with a Coinstar self-service coin-counting machine and/or a Coinstar electronic money transfer service) and better optimize revenue per square foot. Inside-the-store Redbox kiosks occupied an area of less than 10 square feet; outside locations were slightly larger.

The ease with which Redbox had, so far, been able to secure additional retail locations for its DVD rental kiosks went beyond just the attractive revenue stream that a Redbox kiosk produced for the retailer and the buzz that Redbox was generating among retailers interested in boosting customer traffic in their stores. It also had to do with Coinstar's ability to capitalize on the relationships it had previously established with many retail chains and its expertise in developing, deploying, and operating kiosks in retail settings. Prior to Coinstar's acquisition of Redbox, Coinstar had been well-known among many multistore retailers because of its track record in supplying them with other proven ways to generate revenues from the area between their cash registers and front entrances and also to boost store traffic. For example, Coinstar had 19,200 self-service coin-counting kiosks and 49,000 automated money transfer service locations at year-end 2009, a substantial fraction of which were in retail establishments. Coinstar had built productive business relationships with many chain retailers in the course of securing these locations, and the data from its coin-counting kiosks and money transfer locations provided valuable insight into which of its current retail partners and which of their locations were likely to be the most revenue-productive places to deploy a Redbox kiosk. The recent deployment of Redbox kiosks at the locations of retailers that also had coin-counting and/or money transfer services in some of their stores had made some of its partnerships with retailers of prime importance. For instance, Walmart, Walgreens, Kroger, and Supervalu (the parent company of Albertsons and other grocery chains) accounted for a combined 44.7 percent of Coinstar's total revenues in 2009; McDonald's accounted for an additional 9.0 percent of Coinstar's 2009 revenues.

Redbox management foresaw opportunities to deploy thousands of additional kiosks and to capture a meaningful portion of the customers displaced by the closing of so many Blockbuster, Movie Gallery, Hollywood Video, and other movie rental outlets. The store closures meant that Redbox's growth was not dependent on the DVD rental market continuing to grow or even remain flat—Redbox could grow in a stagnating market by simply getting many DVD rental outlet customers to patronize a Redbox kiosk instead.

KIOSK ECONOMICS

Each Redbox kiosk had an installed cost of about $15,000. Requests from retailers for Redbox installations far exceeded the numbers that Redbox actually installed, chiefly because the estimated rental revenues at some retailer locations were not deemed high enough to cover operating costs and also meet Redbox management's strict internal rate of return (IRR) hurdle. Redbox executives closely monitored the density of kiosk locations in each geographic market where kiosks had been installed. Even in markets with the densest number of kiosk locations, the deployed machines generated internal rates of return on investment well above the company's cost of capital, although high-density geographic markets did have slightly lower IRRs than the average kiosk.[7]

Experience indicated that annual rental revenues at machines installed in a location for three years or more tended to top out at around $50,000. Retailers were paid a percentage of the revenue collected at kiosks located in their stores. Redbox vending machines were assigned a useful life of five years and were depreciated on a straight-line basis.

Redbox paid about $18 for a DVD and rented a DVD about 15 times at an average of $2 per transaction.[8] Redbox sold about 3 percent of its previously rented DVDs to customers for about $7. It typically sold about half of its used DVD copies at the end of their rental life to certain wholesale distributors at a negotiated price; the sell-back prices averaged about $4 per disc in 2009. The rest were destroyed. The DVD discs that Redbox acquired for its library were initially recorded at cost and were amortized over an assumed useful life to their estimated salvage value. Estimated salvage value was based on the amounts that Redbox had historically recovered on selling DVDs at the end of their useful rental lives. The amortization charges were accelerated to reflect higher rentals of the DVD in the first few weeks after release, and substantially all of the amortization expense was recognized within one year of the assumed life of the DVDs.

CONTENT ACQUISITION AND LICENSE AGREEMENTS

Redbox obtained copies of DVD titles through licensing arrangements with movie studios, wholesale distributors, and third-party retailers. Redbox's relationships with several movie studios had been contentious, in some cases resulting in Redbox instituting litigation to combat the refusal of Universal Studios, 20th Century Fox, and Warner Bros. to sell their movie DVDs to Redbox for rental purposes until 30 to 45 days after the release of movie DVDs to retailers. Such delays forced Redbox to try to obtain those DVD titles from alternative sources—including buying copies from retailers at the regular retail price. The delayed rental window imposed on Redbox by these movie studios raised Redbox's title acquisition costs and impaired its ability to stock its vending machines with ample copies of new releases; indeed, some retailers (Walmart, for example) had limited the number of copies of new releases they would sell to Redbox.

Redbox management estimated that during 2009 its inability to secure ample copies of certain titles resulted in lost rental revenues of $15 million to $25 million.[9] The revenue loss would have been greater had it not been for Redbox's ability to track disc title inventories in real time at each vending location and use this information to guide Redbox's field staff in moving copies of discs from machine to machine in order to improve title availability rates at particular Redbox locations. In addition to the revenue losses associated with not having enough copies of certain titles, Redbox incurred incremental costs of $1 to $2 per DVD to purchase the disc copies it was able to obtain. However, Redbox had recently succeeded in negotiating license agreements with six prominent movie studios establishing the terms on which Redbox would be entitled to obtain copies of their DVDs:[10]

- *Sony agreement:* In July 2009, Redbox entered into a licensing agreement with Sony Pictures Home Entertainment that called for Redbox to receive deliveries of new releases by the "street date," defined in the agreement as the initial date the titles became available on a rental basis to the general public for in-home entertainment viewing. Under terms of the agreement, Redbox would license specified minimum quantities of each new release and would pay Sony an estimated $487 million during the term of the agreement, which was expected to last from July 1, 2009, until September 30, 2014. However, at Sony's discretion, the agreement was subject to termination as early as September 30, 2011. In addition to the $487 million payment by Redbox over the expected five-year life of the agreement, Coinstar granted 193,348 shares of restricted common stock to Sony. Sony became entitled to 19,335 of these shares on December 31, 2009, and was scheduled to receive additional portions of the 193,348-share total at specified times during the remainder of the agreement.

- *Lionsgate agreement:* In August 2009, Redbox entered into an agreement with Lions Gate Entertainment Corporation (known commonly as Lionsgate) to license minimum quantities of Lionsgate's new releases for rental in each location that Redbox had a DVD kiosk in the United States. Like the Sony agreement, Redbox would receive delivery of Lionsgate's new releases on the initial date the titles became available for rental by the general public for in-home entertainment viewing. Redbox estimated that it would pay Lionsgate approximately $160 million during the term of the agreement, which was expected to last from September 1, 2009, until August 31, 2014. However, Lionsgate had the option of terminating the agreement as early as August 31, 2011.

- *Paramount agreement:* Also in August 2009, Redbox entered into a revenue-sharing licensing agreement with Paramount Home Entertainment that originally ran from August 25, 2009, through December 31, 2009. But in early December 2009, Redbox and Paramount agreed to extend the term of the agreement until June 30, 2010, with the proviso that prior to June 15, 2010, Paramount had the unilateral right to extend the term of the agreement to December 31, 2014. If Paramount exercised its option to extend the agreement through December 2014, Paramount could unilaterally elect to terminate the agreement as early as December 31, 2011. Redbox estimated that it would pay Paramount approximately $56 million during the period August 25, 2009, to June 30, 2010, and approximately $494 million during the period August 25, 2009, to December 31, 2014, for licensing minimum quantities of Paramount's DVDs in each location in the United States where Redbox had a DVD kiosk. Coinstar was required to provide a $28 million letter of credit to Paramount for the period October 1, 2009, through January 31, 2010; during the remainder of the agreement period, the letter of credit was replaced with a Coinstar guarantee to Paramount of up to $25 million. As was the case with the Sony and Lionsgate agreements, Redbox would receive delivery of Paramount's new releases on the initial date the titles were distributed on a rental basis to the general public for home entertainment purposes, whether on a rental or sell-through basis.

- *Warner Bros. agreement:* In February 2010, Redbox entered into a rental revenue-sharing agreement with Warner Home Video, a division of Warner Bros. Home Entertainment Inc., whereby Redbox would license minimum quantities of Warner's DVDs for rental at each location that had a DVD-rental kiosk owned and/or operated by Redbox in the United States. Under the agreement, Redbox could begin renting Warner-released DVDs 28 days after the "street date," defined as the earliest date on which Warner made its new releases available on physical home video formats to consumers, whether on a rental or sell-through basis. The agreement further called for Redbox to dismiss its lawsuit against Warner relating to Redbox's access to Warner titles. Redbox estimated that it would pay Warner approximately $124 million during the term of the agreement, which was expected to last from February 1, 2010, through January 31, 2012.

- *Universal Studios and 20th Century Fox agreements:* In April 2010, Redbox entered into multiyear licensing and distribution agreements with both Universal Studios and 20th Century Fox. The terms on which Redbox would be able to obtain access to rent new DVDs released by these studios were essentially identical to those in the Warner agreement, with Redbox also agreeing to dismiss its lawsuit against Universal and 20th Century Fox.

These recent agreements gave Redbox access to about 90 percent of the DVD content the company needed for 2010.[11]

Redbox's agreements with some of the movie studios called for Redbox to destroy the discs of their titles following their useful life in Redbox's rental kiosk rather than selling them to customers or to wholesale distributors. This was beneficial to the studios because it reduced the number of used movie DVDs in circulation, potentially enhancing retail sales of new DVDs for these titles.

REDBOX'S FINANCIAL PERFORMANCE

Exhibit 3 shows all of the data from Coinstar's financial reports regarding the recent performance of Coinstar's DVD services business, which includes the operations of both

▶EXHIBIT 3

Combined Operations of Redbox-Branded and DVDXpress-Branded Kiosks	Three Months Ending		Years Ended December 31		
	March 31, 2010	March 31, 2009	2009	2008	2007
Revenues	$263.1	$154.7	$773.5	$399.5*	$143.6*
Operating income (before depreciation/amortization and stock-based compensation/share-based payments)	44.8	20.8	128.3	72.3	Not available
Operating income as a percent of revenues	17.0%	13.4%	16.6%	18.6%	—
Total assets	$482.6	$445.2	$491.8	$378.1	Not available

Financial Performance of Coinstar's DVD Services Business (includes the operations of both Redbox-branded and DVDXpress-branded kiosks), 2007–2009 ($ millions)

*Includes revenues of $11.0 million for the period January 1, 2008, through January 17, 2008, and revenues of $134.1 million for full-year 2007 when Coinstar did not consolidate the operating results of Redbox, owing to its minority ownership of Redbox.

Sources: Coinstar's 10-K reports for 2008 and 2009.

Redbox-branded and DVDXpress-branded kiosks. Coinstar reported that $105 million of the $374 million in revenue growth at Redbox and DVD Express in 2009 was due to increased sales at kiosks in operation at least 12 months. Coinstar management said the following about the reasons for the decline in operating income as a percentage of revenues from 18.6 percent in 2008 to 16.6 percent in 2009:

> The decline in DVD services segment operating income as a percentage of revenue for the year ended December 31, 2009, compared to the prior year was mostly driven by higher product costs, offset in part by the favorable effects of leveraging general and administrative expenses. The higher product costs resulted from the decrease in DVD salvage values, as well as the increased cost associated with purchasing certain DVD titles from alternative procurement sources. Throughout 2009, one movie studio has restricted the distribution of DVDs to our DVD services segment. During October 2009, two additional movie studios began restricting the distribution of DVDs to our DVD services segment. The increased restriction of DVDs has had a negative impact on the operating income margins in our DVD services business, because in these situations we must

obtain DVD titles from alternative sources including certain wholesale distributors and third party retailers, often at a higher cost and often not in advantageous quantities.[12]

REDBOX'S FUTURE OUTLOOK

In February 2010, Gregg Kaplan, Coinstar's chief operating officer, said the following:

> The future looks extremely bright for Redbox. We strongly believe that physical DVDs will be the preferred medium of home entertainment for many years to come. As studios continue to develop high content entertainment such as Blu-ray and 3-D movies, Redbox is well positioned to be the delivery mechanism of choice due to our ability to deliver content to a broad base of consumers very inexpensively through our physical kiosk presence. Our kiosks eliminate the challenges of time and bandwidth that would be necessary for consumers to directly access this content in their homes.
>
> We should also point out that Redbox's growth is not dependent upon a flat or growing DVD rental market. We believe that Redbox will continue to take share and be a leader in the DVD rental market, even as that market eventually plateaus and as

our competitors continue to close the doors of their retail stores.

Despite our confidence that Redbox's physical DVD rental business will sustain it for quite a long time, we recognize that there will be a gradual shift to digital, and we will not be watching from the sidelines. We believe digital represents a great way for loyal Redbox customers to access a wider variety of titles than we can effectively offer in our kiosks. Over time, Redbox customers have said to us, we love Redbox and usually rent new releases, but there are times when we want to watch an old classic, can you offer that? Digital is a great way for us to offer that alternative. We began testing digital downloads in 2009 and will use 2010 to continue testing.[13]

In his 2009 letter to stockholders, Coinstar CEO Paul Davis said:

> Over the years, we have developed an expertise in kiosk development, deployment, and operations, and in building solid relationships with the best-known retailers in the world. These core competencies combined with our strong market presence will continue to drive our automated retail strategy. Looking ahead we will focus on three areas: delight and engage our customers, strengthen partner relationships, and generate profitable growth.

ENDNOTES

[1] Coinstar, 2009 10-K report, p. 2.

[2] Coinstar, Q4 2008 earnings call transcript, February 13, 2009, www.seekingalpha.com, accessed May 24, 2010.

[3] David Lieberman, "Video Kiosks Have Rivals Seeing Red," *USA Today,* August 12, 2009, p. 3B.

[4] Ibid.

[5] Ibid.

[6] Coinstar, Q4 2009 earnings call transcript, February 11, 2010, www.seekingalpha.com, accessed May 25, 2010.

[7] Ibid.

[8] Lieberman, "Video Kiosks Have Rivals Seeing Red," p. 3B.

[9] Coinstar, Q4 2009 earnings call transcript.

[10] Coinstar, 2009 10-K report, p. 4 and pp. 26–27; Coinstar news releases, April 22, 2010.

[11] Statement by Coinstar CEO Paul Davis in his letter to stockholders, in Coinstar, 2009 annual report.

[12] Coinstar, 2009 10-K report, p. 37.

[13] Coinstar, Q4 2009 earnings call transcript.

SIFT CUPCAKE AND DESSERT BAR

Rui Gregorio
Sonoma State University
Andy Kiehl
Sonoma State University

Mark Mathewson
Sonoma State University
Meredith Nicklas
Sonoma State University

Cynthia Riggs
Sonoma State University
Armand Gilinsky, Jr.
Sonoma State University

Gathered around a bright pink table in the party room of her third successful cupcake shop in Santa Rosa, California, Sift founder Andrea Ballus, seated along with her husband, Jeff, and manager Corey Fanfa, contemplated the future of her company in late October 2010:

> We pride ourselves on the fact that we are very team oriented, more like a family, and that we develop from within, yet I want to be the premier cupcake shop in the San Francisco Bay Area. To do this we need to hire smart experienced people to help us grow beyond the capacity of the three of us. How do we do this and continue to deliver the "OMG" experience every day?

As they reflected on their past successes, another issue loomed: Sift's line of credit (LOC) was maxed out and Sift had burned through the money that it had saved to pay income taxes. Jeff and Andrea had recently asked their banker for an increase in the company's LOC; however, the loan officer recommended against this idea. Instead, he offered to float their cash flow shortages in the short term, explaining that increasing Sift's current LOC could negatively impact their ultimate success in securing a much-needed $340,000 Small Business Administration (SBA) loan. Creating a business plan to obtain the SBA loan and a strategic plan for 2011 would be necessary to realize Andrea's dream of becoming the premier cupcake shop in the San Francisco Bay Area.

THE SPECIALTY BAKING MARKET

With the exception of cakes and cupcakes industry-wide sales, all other categories of bakery products declined in 2009.[1] Despite negative factors facing the baking industry, such as grocery and "big box" in-store bakeries, high unemployment, and a sputtering economy, retail bakery sales were expected to grow 8.1 percent per year on average through 2014.[2]

Capitalizing on a national trend started at New York's Magnolia Bakery in 2005 and popularized on the hit television program "Sex in the City," specialty cupcake bakeries had been opening across the country. According to the market research firm Mintel, nationwide cupcake sales were projected to rise another 20 percent between 2009 and 2014.[3] The specialty cupcake trend is so popular it has spawned its own Food Network® show, *Cupcake Wars*®, where top cupcake bakers around the country compete. According to Pam Nelson, owner of Butter Lane Bakery in New York:

> People still want a cupcake. I think it's kind of an indulgence and the price point is still low. For $3 people can buy something for themselves instead of spending 100 bucks on a dinner and still feel like they are treating themselves.[4]

Consumer trends focusing more on healthful choices could pose a risk to specialty cupcake bakeries. However, the National Association for the Specialty Food Trade (NASFT) reported that the next big food trend will be: "Back to the future—a reaction against organic/healthful, etc., and a realization that old fashioned in moderation is a joy. Food will play the role of a necessity, a pleasure, and an indulgence."[5] The NASFT also reported that consumers were responding to an improving economy by purchasing specialty foods. According to the 2010 research, 63 percent of consumers had purchased a specialty food product in the last six months. This compared with 46 percent in 2009, which was approaching the pre-recession specialty food consumption levels of 2005.[6] One of the benefits of cupcakes was that they came in relatively small portions and were a good snack for getting a sugar fix while assisting with portion control.[7]

According to the Bureau of Labor Statistics, in 2009, the 35-to-44 and the 45-to-54 age brackets spent the most on bakery products, spending, on average, $357 and $346, respectively, per year (see Exhibit 1). In November 2010, Sift conducted an online survey of 1,629 customers resulting in a 32 percent response rate. Of the respondents, the majority fell within the higher spending age brackets (see Exhibit 2), as well as higher income brackets (see Exhibit 3). Of the customer respondents, 93.4 percent were women and 6.6 percent were men. When sorted by parenting group, 28.2 percent of Sift customers had children under 10, while 35.8 percent had no children at all (see Exhibit 4). Specialty food consumers also spent quite a bit of time online: More than 90 percent were online two hours per day away from work (see Exhibit 5).[8]

COMPANY HISTORY

In 2006, Andrea became obsessed with cupcakes. As a high-energy, successful sales rep for Nestlé Waters, Andrea sold San Pellegrino products to fine-dining establishments in the greater Las Vegas area. She found cupcakes provided the perfect "wow" factor; getting her

▶ EXHIBIT 1

U.S. Annual Consumer Spending on Bakery Products

Age Group	2009 Actual	2014 Projected	% Change
Under 25	$167.75	$213.75	27%
25–34	269.75	218.00	(19)
35–44	357.00	404.50	13
45–54	346.00	394.25	14
55–64	313.50	361.75	15
65 and Over	275.25	322.75	17
All Consumers	$303.75	$351.50	16

Source: Bureau of Labor Statistics and Sundale Research.

in the door of high-end dining establishments and taking her directly to decision makers.

When planning her northern California wine country wedding the next year, serving cupcakes rather than the traditional wedding cake seemed an obvious choice. However, she found the area disappointingly void of "designer" cupcakes, forcing her to drive her wedding cupcakes from Las Vegas to California. This got Andrea thinking.

In December 2007, Andrea and Jeff decided to move back to California to be closer to their families. Jeff's company was willing to transfer him to California, yet Andrea's was not. With the wedding experience fresh in her mind, Andrea leveraged her enterprising nature and

▶ EXHIBIT 2

Sift's Customers by Age Group, November 2010

Age Group	% of Sift Customers	2009 Bakery Product Spending
Under 25	9.9%	$167.75
25–34	35.3	269.75
35–44	26.5	357.00
45–54	18.0	346.00
55–64	8.7	313.50
65 and Over	1.7	275.25

Source: Sift Customer Survey, Bureau of Labor Statistics, and Sundale Research.

▶ EXHIBIT 3

Sift's Customers by Family Income, November 2010		
Total Family Income	**% of Sift Customers**	**2009 Bakery Product Spending**
Under $15,000	2.7%	Not Available
$15,000–$29,999	5.9	$201.25
$30,000–$39,999	5.7	249.75
$40,000–$49,000	7.0	290.50
$50,000–$69,999	14.9	332.00
$70,000–$79,999	6.3	355.50
$80,000–$99,999	10.7	404.75
$100,000 and over	20.6	473.75

Source: Sift, Bureau of Labor Statistics, and Sundale Research.

▶ EXHIBIT 4

Sift's Customers by Parenting Group, November 2010	
Parenting Group	**% of Sift Customers**
Pregnant, No Children	1.9%
Children under 10	28.2
Children 10–18	17.0
Children Over 18 Living at Home	6.1
Children Over 18 Not at Home	11.0
No Children	35.8

Source: Sift Customer Survey.

decided to open a cupcake shop somewhere in wine country. Not knowing where to start, she found a "good opportunity" and began there.

Searching online, she found her first location. Site unseen, Andrea purchased an existing 1,000-square-foot coffee shop, located in a small strip mall in the college town of Cotati, California. Her friend Corey sent pictures of the location from California. Andrea soon closed the deal—without visiting the location—negotiating the purchase price from $13,000 down to $9,000.

▶ EXHIBIT 5

U.S. Consumer Internet and Social Media Use in the Specialty Food Segment		
	% All Consumers	**% Specialty Food Consumers**
Online at least two hours per day away from work	90%	91%
Facebook	59	65
YouTube	26	33
Twitter	14	17
LinkedIn	8	11
Other	8	9
None	32	24

Base: 1,500 adults aged 18 + with Internet access.
Source: Mintel.

Using a $15,000 bonus from her job at Nestlé, $14,000 from Jeff's 401(k) and a $20,000 investment by Andrea's mother as start-up money, the three became shareholders of Sift A Cupcakery, LLC, in early 2008. In March of that year Andrea moved back to California and the Cotati store opened six weeks later. Andrea was the baker, the decorator, the "everything" gal. She relied heavily on family, friends, and her best friend Corey who became a Sift employee and ultimately their first manager. In 2009, Jeff left his sales job to join Sift. He taught himself what he needed to learn to fill the much-needed roles of working out logistics, addressing supply chain issues, as well as assisting with the day-to-day financial management of the company.

The company was profitable during its first year of operation, and retained earnings from initial operations made it possible for Andrea to achieve her goal of opening a store in Napa during the company's second year. The 500-square-foot Napa store occupied sublet space in a women's clothing store operating under the name Cake Plate, providing retail sales without on-site baking.

During its third year of operation, Sift internally financed the opening of a third 2,260-square-foot full-service bakery with a party room in downtown Santa Rosa. The 200-square-foot party room introduced a new concept to the Sift business model and an additional revenue stream by providing decorating classes and parties for children and adults. The Santa Rosa kitchen was set up for production baking and supplied product to the Napa location. None of the three stores were exactly alike: Each location adapted to the environment and opportunity that were available in that market at the time.

MARKETING STRATEGY

With disappointing results from print advertising and her background in radio advertising sales, Andrea preferred to use local radio to promote the business. In addition, Sift used social media platforms such as Facebook and Twitter as communication and promotional tools. Sift had close to 5,000 "fans" on Facebook and ran weekly Facebook promotions to drive traffic to the stores.

In addition to radio and social media, Sift was very active within the community. In exchange for promotional benefit, Sift donated to local school fund-raisers and nonprofit organizations. Sift also participated in large local community events, such as Levi's Grand Fondo and the Relay for Life, to promote consumer trial and enhance brand recognition. Sift's management team saw growth potential in developing the wedding side of the business in both Napa and Sonoma. To take advantage of this opportunity, Sift secured booth space at seasonal wedding expos to promote cupcakes as a replacement for the traditional wedding cake.

In the early stages of her business, Andrea created a website for Sift. As the company grew, both Andrea and Jeff recognized they needed a more polished representation of the business. To that end, they hired a professional marketing company to develop a new website and to assist with branding and promotional material development.

In October of 2010, Andrea and Jeff decided to shift strategy and focus not only on cupcakes, but also on a variety of complementary desserts in hopes of creating even broader appeal. They rebranded the business from Sift a Cupcakery to Sift Cupcake and Dessert Bar. The repositioning allowed for the creation of new desserts such as cruffles and whoopie cookies,

ice cream sandwiches, macaroons, and profiteroles, in addition to cupcakes and frosting shots. Andrea and Jeff believed that repositioning the business would establish Sift as a family dessert destination, the likes of which did not exist in the local marketplace.

HUMAN RESOURCE ISSUES

Most of Andrea's employees were high school and college students with an average age of 20 years old. Many employees had been with Sift from the beginning. Her employees were excited about working at Sift and indicated that they looked forward to working there for the foreseeable future. Andrea commented:

> We have many long-term employees. Our turnover is very low compared to other retailers. If our turnover had been higher, it would not have allowed our growth. So my employees are important to me and we work hard to create a family culture among us.

Andrea believed that a happy employee equaled a happy customer. She sought to nurture her employees through hiring and promoting from within. She supported staff in learning new skills and provided them with opportunities for individual growth. (See Sift's Mission and Values Statement in Exhibit 6.) Although Andrea desired to promote from within, training employees for new positions presented challenges. Sometimes an individual staff member just didn't possess the necessary skills to get the job done. Chain of command and effective communication about processes and their implementation also proved to be problematic. While everyone was eager to get things accomplished, because there were no processes in place to guide decisions, more work was created.

In 2010, Andrea hired Robert Evans, a former store manager from Peet's Coffee, a nationwide chain of coffee emporia that had been founded in Berkeley, California, to oversee Sift's Santa Rosa location. With a breadth of experience in a related industry, Robert was able to remove day-to-day tasks from Andrea and allow her to devote her time to larger business objectives.

EXHIBIT 6

Sift's Mission and Values

Sift Mission Statement

At Sift Cupcake and Dessert Bar we do what it takes to deliver the OMG factor to all our customers. Our unique variety of outstanding house-made treats is accompanied with exceptional customer service and a bright trendy décor. This provides our customers with their most positive and memorable cupcake and dessert experience. We want our customers to fall in love with us and will do whatever it takes to make that happen.

Sift Core Values

1. Deliver the OMG Factor everyday.
2. Smile and be kind to everyone . . . ALWAYS!
3. Quality products, a clean environment, and OVER THE TOP customer service rule!
4. Create a fun place to work, learn, and grow.
5. Be Innovative, Creative, and Passionate.
6. Build Team Spirit through Open and Honest Communication.
7. Be accountable and learn from mistakes.
8. Be empowered. YOU have the power to create loyal Sift customers.
9. Challenge yourself to get 1% better each day.
10. Support our Community.

Andrea hoped that Robert would also take on the task of creating a more efficient baking space and streamlined processes.

Employing Robert signaled a change in Andrea's hiring policy, that is, toward improving her "business IQ," beginning with each new hire. Andrea and her management team admitted that finding the right people for the job was a daunting task, and being able to offer enough compensation to attract that talent and finding the right incentives to motivate both new and existing employees was one of their biggest challenges. While their cupcake business was profitable and employees were making more than the California minimum wage, there was not enough revenue to support manager wages. However, additional store managers were necessary as Andrea looked to expand beyond her existing three stores and beyond the capability of her management team (see Exhibit 7).

COMPETITION

There was no specialty cupcake trade association tracking the industry as it expanded across the United States. The industry segment relied on passionate cupcake bloggers such as cupcaketakesthecake.blogspot.com and allthingscupcake.com, or the review site Yelp.com to stay up with industry trends and keep an eye on the competition.

As of November 1, 2010, there were 106 known "cupcakeries" in the Bay Area, according to Yelp.com. Most of them were single-store operations. In addition, there were hundreds of additional bakeries, dessert bars, and other commercial venues selling cupcakes (see Exhibit 8). Andrea and Jeff viewed Kara's Cupcakes as their primary competitor. Kara's had six Bay Area

EXHIBIT 7

Sift's Store Staffing Levels, November 2010

Job Title	Cotati	Santa Rosa	Napa	Total
Manager	1	1	0	2
Assistant Manager	1	0	1	2
Baker	2	1	0	3
Baker's Assistant	0	2	0	2
Frosting Maker	0	1	0	1
Counter Staff/ Decorator	7	7	4	18
Delivery Driver	0	1	0	1
Wedding Coordinator	0	1	0	1
Total Staff	11	14	5	30

EXHIBIT 8   Statistics for the San Francisco Bay Area Specialty Bakery Market, November 2010

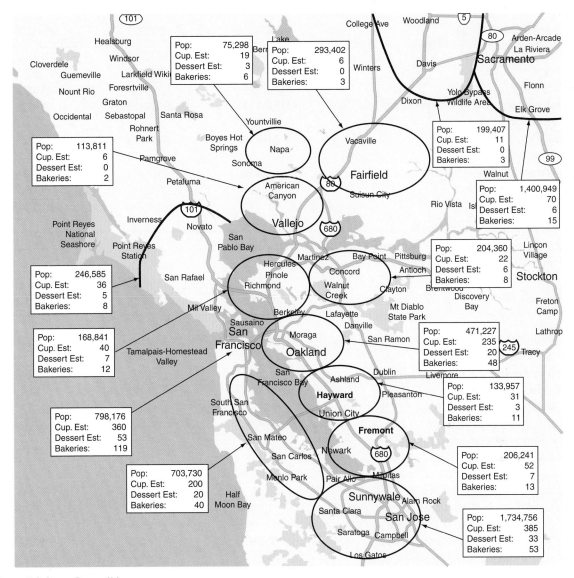

Source: U.S. Census Bureau, Yelp.com.
Pop: Population of area indicated
Cup Est.: Any retailer that sells cupcakes
Dessert Est.: Retailers specializing in desserts
Bakeries: Stand-alone bakeries

locations: two in San Francisco, and one in Palo Alto, San Jose, Napa, and Walnut Creek. On a national level, Sprinkles had emerged as the retail specialty cupcake leader. With 10 locations in major metropolitan areas around the United States, one of which was in Palo Alto, Sprinkles announced plans to open 15 more locations in 2011, including a store in San Francisco.

SIFT FINANCIALS

Andrea started Sift with relatively little capital: founding the business with what she and Jeff could piece together plus a small investment from Andrea's mother, who remained a silent partner. The company grew by reinvesting its earnings and from Andrea's ability to find a "good deal."

▶ EXHIBIT 9

Sift Cupcake and Dessert Bar Financial Statements, 2008–2010

Year Ending Dec. 31	2008	2009	2010**
Net sales	$220,904.46	$508,357.99	$961,118.23
Cost of goods sold*	58,067.35	137,036.98	607,085.68
Gross profit	162,837.11	371,321.01	354,032.56
Operating expenses (exc. depreciation)	155,667.77	335,257.86	190,843.67
Depreciation	0	0	0
EBIT	7,169.34	36,063.15	163,188.89
Interest expenses	0	0	0
Income before taxes	7,169.34	36,063.15	163,188.89
Federal income taxes	994.94	5,673.91	26,110.22
Net Income	$ 6,174.40	$ 30,389.25	$137,078.67

*In 2010, Labor expense was moved from the Operating Expense line to Cost of Goods Sold.

**Full Year forecast based on Actuals through October 2010.

Balance Sheet at Dec. 31	2008	2009	2010
Assets			
Cash	$29,507	$ 27,175	$ 46,474
Accounts receivable	0	0	185
Inventories	185	15,757	17,669
Total current assets	29,692	42,932	64,328
Net fixed assets	29,917	93,433	215,341
Total assets	59,609	136,365	279,669
Liabilities and Stockholders' Equity			
Notes payable—banks	0	0	0
Accounts payable	4,452	1,950	17,473
Accrued expenses and taxes	1,307	11,138	28,455
Total current liabilities	5,760	13,088	45,928
Long-term debt	0	11,654	88,122
Stockholders' equity/Retained earnings	53,849	111,622	145,619
Total liabilities and stockholders' equity	$59,609	$136,365	$279,669

Financial statements for Sift's first three years of operation are shown in Exhibit 9.

Despite the fact that Sift had been profitable from its opening year, store managers were still expected to control their costs and payroll. However, store managers were not trained to read and utilize the new POS reports and had not been given clear financial guidelines to follow. Day-to-day financial monitoring seldom took place, negatively impacting profitability.

THE FUTURE

At the end of the October 2010 meeting, Andrea, Jeff, and Corey agreed that a clear growth strategy needed to be developed in order to continue moving forward. Sift was in the process of relocating the Napa store to a larger location with more foot traffic in a nearby shopping center. While reviewing future growth options, they observed that Sift

▶ EXHIBIT 10

Sift's Growth Options and Forecasted Income Statements for Each Option, 2011–2013

Option 1: Maintain Current Locations

Year Ending Dec. 31	Forecast 2011	Forecast 2012	Forecast 2013
Net Sales	$1,057,230	$1,162,953	$1,279,248
Cost of Goods Sold	667,794	734,574	808,031
Gross Profit	389,436	428,379	471,217
Operating Expense (excl. dep.)	194,661	198,554	202,525
Depreciation	0	0	0
EBIT	194,775	229,826	268,693
Interest Expense	0	0	0
Income Before Taxes	194,775	229,826	268,693
Federal Income Taxes @ 20%	38,955	45,965	53,739
Net Income	$ 155,820	$ 183,861	$ 214,954

Option 2: Rapid Expansion with Retail-Only Stores/Commissary

Year Ending Dec. 31	Forecast 2011	Forecast 2012	Forecast 2013
Net Sales	$2,122,136	$4,250,723	$7,068,337
Cost of Goods Sold	1,363,216	2,028,020	3,123,599
Gross Profit	748,920	2,222,703	3,944,738
Operating Expense (excl. dep.)	574,641	1,166,407	2,170,779
Depreciation	53,321	94,892	140,378
EBIT	120,958	961,404	1,633,581
Interest Expense	18,802	13,579	2,748
Income Before Taxes	102,156	947,825	1,630,833
Federal Income Taxes @ 20%	22,431	189,565	326,167
Net Income	$ 81,725	$ 758,260	$1,304,666

Option 3: Expansion with Retail/Baking Stores

Year Ending Dec. 31	Forecast 2011	Forecast 2012	Forecast 2013
Net Sales	$1,691,730	$2,283,903	$2,935,293
Cost of Goods Sold	1,068,573	1,442,616	1,854,064
Gross Profit	623,157	841,287	1,081,229
Operating Expense (excl. dep.)	194,661	198,554	202,525
Depreciation	0	0	0
EBIT	428,496	642,733	878,704
Interest Expense	18,802	13,579	2,748
Income Before Taxes	409,694	629,154	875,956
Federal Income Taxes @ 20%	81,939	125,831	175,191
Net Income	$ 327,775	$ 503,323	$ 700,765

was simultaneously in an expansion mode and in the process of rebranding. Doing both had increased expenses, and for the first time since opening the business, Sift had begun to experience serious cash flow challenges. To prepare a business plan for the SBA loan application, Andrea hired a consultant to help her prepare a formal three-year financial forecast for three separate scenarios, as described on the next page and detailed above in Exhibit 10.

Option 1: Maintain Current Locations:
Maintain current stores and small business model while improving operational issues and strengthening infrastructure. Further develop brand identity and own the local marketplace.

Option 2: Rapid Expansion with Retail-Only Stores/Commissary: Open a central baking commissary along the I-80 freeway corridor. This commissary would service four additional 500-to-600-square-foot storefront locations in 2011 in affluent communities without existing specialty cupcake shops. Additional storefronts would be added at a rate of two storefronts per year. These storefronts will only decorate and sell cupcakes; all baking will be completed at the central commissary.

Option 3: Expansion with Retail/Baking Stores:
Expand on current business model of baking, decorating, and selling in each new 1,500-to-2,000-square-foot store. Move into targeted locations as the opportunity arises with controlled growth based on the financial health of the business. The plan was based on three stores opening in the last three quarters of 2011 followed by two additional stores opening each year following.

In the back of her mind, Andrea also wondered if now was the right time to establish a mail-order division. Many of Sift's competitors had already diversified into similar operations. Developing this new channel could expand Sift's potential customer base well beyond the reach of its brick-and-mortar stores.

ENDNOTES

[1] Sundale Research; and U.S. Department of Commerce data.

[2] Ibid.

[3] Elizabeth Olsan, "The Latest Entrepreneurial Fantasy Is Selling Cupcakes," *The New York Times,* www.nytimes.com/2009/11/26/business/smallbusiness/26cupcake.html.

[4] "New York City's Cupcake Economy," *The Wall Street Journal,* July 16, 2010, http://blogs.wsj.com/metropolis/2010/07/16/new-york-citys-cupcake-economy/.

[5] "Today's Specialty Food Consumer Report 2010," *Specialty Food Magazine.*

[6] Ibid.

[7] Hubert Vigilla, "Let them Eat Cupcakes: Why Cupcakes are such Trendy Snacks," October 1, 2008, www.docshop.com/2008/10/01/let-them-eat-cupcakes-why-cupcakes-are-such-trendy-snacks.

[8] Ibid.

BLUE NILE INC. IN 2011: WILL ITS STRATEGY TO REMAIN NUMBER ONE IN ONLINE DIAMOND RETAILING WORK?

Arthur A. Thompson
The University of Alabama

Ronald W. Eastburn
University of South Alabama

A 2009 issue of *Forbes* cited the experience of a Cleveland couple, Sanjay and Amy Bhargave, who were shopping for an engagement ring.[1] During a trip to New York City, Amy, 33, led Sanjay into a Tiffany store. But while this gave the soon-to-be-married couple a chance to scout diamonds, neither was happy with the service or the inventory. Back at home, they visited several local jewelry stores, but again, quality was a concern. Then one of Sanjay's clients suggested Blue Nile, the world's largest online jeweler. After viewing Blue Nile's extensive diamond inventory and spending six hours over the course of three weeks talking to his diamond consultant, Sanjay placed an order for a 2.2 carat princess cut in a Petite Trellis platinum setting for $20,000.

Once Blue Nile received an online order from a customer such as Sanjay Bhargave, the company secured the selected diamond from one of their exclusive suppliers, who then shipped the diamond overnight to Blue Nile's 27,000-square-foot warehouse in Seattle. There, a bench jeweler created the finished product. The ring was then steam-cleaned and packaged in a Blue Nile signature blue-and-silver box and shipped overnight to the customer. The purchase process typically took just three days. Furthermore, the satisfaction guarantee allowed dissatisfied customers to return items within 30 days of shipment for a full refund. Sanjay's ring arrived in time for his planned New Year's Eve proposal.

Founded in 1999, and taken public in 2004, Blue Nile had grown to become the world's largest online retailer of certified diamonds and fine jewelry, with sales of $332.9 million in 2010 (up from $169.2 million in 2004). The vast majority of Blue Nile's sales were diamond engagement rings—the company had sold more than 230,000 engagement rings by 2010. Blue Nile was ranked 60th in *Internet Retailer*'s "Top 500 Guide to Retail Web Sites" in 2010 and had been named best online retailer by *Kiplinger Personal Finance* each year between 2006 and 2009 and had been listed as a Forbes Favorite by *Forbes* magazine every year since 2000. In addition, Blue Nile had received the BizRate.com Circle of Excellence Platinum Award, which recognized the best in online customer service as ranked by actual consumers. The only jeweler to have ever received this annual award, Blue Nile and had won it nine times since 2002. A March 2008 article in *The Economist* said, "Creating a website that looks good and makes it easy for men to learn about diamonds before buying has turned Blue Nile into the leading online seller of jewelry, confounding predictions that luxury and e-commerce would never mix."[2]

In 2010, jewelry sales in the United States were estimated at $63.2 billion, up 5.3 percent over 2009 and surpassing the previous highest level of $60 billion in 2007. Industry revenues had grown by approximately 5.5 percent annually since the mid-1980s to reach the $60 billion level before declining after the onset of the U.S. recession in 2008. Blue Nile's revenues fell by nearly 8 percent between 2007 and 2008 before improving by 2.5 percent between 2008 and 2009, with sales growing to $332.9 million in 2010 to record a staggering 10.2 percent growth over the previous year. The company's strategy—which was keyed to having a large inventory of high-quality diamonds, exceptional customer service, and low prices (20 to 40 percent less than traditional jewelry stores)—had allowed it to weather the effects of the U.S. recession far better than most of its rivals in the industry and to capitalize on the economic rebound.

In 2011, Blue Nile management remained concerned about the lingering effects of poor economic conditions in the United States on the diamond jewelry industry, the increasing number of brick-and-mortar jewelers that had begun selling online, and weaknesses in the company's strategy that might limit its growth and competitiveness. Also of concern was how the company might encourage a greater percentage of jewelry consumers to shop online for jewelry purchases, how it should go about increasing its sales of diamond jewelry other than engagement rings, and how aggressively it should pursue expansion in international markets.

BLUE NILE'S BUSINESS MODEL AND STRATEGY

In an industry famous for big markups, frequent "closeout" sales, and a myriad of ill-understood ways of judging the caliber and value of its product offering, online jewelers faced the marketing challenge of convincing understandably skittish shoppers to purchase diamonds and fine jewelry online. It was one thing to shop for diamonds in a reputable jewelry store where one could put on a ring or other jewelry item to see how it looked, perhaps inspect the stones with a magnifying glass or microscope, and have a qualified jeweler explain the caliber of the stones and address concerns about pricing, characteristics of the stones, and jewelry settings. It was quite another thing to commit to buying expensive jewelry sight-unseen on the Internet.

Blue Nile's strategy to attract customers had two core elements. The first was offering high-quality diamonds and fine jewelry at competitively attractive prices. The second entailed providing jewelry shoppers with a host of useful information and trusted guidance throughout their purchasing process. Top management believed that Blue Nile's strategy of providing educational information, in-depth product information, and grading reports, coupled with its wide product selection and attractive prices, were the key drivers of the company's success and, ideally, would lead to customers looking on Blue Nile as their jeweler for life:

> We have established and are continuing to develop a brand based on trust, guidance and value, and we believe our customers view Blue Nile as a trusted authority on diamonds and fine jewelry. Our goal is for consumers to seek out the Blue Nile brand whenever they purchase high quality diamonds and fine jewelry.[3]

COMPETITIVE PRICING, LEAN COSTS, AND SUPPLY CHAIN EFFICIENCY

Blue Nile's websites showcased as many as 70,000 independently certified diamonds and styles of fine jewelry, including rings, wedding bands, earrings, necklaces, pendants, bracelets, and watches. The product offerings ranged from simple classic designs suitable for wearing every day to an impressive signature collection of some of the finest diamonds in the world. Diamonds were the most significant component of Blue Nile's merchandise offerings, but the selection was limited chiefly to high-quality stones in terms of shape, cut, color, clarity, and carat weight. Complementing the large diamond selection was a broad range of diamond, platinum, gold, pearl, and sterling silver jewelry that included settings, rings, wedding bands, earrings, necklaces, pendants, bracelets, and watches.

Blue Nile specialized in the customization of diamond jewelry with a Build Your Own feature that offered customers the ability to customize diamond rings, pendants, and earrings. The company's product offerings included more than 70,000 diamonds and hundreds of settings. Customers could select a diamond and then choose from a variety of ring, earring, and pendant settings that were designed to match the characteristics of each individual diamond.

Blue Nile's economical supply chain and comparatively low operating costs allowed it to sell comparable-quality diamonds, gemstones, and fine jewelry pieces at substantially lower prices than those of reputable local jewelers. The supply chain bypassed the markups of traditional layers of diamond wholesalers and brokers, thus generally allowing Blue Nile to obtain most of its product offerings more cost-efficiently than traditional brick-and-mortar jewelers. The distinctive feature of Blue Nile's supply chain was its set of exclusive arrangements that allowed it to display leading diamond and gem suppliers' products on its website; some of these arrangements entailed multiyear agreements whereby designated diamonds were offered only at Blue Nile. Blue Nile did not actually purchase a diamond or gem from these suppliers until a customer placed an order for it; this enabled Blue Nile to minimize the costs associated with carrying large inventories and limited its risk of potential markdowns. However, Blue Nile did selectively purchase jewelry merchandise (usually bracelets, necklaces, earrings, pendants, wedding bands, and watches), stocking them in its own inventory until they were ordered and delivered to customers. Blue Nile's inventory was $20.24 million at year-end 2010. In contrast, traditional jewelers had far bigger inventories relative to annual sales. For example, Zale Corporation—which not only

sold online but also was the parent of Zales Jewelers (700 stores in the United States and Puerto Rico), Zales Outlet, Gordon's Jewelers, Peoples Jewelers (the largest Canadian jeweler), Mappins Jewelers (another Canadian jewelry chain), and Piercing Pagoda—reported year-end inventories of $703.1 million on 2010 sales of $1.6 billion. Luxury jewelry retailer Tiffany & Co. reported year-end inventories of $1.5 billion on 2010 sales of $3.1 billion.

Blue Nile's supply chain savings gave it a significant pricing advantage: purchasing diamonds on a "just-in-time" basis from their suppliers when a customer places an order for a specific diamond. In 2010, for every dollar that Blue Nile paid suppliers for stones, settings, and other purchased items, it sold its finished jewelry for a markup of about 28 percent over cost. In contrast, Tiffany sold at an average markup of 144 percent over cost of goods sold and Zale sold at an average markup over cost of goods sold of 103 percent. In terms of gross profit margin (pre-tax) for 2010 Blue Nile was 6.5 percent; Tiffany & Co. was 17.7 percent, while Zale was unprofitable.

While much of Blue Nile's competitiveness was dependent on maintaining favorable arrangements with its suppliers, the company was somewhat protected by having negotiated agreements with a variety of suppliers, thus limiting its dependence on particular suppliers—the top three suppliers accounted for only 22 percent of the company's purchases in 2008, 24 percent of its purchases in 2009, increasing to 28 percent in 2010. Moreover, the supply arrangements were favorable to suppliers, providing them with real-time market intelligence about what items were selling, the potential of high sales volume through a single account, and a way to achieve more inventory turns and otherwise manage their own inventories more efficiently.

Another cost-saving element of Blue Nile's strategy was lean operating costs. At year-end 2010 the company had only 191 full-time employees and 2 part-time employees, and they also utilized temporary personnel on a seasonal basis. Operations were conducted via a combination of proprietary and licensed technologies. Blue Nile licensed third-party information technology systems for financial reporting, inventory management, order fulfillment, and merchandising. Redundant Internet carriers were used to minimize service interruptions and downtime at its website. Various operating systems were monitored continuously using third-party software, and an on-call team responded to any emergencies or technology issues. Management continuously explored avenues to improve operating efficiency, refine its supply chain, and leverage its investment in fixed-cost technology. In 2010, Blue Nile's selling, general, and administrative (SG&A) expenses were only 15.2 percent of annual sales; in contrast, SG&A expenses were 40.2 percent of 2010 sales at Tiffany & Co. and 52.4 percent of 2010 sales at Zale Corporation. The strength of Blue Nile's business model and its efficient operations provided a net profit margin of 4.2 percent in 2010, compared to a 2010 net profit margin of 11.9 percent at Tiffany and a 2010 net loss at Zale.

EDUCATIONAL INFORMATION AND CERTIFICATION

Blue Nile went to considerable lengths to put to rest any concerns shoppers might have about buying fine jewelry online. It employed an informative sales process, striving to demystify and simplify the process of choosing a diamond or some other gemstone. Blue Nile's website provided a wealth of easy-to-understand information about the five Cs (cut shape, cut, color, clarity, and carat weight—see Exhibit 1), allowing shoppers to educate themselves about what characteristics determined the quality and value of various stones. In addition to providing substantial educational information, Blue Nile's website and its extensively trained customer service representatives provided detailed product information that enabled customers to objectively compare diamonds and fine jewelry products and to make informed decisions in choosing a stone of suitable size/weight, cut, color, clarity, look, and price.

Blue Nile management believed that having reputable industry professionals certify and grade each diamond/gemstone offered for sale had many advantages. The grading reports provided valuable guidance to consumers in choosing a stone that was right for them and their pocketbook—the carat weight, color, cut, and clarity of a diamond were critical in providing the buyer with the desired sparkle, brilliance, and dazzling or sophisticated look. In addition, a jewelry shopper's ability to immediately review professionally prepared grading reports for a diamond/gemstone of particular interest instilled confidence in shopping for fine jewelry at Blue Nile, typically quelling any fears that the stone(s) might not live up to expectations. Furthermore, the grading reports that Blue Nile provided facilitated comparison shopping, allowing jewelry shoppers not only to compare alternative Blue Nile diamonds/gems but also to see how Blue Nile's products stacked up against the products they might be considering at competing jewelers.

Customers interested in a particular diamond displayed at Blue Nile's websites could view or print out an accompanying diamond grading or certification report that documented the specific characteristics of the diamond and that was prepared by an independent team of professional gemologists (see Exhibit 2). A Diamond Dossier (also called a diamond quality document or diamond grading report) was a report created by a team of gemologists who evaluated, measured, and scrutinized the diamond using trained eyes, a jeweler's loupe, a microscope, and other industry tools. A completed certificate included an analysis of the diamond's dimensions, clarity, color, polish, symmetry, and other characteristics. Many round diamonds had a cut grade on the report. Every loose diamond sold by Blue Nile was analyzed and graded by either the Gemological Institute of America (GIA) or the American Gem Society Laboratories (AGSL).

- The GIA was regarded as the world's foremost authority in gemology; its mission was to promote public trust in gems and jewelry. In the 1950s, the GIA had created the International Diamond Grading System and established standards that revolutionized the diamond industry. Most recently, the GIA had introduced its new Diamond Cut Grading System, which used computer modeling to assess and predict the cut quality in round brilliant cut diamonds. The GIA's research revealed that there was no single set of proportions that defined a well-cut round brilliant diamond; many different proportions could produce attractive diamonds. The GIA had also developed software that provided a method of estimating a cut grade—and a database that was embedded into a number of leading diamond-measuring devices so that cut grade estimation could be automated. As a result, manufacturers could plan and, in effect, predict cut grades; buyers

EXHIBIT 1

Determining a Diamond's Value: The Five Cs

CARAT: Refers to a diamond's weight, not its size. One carat equals one-fifth of a gram. While lighter diamonds often carry a lower price per carat, a 1.0 carat diamond might sparkle more than a 1.25 carat diamond if it is cut differently or has better color and clarity.

CLARITY: Concerns the degree to which a diamond is free of inclusions (i.e., flaws)—blemishes, internal imperfections, scratches, trace minerals, or other tiny characteristics that can detract from a diamond's beauty. Diamonds that are absolutely clear are the most sought-after and therefore the most expensive. The lower the clarity (and the greater the inclusions), the lower the value of the diamond. The naked eye can see flaws in diamonds with very poor clarity, but even using a magnifying glass untrained eyes would have trouble seeing flaws in a high-clarity diamond. There are 11 grades of clarity ranging from "flawless" to "included," based on the number, location, size, and type of inclusions present in a diamond. Inclusions were more visible to the naked eye in lower-grade emerald cuts than in lower-grade round diamonds.

COLOR: Concerns a diamond's transparency. Acting as a prism, a diamond can divide light into a spectrum of colors and reflect this light as colorful flashes called fire. Just as when looking through colored glass, color in a diamond will act as a filter and will diminish the spectrum of color emitted. The less color in a diamond, the more colorful the fire and the better the color grade. A little color in a white diamond could diminish its brilliance. White diamonds with very little color are the most highly valued and are priced accordingly. Color grades range from D (absolutely colorless and extremely rare) to Z. White diamonds with a grade of D, E, or F are considered "colorless" grade and very high quality; diamonds with grades of G or H are near-colorless and offer excellent value: diamonds with grades of I or J have slightly detectable color but still represent good value; the color in diamonds graded K–Z detracts from the beauty of a diamond and is especially noticeable in platinum or white gold settings. (Blue Nile only sold diamonds with color grades of J or higher.) Yellow diamonds (some of which were fancy and highly valued) are graded on a different scale than white diamonds are.

CUT: Concerns a diamond's shape (round, square, oval, pear, heart, marquise, and so on) and style (width, depth, symmetry, polish, and number/position of flat surfaces). Most diamonds are cut with 58 facets, or separate flat surfaces; it is the diamond cutter's job, utilizing precise mathematical formulas, to align the facets at precise angles in relation to each other to maximize the reflection and refraction of light. Cut style affects how light travels within a diamond, thus determining its brightness, fire, and face-up appearance. The cutter's goal is to transform a diamond in the rough into a sparkling, polished stone of the largest possible size and greatest optical beauty; a poor or less desirable cut can dull the look and brilliance of diamonds with excellent color and clarity. There is no single measurement of a diamond that defines its cut, but rather a collection of measurements and observations that determine the relationship between a diamond's light performance, dimensions, and finish.

CUT GRADE: This newest of the five Cs is perhaps the overall best measure or indicator of a diamond's brilliance, sparkle, and "wow effect." Fewer than 5% of diamonds on the market qualify for the highest cut grade rating. Cut grade is a summary rating that takes into account such measures as the diamond's table size (the flat surface at the top of the diamond) as a percentage of the diamond's girth (the widest part of the diamond), the crown of the diamond (the portion above the girth) and the crown angle, the pavilion (the portion of the diamond below the girth)—the height of the pavilion contributes to its brilliance, the pavilion angle, the depth of the diamond (from the top facet to the culet), culet size, the diamond's polish and symmetry, and several other factors affecting sparkle, radiance, and brilliance.

(continued)

▶EXHIBIT 1 (*concluded*)

The following table shows price variations in diamonds with varying clarity but the same carat weight and color grade with excellent polish and delivery date of September 1, 2011:

	Price comparison: 1 carat, H-color, ideal cut diamond		
Clarity Grade	**Description**	**Price**
FL	**Flawless** No internal or external finish flaws.	$13,700
IF	**Internally Flawless** No internal flaws.	$12,400
VVS1 VVS2	**Very Very Slightly Included** Very difficult to see inclusions under 10x magnification.	$11,400 $10,500
VS1 VS2	**Very Slightly Included** Difficult to see inclusions under 10x magnification, typically unable to see inclusions with unaided eye.	$ 9,000 $ 7,500
SI1 SI2	**Slightly Included** Easy to see inclusions under 10x magnification, may not be able to see inclusions with unaided eye.	$ 6,800 $ 6,000

The following table compares the prices of diamonds with varying color grades but the same clarity grade (VS1) and carat weight:

	Price comparison: 1–1.09 carat VS1 round diamond						
	Colorless			**Near-Colorless**			
Cut	**D**	**E**	**F**	**G**	**H**	**I**	**J**
Ideal	$16,000	$13,400	$12,200	$10,500	$9,500	$7,900	$6,700
Very Good	$13,700	$12,000	$10,700	$ 9,800	$8,900	$7,300	$6,400
Good	$12,400	$10,500	$ 9,300	$ 8,200	$7,400	$6,500	$5,400
Fair	$11,600	$9,900	$ 7,600	$ 7,500	$7,700	$5,700	$5,700

Source: Compiled from a variety of sources, including the educational information posted at www.bluenile.com and www.diamonds.com, accessed August 23, 2006. The two price tables are from Blue Nile, www.bluenile.com, accessed August 25, 2011. Prices are based on diamonds of approximately 1.0 carrot with excellent polish and for delivery date of August 30 to September 1, 2011. Figures are rounded to nearest hundred.

could compare cut qualities; and retailers could communicate the effects of cut on round brilliant diamonds. In 2006, the GIA Laboratory introduced new versions of the GIA Diamond Grading Report and Diamond Dossier that provided a single, comprehensive cut grade for all standard round brilliant diamonds falling in the GIA D-to-Z color scale and Flawless-to-I3 clarity scale. Diamonds received one of five cut grades, from Excellent to Poor.

- Founded in 1996, the AGSL was the only diamond-grading laboratory to offer a unique 0 to 10 grading system that

provided easy-to-read, clear, and accurate information about each diamond it graded. A cut grade of 10 was the lowest quality, and a grade of 000 was the absolute finest or ideal quality, but so far the AGSL had only awarded cut grades to select round and square-cut diamonds (it was considering expanding the grading system to other cuts). AGSL grading reports were based on the gemological industry's highest standards of evaluating the four Cs of cut, color, clarity, and carat weight. AGSL grades allowed a shopper to compare the quality of the diamond against the price.

▶ EXHIBIT 2

Diamond Characteristics Documented in a GIA Diamond Grading Report

Shape and Cutting Style: The diamond shape and cutting style.

Measurement: The diamond's dimensions in millimeters.

Carat Weight: The weight of the diamond listed to the nearest hundredth of a carat.

Color Grade: The absence of color in the diamond.

Clarity Grade: The degree of clarity determined under 10x magnification.

Cut Grade: A grade of cut as determined by a diamond's face-up appearance, design, and craftsmanship. A GIA cut grade was available on round diamonds graded after January 1, 2006.

Finish: The diamond's surface and facet placement.

Polish: The overall smoothness of the diamond's surface.

Symmetry: The shape, alignment, and placement of the diamond's facets in relation to one another as well as the evenness of the outline.

Fluorescence: The color and strength of color when the diamond is viewed under ultraviolet light.

Clarity: The approximate size, type, and position of inclusions as viewed under a microscope.

Proportion: A map of the diamond's actual proportions, typically with information about the following:

- **Culet:** Appearance, or lack thereof, of the culet facet. The culet (pronounced "que-let" or the French-sounding "que-lay") was a tiny flat surface formed by polishing off the tip at the bottom of a diamond. A culet protects the fragile tip of the diamond from chipping during the cutting, handling, and setting of the diamond. However, Asians often prefer diamonds without a culet, so the practice of downgrading diamonds without culets has been discontinued.
- **Table:** The largest facet (or flat surface), located at the top of the diamond.
- **Depth:** The height of the diamond measured from the culet to the table.
- **Girdle:** The range of thickness.

Comments: A description of additional diamond characteristics not already mentioned in the report.

Source: Blue Nile, www.bluenile.com, accessed August 27, 2011.

These two laboratories were among the most respected laboratories in the diamond industry and were known for their consistency and unbiased diamond-grading systems. Diamonds that were accompanied by GIA and ASGL grading reports were the most highly valued in the industry.

All diamonds in Blue Nile's signature collection also were certified by the Gem Certification and Appraisal Lab (GCAL) in addition to being graded by the GIA or AGSL. This provided a second authoritative analysis of the diamond. The GCAL verified that a diamond met all the specific quality requirements of the Blue Nile Signature Collection (see Exhibit 3).

MARKETING

Blue Nile's marketing strategy was designed to increase Blue Nile brand recognition, generate consumer traffic, acquire customers, build a loyal customer base, and promote repeat purchases. Top executives at Blue Nile believed that jewelry shoppers preferred to seek out high-quality diamonds and fine jewelry from a trusted source in a nonintimidating environment, where information, guidance, reputation, convenience, and value were important characteristics. Hence, a major portion of Blue Nile's marketing effort was focused on making sure that site visitors had a positive, informative experience, one that inspired their confidence to buy diamonds and fine jewelry from the company. One key initiative to provide a good customer experience was the development of a user-friendly interactive search tool that allowed shoppers to customize their search and quickly identify diamonds with the characteristics they were looking for. Blue Nile's website was redesigned in 2009 to improve the site's appeal with women and allow site visitors to more easily search Blue Nile's diamond

▶ EXHIBIT 3

Contents of a Certificate of Authenticity Issued by the Gem Certification and Appraisal Lab (GCAL)

Actual Size Photo: A photo of the diamond at its true size.

Laser Inscription Photo: A close-up shot of the laser inscription on the diamond taken at 50x magnification.

Proportion Diagram: The actual scale and specific measurements of the diamond are noted on a diagram. These measurements are used to determine the cut grade.

Enlarged Photomicrograph: A photo of the diamond viewed from top and bottom.

An Optical Brilliance Analysis: Images of the diamond are captured using a controlled lighting environment and carefully calibrated amounts of light at specific viewing angles. These tests show the amount of light return or brilliance as it exited the diamond's crown.

Optical Symmetry Analysis: A test analyzing the light exiting the diamond and showing the discrepancies in the balance of the diamond. An even and symmetrical pattern shows that the light is well balanced and indicates exceptional diamond quality.

Certification Statement: A statement signed by the GCAL laboratory director verifying the quality of the graded diamond.

Diamond Grading Analysis: Notes on the diamond's shape, measurements, carat weight, and cut grade based on its proportions, polish, symmetry, color, and clarity grades. The analysis also contains any comments regarding the diamond.

Source: Blue Nile, www.bluenile.com, accessed August 27, 2011.

collection according to any of 12 criteria—price, carat weight, cut, color, clarity, polish, symmetry, fluorescence, culet, diamond grading report, depth percentage, and table percentage. Blue Nile's redesigned website also included a blog page where customers could write about their proposal stories. Site visitors could browse approximately 1,100 stories (broken down by adventurous, extravagant, romantic, creative, humorous, and so on) to get ideas and inspiration on how others had popped the question.

Blue Nile's website also emphasized that the company did not market "blood" or "conflict" diamonds, which were gems that had been traded for money or guns to fight wars in parts of Africa. Blue Nile and all other major sellers of diamond jewelry had entered into partnerships with the United Nations, governments, and nongovernmental organizations to prevent the trade of illegal diamonds through measures such as the Kimberley Process, which tracked diamonds from mine to market. A goal of Blue Nile's communications with its customers was to empower them with knowledge and confidence as they evaluated, selected, and purchased diamonds and fine jewelry.

The company's efforts to draw more shoppers to its site and boost awareness of Blue Nile included both online and offline marketing and advertising efforts. Most of Blue Nile's advertising dollars went for banner ads at Web portals (Yahoo, Google, Facebook, YouTube, and MSN), search engine sites (Google and Bing), and select other sites. As competition for online advertising had increased, the cost for these services had also increased. The company also did some direct online marketing. Marketing expenses were $6.5 million in 2004, growing to $11.9 million in 2007, $12.4 million in 2008, $11.6 million in 2009, and $14.5 million in 2010.

CUSTOMER SERVICE AND SUPPORT

Blue Nile strove to provide a high level of customer service and was continuously engaged in refining the customer service aspects in every step of the purchase process. Complementing the extensive information resources on its website was a call center staffed with knowledgeable, highly trained support personnel. Blue Nile diamond and jewelry consultants were trained to provide guidance on all steps in the process of buying diamonds and fine jewelry, including the processes for selecting an appropriate item, purchasing that item, financing the purchase, and having the item shipped. The company further boosted service quality by adopting a salary-based compensation plan for sales personnel that did not create incentives to put undue pressure on customers to purchase products that had the highest margins or highest commissions.

Blue Nile customers with questions could call a prominently displayed toll-free number or send an e-mail to service@bluenile.com; most calls to the Blue Nile call center were answered within 10 seconds.[4] Policies relating to privacy, security, product availability, pricing, shipping, refunds, exchanges, and special orders were readily accessed at the company's website. In 2009, Blue Nile released mobile applications for the iPhone and Android-equipped smartphones to make comparison shopping easier when customers were visiting brick-and-mortar jewelry stores operated by its competitors. Blue Nile reported that over 200,000 consumers have used the service for comparison shopping. A new and more robust Shopping App was made available on Apple's App store effective July 2011.

ORDER FULFILLMENT OPERATIONS

Order fulfillment at Blue Nile was designed to enhance customer value and confidence by filling customer orders accurately and delivering them quickly and securely. When an order for a customized diamond jewelry piece was received, the supplier holding the diamond in inventory generally shipped it to Blue Nile (or an independent third-party jeweler with whom Blue Nile maintained an ongoing relationship for assembly) within one business day. Upon receipt at Blue Nile, the diamond was sent to assembly for setting and sizing, tasks performed by either Blue Nile bench jewelers or independent third-party bench jewelers. Each diamond was inspected upon arrival from suppliers; additionally, each finished setting or sizing was inspected prior to shipment to a customer. Prompt and secure delivery was a high priority, and Blue Nile shipped nearly all diamond and fine jewelry products via FedEx. The company had an on-time order delivery rate of 99.96 percent, which it was striving to push to 100 percent.[5] Shipping and handling costs totaled $2.8 million and $3.2 million in 2009 and 2010, respectively.

Blue Nile's order fulfillment costs, included as part of SG&A expenses, totaled $3.1 million in 2010, up slightly from $3.0 million reported in 2009 and up from $1.6 million in 2004, reflecting the increase in sales. These costs included all expenses associated with operating and staffing the Seattle warehouse and order fulfillment center, including costs attributable to receiving, inspecting, and warehousing inventories and picking, preparing, and packaging customers' orders for shipment.

PRODUCT LINE EXPANSION

Blue Nile was selectively expanding its product offerings in terms of both price points and product mix. New product offerings included both customized and noncustomized jewelry items. Management believed that the online nature of Blue Nile's business, coupled with its supply arrangements and just-in-time inventory management, allowed it to readily test shopper response to new diamond and gemstone offerings and to efficiently add promising new merchandise to its overall assortment of fine jewelry.

EXPANSION INTO INTERNATIONAL MARKETS

Blue Nile was selectively pursuing opportunities in international markets where management believed the company could leverage its existing infrastructure and deliver compelling customer value. Blue Nile's international business began in August 2004 when Blue Nile launched a website in the United Kingdom (www.bluenile.co.uk), offering a limited number of products; in September 2005, Blue Nile began providing customers at its UK website with the ability to customize their diamond jewelry purchases and to buy wedding bands. A website in Canada (www.bluenile.ca) was launched in January 2005. Blue Nile opened a fulfillment center in Dublin, Ireland, to serve the company's UK and European Union customers in 2007. The company launched its Chinese-language site in April 2010, which increased its number of international markets to 40. Customers in 35 international markets could complete transactions in their local currency. Blue Nile revenues generated outside the United States had grown from $8.3 million in 2006 to $43.3 million in 2010. International sales now represent 13.0 percent of total sales. Blue Nile's CEO, Diane Irvine, stated in a 2008 *Forbes* video interview that "over the long term, we believe international will be half or more of our total business."[6]

OTHER STRATEGY ELEMENTS

Blue Nile's strategy had several other key elements:

- Blue Nile had a 30-day return policy that gave customers plenty of time to consider their purchase and make sure they had made a good decision. If customers were not satisfied for any reason, they could return any item without custom engraving in its original condition within 30 days of the date of shipment for a refund or an exchange. Requests for a refund or a different item were processed within a few days.
- Blue Nile offered free shipping with every order delivered to a U.S. address; orders were shipped via FedEx Express, FedEx Ground, or U.S. Postal Service, depending on order value and destination. All orders under $250 were shipped via FedEx Ground if within the 48 contiguous states or by U.S. Postal Service for destinations in Hawaii and Alaska. Orders between $250 and $1,000 were shipped via FedEx two-day delivery. All orders over $1,000 and all loose diamond orders were shipped via

FedEx Priority Overnight. Customers had the option to upgrade the delivery of items under $1,000 to FedEx Priority Overnight for a $15 charge.

- Blue Nile automatically provided an appraisal stating the approximate retail replacement value of the item to customers who bought (1) a preset engagement ring priced under $2,500; (2) a diamond jewelry item priced $1,000 or over (except preset solitaire engagement rings, preset earrings, or preset solitaire pendants priced $2,500 or over, all of which came with International Gemological Institute appraisals); or (3) any custom diamond ring, earring, or pendant. The appraisal value was based on current market data; typical retail prices; the weight of the precious metal included in the item; craftsmanship; and the cut, color, clarity, and carat weight of the gemstone(s). Included with the appraisal was a brief description of the item being appraised; a photograph of the item; and the cut, color, clarity, and either carat weight (for diamonds) or millimeter dimensions (for gemstones). An appraisal represented value-added to customers because it was necessary to obtain insurance coverage and determine what constituted equal replacement in case of loss, theft, or damage.

BLUE NILE'S FINANCIAL PERFORMANCE

Between 2005 and 2007, Blue Nile's revenues grew from $203 million to $319 million and its net earnings increased from $13.1 million to nearly $17.5 million. The company's stellar performance pushed its stock price over the $100 mark just weeks before U.S. consumers began feeling the effects of the deep recession that began in late 2007. The recession caused consumers to rapidly cut back on discretionary spending, which directly affected the sales of almost every business operating in the United States. Blue Nile's revenues and earnings declined to

EXHIBIT 4 The Cash-Generating Capability of Blue Nile's Business Model

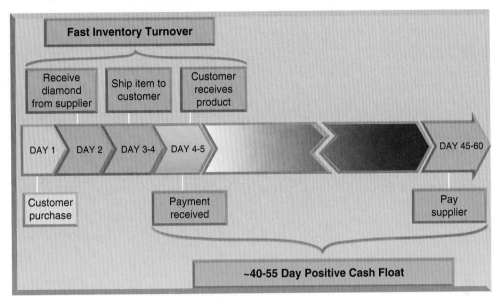

Source: Blue Nile Management Presentation, Goldman Sachs Seventh Annual Internet Conference, May 24, 2006.

$295 million and $11.6 million, respectively, in 2008 before increasing slightly in 2009. However, in 2010 Blue Nile's financial performance rebounded, with net sales increasing by 10 percent from the previous year to reach a record $332.9 million and net income improving to $14.1 million.

Blue Nile's business model continued to generate cash 40 to 55 days ahead of the need to pay suppliers; in a very real sense, Blue Nile's business model was self-funding because suppliers financed Blue Nile's sales growth (see Exhibit 4). The company generated $36.7 million in free cash flow in 2009 and $39.8 million in 2010. Since 2001, Blue Nile had generated more than $240 million in cumulative free cash. At year-end 2010, the firm had a cash balance of $113.1 million, total assets of $151.8 million, and minimal debt outstanding. Moreover, the company's business model was readily scalable to substantially higher sales volumes with minimal additional capital investment. Blue Nile's capital expenditures for facilities and equipment were a meager $1.8 million in 2010, $2.3 million in 2009, $2.0 million in 2008, and

$4.9 million in 2007. Exhibit 5 presents a summary of Blue Nile's financial results from 2006 through 2010.

STOCK ISSUES AND REPURCHASES

Blue Nile became a public company in 2004, selling some 2.3 million shares of common stock at $20.50 per share and realizing proceeds of $42.5 million after expenses. Trading of the company's stock began on May 20, 2004, on the NASDAQ exchange under the symbol NILE. Since trading began, the stock had traded as low as $22.50 (August 2004) and as high as $104.25 (September 2007); the stock price had steadily declined from $65 in January 2010 to a low of $30.44 (August 19, 2010) and a year later has climbed to $36.45 (August 26, 2011).

Blue Nile had not paid any cash dividends on the common stock since the inception of the company and, in February 2006, had authorized the repurchase of $100 million of its common stock

▶ EXHIBIT 5

Selected Financial Data, Blue Nile Inc., 2006–2010 ($ thousands, except per share data)

	2010	2009	2008	2007	2006
Revenue	$332,889	$302,134	$295,329	$319,264	$251,600
Cost of goods sold	260,949	236,790	235,333	254,060	200,700
Gross profit	71,940	65,344	59,996	65,204	50,900
SG&A	50,654	45,997	44,005	42,792	34,300
EBIT	21,286	19,347	15,991	22,412	16,600
Interest	—	—	—	—	—
Other items	252	331	1,865	4,175	3,400
Taxes	7,396	6,878	6,226	9,128	6,916
Net income	14,142	12,800	11,630	17,459	13,084
Average shares outstanding (000s)					
Basic	14,446	14,534	14,925	15,919	16,563
Diluted	15,080	15,216	15,505	16,814	17,278
EPS (diluted)	$ 0.94	$ 0.84	$ 0.75	$ 1.04	$0.76
Dividends/share	—	—	—	—	—

Balance Sheet Data

	2010	2009	2008	2007	2006
Cash and cash equivalents	$113,261	$ 78,149	$ 54,451	$122,793	$ 78,659
Short-term investments	—	15,000	—	—	19,767
Accounts receivable	1,771	1,835	1,709	3,576	1,640
Inventories	20,166	19,434	18,834	20,906	14,616
Other current assets	1,640	1,426	1,739	1,871	1,338
Total current assets	136,838	115,844	76,733	149,146	116,020
Property and equipment	6,157	7,332	7,558	7,601	3,391
Other assets (including intangibles)	8,816	7,239	5,374	3,839	2,697
Total assets	151,811	130,415	89,665	160,586	122,108
Accounts payable	90,296	76,128	62,291	85,866	66,625
Total current liabilities	101,920	86,182	69,103	95,691	74,137
Long-term financing obligations	830	964	1,213	1,418	666
Retained earnings	49,061	48,999	36,199	24,569	7,110
Treasury stock at cost	(187,177)	(161,841)	(161,841)	(95,391)	(75,395)
Stockholders' equity	49,061	43,269	19,290	63,477	47,303

Cash Flow Data

	2010	2009	2008	2007	2006
Net cash provided by operating activities	$ 41.608	$ 39,018	($ 2,927)	$ 41,455	$ 40,518
Net cash used in investing activities	13,157	(17,345)	(2,000)	15,016	21,065
Net cash provided (used) in financing activities	(19,157)	1,981	(63,357)	(12,296)	(54,964)

Source: Blue Nile Inc., 10-K reports and annual reports for 2006, 2007, 2009, and 2010.

over a two-year period. Blue Nile repurchased 438,755 shares for approximately $20 million in 2007 and another 1.6 million shares of stock for approximately $66.5 million in 2008. In February 2010, the company reauthorized its repurchase plan to acquire up to $100 million of its common stock within a 24-month period. In 2010, the company repurchased 0.5 million shares at a cost of $25.3 million.

Blue Nile had several stock-based compensation plans, under which stock options could be issued to officers, employees, non-employee directors, and consultants. Going into 2011, stock options for just over 2.4 million shares were outstanding; of those, 1.7 million were exercisable. Blue Nile also had an employee stock purchase plan, but no shares had been issued as of January 2011.

OVERVIEW OF THE JEWELRY INDUSTRY

The worldwide jewelry and watch market in 2010 was estimated to be between $140 billion and $145 billion and, according to the U.S. Department of Commerce, U.S. jewelry and watch sales for the same period represented $61.5 billion, which equates to approximately 43 percent of the world market. Jewelry sales represent approximately 89 percent of total sales (see Exhibit 6).

Industry revenues had grown by approximately 5.5 percent annually since the mid-1980s before reaching a peak at $65.3 billion in 2007 and then declining with the onset of the U.S. recession in 2008. In fact peak to valley, U.S. jewelry sales fell by approximately 11 percent in the great recession. Diamond jewelry sales were particularly hard hit by the recession, with industry sales declining from $32.5 billion in 2005 to an estimated $29.5 billion in 2009. The 2008–2009 drop in sales was the steepest decline in industry revenues since the recession of the early 1980s. In addition to being cyclical, diamond jewelry sales were also somewhat seasonal, with relatively higher sales in February (Valentine's Day), May (Mother's Day), and the October–December holiday shopping season. As such, jewelry sales are both seasonal and cyclical in nature. About 40 percent of revenue is generated in the fourth quarter, and 25 percent of annual jewelry sales occur in the Christmas season. Sales are also influenced by mineral availability, fashion trends, environmental regulations, and international tariffs.

Another factor influencing jewelry sales relates to the need for carrying high inventories as jewelers believe it is much easier to sell product "in-hand." An average specialty jeweler may sell $1 million in product annually, half of which is inventoried on site at a given time.

For the past year, retailers have been under pressure to raise jewelry prices to reflect two years of sharply rising prices for diamonds and precious metals (gold, silver, and platinum). Fluctuation in prices of these precious metals can adversely affect sales and profit margins by increasing the prices of products. This is particularly true for Blue Nile because of its virtual inventory model.

Overall, 2010 was a solid year for jewelry sales. Of the 37 companies on National Jewelers 2011 list of $100 million Super-Sellers, 25 reported increased sales over the prior year and 12 reported declines. The best performers: Tiffany & Co experienced 12 percent growth; Cartier and Van Cleef Arpels, 20 percent; Sterling Jewelers reported an 8 percent increase. Many shoppers found Walmart and Costco where sales were up 2 to 5 percent. The department stores overall saw 1 to 2 percent increases, with Saks Fifth Avenue experiencing a 6 percent gain and Macy's a 7 percent sales gain. Online stores: Blue Nile grew 10 percent and Amazon reached the top 20 Super-Seller list for the first time with a 20 percent gain. The multimedia groups also saw increased sales; both Jewelry Television and QVC were up 14 percent. As for the declines, Zales continued its poor performance, losing ground for three consecutive years.

The diamond and fine jewelry retail market was intensely competitive, with sales highly fragmented among locally owned specialty jewelry stores, retail jewelry store chains with 100+ stores, numerous chain department stores, online

EXHIBIT 6

Annual Jewelry Sales in the United States

Year	U.S. Watch & Jewelry Sales $ billions	Percent Change Year-to-Year
2003	$51.4	—
2004	55.3	7.06%
2005	58.1	5.06
2006	62.3	7.23
2007	65.3	4.82
2008	63.4	(2.91)
2009	58.1	(8.36)
2010	61.5	5.85

Source: U.S. Department of Commerce, Bureau of Economic Analysis, Table 2.4.5 Personal Consumption Expenditure by Type of Product.

retailers that sold fine jewelry, online auction sites, television shopping retailers, and mass merchants such as discount superstores and wholesale clubs whose merchandise offerings included fine jewelry. Also, the majority of sellers (115,000) consists of those merchants without employees, including jewelry designers, repair shops, and other owner/operater merchants. The Jewelry Board of Trade estimated that there were some 22,164 specialty jewelry firms in the United States in 2010, down from 26,750 in 1999. Most specialty retailers operated only one or two stores and recorded annual sales of about $0.9 million. However, while the number of jewelers was in decline, the number of jewelry stores in the United States remained relatively stable at about 27,000. According to the *National Jeweler*, the top 40 jewelry chain stores operated 6,405 stores in 2008, up from 4,537 a decade earlier. For example, Zale Corporation increased its stores from 1,100 to 1,937 (although it closed some stores in early 2011 to 1,870 stores), and Sterling Jewelers increased its stores from 768 to 1,360 over the decade and closed 44 in 2011. The five largest specialty jewelry retailers in the United States had increased their collective share from about 18 percent to about 24 percent of specialty jewelry sales since 1999—reflecting a continuing industry trend toward consolidation. Nonetheless, independent jewelers, including those with fewer than 100 stores, accounted for about 72 percent of the sales made by specialty jewelry retailers. Exhibit 7 presents revenues and market shares for the top 20 U.S. jewelry retailers in 2010.

COMPETITION IN JEWELRY RETAILING

The principal competitive factors in the fine jewelry market were product selection and quality; price; customer service and support; brand recognition; reputation; reliability and trust; and, in the case of online retailers, website features and functionality, convenience, and speed of delivery. Blue Nile's primary competition came from both online and offline retailers that offered products within the higher value

segment of the jewelry market. Many brick-and-mortar jewelry retailers (including market leaders Zale, Sterling, Tiffany, and Helzberg, among many others) had recently begun selling jewelry online at their websites, although the online category represented a small portion of their total sales. For example, only 3.6 percent of Zale Corporation's sales were made online. The U.S. Department of Commerce data for 2009 showed e-commerce represented 4.0 percent of total retail sales compared to 2.1 percent in 2008. According to IDEX Online e-commerce sales of jewelry in 2009 were $2.7 billion, which equated to 4.65 percent of total jewelry sales and was a 10.7 percent increase from 2008. Overall, IDEX reported that e-commerce jewelry sales grew from 1.6 percent of total jewelry sales in 2000 to nearly 6 percent in 2010 ($0.8 billion to $3.8 billion, respectively).

BLUE NILE'S CHIEF RIVALS IN ONLINE JEWELRY RETAILING

There were dozens of online retailers of diamonds in 2010. Most online jewelry retailers employed a business model similar to Blue Nile's, keeping their inventories lean, purchasing stones from suppliers only when an order for a specific stone was received, and delivering the merchandise a few days after the order was placed. The most popular sites, in addition to market leader Blue Nile, included Diamonds.com, Whiteflash.com, Ice.com, JamesAllen.com, Overstock.com, and Amazon.com.

Diamonds.com

Diamonds.com was founded in 2000 and headquartered in Las Vegas; the principal owners had more than 25 years' experience in all areas of the diamond industry. The company's product offering included more than 40,000 loose diamonds sourced from New York City's famed 47th Street diamond district, along with a selection of settings, rings, bracelets, necklaces, and earrings. There was extensive educational information on the Diamonds.com website; the discussion of the four Cs of purchasing a diamond

▶ EXHIBIT 7

Revenues and Market Shares for the 20 Largest U.S. Jewelry Retailers, 2010 ($ millions)

Rank	Marketer	Sales	Market Share (%)
1	Walmart	$ 2,800	4.6%
2	Sterling Jewelers*	2,744	4.5
3	Zale Corporation**	1,616	2.6
4	Tiffany & Co.	1,575	2.6
5	Macy's	1,500	2.4
6	QVC	1,015	1.7
7	Sears	860	1.4
8	JC Penney	710	1.2
9	Costco Wholesale	500	0.8
10	Target stores	465	0.8
11	Neiman Marcus	406	0.7
12	Jewelry Television	400	0.7
13	Helsberg Diamonds	380	0.6
14	Cartier	360	0.6
16	Blue Nile	332	0.5
17	Ross-Simon	330	0.5
18	HSN	309	0.5
19	Tourneau***	305	0.5
20	Amazon.com	300	0.5
Subtotal	Top 20 firms	16,907	27.5
Others	Other firms and individuals****	44,593	72.5
Total		$61,500	100.0%

*Sterling was a wholly owned subsidiary of Britain-based Signet Group, PLC; Sterling operated 925 Kay's Jewelry stores in 50 states, 175 Jared Galleria of Jewelry showrooms in 26 states, and 260 other regional stores under a variety of brand names in 31 states.

**Zale Corporation operated Gordon Jewelers, Zales Outlet, Mappins Jewellers, Peoples Jewellers and ***Tourneau's sales were heavily concentrated in fine watches.

**** Excluding the top 20 major retailers reported in Exhibit 7, the Other category is broken down, according to IDEX Online, as: Other Specialty Jewellers—22,800 firms; Other sellers without employees—41,000; and Other Multi-line/ Other Retailers—115,000 firms.

Source: National Jeweller.com; company websites and annual reports; and IDEX online.

was lucid and informative. There was a search function that allowed site visitors to search the loose diamond inventory based on shape, carat size, cut, color, clarity, and price. Shoppers had the ability to customize their purchase by choosing a stone and a setting. Online shoppers could view diamond grading reports issued by either the Gemological Institute of America or the American Gemological Society Laboratory for all loose diamonds, shipping was free, and orders came with an identifying grading report and a warranty document. Customers could return noncustomized orders for a full refund (excluding shipping, handling, and insurance) for up to 30 days after delivery; returns were not accepted on custom work or special orders unless an error had been made. The staff at Diamonds.com included expert gemologists trained at the world's leading gemological laboratories; shoppers could call a toll-free number to receive assistance or to place a phone order.

Whiteflash.com

About half of Whiteflash's sales involved orders for customized jewelry. Whiteflash could tap a pool of about 50,000 stones, most of which were also available for sale at other online retailers.[7] Of particular interest was a trade-up program that Blue Nile and most other online rivals didn't match: A customer could swap a Whiteflash rock for a higher-priced one at any time, paying the difference between the new diamond and the original purchase price, less shipping. Whiteflash had a policy of not accepting returns on customized jewelry products unless an error had been made in doing the custom work; for loose stones and standard settings, Whiteflash offered a risk-free 10-day return policy. The education materials at the Whiteflash website included video tutorials.

Ice.com

More than 500,000 customers had made purchases at Ice.com since the company began online operations in 2001. Its product offerings were all finished products; no customization options were available. The company had a monthly payment option, provided free shipping on orders over $150, and had an unconditional 30-day money-back guarantee. Bridal and engagement rings came with an appraisal certificate. There was no educational information on the company's website, and the information provided about the quality of its diamond jewelry was limited. Customers could make inquiries via a toll-free number or e-mail.

JamesAllen.com

Founded in 1998, JamesAllen.com had grown to be one of the largest online diamond retailers. The firm claimed to offer "the world's most beautiful engagement rings coupled with the finest laboratory graded diamonds, all at an extraordinary value." It had been featured in such trade magazines as *National Jeweler* and profiled by the *Washington Post, U.S. News & World Report*, NBC News, and National Public Radio. While an estimated 3 percent of the round diamonds sold in the United States qualified as "Ideal" under AGSL grading standards, more than 90 percent of the customers shopping at JamesAllen.com chose diamonds from the retailer's Signature Ideal, Ideal, or Premium categories. All stones came with grading reports from either the Gemological Institute of America or the American Gemological Society Laboratory.

The product offerings at JamesAllen.com included 55,000 loose diamonds; preset engagement rings; preset wedding and anniversary rings; diamond studs; other diamond jewelry; and designer jewelry by Amy Levine, Danhov, and Leo Popov. Shoppers could customize their own diamond rings, studs, and pendants. The JamesAllen.com website had a comprehensive Education section that featured an interactive demonstration of the importance of diamond cut, three-dimensional viewing, and tips and search tools. An expert staff answered questions via phone or e-mail. JamesAllen.com provided free overnight shipping via FedEx or UPS on all orders within the United States. Orders outside the United States had to be prepaid via wire transfer and carried a shipping fee of $100. The company had a full 30-day return policy, but loose diamond returns that did not include the original laboratory grading report were subject to a charge of $150.

ENDNOTES

[1] Kiri Blakeley, "Are Diamonds Still a Girl's Best Friend?" *Forbes*, April 17, 2009, www.forbes.com/2009/04/17/engagement-weddings-diamonds-forbes-woman-style-retail.html, accessed August 19, 2010.

[2] Quoted in "A Boy's Best Friend: Internet Jewelers," *The Economist* 386, no. 8572 (March 22, 2008), p. 7.

[3] Blue Nile, 2007 10-K report, p. 4.

[4] Sean O'Neill, "Clicks and Stones," *Kiplinger's Personal Finance*, February 2006, www.kiplinger.com/personalfinance/magazine/archives/2006/02/diamonds.html, accessed August 27, 2010.

[5] As cited in "Internet Retailer Best of the Web 2007," *Internet Retailer*, December 2006, www.internetretailer.com, accessed February 27, 2010.

[6] *Forbes*, http://video.forbes.com/fvn/lifestyle/blue-nile, accessed August 18, 2010.

[7] Kiplinger.com, accessed February 2010.

PANERA BREAD COMPANY IN 2011—PURSUING GROWTH IN A DIFFICULT ECONOMY

Arthur A. Thompson
The University of Alabama

In mid-2011, Panera Bread Company was continuing to pursue an aggressive strategy to expand its market presence across North America and improve the quality of the dining experience it provided to customers. It already operated 1,493 company-owned and franchised bakery-cafés in 40 states, the District of Columbia, and Ontario, Canada, under the Panera Bread, Saint Louis Bread Co., and Paradise Bakery & Café names. The number of locations was up from 1,027 units in 36 states at the end of 2006, but well short of the ambitious target the company set in 2006 to have 2,000 outlets in operation by the end of 2010. The recession of 2008–2009 had forced management to scale back Panera's expansion plans, but the company expected to open 95 to 105 new company-operated and franchised units in 2011, versus just 76 units in 2010. Management was confident that Panera Bread's attractive menu and the dining ambience of its bakery-cafés provided significant growth opportunity—despite sluggish economic conditions and the fiercely competitive nature of the restaurant industry—and that the company's targeted long-term earnings per share (EPS) growth rate of 15 to 20 percent annually was achievable.

Panera Bread baked more specialty breads daily than any other bakery-café enterprise in North America, and it was widely regarded as the clear leader of the "fast-casual" segment of the restaurant industry. In 2010, it had corporate revenues of $1.5 billion, systemwide store revenues of $3.1 billion, and average sales of $2.2 million per store location. An average of nearly 6 million customers patronized Panera locations systemwide each week.

The company was the recipient of many honors and awards. It had scored the highest level of customer loyalty among quick-casual restaurants, according to research conducted by TNS Intersearch.[1] For eight consecutive years, customers had rated Panera Bread tops among chain restaurants in Sandleman & Associates Quick-Track Awards of Excellence. Additionally, in 2010, Panera Bread had been named Most Popular (for chain restaurants with less than 5,000 outlets) by Zagat, a highly regarded restaurant review service; Zagat had also awarded Panera a number 1 ranking for Best Salad and Best Facilities and number 2 rankings for Healthy Options, Best Value, and Best Breakfast Sandwich. Panera Bread was named to *BusinessWeek*'s 2010 list of top 25 "Customer Service Champs" and to *Fortune* magazine's 2010 list of the 100 Fastest-Growing

Companies. In a 2011 Harris Poll, Panera Bread was named Casual Dining Brand of the Year.

COMPANY BACKGROUND

In 1981 Louis Kane and Ron Shaich founded a bakery-café enterprise named Au Bon Pain Co., Inc. Units were opened in malls, shopping centers, and airports along the East Coast of the United States and internationally throughout the 1980s and 1990s; the company prospered and became the dominant operator within the bakery-café category. In 1993, Au Bon Pain Co. purchased Saint Louis Bread Company, a chain of 20 bakery-cafés located in the St. Louis area. Ron Shaich and a team of Au Bon Pain managers then spent considerable time in 1994 and 1995 traveling the country and studying the market for fast food and quick-service meals. They concluded that many patrons of fast-food chains such as McDonald's, Wendy's, Burger King, Subway, Taco Bell, Pizza Hut, and KFC could be attracted to a higher-quality quick-dining experience. Top management at Au Bon Pain then instituted a comprehensive overhaul of the newly acquired Saint Louis Bread locations, altering the menu and the dining atmosphere. The vision was to create a specialty café anchored by an authentic, fresh dough, artisan bakery and upscale, quick-service menu selections. Between 1993 and 1997 average unit volumes at the revamped Saint Louis Bread units increased by 75 percent, and more than 100 additional Saint Louis Bread units were opened. In 1997, the Saint Louis Bread bakery-cafés were renamed Panera Bread in all markets outside St. Louis.

By 1998, it was clear the re-concepted Panera Bread units had connected with consumers. Au Bon Pain management concluded the Panera Bread format had broad market appeal and could be rolled out nationwide. Ron Shaich believed Panera Bread had the potential to become one of the leading "fast-casual" restaurant chains in the nation. Shaich also believed that growing Panera Bread into a national chain required significantly more management attention and financial resources than the company

could marshal if it continued to pursue expansion of both the Au Bon Pain and Panera Bread chains. He convinced the Au Bon Pain Board of Directors that the best course of action was for the company to go exclusively with the Panera Bread concept and divest the Au Bon Pain cafés. In August 1998, the company announced the sale of its Au Bon Pain bakery-café division for $73 million in cash to ABP Corp.; the transaction was completed in May 1999. With the sale of the Au Bon Pain division, the company changed its name to Panera Bread Company. The restructured company had 180 Saint Louis and Panera Bread bakery-cafés and a debt-free balance sheet.

Between January 1999 and December 2006, close to 850 additional Panera Bread bakery-cafés were opened, some company-owned and some franchised. As of June 28, 2011, Panera had 703 company-owned and 790 franchised bakery-cafés in operation. In February 2007, Panera purchased a 51 percent interest in Arizona-based Paradise Bakery & Café, which operated 70 company-owned and franchised units in 10 states (primarily in the West and Southwest) and had sales close to $100 million. At the time, Paradise Bakery units had average weekly sales of about $40,000 and an average check size of $8 to $9. Panera purchased the remaining 49 percent ownership of Paradise Bakery in June 2009. In 2008, Panera expanded into Canada, opening two locations in Ontario; since then, an additional unit in Canada had been opened.

In May 2010, William W. Moreton, Panera's executive vice president and co-chief operating officer, was appointed president and CEO and a member of the company's board. Ron Shaich, who had served as Panera's president and CEO since 1994 and as chairman or co-chairman of the Board of Directors since 1988, transitioned to the role of executive chairman of the board. In addition to the normal duties of board chairman, Shaich planned to maintain an active strategic role, with a particular focus on how Panera Bread could continue to be the best competitive alternative in the market segments the company served.

A summary of Panera Bread's recent financial performance is shown in Exhibit 1.

►EXHIBIT 1

Selected Consolidated Financial Data for Panera Bread, 2002–2010 (in thousands, except for per share amounts)

	2010	2009	2008	2007	2002
Income Statement Data					
Revenues:					
Bakery-café sales	$1,321,162	$1,153,255	$1,106,295	$ 894,902	$212,645
Franchise royalties and fees	86,195	78,367	74,800	67,188	27,892
Fresh dough and other product sales to franchisees	135,192	121,872	117,758	104,601	41,688
Total revenues	1,542,549	1,353,494	1,298,853	1,066,691	282,225
Bakery-café expenses:					
Food and paper products	374,816	337,599	332,697	271,442	63,370
Labor	419,140	370,595	352,462	286,238	63,172
Occupancy	100,970	95,996	90,390	70,398	15,408
Other operating expenses	177,059	155,396	147,033	121,325	27,971
Total bakery-café expenses	1,071,985	959,586	922,582	749,403	169,921
Fresh dough and other product costs of sales to franchisees	110,986	100,229	108,573	92,852	38,432
Depreciation and amortization	68,673	67,162	67,225	57,903	13,794
General and administrative expenses	101,494	83,169	84,393	68,966	24,986
Pre-opening expenses	4,282	2,451	3,374	8,289	1,051
Total costs and expenses	1,357,420	1,212,597	1,186,147	977,413	248,184
Operating profit	185,069	140,897	112,706	89,278	34,041
Interest expense	675	700	1,606	483	32
Other (income) expense, net	4,232	273	883	333	467
Income taxes	68,563	53,073	41,272	31,434	12,242
Less net income (loss) attributable to non-controlling interest	(267)	801	1,509	(428)	—
Net income to shareholders	$ 111,866	$ 86,050	$ 67,436	$ 57,456	$ 21,300
Earnings per share					
Basic	$3.65	$2.81	$2.24	$1.81	$0.74
Diluted	3.62	2.78	2.22	1.79	0.71
Weighted average shares outstanding					
Basic	30,614	30,667	30,059	31,708	28,923
Diluted	30,922	30,979	30,422	32,178	29,891
Balance Sheet Data					
Cash and cash equivalents	$229,299	$246,400	$74,710	$68,242	$29,924
Short-term investments	152	—	2,400	23,198	9,149
Current assets	330,685	322,084	138,413	152,121	59,262
Total assets	924,581	837,165	673,917	698,752	195,431
Current liabilities	211,516	142,259	114,014	127,766	32,325
Total liabilities	328,973	240,129	175,231	250,573	32,587
Stockholders' equity	595,608	597,036	495,162	446,164	151,503
Cash Flow Data					
Net cash provided by operating activities	$ 237,634	$ 214,904	$ 157,324	$ 154,014	$ 46,323
Net cash used in investing activities	(132,199)	(49,219)	(48,705)	(197,262)	(40,115)
Net cash provided by financing activities	(122,536)	6,005	(102,151)	59,393	5,664

(continued)

EXHIBIT 1 *(concluded)*

	2010	2009	2008	2007	2002
Net (decrease) increase in cash and cash equivalents	(17,101)	171,690	6,468	16,145	11,872

Sources: 2010 10-K Report, pp. 29-30 and pp. 46-48; 2008 10-K Report, pp. 48-50; and 2003 10-K Report, pp. 29-31.

PANERA BREAD'S CONCEPT AND STRATEGY

Panera Bread's identity was rooted in its fresh-baked, artisan breads made with a craftsman's attention to quality and detail, and its breads and baked products were the platform for the dining experience at its bakery-cafés and a major basis for differentiating Panera from competitors. The featured menu offerings at Panera locations included breads and pastries baked in-house, breakfast items and smoothies, made-to-order sandwiches, signature soups and salads, and café beverages. Recognizing that diners chose a dining establishment based on individual food preferences and mood, Panera strived to be the first choice for diners craving fresh-baked goods, a sandwich, soup, a salad, or a beverage served in a warm, friendly, comfortable dining environment. Its target market was urban workers and suburban dwellers looking for a quick service meal

EXHIBIT 2

Selected Operating Statistics, Panera Bread Company, 2002–2010

	2010	2009	2008	2007	2006	2002
Revenues at company-operated stores (in millions)	$1,321.1	$1,153.3	$1,106.3	$894.9	$666.1	$212.6
Revenues at franchised stores (in millions)	$1,802.1	$1,640.3	$1,542.8	$1,376.4	$1,245.5	$542.6
Systemwide store revenues (in millions)	$3,123.2	$2,793.6	$2,649.1	$2,271.3	$1,911.6	$755.2
Average annualized revenues per company-operated bakery-café (in millions)	$2.179	$2.031	$1.979	$1.952	$1.967	$1.764
Average annualized revenues per franchised bakery-café (in millions)	$2.266	$2.109	$2.087	$2.051	$2.074	$1.872
Average weekly sales, company-owned cafés	$41,899	$39,050	$38,066	$37,548	$37,833	$33,924
Average weekly sales, franchised cafés	$43,578	$40,566	$40,126	$39,438	$39,894	$35,997
Comparable bakery-café sales percentage increases:*						
Company-owned outlets	7.5%	2.4%	3.8%	1.7%	3.2%	4.1%
Franchised outlets	8.2%	2.0%	3.5%	1.7%	4.3%	6.1%
Company-owned bakery-cafés open at year-end	662	585	562	532	391	132

(continued)

	2010	2009	2008	2007	2006	2002
Franchised bakery-cafés open at year-end	791	795	763	698	636	346
Total bakery-cafés open	1,453	1,380	1,325	1,230	1,027	478

*The percentages for comparable store sales are based on annual changes at stores open at least 18 months.

Sources: Company 10-K Reports 2010, 2008, and 2003.

or light snack and an aesthetically pleasing dining experience. Management's long-term objective and strategic intent was to make Panera Bread a nationally recognized brand name and to be the dominant restaurant operator in upscale, quick-service dining. Top management believed that success depended on "being better than the guys across the street" and making the experience of dining at Panera so attractive that customers would be willing to pass by the outlets of other fast-casual restaurant competitors to dine at a nearby Panera Bread bakery-café.[2]

Panera management's blueprint for attracting and retaining customers was called Concept Essence. Concept Essence underpinned Panera's strategy and embraced several themes that, taken together, acted to differentiate Panera from its competitors:

- Offering an appealing selection of artisan breads, bagels, and pastry products that were handcrafted and baked daily at each café location.
- Serving high-quality food at prices that represented a good value.
- Developing a menu with sufficiently diverse offerings to enable Panera to draw customers from breakfast through the dinner hours each day.
- Providing courteous, capable, and efficient customer service.
- Designing bakery cafés that were esthetically pleasing and inviting.
- Offering patrons such a sufficiently satisfying dining experience that they were induced to return again and again.

Panera Bread's menu, store design and ambience, and unit location strategies enabled it to compete successfully in multiple segments of the restaurant business: breakfast, a.m. "chill" (when customers visited to take a break from morning hour activities), lunch, p.m. "chill" (when customers visited to take a break from afternoon activities), dinner, and take home, through both on-premise sales and off-premise catering. It competed with a wide assortment of specialty food, casual dining, and quick-service establishments operating nationally, regionally, and locally. Its close competitors varied according to the menu item, meal, and time of day. For example, breakfast and a.m. "chill" competitors included Starbucks and McDonald's; close lunch and dinner competitors included such chains as Chili's, Applebee's, California Pizza Kitchen, Jason's Deli, Cracker Barrel, Ruby Tuesday, T.G.I. Friday's, and Fazoli's. In the bread and pastry segment, Panera competed with Corner Bakery Café, Atlanta Bread Company, Au Bon Pain, local bakeries, and supermarket bakeries. Exhibit 3 provides information on prominent national and regional dining chains that competed against Panera Bread in some or many geographical locations.

Except for bread and pastry products, Panera's strongest competitors were dining establishments in the so-called fast-casual restaurant category. Fast-casual restaurants filled the gap between fast-food outlets and casual, full table service restaurants. A fast-casual restaurant provided quick-service dining (much like fast-food enterprises) but was distinguished by enticing menus, higher food quality,

▶EXHIBIT 3

Representative Fast-Casual Restaurants Chains and Selected Full-Service Restaurant Chains in the United States

Company	Number of Locations, 2010–2011	Select 2010 Financial Data	Key Menu Categories
Atlanta Bread Company	About 100 bakery-cafés mainly in the southeastern U.S.	Not available (privately held company)	Fresh-baked breads, salads, sandwiches, soups, wood-fired pizza and pasta (select locations only), baked goods, desserts
Applebee's Neighborhood Grill and Bar*	2,010 locations in the U.S. and 16 other countries	2010 average annual sales of $2.1 million per location; alcoholic beverages accounted for about 12 percent of sales	Beef, chicken, pork, seafood, and pasta entrees plus appetizers, salads, sandwiches, a selection of Weight Watchers branded menu alternatives, desserts, and alcoholic beverages
Au Bon Pain	200+ company-owned and franchised bakery-cafés in 23 states, South Korea, Thailand, and Taiwan	Not available (privately held company)	Baked goods (with a focus on croissants and bagels), soups, salads, sandwiches and wraps, and coffee drinks
Bruegger's	300+ bakery-cafés in 26 states	2005 revenues of $155.2 million; 3,500 full-time employees	Fresh-baked bagels and breads, sandwiches, salads, soups, and desserts
California Pizza Kitchen* (a subsidiary of Golden Gate Capital)	265 locations in 32 states and 10 other countries	2010 revenues of $642 million; average annual sales of $3.2 million per location	Signature California-style hearth-baked pizzas; salads, pastas, soups, and sandwiches; appetizers; desserts, beer, wine, coffees, teas, and assorted beverages
Chili's Grill and Bar* (a subsidiary of Brinker International**)	1,300 locations in 50 states and 221 locations in 31 foreign countries	2010 average revenues of $3 million per location; average check size per customer of $13.30	Chicken, beef, and seafood entrees, steaks, appetizers, salads, sandwiches, desserts, and alcoholic beverages (13 percent of sales)
Chipotle Mexican Grill	1,080+ units	2010 revenues of $1.84 billion; average unit sales of $1.8 million	Gourmet burritos and tacos, salads, beverages
Corner Bakery Café (a subsidiary of Roark Capital Group)	119 locations in 10 states and District of Columbia	Menu price range: $0.99 to 7.99	Specialty breads, hot breakfasts, sandwiches, soups, salads, sweets, coffees, and teas
Cracker Barrel*	600 combination retail stores and restaurants in 42 states	Restaurant sales of $1.9 billion in 2010; average restaurant sales of $3 million; serves an average of 6,900 customers per week per location	Two menus (breakfast and lunch/dinner); rated in Zagat's 2010 Consumer Survey as "Best Breakfast" among family dining chains and by Technomics as "Top of the Full-Service Restaurants in family and casual dining"
Culver's	428 locations in 19 states	Not available (a privately held company)	Signature hamburgers served on buttered buns, fried battered cheese curds, value dinners (chicken, shrimp, cod with potato and slaw), salads, frozen custard, milk shakes, sundaes, and fountain drinks

(continued)

▶ EXHIBIT 3   *(continued)*

Company	Number of Locations, 2010–2011	Select 2010 Financial Data	Key Menu Categories
Einstein Bros. Bagels (a unit of the Einstein Noah Restaurant Group)	330 company-owned and 100 licensed locations in 34 states and the District of Coumbia	2010 revenues of about $330 million; annual sales revenues per unit of $1 million	Fresh-baked bagels, hot breakfast sandwiches, made-to-order lunch sandwiches, creamed cheeses and other spreads, salads, soups, and gourmet coffees and teas.
Fazoli's (a subsidiary of Sun Capital Partners)	230 locations in 26 states	Not available (a privately held company)	Spaghetti and meatballs, fettuccine Alfredo, lasagna, ravioli, submarines and panini sandwiches, pizza, entrée salads, garlic breadsticks, and desserts
Firehouse Subs	402 locations in 21 states	2010 total revenues of $233 million; average unit sales of $604,000	Hot and cold subs, salads, sides, drinks, catering
Five Guys Burgers and Fries	725+ locations in 40 states and 4 Canadian provinces	Not available (a privately held company)	Hamburgers (with choice of 15 toppings), hot dogs, fries, Coca-Cola, and beverages
Fuddruckers	190 locations in 31 states, Puerto Rico and Canada	Not available (a privately held company)	Exotic hamburgers (the feature menu item), chicken and fish sandwiches, French fries and other sides, soups, salads, desserts
Jason's Deli	214+ locations in 28 states	Not available (a privately held company)	Sandwiches, extensive salad bar, soups, loaded potatoes, desserts; catering services, party trays, and box lunches
McAlister's Deli (a subsidiary of Roark Capital Group)	200+ locations in 22 states	Not available (a privately held company)	Deli sandwiches, loaded baked potatoes, soups, salads, and desserts, plus sandwich trays, lunch boxes, and catering
Noodles & Company	260+ urban and suburban locations in 22 states	Not available (a privately held company); designated by *Parents* magazines as one of the 10 best restaurant chains in 2011; typical price point of $7	Asian, Mediterranean and American noodle/pasta entrees, soups, salads, sandwiches, alcoholic beverages
Qdoba Mexican Grill (a subsidiary of Jack in the Box, Inc.)	500+ locations in 43 states and District of Columbia	Average unit sales of $923,000 in 2010; Jack in the Box had 2010 revenues of $2.3 billion	Signature burritos, tacos, taco salads, quesadillas, 3-cheese nachos, Mexican gumbo, tortilla soup, five signature salsas, and breakfast selections at some locations
Ruby Tuesday*	793 company-owned and franchised locations in 47 states and 53 franchised locations in 14 foreign countries and Guam	Fiscal 2011 sales of $1.26 billion; average revenues of $1.2 million per company-operated unit in 2010. Entree price ranges of $6.99 to $18.99.	Appetizers, handcrafted burgers, 40-item salad bar, steaks, fresh chicken, crab cakes, lobster, salmon, tilapia, ribs, desserts, nonalcoholic and alcoholic beverages, and catering
Starbucks	10,930+ company-operated and licensed locations in U.S. and 5,900+ international locations	2010 revenues of $10.7 billion; estimated retail sales of $1.1 million per company-operated location in U.S.	Italian-style espresso beverages, teas, sodas, juices, assorted pastries and confections; some locations offer sandwiches and salads

(continued)

▶ **EXHIBIT 3** *(concluded)*

Company	Number of Locations, 2010–2011	Select 2010 Financial Data	Key Menu Categories
T.G.I. Friday's* (a subsidiary of Carlson's Restaurants)	588 company-owned and franchised locations in 44 states and 341 locations in 60 foreign countries	Not available (a privately held company)	Appetizers, salads, soups, burgers and other sandwiches, chicken, seafood, steaks, pasta, desserts, nonalcoholic and alcoholic beverages, party platters

*Denotes a full-service restaurant

**Brinker International is a multi-concept restaurant operator with two principal brands: Chili's Grill & Bar and Maggiano's Little Italy; it also owned a minority stake in Romano's Macaroni Grill. Brinker had 2010 sales of $2.9 billion.

Sources: Company websites; and FastCasual.com's "Top 100 2011 Movers and Shakers," accessed at www.fastcasual.com on July 17, 2011.

and more inviting dining environments; typical meal costs per guest were in the $7 to $12 range. Some fast-casual restaurants had full table service, some had partial table service (with orders being delivered to the table after ordering and paying at the counter), and some were self-service (like fast-food establishments).

Panera Bread's growth strategy was to capitalize on Panera's market potential by opening both company-owned and franchised Panera Bread locations as fast as was prudent. So far, working closely with franchisees to open new locations had been a key component of the company's efforts to broaden its market penetration. Panera Bread had organized its business around company-owned bakery-cafe operations, franchise operations, and fresh dough operations; the fresh bread unit supplied dough and other products to all Panera Bread stores, both company-owned and franchised.

PANERA BREAD'S PRODUCT OFFERINGS AND MENU

Panera Bread's artisan signature breads were made from four ingredients—water, natural yeast, flour, and salt; no preservatives or chemicals were used. Carefully trained bakers shaped every step of the process, from mixing the ingredients, to kneading the dough, to placing the loaves on hot stone slabs to bake in a traditional European-style stone deck bakery oven. Breads, as well as bagels, cookies, and

other pastries, were baked fresh throughout the day at each café location. Exhibit 4 shows Panera's lineup of breads.

The Panera Bread menu was designed to provide target customers with products built on the company's bakery expertise, particularly its varieties of breads and bagels baked fresh throughout the day at each café location. The key menu groups were fresh baked goods, made-to-order sandwiches and salads, soups, light entrées, fruit smoothies, and café beverages. Exhibit 5 summarizes the menu offerings at Panera Bread locations as of mid-2011.

Menu offerings were regularly reviewed and revised to sustain the interest of regular customers, satisfy changing consumer preferences, and be responsive to various seasons of the year. Special soup offerings, for example, appeared seasonally. Product development was focused on providing food that customers would crave and trust to be tasty. New menu items were developed in test kitchens and then introduced in a limited number of the bakery-cafés to determine customer response and verify that preparation and operating procedures resulted in product consistency and quality standards. If successful, they were then rolled out systemwide. New-product introductions were integrated into periodic or seasonal menu rotations, referred to as "Celebrations." Ten new menu items were introduced in 2010.

Over the past seven years, Panera had responded to growing consumer interest in

EXHIBIT 4

Panera's Line of Fresh-Baked Breads, 2011

Artisan Breads	**Specialty Breads**
Country A crisp crust and nutty flavor. *Available in Loaf, Miche.*	**Sourdough** Panera's signature sourdough bread that featured a golden, crackled crust and firm, moderately structured crumb with a satisfying, tangy flavor. *Available in Loaf, XL Loaf, Roll, Bread Bowl.*
French Slightly blistered crust, wine-like aroma. *Available in Baguette, Miche.*	**Asiago Cheese** Chunks of Asiago cheese were added to the standard sourdough recipe and baked right in, with more Asiago cheese sprinkled on top. *Available in Demi, Loaf.*
Ciabatta A moist, chewy crumb with a thin crust and light olive oil flavor. *Available in Loaf.*	**Honey Wheat** A mild wheat bread with tastes of honey and molasses; the soft crust and crumb made it great for sandwiches. *Available in Loaf.*
Focaccia Italian flatbread baked with olive oil and topped with salt; two varieties—Asiago Cheese and Sea Salt. *Available in Loaf.*	**White Whole Grain** A thin crust and a soft crumb sweetened with honey and molasses. *Available in Loaf.*
Stone-Milled Rye With chopped rye kernels and caraway seeds. *Available in Loaf, Miche.*	**Tomato Basil** Sourdough bread made with tomatoes and basil, topped with a sweet streusel topping. *Available in Loaf.*
Three Cheese Made with Parmesan, Romano, and Asiago cheeses. *Available in Demi, Loaf, Miche.*	**Cinnamon Raisin** Made from sweet dough, egg, Korintje cinnamon, plump raisins, and brown sugar, topped with Panera's cinnamon crunch topping. *Available in Loaf.*
Three Seed Sesame, poppy, and fennel seeds. *Available in Demi.*	
Whole Grain Moist and hearty, sweetened with honey. *Available in Loaf, Miche, Baguette.*	
Sesame Semolina Delicate and moist, topped with sesame seeds. *Available in Loaf, Miche.*	

Source: www.panerabread.com, accessed July 20, 2011.

healthier, more nutritious menu offerings. In 2004, whole-grain breads were introduced, and in 2005 Panera switched to the use of natural, antibiotic-free chicken in all of Panera's chicken-related sandwiches and salads. Other recent health-related changes included using organic and all-natural ingredients in selected items, using unbleached flours in its breads, adding a yogurt-granola-fruit parfait and reduced-fat spreads for bagels to the menu, introducing fruit smoothies, and revising ingredients and preparation methods to yield 0 grams of artificial trans fat per serving. Panera's website had detailed nutritional information for individual products and a nutritional calculator that could be used to determine the nutritional content of an entire meal or combination of menu selections.

Off-Premise Catering

In 2004–2005 Panera Bread introduced a catering program to extend its market reach into the workplace, schools, and parties and gatherings held in homes and to grow breakfast, lunch, and dinner sales without making capital investments in additional physical facilities. A

► EXHIBIT 5

Panera Bread's Menu Selections, July 2011

Bakery
Artisan and Specialty Breads (15 varieties), Bagels (12 varieties), Scones (4 varieties), Sweet Rolls (4 varieties), Cinnamon Crumb Coffee Cake, Muffins (5 varieties), Artisan Pastries (5 varieties), Brownies, Cookies (6 varieties)

Bagels & Cream Cheese Spreads (12 varieties of bagels, 7 varieties of spreads)

Hot Breakfast
Signature Breakfast Sandwiches (3 varieties), Baked Egg Soufflés (4 varieties), Breakfast Power Sandwich on Whole Grain Ciabatta Breakfast Sandwiches (2 varieties)

Strawberry Granola Parfait

Fruit Smoothies (4 varieties)

Signature Hot Paninis
Steakhouse and White Cheddar, Turkey Artichoke, Frontega Chicken, Cuban Chicken, Smokehouse Turkey, Tomato and Mozzarella

Signature Sandwiches
Napa Almond Chicken Salad, Asiago Roast Beef, Italian Combo, Bacon Turkey Bravo

Café Sandwiches
Smoked Ham and Swiss, Smoked Turkey Breast, Tuna Salad, Mediterranean Veggie

Signature Hot Entrées
Mac & Cheese

Soups (5 selections varying daily, plus seasonal specialties)
Options include: Broccoli Cheddar, French Onion, Baked Potato, Low Fat All-Natural Chicken Noodle, Cream of Chicken and Wild Rice, New England Clam Chowder, Low Fat Garden Vegetable with Pesto, Low Fat Vegetarian Black Bean, Low Fat Lemon Chicken Orzo, Vegetarian Creamy Tomato, Steak Chili

Signature Salads
Strawberry Poppyseed & Chicken, Steak and Blue Cheese, BBQ Chopped Chicken, Grilled Chicken Caesar, Asian Sesame Chicken, Fuji Apple Chicken, Thai Chopped Chicken

Café Salads
Chicken, Caesar, Classic

Panera Kids
Grilled Cheese, Peanut Butter and Jelly, Mac & Cheese, Kids Deli (Organic American cheese and choice of smoked ham, turkey breast or roast beef)

Beverages
Coffee (4 varieties), Hot Teas, Iced Tea, Iced Green Tea, Pepsi beverages, Bottled Water, Organic Milk, Organic Chocolate Milk, Orange Juice, Organic Apple Juice, Lemonade

Frozen Drinks (5 varieties)

Espresso Bar
Espresso, Cappuccino, Caffe Latte, Caffe Mocha, Caramel Latte, Chai Tea Latte (hot or iced), Hot Chocolate

Source: Menu posted at www.panerabread.com, accessed July 20, 2011.

catering menu that drew upon items appearing on the regular menu was created and posted for viewing at the company's website. Selections included an assortment of bagels and morning pastries (with butter, cream cheeses, and preserves), a fruit bowl, hot breakfast sandwiches and egg soufflés, sandwich assortments, boxed lunches, salads and soups for a group, and beverages. A catering coordinator was available to help customers make menu selections, choose between assortments or boxed meals, determine appropriate order quantities, and arrange pickup or delivery times. Orders came complete with plates, napkins, and utensils, all packaged and presented in convenient, ready-to-serve-from packaging.

In 2010, Panera boosted the size of its catering sales staff and introduced sales training programs and other tools—factors that helped drive a 26 percent increase in catering sales in 2010. In 2011, Panera introduced an online catering system that catering customers could use to view the catering menu, place orders, and pay for purchases. Going forward, top executives at Panera believed that continuing to develop the company's off-premise catering capabilities and provide even more convenient catering options for customers would lead to significantly higher catering revenues at both company-operated and franchised locations.

The MyPanera Loyalty Program

In 2010, Panera initiated a loyalty program to reward customers who dined frequently at Panera Bread locations. The introduction of the MyPanera program was completed systemwide in November and, by the end of December, some 4.5 million customers had signed up and become registered card members. Members presented their MyPanera card when ordering; when the card was swiped, the specific items being purchased were automatically recorded to learn what items a member liked. As Panera got an idea of a member's preferences over the course of several visits, a member's card was "loaded" with such "surprises" as complimentary bakery-cafe items, exclusive previews and tastings, cooking and baking tips, invitations to special events, ideas for entertaining, or recipe books. On a member's next visit, when an order was placed and the card swiped, order-taking personnel informed the member of the surprise award. Members could also go online at www.MyPanera.com and see if a reward was waiting on their next visit.

Management believed that the loyalty program had two primary benefits. One was to entice members to dine at Panera more frequently and thereby deepen the bond between Panera Bread and its most loyal customers. The second was to provide Panera management with better marketing research data on the purchasing behavior of customers and enable Panera to "get as close to one on one marketing with our customers as possible."[3]

Panera's Nonprofit Pay-What-You-Want Bakery-Café Locations

In May 2010, Panera Bread converted one of its restaurants in a wealthy St. Louis suburb into a nonprofit pay-what-you-want Saint Louis Bread Cares bakery-café with the idea of helping to feed the needy and raising money for charitable work. A sign in the bakery-café said, "We encourage those with the means to leave the requested amount or more if you're able. And we encourage those with a real need to take a discount." The menu board listed "suggested funding levels," not prices. Payments went into a donation box, with the cashiers providing change and handling credit card payments. The hope was that enough generous customers would donate money above and beyond the menu's suggested funding levels to subsidize discounted meals for those who were experiencing economic hardship and needed help. The restaurant was operated by Panera's charitable Panera Bread Foundation; all profits from the store were donated to community programs.

After several months of operation, the Saint Louis Bread Cares store was judged to be successful enough that Ron Shaich, who headed the Panera Bread Foundation, opted to open two similar Panera Cares cafés—one in the Detroit suburb of Dearborn, Michigan, and one in Portland, Oregon. At one juncture, Panera statistics indicated that roughly 60 percent of store patrons left the suggested amount; 20 percent left more, and 20 percent less.[4] Of course, there were occasional instances where a patron tried to game the system. Ron Shaich cited the case of a college student who ordered more than $40 worth of food and charged only $3 to his father's credit card; Shaich, who happened to be working in the store behind the counter, had to restrain himself, saying, "I wanted to jump over the counter."[5] One person paid $500 for a meal, the largest single payment. As of May 2011, Panera was planning to add a new pay-what-you-want store every three months or so.

MARKETING

In the company's early years, marketing had played only a small role in Panera's success. Brand awareness had been built on customers' satisfaction with their dining experience at Panera and their tendency to share their positive experiences with friends and neighbors. From time to time, Panera had utilized focus groups to determine customer food and drink preferences and price points In 2006, Panera's marketing research indicated that about 85 percent of consumers who were aware that there was a Panera Bread bakery-café in their community or neighborhood had dined at Panera on at least one occasion; 57 percent of consumers who had "ever tried" dining at Panera Bread had been customers in the past 30 days.[6] Panera's research also showed that people who dined at Panera Bread very frequently or moderately frequently typically did so for only one part of the day, although 81 percent indicated "considerable willingness" to try dining at Panera Bread at other parts of the day.

This data prompted management to pursue three marketing initiatives during 2006–2007. One aimed at raising the quality of awareness about Panera by continuing to feature the caliber and appeal of its breads and baked goods, by hammering the theme "food you crave, food you can trust," and by enhancing the appeal of its bakery-cafés as a neighborhood gathering place. A second initiative sought to raise awareness and boost customer trials of dining at Panera Bread at multiple meal times (breakfast, lunch, "chill out" times, and dinner). The third initiative was to increase perception of Panera Bread as a viable evening meal option by introducing a number of new entrée menu selections. Panera avoided hard-sell or "in your face" marketing approaches, preferring instead to employ a range of ways to softly drop the Panera Bread name into the midst of consumers as they moved through their lives and let them "gently collide" with the brand. The idea was to let consumers "discover" Panera Bread and then convert them into loyal, repeat customers by providing a very satisfying dining experience when they tried Panera bakery-cafés for the first time or opted to try dining at Panera at a different part of the day particularly during breakfast or dinner as opposed to the busier lunchtime hours. These initiatives were only partially successful, partly because of the difficult economic environment that emerged in 2008–2009 and partly because the new dinner entrées that were introduced did not prove popular enough to significantly boost dinner-hour traffic and were dropped from the menu.

In 2011, the only hot entrée on the menu was Mac & Cheese (see Exhibit 5).

Panera management was committed to growing sales at existing and new unit locations, continuously improving the customer experience at its restaurants, and encouraging more frequent customer visits via the newly instituted MyPanera loyalty programs and efforts to build a deeper and lasting relationship with customers who, management believed, would then recommend dining at Panera to their friends and acquaintances.

To reach target customer groups, Panera employed a mix of radio, billboards, social networking, television, and in-store sampling days. Advertising expenses totaled $27.4 million in 2010, $15.3 million in 2009, and $14.2 million in 2008. In 2010, Panera continued its multiple-year initiative to refine its media and advertising strategy. Although the company increased its media spending in 2010, it nonetheless spent only 1.1 percent of system-wide sales on direct media advertising; many national restaurant chains spend 3 to 5 percent of revenues on media advertising. Much effort had also gone into improving Panera's advertising messages to better capture the points of difference and the soul of the Panera concept and doing a better job of optimizing the media mix by market. Management planned to increase media spending modestly in 2011 but exercise care in generating a positive payback on its media expenditures.

Franchise-operated bakery-cafés were required, as part of their franchising agreement, to contribute 1.2 percent of their sales to a national advertising fund and 0.4 percent of their sales as a marketing administration fee and were also required to spend 2.0 percent of their sales in their local markets on advertising. Panera contributed similar amounts from company-owned bakery-cafés toward the national advertising fund and marketing administration. The national advertising fund contribution of 1.2 percent had been increased from 0.7 percent starting in July 2010; the 0.7 percent contribution became effective in January 2006 when it was raised from 0.4 percent. According to the franchise agreement, Panera could opt to raise the national advertising fund contributions as high as 2.6 percent of sales.

Panera had recently hired a new chief marketing officer and a new vice president of marketing. Both had considerable consumer marketing experience and were playing an important role in crafting the company's long-term marketing strategy to boost customer traffic and grow revenues at all of Panera's restaurant locations. Efforts were underway to refine marketing initiatives aimed at increasing brand awareness, continuously improving the customer experience at the company's restaurants, expanding customer participation in the MyPanera loyalty program, and developing and promoting appealing new menu selections.

FRANCHISE OPERATIONS

Opening additional franchised bakery-cafés was a core element of Panera Bread's strategy and management's initiatives to achieve the company's revenue growth and earnings targets. Panera Bread did not grant single-unit franchises, so a prospective franchisee could not open just one bakery-café. Rather, Panera Bread's franchising strategy was to enter into franchise agreements that required the franchise developer to open a number of units, typically 15 bakery-cafes in a period of six years. Franchisee candidates had to be well capitalized, have a proven track record as excellent multi-unit restaurant operators, and agree to meet an aggressive development schedule. Applicants had to meet eight stringent criteria to gain consideration for a Panera Bread franchise:

- Experience as a multi-unit restaurant operator.
- Recognition as a top restaurant operator.
- Net worth of $7.5 million.
- Liquid assets of $3 million.
- Infrastructure and resources to meet Panera's development schedule for the market area the franchisee was applying to develop.

- Real estate experience in the market to be developed.
- Total commitment to the development of the Panera Bread brand.
- Cultural fit and a passion for fresh bread.

Exhibit 6 shows estimated costs of opening a new franchised Panera Bread bakery-café. The franchise agreement typically required the payment of a franchise fee of $35,000 per bakery-café (broken down into $5,000 at the signing of the area development agreement and $30,000 at or before a bakery-café opened) and continuing royalties of 5 percent on gross sales at each franchised bakery-café. Franchise-operated bakery-cafés followed the same standards for in-store operating standards, product quality, menu, site selection, and bakery-café construction as did company-owned bakery-cafés. Franchisees were required to purchase all of their dough products from sources approved by Panera Bread. Panera's fresh dough facility system supplied fresh dough products to substantially all franchise-operated bakery-cafes. Panera did not finance franchisee construction or area development agreement payments or hold an equity interest in any of the franchise-operated bakery-cafes. All area development agreements executed after March 2003 included a clause allowing Panera Bread the right to purchase all bakery-cafés opened by the franchisee at a defined purchase price, at any time five years after the execution of the franchise agreement. In 2010, Panera purchased 37 bakery-cafés from the franchisee in the New Jersey market and sold 3 bakery-cafés in the Mobile, Alabama, market to an existing franchisee. In 2011, Panera completed the purchase of 25 bakery-cafés owned by its Milwaukee franchisee and sold two Paradise Bakery & Café units to a Texas franchisee.

As of July 2011, Panera Bread had agreements with 47 franchise groups that operated 790 bakery-cafés. Panera's largest franchisee operated nearly 200 bakery-cafés in Ohio, Pennsylvania, West Virginia, Kentucky, and Florida. The company's franchise groups had committed to open an additional 160 bakery-cafés during

► EXHIBIT 6

Estimated Initial Investment for a Franchised Panera Bread Bakery-Café, 2011

Investment Category	Actual or Estimated Amount	To Whom Paid
Franchise fee	$35,000	Panera
Real property	Varies according to site and local real estate market conditions	
Leasehold improvements	$245,000 to $1,160,000	Contractors
Equipment	$184,000 to $310,000	Equipment vendors, Panera
Fixtures	$35,000 to $77,000	Vendors
Furniture	$35,000 to $88,000	Vendors
Consultant fees and municipal impact fees (if any)	$52,500 to $153,500	Architect, engineer, expeditor, others
Supplies and inventory	$19,000 to $24,350	Panera, other suppliers
Small wares	$24,000 to $29,000	Suppliers
Signage	$13,000 to $94,000	Suppliers
Additional funds (for working capital and general operating expenses for 3 months)	$175,000 to $245,000	Vendors, suppliers, employees, utilities, landlord, others
Total	$817,500 to $2,215,500, plus real estate and related costs	

Source: www.panerabread.com, accessed July 7, 2010.

the next four to five years. If a franchisee failed to develop bakery-cafés on schedule, Panera had the right to terminate the franchise agreement and develop its own company-operated locations or develop locations through new franchisees in that market. However, Panera from time to time agreed to modify the commitments of franchisees to open new locations when unfavorable market conditions or other circumstances warranted the postponement or cancellation of new unit openings.

The typical franchise-operated bakery-café averaged somewhat higher average weekly and annual sales volumes than company-operated cafés (see Exhibit 2). Also, franchised cafés tended to be equal to or slightly more profitable than company-operated locations and produced a slightly higher return on equity investment than company-operated cafés (partly because many franchisees made greater use of long-term debt in financing their operations than did Panera).[7] In 2009, annual sales at franchised bakery-cafés ranged from a low of $666,400 to a high of $4,312,900, with an average of $2,141,000; this compared very favorably with the sales range of $1,000,900 to $3,809,000 and unit average of $2,047,500 for company-operated bakery-cafés.[8]

Panera provided its franchisees with support in a number of areas: market analysis and site selection assistance, lease review, design services and new-store opening assistance, a comprehensive 10-week initial training program, a training program for hourly employees, manager and baker certification, bakery-café certification, continuing education classes, benchmarking data regarding costs and profit margins, access to company-developed marketing and advertising programs, neighborhood marketing assistance, and calendar planning assistance.

SITE SELECTION AND CAFÉ ENVIRONMENT

Bakery-cafés were typically located in suburban, strip mall, and regional mall locations. In evaluating a potential location, Panera studied the surrounding trade area, demographic information within that area, and information on nearby competitors. Based on analysis of this information, including utilization of predictive modeling using proprietary software, Panera developed projections of sales and return on investment for candidate sites. Cafés had proven successful as freestanding units and as both in-line and end-cap locations in strip malls and large regional malls.

The average Panera bakery-café size was approximately 4,600 square feet. All company-operated locations were leased. Lease terms were typically for 10 years with one, two, or three 5-year renewal option periods at most locations. Leases typically entailed charges for minimum base occupancy, a proportionate share of building and common area operating expenses and real estate taxes, and a contingent percentage rent based on sales above a stipulated amount. Some lease agreements provided for scheduled rent increases during the lease term. The average construction, equipment, furniture and fixture, and signage cost for the 42 company-owned bakery-cafés opened in 2010 was $750,000 (net of landlord allowances and capitalized development overhead expenses), compared to a cost of $920,000 per bakery-café for the 66 company-owned bakery-cafes opened in 2005.

Each bakery-café sought to provide a distinctive and engaging environment (what management referred to as "Panera Warmth"), in many cases using fixtures and materials complementary to the neighborhood location of the bakery-café. All Panera cafés used reusable dishes and stainless-steel silverware, instead of paper plates and plastic utensils. In 2005–2006, the company had introduced a new café design aimed at further refining and enhancing the appeal of Panera bakery-cafés as a warm and appealing neighborhood gathering place. The design incorporated higher-quality furniture, cozier seating, comfortable gathering areas, and relaxing décor. A number of locations had fireplaces to further create an alluring and hospitable atmosphere that patrons would flock to on a regular basis,

sometimes for a meal with or without friends and acquaintances and sometimes to take a break for a light snack or beverage. Many locations had outdoor seating, and all company-operated and most franchised locations had free wireless Internet to help make the bakery-cafés community gathering places where people could catch up on some work, hang out with friends, read the paper, or just relax (a strategy that Starbucks had used with great success).

In 2006, Panera began working on store designs and operating systems that would enable freestanding and end-cap locations to incorporate a drive-thru window. In 2010–2011, increasing numbers of newly opened locations, both company-owned and franchised, featured drive-thru windows. Some existing units had undergone renovation to add a drive-thru window. By the end of 2011, some 50 or more Panera Bread locations were expected to have drive-thru windows. Sales at these locations were running about 20 percent higher on average than units without drive-thru capability.

BAKERY-CAFÉ OPERATIONS

Panera's top executives believed that operating excellence was the most important element of Panera Warmth and that without strong execution and operational skills and energized café personnel who were motivated to provide pleasing service, it would be difficult to build and maintain a strong relationship with the customers patronizing its bakery-cafés. Additionally, top management believed high-quality restaurant management was critical to the company's long-term success. Bakery-café managers were provided with detailed operations manuals and all café personnel received hands-on training, both in small group and individual settings. The company had created systems to educate and prepare café personnel to respond to a customer's questions and do their part to create a better dining experience. Management strived to maintain adequate staffing at each café and had instituted competitive compensation for café managers and both full-time and part-time café personnel (who were called associates).

Going into 2011, Panera Bread had approximately 800 full-time associates (defined as associates who worked an average of 25 hours or more per week) employed in general or administrative functions, principally at the company's support centers; approximately 13,900 full-time people employed in company-operated bakery-cafés as bakers, managers, and associates; and approximately 9,700 part-time hourly associates that worked at its bakery-cafés. Panera had no collective bargaining agreements with its associates and considered its employee relations to be good.

PANERA'S BAKERY-CAFÉ SUPPLY CHAIN

Panera operated a network of 26 regional facilities (22 company-owned and 4 franchise-operated) to supply fresh dough for breads and bagels on a daily basis to substantially all of its company-owned and franchised bakery-cafés. All these facilities were leased. Most of the 1,200 employees at the regional facilities were engaged in preparing dough for breads and bagels, a process that took about 48 hours. The dough-making process began with the preparation and mixing of starter dough, which then was given time to rise; other all-natural ingredients were then added to create the dough for each of the different bread and bagel varieties (no chemicals or preservatives were used). Another period of rising then took place. Next, the dough was cut into pieces, shaped into loaves or bagel shapes, and readied for shipment in fresh dough form. There was no freezing of the dough, and no partial baking was done at the fresh dough facilities. Trained bakers at each bakery-café performed all of the baking activities, using the fresh doughs delivered daily.

Distribution of the fresh bread and bagel doughs (along with tuna, cream cheese spreads, and certain fresh fruits and vegetables) was accomplished through a leased fleet of about 196 temperature-controlled trucks operated

by Panera personnel. The optimal maximum distribution route was approximately 300 miles; however, routes as long as 500 miles were sometimes necessary to supply cafés in outlying locations with only a few Panera restaurants. New regional facilities and trucks were added once the number of locations in an area was sufficient to support efficient production and distribution of fresh dough and other products to surrounding bakery-cafés. In 2010, the various distribution routes for regional facilities entailed making daily deliveries to an average of seven bakery-cafés.

Panera obtained ingredients for its doughs and other products manufactured at its regional facilities. While some ingredients used at these facilities were sourced from a single supplier, there were numerous suppliers of each needed fresh dough and cheese spread ingredient and Panera could obtain ingredients from another supplier when necessary. Panera contracted externally for the manufacture and distribution of sweet goods to its bakery-cafés. After delivery, sweet good products were finished with fresh toppings and other ingredients (based on Panera's own recipes) and baked to Panera's artisan standards by professionally trained bakers at each café location.

Panera had arrangements with several independent distributors to handle the delivery of sweet goods products and other items to its bakery-cafés, but the company had contracted with a single supplier to deliver the majority of ingredients and other products to its bakery-cafés two or three times per week. Virtually all other food products and supplies for bakery-cafés, including paper goods, coffee, and small wares, were contracted for by Panera and delivered by the vendors to designated independent distributors for delivery to the bakery-cafés. Individual bakery-cafés placed orders for the needed supplies directly with a distributor; distributors made deliveries to bakery-cafés two to three times per week. Panera maintained a list of approved suppliers and distributors that all company-owned and franchised cafes could select from in obtaining food products and other supplies not sourced from the company's regional facilities or delivered directly by contract suppliers.

Although many of the ingredients and menu items sourced from outside vendors were prepared to Panera's specifications, the ingredients for a big majority of menu selections were generally available and could be obtained from alternative sources when necessary. In a number of instances, Panera had entered into annual and multiyear contracts for certain ingredients in order to decrease the risks of supply interruptions and cost fluctuation. Antibiotic-free chicken was currently obtained from three different suppliers; however, alternative sources of antibiotic-free chicken—as well as certain other organically grown items—in the quantities needed were limited.

Management believed the company's fresh dough-making capability provided a competitive advantage by ensuring consistent quality and dough-making efficiency (it was more economical to concentrate the dough-making operations in a few facilities dedicated to that function

than it was to have each bakery-café equipped and staffed to do all of its baking from scratch). Management also believed that the company's growing size and scale of operations gave it increased bargaining power and leverage with suppliers to improve ingredient quality and cost and that its various supply-chain arrangements entailed small risk that its bakery-cafés would experience significant delivery interruptions from weather conditions or other factors that would adversely affect café operations.

The fresh dough made at the regional facilities was sold to both company-owned and franchised bakery-cafés at a delivered cost not to exceed 27 percent of the retail value of the product. Exhibit 7 provides financial data relating to each of Panera's three business segments: company-operated bakery-cafés, franchise operations, and the operations of the regional facilities that supplied fresh dough and other products. The sales and operating profits of the fresh dough and other products segment shown in Exhibit 7 represent only

▶ EXHIBIT 7

Business Segment Information, Panera Bread Company, 2008–2010 (in thousands of dollars)			
	2010	**2009**	**2008**
Segment revenues:			
Company bakery-café operations	$1,321,162	$1,153,255	$1,106,295
Franchise operations	86,195	78,367	74,800
Fresh dough and other product operations at regional facilities	252,045	216,116	213,620
Intercompany sales eliminations	(116,913)	(94,244)	(95,862)
Total revenues	$1,542,489	$1,353,494	$1,298,853
Segment operating profit:			
Company bakery-café operations	$249,177	$193,669	$183,713
Franchise operations	80,397	72,381	65,005
Fresh dough and other product operations at regional facilities	24,146	21,643	9,185
Total segment operating profit	$353,720	$287,693	$257,903
Depreciation and amortization:			
Company bakery-café operations	$57,031	$55,726	$54,814
Fresh dough and other product operations at regional facilities	7,495	7,620	8,072
Corporate administration	4,147	3,816	4,339
Total	$68,673	$67,162	$67,225

(continued)

▶ EXHIBIT 7   (*concluded*)

	2010	2009	2008
Capital expenditures:			
Company bakery-café operations	$66,961	$46,408	$56,477
Fresh dough and other product operations at regional facilities	6,452	3,681	3,872
Corporate administration	8,813	4,595	2,814
Total capital expenditures	$82,226	$54,684	$63,163
Segment assets:			
Company bakery-café operations	$581,193	$498,806	$503,928
Franchise operations	6,679	3,850	5,951
Fresh dough and other product operations at regional facilities	48,393	48,616	50,699
Total segment assets	$636,265	$551,272	$560,578

Source: Company 10-K Report, 2010, pp. 80-81.

those transactions with franchised bakery-cafés. The company classified any operating profit of the regional facilities stemming from supplying fresh dough and other products to company-owned bakery-cafés as a reduction in the cost of food and paper products—the costs of food and paper products for company-operated bakery-cafés are shown in Exhibit 1.

PANERA BREAD'S MANAGEMENT INFORMATION SYSTEMS

Each company-owned bakery-café had programmed point-of-sale registers that collected transaction data used to generate transaction counts, product mix, average check, and other pertinent statistics. The prices of menu selections at all company-owned bakery-cafés were programmed into the point-of-sale registers from the company's data support centers. Franchisees were allowed access to certain of Panera's proprietary bakery-café systems and systems support. Franchisees were responsible for providing the appropriate menu prices, discount rates, and tax rates for system programming.

The company used in-store enterprise application tools to (1) assist café managers in scheduling work hours for café personnel and

controlling food costs, (2) provide corporate and retail operations management quick access to retail data, (3) enable café managers to place on-line orders with distributors, and (4) reduce the time café managers spent on administrative activities. The information collected electronically at café registers was used to generate daily and weekly consolidated reports regarding sales, transaction counts, average check size, product mix, sales trends and other operating metrics, as well as detailed profit and loss statements for company-owned bakery-cafés. This data was incorporated into the company's "exception-based reporting" tools.

Panera's regional facilities had software that accepted electronic orders from bakery-cafés and monitored delivery of the ordered products back to the bakery-cafés. Panera also had developed proprietary digital software to provide online training to employees at bakery-cafés and online baking instructions for the baking personnel at each café.

THE RESTAURANT INDUSTRY IN THE UNITED STATES

According to the National Restaurant Association, total food and drink sales at all types of food service locations in the United States were projected to reach a record $604 billion in 2011, up 3.6 percent over 2010 and up from $379 billion in 2000 and $239 billion in 1990.[9] Of the projected $604 billion in forecasted sales industrywide in 2011, $550.8 billion were expected to occur in commercial establishments of various kinds. The nation's 960,000 eating place establishments were expected to account for $404.5 billion in sales, with the remainder divided among bars and taverns, lodging place restaurants, managed food service locations, and other types of retail, vending, recreational, and mobile operations with food service capability. Quick-service restaurants were expected to grow slightly faster than full-service restaurants and post 2011 sales of about $168 billion, a gain of 3.3 percent over 2010; sales at full-service restaurants were forecast to be $195 billion in 2011, an increase of 3.1 percent over 2010. Within the various commercial establishment segment, the category expected to show the strongest growth in 2011 was catering, with forecasted sales growth of 6.2 percent.

As of April 2011, the operators of fast-casual establishments had reported increases in year-over-year store sales for eight consecutive months. The National Restaurant Association expected the top trends on quick-service menus in 2011 would be healthy options in kids' meals, gluten-free items, spicy items, locally sourced produce, and smoothies.

In 2010, the restaurant industry in the United States added a net of nearly 7,700 establishments, a solid improvement over the 2,600 establishments in 2009 but substantially below the 13,000 new locations added in 2006 and 2007. The full-service segment had a net gain of 3,968 establishments in 2010, after adding just 753 locations in 2009. The quick-service segment added a net 2,973 locations in 2010, nearly double the 1,512 establishments added in 2009. The snack and nonalcoholic beverage bar segment—including coffee, donut, and ice cream shops—added only 162 locations, after expanding by at least 1,000 locations in each of the previous eight years.

Restaurants were the nation's second-largest private employer with 12.8 million employees. While the restaurant industry had shed 366,000 jobs from January 2008 to January 2010 because of the effects of recessionary forces, by May 2011, some 226,000 jobs had been added since January 2010, and the industry was on track to reach prerecession employment levels by early 2012. Nearly half of all adults in the United States had worked in the restaurant industry at some point in their lives, and more than one out of four adults got their first job experience in a restaurant. About 93 percent of all eating-and-drinking place businesses had fewer than 50 employees.

Even though the average U.S. consumer ate 76 percent of meals at home, on a typical day, about 130 million U.S. consumers were food service patrons at an eating establishment—sales at commercial eating places averaged about $1.5 billion daily in 2010. Average household expenditures for food away from home in 2009 were $2,619, equal to about 49 percent of total household expenditures for food and drink in 2010. In 2008, unit sales averaged $862,000 at full-service restaurants and $737,000 at quick-service restaurants; however, very popular restaurant locations achieved annual sales volumes in the $2.5 million to $5 million range. The profitability of a restaurant location ranged from exceptional to good to average to marginal to money-losing.

The restaurant business was labor-intensive, extremely competitive, and risky. Industry members pursued differentiation strategies of one variety of another, seeking to set themselves apart from rivals via pricing, food quality, menu theme, signature menu selections, dining ambience and atmosphere, service, convenience, and location. To further enhance their appeal, some restaurants tried to promote greater customer traffic via happy hours, lunch and dinner specials, children's menus, innovative or trendy dishes, diet-conscious menu selections, and beverage/appetizer specials during televised sporting events (important at restaurants/bars with big-screen TVs). Most restaurants were quick to adapt their menu offerings to changing consumer tastes and eating preferences, frequently featuring heart-healthy, vegetarian, organic, low-calorie, and/or low-carb items on their menus. Research conducted by the Natural Restaurant Industry in 2010–2011 indicated:

- 71 percent of adults were trying to eat healthier at restaurants than they did two years earlier.
- 69 percent of adults were more likely to visit a restaurant that offered locally produced food items.
- 57 percent were more likely to visit a restaurant that offered food that was grown in an organic or environmentally friendly way.

It was the norm at many restaurants to rotate some menu selections seasonally and to periodically introduce creative dishes in an effort to keep regular patrons coming back, attract more patrons, and remain competitive.

Consumers (especially those that ate out often) were prone to give newly opened eating establishments a trial, and if they were pleased with their experience to return, sometimes frequently—loyalty to existing restaurants was low when consumers perceived there were better dining alternatives. It was also common for a once-hot restaurant to lose favor and confront the stark realities of a dwindling clientele, forcing it to either reformat its menu and dining environment or go out of business. Many restaurants had fairly short lives; there were multiple causes for a restaurant's failure—a lack of enthusiasm for the menu or dining experience, inconsistent food quality, poor service, a poor location, meal prices that patrons deemed too high, and being outcompeted by rivals with comparable menu offerings.

PANERA BREAD'S PERFORMANCE IN THE FIRST SIX MONTHS OF 2011

Panera Bread reported strong financial and operating results for the first two quarters of 2011. Highlights for the first 26 weeks of 2011 included the following:

- An 18 percent increase in sales revenues, from $743.3 million to $873.2 million.
- A 30 percent increase in net income, from $52.5 million to $68.5 million.
- A 36 percent increase in diluted earnings per share, from $1.67 to $2.27. (The 39 percent gain in diluted EPS reported for the second quarter of 2011 marked the 12th out of the last 13 quarters that diluted EPS had grown more than 20 percent.)
- Second-quarter sales increases of 4.4 percent at existing company-owned bakery-cafés, 3.6 percent at existing franchise-operated bakery-cafés, and 3.9 percent at bakery-cafés systemwide—all as compared to the second quarter of 2010. First-quarter 2011 sales increases (compared to the first quarter of 2010) averaged 3.3 percent at existing company-owned bakery-cafés, 3.4 percent at existing franchise-operated bakery-cafés, and 3.3 percent at existing bakery-cafés systemwide.
- The 4.4 percent sales increase in company-owned bakery-cafés sales in the second quarter of 2011 was comprised of year-over-year transaction growth of 2.9 percent and average check growth of 1.5 percent.
- Since January 1, 2011, a net of 40 new company-operated and franchised bakery-cafés were opened, boosting the systemwide total to 1,493 locations. Management expected that a net of 100 to 105 new bakery-cafés would be opened in 2011.

In its second-quarter 2011 release, Panera Bread management announced it was raising targeted earnings per diluted share for full-year 2011 to the $4.54 to $4.58 range; if the company met its target, it would generate diluted earnings per share growth of 25 percent to 26 percent in fiscal 2011. Management also said it was lowering its full-year 2011 forecast of average sales growth at existing bakery-café locations to 4.5 percent, chiefly because of weaker economic conditions than previously anticipated.

During the first three weeks of July 2011, Panera Bread's stock price traded between $129.00 and $132.00 per share, up from a closing price of $101.21 on December 31, 2010, and a closing price of $66.94 on December 31, 2009. However, in the days following the release of the company's second-quarter 2011 performance (which happened to coincide with a 3 percent decline in the S&P 500 and the Dow Jones Industrial Average stemming from uncertainties surrounding the Congressional debate over raising the debt ceiling), Panera's stock price dropped sharply and traded in the $112 to $115 range.

Top management at Panera expected to open a net of 100 to 110 new bakery-cafés systemwide, achieve average sales gains of 4 to 5 percent, and grow diluted earnings per share at the low end of its long-term target of 15 to 20 percent in 2012.

ENDNOTES

[1] According to information posted at Panera Bread's website, www.panerabread.com, accessed July 7, 2011.

[2] As stated in a presentation to securities analysts, May 5, 2006.

[3] CEO William Moreton's letter to the stockholders, Panera's *2010 Annual Report*, April 18, 2011.

[4] Ron Ruggless, "Panera Cares: One Year Later," *Nation's Restaurant News*, May 16, 2011, posted at www.nrn.com, accessed July 19, 2011.

[5] Sean Gregory-Clayton, "Sandwich Philanthropy," *Time*, August 2, 2010, posted at www.time.com, accessed July 19, 2011.

[6] As cited in Panera Bread's presentation to securities analysts on May 5, 2006.

[7] Ibid.

[8] Information posted in the franchise section at www.panerabread.com, accessed July 23, 2011.

[9] The statistical data in this section is based on information posted at www.restaurant.org, accessed July 26, 2011.

APPLE INC. IN 2011: CAN IT PROSPER WITHOUT STEVE JOBS?

John E. Gamble
University of South Alabama

Lou Marino
The University of Alabama

Despite the effects of ongoing poor economic conditions in the United States, Apple Inc. celebrated record quarterly revenues and profits during its third quarter of 2011, which resulted in its stock price catapulting to a level that made it the world's most valuable company as measured by market capitalization. The record growth in revenues and profits came primarily from volume increases in the sale of iPhones and iPads, which increased by 142 percent and 183 percent, respectively, from the same period in 2010. The sales of Mac computers increased by 14 percent from the third quarter of 2010 to reach a record 3.95 million units. The only sales disappointment for the company was a 20 percent year-over-year decline in iPod sales. The company sold 7.54 million iPods during the third quarter of 2011 compared to 9.41 million units during the third quarter of 2010.

However, the excitement generated by news of Apple's record third quarter performance would soon be replaced by deep sadness among many as they would learn of Steve Jobs' illness-forced resignation in late-August and then his death on October 5, 2011. Steve Jobs had battled a variety of health issues including pancreatic cancer since 2004 and had taken medical leaves of absence from his CEO position in 2004, 2009, and earlier in 2011, but despite his absence, he had been able to provide inspiration for the company's hottest new products such as the iPhone, iPad, and iPod.

During all three medical leaves, Apple's chief operating officer, Tim Cook, took the helm of the company. He oversaw the successful launch of the company's most successful new products while also revamping the company's supply chain and improving overall operating efficiency. Tim Cook's successful performance during Steve Jobs' absences led to his appointment as successor to Jobs as CEO of Apple Inc.

But many challenges faced the new CEO and his chief managers as the company approached the end of 2011. Analysts were concerned with the general decline in iPod unit sales and worried that Apple might have to struggle to sustain its growth in the smartphone market. Continuing growth in iPhone sales was critical to the company's financial performance, since iPhone sales accounted for $13.3 billion of the company's third-quarter 2011 revenues of $28.6 billion. Apple's iPad tablet computers were the company's second-largest contributor to total revenues with sales of more than $6 billion during the third quarter of 2011.

The company's success in smartphones and tablet computers had not gone unnoticed, with Google announcing in August 2011 its intention to enter the market for smartphone handsets and tablet computers through a planned $12.5 billion acquisition of Motorola Mobility.

Google's Android was the number-one smartphone platform in 2011, which would allow it to quickly begin production of smartphones and tablet computers running on the Android operating system. Also in late 2011, Research in Motion (the producer of BlackBerry smartphones and tablet computers), Nokia, Samsung, and HTC were introducing new models equipped with more powerful microprocessors and improved operating systems that might surpass the capabilities of the iPhone and iPad. Dell, HP, Acer, and other computer manufacturers were also rolling out new tablet computers to compete against the iPad. With competitive rivalry heating up and technological change accelerating, Apple's new managers would be forced to work creatively and expeditiously to sustain the company's success achieved under Steve Jobs.

STEVE JOBS' STRATEGIC LEADERSHIP AT APPLE

Stephen Wozniak and Steve Jobs founded Apple Computer in 1976 when they began selling a crudely designed personal computer called the Apple I to Silicon Valley computer enthusiasts. Two years later, the partners introduced the first mass-produced personal computer (PC), the Apple II, which eventually sold more than 10,000 units. While the Apple II was relatively successful, the next revision of the product line, the Macintosh (Mac), would dramatically change personal computing through its user-friendly graphical user interface (GUI), which allowed users to interact with screen images rather than merely type text commands.

The Macintosh that was introduced in 1984 was hailed as a breakthrough in personal computing, but it did not have the speed, power, or software availability to compete with the PC that IBM had introduced in 1981. One of the reasons the Macintosh lacked the necessary software was that Apple put very strict restrictions on the Apple Certified Developer Program, which made it difficult for software developers to obtain Macs at a discount and receive informational materials about the operating system.

With the Mac faring poorly in the market, founder Steve Jobs became highly critical of the company's president and CEO, John Sculley, who had been hired by the board in 1983. Finally, in 1985, as Sculley was preparing to visit China, Jobs devised a boardroom coup to replace him. Sculley found out about the plan and canceled his trip. After Apple's board voted unanimously to keep Sculley in his position, Jobs, who was retained as chairman of the company but stripped of all decision-making authority, soon resigned. During the remainder of 1985, Apple continued to encounter problems and laid off one-fifth of its employees while posting its first ever quarterly loss.

Despite these setbacks, Apple kept bringing innovative products to the market, while closely guarding the secrets behind its technology. In 1987, Apple released a revamped Macintosh computer that proved to be a favorite in K–12 schools and with graphic artists and other users needing excellent graphics capabilities. However, by 1990, PCs running Windows 3.0 and Word for Windows were preferred by businesses and consumers and held a commanding 97+ percent share of the market for personal computers.

In 1991, Apple released its first-generation notebook computer, the PowerBook, and, in 1993, Apple's board of directors opted to remove Sculley from the position of CEO. The board chose to place the chief operating officer, Michael Spindler, in the vacated spot. Under Spindler, Apple released the PowerMac family of PCs in 1994, the first Macs to incorporate the PowerPC chip, a very fast processor co-developed with Motorola and IBM. Even though the PowerMac family received excellent reviews by technology analysts, Microsoft's Windows 95 matched many of the capabilities of the Mac OS and prevented the PowerMac from gaining significant market share. In January 1996, Apple asked Spindler to resign and chose Gil Amelio, former president of National Semiconductor, to take his place.

During his first 100 days in office, Amelio announced many sweeping changes for the company. He split Apple into seven distinct divisions, each responsible for its own profit or loss, and he tried to better inform the developers and consumers of Apple's products and projects. Amelio acquired NeXT, the company Steve Jobs had founded upon his resignation from Apple in 1985. Steve Jobs was rehired by Apple as part of the acquisition. In 1997, after recording additional quarterly losses, Apple's board terminated Amelio's employment with the company and named Steve Jobs interim CEO.

Under Jobs' leadership, Apple introduced the limited feature iMac in 1998 and the company's iBook line of notebook computers in 1999. The company was profitable in every quarter during 1998 and 1999, and its share price reached an all-time high in the upper $70 range. Jobs was named permanent CEO of Apple in 2000 and, in 2001, oversaw the release of the iPod. The iPod recorded modest sales until the 2003 launch of iTunes—the online retail store where consumers could legally purchase individual songs. By July 2004, 100 million songs had been sold and iTunes had a 70 percent market share among all legal online music download services. The tremendous success of the iPod helped transform Apple from a struggling computer company into a powerful consumer electronics company.

By 2005, consumers' satisfaction with the iPod had helped renew interest in Apple computers, with its market share in personal computers growing from a negligible share to 4 percent. The company also exploited consumer loyalty and satisfaction with the iPod to enter the market for smartphones with the 2007 launch of the iPhone. The brand loyalty developed through the first iPod, and then the iPhone, made the company's 2010 launch of the iPad a roaring success with 3.3 million units sold during its first three months on the market. Much of Apple's turnaround could be credited to Steve Jobs, who had idea after idea for how to improve the company and turn its performance around. He not only consistently pushed for innovative new ideas and products but also enforced several structural changes, including ridding the company of unprofitable segments and divisions.

The success of the turnaround could also be attributed to the efforts of Tim Cook, Apple's chief operating officer, who oversaw the company's operations at various times between 2004 and 2011. Tim Cook was first asked to act as the company's chief manager in 2004 when Steve Jobs was recovering from pancreatic cancer surgery, later in 2009 when Jobs took a six-month medical leave for a liver transplant, and again in early 2011 when Jobs left the company for another medical leave. Analysts and key Apple managers viewed Cook as an "operational genius" who was responsible for overhauling Apple's supply chain system and transforming it into one of the lowest cost electronics manufacturers.[1] Prior to coming to Apple in 1998, Tim Cook was a rising star among Compaq Computer's management team.

A summary of Apple's financial performance for fiscal years 2006 through 2010 is provided in Exhibit 1. The company's net sales by operating segment and product line and unit sales by product line for 2008 through 2010 are provided in Exhibit 2.

▶ **EXHIBIT 1**

Summary of Apple Inc.'s Financial Performance, 2006–2010 ($ millions, except share amounts)					
	2010	**2009**	**2008**	**2007**	**2006**
Net sales	$65,225	$42,905	$37,491	$24,006	$19,315
Costs and expenses					
Cost of sales	39,541	25,683	24,294	15,852	13,717
Research and development	1,782	1,333	1,109	782	712
Selling, general and administrative	5,517	4,149	3,761	2,963	2,433
Total operating expenses	$ 7,299	$ 5,482	$ 4,870	$ 3,745	$ 3,145

(continued)

EXHIBIT 1 *(concluded)*

	2010	2009	2008	2007	2006
Operating income	$18,385	$11,740	$8,327	$4,409	$2,453
Other income and expenses	155	326	620	599	365
Income before provision for income taxes	18,540	12,066	8,947	5,008	2,818
Provision for income taxes	4,527	3,831	2,828	1,512	829
Net income	$14,013	$8,235	$6,119	$3,496	$1,989
Earnings per common share:					
Basic	$15.41	$9.22	$6.94	$4.04	$2.36
Diluted	15.15	9.00	6.78	3.93	2.27
Cash dividends declared per common share	0.00	0.00	0.00	0.00	0.00
Shares used in computing earnings per share:					
Basic	909,461	893,016	881,592	864,595	844,058
Diluted	924,712	907,005	902,139	889,292	877,526
Total cash, cash equivalents, and marketable securities	$ 51,011	$ 33,992	$ 24,490	$ 15,386	$ 10,110
Total assets	75,183	47,501	36,171	24,878	17,205
Total long-term obligations	5,531	3,502	1,745	687	395
Total liabilities	27,392	15,861	13,874	10,347	7,221
Total shareholders' equity	47,791	31,640	22,297	14,531	9,984

Sources: Apple Inc., 2008 and 2010 10-K reports.

EXHIBIT 2

Apple Inc.'s Net Sales by Operating Segment, Net Sales by Product, and Unit Sales by Product, 2008–2010 ($ in millions)

	2010	Change(%)	2009	Change(%)	2008
Net Sales by Operating Segment:					
Americas net sales	$24,498	29%	$18,981	15%	$16,552
Europe net sales	18,692	58	11,810	28	9,233
Japan net sales	3,981	75	2,279	32	1,728
Asia-Pacific net sales	8,256	160	3,179	18	2,686
Retail net sales	9,798	47	6,656	-9	7,292
Total net sales	$65,225	52%	$42,905	14%	$37,491
Mac Unit Sales by Operating Segment:					
Americas Mac unit sales	$ 4,976	21%	$ 4,120	4%	$ 3,980
Europe Mac unit sales	3,859	36	2,840	13	2,519
Japan Mac unit sales	481	22	395	2	389
Asia-Pacific Mac unit sales	1,500	62	926	17	793
Retail Mac unit sales	2,846	35%	2,115	4%	2,034
Total Mac unit sales	$13,662	31%	$10,396	7%	$ 9,715

(continued)

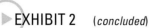

► EXHIBIT 2 *(concluded)*

	2010	Change(%)	2009	Change(%)	2008
Net Sales by Product:					
Desktops [a]	$ 6,201	43%	$ 4,324	-23%	$ 5,622
Portables [b]	11,278	18	9,535	9	8,732
Total Mac net sales	$17,479	26%	$13,859	-3%	$14,354
iPod	8,274	2	8,091	-12	9,153
Other music-related products and services [c]	4,948	23	4,036	21	3,340
iPhone and related products and services [d]	25,179	93	13,033	93	6,742
iPad and related products and services [e]	4,958	n.m.	0	n.m.	0
Peripherals and other hardware [f]	1,814	23	1,475	-13	1,694
Software, service and other sales [g]	2,573	7	2,411	9	2,208
Total net sales	$65,225	52%	$42,905	14%	$37,491
Unit Sales by Product:					
Desktops [a]	4,627	45%	3,182	-14%	3,712
Portables [b]	9,035	25	7,214	20	6,003
Total Mac unit sales	13,662	31%	10,396	7%	9,715
Net sales per Mac unit sold [h]	$ 1,279	-4	$ 1,333	-10	$ 1,478
iPod unit sales	50,312	-7	54,132	-1	54,828
Net sales per iPod unit sold [h]	$ 164	10	$ 149	-11	$ 167
iPhone units sold	39,989	93	20,731	78	11,627
iPad units sold	7,458	n.m.	0	n.m.	0

n.m.: Not meaningful

[a]Includes iMac, Mac mini, Mac Pro, and Xserve product lines.

[b]Includes MacBook, MacBook Pro, iBook, and PowerBook product lines.

[c]Consists of iTunes Store sales, iPod services, and Apple-branded and third-party iPod accessories.

[d]Includes revenue recognized from iPhone sales, carrier agreements, and Apple-branded and third-party iPhone accessories.

[e]Includes revenue recognized from iPad sales, services and Apple-branded and third-party iPad accessories.

[f]Includes sales of displays, wireless connectivity and networking solutions, and other hardware accessories.

[g]Includes sales of Apple-branded operating system and application software, third-party software, Mac and Internet services.

[h]Derived by dividing total product-related net sales by total product-related unit sales.

Source: Apple Inc., 2010 10-K report.

OVERVIEW OF THE PERSONAL COMPUTER INDUSTRY

The personal computer industry was relatively consolidated, with five sellers accounting for 77.3 percent of the U.S. shipments and 59.7 percent of worldwide shipments in 2010 (see Exhibit 3). Prior to the onset of the recession that began in 2008, the PC industry was expected to grow at a rate of 5–6 percent, to reach $354 billion by 2012. However, the effects of the recession caused a dramatic decline in industry revenues in 2008 and 2009.

PC industry shipments grew by 13.6 percent during 2010 as businesses were forced to replace aging computers and demand in some developing countries accelerated. However, worldwide PC shipments declined by 3.2 percent

▲ EXHIBIT 3

U.S. and Global Market Shares of Leading PC Vendors, 2000 and 2006–2010

A. U.S. Market Shares of the Leading PC Vendors, 2000 and 2006–2010

2010 Rank	Vendor	2010 Shipments (in 000s)	2010 Market Share	2009 Shipments (in 000s)	2009 Market Share	2008 Shipments (in 000s)	2008 Market Share	2007 Shipments (in 000s)	2007 Market Share	2006 Shipments (in 000s)	2006 Market Share	2000 Shipments (in 000s)	2000 Market Share
1	Hewlett-Packard[1]	19,488	25.9%	18,781	26.9%	16,218	24.7%	16,759	23.9%	11,600	21.5%	5,630	11.5%
2	Dell	17,352	23.1	17,099	24.5	19,276	29.4	19,645	28.0	20,472	31.2	9,645	19.7
	Compaq[1]	—	—	—	—	—	—	—	—	—	—	7,761	15.9
3	Acer[2]	8,012	10.7	7,983	11.4	6,106	9.3	3,880	5.5	1,421	2.2	n.a.	n.a.
4	Toshiba	6,624	8.8	5,379	7.7	3,788	5.8	3,509	5.0	2,843	4.3	n.a.	n.a.
5	Apple	6,586	8.8	5,579	8.0	5,158	7.9	4,081	5.8	3,109	4.7	n.a.	n.a.
	Others	17,038	22.7	15,008	21.5	15,026	22.9	22,235	31.7	23,350	35.7	18,959	38.8
	All vendors	75,101	100.0%	69,829	100.0%	65,571	100.0%	70,088	100.0%	65,481	100.0%	48,900	100.0%

(continued)

▲ EXHIBIT 3 *(concluded)*

B. Worldwide Market Shares of the Leading PC Vendors, 2000 and 2006–2010

2010 Rank	Vendor	2010 Shipments (in 000s)	2010 Market Share	2009 Shipments (in 000s)	2009 Market Share	2008 Shipments (in 000s)	2008 Market Share	2007 Shipments (in 000s)	2007 Market Share	2006 Shipments (in 000s)	2006 Market Share	2000 Shipments (in 000s)	2000 Market Share
1	Hewlett-Packard[1]	64,213	18.5%	59,942	20.3%	54,293	18.9%	50,526	18.8%	38,838	16.5%	10,327	7.4%
2	Dell	43,403	12.5	38,416	13.1	42,388	14.7	39,993	14.9	39,094	16.6	14,801	10.6
	Compaq[1]	—	—	—	—	—	—	—	—	—	—	17,399	12.5
3	Acer[2]	42,430	12.3	38,377	13.0	31,377	13.0	21,206	7.9	13,594	5.8	n.a.	n.a.
4	Lenovo/IBM[3]	34,182	9.9	24,887	8.5	21,870	7.6	20,224	7.5	16,609	7.1	9,308	6.7
5	Toshiba	19,095	5.5	15,878	5.4	13,727	4.8	10,936	4.1	9,292	3.9	n.a.	n.a.
	Others	142,874	41.3	116,709	39.7	123,910	43.1	126,075	46.9	117,971	50.1	80,640	5.8%
	All vendors	346,198	100.0%	294,208	100.0%	287,566	100.0%	268,960	100.0%	235,397	100.0%	139,057	100.0%

n.a. = not available; sales and market shares for these companies in the years where *n.a.* appears are included in the "Others" category because the company was not in the top 5 in shipments or market share.

[1]Compaq was acquired by Hewlett-Packard in May 2002.

[2]Acer acquired Gateway in 2007 and Packard Bell in 2008. Data for Acer includes shipments for Gateway starting in Q4 2007 and shipments for Packard Bell starting in Q1 2008, and only Acer data for prior periods.

[3]Lenovo, a Chinese computer company, completed the acquisition of IBM's PC business in 2005. The numbers for Lenovo/IBM for 2000 reflect sales of IBM branded PCs only; the numbers for 2005–2009 reflect their combined sales beginning in the second quarter of 2005. In 2007, Lenovo rebranded all IBM PCs as Lenovo.

Sources: International Data Corp.

during the first quarter of 2011, with the steepest declines occurring in the United States and Japan. Modest single-digit growth in emerging markets allowed China to become the world's largest market for PCs during the second quarter of 2011. The United States was expected to remain the largest global market for PCs for the entire 2011 calendar year.

The poor growth in worldwide PC shipments was attributable to poor economic conditions in the United States and many other countries, a lack of compelling new PC applications, and the rise in popularity of tablet computers. Tablet computers, such as the iPad, had yet to become widely adopted by businesses, but were commonly becoming replacements for laptops and PCs among consumers. The market for tablet computers was expected to increase from 17 million units in 2010 to an estimated 44 million to 50 million units in 2011 to 77 million to 100 million units in 2012.

APPLE'S COMPETITIVE POSITION IN THE PERSONAL COMPUTER INDUSTRY

Apple's proprietary operating system and strong graphics-handling capabilities differentiated Macs from PCs, but many consumers and business users who owned PCs were hesitant to purchase a Mac because of Apple's premium pricing and because of the learning curve involved with mastering its proprietary operating system. The company's market share in the United States had improved from 4.7 percent in 2006 to 8.8 percent in 2010 primarily because of the success of the iPod and iPhone. These products created a halo effect whereby some consumers (but not business users) switched to Apple computers after purchasing an iPod or iPhone.

Apple's computer product line consisted of several models in various configurations. Its desktop lines included the Mac Pro (aimed at professional and business users); the iMac (targeted toward consumer, educational, and business use); and Mac mini (made specifically for consumer use). Apple had two notebook product lines: MacBook Pro (for professional and advanced consumer users) and MacBook Air (designed for education users and consumers). All Apple computers were priced at a steep premium compared to PCs and laptops offered by Dell, HP, and other rivals. In September 2011, Mac Pro pricing started at $2,499, iMac and MacBook Pro pricing began at $1,199, the MacBook Air was offered from $999, and Mac mini pricing started at $599.

APPLE'S ENTRY INTO THE MARKET FOR TABLET COMPUTERS

Apple entered the market for tablet computers with its April 3, 2010, launch of the iPad. Tablet computers had been on the market since the late 1990s, but only Apple's version had gained any significant interest from consumers and business users. Previous-generation tablet computers required the use of a stylus to launch applications and enter information. Most users found the stylus interface to be an annoyance and preferred to use a smartphone or laptop when portability was required. Dell, Acer, Hewlett-Packard, and RIM had all raced to get touch-screen tablet computers to market but were unable to do so until very late 2010 and early 2011 because of the technological differences between tablet computers and PCs. Tablet computers were technologically similar to smartphones and shared almost no components with PCs. HP acquired Palm for $1.2 billion in May 2010 to accelerate its entry into tablet computers. By year-end 2010, Apple had sold more than 14 million iPads and held an 85 percent share of the market for tablet computers.

Intel's Atom microprocessor and Microsoft's Windows Phone 7 were both launched in 2010 and were suitable for use in tablet computers. Some PC manufacturers chose to utilize smartphone microprocessors and Google's Android operating system in their tablet computer models. Apple's iPad 2 that was launched in

March 2011 contained a dual-core processor that was far more powerful than the first-generation iPad and most competing tablet computers. The iPad 3, planned for an October 2011 launch, would utilize the iPad 2's dual-core processor, but would feature an ultra-high-resolution 9.7-inch display. E-readers such as Amazon's Kindle were not considered direct competitors to the iPad since dedicated reading devices could not browse the Internet, view videos, play music, or perform other media tasks.

APPLE'S RIVALS IN THE PERSONAL COMPUTER INDUSTRY

Hewlett-Packard

Hewlett-Packard (HP) was broadly diversified across segments of the computer industry with business divisions focused on information technology consulting services, large enterprise systems, software, personal computers, printers and other imaging devices, and financial services. The company's Personal Systems Group (PSG), which manufactured and marketed HP and Compaq desktop computers and portable computers, was its largest division, accounting for revenues of $40.7 billion in 2010. HP recorded total net revenues of $126 billion in 2010, with information technology services

contributing $34.9 billion, imaging and printing devices contributing nearly $25.8 billion, and enterprise systems accounting for about $18.7 billion. The company's software business units accounted for sales of nearly $3.6 billion and its financial services unit contributed net revenue of about $3 billion in 2010.

HP's sales of personal computers declined by 16.5 percent between 2008 and 2009 as the recession forced consumers and businesses to reduce expenditures and capital investments. Handheld computers and workstations were affected most by the recession, with sales declining by 52.2 percent and 33.7 percent, respectively, during 2009. The company's sales of desktop computers were affected not only by the recession but also by business users' and consumers' growing preference for portable computers over desktop models. HP portable computers were harmed least by the recession, with a 10.8 percent decline in sales between 2008 and 2009. HP did sustain some growth in emerging markets despite the recession in developed countries. The company's sales of personal computers improved by 15.4 percent in 2010 as businesses upgraded desktop computers and workstations and as consumers replaced home desktop PCs with laptops. In 2011, HP was considering the divestiture of its Personal Systems Group because of the division's weak operating profit margins relative to its other business units. Exhibit 4 provides the

▶ EXHIBIT 4

Hewlett-Packard Personal Systems Group, Net Revenue ($ millions)					
Product	**2010**	**2009**	**2008**	**2007**	**2006**
Notebooks	$22,545	$20,210	$22,657	$17,650	$12,005
Desktop PCs	15,478	12,864	16,626	15,889	14,641
Workstations	1,786	1,261	1,902	1,721	1,368
Handhelds	87	172	360	531	650
Other	845	798	750	618	502
Total	$40,741	$35,305	$42,295	$36,409	$29,166

Sources: Hewlett-Packard, 2007 and 2010 10-K reports.

revenue contribution by PSG product line for 2006 through 2010.

Dell Inc.

Dell Inc. was the world's second-largest seller of personal computers, with revenues of about $61.59 billion for the fiscal year ending January 28, 2011. Exhibit 5 presents Dell's revenues by product category for fiscal 2009 through fiscal 2011. The recession significantly affected Dell's financial performance, with its revenues declining from $61.1 billion in fiscal 2008 to $52.9 billion in fiscal 2010. The revenue decline was a result of an overall decline in unit sales and strong price competition in both desktop PCs and portables. In addition, Dell's net earnings fell from $2.9 billion in fiscal 2008 to $2.5 billion in fiscal 2009 to $1.4 billion in fiscal 2010. In fiscal 2011, the company's revenues and net income had improved to $61.5 billion and $2.6 billion, respectively, as the technology sector of the economy began to improve. The company offered a wide range of desktop computers and portables, ranging from low-end, low-priced models to state-of-the-art, high-priced models. The company also offered servers; workstations; peripherals such as printers, monitors, and projectors; and Wi-Fi products. Dell also offered an Android-based Streak tablet computer line and a Windows Phone 7 smartphone in 2011.

Acer

Taiwan-based Acer was the world's second-largest portable computer and desktop computer manufacturer in 2011. Acer's 2010 consolidated revenues rose by approximately 10 percent from the previous year to reach $19.9 billion, while operating income increased by 18.7 percent to reach $575 million. Its 32.9 percent annual growth in global PC shipments between 2006 and 2010 ranked first among the industry's leading sellers. The company's largest and one of its fastest-growing geographic segments was the Europe/Middle East/Africa segment, which accounted for 50 percent of the company's PC, desktop, and notebook sales. A summary of the company's financial performance between 2006 and 2010 is presented in Exhibit 6.

Acer's multibrand strategy—which positioned Acer, Gateway, eMachines, and Packard Bell at distinct price points in the market for PCs—had helped it become one of the fastest-growing vendors in the United States. The company based its competitive strategy on its four pillars of success: a winning business model, competitive products, an innovative marketing strategy, and an efficient operation model.

▶EXHIBIT 5

Dell's Revenues by Product Category, Fiscal 2008–Fiscal 2011 ($ millions)

FISCAL YEAR ENDED:	JANUARY 28, 2011		JANUARY 29, 2010		JANUARY 30, 2009	
	Dollars	% of Revenue	Dollars	% of Revenue	Dollars	% of Revenue
Servers and networking	$ 7,609	12%	$ 6,032	11%	$ 6,512	11%
Storage	2,295	4	2,192	4	2,667	4
Services	7,673	12	5,622	11	5,351	9
Software and peripherals	10,26	17	9,499	18	10,603	17
Mobility	18,971	31	16,610	31	18,604	30
Desktop PCs	14,685	24	12,947	25	17,364	29
Total net revenue	$61,494	100%	$52,902	100%	$61,101	100%

Source: Dell Inc., 2011 10-K report.

▶ EXHIBIT 6

Financial Summary for Acer Incorporated, 2006–2010 ($ thousands)					
	2010	**2009**	**2008**	**2007**	**2006**
Revenue	$21,594,884	$18,264,125	$16,186,102	$15,252,801	$10,577,113
Gross profit	2,213,569	1,855,993	1,697,374	1,565,278	1,150,865
Operating income	624,920	488,102	416,962	336,211	224,993
Operating margin	2.9%	2.7%	2.6%	2.2%	2.1%
Income before income taxes	663,556	476,759	438,723	498,736	408,481
Net income	$ 518,989	$ 361,248	$ 347,919	$ 427,774	$ 308,080

Sources: Acer Incorporated 2010 Annual Report; and Acer Incorporated Financial Snapshot, www.acer-group.com/public/Investor_Relations/financial_snapshot.htm.

The company's computer offering included desktop and mobile PCs, LCD monitors, servers and storage, and high-definition TVs and projectors. In 2009, the company entered the market for smartphones with the launch of its Liquid line of stylish, high-end smartphones, which used Google's Android operating system. The company's tablet computer line introduced in 2011 also used the Android platform.

APPLE'S COMPETITIVE POSITION IN THE PERSONAL MEDIA PLAYER INDUSTRY

Although Apple didn't introduce the first portable digital music player, the company held a 73 percent market share for digital music players in 2010, and the name iPod had become a generic term used to describe digital media players. When Apple launched its first iPod, many critics did not give the product much of a chance for success, given its fairly hefty price tag of $399. However, the iPod's sleek styling, ease of use, and eventual price decreases allowed it to develop such high levels of customer satisfaction and loyalty that rivals found it difficult to gain traction in the marketplace.

The most popular portable players in 2011 not only played music but also could be connected to Wi-Fi networks to play videos, access the Internet, view photos, or listen to FM high-definition radio. The iPod Touch was the best-selling media player in 2011, but electronics sector reviewers generally agreed that Microsoft's Zune, Archos's Vision models, and Sony's X-series media players compared quite favorably to the iPod Touch. In addition, electronics reviewers found that inexpensive MP3 music players offered by SanDisk, Creative, iRiver, and others generally performed as well as Apple's more basic iPod models. However, none of Apple's key rivals in the media player industry had been able to achieve a market share greater than 5 percent in 2010. Most consumers did not find many convincing reasons to consider any brand of media player other than Apple.

In 2011, Apple offered four basic styles in the iPod product line: the iPod shuffle, iPod nano, iPod Touch, and iPod classic. Apple also sold an Apple TV device that would allow users to play iPod content, including HD movies and television programming purchased at iTunes on their televisions. The Apple TV device also allowed users to watch streaming movies and other content provided by Netflix, YouTube, or other Internet sources.

ITUNES

Aside from the iPod's stylish design and ease of use, another factor that contributed to the popularity of the iPod was Apple's iPod/iTunes combination. In 2011, more than 50 million customers visited the iTunes Store to purchase and download music, videos, movies, and television shows that could be played on iPods, iPhones, or Apple TV devices. Also in 2010, Apple's iTunes Store recorded its 10 billionth download since its launch in 2003. Additionally, iTunes was the world's most popular online movie store, with customers purchasing and renting more than 50,000 movies each day.

The success of the iPod/iTunes combination gave iTunes a 69 percent share of the U.S. digital music market in 2010. Since downloads accounted for about 40 percent of all music sales in the United States, iTunes' commanding share of the digital music sales also gave it a 27 percent share of total U.S. music sales. Amazon.com was the second-largest seller of digital music in the United States, with an 8 percent share of the market. Amazon.com and Walmart were tied for second in total U.S. music sales, with 12 percent market shares.

APPLE'S COMPETITIVE POSITION IN THE MARKET FOR SMARTPHONES

The first version of the iPhone was released on June 29, 2007, and had a multitouch screen with a virtual keyboard, a camera, and a portable media player (equivalent to the iPod) in addition to text messaging and visual voice mail. It also offered Internet services including e-mail, Web browsing (using access to Apple's Safari Web browser), and local Wi-Fi connectivity. More than 270,000 first-generation iPhones were sold during the first 30 hours of the product's launch. The iPhone was named *Time* magazine's Invention of the Year in 2007.

The iPhone 3G was released in 70 countries on July 11, 2008, and was available in the United States exclusively through AT&T Mobility. The iPhone 3G combined the functionality of a wireless phone and an iPod, and allowed users to access the Internet wirelessly at twice the speed of the previous version of the iPhone.

Apple's new phone also featured a built-in global positioning system (GPS) and, in an effort to increase adoption by corporate users, was compatible with Microsoft Exchange.

The iPhone 3GS was introduced on June 19, 2009, and included all of the features of the iPhone 3G but could also launch applications and render Web pages twice as fast as the iPhone 3G. The iPhone 4 was launched on June 24, 2010, with the 16 GB model priced at $199 on a two-year AT&T contract and the 32 GB model priced at $299 on a two-year AT&T contract. Upgrades over the 3GS included video-calling capabilities (only over a Wi-Fi network), a higher resolution display, a 5-megapixel camera including flash and zoom, 720p video recording, a longer-lasting battery, and a gyroscopic motion sensor to enable an improved gaming experience. The iPhone 4 sold more than 1.7 million units within three days of its launch. In 2010, Apple expanded its carrier network beyond AT&T to include Verizon. The iPhone 5 would be available for AT&T and Verizon subscribers as well as Sprint mobile phone customers. The iPhone 5 was set for an October 2011 launch.

APP STORE

Like the iPod/iTunes combination, the 425,000 iPhone applications and 100,000 iPad applications available at Apple's App Store helped the company build strong competitive positions in the markets for smartphones and tablet computers. In 2011, more than 15 billion iPhone and iPad apps had been downloaded from the App Store. Third-party developers had earned more than $2.5 billion from the sale of their applications at the App Store since the site's launch in 2007. Users of Apple's iPods, iPhones, iPads, or Macs could also use the company's iMatch or iCloud services that integrated apps, iBooks, and iTunes purchased at the App Store to all devices owned by the individual. The iCloud service also allowed users to share calendars and contacts, wirelessly push photographs to all devices, and back up data from Apple devices.

DEMAND AND COMPETITION IN THE SMARTPHONE MARKET

Worldwide shipments of mobile phones increased from 1.19 billion units in 2008 to 1.36 billion units in 2010, with smartphones accounting for much of the growth in shipments. The shipments of smartphones increased by 74 percent between the second quarter of 2010 to the second quarter of 2011, while shipments of all mobile phones increased by 16.5 percent between the second quarter of 2010 and the second quarter of 2011. Smartphones accounted for 25 percent of all mobile phone shipments in August 2011.

Developing countries such as China offered the greatest growth opportunities but also presented challenges to smartphone producers. For example, there were 700 million mobile phone users in China, but popular-selling models were quickly counterfeited, it was difficult to develop keyboards that included the thousands of commonly used characters in the Chinese language, and most consumers preferred inexpensive feature phones over smartphones. Nevertheless, many analysts expected China to account for 10 percent of worldwide smartphone shipments within the near term. Apple began selling the iPhone 4 in China in 2010 through its partnership with China Telecom, the country's second-largest wireless provider and its network of 25 flagship stores located in the country's largest cities. The iPhone was available in 100 countries in 2011.

With the market for smartphones growing rapidly and supporting high average selling prices, competition was becoming more heated. Google's entry into the market with its Android operating system had allowed vendors such as HTC, Motorola, Acer, and Samsung to offer models that matched many of the features of the iPhone. In addition, Microsoft's Windows Phone 7 features compared favorably to the capabilities of the iPhone operating system with live tiles of rotating pictures, e-mail messages, and social-networking feeds. While iPhones and Android phones primarily targeted consumers enthralled with clever and helpful Web apps, RIM had built its position in the smartphone market by appealing to businesspeople who needed the ability to check e-mail; maintain appointment calendars; receive fax transmissions; and open, edit, and save Microsoft Office and Adobe PDF files. In August 2011, Android was the leading smartphone platform followed by the iPhone, RIM's BlackBerry, and

▶ EXHIBIT 7

Top Five Worldwide Smartphone Vendors, Shipment Volumes and Market Shares, 2009 to Second Quarter 2011

Q2 2011 Rank	Vendor	Q2 2011		2010		2009	
		Shipments (in millions)	Market Share	Shipments (in millions)	Market Share	Shipments (in millions)	Market Share
1	Apple	20.3	19.1%	47.5	15.7%	25.1	14.5%
2	Samsung	17.3	16.2	23.0	7.6	5.5	3.2
3	Nokia	16.7	15.7	100.3	33.1	67.7	39.0
4	Research in Motion	12.4	11.6	48.8	16.1	34.5	19.9
5	HTC	11.7	11.0	21.5	7.1	8.1	4.7
	Others	28.1	26.4	61.5	20.3	32.6	18.8
	All vendors	106.5	100.0%	302.6	100.0%	173.5	100.0%

Source: International Data Corporation Worldwide Mobile Phone Tracker, January 27, 2011, August 4, 2011.

Windows Phone 7. The success of Android and the iPhone in the market for smartphones came largely at the expense of Nokia and BlackBerry, which had seen substantial market share erosion since 2009. Android's quick rise to the top spot among smartphone platforms led to the August 2011 announcement by Google that the company would enter the handset segment of the smartphone industry and the tablet computer business through the $12.5 billion acquisition of Motorola Mobility. Exhibit 7 presents shipments and market shares for the leading smartphone producers between 2009 and the second quarter of 2011.

APPLE'S PERFORMANCE GOING INTO THE FOURTH QUARTER OF 2011

Apple set a number of records with its third-quarter 2011 performance. The company's quarterly revenue of $28.6 billion was its highest-ever quarterly sales figure, and the company set a new record for quarterly shipments of computers, with 3.95 million Macs shipped during the quarter. The company also sold 9.25 million iPads and 20.34 million iPhones during the third quarter of 2011, which were also quarterly sales records. Unit sales for the iPod fell to 7.54 million, which was a 20 percent decline from the third quarter of 2010.

The biggest concerns for the company going into the fourth quarter of 2011 were how the loss of Steve Jobs would affect the company's strategy and performance and how Google's entry into the market for smartphone handsets and tablet computers would impact the company's sales of iPhones and iPads. Clearly, iPad sales and iPhone sales were the largest contributors to the company's record third-quarter 2011 performance and its August 11, 2011, standing as the world's most valuable company in terms of market capitalization. Jobs was widely recognized as the visionary force behind the development of the iPod, iPhone, and iPad and there was little doubt that Google intended to exploit its status as the number-one smartphone platform to build a commanding share in the market for smartphones and tablet computers. Also, RIM, Nokia, HTC, and Samsung were making moves to recapture market share lost to the iPhone, and Dell, HP, Acer, and others were intent on capturing significant shares of the tablet computer market.

ENDNOTES

[1] Yukari Iwatani Kane and Nick Wingfield, "Apple's Deep Bench Faces Challenges," *Wall Street Journal Online*, August 24, 2011.

GOOGLE'S STRATEGY IN 2011

John E. Gamble
University of South Alabama

Google was the leading Internet search firm in 2011, with 65 percent market shares in both searches performed on computers and searches performed on mobile devices. Google's business model allowed advertisers to bid on search terms that would describe their product or service on a cost-per-impression (CPI) or cost-per-click (CPC) basis. Google's search-based ads were displayed near Google's search results and generated advertising revenues of more than $28.2 billion in 2010. The company also generated revenues of about $1.1 billion in 2010 from licensing fees charged to businesses that wished to install Google's search appliance on company intranets and from a variety of new ventures. New ventures were becoming a growing priority with Google management since the company dominated the market for search-based ads and sought additional opportunities to sustain its extraordinary growth in revenues, earnings, and net cash provided by operations.

In 2008, Google had launched its Android operating system for mobile phones, which allowed wireless phone manufacturers such as LG, HTC, and Nokia to produce Internet-enabled phones boasting features similar to those available on Apple's iPhone. Widespread use of the Internet-enabled Android phones would not only help Google solidify its lead in mobile search but also allow the company to increase its share of banner ads and video ads displayed on mobile phones. In 2011, Android was the leading smartphone platform with a 38.1 percent market share. Google had also

entered into alliances with Intel, Sony, DISH Network, Logitech, and other firms to develop the technology and products required to launch Google TV. Google TV was launched in the United States in 2011 and would allow users to search live network and cable programming; streaming videos from providers such as Netflix, Amazon Video On Demand, and YouTube; and recorded programs on a DVR. The company was also pursuing a cloud computing initiative that was intended to change the market for commonly used business productivity applications such as word processing, spreadsheets, and presentation software from the desktop to the Internet. Information technology analysts believed that the market for such applications—collectively called cloud computing—could grow to $95 billion by 2013. Perhaps the company's most ambitious strategic initiative in 2011 was its agreement to acquire Motorola Mobility for $12.5 billion, which would put it in the hardware segment of the smartphone and tablet computer industries. Analysts following the transaction saw the move to acquire Motorola Mobility as a direct attempt to mimic Apple's strategy used for the iPhone and iPad that tightly integrated hardware and software for its most profitable and fastest-growing products.

While Google's growth initiatives seemed to take the company into new industries and thrust it into competition with companies ranging from AT&T to Microsoft to Apple, its CEO, Eric Schmidt, saw the new ventures as natural extensions of the company's mission to "organize the world's information and make it universally accessible and useful."[1] In September 2011, it was yet to be determined to what extent Google's new initiatives would contribute to the company's growth. Some industry analysts preferred that Google focus on improving its search technology to protect its competitive advantage in search and thereby its key revenue source. There was also a concern among some that, as the company pushed harder to sustain its impressive historical growth rates, it had backed away from its commitment to "make money without doing evil."[2] While free-speech advocates had criticized Google for aiding China in its Internet censorship practices since its 2006 entry into China, authorities in the United States, Canada, Australia, Germany, Italy, the United Kingdom, and Spain were conducting investigations into Google's Street View data collection practices. It had been discovered that while Google's camera cars photographed homes and businesses along city streets, the company also captured personal data from Wi-Fi networks in the photographed homes and businesses. The practice had resulted in a class-action suit in the United States tied to allegations that the company violated federal wiretapping statutes. Also, in late 2011, Google entered into a $500 million settlement agreement with the U.S. Justice Department to avoid prosecution on charges that it knowingly accepted hundreds of millions of dollars in advertising from online pharmacies in Canada that unlawfully shipped controlled substances to U.S. consumers.

COMPANY HISTORY

The development of Google's search technology began in January 1996 when Stanford University computer science graduate students Larry Page and Sergey Brin collaborated to develop a new search engine. They named the new search engine BackRub because of its ability to rate websites for relevancy by examining the number of back links pointing to the website. The approach for assessing the relevancy of websites to a particular search query used by other websites at the time was based on examining and counting meta tags and keywords included on various websites. By 1997, the search accuracy of BackRub had allowed it to gain a loyal following among Silicon Valley Internet users. Yahoo cofounder David Filo was among the converted, and in 1998 he convinced Brin and Page to leave Stanford to focus on making their search technology the backbone of a new Internet company.

BackRub would be renamed Google, which was a play on the word *googol*—a mathematical term for a number represented by the numeral 1 followed by 100 zeros. Brin and Page's adoption of the new name reflected their mission to organize a seemingly infinite amount of information on the Internet. In August 1998, a Stanford professor arranged for Brin and Page to meet at his home with a potential angel investor to demonstrate the Google search engine. The investor, who had been a founder of Sun Microsystems, was immediately impressed with Google's search capabilities but was too pressed for time to hear much of their informal presentation. The investor stopped the two during the presentation and suggested, "Instead of us discussing all the details, why don't I just write you a check?"[3] The two partners held the investor's $100,000 check, made payable to Google Inc., for two weeks while they scrambled to set up a corporation named Google Inc. and open a corporate bank account. The two officers of the freshly incorporated company went on to raise a total of $1 million in venture capital from family, friends, and other angel investors by the end of September 1998.

Even with a cash reserve of $1 million, the two partners ran Google on a shoestring budget, with its main servers built by Brin and Page from discounted computer components and its four employees operating out of a garage owned by a friend of the founders. By year-end 1998, Google's beta version was handling 10,000 search queries per day and *PC Magazine* had named the company to its list of "Top 100 Web Sites and Search Engines for 1998."

The new company recorded successes at a lightning-fast pace, with the search kernel answering more than 500,000 queries per day and Red Hat agreeing to become the company's first search customer in early 1999. Google attracted an additional $25 million in funding from two leading Silicon Valley venture capital firms by mid-year 1999 to support further growth and enhancements to Google's search technology. The company's innovations in 2000 included wireless search technology, search capabilities in 10 languages, and a Google Toolbar browser plug-in that allowed computer users to search the Internet without first visiting a Google-affiliated web portal or Google's home page. Features added through 2004 included Google News, Google Product Search, Google Scholar, and Google Local. The company also expanded its index of web pages to more than 8 billion and increased its country domains to more than 150 by 2004. Google also further expanded its products for mobile phones with a short message service (SMS) feature that allowed mobile phone users to send a search request to Google as a text message. After submitting the search request to 466453 (google), a mobile phone user would receive a text message from Google providing results to his or her query.

THE INITIAL PUBLIC OFFERING

Google's April 29, 2004, initial public offering (IPO) registration became the most talked-about planned offering involving an Internet company since the dot-com bust of 2000. The registration announced Google's intention to raise as much as $3.6 billion from the issue of 25.7 million shares through an unusual Dutch auction. Among the 10 key tenets of Google's philosophy (see Exhibit 1) was "You can make money without doing evil."[4] The choice of a Dutch auction stemmed from this philosophy, since Dutch auctions allowed potential investors to place bids for shares regardless of size. The choice of a Dutch auction was also favorable to Google since it involved considerably lower investment banking and underwriting fees and few or no commissions for brokers.

At the conclusion of the first day of trading, Google's shares had appreciated by 18 percent to make Brin and Page each worth approximately $3.8 billion. Also, an estimated 900 to 1,000 Google employees were worth at least $1 million, with 600 to 700 holding at least $2 million in Google stock. On average, each of Google's 2,292 staff members held approximately $1.7 million in company stock, excluding the holdings of the top five executives. Stanford University also enjoyed a $179.5 million windfall from its stock holdings granted for its early investment in Brin and Page's search engine. Some of Google's early contractors and consultants also profited handsomely from forgoing fees in return for stock options in the company. One such contractor was Abbe Patterson, who took options for 4,000 shares rather than a $5,000 fee for preparing a PowerPoint presentation and speaking notes for one of Brin and Page's first presentations to venture capitalists. After two splits and four days of trading, her 16,000 shares were worth $1.7 million.[5] The company executed a second public offering of 14,159,265 shares of common stock in September 2005. The number of shares issued represented the first eight digits to the right of the decimal point for the value of π (pi). The issue added more than $4 billion to Google's liquid assets.

Exhibit 2 tracks the performance of Google's common shares between August 19, 2004, and August 2011.

GOOGLE FEATURE ADDITIONS BETWEEN 2005 AND 2011

Google used its vast cash reserves to make strategic acquisitions that might lead to the development of new Internet applications offering advertising opportunities. Google Earth was launched in 2005 after the company acquired Keyhole, a digital mapping company, in 2004. Google Earth and its companion software Google Maps allowed Internet users to search and view satellite images of any location in the world. The feature was enhanced in 2007 with the addition of street-view images taken by traveling Google camera cars. Digital images, webcam feeds, and videos captured by Internet users could be linked to locations displayed by Google Maps. Real estate listings and short personal messages could also be linked to Google Maps locations. In 2010, Google further enhanced Google Maps with the inclusion of

▶ EXHIBIT 1

The 10 Principles of Google's Corporate Philosophy

1. **Focus on the user and all else will follow.**

   From its inception, Google has focused on providing the best user experience possible. While many companies claim to put their customers first, few are able to resist the temptation to make small sacrifices to increase shareholder value. Google has steadfastly refused to make any change that does not offer a benefit to the users who come to the site:
   - The interface is clear and simple.
   - Pages load instantly.
   - Placement in search results is never sold to anyone.
   - Advertising on the site must offer relevant content and not be a distraction.

   By always placing the interests of the user first, Google has built the most loyal audience on the web. And that growth has come not through TV ad campaigns, but through word of mouth from one satisfied user to another.

2. **It's best to do one thing really, really well.**

   Google does search. With one of the world's largest research groups focused exclusively on solving search problems, we know what we do well, and how we could do it better. Through continued iteration on difficult problems, we've been able to solve complex issues and provide continuous improvements to a service already considered the best on the web at making finding information a fast and seamless experience for millions of users. Our dedication to improving search has also allowed us to apply what we've learned to new products, including Gmail, Google Desktop, and Google Maps.

3. **Fast is better than slow.**

   Google believes in instant gratification. You want answers and you want them right now. Who are we to argue? Google may be the only company in the world whose stated goal is to have users leave its website as quickly as possible. By fanatically obsessing on shaving every excess bit and byte from our pages and increasing the efficiency of our serving environment, Google has broken its own speed records time and again.

4. **Democracy on the web works.**

   Google works because it relies on the millions of individuals posting websites to determine which other sites offer content of value. Instead of relying on a group of editors or solely on the frequency with which certain terms appear, Google ranks every web page using a breakthrough technique called PageRank™. PageRank evaluates all of the sites linking to a web page and assigns them a value, based in part on the sites linking to them. By analyzing the full structure of the web, Google is able to determine which sites have been "voted" the best sources of information by those most interested in the information they offer.

5. **You don't need to be at your desk to need an answer.**

   The world is increasingly mobile and unwilling to be constrained to a fixed location. Whether it's through their PDAs, their wireless phones, or even their automobiles, people want information to come to them.

6. **You can make money without doing evil.**

   Google is a business. The revenue the company generates is derived from offering its search technology to companies and from the sale of advertising displayed on Google and on other sites across the web. However, you may have never seen an ad on Google. That's because Google does not allow ads to be displayed on our results pages unless they're relevant to the results page on which they're shown. So, only certain searches produce sponsored links above or to the right of the results. Google firmly believes that ads can provide useful information if, and only if, they are relevant to what you wish to find.

   Advertising on Google is always clearly identified as a "Sponsored Link." It is a core value for Google that there be no compromising of the integrity of our results. We never manipulate rankings to put our partners higher in our search results. No one can buy better PageRank. Our users trust Google's objectivity and no short-term gain could ever justify breaching that trust.

(continued)

EXHIBIT 1 *(concluded)*

7. There's always more information out there.

Once Google had indexed more of the HTML pages on the Internet than any other search service, our engineers turned their attention to information that was not as readily accessible. Sometimes it was just a matter of integrating new databases, such as adding a phone number and address lookup and a business directory. Other efforts required a bit more creativity, like adding the ability to search billions of images and a way to view pages that were originally created as PDF files. The popularity of PDF results led us to expand the list of file types searched to include documents produced in a dozen formats such as Microsoft Word, Excel, and PowerPoint. For wireless users, Google developed a unique way to translate HTML formatted files into a format that could be read by mobile devices. The list is not likely to end there as Google's researchers continue looking into ways to bring all the world's information to users seeking answers.

8. The need for information crosses all borders.

Though Google is headquartered in California, our mission is to facilitate access to information for the entire world, so we have offices around the globe. To that end we maintain dozens of Internet domains and serve more than half of our results to users living outside the United States. Google search results can be restricted to pages written in more than 35 languages according to a user's preference. We also offer a translation feature to make content available to users regardless of their native tongue and for those who prefer not to search in English, Google's interface can be customized into more than 100 languages.

9. You can be serious without a suit.

Google's founders have often stated that the company is not serious about anything but search. They built a company around the idea that work should be challenging and the challenge should be fun. To that end, Google's culture is unlike any in corporate America, and it's not because of the ubiquitous lava lamps and large rubber balls, or the fact that the company's chef used to cook for the Grateful Dead. In the same way Google puts users first when it comes to our online service, Google Inc. puts employees first when it comes to daily life in our Googleplex headquarters. There is an emphasis on team achievements and pride in individual accomplishments that contribute to the company's overall success. Ideas are traded, tested and put into practice with an alacrity that can be dizzying. Meetings that would take hours elsewhere are frequently little more than a conversation in line for lunch and few walls separate those who write the code from those who write the checks. This highly communicative environment fosters a productivity and camaraderie fueled by the realization that millions of people rely on Google results. Give the proper tools to a group of people who like to make a difference, and they will.

10. Great just isn't good enough.

Always deliver more than expected. Google does not accept being the best as an end point, but a starting point. Through innovation and iteration, Google takes something that works well and improves upon it in unexpected ways. Google's point of distinction however, is anticipating needs not yet articulated by our global audience, then meeting them with products and services that set new standards. This constant dissatisfaction with the way things are is ultimately the driving force behind the world's best search engine.

Source: Google.com.

an Earth View mode that allowed users to view three-dimensional images of various locations from the ground level. Other search features added to Google between 2005 and 2010 that users found particularly useful included Book Search, Music Search, Video Search, and the expansion of Google News to include archived news articles dating to 1900.

Google also expanded its website features beyond search functionality to include its Gmail software, a web-based calendar, web-based document and spreadsheet applications, its Picasa web photo albums, and a translation feature that accommodated 51 languages. The company also released services for mobile phone uses such as Mobile Web Search, Blogger Mobile, Gmail, Google News, and Maps for Mobile. A complete list of Google services and tools for computers and mobile phones in 2011 is presented in Exhibit 3.

► EXHIBIT 2   Performance of Google's Stock Price, August 19, 2004, to August 2011

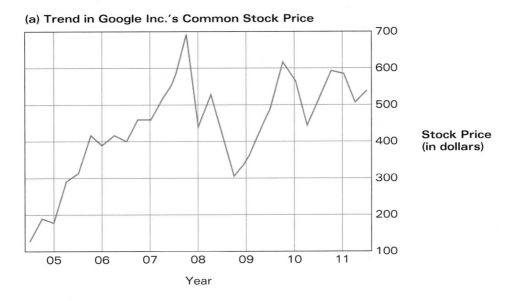

(a) Trend in Google Inc.'s Common Stock Price

Stock Price
(in dollars)

Year

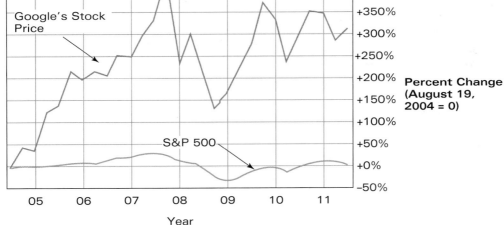

**(b) Performance of Google Inc.'s Stock Price
versus the S&P 500 Index**

Google's Stock
Price

S&P 500

Percent Change
**(August 19,
2004 = 0)**

Year

GOOGLE'S BUSINESS MODEL

Google's business model had evolved since the company's inception to include revenue beyond the licensing fees charged to corporations needing search capabilities on company intranets or websites. The 2000 development of keyword-targeted advertising expanded its business model to include revenues from the placement of highly targeted text-only sponsor ads adjacent to its search results. Google was able to target its ads to specific users based on the user's browsing history. The addition of advertising-based revenue allowed Google to increase annual revenues from $220,000 in 1999 to more than $86 million in 2001. A summary

EXHIBIT 3

Google Services and Tools in 2011

Search Features

Alerts
Get email updates on the topics of your choice

Blog Search
Find blogs on your favorite topics

Books
Search the full text of books

Checkout
Complete online purchases more quickly and securely

Google Chrome
A browser built for speed, stability and security

Custom Search
Create a customized search experience for your community

Desktop
Search and personalize your computer

Directory
Search the web, organized by topic or category

Earth
Explore the world from your computer

Finance
Business info, news, and interactive charts

GOOG-411
Find and connect with businesses from your phone

Google Health
Organize your medical records online

iGoogle
Add news, games and more to your Google homepage

Images
Search for images on the Web

Maps
View maps and directions

News
Search thousands of news stories

Patent Search
Search the full text of U.S. Patents

(continued)

 EXHIBIT 3 *(continued)*

Search Features

Product Search
Search for stuff to buy

Scholar
Search scholarly papers

Toolbar
Add a search box to your browser

Trends
Explore past and present search trends

Videos
Search for videos on the Web

Web Search
Search billions of Web pages

Google Tools and Web Applications

Code
Developer tools, APIs and resources

Labs
Explore Google's technology playground

Blogger
Share your life online with a blog—it's fast, easy, and free

Calendar
Organize your schedule and share events with friends

Docs
Create and share your online documents, presentations, and spreadsheets

Google Mail
Fast, searchable email with less spam

Groups
Create mailing lists and discussion groups

Knol
Share what you know

orkut
Orkut
Meet new people and stay in touch with friends

Picasa
Find, edit and share your photos

Reader
Get all your blogs and news feeds fast

(continued)

▶ EXHIBIT 3 (*concluded*)

Google Tools and Web Applications

<u>Sites</u>
Create Web sites and secure group wikis

<u>SketchUp</u>
Build 3D models quickly and easily

<u>Talk</u>
IM and call your friends through your computer

<u>Translate</u>
View Web pages in other languages

<u>YouTube</u>
Watch, upload and share videos

Google Mobile Applications

<u>Maps for mobile</u>
View maps, your location and get directions on your phone

<u>Search for mobile</u>
Search Google wherever you are

Source: Google.com.

of Google's financial performance for selected years between 2001 and 2010 is presented in Exhibit 4. The company's balance sheets for 2009 and 2010 are presented in Exhibit 5.

GOOGLE SEARCH APPLIANCE

Google's search technology could be integrated into a third party's website or intranet if search functionality was important to the customer. Google's Site Search allowed enterprises ranging from small businesses to public companies to license Google's search appliance for use on their websites for as little as $100 per year. The Google Search Appliance was designed for use on corporate intranets to allow employees to search company documents. The Search Appliance included a variety of security features to ensure that only employees with proper authority were able to view restricted documents. The Google Mini Search Appliance

was designed for small businesses with 50,000 to 300,000 documents stored on local PCs and servers. The Google Mini hardware and software package could be licensed online (at www.google.com/enterprise/mini) at prices ranging from $2,990 to $9,900, depending on document count capability. Google's more robust search appliance had a document count capability of up to 30 million documents and was designed for midsized to global businesses. Licensing fees for the Google Search appliance ranged from $30,000 to $600,000, depending on document count capability.

ADWORDS

Google AdWords allowed advertisers, either independently through Google's automated tools or with the assistance of Google's marketing teams, to create text-based ads that would appear alongside Google search results.

▶ EXHIBIT 4

Financial Summary for Google, 2001, 2004–2010 ($ millions, except per share amounts)								
	2010	2009	2008	2007	2006	2005	2004	2001
Revenues	$29,321	$23,651	$21,796	$16,594	$10,605	$6,139	$ 3,189	$ 86
Costs and expenses:								
Cost of revenues	10,417	8,844	8,622	6,649	4,225	2,577	1,458	14
Research and development	3,762	2,843	2,793	2,120	1,229	600	226	17
Sales and marketing	2,799	1,984	1,946	1,461	850	468	246	20
General and administrative	1,962	1,667	1,803	1,279	76	387	188	25
Contribution to Google Foundation	—	—	—	—	—	90,000	—	—
Non-recurring portion of settlement of disputes with Yahoo	—	—	—	—	—	—	201,000	—
Total costs and expenses	18,940	15,338	15,164	11,510	7,055	4,121	2,549	75
Income (loss) from operations	10,381	8,312	6,632	5,084	3,550	2,017	640	11
Impairment of equity investments	—	—	(1,095)	—	—	—	—	—
Interest income (expense) and other, net	415	69	316	590	461	124	10	(1)
Income (loss) before income taxes	10,796	8,381	5,854	5,674	4,011	2,142	650	10
Provision for income taxes	2,291	1,861	1,627	1,470	934	676	251	3
Net income (loss)	$ 8,505	$ 6,520	$ 4,227	$ 4,204	$ 3,077	$1,465	$ 399	$ 7
Net income (loss) per share:								
Basic	$ 26.69	$ 20.62	$ 13.46	$ 13.53	$ 10.21	$ 5.31	$ 2.07	$0.07
Diluted	$ 26.31	$ 20.41	$ 13.31	$ 13.29	$ 9.94	$ 5.02	$ 1.46	$0.04
Number of shares used in per share calculations:								
Basic	319	316	314	311	301	276	193	95
Diluted	323	319	318	316	310	292	273	187
Net cash provided by operating activities	$11,081	$ 9,316	$ 7,853	$ 5,775	$ 3,581	$2,459	$ 977	N/A
Cash, cash equivalents, and marketable securities	34,975	24,485	15,846	14,219	11,244	8,034	2,132	N/A
Total assets	57,851	40,497	31,768	25,336	18,473	10,272	3,313	N/A
Total long-term liabilities	1,614	1,745	1,227	611	129	107	447	N/A
Total stockholders' equity	46,241	36,004	28,239	22,690	17,040	9,419	2,929	N/A

Sources: Google, Form S-1, filed April 29, 2004; Google, 2009 and 2010 10-K reports.

AdWords users could evaluate the effectiveness of their advertising expenditures with Google through the use of performance reports that tracked the effectiveness of each ad. Google also offered a keyword targeting program that suggested synonyms for keywords entered by advertisers, a traffic estimator that helped potential advertisers anticipate charges, and multiple payment options that included charges to credit cards, debit cards, and monthly invoicing.

Larger advertisers were offered additional services to help run large, dynamic advertising campaigns. Such assistance included the availability of specialists with expertise in various industries to offer suggestions for targeting potential customers and identifying relevant keywords. Google's advertising specialists helped develop ads for customers that would increase click-through rates and purchase rates. Google also offered its large advertising customers bulk posting services that helped launch and manage campaigns including ads using hundreds or thousands of keywords.

Google's search-based ads were priced using an auction system that allowed advertisers to

▶ EXHIBIT 5

Google's Balance Sheets, 2009–2010 ($ millions, except per share amounts)

	As of December 31	
	2010	2009
Assets		
Current assets:		
Cash and cash equivalents	$13,630	$10,198
Marketable securities	21,345	14,287
Accounts receivable, net of allowance of $101 and $79	4,252	3,178
Deferred income taxes, net	750	644
Income taxes receivable	259	23
Prepaid revenue share, expenses and other assets	1,326	836
Total current assets	41,562	29,166
Prepaid revenue share, expenses and other assets, non-current	442	416
Deferred income taxes, net, non-current	265	263
Non-marketable equity securities	523	129
Property and equipment, net	7,759	4,845
Intangible assets, net	1,044	775
Goodwill	6,256	4,903
Total assets	$57,851	$40,497
Liabilities and Stockholders' Equity		
Current liabilities:		
Accounts payable	$ 483	$ 216
Short-term debt	3,465	—
Accrued compensation and benefits	1,410	982
Accrued expenses and other current liabilities	961	570
Accrued revenue share	885	694
Securities lending payable	2,361	0
Deferred revenue	394	285
Income taxes payable, net	37	—
Total current liabilities	9,996	2,747
Deferred revenue, long-term	35	42
Income taxes payable, long-term	1,200	1,392
Other long-term liabilities	379	312
Commitments and contingencies		
Stockholders' equity:		
Convertible preferred stock, $0.001 par value, 100,000 shares authorized; no shares issued and outstanding	—	—
Class A and Class B common stock and additional paid-in capital, $0.001 par value per share: 9,000,000 shares authorized; 317,772 (Class A 243,611, Class B 74,161) and par value of $318 (Class A $244, Class B $74) and 321,301 (Class A 250,413, Class B 70,888) and par value of $321 (Class A $250, Class B $71) shares issued and outstanding	18,235	15,816
Accumulated other comprehensive income	138	105
Retained earnings	27,868	20,082
Total stockholders' equity	46,241	36,004
Total liabilities and stockholders' equity	$57,851	$40,497

Source: Google, 2010 10-K report

bid on keywords that would describe their product or service. Bids could be made on a cost-per-impression (CPI) or cost-per-click (CPC) basis. Most Google advertisers placed bids based on CPC frequency rather than how many times an ad was displayed by Google. Google's auction pricing model assigned each bidder a Quality Score, which was determined by the advertiser's past keyword click-through rate and the relevance of the ad text. Advertisers with high Quality Scores were offered lower minimum bids than advertisers with poor quality scores.

Google allowed users to pay a CPC rate lower than their bid price if their bid was considerably more than the next highest bid. For example, an advertiser who bid $0.75 per click for a particular keyword would be charged only $0.51 per click if the next highest bid was only $0.50. The AdWords discounter ensured that advertisers paid only 1 cent more than the next highest bid, regardless of the actual amount of their bid.

ADSENSE

Google's AdSense program allowed web publishers to share in the advertising revenues generated by Google's text ads. The AdSense program served content-relevant Google text ads to pages on Google Network websites. For example, an Internet user reading an article about the state of the economy at Reuters. com would see Google text ads by investment magazines and companies specializing in home business opportunities. Google Network members shared in the advertising revenue whenever a site visitor clicked on a Google ad displayed on their sites. The more than 1 million Google Network members did not pay a fee to participate in the program and received about 60 percent of advertising dollars generated from the ads. Google's AdSense program also allowed mobile phone operators to share in Google revenues if text and image ads were displayed on mobile handsets. Also, owners of dormant domain names, web-based game sites, video sites, and news feed services could also participate in the AdSense program. The breakdown of Google's revenues by source for 2004 through 2010 is presented in Exhibit 6.

OTHER REVENUE SOURCES

The company's 2006 acquisition of YouTube allowed it to receive advertising revenues for ads displayed during Internet videos, while its 2008 acquisition of DoubleClick allowed the company to generate advertising revenues through banner ads. The company's 2008 launch of Google Checkout generated fees of as much as 2 percent of the transaction amount for purchases made at participating e-retailer sites. Google's business model was further expanded in 2008 to include licensing fees paid by users of its web-based Google Apps document and spreadsheet software.

► EXHIBIT 6

Google's Revenues by Source, 2004–2010 ($ millions)

	2010	2009	2008	2007	2006	2005	2004
Advertising revenues:							
Google websites	$19,444	$15,722	$14,414	$10,625	$6,333	$3,377	$1,589
Google Network websites	8,792	7,166	6,715	5,788	4,160	2,688	1,554
Total advertising revenues	28,236	22,889	21,129	16,413	10,493	6,065	3,143
Licensing and other revenues	1,085	762	667	181	112	74	50
Net revenues	$29,321	$23,651	$21,796	$16,594	$10,605	$6,139	$3,193

Sources: Google, 2007, 2009, and 2010 10-K reports.

GOOGLE'S STRATEGY AND COMPETITIVE POSITION IN 2011

Google's Strategies to Dominate Internet Advertising

Google's multiple acquisitions since its 2004 IPO and its research and development activities were directed at increasing the company's dominance in Internet advertising. The addition of Google Maps, local search, airline travel information, weather, Book Search, Gmail, Blogger, and other features increased traffic to Google sites and gave the company more opportunities to serve ads to Internet users. Also, the acquisition of DoubleClick in 2008 allowed Google to diversify its Internet advertising beyond search ads to include banner ads. However, not all of Google's acquisitions and innovations had resulted in meaningful contributions to the company's revenues. Even though more than 12 billion videos were watched on YouTube each month, the online video site's advertising revenues in 2009 were estimated at less than $300 million. Also, the company's internally developed social networking site, Orkut, had failed to match the success of competing social networking sites Facebook.com and MySpace.com.

Google's strategy to dominate Internet advertising also entailed becoming the number one search engine used not only in the United States but also across the world. In 2011, Google's search-based ads could be delivered to Internet users in 41 different languages. More than 50 percent of the company's 2010 revenues and traffic were generated from outside the United States, and the percentage of sales from outside the United States was expected to grow as Google entered emerging markets such as Russia and China. China was a particularly attractive market for Google since it had more Internet users (300+ million) than any other country in the world. However, Google's 2006 entry into China was accompanied by challenges, including strong competition from local search provider Baidu and requirements by the Chinese government to censor search results that were critical of the government. Google complied with government censorship requirements until early 2010, when cyberattacks originating in China stole proprietary computer code from Google and information from the Gmail accounts of several Chinese human rights activists. Google first responded to the hacking incidents by stating that it would withdraw from the Chinese search market and then shifted to a strategy of redirecting users of its censored Google.cn site in China to its uncensored Hong Kong search site, Google.com.hk. The Chinese government was able to block search results from Google's Hong Kong site, but the new policy ended Google's involvement in China's censorship practices. To avoid breaking Chinese law prohibiting the distribution of information not authorized by the government, Google agreed in June 2010 to stop the automatic redirects to its Hong Kong site. Instead, it presented Google.cn users with a link to Google.com.hk. In 2009, 64 percent of Internet searches in China were performed by Baidu, while Google held a 31 percent share of searches in that country. A breakdown of Google's revenues and long-lived assets by geographic region for 2006 through 2010 is presented in Exhibit 7.

Mobile Search and Google's Emerging Rivalry with Apple in Smartphones and Tablet Computers

In 2010, more than 5 billion people worldwide and 234 million Americans ages 13 and older owned and used mobile phones. More than 35 percent of Americans and a growing percentage worldwide accessed the Internet from mobile devices, and a rapidly growing number of mobile phone users were exchanging basic mobile phones for smartphones. Smartphones such as Apple's iPhone could connect to the networks of wireless carriers to make phone calls, access the Internet, or run various Internet applications. Between March 2011 and June 2011, the number of smartphone users in the United States had grown by 10 percent to reach 82.2 million.

► EXHIBIT 7

Google's Revenues and Long-Lived Assets by Geographic Region, 2006–2010 (in $ millions)

	Year Ended December 31				
Revenues	**2010**	**2009**	**2008**	**2007**	**2006**
United States	$14,056	$11,194	$10,636	$ 8,698	$ 6,030
United Kingdom	3,329	2,986	3,038	2,531	1,604
Rest of the world	11,936	9,471	8,122	5,365	2,971
Total revenues	$29,321	$23,651	$21,796	$16,594	$10,605
	As of December 31				
Long-Lived Assets	**2010**	**2009**	**2008**	**2007**	**2006**
United States	$14,000	$ 9,432	$ 9,783	$ 7,335	$ 5,071
Rest of the world	2,289	1,898	1,807	712	363
Total long-lived assets	$16,289	$11,330	$11,589	$ 8,047	$ 5,434

Sources: Google, 2007, 2009, and 2010 10-K reports.

Apple Inc. built its early reputation in the 1980s and 1990s on its innovative Mac computer lines, but in 2010, only $17.5 billion of its net sales of $65.2 billion came from the sale of computers. In 2011, Apple was the world's largest seller of smartphones, tablet computers, and personal media players with market shares of 19.1 percent, 85 percent, and 73 percent, respectively. In 2010, the iPhone accounted for $25.2 billion of its total sales of $65.2 billion. The iPad contributed revenues of nearly $5 billion, and iPod and related music products accounted for sales of more than $13 billion in 2010. The company's hefty profit margins on its electronic devices allowed the company to record net income of more than $14 billion in 2010. Apple's performance accelerated in 2011, with the company setting revenue and profit records during the third quarter of 2011. The record sales and earnings were driven largely by the iPhone, which saw a year-over-year revenue increase of 142 percent, and iPad, which increased by 183 percent from the same period in 2010. The company's strong performance allowed its stock price to increase to a price that made it the most valuable company in the world as measured by market capitalization in August 2011. A summary of Apple's financial performance between 2006 and 2010 is presented in Exhibit 8.

Google's introduction of its Android operating system for smartphones in 2008 was expected to allow it to increase its 60-plus percent share of mobile searches and expand the market for other types of Internet ads delivered on mobile devices. Android was not a phone but an operating system that Google made available free to any phone manufacturer wishing to market mobile devices with Internet capability. Android's core applications included Wi-Fi capability, e-mail, a web-based calendar, Google Earth maps, a browser, and GPS. T-Mobile was the first wireless provider to market an Android phone. Its $179 G1 was launched in September 2008 and included essentially the same features found on the more expensive Apple iPhone. By 2010, all major mobile phone providers had added smartphone models running Android software to their lineup of handsets, and despite Google's late entry into the market, Android's market share had increased from zero in 2008 to 38.1 percent in May 2011 (see Exhibit 9).

Similar to its relationship with mobile phone manufacturers, Google allowed mobile app developers to use the Android operating system free of licensing fees. The worldwide market for mobile apps was expected to increase from $4.1 billion in 2009 to $17.5 billion by 2012. In 2011, more than 28,000 free and paid

EXHIBIT 8

Financial Summary for Apple Inc., 2006–2010 ($ millions)

	Fiscal Year Ended June 30				
	2010	**2009**	**2008**	**2007**	**2006**
Net sales	$65,225	$42,905	$37,491	$24,006	$19,315
Operating income	18,385	11,740	8,327	4,409	2,453
Net income	14,013	8,235	6,119	3,496	1,989
Cash, cash equivalents, and marketable securities	$51,011	$33,992	$24,490	$15,386	$10,110
Total assets	75,183	47,501	36,171	24,878	17,205
Long-term obligations	5,531	3,502	1,745	687	395
Stockholders' equity	47,791	31,640	22,297	14,531	9,984

Sources: Apple Inc. 2008 and 2010 10-K report.

smartphone apps were available at Google's Android Market. However, fewer than 1,000 apps for tablet computers running Android were available at the Android Market in 2011. By comparison, Apple offered 475,000 smartphone apps and 90,000 apps for iPads at its App Store in 2011. In 2010, Google briefly marketed its own Nexus One smartphone, which was produced by HTC and was compatible with all major wireless carrier 3G and 4G networks. In August 2011, Google announced a planned $12.5 billion acquisition of Motorola Mobility, which would allow it to design and market its own line of smartphones and tablet computers.

Google's Strategic Offensive to Control the Desktop

Google's senior management believed that, in the very near future, most computer software programs used by businesses would move from local hard drives or intranets to the Internet. Many information technology analysts agreed that cloud computing would become a common software platform and could grow to a $95 billion market by 2013. Moving software applications to the cloud offered many possible benefits to corporate users, including lower software acquisition costs, lower computing support costs, and easier collaboration among employees in different locations. The beta version of Google Apps was launched in 2006 as a free word processing and spreadsheet package for individuals, but was relaunched in 2008 as a competing product to Microsoft Office. Google Apps was hosted on computers in Google's data centers and included Gmail, a calendar, instant messaging, word processing, spreadsheets, presentation software, and file storage space. Google Apps could be licensed by corporate customers at $50 per user per year. The licensing fee for the Microsoft Office and Outlook package was

EXHIBIT 9

U.S. Smartphone Platform Market Share Rankings, Selected Periods, September 2009–May 2011

Smartphone Platform	September 2009	May 2010	May 2011
Google Android	2.5%	13.0%	38.1%
Apple iPhone	24.1	24.4	28.6
RIM (Blackberry)	42.6	41.7	24.7
Microsoft Windows for Mobile	19.0	13.2	5.8
Palm	8.3	4.8	—
Others	3.5	2.9	2.8
Total	100.0%	100.0%	100.0%

Sources: ComScore.com.

typically $350 per user per year. Industry analysts estimated Google Apps users at about 25 million and paid subscribers at about 1.5 million in 2010. Microsoft estimated Microsoft Office users at about 500 million in 2010.

Google's Chrome browser, which was launched in September 2008, and Chrome operating system (OS) launched in July 2009 were developed specifically to accommodate cloud computing applications. The bare-bones Chrome browser was built on a multiprocessor design that would allow users to operate spreadsheets, word processing, video editing, and other applications on separate tabs that could be run simultaneously. Each tab operated independently so that if one tab crashed, other applications running from Google's data centers were not affected. The Chrome browser also provided Google with a defense against moves by Microsoft to make it more difficult for Google to deliver relevant search-based ads to Internet users. Microsoft's Internet Explorer 8 allowed users to hide their Internet address and viewing history, which prevented Google from collecting user-specific information needed for ad targeting. Mozilla's Firefox browser employed a similar feature that prevented third parties from tracking a user's viewing habits. The clean-running Chrome OS was an open source operating system specifically designed as a platform for cloud computing applications. Google had entered into agreements with Acer, Hewlett-Packard, and Lenovo to begin producing netbooks that would use the Chrome OS and Chrome browser to access the cloud-based Google Apps productivity software. Worldwide market share statistics for the leading browsers for selected periods between September 2008 and August 2011 are presented in Exhibit 10.

Google's Initiatives to Expand Search to Television

In mid-2010, Google entered into an alliance with Intel, Sony, Logitech, Best Buy, DISH Network, and Adobe to develop Google TV. Google TV would be built on the Android platform and would run the Chrome browser

▶ **EXHIBIT 10**

Worldwide Browser Market Share Rankings, Selected Periods, September 2008–August 2011			
Browser	**September 2008**	**June 2010**	**August 2011**
Internet Explorer	74%	60%	42%
Firefox	19	24	27
Chrome	1	7	23
Safari	3	5	5
Opera	2	3	2
Others	1	1	1
Total	100%	100%	100%

Sources: "Google Rekindles Browser War," *Wall Street Journal Online*, July 7, 2010; and gs.statcounter.com.

software to search live network and cable programming; streaming videos from providers such as Netflix, Amazon Video On Demand, and YouTube; and recorded programs on a DVR. Google TV users would also be able to use their televisions to browse the web and run cloud-based applications such as Google Apps. Google TV was expected to be integrated into DISH Network's satellite service by fall 2010, while Sony was on schedule for fall 2010 shipments of Google TV–compatible high-definition televisions (HDTVs). Logitech was also on track for fall 2010 shipments of Google TV set-top boxes that would be compatible with all brands of HDTVs and Google TV accessories such as HD cameras that could be used for video chats.

Google acquired On2 Technologies, which was the leading developer of video compression technology, in February 2010 in a $124 million stock and cash transaction. The acquisition of On2 was expected to improve the video streaming capabilities of Google TV. Google also lobbied heavily during 2009 and 2010 to encourage the Obama administration to adopt a "Net neutrality" policy that would require Internet providers to manage traffic in a manner that would not restrict high-bandwidth services such as Internet television. The company was also testing an ultrafast broadband network in several cities across the United States that was as much as 100 times faster than what was offered by competing Internet providers. Google management had stated that the company did not intend to launch a nationwide Internet service, but did want to expose consumers to Internet applications and content that would be possible with greater bandwidth and faster transmission speeds.

GOOGLE'S INTERNET RIVALS

Google's ability to sustain its competitive advantage among search companies was a function of its ability to maintain strong relationships with Internet users, advertisers, and websites. In 2011, Google was the world's most-visited Internet site, with more than 1 billion unique Internet users going to Google sites each month to search for information. Google management believed its primary competitors to be Microsoft and Yahoo. A comparison of the percentage of Internet searches among websites offering search capabilities for selected periods between July 2006 and July 2011 is shown in Exhibit 11.

Microsoft Online Services

Microsoft Corporation recorded fiscal 2011 revenues and net income of approximately $70 billion and $23.2 billion, respectively, through the sales of computer software, consulting services, video game hardware, and online services. Windows 7 and Microsoft Office accounted for more than one-half of the company's 2011 revenues and nearly all of its operating profit. The company's online services business recorded sales of nearly $2.5 billion and an operating loss of almost $2.6 billion during fiscal 2011. Microsoft's online services business generated revenues from banner ads displayed at the company's MSN web portal and its affiliated websites, search-based ads displayed with Bing results, and subscription fees from its MSN dial-up service. Microsoft's websites made the company the second-most-visited Internet destination worldwide in 2011,

► **EXHIBIT 11**

U.S. Search Engine Market Share Rankings, Selected Periods, July 2006–July 2011

Percent of Searches

Search Entity	July 2006	June 2009	May 2010	July 2011
Google Sites	43.7%	65.0%	63.7%	65.1%
Yahoo Sites	28.8	19.6	18.3	16.1
Microsoft Sites	12.8	8.4	12.1	14.4
Ask.com	5.4	3.9	3.6	2.9
AOL	5.9	3.1	2.3	1.5
Others	3.4	n.m.	n.m.	n.m.
Total	100.0%	100.0%	100.0%	100.0%

n.m. = not material.

Sources: ComScore.com.

with approximately 900 million unique visitors each month. A financial summary for Microsoft Corporation and its Online Services Division is provided in Exhibit 12.

Microsoft's search business was launched in November 2004 as Live Search to compete directly with Google and slow whatever intentions Google might have to threaten Microsoft in its core operating system and productivity software businesses. Microsoft's concern with threats posed by Google arose shortly after Google's IPO, when Bill Gates noticed that many of the Google job postings on its site were nearly identical to Microsoft job specifications. Recognizing that the position announcements had more to do with operating-system design than search, Gates e-mailed key Microsoft executives, warning, "We have to watch these guys. It looks like they are building something to compete with us."[6] Gates later commented that Google was "more like us than anyone else we have ever competed with."[7]

Gates speculated that Google's long-term strategy involved the development of web-based software applications comparable to Word, Excel, PowerPoint, and other Microsoft products. Microsoft's strategy to compete with Google was keyed to making Live Search more effective than Google at providing highly

► EXHIBIT 12

Financial Summary for Microsoft Corporation and Microsoft's Online Services Business Unit, 2007–2011 ($ millions)

Financial Summary for Microsoft Corporation

	2011	2010	2009	2008	2007
Revenue	$69,943	$62,484	$58,437	$60,420	$51,122
Operating income	27,161	24,098	20,363	22,492	18,524
Net income	23,150	18,760	14,569	17,681	14,065
Cash, cash equivalents, and short-term investments	$52,772	$36,788	$31,447	$23,662	$23,411
Total assets	108,704	86,113	77,888	72,793	63,171
Long-term obligations	22,847	13,791	11,296	6,621	8,320
Stockholders' equity	57,083	46,175	39,558	36,286	31,097

Financial Summary for Microsoft's Online Services Business Unit

	2011	2010	2009	2008	2007
Revenue	$ 2,528	$ 2,201	$ 2,121	$ 3,214	$ 2,441
Operating income (loss)	(2,557)	(2,337)	(1,641)	(1,233)	(617)

Sources: Microsoft, 2007, 2009, and 2011 annual reports.

relevant search results. Microsoft believed that any conversion of Google users to Live Search would reduce the number of PC users who might ultimately adopt Google's web-based word processing, spreadsheet, and presentation software packages. In 2008, Microsoft paid more than $100 million to acquire Powerset, which was the developer of a semantic search engine. Semantic search technology offered the opportunity to surpass the relevancy of Google's search results since semantic search evaluated the meaning of a word or phrase and considered its context when returning search results. Even though semantic search had the capability to answer questions stated in common language, semantic search processing time took several seconds to return results. The amount of time necessary to conduct a search had caused Microsoft to limit Powerset's search index to only articles listed in Wikipedia. Microsoft's developers were focused on increasing the speed of its semantic search capabilities so that its search index could be expanded to a greater number of Internet pages. The company's developers also

incorporated some of Powerset's capabilities into its latest-generation search engine, Bing, which was launched in June 2009. Banner ads comprised the bulk of Microsoft's online advertising revenues, since its Bing search engine accounted for only 14.4 percent of online searches in July 2011. Even though the market for display ads was only about one-half the size of the search ad market in 2009, the advertising spending on banner ads was expected to double by 2012 to reach $15 billion.

Microsoft was also moving forward with its own approach to cloud computing. The company's 2008 launch of Windows Live allowed Internet users to store files online at its password-protected SkyDrive site. SkyDrive's online file storage allowed users to access and edit files from multiple locations, share files with co-workers who might need editing privileges, or make files available in a public folder for wide distribution. Azure was Microsoft's most ambitious cloud computing initiative in 2010 and was intended to allow businesses to reduce computing costs by allowing Microsoft to host its operating programs and data files.

In addition to reducing capital expenditures for software upgrades and added server capacity, Azure's offsite hosting provided data security in the event of natural disasters such as fires or hurricanes.

Yahoo

Yahoo was founded in 1994 and was the fourth-most-visited Internet destination worldwide in 2011, with nearly 700 million unique visitors each month. Facebook was the third-most-visited website, with more than 700 million unique visitors each month in 2011. Almost any information available on the Internet could be accessed through Yahoo's web portal. Visitors could access content categorized by Yahoo or set up an account with Yahoo to maintain a personal calendar and e-mail account, check the latest news, check local weather, obtain maps, check TV listings, watch a movie trailer, track a stock portfolio, maintain a golf handicap, keep an online photo album, or search personal ads or job listings.

Yahoo also hosted websites for small businesses and Internet retailers and had entered into strategic partnerships with 20 mobile phone operators in the United States and Europe to provide mobile search and display ads to their customers. Yahoo accounted for about 35 percent of searches performed on mobile phones in 2010. Yahoo's broad range of services allowed it to generate revenues from numerous sources—it received fees for banner ads displayed at Yahoo.com, Yahoo! Messenger, Yahoo! Mail, Flickr, or mobile phone customers; it received listing fees at Yahoo! Autos, Cars.com, and Yahoo! Real Estate; it received revenues from paid search results at Yahoo! Search; it shared in travel agency booking fees made at Yahoo! Travel; and it received subscription fees from its registered users at Rivals.com, Yahoo! Games, Yahoo! Music, and Yahoo! Personals.

Yahoo's relationship with Google dated to 2000 and, since that time, had oscillated between cooperative and adversarial. Yahoo was among Google's earliest customers for its search appliance, but Yahoo began to distance itself from Google in 2002 when it began acquiring companies with developed search technologies. Yahoo replaced Google with its own search capabilities in February 2004. Yahoo later levied a patent infringement charge against Google that resulted in a settlement that gave Google ownership of the technology rights in return for 2.7 million shares of Google stock. Yahoo attempted to renew its relationship with Google in 2008 in hopes of reversing a decline in profitability and liquidity that began in 2006. After averting a hostile takeover by Microsoft in June 2008, Yahoo reached an agreement with Google that would allow Yahoo to host Google search ads. The partnership would provide Yahoo with an estimated $800 million in additional revenues annually, most of which would go directly to its bottom line. However, Google withdrew from the agreement in November 2008 after receiving notification from the U.S. Justice Department that the alliance would possibly violate antitrust statutes. Shortly after being notified that Google was withdrawing from the deal, Yahoo's chief managers told business reporters that the company was "disappointed that Google has elected to withdraw from the agreement rather than defend it in court."[8] In July 2009, Microsoft and Yahoo finally came to an agreement that would make Microsoft Bing Yahoo's imbedded search engine for a period of 10 years. A summary of Yahoo's financial performance between 2006 and 2010 is presented in Exhibit 13.

ISSUES CONCERNING GOOGLE'S PERFORMANCE AND BUSINESS ETHICS IN 2011

During its second quarter of fiscal 2011, Google had been able to achieve year-over-year revenue growth of 32 percent, while many companies in almost every industry struggled as the U.S. economy continued to falter. So far, it appeared that Google's business model and strategy had insulated it from the effects of the prolonged economic malaise in the United States and it was in position to pursue its growth strategies. The company's strategic

EXHIBIT 13

Financial Summary for Yahoo, 2006–2010 ($ thousands)

	2010	2009	2008	2007	2006
Revenues	$ 6,324,651	$ 6,460,315	$ 7,208,502	$ 6,969,274	$ 6,425,679
Income from operations	772,524	386,692	12,963	695,413	940,966
Net income	1,231,663	597,992	418,921	639,155	731,568
Cash and cash equivalents	$ 1,526,427	$ 1,275,430	$ 2,292,296	$ 1,513,930	$ 1,569,871
Marketable debt securities	2,102,255	3,242,574	1,229,677	849,542	1,967,414
Working capital	2,719,676	2,877,044	3,040,483	937,274	2,276,148
Total assets	14,928,104	14,936,030	13,689,848	12,229,741	11,513,608
Long-term liabilities	705,822	699,666	715,872	384,208	870,948
Total stockholders' equity	12,558,129	12,493,320	11,250,942	9,532,831	9,160,610

Sources: Yahoo, 2007, 2009, and 2010 10-K reports.

priorities in 2011 focused on expanding its share of mobile search and smartphone platforms, expanding into the design and sale of smartphone handsets, pushing forward with its plans to become the dominant provider of cloud computing solutions, increasing search advertising revenues from markets outside the United States, and extending search to television. Some analysts believed the company's priorities should also include the development of semantic search capabilities, while others were concerned that the company had strayed from its 10 Principles—specifically, Principle 6, "You can make money without doing evil."

Free-speech advocates had criticized Google for its complicity in China's censorship of Internet content since it launched its Chinese site in 2006, while privacy advocates complained that Google Map's street-view mode violated privacy rights. The company also agreed to a $500 million legal settlement with the U.S. Justice Department to avoid prosecution on charges that it accepted hundreds of millions of dollars in illegal ads from unlicensed online Canadian pharmacies selling controlled substances in the United States. Among the most disturbing aspect of the case against Google related to the Justice Department's assertion that Larry Page knew of the practice and had allowed it for years. In commenting about the case, Rhode Island U.S. Attorney Peter Neronha, stated, "We simply know it from the

documents we reviewed, the witnesses that we interviewed, that Larry Page knew what was going on."[9] Perhaps the most serious legal issue facing the company involved its decision by management to allow its Street View camera cars to capture Wi-Fi data emitted from homes and businesses while photographing the route. Data collected by Google included e-mails, user names, passwords, and other private data. In 2011 authorities in the United States, Canada, Australia, Germany, Italy, the United Kingdom, and Spain were conducting investigations into Google's data collection activities to determine if prosecution of company managers was warranted. In 2010, Google cofounder Sergey Brin said the company "screwed up" by collecting personal data through wireless networks in an attempt to improve its mapping system, but a federal judge ruled in June 2011 that Google's Street View data collection policies may have violated federal wiretap laws and allowed a class-action suit against the company to go forward.[10]

Also, the company's lobbying efforts to encourage the Obama administration to institute policies to promote Net neutrality had drawn the scrutiny of the U.S. House Oversight Committee. The primary concern of the House Oversight Committee involved communications between the company and its former head of public policy and government affairs, Andrew McLaughlin, who had been appointed to the position of White House deputy chief technology officer. Ethics rules created by an executive order signed by President Obama barred all White House officials from communicating with lobbyists or a company potentially affected by pending policy matters. A Freedom of Information Act (FOIA) request by a consumer group found that McLaughlin regularly communicated with Google executives to discuss the administration's push to have the Internet regulated by the Federal Communications Commission to promote Net neutrality. McLaughlin's e-mails could be obtained under the FOIA since all White House e-mail accounts were required to be archived under federal law. The House Oversight Committee was particularly disturbed by McLaughlin's alleged use

of a personal Gmail account to avoid having his communications with Google executives archived and subject to FOIA requests.

Some analysts believed that pressure to achieve the revenue and earnings growth necessary to maintain Google's lofty stock price may have caused Google management to make decisions that pushed the bounds of its corporate philosophy. The company's revenues and earnings growth had begun to slow in recent years, and the sluggish U.S. economy seemed unlikely to give Google a dramatic boost in revenues in 2010. It remained to be determined if Google's strategies could sustain its growth and stock performance in a manner that would adhere to the company founders' early beliefs.

ENDNOTES

[1] Google, www.google.com/corporate/, accessed July 13, 2010.

[2] Google, www.google.com/corporate/tenthings.html, accessed July 13, 2010.

[3] Quoted in Google's Corporate Information, www.google.com/corporate/history.html.

[4] Google, "Our Philosophy," www.google.com/corporate/tenthings.html.

[5] "For Some Who Passed on Google Long Ago, Wistful Thinking," *Wall Street Journal Online*, August 23, 2004.

[6] Quoted in "Gates vs. Google," *Fortune*, April 18, 2005.

[7] Ibid.

[8] Quoted in "With Google Gone, Will Microsoft Come Back to Yahoo?" *Fortune*, November 5, 2008.

[9] Quoted in "New Heat for Google CEO," *Wall Street Journal Online*, August 27, 2011.

[10] Quoted in "Google Faces European Probes on Wi-Fi Data," *Wall Street Journal Online*, May 20, 2010; and "Google Loses Bid to Dismiss Street View Suit Over Privacy-Violation Claims," *Bloomberg Online*, June 30, 2011.

SARA LEE CORPORATION IN 2011: HAS ITS RETRENCHMENT STRATEGY BEEN SUCCESSFUL?

Arthur A. Thompson
The University of Alabama

John E. Gamble
University of South Alabama

In February 2005, Brenda Barnes, Sara Lee Corporation's newly appointed president and CEO, announced a bold and ambitious multi-year strategic plan to transform Sara Lee into a more tightly focused food, beverage, and household products company. The centerpiece of Barnes's transformation plan was the divestiture of weak-performing business units and product categories accounting for $7.2 billion in sales (37 percent of Sara Lee's annual revenues). While the divestitures would cut Sara Lee's revenues from $19.6 billion to about $12.3 billion, Barnes believed that Sara Lee would be better off concentrating its financial and managerial resources on a smaller number of business segments in which market prospects were promising and Sara Lee's brands were well positioned.[1] Once the retrenchment initiatives were completed, the plan was to drive the company's growth via initiatives to boost the sales, market shares, and profitability of the key remaining brands: Sara Lee breads and bakery products, Ball Park meats, Douwe Egberts coffees, Hillshire Farm meats, Jimmy Dean sausage, and Senseo single-serve coffee products. Company executives believed that the retrenchment would allow revenues to increase to $14 billion by fiscal 2010 and that the company's operating profit margin in 2010 would increase to at least 12 percent (versus an 8.1 percent operating profit margin in fiscal 2004).[2]

By fiscal year-end 2010, it remained unclear to what extent the retrenchment strategy had benefited shareholders. The company had missed both revenue and operating profit margin projections for 2010. Revenues had increased to only $10.8 billion in fiscal 2010, and the company's operating profit margin during the year had improved to only 8.5 percent. During 2010, Sara Lee had engaged in further retrenchment with the divestiture of its International Household and Body Care business, which produced and marketed Kiwi shoe care products, Sanex personal care products, Ambi Pur air fresheners, and various insecticides and cleaning products sold outside North America. The company was also well under way with Project Accelerate, a company-wide cost savings and productivity initiative launched in 2008 that focused on outsourcing, supply chain efficiencies, and overhead reduction. Project Accelerate had produced savings of $180 million by 2010 and was expected to produce cumulative savings of $350 million to $400 million by the end of fiscal 2012. Management also launched a share buyback plan in 2010 that would repurchase $2.5 billion to $3 billion of shares over a three-year period. Also during 2010, Brenda Barnes had been forced to step down as CEO in August after suffering a stroke in May. The company's chief financial officer, Marcel Smits, had been named interim CEO while the board searched for a permanent replacement. Smits's strategies for 2011 focused on increasing share in the company's most powerful brands, pursuing growth in attractive geographic markets, and fully capturing the anticipated benefits of Project Accelerate.

COMPANY BACKGROUND

The origins of Sara Lee Corporation date to 1939, when Nathan Cummins acquired C. D. Kenny Company, a small wholesale distributor of sugar, coffee, and tea that had net sales of $24 million. The purchase of Sprague, Warner & Company in 1942 prompted a name change to Sprague Warner–Kenny Corporation and a shift in the headquarters location from Baltimore to Chicago; the company's shares began trading on the New York Stock Exchange in 1946. In 1954, the company's name was changed to Consolidated Foods Corporation to emphasize its diversified role in food processing, packaging, and distribution. In 1956, Consolidated Foods acquired Kitchens of Sara Lee and also entered the retail food business by acquiring 34 Piggly Wiggly supermarkets (later divested in 1966). The next 40 years were marked by a series of related and unrelated acquisitions:

John H. Bryan, former head of Bryan Meats (which the company acquired in 1968), became president and CEO of Consolidated Foods

Year	Acquisitions
1962	Jonker Fris, a Dutch producer of canned goods
1966	Oxford Chemical Corporation
	E. Kahn's Sons Company, a producer of meats
1968	Bryan Foods, a meat products producer
	Electrolux, a direct seller of vacuum cleaners
	Gant, an apparel producer
	Country Set, an apparel producer
	Canadelle, a producer of women's intimate apparel
1969	Aris Gloves (later renamed Aris Isotoner)
1971	Hillshire Farm, a meat producer
	Rudy's Farm, a meat producer
1972	Erdal, a Dutch company that produced and marketed personal care products (later renamed Intradal)
1978	Chef Pierre, a manufacturer/distributor of frozen prepared desserts
	Douwe Egberts, a Dutch coffee and grocery company
1980	Productos Cruz Verde, a Spanish household products company
1982	Standard Meat Company, a processor of meat products
1984	Jimmy Dean Meats, a manufacturer of various meat, food, and leather products
	Nicholas Kiwi Limited, an Australian-based manufacturer and marketer of personal, household, shoe and car care products and home medicines
1987	Bil Mar Foods, a producer of turkey-based products
	Dim, S.A., the leading hosiery brand in France
1988	Adams-Millis Corporation, a manufacturer of hosiery products (provided an entry into the men's basic sock business)
1989	Champion Products, manufacturer of professional-quality knit athletic wear
	Van Nelle, a Dutch company active in coffee and tea
	Hygrade Food Products, a manufacturer of hot dogs, luncheon meats, bacon, and ham (which included the Ball Park and Hygrade hot dog brands)
1990	Henson-Kickernick Inc., a manufacturer of high-quality foundations and daywear

(continued)

Year	Acquisitions *(concluded)*
1991	Playtex Apparel Inc., an international manufacturer and marketer of intimate apparel products
	Rinbros, a manufacturer/marketer of men's and boys' underwear in Mexico
1992	BP Nutrition's Consumer Foods Group
	Giltex Hosiery
	Bessin Corporation
	The furniture care businesses of SC Johnson Wax
	A majority interest in Maglificio Bellia SpA
	Select assets of Mark Cross Inc.
1993	SmithKline Beecham's European bath and body care brands
1997	Aoste, a French meats company
	Lovable Italiana SpA, an Italian intimate apparel manufacturer
	Brossard France SA, a French manufacturer of bakery products
1998	NutriMetics
	Café do Ponto
1999	Wechsler Coffee
	Chock full o'Nuts
	Continental Coffee
2000	Hills Bros., MJB, and Chase & Sanborn coffee brands (acquired from Nestlé USA)
	Courtaulds Textiles, UK-based producer of intimate apparel brands Gossard and Berlei
	Café Pilão, the number one coffee company in Brazil
	Sol y Oro, the leading company in women's underwear in Argentina,
2001	The EarthGrains Company, the number two player in the U.S. bakery market
	A major European bakery company

in 1975 and served as CEO until 2000; Bryan was appointed chairman in 1976, a position he held until 2001. Bryan was the chief architect of the company's acquisition strategy during 1975–2000, guiding both its diversification efforts and its emergence as a global corporation. By 1980, sales had reached $5 billion. In 1985, Consolidated Foods changed its name to Sara Lee Corporation. Sales reached $10 billion in 1988, $15 billion in 1994, and $20 billion in 1998. But revenues peaked at the $20 billion level in 1998–1999 as management struggled to manage the company's broadly diversified and geographically scattered operations.

In 2000, C. Steven McMillan succeeded John Bryan as CEO and president of Sara Lee; Bryan remained chairman until he retired a year later, at which time McMillan assumed the additional title. McMillan launched strategic initiatives to narrow Sara Lee's focus on a smaller number of global branded consumer packaged-goods segments—Food and Beverage, Intimates and

Year	Divestitures
1966	Piggly Wiggly supermarket chains
2000	PYA/Monarch (sold to Royal Ahold's U.S. food service for nearly $1.6 billion)
	Champion Europe
	Coach
	The International Fabrics division of Courtaulds
	The international bakery businesses in France, India, China, and the United Kingdom
2004	Filodoro, an Italian intimate apparel business

Underwear, and Household Products. McMillan orchestrated several divestitures to begin the process of sharpening Sara Lee's business focus.

Brenda C. Barnes, who had been president of PepsiCola North America from 1996 to 1998, joined Sara Lee as president and chief operating officer in July 2004. At the time of her appointment, Barnes, age 50, was a member of the board of directors at Avon Products, the New York Times Company, Sears Roebuck, and Staples. During her 22-year career at PepsiCo, Barnes had held a number of senior executive positions in operations, general management, manufacturing, sales, and marketing. From November 1999 to March 2000, she served as interim president and chief operating officer of Starwood Hotels & Resorts. Barnes's appointment as president and CEO of Sara Lee was announced on February 10, 2005, the same day as the announcement of the plan to transform Sara Lee into an even more tightly focused company.

SARA LEE'S RETRENCHMENT INITIATIVES

The first phase of Brenda Barnes's transformation plan for Sara Lee was to exit eight businesses that had been targeted as nonstrategic:

- *Direct selling*—a $450 million business that sold cosmetics, skin care products, fragrances, toiletries, household products, apparel, and other products to consumers through a network of independent salespeople in 18 countries around the world, most notably in Mexico, Australia, the Philippines, and Japan. In August 2005, Sara Lee announced a definitive agreement to sell its direct selling business to Tupperware Corporation for $547 million in cash.[3] The sale included products being sold under such brands as Avroy Shlain, House of Fuller, House of Sara Lee, NaturCare, Nutrimetics, Nuvó Cosméticos, and Swissgarde.

- *U.S. retail coffee*—a $213 million business that marketed the well-known Chock full o'Nuts, Hills Bros., MJB, and Chase & Sanborn coffees plus several private-label coffees. Not included in the divestiture plan was the sale of Sara Lee's fast-growing global coffee brand, Senseo, which had sales of approximately $85 million. The U.S. retail coffee business was sold to Italy-based Segafredo Zanetti Group for $82 million in late 2005.[4]

- *European apparel*—a Sara Lee business unit that marketed such well-known brands as Dim, Playtex, Wonderbra, Abanderado, Nur Die, and Unno in France, Germany, Italy, Spain, the United Kingdom, and much of Eastern Europe; it also included Sara Lee Courtaulds, a UK-based maker of private-label clothing for retailers. The branded European apparel business had nearly $1.2 billion in sales in fiscal year 2005, ending July 2, 2005; the Sara Lee Courtaulds business had fiscal 2005 sales of about $560 million. In November 2005, Sara Lee sold the branded apparel portion of the European apparel business unit to an affiliate of Sun Capital Partners, a U.S. private equity company, based in Boca Raton, Florida, for about $115 million plus possible contingent payments based on future performance.[5] In May 2006, a big fraction of Sara Lee Courtaulds was sold to PD Enterprise Ltd., a global garment producer with nine facilities that produced more than 120 million garments annually, including bras, underwear, nightwear, swim- and beachwear, formal wear, casual wear, jackets and coats, baby clothes, and socks; the deal with PD Enterprise did not include three Sara Lee Courtaulds facilities in Sri Lanka (Sara Lee was continuing its efforts to find a buyer for the Sri Lanka operations). Sara Lee received no material consideration as a result of the sale and remained liable for certain obligations of Sara Lee Courtaulds after the disposition, the most significant of which was the defined benefit pension plans that were underfunded by $483 million at the end of 2005.

- *European nuts and snacks*—a business with approximately €88 million in annual sales in fiscal 2005 that marketed products under the Duyvis brand in the Netherlands and Belgium as well as the Bénénuts brand in France. Sara Lee sold its European nuts and snacks business in the Netherlands, Belgium, and France to PepsiCo for approximately $160 million in November 2005.[6]

- *European rice*—a small business that packaged Lassie brand rice sold in the Netherlands and other European countries. The business unit was sold to Grupo SOS of Spain for $62 million in November 2005.
- *U.S. meat snacks*—a small unit with annual sales of $33 million in fiscal 2005 and $25 million in fiscal 2006. This business was sold in June 2006 for $9 million.[7]
- *European meats*—a $1.1 billion packaged meats business in Europe that had respectable market positions in France, the Benelux region, and Portugal and included such brands as Aoste, Justin Bridou, Cochonou, Nobre, and Imperial. Headquartered in Hoofddorp, the Netherlands, Sara Lee's European meats operation generated $1.1 billion in sales in fiscal 2005, and employed approximately 4,500 people. In June 2006, Sara Lee completed the sale of this unit to Smithfield Foods for $575 million in cash; based in Smithfield, Virginia, Smithfield Foods was the world's largest grower of hogs and producer of pork products and had subsidiaries in France, Poland, Romania, and the United Kingdom that marketed meats under the Krakus and Stefano's brands as well as other brands.[8]

- *Sara Lee branded apparel*—a business that consisted of producing and marketing 10 brands of apparel: Hanes, L'eggs, Champion, Bali, Barely There, Playtex, Wonderbra, Just My Size, Duofold (outdoor apparel), and Outer Banks (golf, corporate, and stylish sportswear); sales of these brands were chiefly in North America, Latin America, and Asia. Sara Lee's strategy for exiting branded apparel (2004 sales of $4.5 billion) was to spin the entire business off as an independent company named Hanesbrands Inc. Two top executives of the Sara Lee branded apparel business were named to head the new company. The spin-off was completed in September 2006 when Sara Lee distributed 100 percent of the common stock of Hanesbrands to Sara Lee shareholders; shares were traded on the New York Stock Exchange under the symbol HBI.

Sara Lee management expected the retrenchment initiatives to generate combined net after-tax proceeds in excess of $3 billion. Exhibit 1 provides financial data relating to the divested businesses. The next section provides additional details about the Hanesbrands spin-off.

▶ EXHIBIT 1

Financial Data for Sara Lee's Divested Businesses, Fiscal Years 2004–2006

(a) Sales and Income of Divested Businesses, Fiscal Years 2004–2006 ($ millions)

	Fiscal Years		
	2006	**2005**	**2004**
Net Sales of Divested Businesses			
Direct selling	$ 202	$ 473	$ 447
U.S. retail coffee	122	213	206
European branded apparel	641	1,184	1,276
European nuts and snacks	54	64	66
Sara Lee Courtaulds	437	558	536
European rice	n/a	n/a	n/a
U.S. meat snacks	25	30	33
European meats	1,114	1,176	1,111
Total net sales	$2,595	$3,698	$3,675

(continued)

▶ EXHIBIT 1   *(concluded)*

	Fiscal Years		
	2006	**2005**	**2004**
Pretax Income (Loss) of Divested Businesses			
Direct selling	$ 14	$ 55	$ 55
U.S. retail coffee	(46)	(39)	(2)
European branded apparel	(186)	(302)	67
European nuts and snacks	8	7	12
Sara Lee Courtaulds	(69)	—	14
European rice	n/a	n/a	n/a
U.S. meat snacks	(14)	(1)	(1)
European meats	(57)	90	101
Total pretax income (loss)	$(350)	$(190)	$ 246
After-Tax Income (Loss) of Divested Businesses			
Direct selling	$ 54	$ (12)	$ 34
U.S. retail coffee	(39)	(33)	—
European branded apparel	(153)	(296)	68
European nuts and snacks	3	3	7
Sara Lee Courtaulds	(71)	(1)	26
European rice	n/a	n/a	n/a
U.S. meat snacks	(9)	(1)	—
European meats	(41)	(22)	86
Total after-tax income (loss)	$(256)	$(362)	$ 221

(b) Proceeds Realized from the Sales of the Divested Businesses ($ millions)

	Sale Price	Pretax Gain on Sale	Tax Benefit (Charge)	After-Tax Gain
Direct selling	$ 547	$327	$(107)	$220
U.S. retail coffee	82	5	(2)	3
European branded apparel	~115	45	41	86
European nuts and snacks	160	66	4	70
Sara Lee Courtaulds	No material consideration**	22	—	22
European rice	62	n/a	n/a	n/a
U.S. meat snacks	9	1	(1)	—
European meats*	575	42	(2)	40
Totals	$1,550***	$508	$ (67)	$441

*This unit was divested in early fiscal 2007; data regarding the gains from the sale is from a company press release of November 7, 2006, reporting results for the first quarter of fiscal 2007.

**Sara Lee retained liability for unfunded pension benefits of $483 million at Sara Lee Courtaulds and made payments of approximately $93 million to remedy its liability during 2006.

***The actual amount realized from the sales of these businesses was closer to $1.3 billion after taking into account the payments made to remedy unfunded pension liabilities at Sara Lee Courtaulds and other costs incurred in discontinuing the operations of all these businesses.

n/a = not available

Sources: Sara Lee, 2006 10-K report, p. 56, and various company press releases announcing the sale and disposition of the businesses.

THE SPIN-OFF OF HANESBRANDS

Sara Lee management's decision to exit the branded apparel business was driven principally by eroding sales and weak returns on its equity investment in branded apparel—see Exhibit 2. But rather than sell the business, management determined that shareholders would be better served by spinning off the branded apparel business as a stand-alone company. Sara Lee shareholders received one share of Hanesbrands stock for every eight shares owned. Hanesbrands began independent operations in September 2006 and organized its business around four product/geographic segments, as shown in Exhibit 3.

However, the spin-off of Hanesbrands had some unique financial features. The terms of the spin-off called for Hanesbrands to make a one-time "dividend" payment of $2.4 billion to Sara Lee immediately following the commencement of independent operations. But in order to make the $2.4 billion payment to Sara Lee and to fund its own operations, Hanesbrands borrowed $2.6 billion, thus saddling itself with a huge debt that prompted Standard & Poor's to assign the company a B+ credit rating (which put Hanesbrands in the bottom half of apparel companies from a credit rating standpoint). The company's debt-to-equity ratio was extraordinarily high, raising some questions about whether the interest expenses associated with the high debt would still leave

► EXHIBIT 2

Performance of Hanesbrands Prior to Spin-Off by Sara Lee, Fiscal Years 2002–2006 ($ thousands)

	Fiscal Years Ending				
	July 1, 2006	July 3, 2005	July 3, 2004	June 28, 2003	June 29, 2002
Statements of Income Data					
Net sales	$4,472,832	$4,683,683	$4,632,741	$4,669,665	$4,920,840
Cost of sales	2,987,500	3,223,571	3,092,026	3,010,383	3,278,506
Gross profit	1,485,332	1,460,112	1,540,715	1,659,282	1,642,334
Selling, general and administrative expenses	1,051,833	1,053,654	1,087,964	1,126,065	1,146,549
Charges for (income from) exit activities	(101)	46,978	27,466	(14,397)	27,580
Income from operations	433,600	359,480	425,285	547,614	468,205
Interest expense	26,075	35,244	37,411	44,245	2,509
Interest income	(8,795)	(21,280)	(12,998)	(46,631)	(13,753)
Income before income taxes	416,320	345,516	400,872	550,000	479,449
Income tax expense (benefit)	93,827	127,007	(48,680)	121,560	139,488
Net income	$ 322,493	$ 218,509	$ 449,552	$ 428,440	$ 339,961
Balance Sheet Data					
Cash and cash equivalents	$ 298,252	$1,080,799	$ 674,154	$ 289,816	$ 106,250
Total assets	4,891,075	4,237,154	4,402,758	3,915,573	4,064,730
Noncurrent liabilities:					
Noncurrent capital lease obligations	2,786	6,188	7,200	10,054	12,171
Noncurrent deferred tax liabilities	5,014	7,171	—	6,599	10,140
Other noncurrent liabilities	42,187	40,200	28,734	32,598	37,660
Total noncurrent liabilities	49,987	53,559	35,934	49,251	59,971
Total Sara Lee equity investment	3,229,134	2,602,362	2,797,370	2,237,448	1,762,824

Source: Hanesbrands, fiscal 2006 10-K report.

▶ EXHIBIT 3

Hanesbrands' Lineup of Products and Brands, 2006

Product/Geographic Segments	Primary Products	Primary Brands
Innerwear	Intimate apparel, such as bras, panties and bodywear	Hanes, Playtex, Bali, barely there, Just My Size, Wonderbra
	Men's underwear and kids' underwear	Hanes, Champion, Polo Ralph Lauren**
	Socks	Hanes, Champion
Outerwear	Activewear, such as performance T-shirts and shorts	Hanes, Champion, Just My Size
	Casual wear, such as T-shirts, fleece and sport shirts	Hanes, Just My Size, Outerbanks, Hanes Beefy-T
Hosiery	Hosiery	L'eggs, Hanes, Just My Size
International	Activewear, men's underwear, kids' underwear, intimate apparel, socks, hosiery and casual wear	Hanes, Wonderbra,* Playtex,* Champion, Rinbros, Bali

*Terms of the February 2006 sale of Sara Lee's European branded apparel business prevented Hanesbrands from selling Wonderbra and Playtex branded products in the European Union, several other European countries, and South Africa.

**Hanesbrands had a license agreement to sell men's underwear and kids' underwear under the Polo Ralph Lauren label.

Source: Hanesbrands, fiscal 2006 10-K report.

Hanesbrands with sufficient funds and financial flexibility to invest in revitalizing its brands and growing its business.

A *BusinessWeek* reporter speculated that the reason for the unusually outsized dividend payment to Sara Lee was that the proceeds Sara Lee realized from the sales of the divested units fell far short of the hoped-for $3 billion that was an integral part of the retrenchment strategy and restructuring announced by CEO Brenda Barnes in February 2005.[9] To make up for the shortfall, Sara Lee supposedly opted to get more cash out of the Hanesbrands spin-off.

SARA LEE'S POST-RETRENCHMENT STRATEGY: INITIATIVES TO REVITALIZE SALES AND BOOST PROFITABILITY

Upon the completion of Sara Lee Corporation's disposition of nonstrategic businesses in September 2006, Sara Lee management turned its full attention to increasing the sales, market shares, and profitability of its remaining businesses. The two chief financial goals were to boost top line sales by 2–4 percent annually to reach $14 billion by 2010 and to achieve a 12 percent operating profit margin by 2010. Sara Lee planned to achieve its objectives by developing three competitive capabilities in all of its remaining businesses. The company's management believed that competitive pricing, innovative new products, and brand-building capabilities were essential to its efforts to please consumers. Category management and leverage through size were also thought to be necessary for the company to win new accounts with supermarket and discount store customers. Operating excellence was the third key element of its corporate strategy, which was critical to competitive pricing. Major operations initiatives at Sara Lee included lean manufacturing, centralized purchasing to achieve economies of scope, and the implementation of a common corporate-wide information systems platform.

While the company was making headway in focusing on consumer needs and category management, its efforts to improve operating efficiency and increase operating margins were showing little progress by year-end 2007. Top management launched Project Accelerate in March 2008 to strengthen the company's ability to meet its objective of achieving an operating profit margin of 12 percent by 2010. Project Accelerate included additional business process outsourcing, operating segment restructuring, new supply chain efficiencies, reductions in corporate overhead, and reductions in employee benefit costs. By the end of fiscal 2010, Project Accelerate had produced total cumulative benefits of $180 million. Management expected cumulative benefits for Project Accelerate to reach $350 million to $400 million by the end of fiscal 2012.

The organizational structure developed by Brenda Barnes and other key Sara Lee managers that would best enable the company's businesses to contribute to corporate goals was a six-division structure built around product similarities, customer types, and geographic regions. The North American Retail division included such products sold in supermarkets and discount stores as lunch meats, breakfast sausage, smoked sausage, frozen desserts, and single-serve coffee; its North American Fresh Bakery division included fresh breads, buns, and bagels sold in supermarkets; and North American Foodservice included the sales of meat products, bakery products, and coffee and tea products sold to food service accounts in North America. The International Beverage division included the sales of coffee and tea products in Europe, while the International Bakery division included sales of bakery goods in Europe. The company's International Household and Body Care division included insecticides, personal hygiene products, and cleaning brands sold outside North America. The Household and Body Care division was discontinued in 2010, with all but shoe care products and cleaning brands divested during the year. In fiscal 2011, Sara Lee was negotiating with a number of potential buyers for the sale of these remaining businesses. Exhibit 4 presents a summary of Sara Lee's financial performance for 2004 through 2010 that includes all businesses operated in each reporting year. A summary of the financial performance between 2006 and 2010 for the company's

continuing operations in 2010 is presented in Exhibit 5. Exhibit 6 presents sales and operating profits for Sara Lee's major business segments for 2008 through 2010.

North American Retail

Sara Lee's North American Retail division had limited its product lineup to food categories that offered retailers high margins, were growing faster than the overall industry, and showed consumer preferences for branded products versus private-label brands. In 2010, the division had a number of market-leading brands such as Ball Park franks, Jimmy Dean sausage, Hillshire Farm smoked sausage, State Fair corn dogs, Sara Lee frozen desserts, and Senseo single-serving coffeemakers and coffee pods. Sara Lee was the second-largest seller of lunch meats and frozen desserts in North America. In 2010, Sara Lee North American Retail businesses held market shares of 30 percent in smoked sausage, 23 percent in hot dogs, 14 percent in lunch meat, 58 percent in breakfast sausage, 22 percent in frozen desserts, and 55 percent in single-serve coffee. Ten of the division's 12 core products increased market share in 2010. Between 2008 and 2010, the division's sales had grown faster than the sales of any other processed food company. Also, the operating profit margin for the division improved from 9.2 percent in 2009 to 12.3 percent in 2010. Going into 2011, Sara Lee's North American Retail meats business unit was near completion of a state-of-the art meat-slicing plant and the planned divestiture of its kosher hot dog brands and commodity meat business.

The division's Senseo single-serving coffee pods were also the number one brand in North America, with a 55 percent share of the market for single-serving coffees in 2008. However, the division's Senseo coffeemakers and coffee pods had experienced little growth in the United States and achieved U.S. sales of only $26 million in 2008. Single-serve coffee accounted for less than 6 percent of the global retail coffee market in 2009, but was expected to increase to 8.5 percent of industry sales by 2013.

EXHIBIT 4

Summary of Sara Lee Corporation's Annual Financial Performance, 2004–2010 ($ millions, except per share data)

	Years Ended						
	July 3, 2010	June 27, 2009	June 28, 2008	June 30, 2007	July 1, 2006	July 2, 2005	July 3, 2004
Results of Operations							
Continuing and discontinued operations							
Net sales	$10,793	$12,881	$13,212	$12,278	$15,944	$19,254	$19,566
Operating income	918	713	260	566	911	1,120	1,723
Income before income taxes	795	588	160	419	683	934	1,542
Income (loss)	642	364	(41)	426	410	731	1,272
Income (loss) per share of common stock							
Basic	$0.92	$0.52	($0.06)	$0.58	$0.54	$0.93	$1.61
Diluted	$0.92	$0.52	($0.06)	$0.57	$0.53	$0.92	$1.59
Income (loss) from discontinued operations	(199)	—	(14)	62	(256)	(12)	—
Gain (loss) on sale of discontinued operations	84	—	(24)	16	401	—	—
Net income (loss)	527	364	(79)	504	555	719	1,272
Net income (loss) per share of common stock							
Basic	$0.74	$0.52	($0.11)	$0.68	$0.72	$0.91	—
Diluted	$0.73	$0.52	($0.11)	$0.68	$0.72	$0.90	—
Financial Position							
Total assets	$8,836	$9,417	$10,830	$12,190	$14,522	$14,412	$14,883
Total debt	2,781	2,820	3,188	4,267	5,959	4,754	5,295
Per Common Share							
Dividends declared	$0.44	$0.44	$0.42	$0.40	$0.79	$0.78	$0.75
Book value at year-end	2.25	2.93	3.98	3.61	3.22	3.74	3.71
Market value at year-end	13.99	9.58	12.18	17.4	16.02	19.65	23.17
Shares used in the determination of net income per share							
Basic (in millions)	688	701	715	741	766	789	788
Diluted (in millions)	691	703	715	743	768	796	798
Other Information—Continuing Operations Only							
Net cash flow from operating activities	$ 631	$ 900	$ 596	$ 492	$ 1,232	$ 1,314	$ 2,042
Depreciation	361	383	398	420	541	563	561
Capital expenditures	375	379	509	631	625	538	530
Number of employees	33,000	41,000	44,000	52,000	109,000	137,000	150,400

Source: Sara Lee Corporation Annual Reports, various years.

EXHIBIT 5

Financial Summary for Sara Lee Corporation's Continuing Operations, 2006–2010 ($ millions, except per share data)

	Years Ended				
	July 3, 2010	June 27, 2009	June 28, 2008	June 30, 2007	July 1, 2006
Results of Operations, Continuing Operations Only					
Continuing operations only					
Net sales	$10,793	$10,882	$10,949	$ 9,964	$ 9,371
Operating income	918	487	(51)	305	211
Income before income taxes	795	358	(156)	161	(26)
Income (loss)	642	225	(276)	258	(18)
Income (loss) per share of common stock					
Basic	$0.92	$0.31	$(0.39)	$0.35	$(0.02)
Diluted	$0.92	$0.31	$(0.39)	$0.34	$(0.02)
Income (loss) from discontinued operations	(199)	155	236	228	184
Gain (loss) on sale of discontinued operations	84	—	(24)	16	401
Net income (loss)	527	380	(64)	502	568
Net income (loss) attributable to Sara Lee	506	364	(79)	504	555
Net income (loss) per share of common stock					
Basic	$0.74	$0.52	$(0.11)	$0.68	$0.72
Diluted	$0.73	$0.52	$(0.11)	$0.68	$0.72
Financial Position					
Total assets	$ 8,836	$ 9,419	$10,831	$11,755	$ 14,660
Total debt	2,781	2,804	3,164	4,204	5,898
Per Common Share					
Dividends declared	$0.44	$0.44	$0.42	$0.50	$0.59
Book value at year-end	2.25	2.93	3.98	3.51	3.22
Market value at year-end	13.99	9.58	12.18	17.4	16.02
Shares used in the determination of net income per share					
Basic (in millions)	688	701	715	741	766
Diluted (in millions)	691	703	715	743	768
Other Information—Continuing Operations Only					
Net cash flow from operating activities	$ 631	$ 640	$ 385	$ 268	$ 122
Depreciation	361	351	367	363	351
Capital expenditures	375	359	490	568	396
Number of employees	33,000	35,000	37,000	38,000	41,000

Source: Sara Lee Corporation 2010 Annual Report.

EXHIBIT 6

Net Sales and Operating Profits for Sara Lee Corporation's Business Units, 2008–2010 ($ millions)			
	2010	**2009**	**2008**
Net Sales			
North American Retail	$ 2,818	$ 2,767	$ 2,613
North American Fresh Bakery	2,128	2,200	2,028
North American Foodservice	1,873	2,092	2,186
International Beverage	3,221	3,062	3,238
International Bakery	785	795	934
Total business segments	10,825	10,916	10,999
Intersegment sales	(32)	(34)	(50)
Net sales	$10,793	$10,882	$10,949
Income (Loss) from Continuing Operations before Income Taxes			
North American Retail	$ 346	$253	$ 149
North American Fresh Bakery	44	26	55
North American Foodservice	125	36	(324)
International Beverage	592	493	551
International Bakery	(14)	(194)	(346)
Total operating segment income	$ 1,093	$ 614	$ 85

Source: Presentations by Sara Lee, 2010 annual report.

North American Fresh Bakery

Sara Lee's entry into the fresh bakery business in 2002 had produced phenomenal results, with its sales increasing from $91 million in 2003 to $2.1 billion in 2008. In 2010, Sara Lee was the best-selling brand of packaged bread sold in the United States, with an 8.3 percent market share. Arnold's, Nature's Own, and Pepperidge Farm were the three next best-selling brands in U.S. supermarkets and discount stores. The North American Fresh Bakery division held a number one ranking in hot dog and hamburger buns, and produced and marketed the EarthGrains brand of packaged bread. The company's ability to negotiate with supermarket buyers to increase shelf space allocated for its bakery products accounted for much of the growth in bakery sales. In several cases, Sara Lee's fresh bakery division had been able to increase space on the bread aisle from 1.5 feet to 4.0 feet. Average weekly sales tripled in stores where Sara Lee gained shelf space. Poor economic conditions in the United States had slowed the division's growth in revenues considerably, but the company had been able to improve operating income through pricing discipline and Project Accelerate productivity gains.

North American Foodservice

Sara Lee's North American Foodservice division marketed and sold products available to consumers in North American supermarkets to food service distributors such as U.S. Foodservice and Sodexho. North American Foodservice also sold meat, bakery, and coffee products to national restaurant chains like Sonic, Dunkin' Donuts, Waffle House, Quiznos, and Burger King. Most of the division's sales were standard Sara Lee, Jimmy Dean, Hillshire Farm, Ball Park, and State Fair branded products, although the division did customize meat and bakery products for its largest customers. Coffee brands sold to North American food service accounts included Douwe Egberts and Superior Coffee. North American Foodservice also provided commercial-grade coffee machines and espresso makers to food service customers.

The food service industry was expected to be a considerable growth opportunity for Sara Lee as Americans continued to eat a higher percentage of meals away from home. However, the recession that began in late 2007 and resulting reduced consumer spending that continued into 2010 had dramatically decreased spending at restaurants. Even though division sales had declined from nearly $2.2 billion in sales in 2008 to approximately $1.9 billion in sales in 2010, the division had preserved market share in key product categories. North American Foodservice held a 65 percent market share in liquid coffee and tea sold to food service customers, a 52 percent market share in pies, a 19 percent market share in cakes, and a 20 percent share of refrigerated dough sold to food service customers. The division also operated a route sales coffee business and distributed a number of low-margin sauces and dressings sold to restaurants that were both slated for divestiture.

Sara Lee's food service division had benefited from the innovations developed by Sara Lee's retail divisions since the food service trends mirrored those in the grocery industry. For example, presliced deli meats that were intended to satisfy consumers' desire for convenience also made sense for food service accounts. Food service customers had found that it was more cost-effective and more sanitary to purchase presliced meat than to purchase bulk meat for restaurant employees to slice. Sara Lee's dessert and bakery brands like Sara Lee, Bistro Collection, and Chef Pierre also benefited from innovations developed for consumers.

International Beverage

Sara Lee's International Beverage business included teas and coffee products marketed in Europe, Australia, New Zealand, and Brazil. The strength of the company's coffee brands—which included Douwe Egberts, Maison du Café, Marcilla, and Senseo—made it the leader in retail sales of coffee in the Netherlands, Belgium, Hungary, Denmark, and Brazil in 2010. Sara Lee's coffee brands were ranked second in retail coffee sales in France and Spain in 2010. The company was also the number one seller of coffee to food service customers in the United States, the Netherlands, Belgium, Hungary, Denmark, and Norway in 2010.

The global retail coffee market was expected to grow from $51 billion in 2009 to $62 billion in 2013, with instant coffee retail sales projected to increase from $19.6 billion to $23.6 billion, espresso expected to grow from $4.3 billion in 2009 to $9.9 billion in 2013, and single-serving coffee pods expected to increase from $2.9 billion to $5.3 billion between 2009 and 2013. Retail sales of traditional roast and ground coffee were projected to decline from $24.3 billion in 2009 to $23.5 billion in 2013. In 2010, Sara Lee's Senseo single-serving coffeemakers were the best-selling brand of single-serving coffee machines in Europe, with a 40 percent market share, and the sales of its coffee pods had increased from about 15,000 tons in 2004 to approximately 28,000 tons in 2009. The company launched nine new Senseo coffeemaker models in 2009 and expanded its lineup of single-serving coffees to include L'OR Espresso capsules. L'OR Espresso capsules were compatible with Nestlé's Nespresso espresso makers, which were the second-best-selling brand of single-serve coffeemaker in Europe, with a 27 percent market share in 2009.

International Bakery

Sara Lee's International Bakery division primarily consisted of the Bimbo brand of fresh, frozen, and refrigerated bread products. Bimbo fresh bread was sold in Spain and accounted for 63 percent of division sales; Bimbo frozen bread was sold only in Australia and accounted for 12 percent of division sales; and Bimbo refrigerated bread sold in France accounted for 25 percent of division sales. Bimbo was the market leader among packaged breads sold in Spain in 2010, with a 37 percent market share—private-label brands collectively ranked as the second-best-selling packaged bread in Spain. Even though Bimbo was the best-selling brand of packaged bread in Spain, the deep long-term economic recession in Spain, which included an unemployment rate higher than 20 percent, had caused division sales declines and operating losses every year since 2007. The division had met with limited success marketing packaged bread in European countries outside of Spain because of a consumer preference for fresh-baked bread. Sara Lee hoped to improve financial performance within the division by introducing new products, adopting an everyday low pricing strategy and increasing bakery capacity utilization from 58 percent in 2009 to more than 80 percent in

2011 and beyond. Increased capacity utilization would be achieved through the sale or closing of underutilized facilities.

International Household & Body Care

Sara Lee's International Household & Body Care unit's Kiwi brand was the number one shoe care brand worldwide, with distribution in 200 countries and a global market share of 30 percent in 2008. Sanex was the number one brand of bath and shower products in Denmark, Spain, and France, and Ambi Pur was the best-selling air freshener in the Netherlands and Spain and the third best-selling air freshener brand in the United Kingdom, Italy, and France. The division also included various insecticide brands sold primarily in India, Malaysia, Spain, and France.

In 2009, Sara Lee announced its intention to divest its entire Household and Body Care business. During 2010, the company sold its household insecticides business in India to Godrej Consumer Products Ltd. for €185 million and its Ambi Pur air care business to Procter & Gamble for €320. Also during fiscal 2010, Sara Lee agreed to sell its global body care and European detergents business to Unilever for €1.275 billion. The transaction was expected to close by the end of the 2010 calendar year. The sale of the company's remaining insecticide brands to S. C. Johnson and Son for €153.5 million was also expected to close by the end of the 2010 calendar year. The company had identified several potential buyers for the remainder of its Household and Body Care unit, which included Kiwi shoe care products sold internationally and Endust and Ty-D-Bol cleaning products sold in the Asia-Pacific region. Analysts believed that Sara Lee could expect $300 million to $400 million from the sale of Kiwi. The amount Sara Lee might receive for the Endust and Ty-D-Bol brands was less definite.

EXPECTATIONS IN EARLY 2011

Sara Lee's top management believed that the company's restructured business lineup and corporate strategy initiatives—both those planned and those under way—would deliver strong increases in shareholder value in 2011 and 2012. Sara Lee's interim CEO, Marcel Smits, expected that the company's divestiture of its Household and Body Care businesses, the repurchase of $360 million of shares of common stock in 2011, and cumulative Project Accelerate benefits of $350 million to $400 million expected by 2012 would lead to improvements in earnings per share of $0.15 to $0.20. In addition, the company planned to restructure the corporate functions of its International Beverage and Bakery businesses to eliminate 390 positions and reduce overhead by €30 million by fiscal 2013. The company intended for most of its growth to come from the further development and growth of its premium brands such as L' OR Espresso and Senseo as well as its market-leading brands like Ball Park, Hillshire Farm, Jimmy Dean, and Sara Lee. The company also expected that an increased emphasis on wellness and nutrition would allow it to increase sales of its meat and bakery products in North America and Europe. The company expected to contain growth in operating expenses through a continued emphasis on efficiency, focusing on its most promising markets, and by reducing inventories. Smits and his chief lieutenants believed that the company was fully capable of delivering significant gains in shareholder value as the search continued for a permanent CEO.

ENDNOTES

[1] Sara Lee, press release, February 10, 2005.

[2] Sara Lee, press releases on February 10, 2005, and February 25, 2005.

[3] Sara Lee, press release, August 10, 2005.

[4] Sara Lee, press release, October 26, 2005.

[5] Sara Lee, press release, November 14, 2005.

[6] Sara Lee, press release, November 22, 2005.

[7] Sara Lee, fiscal 2006 10-K report.

[8] Sara Lee, press release, June 27, 2006.

[9] Jane Sasseen, "How Sara Lee Left Hanes in Its Skivvies," *BusinessWeek,* September 18, 2006, p. 40.

ROBIN HOOD

Joseph Lampel
New York University

It was in the spring of the second year of his insurrection against the High Sheriff of Nottingham that Robin Hood took a walk in Sherwood Forest. As he walked he pondered the progress of the campaign, the disposition of his forces, the Sheriff's recent moves, and the options that confronted him.

The revolt against the Sheriff had begun as a personal crusade. It erupted out of Robin's conflict with the Sheriff and his administration. However, alone Robin Hood could do little. He therefore sought allies, men with grievances and a deep sense of justice. Later he welcomed all who came, asking few questions and demanding only a willingness to serve. Strength, he believed, lay in numbers.

He spent the first year forging the group into a disciplined band, united in enmity against the Sheriff and willing to live outside the law. The band's organization was simple. Robin ruled supreme, making all important decisions. He delegated specific tasks to his lieutenants. Will Scarlett was in charge of intelligence and scouting. His main job was to shadow the Sheriff and his men, always alert to their next move. He also collected information on the travel plans of rich merchants and tax collectors. Little John kept discipline among the men and saw to it that their archery was at the high peak that their profession demanded. Scarlock took care of the finances, converting loot to cash, paying shares of the take, and finding suitable hiding places for the surplus. Finally, Much the Miller's son had the difficult task of provisioning the ever-increasing band of Merrymen.

The increasing size of the band was a source of satisfaction for Robin, but also a source of concern. The fame of his Merrymen was spreading, and new recruits were pouring in from every corner of England. As the band grew larger, their small bivouac became a major encampment. Between raids the men milled about, talking and playing games. Vigilance was in decline, and discipline was becoming harder to enforce. "Why," Robin reflected, "I don't know half the men I run into these days."

The growing band was also beginning to exceed the food capacity of the forest. Game was becoming scarce, and supplies had to be obtained from outlying villages. The cost of buying food was beginning to drain the band's financial reserves at the very moment when revenues were in decline. Travelers, especially those with the most to lose, were now giving the forest a wide berth. This was costly and inconvenient to them, but it was preferable to having all their goods confiscated.

Robin believed that the time had come for the Merrymen to change their policy of outright confiscation of goods to one of a fixed transit tax. His lieutenants strongly resisted this idea. They were proud of the Merrymen's famous motto: "Rob the rich and give to the poor." "The farmers and the townspeople," they argued, "are our most important allies. How can we tax them, and still hope for their help in our fight against the Sheriff?"

Robin wondered how long the Merrymen could keep to the ways and methods of their early days. The Sheriff was growing stronger and becoming better organized. He now had the money and the men and was beginning to harass the band, probing for its weaknesses. The tide of events was beginning to turn against the Merrymen. Robin felt that the campaign must be decisively concluded before the Sheriff had a chance to deliver a mortal blow. "But how," he wondered, "could this be done?"

Robin had often entertained the possibility of killing the Sheriff, but the chances for this seemed increasingly remote. Besides, killing the Sheriff might satisfy his personal thirst for revenge, but it would not improve the situation. Robin had hoped that the perpetual state of unrest, and the Sheriff's failure to collect taxes, would lead to his removal from office. Instead, the Sheriff used his political connections to obtain reinforcement. He had powerful friends at court and was well regarded by the regent, Prince John.

Prince John was vicious and volatile. He was consumed by his unpopularity among the people, who wanted the imprisoned King Richard back. He also lived in constant fear of the barons, who had first given him the regency but were now beginning to dispute his claim to the throne. Several of these barons had set out to collect the ransom that would release King Richard the Lionheart from his jail in Austria. Robin was invited to join the conspiracy in return for future amnesty. It was a dangerous proposition. Provincial banditry was one thing, court intrigue another. Prince John had spies everywhere, and he was known for his vindictiveness. If the conspirators' plan failed, the pursuit would be relentless, and retributions swift.

The sound of the supper horn startled Robin from his thoughts. There was the smell of roasting venison in the air. Nothing was resolved or settled. Robin headed for camp promising himself that he would give these problems his utmost attention after tomorrow's raid.

SOUTHWEST AIRLINES IN 2010: CULTURE, VALUES, AND OPERATING PRACTICES

Arthur A. Thompson
The University of Alabama

John E. Gamble
University of South Alabama

In 2010, Southwest Airlines was the market share leader in domestic air travel in the United States; it transported more passengers from U.S. airports to U.S. destinations than any other airline, and it offered more regularly scheduled domestic flights than any other airline. Southwest also had the enviable distinction of being the only major U.S. air carrier that was consistently profitable. The U.S. airline industry had lost money in 15 of the 30 years from 1980 through 2009, with combined annual losses exceeding combined annual profits by $43.2 billion. Yet Southwest had reported a profit every year since 1973, chiefly because of its zealous pursuit of low operating costs, low fares, and customer-pleasing service.

From humble beginnings as a quirky but scrappy underdog that flew mainly to secondary airports (rather than high-traffic airports like Chicago O'Hare, Dallas–Fort Worth, Atlanta Hartsfield, and New York's LaGuardia and Kennedy airports), Southwest had climbed up through the industry ranks to become a major competitive force in the domestic segment of the U.S. airline industry. It had weathered industry downturns, dramatic increases in the prices of jet fuel, cataclysmic falloffs in airline traffic due to terrorist attacks and economy-wide recessions, and fare wars and other attempts by rivals to undercut its business, all the while adding more and more flights to more and more airports. Since 2000, the number of passengers flying Southwest had increased by more than 28 million annually, whereas passenger traffic on domestic routes had declined at such carriers as American Airlines, Delta, Continental, United, and US Airways—see Exhibit 1.

COMPANY BACKGROUND

In late 1966, Rollin King, a San Antonio entrepreneur who owned a small commuter air service, marched into Herb Kelleher's law office with a plan to start a low-cost/low-fare airline that would shuttle passengers between San Antonio, Dallas, and Houston.[1] Over the years, King had heard many Texas businesspeople complain about the length of time that it took to drive between the three cities and the expense of flying the airlines currently serving these cities. His business concept for the airline was simple: attract passengers by flying convenient schedules, get passengers to their destination on time, make sure they have a good experience, and charge fares competitive with travel by automobile. Kelleher, skeptical that King's business idea was viable, dug into the possibilities during the next few weeks and concluded that a new airline was feasible; he agreed to handle the necessary legal work and also to invest $10,000 of his own funds in the venture.

▶ EXHIBIT 1

Total Number of Domestic and International Passengers Traveling on Selected U.S. Airlines, 2000–2009 (in thousands)

Carrier	Total Number of Enplaned Passengers (including both passengers paying for tickets and passengers traveling on frequent flyer awards)						
	2000	2002	2004	2006	2007	2008	2009
American Airlines							
Domestic	68,319	77,489	72,648	76,813	76,581	71,539	66,142
International	17,951	16,580	18,858	21,313	21,562	21,233	19,578
Total	86,270	94,069	91,506	98,126	98,143	92,772	85,720
Continental Airlines[1]							
Domestic	36,591	31,653	31,529	35,795	37,117	34,501	31,915
International	8,747	8,247	9,146	10,994	11,859	12,418	12,031
Total	45,338	39,900	40,675	46,789	48,976	46,919	43,946
Delta Airlines[2]							
Domestic	97,965	83,747	79,374	63,496	61,599	59,276	55,627
International	7,596	7,036	7,416	10,020	11,435	12,339	12,118
Total	105,561	90,783	86,790	73,516	73,034	71,615	67,745
JetBlue Airways							
Domestic	1,128	5,672	11,616	18,098	20,528	20,479	20,008
International	—	—	116	408	777	1,345	2,370
Total	1,128	5,672	11,732	18,506	21,305	21,824	22,378
Northwest Airlines[2]							
Domestic	48,462	43,314	45,959	45,141	43,812	38,449	32,542
International	8,228	7,454	7,576	7,831	8,042	10,323	8,323
Total	56,690	50,768	53,535	52,972	51,854	48,772	40,865
Southwest Airlines (Domestic only, has no international flights)	**72,568**	**72,459**	**81,121**	**96,330**	**101,948**	**101,921**	**101,338**
United Airlines[1]							
Domestic	72,450	57,830	60,081	57,229	56,402	51,661	45,571
International	10,625	9,532	9,490	10,770	11,011	11,409	10,454
Total	83,075	67,362	69,571	67,999	67,413	63,071	56,025
US Airways[3]							
Domestic	56,667	43,480	37,810	31,886	51,895	48,504	44,515
International	3,105	3,679	4,598	4,609	4,978	6,272	6,460
Total	59,772	47,159	42,408	36,495	56,873	54,776	50,975

[1]Continental and United agreed to merge in May 2010; the deal became effective on October 1, 2010.

[2]Delta Air Lines and Northwest Airlines announced their intent to merge in October 2008; however, the merger did not clear all regulatory hurdles until 2010 and combined reporting did not begin until 2010.

[3]US Airways and America West merged in September 2005; beginning in 2007, traffic data for US Airways includes the results of the merger.

Source: U.S. Department of Transportation, Bureau of Transportation Statistics, Air Carrier Statistics, Form T-100.

In 1967, Kelleher filed papers to incorporate the new airline and submitted an application to the Texas Aeronautics Commission for the new company to begin serving Dallas, Houston, and San Antonio.[2] But rival airlines in Texas pulled every string they could to block the new airline from commencing operations, precipitating a contentious four-year parade of legal and regulatory proceedings. Herb Kelleher led the fight on the company's behalf, eventually prevailing in June 1971 after winning two appeals to the Texas Supreme Court and a favorable ruling from the U.S. Supreme Court. Kelleher recalled, "The constant proceedings had gradually come to enrage me. There was no merit to our competitors' legal assertions. They were simply trying to use their superior economic power to squeeze us dry so we would collapse before we ever got into business. I was bound and determined to show that Southwest Airlines was going to survive and was going into operation."[3]

In January 1971, Lamar Muse was brought in as Southwest's CEO to get operations under way. Muse was an aggressive, self-confident airline veteran who knew the business well and who had the entrepreneurial skills to tackle the challenges of building the airline from scratch and then competing head-on with the major carriers. Through private investors and an initial public offering of stock in June 1971, Muse raised $7 million in new capital to purchase planes and equipment and provide cash for start-up. Boeing agreed to supply three new 737s from its inventory, discounting its price from $5 million to $4 million and financing 90 percent of the $12 million deal. Muse was able to recruit a talented senior staff that included a number of veteran executives from other carriers. He particularly sought out people who were innovative, wouldn't shirk from doing things differently or unconventionally, and were motivated by the challenge of building an airline from scratch. Muse wanted his executive team to be willing to think like mavericks and not be lulled into instituting practices at Southwest that imitated what was done at other airlines.

Southwest's Struggle to Gain a Market Foothold

In June 1971, Southwest initiated its first flights with a schedule that soon included 6 round-trips between Dallas and San Antonio and 12 round-trips between Houston and Dallas. But the introductory $20 one-way fares to fly the Golden Triangle, well below the $27 and $28 fares charged by rivals, attracted disappointingly small

numbers of passengers. Southwest's financial resources were stretched so thin that the company bought fuel for several months on Lamar Muse's personal credit card. Money for parts and tools was so tight that, on occasion, company personnel got on the phone with acquaintances at rival airlines operating at the terminal and arranged to borrow what was needed. Nonetheless, morale and enthusiasm remained high; company personnel displayed can-do attitudes and adeptness at getting by on whatever resources were available.

To try to gain market visibility and drum up more passengers, Southwest decided it had to do more than run ads in the media publicizing its low fares:

- Southwest decided to have its flight hostesses dress in colorful hot pants and white knee-high boots with high heels. Recruiting ads for Southwest's first group of hostesses were headlined "Attention, Raquel Welch: You can have a job if you measure up." Two thousand applicants responded, and those selected for interviews were asked to come dressed in hot pants to show off their legs—the company wanted to hire long-legged beauties with sparkling personalities. More than 30 of Southwest's first graduating class of 40 flight attendants consisted of young women who were cheerleaders and majorettes in high school and thus had experience performing in front of people while skimpily dressed.

- A second attention-getting action was to give passengers free alcoholic beverages during daytime flights. Most passengers on these flights were business travelers. Management's thinking was that many passengers did not drink during the daytime and that with most flights being less than an hour's duration it would be cheaper to simply give the drinks away rather than collect the money.

- Taking a cue from being based at Dallas Love Field, Southwest began using the tag line "Now There's Somebody Else Up There Who Loves You." The routes between Houston, Dallas, and San Antonio became known as the Love Triangle. Southwest's planes were referred to as Love Birds, drinks became Love Potions, peanuts were called Love Bites, drink coupons were Love Stamps, and tickets were printed on Love Machines. The "Love" campaign set the tone for Southwest's approach to its customers and company efforts to make flying Southwest an enjoyable, fun, and differentiating experience. (Later, when the company went public, it chose LUV as its stock-trading symbol.)

- In order to add more flights without buying more planes, the head of Southwest's ground operations came up with a plan for ground crews to off-load passengers and baggage, refuel the plane, clean the cabin and restock the galley, on-load passengers and baggage, do the necessary preflight checks and paperwork, and push away from the gate in 10 minutes. The 10-minute turn became one of Southwest's signatures during the 1970s and 1980s. (In later years, as passenger volume grew and many flights were filled to capacity, the turnaround time gradually expanded to 25 minutes—because it took more time to unload and load a plane with 125 passengers, as compared with a half-full plane with just 60–65 passengers. Even so, the 25-minute average turnaround time at Southwest during the 2000–2009 period was shorter than the 30- to 50-minute turnaround times typical at other major airlines.)

- In late November 1971, Lamar Muse came up with the idea of offering a $10 fare to passengers on the Friday-night Houston–Dallas flight. With no advertising, the 112-seat flight sold out. This led Muse to realize that Southwest was serving two quite distinct types of travelers in the Golden Triangle market: (1) business travelers who were more time-sensitive than price-sensitive and wanted weekday flights at times suitable for conducting business and (2) price-sensitive leisure travelers who wanted lower fares and had more flexibility about when to fly.[4] He came up with a two-tier on-peak/off-peak pricing structure in which all seats on weekday flights

departing before 7:00 p.m. were priced at $26 and all seats on other flights were priced at $13. Passenger traffic increased significantly—and system-wide on-peak/off-peak pricing soon became standard across the whole airline industry.

- In 1972, the company decided to move its flights in Houston from the newly opened Houston Intercontinental Airport (where it was losing money and where it took 45 minutes to get to downtown) to the abandoned Houston Hobby Airport located much closer to downtown Houston. Despite being the only carrier to fly into Houston Hobby, the results were spectacular—business travelers who flew to Houston frequently from Dallas and San Antonio found the Houston Hobby location far more convenient, and passenger traffic doubled almost immediately.

- In early 1973, in an attempt to fill empty seats on its San Antonio–Dallas flights, Southwest cut its regular $26 fare to $13 for all seats, all days, and all times. When Braniff International, at that time one of Southwest's major rivals, announced $13 fares of its own, Southwest retaliated with a two-page ad, run in the Dallas newspapers, headlined "Nobody is going to shoot Southwest Airlines out of the sky for a lousy $13" and containing copy saying Braniff was trying to run Southwest out of business. The ad announced that Southwest would not only match Braniff's $13 fare but that it would also give passengers the choice of buying a regular-priced ticket for $26 and receiving a complimentary fifth of Chivas Regal scotch, Crown Royal Canadian whiskey, or Smirnoff vodka (or, for nondrinkers, a leather ice bucket). More than 75 percent of Southwest's Dallas-Houston passengers opted for the $26 fare, although the percentage dropped as the two-month promotion wore on and corporate controllers began insisting that company employees use the $13 fare. The local and national media picked up the story of Southwest's offer, proclaiming the battle as a David-versus-Goliath struggle in which the upstart Southwest did not stand much of a chance against the much larger and well-established Braniff; grassroots sentiment in Texas swung to Southwest's side.

All these moves paid off. The resulting gains in passenger traffic enabled Southwest to report its first-ever annual profit in 1973.

More Legal and Regulatory Hurdles

During the rest of the 1970s, Southwest found itself embroiled in another round of legal and regulatory battles. One involved Southwest's refusal to move its flights from Dallas Love Field, located 10 minutes from downtown, to the newly opened Dallas–Fort Worth (DFW) Regional Airport, which was 30 minutes from downtown Dallas. Local officials were furious because they were counting on fees from Southwest's flights in and out of DFW to help service the debt on the bonds issued to finance the construction of DFW. Southwest's position was that it was not required to move because it had not agreed to do so or been ordered to do so by the Texas Aeronautics Commission—moreover, the company's head-quarters were located at Love Field. The courts eventually ruled that Southwest's operations could remain at Love Field.

A second battle ensued when rival airlines protested Southwest's application to begin serving several smaller cities in Texas; their protest was based on arguments that these markets were already well served and that Southwest's entry would result in costly over-capacity. Southwest countered that its low fares would allow more people to fly and grow the market. Again, Southwest prevailed and its views about low fares expanding the market proved accurate. In the year before Southwest initiated service, 123,000 passengers flew from Harlingen Airport in the Rio Grande Valley to Houston, Dallas, or San Antonio; in the 11 months following Southwest's initial flights, 325,000 passengers flew to the same three cities.

Believing that Braniff and Texas International were deliberately engaging in tactics to harass Southwest's operations, Southwest convinced the U.S. government to investigate what it considered predatory tactics by its chief rivals. In February 1975, Braniff and Texas International were indicted by a federal grand jury for conspiring to put Southwest out of business—a violation of the Sherman Antitrust Act. The two airlines pleaded "no contest" to the charges, signed cease-and-desist agreements, and were fined a modest $100,000 each.

When Congress passed the Airline Deregulation Act in 1978, Southwest applied to the Civil Aeronautics Board (now the Federal Aviation Administration) to fly between Houston and New Orleans. The application was vehemently opposed by local government officials and airlines operating out of DFW because of the potential for passenger traffic to be siphoned away from DFW. The opponents solicited the aid of Fort Worth congressman Jim Wright, then the majority leader of the U.S. House of Representatives, who took the matter to the floor of the House of Representatives; a rash of lobbying and maneuvering ensued. What emerged came to be known as the Wright Amendment of 1979: no airline may provide nonstop or through-plane service from Dallas Love Field to any city in any state except for locations in Texas, Louisiana, Arkansas, Oklahoma, and New Mexico. Southwest was prohibited from advertising, publishing schedules or fares, or checking baggage for travel from Dallas Love Field to any city it served outside the five-state "Wright Zone." The Wright Amendment continued in effect until 1997, when Alabama, Mississippi, and Kansas were added to the Wright Zone; in 2005, Missouri was added to the Wright Zone. In 2006, after a heated battle in Congress, legislation was passed and signed into law that repealed the Wright Amendment beginning in 2014.

The Emergence of a Combative Can-Do Culture at Southwest

The legal, regulatory, and competitive battles that Southwest fought in its early years produced a strong esprit de corps among Southwest personnel and a drive to survive and prosper despite the odds. With newspaper and TV stories reporting Southwest's difficulties regularly, employees were fully aware that the airline's existence was constantly on the line. Had the company been forced to move from Love Field, it would most likely have gone under, an outcome that employees, Southwest's rivals, and local government officials understood well. According to Southwest's former president Colleen Barrett, the obstacles thrown in Southwest's path by competitors and local officials were instrumental in building Herb Kelleher's passion for Southwest Airlines and ingraining a combative, can-do spirit into the corporate culture:

> They would put twelve to fifteen lawyers on a case and on our side there was Herb. They almost wore him to the ground. But the more arrogant they were, the more determined Herb got that this airline was going to go into the air—and stay there.
> The warrior mentality, the very fight to survive, is truly what created our culture.[5]

When Lamar Muse resigned in 1978, Southwest's board wanted Herb Kelleher to take over as chairman and CEO. But Kelleher enjoyed practicing law and, while he agreed to become chairman of the board, he insisted that someone else be CEO. Southwest's board appointed Howard Putnam, a group vice president of marketing services at United Airlines, as Southwest's president and CEO in July 1978. Putnam asked Kelleher to become more involved in Southwest's day-to-day operations, and over the next three years, Kelleher got to know many of the company's personnel and observe them in action. Putnam announced his resignation in the fall of 1981 to become president and chief operating officer at Braniff International. This time, Southwest's board succeeded in persuading Kelleher to take on the additional duties of CEO and president.

Sustained Growth and the Emergence of a New Industry Leader, 1981–2009 When Herb Kelleher took over in 1981, Southwest was flying 27 planes to 14 destination cities and had $270 million in revenues and 2,100 employees. Over the next 20 years, Southwest Airlines prospered under Kelleher's leadership. When Kelleher stepped down as CEO

in mid-2001, the company had 350 planes flying to 58 U.S. airports, annual revenues of $5.6 billion, more than 30,000 employees, and 64 million fare-paying passengers annually. Under the two CEOs who succeeded Kelleher, Southwest continued its march to becoming the market share leader in domestic air travel; by 2009, it was earning annual revenues of $10.4 billion, employing 34,874 people, flying 537 planes to 69 airports in 36 states, and transporting some 86 million fare-paying passengers and some 100 million passengers (including those traveling on frequent flyer awards) annually. In the process, the company won more industry Triple Crown Awards for best on-time record, best baggage handling, and fewest customer complaints than any other U.S. airline.

Exhibit 2 provides a five-year summary of Southwest's financial and operating performance. Exhibit 3 provides selected financial and operating data for major U.S. air carriers during 1995–2009.

HERB KELLEHER: SOUTHWEST'S CELEBRATED CEO

Herb Kelleher majored in philosophy at Wesleyan University in Middletown, Connecticut, graduating with honors. He earned his law degree at New York University, again graduating with honors and also serving as a member of the law review. After graduation, he clerked for a New Jersey Supreme Court justice for two years and then joined a law firm in Newark. Upon marrying a woman from Texas and becoming enamored with Texas, he moved to San Antonio, where he became a successful lawyer and came to represent Rollin King's small aviation company.

When Herb Kelleher took on the role of Southwest's CEO in 1981, he made a point of visiting with maintenance personnel to check on how well the planes were running and of talking with the flight attendants. Kelleher did not do much managing from his office, preferring instead to be out among the troops as much as he could. His style was to listen and observe and to offer encouragement. Kelleher attended

▶ EXHIBIT 2

Summary of Southwest Airlines' Financial and Operating Performance, 2005–2009

	Years Ended December 31				
	2009	**2008**	**2007**	**2006**	**2005**
Financial Data ($ millions, except per share data)					
Operating revenues	$10,350	$11,023	$ 9,861	$ 9,086	$ 7,584
Operating expenses	10,088	10,574	9,070	8,152	6,859
Operating income	262	449	791	934	725
Other expenses (income) net	98	171	(267)	144	(54)
Income before taxes	164	278	1,058	790	779
Provision for income taxes	65	100	413	291	295
Net income	$ 99	$ 178	$ 645	$ 499	$ 484
Net income per share, basic	$0.13	$0.24	$0.85	$0.63	$0.61
Net income per share, diluted	$0.13	$0.24	$0.84	$0.61	$0.60
Cash dividends per common share	$0.018	$0.018	$0.018	$0.018	$0.018
Total assets at period-end	$14,269	$14,068	$16,772	$13,460	$14,003
Long-term obligations at period-end	$ 3,325	$ 3,498	$ 2,050	$ 1,567	$ 1,394
Stockholders' equity at period-end	$ 5,466	$ 4,953	$ 6,941	$ 6,449	$ 6,675
Operating Data					
Revenue passengers carried	86,310,229	88,529,234	88,713,472	83,814,823	77,693,875
Enplaned passengers[1]	101,338,228	101,920,598	101,910,809	96,276,907	88,379,900
Revenue passenger miles (RPMs) (000s)	74,456,710	73,491,687	72,318,812	67,691,289	60,223,100
Available seat miles (ASMs) (000s)	98,001,550	103,271,343	99,635,967	92,663,023	85,172,795
Load factor[2]	76.0%	71.2%	72.6%	73.1%	70.7%
Average length of passenger haul (miles)	863	830	815	808	775
Average aircraft stage length (miles)	639	636	629	622	607
Trips flown	1,125,111	1,191,151	1,160,699	1,092,331	1,028,639
Average passenger fare	$114.61	$119.16	$106.60	$104.40	$ 93.68
Passenger revenue yield per RPM	13.29¢	14.35¢	13.08¢	12.93¢	12.09¢
Operating revenue yield per ASM	10.56¢	10.67¢	9.90¢	9.81¢	8.90¢
Operating expenses per ASM	10.29¢	10.24¢	9.10¢	8.80¢	8.05¢
Fuel costs per gallon (average)	$ 2.12	$ 2.44	$ 1.80	$ 1.64	$ 1.13
Fuel consumed, in gallons (millions)	1,428	1,511	1,489	1,389	1,287
Full-time equivalent employees at year-end	34,726	35,499	34,378	32,664	31,729
Size of fleet at year-end[3]	537	537	520	481	445

[1]Includes passengers traveling on free travel award tickets.
[2]Revenue passenger miles divided by available seat miles.
[3]Includes leased aircraft.

Source: Southwest Airlines, 2009 10-K report, p. 23.

▶ EXHIBIT 3

Selected Operating and Financial Data for Major U.S. Airline Carriers, 1995–2009 (selected years)

	1995	2000	2005	2007	2008	2009
Passengers (in millions)	559.0	666.2	738.3	769.6	743.3	703.9
Flights (in thousands)	8,062	9,035	11,564	11,399	10,841	10,373
Revenue passenger miles (in billions)	603.4	692.8	778.6	829.4	812.4	769.5
Available seat miles (in billions)	807.1	987.9	1,002.7	1,037.7	1,021.3	957.2
Load factor	67.0	72.4	77.7	79.9	79.5	80.4
Passenger revenues (in millions)	$69,470	$93,622	$93,500	$107,678	$111,542	$91,331
Operating profit (loss) (in millions)	$ 5,852	$ 6,999	$ 427	$ 9,344	($ 3,348)	$ 2,409
Net profit (loss) excluding one-time charges and gains (in millions)	$ 2,283	$ 2,486	($5,782)	$ 4,998	($ 9,464)	($2,799)
Total employees	546,987	679,967	562,467	560,997	556,920	536,200

Sources: Air Transport Association, *2010 Economic Report,* pp. 8, 19, 23, and 30; *2009 Economic Report,* p. 19; Air Transport Association, *2008 Economic Report,* p. 19; and Air Transport Association, *2005 Economic Report,* p. 7.

most graduation ceremonies of flight attendant classes, and he often helped load bags on "Black Wednesday," the busy travel day before Thanksgiving. He was held in the highest regard by Southwest employees and knew thousands of their names. When he attended a Southwest employee function, he was swarmed like a celebrity.

Kelleher had an affinity for bold-print Hawaiian shirts, owned a tricked-out motorcycle, and made no secret of his passion for cigarettes and Wild Turkey whiskey. He loved to make jokes and engage in pranks and corporate antics, prompting some people to refer to him as the "clown prince" of the airline industry. He once appeared at a company gathering dressed in an Elvis costume and had arm-wrestled a South Carolina company executive at a public event in Dallas for rights to use "Just Plane Smart" as an advertising slogan.[6] Kelleher was well known inside and outside the company for his combativeness, particularly when it came to beating back competitors. On one occasion, he reportedly told a group of veteran employees, "If someone says they're going to smack us in the face—knock them out, stomp them out, boot them in the ditch, cover them over, and move on to the next thing. That's the Southwest spirit at work."[7] On another occasion, he said, "I love battles. I think

it's part of the Irish in me. It's like what Patton said, 'War is hell and I love it so.' That's how I feel. I've never gotten tired of fighting."[8]

While Southwest was deliberately combative and flamboyant in some aspects of its operations, when it came to the financial side of the business Kelleher insisted on fiscal conservatism, a strong balance sheet, comparatively low levels of debt, and zealous attention to bottom-line profitability. While believing strongly in being prepared for adversity, Kelleher had an aversion to Southwest personnel spending time drawing up all kinds of formal strategic plans, saying, "Reality is chaotic; planning is ordered and logical. The meticulous nit-picking that goes on in most strategic planning processes creates a mental straitjacket that becomes disabling in an industry where things change radically from one day to the next." Kelleher wanted Southwest managers to think ahead, have contingency plans, and be ready to act when it appeared that the future held significant risks or when new conditions suddenly appeared and demanded prompt responses.

Kelleher was a strong believer in the principle that employees—not customers—came first:

> You have to treat your employees like your customers. When you treat them right, then they will treat your outside customers right.

That has been a very powerful competitive weapon for us. You've got to take the time to listen to people's ideas. If you just tell somebody no, that's an act of power and, in my opinion, an abuse of power. You don't want to constrain people in their thinking.[9]

Another indication of the importance that Kelleher placed on employees was the message he had penned in 1990 that was prominently displayed in the lobby of Southwest's headquarters in Dallas:

> The people of Southwest Airlines are "the creators" of what we have become—and of what we will be.
>
> Our people transformed an idea into a legend. That legend will continue to grow only so long as it is nourished—by our people's indomitable spirit, boundless energy, immense goodwill, and burning desire to excel.
>
> Our thanks—and our love—to the people of Southwest Airlines for creating a marvelous family and a wondrous airline.

In June 2001, Herb Kelleher stepped down as CEO but continued on in his role as chairman of Southwest's board of directors and the head of the board's executive committee; as chairman, he played a lead role in Southwest's strategy, expansion to new cities and aircraft scheduling, and governmental and industry affairs. In May 2008, after more than 40 years of leadership at Southwest, Kelleher retired as chairman; he was, however, scheduled to remain a full-time Southwest employee until July 2013.

EXECUTIVE LEADERSHIP AT SOUTHWEST, 2001–2010

In June 2001, responding to anxious investor concerns about the company's leadership succession plans, Southwest Airlines began an orderly transfer of power and responsibilities from Herb Kelleher, age 70, to two of his most trusted protégés: James F. Parker, 54, Southwest's general counsel, succeeded Kelleher as Southwest's CEO, and Colleen Barrett, 56, Southwest's executive vice president–customers and self-described keeper of Southwest's pep-rally corporate culture, became president and chief operating officer.

James Parker, CEO from 2001 to 2004

James Parker's association with Herb Kelleher went back 23 years, to the time when they were colleagues at Kelleher's old law firm. Parker moved over to Southwest from the law firm in February 1986. Parker's profile inside the company as Southwest's vice president and general counsel had been relatively low, but he was Southwest's chief labor negotiator, and much of the credit for Southwest's good relations with employee unions belonged to him. Prior to his appointment as CEO, Parker had been a member of the company's executive planning committee; his experiences ranged from properties and facilities to technical services team to the company's alliances with vendors and partners. Parker and Kelleher were said to think much alike, and Parker was regarded as having a good sense of humor, although he did not have as colorful and flamboyant a personality as Kelleher. Parker was seen as an honest, straight-arrow kind of person who had a strong grasp of Southwest's culture and market niche and who could be nice or tough, depending on the situation. When his appointment was announced, Parker said:

> There is going to be no change of course insofar as Southwest is concerned. We have a very experienced leadership team. We've all worked together for a long time. There will be evolutionary changes in Southwest, just as there have always been in our history. We're going to stay true to our business model of being a low-cost, low-fare airline.[10]

Parker retired unexpectedly, for personal reasons, in July 2004, stepping down as CEO and vice chairman of the board and also resigning from the company's board of directors. He was succeeded by Gary C. Kelly.

Colleen Barrett, Southwest's President from 2001 to 2008

Colleen Barrett began working with Kelleher as his legal secretary in 1967 and had been with Southwest since 1978. As executive vice president–customers, Barrett had a high pro-file among Southwest employees and spent most of her time on culture building, morale building, and customer service; her goal was to ensure that employees felt good about what they were doing and felt empowered to serve the cause of Southwest Airlines.[11] She and Kelleher were regarded as Southwest's guiding lights, and some analysts said she was essentially functioning as the company's chief operating officer (COO) prior to her formal appointment as president. Much of the credit for the company's strong record of customer service and its strong-culture work climate belonged to Barrett.

Barrett had been the driving force behind lining the hallways at Southwest's head-quarters with photos of company events and trying to create a family atmosphere at the company. Believing it was important to make employees feel cared about and important, Barrett had put together a network of contacts across the company to help her stay in touch with what was happening with employees and their families. When network members learned about events that were worthy of acknowledgment, the word quickly got to Barrett—the information went into a database, and an appropriate greeting card or gift was sent. Barrett had a remarkable ability to give gifts that were individualized and that connected her to the recipient.[12]

Barrett was the first woman appointed as president and COO of a major U.S. airline. In October 2001, *Fortune* ranked Colleen Barrett 20th on its list of the 50 most powerful women in American business. Barrett retired as president in July 2008, but was scheduled to remain as a full-time Southwest employee until 2013.

Gary C. Kelly, Southwest's CEO from 2004 Onward

Gary Kelly was appointed vice chairman of the board of directors and CEO of Southwest effective July 15, 2004. Prior to that time, Kelly was executive vice president and chief financial officer (CFO) from 2001 to 2004, and vice

president–finance and CFO from 1989 to 2001. He joined Southwest in 1986 as its controller. In 2008, effective with the retirement of Kelleher and Barrett, Kelly assumed the titles of chairman of the board, CEO, and president.

When Kelly was named CEO in 2004, Herb Kelleher said:

> Gary Kelly is one of our brightest stars, well respected throughout the industry and well known, over more than a decade, to the media, analyst, and investor communities for his excellence. As part of our Board's succession planning, we had already focused on Gary as Jim Parker's successor, and that process has simply been accelerated by Jim's personal decision to retire. Under Gary's leadership, Southwest has achieved the strongest balance sheet in the American airline industry; the best fuel hedging position in our industry; and tremendous progress in technology.[13]

During his tenure as CEO, Kelly and other top-level Southwest executives had sharpened and fine-tuned Southwest's strategy in a number of areas, continued to expand operations (adding both more flights and initiating service to new airports), and worked to maintain the company's low-cost advantage over its domestic rivals.

Kelly saw four factors as keys to Southwest's recipe for success:[14]

- Hire great people, treat 'em like family.
- Care for our Customers warmly and personally, like they're guests in our home.
- Keep fares and operating costs lower than anybody else by being safe, efficient, and operationally excellent.
- Stay prepared for bad times with a strong balance sheet, lots of cash, and a stout fuel hedge.

To help Southwest be a standout performer on these four key success factors, Kelly had established five strategic objectives for Southwest:[15]

- Be the best place to work.
- Be the safest, most efficient, and most reliable airline in the world.

- Offer customers a convenient flight schedule with lots of flights to lots of places they want to go.

- Offer customers the best overall travel experience.

- Do all of these things in a way that maintains a low cost structure and the ability to offer low fares.

During 2008–2009, Kelly initiated a slight revision of Southwest's mission statement and also spearheaded a vision statement that called for a steadfast focus on a triple bottom line of Performance, People, and Planet—see Exhibit 4.

SOUTHWEST AIRLINES' STRATEGY

From day one, Southwest had pursued a low-cost/low-price/no-frills strategy. Its signature low fares made air travel affordable to a wide segment of the U.S. population—giving substance to its tagline "The Freedom to Fly." It employed a relatively simple fare structure, with all of the fare options plainly displayed at the company's website. The lowest fares were usually nonrefundable but could be applied to future travel on Southwest Airlines without incurring a change fee (rival airlines charged a change fee of $100 to $175), and the

▶ **EXHIBIT 4**

Southwest Airlines Mission, Vision, and Triple Bottom Line Commitment to Performance, People, and Planet

THE MISSION OF SOUTHWEST AIRLINES

The mission of Southwest Airlines is dedication to the highest quality of Customer Service delivered with a sense of warmth, friendliness, individual pride, and Company Spirit.

TO OUR EMPLOYEES

We are committed to provide our Employees a stable work environment with equal opportunity for learning and personal growth. Creativity and innovation are encouraged for improving the effectiveness of Southwest Airlines. Above all, Employees will be provided the same concern, respect, and caring attitude within the organization that they are expected to share externally with every Southwest Customer.

TO OUR COMMUNITIES

Our goal is to be the hometown airline of every community we serve, and because those communities sustain and nurture us with their support and loyalty, it is vital that we, as individuals and in groups, embrace each community with the SOUTHWEST SPIRIT of involvement, service, and caring to make those communities better places to live and work.

TO OUR PLANET

We strive to be a good environmental steward across our system in all of our hometowns, and one component of our stewardship is efficiency, which by its very nature, translates to eliminating waste and conserving resources. Using cost-effective and environmentally beneficial operating procedures (including facilities and equipment), allows us to reduce the amount of materials we use and, when combined with our ability to reuse and recycle material, preserves these environmental resources.

TO OUR STAKEHOLDERS

Southwest's vision for a sustainable future is one where there will be a balance in our business model between Employees and Community, the Environment, and our Financial Viability. In order to protect our world for future generations, while meeting our commitments to our Employees, Customers, and Stakeholders, we will strive to lead our industry in innovative efficiency that conserves natural resources, maintains a creative and innovative workforce, and gives back to the Communities in which we live and work.

Source: Southwest Airlines, "One Report, 2009," www.southwest.com, accessed August 20, 2010.

company's advance purchase requirements on tickets were more lenient than those of its rivals. Many Southwest flights had some seats available at deeply discounted fares, provided they were purchased online at the company's website.

In November 2007, Southwest introduced a new Business Select fare to attract economy-minded business travelers; Business Select customers had early boarding privileges, received extra Rapid Rewards (frequent flyer credits), and a free cocktail. In 2008, rival airlines instituted a series of add-on fees—including a fuel surcharge for each flight, fees for checking bags, fees for processing frequent flyer travel awards, fees for buying a ticket in person at the airport or calling a toll-free number to speak with a ticket agent to make a reservation, fees for changing a previously purchased ticket to a different flight, and fees for in-flight snacks and beverages—to help defray skyrocketing costs for jet fuel (which had climbed from about 15 percent of operating expenses in 2000 to 40 percent of operating expenses in mid-2008). Southwest, however, choose to forgo à la carte pricing and stuck with an all-inclusive fare price. During 2009, Southwest ran an ad campaign called "Bags Fly Free" to publicize the cost savings of flying Southwest rather than paying the $20 to $50 fees that rival airlines charged for a first or second checked bag.

When advance reservations were weak for particular weeks or times of the day or on certain routes, Southwest made a regular practice of initiating special fare promotions to stimulate ticket sales on flights that otherwise would have had numerous empty seats. For instance, the company had used fare sales to combat slack air travel during much of the recession of 2008–2009.

The combined effect of Southwest's "Bags Fly Free" ads and periodic fare sales resulted in company-record load factors for every month from July through December 2009. (A load factor was the percentage of all available seats on all flights that were occupied by fare-paying passengers.) Southwest continued to run the "Bags

Fly Free" ads during the first half of 2010. In June 2010, to celebrate its 39 years of flying, Southwest instituted a two-day special promotion of $39 one-way fares for travel up to 450 miles, $79 one-way fares for travel between 451 and 1,000 miles, and $119 one-way fares for travel between 1,001 and 1,500 miles; the fares were good for travel from September 8, 2010, through November 17, 2010, to select destinations.

Southwest was a shrewd practitioner of the concept of price elasticity, proving in one market after another that the revenue gains from increased ticket sales and the volume of passenger traffic would more than compensate for the revenue erosion associated with low fares. When Southwest entered the Florida market with an introductory $17 fare from Tampa to Fort Lauderdale, the number of annual passengers flying that route jumped 50 percent, to more than 330,000. In Manchester, New Hampshire, passenger counts went from 1.1 million in 1997, the year prior to Southwest's entry, to 3.5 million in 2000, and average one-way fares dropped from just over $300 to $129. Southwest's success in stimulating higher passenger traffic at airports across the United States via low fares and frequent flights had been coined the "Southwest effect" by personnel at the U.S. Department of Transportation. Exhibit 5 shows the cities and airports Southwest served in May 2010. Southwest began service to Boston, New York (LaGuardia), Minneapolis–St. Paul, and Milwaukee in 2009. Management had announced plans for Southwest to begin service to Newark, New Jersey, and two South Carolina airports—Charleston and Greenville-Spartanburg—in 2011.

Unlike the hub-and-spoke route systems of rival airlines (where operations were concentrated at a limited number of hub cities and most destinations were served via connections through the hub), Southwest's route system had been carefully designed to concentrate on flights between pairs of cities 150 to 700 miles apart that handled enough passenger traffic to allow Southwest to offer a sizable number of daily flights. As a general rule, Southwest did not initiate service to an airport unless it

EXHIBIT 5

Airports and Cities Served by Southwest Airlines, May 2010

Southwest's Top 10 Airports

	Daily Departures	Number of Gates	Nonstop Cities Served
Chicago Midway	224	29	51
Las Vegas	223	19	57
Baltimore/Washington	181	20	44
Phoenix	177	24	44
Houston (Hobby)	135	17	30
Dallas (Love Field)	131	15	15
Denver	129	14	42
Los Angeles (LAX)	116	11	20
Oakland	114	13	20
Orlando	104	12	33

Other Airports Served by Southwest Airlines

Albany	Fort Myers/Naples	Minneapolis/St. Paul	Reno/Tahoe
Albuquerque	Harlingen/South Padre	Nashville	Sacramento
Amarillo	Island	New Orleans	St. Louis
Austin	Hartford/Springfield	New York (LaGuardia)	Salt Lake City
Birmingham	Indianapolis	Norfolk	San Antonio
Boise	Long Island (MacArthur)	Oklahoma City	San Francisco
Boston Logan	Jackson, MS	Omaha	San Jose
Buffalo	Jacksonville	Ontario, CA	Seattle/Tacoma
Burbank, CA	Kansas City	Orange County, CA	Spokane
Cleveland	Little Rock	Panama City, FL	Tampa
Columbus, OH	Louisville	Philadelphia	Tucson
Corpus Christi, TX	Lubbock	Pittsburgh	Tulsa
Detroit Metro	Manchester, NH	Portland, OR	Washington, DC (Dulles)
El Paso	Midland/Odessa, TX	Providence	West Palm Beach
Fort Lauderdale	Milwaukee	Raleigh-Durham	

Source: Southwest Airlines, www.southwest.com, accessed August 15, 2010.

envisioned the potential for originating at least 8 flights a day there and saw opportunities to add more flights over time—in Denver, for example, Southwest had boosted the number of daily departures from 13 in January 2006 (the month in which service to and from Denver was initiated) to 79 daily departures in May 2008 and to 129 departures in May 2010. Southwest's point-to-point route system minimized connections, delays, and total trip time—its emphasis on nonstop flights between pairs of cities allowed about 75 percent of Southwest's passengers to fly nonstop to their destination. While a majority of Southwest's flights involved actual in-air flight times of less than 90 minutes, in recent years the company had added a significant number of nonstop flights to more distant airports where its low fares could generate profitable amounts of passenger traffic.

Southwest's frequent flyer program, Rapid Rewards, was based on trips flown rather than mileage. Rapid Rewards customers received one credit for each one-way trip or two credits for each round-trip flown and could also earn credits by using the services of Southwest's car rental, hotel, and credit card partners. There were two principal types of travel awards:

- *Standard Awards*—these were for Rapid Rewards members who accumulated one free round-trip after the accumulation of 16 credits within 24 consecutive months. Standard Awards were valid for one free round-trip to any destination available on Southwest Airlines, had to be used within 12 months, and were subject to seat restrictions and blackout dates around certain major holidays.

- *Companion Passes*—these were for Rapid Rewards members who accumulated 100 credits within a 12-month period; these passes provided unlimited free round-trip travel to any destination available on Southwest for a designated companion of a qualifying Rapid Rewards Member who purchased a ticket or used a free travel award ticket. The Rapid Rewards member and designated companion had to travel together on the same flight. Companion Passes were valid for 12 months after issuance and were not subject to seat restrictions or blackout dates.

In addition, Rapid Rewards members who flew 32 qualifying flights within a 12-month period received priority boarding privileges for a year. Southwest customers redeemed 2.4 million free ticket awards during 2009 and 2.8 million free ticket awards in both 2007 and 2008. Free travel award usage accounted for about 8 percent of Southwest's total revenue passenger miles flown during 2007–2009. Since the inception of Rapid Rewards in 1987, approximately 16 percent of all fully earned awards had expired without being used.

Customer Service and Customer Satisfaction

Southwest's approach to delivering good customer service and creating customer satisfaction was predicated on presenting a happy face to passengers, displaying a fun-loving attitude, and doing things in a manner calculated to make sure passengers had a positive flying experience. The company made a special effort to employ gate personnel who enjoyed interacting with customers, had good interpersonal skills, and displayed cheery, outgoing personalities. A number of Southwest's gate personnel let their wit and sense of humor show by sometimes entertaining those in the gate area with trivia questions or contests such as "Who has the biggest hole in their sock?" Apart from greeting passengers coming onto planes and assisting them in finding open seats and stowing baggage, flight attendants were encouraged to be engaging, converse and joke with passengers, and go about their tasks in ways that made passengers smile. On some flights, attendants sang announcements to passengers on takeoff and landing. On one flight while passengers were boarding, an attendant with bunny ears popped out of an overhead bin exclaiming "Surprise!" The repertoires to amuse passengers varied from flight crew to flight crew.

During their tenure, both Herb Kelleher and Colleen Barrett had made a point of sending congratulatory notes to employees when the company received letters from customers complimenting particular Southwest employees; complaint letters were seen as learning opportunities for employees and reasons to consider making adjustments. Employees were provided the following policy guidance regarding how far to go in trying to please customers:

> No Employee will ever be punished for using good judgment and good old common sense when trying to accommodate a Customer—no matter what our rules are.[16]
>
> When you empower People to make a positive difference every day, you allow them to decide. Most guidelines are written to be broken as long as the Employee is leaning toward the Customer. We follow the Golden Rule and try to do the right thing and think about our Customer.[17]

Southwest executives believed that conveying a friendly, fun-loving spirit to customers was the key to competitive advantage. As one Southwest manager put it, "Our fares can be matched; our airplanes and routes can be copied. But we pride ourselves on our customer service."[18]

In 2007, Southwest did an "extreme gate makeover" to improve the airport experience of customers. The makeover included adding

(1) a business-focused area with padded seats, tables with power outlets, power stations with stools, and a flat-screen TV with news programming, and (2) a family-focused area with smaller tables and chairs, power stations for charging electrical devices, and kid-friendly programming on a flat-screen TV.

Marketing and Promotion

Southwest was continually on the lookout for novel ways to tell its story, make its distinctive persona come alive, and strike a chord in the minds of air travelers. Many of its print ads and billboards were deliberately unconventional and attention-getting so as to create and reinforce the company's maverick, fun-loving, and combative image. Some previous campaigns had used the slogans "The Low-Fare Airline" and "The All-Time On-Time Airline"; others had touted the company's Triple Crown Awards. One of the company's billboard campaigns highlighted the frequency of the company's flights with such headlines as "Austin Auften," "Phoenix Phrequently," and "L.A. A.S.A.P." Each holiday season since 1985, Southwest had run a "Christmas Card" ad on TV featuring children and their families from the Ronald McDonald Houses and Southwest employees. Fresh advertising campaigns were launched periodically—Exhibit 6 shows four representative ads.

In 2002, Southwest began changing the appearance of its planes, updating its somewhat drab gold-orange-red scheme to a much fresher and brighter canyon blue/red/gold/orange scheme—see Exhibit 7.

Southwest tended to advertise far more heavily than any other U.S. carrier. According to The Nielsen Company, during the first six months of 2009, Southwest boosted its ad spending by 20 percent, to $112.6 million, to hammer home its "Bags Fly Free" message. Passenger traffic at Southwest subsequently rose, while passenger volumes went in the opposite direction at Southwest's five largest competitors—Delta, American, United, Continental, and US Airways, all of which had recently introduced or increased fees for checked baggage.

Passenger travel on Southwest's domestic flights rose by more than 28 million passengers annually from 2000 through 2009, whereas passenger volume on domestic flights was down by 88 million passengers annually at Delta, American, United, Continental, and US Airways during this same period.

Other Strategy Elements

Southwest's strategy included several other elements:

- *Gradual expansion into new geographic markets.* Southwest generally added one or two new cities to its route schedule annually, preferring to saturate the market for daily flights to the cities/airports it currently served before entering new markets. In selecting new cities, Southwest looked for city pairs that could generate substantial amounts of both business and leisure traffic. Management believed that having numerous flights flying the same routes appealed to business travelers looking for convenient flight times and the ability to catch a later flight if they unexpectedly ran late.

- *Adding flights in areas where rivals were cutting back service.* When rivals cut back flights to cities that Southwest served, Southwest often moved in with more flights of its own, believing its lower fares would attract more passengers. When Midway Airlines ceased operations in November 1990, Southwest moved in overnight and quickly instituted flights to Chicago's Midway Airport. Southwest was a first-mover in adding flights on routes where rivals had cut their offerings following the terrorist attacks of September 11, 2001 (9/11). When American Airlines closed its hubs in Nashville and San Jose, Southwest immediately increased the number of its flights into and out of both locations. When US Airways trimmed its flight schedule for Philadelphia and Pittsburgh, Southwest promptly boosted its flights into and out of those airports. Southwest initiated service to Denver when United, beset

► EXHIBIT 6 **Four Samples of Southwest's Ads**

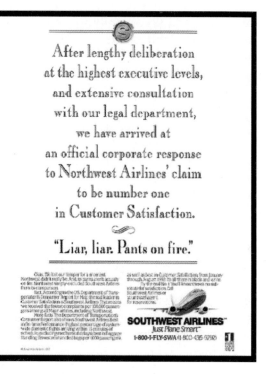

▶ EXHIBIT 7   **Southwest's New Look and Aircraft Equipped with Winglets**

with financial difficulties, cut back operations at its big Denver hub.

- *Curtailing flights on marginally profitable routes where numerous seats often went unfilled and shifting planes to routes with good growth opportunities.* Management was attracted to this strategy element because it enabled Southwest to grow revenues and profits without having to add so many new planes to its fleet. This strategy was aggressively pursued in 2008–2009 as a means of coping with industry-wide declines in passenger air travel during the recession. Management canceled the planned additions to the size of its aircraft fleet in 2009, cut the number of flights in markets where ticket bookings were weak, and redeployed the capacity to support entry into four new markets with promising long-term growth potential: New York's LaGuardia Airport, Minneapolis–St. Paul International Airport, Boston's Logan International Airport, and Milwaukee's General Mitchell International Airport.
- *Putting strong emphasis on safety, high-quality maintenance, and reliable operations.*

Southwest management believed the company's low-fare strategy, coupled with frequent flights and friendly service, delivered "more value for less money" to customers rather than "less value for less money." Kelleher said, "Everybody values a very good service provided at a very reasonable price."[19]

SOUTHWEST'S EFFORTS TO EXECUTE ITS LOW-FARE STRATEGY

Southwest management fully understood that low fares necessitated zealous pursuit of low operating costs and had, over the years, instituted a number of practices to keep its costs below those of rival carriers:

- The company operated only one type of aircraft—Boeing 737s—to minimize the size of spare parts inventories, simplify the training of maintenance and repair personnel, improve the proficiency and speed with which maintenance routines could be done, and simplify the task of scheduling planes for particular flights. Furthermore, as the launch customer for Boeing's 737-300, 737-500, and 737-700 models, Southwest acquired its new aircraft at favorable prices. See Exhibit 8 for statistics on Southwest's aircraft fleet.
- Southwest was the first major airline to introduce ticketless travel (eliminating the need to print and process paper tickets) and also the first to allow customers to make reservations and purchase tickets at the company's website (thus bypassing the need to pay commissions to travel agents for handling the ticketing process and reducing staffing requirements at Southwest's reservation centers). Selling a

▶ EXHIBIT 8

Southwest's Aircraft Fleet as of March 31, 2010			
Type of Aircraft	**Number**	**Seats**	**Comments**
Boeing 737–300	173	137	Southwest was Boeing's launch customer for this model.
Boeing 737–500	25	122	Southwest was Boeing's launch customer for this model.
Boeing 737–700	343	137	Southwest was Boeing's launch customer for this model.
	541		

Other Fleet-Related Facts

Average age of aircraft fleet—10.5 years
Average aircraft trip length—633 miles, with an average duration of 1 hour and 54 minutes
Average aircraft utilization—6.5 flights per day and 12 hours and 15 minutes of flight time
Fleet size—1990: 106   1995: 224   2000: 344   2009: 537
Firm orders for new aircraft—2010: 10   2011: 10   2012: 13   2013–2016: 58

Source: Southwest Airlines, www.southwest.com, accessed August 5, 2010, and 2009 10-K report, p. 18.

ticket on its website cost Southwest roughly $1, versus $3 to $4 for a ticket booked through its own internal reservation system and as much as $15 for tickets for business travelers purchased through travel agents and professional business travel partners. Ticketless travel accounted for more than 95 percent of all sales in 2007, and nearly 74 percent of Southwest's revenues were generated through sales at its website.

• The company stressed flights into and out of airports in medium-sized cities and less congested airports in major metropolitan areas (Chicago Midway, Detroit Metro, Houston Hobby, and Dallas Love Field). This strategy helped produce better-than-average on-time performance and reduce the fuel costs associated with planes sitting in line on crowded taxiways or circling airports waiting for clearance to land. It further allowed the company to avoid paying the higher landing fees and terminal gate costs at such high-traffic airports as Atlanta's Hartsfield International, Chicago's O'Hare, and Dallas–Fort Worth (DFW) where landing slots were controlled and rationed to those airlines willing to pay the high fees. Southwest's strategy of serving less congested airports also helped minimize total travel time for passengers—driving to the airport, parking, ticketing, boarding, and flight time. However, in recent years, to help sustain growth in passenger traffic and revenues, Southwest had initiated service to airports in several large metropolitan cities where air traffic congestion was a frequent problem—such as Los Angeles (LAX), Boston (Logan International, beginning in 2009), New York (LaGuardia), Denver, San Francisco, and Philadelphia.

• Southwest's point-to-point scheduling of flights was more cost-efficient than the hub-and-spoke systems used by rival airlines. Hub-and-spoke systems involved passengers on many different flights coming in from spoke locations (or perhaps another hub) to a central airport or hub within a short span of time and then connecting to an outgoing flight to their destination—a spoke location or another hub. Most flights arrived at and departed from a hub across a two-hour window, creating big peak-valley swings in airport personnel workloads and gate utilization— airport personnel and gate areas were very busy when hub operations were in full swing and then were underutilized in the interval awaiting the next round of inbound/outbound flights. In contrast, Southwest's point-to-point routes permitted scheduling aircraft so as to minimize the time aircraft were at the gate, currently approximately 25 minutes, thereby reducing the number of aircraft and gate facilities that would otherwise be required. Furthermore, with a relatively even flow of incoming/outgoing flights and gate traffic, Southwest could staff its terminal operations to handle a fairly steady workload across a day, whereas hub-and-spoke operators had to staff their operations to serve three to four daily peak periods.

- To economize on the amount of time it took terminal personnel to check passengers in and to simplify the whole task of making reservations, Southwest dispensed with the practice of assigning each passenger a reserved seat. Instead, for many years, passengers were given color-coded plastic cards with the letters A, B, or C when they checked in at the boarding gate. Passengers then boarded in groups, according to the color/letter on their card, sitting in whatever seat was open when they got on the plane—a procedure described by some as a "cattle call." Passengers who were particular about where they sat had to arrive at the gate early to get boarding cards and then had to position themselves near the front when it was their group's turn to board. In 2002, Southwest abandoned the use of plastic cards and began printing a big, bold A, B, or C on the boarding pass when the passenger checked in at the ticket counter; passengers then boarded in groups according to their assigned letter. In 2007–2008, in order to significantly reduce the time that passengers spent standing in line

waiting for their group to board, Southwest introduced an enhanced boarding method that automatically assigned each passenger a specific number within the passenger's boarding group at the time of check-in; passengers then boarded the aircraft in that numerical order. All passengers could check in online up to 24 hours before departure time and print out a boarding pass, thus bypassing counter check-in (unless they wished to check baggage).

- Southwest flight attendants were responsible for cleaning up trash left by deplaning passengers and otherwise getting the plane presentable for passengers to board for the next flight. Rival carriers had cleaning crews come on board to perform this function until they incurred heavy losses in 2001–2005 and were forced to institute stringent cost-cutting measures that included abandoning use of cleaning crews and copying Southwest's practice.

- Southwest did not have a first-class section on any of its planes and had no fancy frequent flyer clubs at terminals.

- Southwest offered passengers no baggage transfer services to other carriers— passengers with checked baggage who were connecting to other carriers to reach their destination were responsible for picking up their luggage at Southwest's baggage claim and then getting it to the check-in facilities of the connecting carrier. (Southwest only booked tickets involving its own flights; customers connecting to flights on other carriers had to book such tickets either through travel agents or the connecting airline.)

- Starting in 2001, Southwest began converting from cloth to leather seats; the team of Southwest employees who investigated the economics of the conversion concluded that an all-leather interior would be more durable and easier to maintain, more than justifying the higher initial costs.

- Southwest was a first-mover among major U.S. airlines in employing fuel hedging and derivative contracts to counteract rising prices for crude oil and jet fuel. From 1998 through 2008, the company's fuel hedging activities produced fuel savings of about $4 billion over what it would have spent had it paid the industry's average price for jet fuel. But unexpectedly large declines in jet fuel prices in late 2008 and 2009 resulted in reported losses of $408 million on the fuel hedging contracts that the company had in place during 2009. Southwest's fuel hedging strategy involved modifying the amount of its future fuel requirements that were hedged based on management's judgments about the forward market prices of crude oil and jet fuel.

- To enhance the performance and efficiency of its aircraft fleet, Southwest had recently added vertical winglets on the wing tips of most all its planes and begun ordering new planes equipped with winglets (see Exhibit 7). These winglets reduced lift drag, allowed aircraft to climb more steeply and reach higher flight levels quicker, improved cruising performance, helped extend engine life and reduce maintenance costs, and reduced fuel burn. In 2007, Southwest entered into an agreement with Naverus, the worldwide leader in performance-based navigation systems, to develop and implement new flight procedures for Southwest planes that would result in lower fuel consumption and greenhouse gas emissions, better on-time reliability, and increased safety in bad weather and at airports situated in mountainous terrain.

- Southwest regularly upgraded and enhanced its management information systems to speed data flows, improve operating efficiency, lower costs, and upgrade its customer service capabilities. In 2001, Southwest implemented use of new software that significantly decreased the time required to generate optimal crew schedules and help improve on-time performance. In 2007–2008, Southwest invested in next-generation technology and software to improve its ticketless system and its

back-office accounting, payroll, and human resource information systems. During 2009, the company replaced or enhanced its point of sale, electronic ticketing and boarding, and revenue accounting systems. During 2010, it completed an initiative to convert to a new SAP enterprise resource planning application that would replace its general ledger, accounts payable, accounts receivable, payroll, benefits, cash management, and fixed asset systems; the conversion was designed to increase data accuracy and consistency, and to lower administrative support costs.

For many decades, Southwest's operating costs had been lower than those of American, Continental, Delta, Northwest, United, US Airways, and other major U.S. airline carriers. Recently, JetBlue, an airline that began operations in 2000 and had grown rapidly with a low-cost, low-fare strategy that was similar to Southwest's strategy, had been able to achieve operating costs that were below those of Southwest—see Exhibit 9 for cost comparisons among the major U.S. airlines during the 1995–2010 period. Exhibit 10 shows a detailed breakdown of Southwest's operating costs based on the number of available seats rather than the number of passenger-occupied seats.

SOUTHWEST'S PEOPLE MANAGEMENT PRACTICES AND CULTURE

Whereas the litany at many companies was that customers come first, at Southwest the operative principle was that "employees come first and customers come second." The high strategic priority placed on employees reflected management's belief that delivering superior service required employees who not only were passionate about their jobs but also knew that the company was genuinely concerned for their well-being and committed to providing them with job security. Southwest's thesis was simple: Keep employees happy—then they will keep customers happy.

EXHIBIT 9

Comparative Operating Cost Statistics, Major U.S. Airlines, 1995–First Quarter 2010 (selected years)

Costs Incurred per Revenue Passenger Mile (in cents)*

	Salaries/Fringe Benefits		Fuel and Oil	Maintenance	Rentals	Landing Fees	Advertising	General and Administrative	Other Operating Expenses	Total Operating Expenses
	Pilots/Copilots	All Employees								
American Airlines										
1995	0.94¢	5.59¢	1.53¢	1.34¢	0.59¢	0.22¢	0.19¢	1.14¢	3.65¢	14.25¢
2000	1.16	5.77	2.04	1.90	0.48	0.23	0.18	0.58	3.30	14.48
2005	0.90	4.65	3.67	1.42	0.41	0.32	0.10	0.95	3.66	15.18
2008	0.87	4.81	6.19	1.72	0.37	0.31	0.12	1.91	4.12	19.54
2009	0.91	5.30	4.10	1.88	0.42	0.35	0.13	1.56	3.47	17.20
Q1 2010	0.98	5.63	4.64	2.16	0.46	0.38	0.14	1.50	3.85	18.76
Continental Airlines										
1995	0.95¢	3.69¢	1.67¢	1.50¢	1.25¢	0.27¢	0.25¢	0.56¢	3.68	12.87¢
2000	1.25	4.43	2.18	1.42	1.17	0.24	0.09	0.59	3.57	13.70
2005	0.79	3.85	3.42	1.18	0.91	0.34	0.13	0.82	5.74	16.38
2008	0.77	3.63	5.90	1.26	0.81	0.33	0.11	1.06	6.04	19.14
2009	0.82	3.89	3.43	1.37	0.79	0.33	0.13	0.98	5.25	16.16
Q1 2010	0.90	4.21	3.75	1.40	0.83	0.35	0.14	1.03	5.80	17.49
Delta Airlines (merged with Northwest Airlines in 2009 and began combined reporting in January 2010)										
1995	1.27¢	4.97¢	1.70¢	1.16¢	0.71¢	0.30¢	0.18¢	0.43¢	4.07¢	13.53¢
2000	1.27	5.08	1.73	1.41	0.54	0.22	0.12	0.74	3.03	12.85
2005	0.93	4.31	3.68	1.10	0.38	0.22	0.16	0.84	6.01	16.68
2008	0.76	3.55	5.99	1.08	0.20	0.21	0.10	0.82	7.85	19.79
2009	0.86	4.04	4.72	1.28	0.19	0.25	0.14	1.10	6.78	18.52
Q1 2010	1.02	4.46	4.60	1.48	0.13	0.31	0.09	0.52	6.96	18.54
JetBlue Airways										
2005	0.51¢	2.31¢	2.42¢	0.68¢	0.38¢	0.25¢	0.16¢	0.51¢	1.44¢	8.13¢
2008	0.74	2.86	5.35	0.86	0.49	0.33	0.18	0.53	2.06	12.67
2009	0.86	3.20	3.64	0.98	0.48	0.40	0.19	0.62	2.13	11.64
Q1 2010	0.97	3.62	3.93	1.04	0.48	0.40	0.14	0.88	2.30	12.80

(continued)

EXHIBIT 9 (concluded)

Costs Incurred per Revenue Passenger Mile (in cents)*

	Salaries/Fringe Benefits		Fuel and Oil	Maintenance	Rentals	Landing Fees	Advertising	General and Administrative	Other Operating Expenses	Total Operating Expenses
	Pilots/Copilots	All Employees								
Northwest Airlines (merged with Delta and began combined reporting in January 2010)										
1995	1.21¢	4.84¢	1.73¢	1.39¢	0.58¢	0.37¢	0.20¢	0.52¢	3.14¢	12.77¢
2000	1.01	4.76	2.35	1.55	0.53	0.31	0.17	0.55	2.77	12.99
2005	0.94	5.07	4.01	1.54	0.57	0.38	0.12	0.58	5.13	17.40
2008	0.73	3.77	7.33	1.30	0.26	0.34	0.08	0.86	6.49	20.43
2009	0.98	4.34	3.79	1.18	0.18	0.32	0.06	1.41	5.22	16.49
Southwest Airlines										
1995	0.92¢	3.94¢	1.56¢	1.21¢	0.79¢	0.35¢	0.41¢	1.09¢	1.56¢	10.91¢
2000	0.86	4.22	1.95	1.22	0.48	0.31	0.35	1.42	0.96	10.91
2005	1.18	4.70	2.44	1.17	0.31	0.34	0.29	0.73	1.23	11.21
2008	1.31	4.81	5.04	1.45	0.26	0.39	0.27	0.84	1.30	14.36
2009	1.33	4.88	4.08	1.43	0.30	0.41	0.27	0.84	1.30	13.53
Q1 2010	1.46	5.27	4.78	1.45	0.34	0.48	0.26	0.95	1.47	14.98
United Airlines										
1995	0.86¢	4.73¢	1.51¢	1.51¢	0.90¢	0.29¢	0.17¢	0.53¢	2.92¢	12.58¢
2000	1.15	5.75	1.98	1.84	0.73	0.28	0.21	0.76	3.09	14.65
2005	0.62	3.72	3.53	1.60	0.35	0.30	0.16	0.60	5.09	15.35
2008	0.69	4.18	7.02	1.88	0.37	0.31	0.06	1.16	5.00	19.97
2009	0.70	4.06	3.39	1.87	0.35	0.37	0.04	0.90	5.06	16.03
Q1 2010	0.73	4.59	4.15	1.92	0.35	0.41	0.05	0.97	5.52	17.95
US Airways (merged with America West in September 2005 and began combined reporting in 2007)										
1995	1.55¢	7.53¢	1.59¢	2.09¢	1.05¢	0.29¢	0.13¢	0.73¢	4.32¢	17.73¢
2000	1.36	7.59	2.44	2.30	0.97	0.28	0.19	1.10	4.81	19.68
2005	0.78	3.74	3.89	1.50	1.06	0.31	0.06	0.66	7.27	18.49
2008	0.80	3.92	5.94	1.94	1.22	0.24	0.02	2.63	7.59	23.50
2009	0.78	3.97	3.20	1.90	1.23	0.27	0.03	1.06	6.77	18.42
Q1 2010	0.84	4.49	4.07	1.99	1.35	0.28	0.03	1.26	7.48	20.94

*Costs per passenger revenue mile represent the costs per ticketed passenger per mile flown; the figures are derived by dividing the company's total expenses in each of the cost categories by the total number of miles flown by all ticketed passengers—thus, if there are 100 ticketed passengers on a flight that travels 500 miles, the number of passenger revenue miles for that flight is 100 × 500, or 50,000).

Source: U.S. Department of Transportation, Bureau of Transportation Statistics, Air Carrier Statistics Form 298C Summary Data and Form 41, Schedules P-6, P-12, P-51, and P-52.

▶ EXHIBIT 10

Southwest Airline's Operating Expenses per Available Seat Mile, 1995–2009 (selected years)

	Costs per Available Seat Mile (in cents)								
Expense Category	**2009**	**2008**	**2007**	**2006**	**2005**	**2004**	**2002**	**2000**	**1995**
Salaries, wages, bonuses, and benefits	3.54¢	3.23¢	3.22¢	3.29¢	3.27¢	3.18	2.89¢	2.81¢	2.40¢
Fuel and oil	3.11	3.60	2.70	2.31	1.58	1.30	1.11	1.34	1.01
Maintenance materials and repairs	0.73	0.70	0.62	0.51	0.52	0.60	0.57	0.63	0.60
Aircraft rentals	0.19	0.15	0.16	0.17	0.19	0.23	0.27	0.33	0.47
Landing fees and other rentals	0.73	0.64	0.56	0.53	0.53	0.53	0.50	0.44	0.44
Depreciation	0.63	0.58	0.56	0.56	0.55	0.56	0.52	0.47	0.43
Other expenses	1.36	1.34	1.28	1.43	1.41	1.37	1.55	1.71	1.72
Total	10.29¢	10.24¢	9.10¢	8.80¢	8.05¢	7.70¢	7.41¢	7.73¢	7.07¢

Note: Figures in this exhibit differ from those for Southwest in Exhibit 9 because the cost figures in Exhibit 9 are based on *cost per passenger revenue mile*, whereas the cost figures in this exhibit are based on *costs per available seat mile.* Costs per revenue passenger mile represent the costs per ticketed passenger per mile flown, whereas costs per available seat mile are the *costs per seat per mile flown (irrespective of whether the seat was occupied or not).*

Source: Southwest Airlines, 10-K reports and annual reports, various years.

In Southwest's 2000 annual report, senior management explained why employees were the company's greatest asset:

> Our people are warm, caring and compassionate and willing to do whatever it takes to bring the Freedom to Fly to their fellow Americans. They take pride in doing well for themselves by doing good for others. They have built a unique and powerful culture that demonstrates that the only way to accomplish our mission to make air travel affordable for others, while ensuring ample profitability, job security, and plentiful Profitsharing for ourselves, is to keep our costs low and Customer Service quality high.
>
> At Southwest, our People are our greatest assets, which is why we devote so much time and energy to hiring great People with winning attitudes. Because we are well known as an excellent place to work with great career opportunities and a secure future, lots of People want to work for Southwest. . . . Once hired, we provide a nurturing and supportive work environment that gives our Employees the freedom to be creative, have fun, and make a positive difference. Although we offer competitive compensation packages, it's our Employees'

> sense of ownership, pride in team accomplishments, and enhanced job satisfaction that keep our Culture and Southwest Spirit alive and why we continue to produce winning seasons.

Gary Kelly, the company's current CEO, echoed the views of his predecessors: "Our People are our single greatest strength and our most enduring long term competitive advantage."[20]

The company changed the Personnel Department's name to the People Department in 1989. Later, it was renamed the People and Leadership Development Department.

Recruiting, Screening, and Hiring

Southwest hired employees for attitude and trained for skills. Herb Kelleher explained:

> We can train people to do things where skills are concerned. But there is one capability we do not have and that is to change a person's attitude. So we prefer an unskilled person with a good attitude . . . [to] a highly skilled person with a bad attitude.[21]

Southwest recruited employees by means of newspaper ads, career fairs, and Internet job listings; a number of candidates applied because of Southwest's reputation as one of the best companies to work for in America and because they were impressed by their experiences as a customer on Southwest flights. Recruitment ads were designed to capture the attention of people thought to possess Southwest's "personality profile." For instance, one ad showed Herb Kelleher impersonating Elvis Presley and had the following copy:

> Work In A Place Where Elvis Has Been Spotted. The qualifications? It helps to be outgoing. Maybe even a bit off center. And be prepared to stay for a while. After all, we have the lowest employee turnover rate in the industry. If this sounds good to you, just phone our jobline or send your resume. Attention Elvis.[22]

Colleen Barrett elaborated on what the company looked for in screening candidates for job openings:

> We hire People to live the Southwest Way. They must possess a Warrior Spirit, lead with a Servant's Heart, and have a Fun-LUVing attitude. We hire People who fight to win, work hard, are dedicated, and have a passion for Customer Service. We won't hire People if something about their behavior won't be a Cultural fit. We hire the best. When our new hires walk through the door, our message to them is you are starting the flight of your life.[23]

All job applications were processed through the People and Leadership Development Department. Exhibit 11 details what the company called the "Southwest Way."

In hiring for jobs that involved personal contact with passengers, the company looked for people-oriented applicants who were extroverted and had a good sense of humor. It tried to identify candidates with a knack for reading peoples' emotions and responding in a genuinely caring, empathetic manner. Southwest wanted employees to deliver the kind of service that showed they truly enjoyed meeting people, being around passengers, and doing their job, as opposed to delivering the kind of service that came across as being forced or taught. Kelleher elaborated: "We are interested in people who externalize, who focus on other people, who are motivated to help other people. We are not interested in navel gazers."[24] In addition to a "whistle while you work" attitude, Southwest was drawn to candidates who it thought would be likely to exercise initiative, work harmoniously with fellow employees, and be community-spirited.

Southwest did not use personality tests to screen job applicants, nor did it ask them what they would or should do in certain hypothetical situations. Rather, the hiring staff at Southwest analyzed each job category to determine the specific behaviors, knowledge, and motivations that job holders needed and then tried to find candidates with the desired traits—a process called targeted selection. A trait common to all job categories was teamwork; a trait deemed critical for pilots and flight attendants was judgment. In exploring an applicant's aptitude for teamwork, interviewers often asked applicants to tell them about a time in a prior job when they went out of their way to help a coworker or to explain how they had handled conflict with a coworker. Another frequent question was "What was your most embarrassing moment?" The thesis here was that having applicants talk about their past behaviors provided good clues about their future behaviors.

To test for unselfishness, Southwest interviewing teams typically gave a group of potential employees ample time to prepare five-minute presentations about themselves; during the presentations in an informal conversational setting, interviewers watched the audience to see who was absorbed in polishing their presentations and who was listening attentively, enjoying the stories being told, and applauding the efforts of the presenters. Those who were emotionally engaged in hearing the presenters and giving encouragement were deemed more apt to be team players than those who were focused on looking good themselves. All applicants for flight attendant positions were put through such a presentation exercise before an interview panel consisting of customers, experienced flight attendants, and members of the People and Leadership Department.

EXHIBIT 11

Personal Traits, Attitudes, and Behaviors That Southwest Wanted Employees to Possess and Display

Living the Southwest Way

Warrior Spirit	Servant's Heart	Fun-LUVing Attitude
• Work hard	• Follow the Golden Rule	• Have FUN
• Desire to be the best	• Adhere to the Basic Principles	• Don't take yourself too seriously
• Be courageous	• Treat others with respect	• Maintain perspective (balance)
• Display a sense of urgency	• Put others first	• Celebrate successes
• Persevere	• Be egalitarian	• Enjoy your work
• Innovate	• Demonstrate proactive Customer Service	• Be a passionate team player
	• Embrace the SWA Family	

Source: Southwest Airlines, www.southwest.com, accessed August 18, 2010.

Flight attendant candidates that got through the group presentation interviews then had to complete a three-on-one interview conducted by a recruiter, a supervisor from the hiring section of the People and Leadership Department, and a Southwest flight attendant; following this interview, the three-person panel tried to reach a consensus on whether to recommend or drop the candidate.

Southwest received 90,043 résumés and hired 831 new employees in 2009. In 2007, prior to the onset of the recession, Southwest received 329,200 résumés and hired 4,200 new employees.

Training

Apart from the FAA-mandated training for certain employees, training activities at Southwest were designed and conducted by Southwest's University for People. The curriculum included courses for new recruits, employees, and managers. Learning was viewed as a never-ending process for all company personnel; the expectation was that each employee should be an "intentional learner," looking to grow and develop not just from occasional classes taken at Southwest's festive University for People learning center but also from their everyday on-the-job experiences.

Southwest's University for People conducted a variety of courses offered to maintenance personnel and other employees to meet the training

and safety requirements of the Federal Aviation Administration, the U.S. Department of Transportation, the Occupational Safety and Health Administration, and other government agencies. And there were courses on written communications, public speaking, stress management, career development, performance appraisal, decision making, leadership, customer service, corporate culture, and employee relations to help employees advance their careers.

Employees wanting to explore whether a management career was for them could take Leadership 101 and 201. One of the keystone course offerings for new frontline managers was a four-session "Leadership Southwest Style" course, which made extensive use of the Myers-Briggs personality assessment to help managers understand the "why" behind coworkers' behaviors and to learn how to build trust, empathize, resolve conflicts, and do a better job of communicating. There was a special "manager-in-training" course for high-potential employees wanting to pursue a long-term career at Southwest. Leadership courses for people already in supervisory or managerial positions emphasized a management style based on coaching, empowering, and encouraging, rather than supervising or enforcing rules and regulations. From time to time, supervisors and executives attended courses on corporate culture, intended to help instill, ingrain, and nurture such cultural themes as teamwork, trust, harmony, and diversity.

All employees who came into contact with customers, including pilots, received customer care training. Southwest's latest customer-related training initiative involved a course called "Every Customer Matters"; by the end of 2009, 14,225 employees had completed the course. Altogether, Southwest employees spent more than 720,000 hours in training sessions of one kind or another in 2009:[25]

Job Category	Amount of Training
Maintenance and support personnel	81,633 hours
Customer support and services personnel	106,480 hours
Flight attendants	109,450 hours
Pilots	199,500 hours
Ground operations personnel	224,799 hours

The OnBoarding Program for Newly Hired Employees Southwest had a program called OnBoarding "to welcome New Hires into the Southwest Family" and provide information and assistance from the time they were selected until the end of their first year. Orientation for new employees included a one-day orientation session, videos on Southwest's history, an overview of the airline industry and the competitive challenges that Southwest faced, and an introduction to Southwest's culture and management practices. The culture introduction included a video called the *Southwest Shuffle,* which featured hundreds of Southwest employees rapping about the fun they had on their jobs (at many Southwest gatherings, it was common for a group of employees to do the Southwest Shuffle, with the remaining attendees cheering and clapping). There were also exercises that demonstrated the role of creativity and teamwork and a scavenger hunt in which new hires were given a timeline with specific dates in Southwest's history and were asked to fill in the missing details by viewing the memorabilia decorating the corridors of the Dallas headquarters and getting information from people work-ing in various offices. During their first 30 days at Southwest, new employees could access an interactive online tool—OnBoarding Online Orientation—to learn about the company.

An additional element of the Onboarding Program involved assigning each new employee to an existing Southwest employee who had volunteered to sponsor a new hire and be of assistance in acclimating the new employee to his or her job and the Southwest Way; each volunteer sponsor received training from Southwest's Onboarding Team in what was expected of a sponsor. Much of the indoctrination of new employees into the company's culture was done by the volunteer sponsor, coworkers, and the new employee's supervisor. Southwest made active use of a one-year probationary employment period to help ensure that new employees fit in with the company's culture and adequately embraced its cultural values.

Promotion

Approximately 80 to 90 percent of Southwest's supervisory positions were filled internally, reflecting management's belief that people who had "been there and done that" would be more likely to appreciate and understand the demands that people under them were experiencing and, also, more likely to enjoy the respect of their peers and higher-level managers. Employees could either apply for supervisory positions or be recommended by their present supervisor. New appointees for supervisor, team leader, and manager attended a three-day class called Leading with Integrity and aimed at developing leadership and communication skills. Employees being considered for managerial positions of large operations (Up and Coming Leaders) received training in every department of the company over a six-month period in which they continued to perform their current job. At the end of the six-month period, candidates were provided with 360-degree feedback from department heads, peers, and subordinates; representatives of the People and Leadership Department analyzed the feedback in deciding on the specific assignment of each candidate.[26]

► **EXHIBIT 12**

Estimated Employee Compensation and Benefits at Selected U.S. Airlines, 2008 and 2009

	Southwest Airlines	American Airlines	Delta	Continental Airlines	JetBlue	United Airlines	US Airways
Average Pilot Wage/Salary							
2008	$172,800	$138,800	$125,600	$136,300	$112,000	$119,500	$113,900
2009	176,200	137,500	137,900	150,200	124,700	125,500	111,300
Average Flight Attendant Wage/Salary							
2008	$ 53,000	$ 49,800	$ 37,000	$ 49,100	$ 33,000	$ 40,100	$ 39,700
2009	46,800	50,900	39,200	51,200	33,800	40,600	40,600
All-Employee Average Wage/Salary							
2008	$ 72,100	$ 60,900	$ 56,100	$ 54,400	$ 54,400	$ 58,100	$ 53,800
2009	75,600	63,000	59,600	56,800	58,600	58,200	55,500
Average Benefits per Employee							
2008	$ 24,200	$ 24,300	$ 45,100	$ 15,800	$ 13,800	$ 25,600	$ 14,500
2009	23,800	30,500	30,100	19,900	14,800	22,700	13,500

Note: The compensation and benefits numbers are estimated from compensation cost and workforce size data reported by the airlines to the Bureau of Transportation Statistics. The number of employees at year-end were used to calculate the averages, which may cause distortions in the event of significant changes in a company's workforce size during the year. In addition, several companies were engaged in mergers and/or major cost restructuring initiatives during 2008–2009, which in some instances (notably Delta) resulted in significant within-company changes from 2008 to 2009.

Source: Derived from data in various airline industry reports published by the Bureau of Transportation Statistics and from information posted at www.airlinefinancials.com.

Compensation

Southwest's pay scales compared quite favorably with other major U.S. airlines (see Exhibit 12). Southwest's average pay for pilots and its all-employee average compensation were the highest of all the major U.S. airlines—sometimes even at or near the top of the industry—and its benefit packages were quite competitive.

Southwest introduced a profit-sharing plan for senior employees in 1973, the first such plan in the airline industry. By the mid-1990s, the plan had been extended to cover most Southwest employees. As of 2010, Southwest had stock option programs for various employee groups (including those covered by collective bargaining agreements), a 401(k) employee savings plans that included company-matching contributions, an employee stock purchase plan, and

a profit-sharing plan covering virtually all employees that consisted of a money purchase defined-contribution plan to which Southwest contributed 15 percent of eligible pretax profits. Company contributions to employee 410(k) and profit-sharing plans totaled $1.3 billion during 2005–2009; in recent years, the annual contribution had represented 6 to 12 percent of base pay. Employees participating in stock purchases via payroll deduction bought 1.3 million shares in 2007, 1.3 million shares in 2008, and 2.2 million shares in 2009 at prices equal to 90 percent of the market value at the end of each monthly purchase period. Southwest employees owned about 10 percent of Southwest's outstanding shares and, as of December 31, 2009, held options to buy some 78.2 million additional shares.

Employee Relations

About 82 percent of Southwest's 34,700 employees belonged to a union, making Southwest one of the most highly unionized U.S. airlines. An in-house union—the Southwest Airline Pilots Association—represented the company's pilots. The Teamsters Union represented Southwest's stock clerks and flight simulator technicians; a local of the Transportation Workers of America represented flight attendants; another local of the Transportation Workers of America represented baggage handlers, ground crews, and provisioning employees; the International Association of Machinists and Aerospace Workers represented customer service and reservation employees; and the Aircraft Mechanics Fraternal Association represented the company's mechanics.

Management encouraged union members and negotiators to research their pressing issues and to conduct employee surveys before each contract negotiation. Southwest's contracts with the unions representing its employees were relatively free of restrictive work rules and narrow job classifications that might impede worker productivity. All of the contracts allowed any qualified employee to perform any function—thus pilots, ticket agents, and gate personnel could help load and unload baggage when needed and flight attendants could pick up trash and make flight cabins more presentable for passengers boarding the next flight.

Except for one brief strike by machinists in the early 1980s and some unusually difficult negotiations in 2000–2001, Southwest's relationships with the unions representing its employee groups were harmonious and nonadversarial for the most part—even though there were sometimes spirited disagreements over particular issues.

In 2000–2001, the company had contentious negotiations with Local 555 of the Transportation Workers of America (TWU) over a new wage and benefits package for Southwest's ramp, baggage operations, provisioning, and freight personnel; the previous contract had become open for renegotiation in December 1999, and a tentative agreement reached at the end of 2000 was rejected by 64 percent of the union members who voted. A memo from Kelleher to TWU representatives said, "The cost and structure of the TWU 555 negotiating committee's proposal would seriously undermine the competitive strength of Southwest Airlines; endanger our ability to grow; threaten the value of our employees' profit-sharing; require us to contract out work in order to remain competitive; and threaten our 29-year history of job security for our employees." In a union newsletter in early 2001, the president of the TWU local said, "We asked for a decent living wage and benefits to support our families, and were told of how unworthy and how greedy we were." The ongoing dispute resulted in informational picket lines in March 2001 at several Southwest locations, the first picketing since 1980. Later in 2001, with the help of the National Mediation Board, Southwest and the TWU reached an agreement covering Southwest's ramp, operations, and provisioning employees.

Prior to 9/11, Southwest's pilots were somewhat restive about their base pay relative to pilots at other U.S. airlines. The maximum pay for Southwest's 3,700+ pilots (before profit-sharing bonuses) was $148,000, versus maximums of $290,000 for United's pilots, $262,000 for Delta's pilots, $206,000 for American's pilots, and $199,000 for Continental's pilots.[27] Moreover, some veteran Southwest employees were grumbling about staff shortages in certain locations (to hold down labor costs) and cracks in the company's close-knit family culture due to the influx of so many new employees over the past several years. A number of employees who had accepted lower pay because of Southwest's underdog status were said to feel entitled to "big airline" pay now that Southwest had emerged as a major U.S. carrier.[28] However, when airline traffic dropped precipitously following 9/11, Southwest's major airline rivals won big wage and salary concessions from unions representing pilots and other airline workers; moreover, about 1 in 5 airline jobs—some 120,000 in all—were eliminated.

In 2006, a senior Boeing 737 pilot at Delta Air Lines working a normal 65-hour month made $116,200 annually, down 26 percent from pre-9/11 wages. A comparable pilot at United Airlines earned $102,200, down 34 percent from before 9/11, and at American Airlines such a pilot made $122,500, 18 percent less than in the days before 9/11.

In 2004, 2007, and 2009, in an attempt to contain rising labor costs and better match workforce size to its operating requirements, Southwest offered voluntary buyout or early retirement packages to selected groups of employees. The 2004 buyout package was offered to approximately 8,700 flight attendants, ramp workers, customer service employees, and those in reservations, operations, and freight who had reached a specific pay scale; the buyout consisted of a $25,000 payment and medical and dental benefits for a specified period. About 1,000 employees accepted the 2004 buyout offer. In 2009, Southwest announced Freedom '09, a one-time voluntary early retirement program offered to older employees, in which the company offered cash bonuses, medical/dental coverage for a specified period of time, and travel privileges based on work group and years of service; some 1,400 employees elected to participate in Freedom '09, resulting in payouts of $66 million.

The No-Layoff Policy

Southwest Airlines had never laid off or furloughed any of its employees since the company began operations in 1971. The company's no-layoff policy was seen as integral to how the company treated its employees and management efforts to sustain and nurture the culture. According to Kelleher:

> Nothing kills your company's culture like layoffs. Nobody has ever been furloughed here, and that is unprecedented in the airline industry. It's been a huge strength of ours. It's certainly helped negotiate our union contracts. . . . We could have furloughed at various times and been more profitable, but I always thought that was shortsighted. You want to show your people you value them

and you're not going to hurt them just to get a little more money in the short term. Not furloughing people breeds loyalty. It breeds a sense of security. It breeds a sense of trust.[29]

Southwest had built up considerable goodwill with its employees and unions over the years by avoiding layoffs. Both senior management and Southwest employees regarded the three recent buyout offers as a better approach to workforce reduction than involuntary layoffs.

Operation Kick Tail

In 2007, Southwest management launched an internal initiative called Operation Kick Tail, a multiyear call to action for employees to focus even more attention on providing high-quality customer service, maintaining low costs, and nurturing the Southwest culture. One component of Operation Kick Tail involved singling out employees for special recognition when they did something to make a positive difference in a customer's travel experience or in the life of a coworker.

Gary Kelly saw this aspect of Operation Kick Tail as a way to foster the employee attitudes and commitment needed to provide "Positively Outrageous Customer Service." He explained:

> One of Southwest's rituals is finding and developing People who are "built to serve." That allows us to provide a personal, warm level of service that is unmatched in the airline industry.

Southwest management viewed Operation Kick Tail as a means to better engage and incentivize employees to strengthen their display of the traits included in the Southwest Way and achieve a competitive edge keyed to superior customer service.

Management Style

At Southwest, management strove to do things in a manner that would make Southwest employees proud of the company they worked for and its workforce practices. Managers were expected to spend at least one-third of their time walking around the facilities under their supervision, observing firsthand what was going on, listening to employees, and being responsive to their concerns. A former director of people development at Southwest told of a conversation he had with one of Southwest's terminal managers:

> While I was out in the field visiting one of our stations, one of our managers mentioned to me that he wanted to put up a suggestion box. I responded by saying, "Sure—why don't you put up a suggestion box right here on this wall and then admit you are a failure as a manager?" Our theory is, if you have to put up a box so people can write down their ideas and toss them in, it means you are not doing what you are supposed to be doing. You are supposed to be setting your people up to be winners. To do that, you should be there listening to them and available to them in person, not via a suggestion box. For the most part, I think we have a very good sense of this at Southwest. I think that most people employed here know that they can call any one of our vice presidents on the telephone and get heard, almost immediately.
>
> The suggestion box gives managers an out; it relinquishes their responsibility to be accessible to their people, and that's when we have gotten in trouble at Southwest—when we can no longer be responsive to our flight attendants or customer service agents, when they can't gain access to somebody who can give them resources and answers.[30]

Company executives were very approachable, insisting on being called by their first names. At new employee orientations, people were told, "We do not call the company chairman and CEO Mr. Kelly, we call him Gary." Managers and executives had an open-door policy, actively listening to employee concerns, opinions, and suggestions for reducing costs and improving efficiency.

Employee-led initiatives were common. Southwest's pilots had been instrumental in developing new protocols for takeoffs and landings that conserved fuel. Another frontline employee had suggested not putting the company logos on trash bags, saving an estimated $250,000 annually. Rather than buy 800 computers for a new reservations center in Albuquerque, company employees determined that they could buy the parts and assemble the PCs themselves for half the price of a new PC, saving the company $1 million. It was Southwest clerks who came up with the idea of doing away with paper tickets and shifting to e-tickets.

There were only four layers of management between a frontline supervisor and the CEO. Southwest's employees enjoyed substantial authority and decision-making power. According to Kelleher:

> We've tried to create an environment where people are able to, in effect, bypass even the fairly lean structures that we have so that they don't have to convene a meeting of the sages in order to get something done. In many cases, they can just go ahead and do it on their own. They can take individual responsibility for it and know they will not be crucified if it doesn't work out. Our leanness requires people to be comfortable in making their own decisions and undertaking their own efforts.[31]

From time to time, there were candid meetings of frontline employees and managers where operating problems and issues between/among workers and departments were acknowledged, openly discussed, and resolved.[32] Informal problem avoidance and rapid problem resolution were seen as managerial virtues.

Southwest's Two Big Core Values—LUV and Fun

Two core values—LUV and fun—permeated the work environment at Southwest. LUV was much more than the company's ticker symbol and a recurring theme in Southwest's advertising campaigns. Over the years, LUV grew into Southwest's code word for treating individuals—fellow employees and customers—with dignity and respect and demonstrating a caring, loving attitude. The code word *LUV* and red hearts commonly appeared on banners and posters at company facilities, as reminders of the compassion that was expected toward customers and other employees. Practicing the Golden Rule, internally and externally, was expected of all employees. Employees who struggled to live up to these expectations were subjected to considerable peer pressure and usually were asked to seek employment elsewhere if they did not soon leave on their own volition.

Fun at Southwest was exactly what the word implies—and it occurred throughout the company in the form of the generally entertaining behavior of employees in performing their jobs, the ongoing pranks and jokes, and frequent company-sponsored parties and celebrations (which typically included the Southwest Shuffle). On holidays, employees were encouraged to dress in costumes. There were charity benefit games, chili cook-offs, Halloween parties, new Ronald McDonald House dedications, and other special events of one kind or another at one location or another almost every week. According to one manager, "We're kind of a big family here, and family members have fun together."

Culture Building

Southwest executives believed that the company's growth was primarily a function of the rate at which it could hire and train people to fit into its culture and consistently display the desired traits and behaviors. CEO Gary Kelly said, "Some things at Southwest won't change. We will continue to expect our people to live what we describe as the 'Southwest Way,' which is to have a Warrior Spirit, Servant's Heart, and Fun-Loving Attitude. Those three things have defined our culture for 36 years."[33]

The Corporate Culture Committee Southwest formed its Corporate Culture Committee in 1990 to promote "Positively Outrageous Service" and devise tributes, contests, and celebrations intended to nurture and perpetuate the Southwest Spirit and Living the Southwest Way. The committee, chaired by Colleen Barrett until mid-2008 and then by Ginger Hardage (who was given lead executive responsibility for cultural aspects at Southwest when Barrett retired), was composed of 100 employees who had demonstrated their commitment to Southwest's mission and values and zeal in exhibiting the Southwest Spirit and Living the

Southwest Way. Members came from a cross-section of departments and locations and functioned as cultural ambassadors, missionaries, and storytellers during their two-year term.

The Corporate Culture Committee had four all-day meetings annually; ad hoc subcommittees formed throughout the year met more frequently. Over the years, the committee had sponsored and supported hundreds of ways to promote and ingrain the traits and behaviors embedded in Living the Southwest Way—examples included promoting the use of red hearts and LUV to embody the spirit of Southwest employees caring about each other and Southwest's customers, showing up at a facility to serve pizza or ice cream to employees or to remodel and decorate an employee break room. Kelleher indicated, "We're not big on Committees at Southwest, but of the committees we do have, the Culture Committee is the most important."[34]

Efforts to Nurture and Sustain the Southwest Culture Apart from the efforts of the Corporate Culture Committee, Southwest management had sought to reinforce the company's core values and culture via its annual Heros of the Heart Award, its CoHearts mentoring program, its Day in the Field program in which employees spent time working in another area of the company's operations, its Helping Hands program in which volunteers from around the system traveled to work two weekend shifts at other Southwest facilities that were temporarily shorthanded or experiencing heavy workloads, and periodic Culture Exchange meetings to celebrate the Southwest Spirit and company milestones. Almost every event at Southwest was videotaped, which provided footage for creating multipurpose videos, such as *Keepin' the Spirit Alive*, that could be shown at company events all over the system and used in training courses. The concepts of LUV and fun were spotlighted in all of the company's training manuals and videos.

Southwest's monthly employee newsletter often spotlighted the experiences and deeds of particular employees, reprinted letters of praise from customers, and reported company celebrations of milestones. A quarterly news video, *As the Plane Turns,* was sent to all facilities to keep employees up to date on company happenings, provide clips of special events, and share messages from customers, employees, and executives. The company had published a book for employees describing "outrageous" acts of service.

Employee Productivity

Management was convinced the company's strategy, culture, esprit de corps, and people management practices fostered high labor productivity and contributed to Southwest's having low labor costs in comparison to the labor costs at its principal domestic rivals. When a Southwest flight pulled up to the gate, ground crews, gate personnel, and flight attendants hustled to perform all the tasks requisite to turn the plane quickly—employees took pride in doing their part to achieve good on-time performance. Southwest's turnaround times were in the range of 25 to 30 minutes, versus an industry average of around 45 minutes. In 2009, Southwest's labor productivity compared quite favorably with its chief domestic competitors (as shown below).

System Operations

Under Herb Kelleher, instituting practices, procedures, and support systems that promoted operating excellence had become a tradition and a source of company pride. Much time and effort over the years had gone into finding the most effective ways to do aircraft maintenance, to operate safely, to make baggage handling more efficient and baggage transfers more accurate, and to improve the percentage of on-time arrivals and departures. Believing that air travelers were more likely to fly Southwest if its flights were reliable and on time, Southwest's managers constantly monitored on-time arrivals and departures, making inquiries when many flights ran behind and searching for ways to improve on-time performance. One initiative to help minimize weather and operational delays involved the development of a state-of-the-art flight dispatch system.

Southwest's current CEO, Gary Kelly, had followed Kelleher's lead in pushing for operating excellence. One of Kelly's strategic objectives for Southwest was "to be the safest, most efficient, and most reliable airline in the world." Southwest managers and employees in all positions and ranks were proactive in offering suggestions for improving Southwest's practices and procedures; those with merit were quickly implemented. Southwest was considered to have one of the most competent and thorough aircraft maintenance programs in the commercial airline industry and, going into 2008, was widely regarded as the best operator among U.S. airlines. Its recent record vis-à-vis rival airlines on four important measures of operating performance was commendable—see Exhibit 13.

The First Significant Blemish on Southwest's Safety Record While no Southwest plane had ever crashed and there

	Productivity Measure	
	Passengers Enplaned per Employee, 2009	**Employees per Plane, 2009**
Southwest Airlines	2,475	65
American Airlines	1,289	109
Continental	1,177	115
Delta	1,430	103
JetBlue	2,121	70
United	1,204	129
US Airways	1,628	90

Source: Calculated from data in Southwest Airlines' 10-K reports.

EXHIBIT 13

Comparative Statistics on On-Time Flights, Mishandled Baggage, Boarding Denials Due to Oversold Flights, and Passenger Complaints for Eight Major U.S. Airlines, 2000 through Quarter 1 of 2010

Percentage of Scheduled Flights Arriving within 15 Minutes of the Scheduled Time (during the previous 12 months ending in May of each year)

Airline	2000	2005	2006	2007	2008	2009	Q1 2010
American Airlines	75.8%	78.0%	75.6%	72.4%	66.9%	75.2%	77.5%
Continental Airlines	76.7	78.7	74.8	73.5	74.1	75.6	80.4
Delta Air Lines	78.3	76.4	76.2	76.6	75.7	76.3	79.3
JetBlue Airways	n.a.	76.3	73.1	69.4	73.3	74.0	77.3
Northwest Airlines*	80.7	79.3	75.1	71.4	71.1	80.5	—
Southwest Airlines	**78.7**	**79.9**	**80.3**	**80.7**	**78.5**	**83.3**	**81.5**
United Airlines	71.6	79.8	75.7	73.0	69.1	76.2	82.5
US Airways	72.7	76.0	78.9	69.7	75.5	79.9	81.9

Mishandled Baggage Reports per 1,000 Passengers (in May of each year)

Airline	2000	2005	2006	2007	2008	2009	Q1 2010
American Airlines	5.44	4.58	4.91	6.40	5.82	4.32	3.87
Continental Airlines	4.11	3.30	3.85	5.02	3.78	2.32	2.27
Delta Air Lines	3.64	6.21	4.75	5.26	3.81	4.33	3.50
JetBlue Airways	n.a.	3.16	2.88	4.38	3.23	2.26	2.15
Northwest Airlines*	4.98	3.58	3.11	3.80	2.97	2.11	—
Southwest Airlines	**4.14**	**3.46**	**3.66**	**5.54**	**4.41**	**3.30**	**3.09**
United Airlines	6.71	4.00	3.89	4.83	4.76	3.67	3.05
US Airways	4.57	9.73	5.69	7.17	3.86	2.91	2.27

Involuntary Denied Boardings per 10,000 Passengers Due to Oversold Flights (January through March of each year)

Airline	2000	2005	2006	2007	2008	2009	Q1 2010
American Airlines	0.59	0.72	1.16	1.06	0.98	0.43	1.28
Continental Airlines	0.50	3.01	2.60	1.93	1.57	1.42	2.73
Delta Air Lines	0.44	1.06	2.68	3.47	1.80	1.64	0.63
JetBlue Airways	n.a.	0.00	0.01	0.04	0.02	0.00	0.01
Northwest Airlines*	0.12	1.70	1.00	1.25	1.15	0.68	—
Southwest Airlines	**1.70**	**0.74**	**1.81**	**1.25**	**1.68**	**1.42**	**2.59**
United Airlines	1.61	0.42	0.88	0.4	0.89	1.30	1.92
US Airways	0.80	1.01	1.07	1.68	2.01	1.50	2.96

Complaints per 100,000 Passengers Boarded (in May of each year)

Airline	2000	2005	2006	2007	2008	2009	Q1 2010
American Airlines	2.77	1.01	1.22	1.44	1.30	1.18	1.61
Continental Airlines	2.25	0.89	0.85	0.75	1.03	1.03	1.36
Delta Airlines	1.60	0.91	0.93	1.50	2.10	1.85	1.57
JetBlue Airways	n.a.	0.00	0.22	0.40	0.56	0.93	1.72
Northwest Airlines*	2.17	0.83	0.69	1.13	0.94	0.88	—
Southwest Airlines	**0.41**	**0.17**	**0.18**	**0.19**	**0.32**	**0.13**	**0.26**
United Airlines	5.07	0.87	1.19	2.00	1.61	1.16	1.67
US Airways	1.63	0.99	1.22	2.65	1.94	1.34	1.19

*Effective January 2010, data of the merged operations of Delta Air Lines and Northwest Airlines were combined and reported as Delta for Q1 2010.

Source: Office of Aviation Enforcement and Proceedings, Air Travel Consumer Report, various years.

had never been a passenger fatality, there was an incident in 2005 in which a Southwest plane landing in a snowstorm with a strong tailwind at Chicago's Midway airport was unable to stop before overrunning a shorter-than-usual runway, rolling onto a highway, crashing into a car, killing one of the occupants, and injuring 22 of the passengers on the plane. A National Traffic Safety Board investigation concluded that "the pilot's failure to use available reverse thrust in a timely manner to safely slow or stop the airplane after landing" was the probable cause.

Belated Aircraft Inspections Further Tarnish Southwest's Reputation In early 2008, various media reported that Southwest Airlines over a period of several months in 2006 and 2007 had knowingly failed to conduct required inspections for early detection of fuselage fatigue cracking on 46 of its older Boeing 737-300 jets. The company had voluntarily notified the Federal Aviation Administration about the lapse in checks for fuselage cracks but continued to fly the planes until the work was done—about eight days. The belated inspections revealed tiny cracks in the bodies of six planes, with the largest measuring four inches; none of the cracks impaired flight safety. According to CEO Gary Kelly, "Southwest Airlines discovered the missed inspection area, disclosed it to the FAA, and promptly re-inspected all potentially affected aircraft in March 2007. The FAA approved our actions and considered the matter closed as of April 2007." Nonetheless, on March 12, 2008, shortly after the reports in the media surfaced about Southwest's failure to meet inspection deadlines, Southwest canceled 4 percent of its flights and grounded 44 of its Boeing 737-300s until it verified that the aircraft had undergone required inspections. Gary Kelly then initiated an internal review of the company's maintenance practices; the investigation raised "concerns" about the company's aircraft maintenance procedures, prompting Southwest to put three employees on leave. The FAA subsequently

fined Southwest $10.2 million for its transgressions. In an effort to help restore customer confidence, Kelly publicly apologized for the company's wrongdoing, promised that such a lapse would not occur again, and reasserted the company's commitment to safety. He said:

> From our inception, Southwest Airlines has maintained a rigorous Culture of Safety—and has maintained that same dedication for more than 37 years. It is and always has been our number one priority to ensure safety.
>
> We've got a 37-year history of very safe operations, one of the safest operations in the world, and we're safer today than we've ever been.

In the days following the public revelation of Southwest's maintenance lapse and the tarnishing of its reputation, an industry-wide audit by the FAA revealed similar failures to conduct timely inspections for early signs of fuselage fatigue at five other airlines—American, Continental, Delta, United, and Northwest. An air travel snafu ensued, with more than a thousand flights subsequently being canceled due to FAA-mandated grounding of the affected aircraft while the overdue safety inspections were performed. Further public scrutiny, including a congressional investigation, turned up documents indicating that, in some cases, planes flew for 30 months after the inspection deadlines had passed. Moreover, high-level FAA officials were apparently aware of the failure of Southwest and other airlines to perform the inspections for fuselage cracks at the scheduled times and chose not to strictly enforce the inspection deadlines—according to some commentators, because of allegedly cozy relationships with personnel at Southwest and the other affected airlines. Disgruntled FAA safety supervisors in charge of monitoring the inspections conducted by airline carriers testified before Congress that senior FAA officials frequently ignored their reports that certain routine safety inspections were not being conducted in accordance with prescribed FAA procedures. Shortly thereafter, the FAA issued more stringent procedures to ensure that aircraft safety inspections were properly conducted.

A SUDDEN SHIFT IN STRATEGY

In September 2010, Southwest announced that it had entered into a definitive agreement to acquire all of the outstanding common stock of AirTran Holdings, Inc. (NYSE: AAI), the parent company of AirTran Airways (AirTran), for a combination of cash and Southwest Airlines' common stock. The transaction was valued at about $1.4 billion; Southwest planned to fund approximately $670 million of the acquisition cost out of cash on hand.[35] For the twelve months ending June 30, 2010, AirTran had revenues of $2.5 billion and operating income (excluding special items) of $128 million. Like Southwest, AirTran was also a low-fare, low-cost airline. AirTran served 70 airports in the United States, Mexico, and the Caribbean; nineteen of these coincided with airports already served by Southwest. AirTran's hub was Atlanta's Hartsfield-Jackson International Airport, the busiest airport in the United States and the largest domestic airport not served by Southwest; AirTran had 202 daily departures out of Atlanta.[36] Some analysts believed that Southwest's entry into the Atlanta market alone could translate into 2 million additional passengers for Southwest annually. AirTran had 8,033 employees, 138 aircraft, and 177 nonstop routes; in 2009 AirTran transported 24.0 million passengers, the seventh largest number of all U.S. airlines. Based on current operations, the combined organization would have nearly 43,000 employees and serve more than 100 million passengers annually. In addition, the combined carriers' all-Boeing fleet consisting of 685 active aircraft would include 401 Boeing 737-700s, 173 Boeing 737-300s, 25 Boeing 737-500s, and 86 Boeing 717s, with an average age of approximately 10 years, one of the youngest fleets in the industry. The companies hoped to close the merger deal in early 2011 and then begin integration of AirTran into the Southwest Airlines brand—a process which Southwest management said might take as long as two years in order to maintain Southwest's standards for customer service.

ENDNOTES

[1] Kevin Freiberg and Jackie Freiberg, *NUTS! Southwest Airlines' Crazy Recipe for Business and Personal Success* (New York: Broadway Books, 1998), p.15.

[2] Ibid., pp. 16–18.

[3] Katrina Brooker, "The Chairman of the Board Looks Back," *Fortune,* May 28, 2001, p. 66.

[4] Freiberg and Freiberg, *NUTS,* p. 31.

[5] Ibid., pp. 26–27.

[6] Ibid., pp. 246–47.

[7] Quoted in the *Dallas Morning News,* March 20, 2001.

[8] Quoted in Brooker, "The Chairman of the Board Looks Back," p. 64.

[9] Ibid., p. 72.

[10] Quoted in *Seattle Times,* March 20, 2001, p. C3.

[11] Speech at Texas Christian University, September 13, 2007, accessed at www.southwest.com on September 8, 2008.

[12] Freiberg and Freiberg, *NUTS!,* p. 163.

[13] Company press release, July 15, 2004.

[14] Speech to Greater Boston Chamber of Commerce, April 23, 2008, www.southwest.com, accessed September 5, 2008.

[15] Speech to Business Today International Conference, November 20, 2007, www.southwest.com, accessed September 8, 2008.

[16] As cited in Freiberg and Freiberg, *NUTS!,* p. 288.

[17] Speech by Colleen Barrett on January 22, 2007, and posted at www.southwest.com, accessed on September 5, 2008.

[18] Brenda Paik Sunoo, "How Fun Flies at Southwest Airlines," *Personnel Journal* 74, no. 6 (June 1995), p. 70.

[19] Statement made in a 1993 Harvard Business School video and quoted in Roger Hallowell, "Southwest Airlines: A Case Study Linking Employee Needs Satisfaction and Organizational Capabilities to Competitive Advantage," *Human Resource Management* 35, no. 4 (Winter 1996), p. 517.

[20] Statement posted in the Careers section at www.southwest.com, accessed August 18, 2010.

[21] Quoted in James Campbell Quick, "Crafting an Organizational Structure: Herb's Hand at Southwest Airlines," *Organizational Dynamics* 21, no. 2 (Autumn 1992), p. 51.

[22] Southwest's ad entitled "Work in a Place Where Elvis Has Been Spotted," and Sunoo, "How Fun Flies at Southwest Airlines," pp. 64–65.

[23] Speech to the Paso Del Norte Group in El Paso Texas, January 22, 2007, www.southwest.com, accessed September 5, 2008.

[24] Quick, "Crafting an Organizational Structure," p. 52.

[25] Southwest's "2009 One Report," p. 20, www.southwest.com, accessed August 19, 2010.

[26] Sunoo, "How Fun Flies at Southwest Airlines," p. 72.

[27] Shawn Tully, "From Bad to Worse," *Fortune,* October 15, 2001, p. 124.

[28] Melanie Trottman, "Amid Crippled Rivals, Southwest Tries to Spread Its Wings," *The Wall Street Journal,* October 11, 2001, p. A10.

[29] Brooker, "The Chairman of the Board Looks Back," p. 72.

[30] Freiberg and Freiberg, *NUTS!,* p. 273.

[31] Ibid., p. 76.

[32] Hallowell, "Southwest Airlines," p. 524.

[33] Speech to Business Today International Conference, November 20, 2007, accessed at www.southwest.com on September 8, 2008.

[34] Freiberg and Freiberg, *NUTS!,* p. 165.

[35] Southwest Airlines press release, September 27, 2010.

[36] Rhonda Cook and Kelly Yamanouchi, "Southwest Buying AirTran for $1.4 Billion," *Atlanta Journal-Constitution,* September 27, 2010, accessed at www.ajc.com on October 26, 2010.

NORTON LILLY INTERNATIONAL: IMPLEMENTING TRANSFORMATIONAL CHANGE IN THE SHIPPING INDUSTRY

James Burton
Norton Lilly International

John E. Gamble
University of South Alabama

At a mid-2010 executive committee meeting, Norton Lilly International's chief financial officer (CFO) and chief operating officer (COO), James (Jim) Burton, introduced the meeting's theme: emphasizing growth. He then shared with the executive committee that the company's top line had grown by only 4 percent since 2006, yet the bottom line had improved by 251 percent since 2007 (2006 had produced a loss). In addition, the company's revenue per full-time employee had increased from $91,000 in 2007 to nearly $113,000 by June 2010.

Norton Lilly was an international shipping agency with 37 regional offices that provided services to ships in 70 ports located in North America, the Caribbean, the Pacific, and the Middle East. Typical services provided by Norton Lilly to the operators of oceangoing cargo ships included booking freight for export, clearing inbound cargo with U.S. Customs, fueling vessels, restocking vessels with supplies and provisions, and arranging cargo handling services. The company's dramatic turnaround since 2006 had come about after Burton, a certified public accountant (CPA) and former management consultant with Ernst & Young, Capgemini, and AlixPartners, arrived on scene to transform Norton Lilly's culture and operating practices from those that sprang from an entrepreneurial mind-set to one focused on execution and value added growth.

At the conclusion of the two-day meeting, Burton worried that after more than three years of restructuring, he was still uncertain whether the execution platform was indeed solidly in place. In addition, he was concerned that the company might not be fully prepared to pursue the disciplined growth that would allow bottom-line performance to match top-line growth. Also, Burton had lingering concerns from the meeting that the company's culture change was incomplete, that some managers were not sufficiently focused on customer needs, and that the company might have trouble developing new solutions around evolving customer needs. During a short debriefing with Larry Baldwin, Norton Lilly's vice president of human resources, Burton summed up his concerns: "Our key executives and managers are looking for revenue growth. Do you think that our foundation is strong enough to support the addition of new business without eroding operational effectiveness? Is our culture ready for disciplined growth? Do our business unit leaders truly understand our value creating processes? Do we have the right team in place? Just how complete is our transformation?"

COMPANY HISTORY AND OVERVIEW

Norton Lilly International was well-known and respected within the shipping industry; its operations in 2010 included 37 regional offices that provided services to ships in 70 ports located in North America, the Caribbean, the Pacific, and the Middle East. The company's ship services first began in 1841, when John Norton booked a shipment of kerosene aboard a small sailing ship bound for South America. The company's ownership expanded in 1907 to include the Lilly family, and in 1925 the company expanded internationally with the opening of a Norton Lilly office in Panama. Panama became an important port in the company's growth over the next several decades, with Norton Lilly remaining the market share leader in handling Panama Canal transits in 2010.

The company grew rapidly after the development of cargo containerization in the early 1970s, with its business shifting almost exclusively to providing services to container vessels. The company was acquired in 1999 by two Mobile, Alabama, entrepreneurs, H. W. (Win) Thurber III and John Rutherford Sr. While Rutherford's previous business experience was in insurance and timber management, Thurber had considerable experience in the shipping industry—so much so that he was inducted in the Maritime Hall of Fame in 2005. Under the leadership of Thurber and Rutherford, Norton Lilly expanded into additional international ports during the early 2000s through a combination of acquisitions, joint ventures, and internal development. By 2005, the company provided cargo handling and other services to nearly 22,000 vessels in ports around the world and was the largest privately held shipping agency based in North America.

SETBACKS AT NORTON LILLY

After five years of steady growth, Norton Lilly found itself handicapped by a number of problems in 2006 that led to a $2.6 million net loss for the year. The series of acquisitions, joint ventures, and internal expansion initiatives led by Thurber and Rutherford had allowed annual revenues to increase to more than $41 million, but acquisitions outside the company's core business, a failure to effectively integrate acquired shipping agencies, an inadequate attention to operational performance, and too little focus on bottom-line performance had put the company in a rather precarious situation.

Realizing the company was in need of a dramatic turnaround and likely in need of fresh ideas from an outsider, Thurber and Rutherford launched a search for an operations-oriented leader who could restore the company's profitability. In February 2007, the two partners settled on Jim Burton to take on the roles of CFO and COO and lead the transformation program. During Burton's 25-year career in public accounting and consulting, he had advised such companies as Exxon, Kellogg's, Sprint, Henkel, and Warner Home Video, but his selection as Norton Lilly's CFO and COO was his first major involvement with a privately held business.

In establishing their expectations for Burton, Rutherford and Thurber stated that their desire was to see the development of a sustainable business platform that would be capable of doubling the company's size, while generating an attractive return on investment. A second objective for Burton was to assist with the gradual handoff of the business to a new generation of family members.

NORTON LILLY INTERNATIONAL'S SCOPE OF BUSINESS OPERATIONS IN 2007

When Burton arrived at Norton Lilly International, the company operated three different business units—Liner, Ship Services, and Overseas. The Liner business unit was headed by Steve Haverstock, an industry veteran with more than 30 years' experience who was supported by H. W. (Winchester) Thurber IV, the eldest son of Win Thurber. The younger Thurber was being groomed to one day take over the Liner unit as Rutherford, Win Thurber, and

Haverstock stepped aside. Norton Lilly's Liner business unit provided various services to container ships that carried dry cargo in and out of U.S. ports of call. These container ships were sometimes referred to as the industry's "bus service" since the oceangoing liners maintained regularly scheduled routes between ports and carried containers of whatever goods had been booked for a particular transportation date.

Norton Lilly's Liner business unit customers were typically foreign-based companies with established ocean trade routes to and from the United States that chose not to set up their own administrative offices within the United States. It was frequently less expensive for foreign shipping firms to outsource support services to a shipping agent. Services performed by Norton Lilly for its outbound liner customers included booking freight, preparing and transmitting bills of lading, and completing shipping manifests for outgoing vessels. Norton Lilly also provided services for inbound ships such as notifying U.S. Customs and consignees of an impending cargo arrival, collecting freight charges from consignees, and clearing all cargo with U.S. Customs before its release from the port. Finally, Norton Lilly arranged truck and/or rail services to move cargo inland.

Norton Lilly's Ship Services business unit was headed by Flemming Buhl, an industry veteran who had more than 20 years' experience and was backed by John Wade Thurber, the youngest son of Win Thurber. Like his older brother, John Wade Thurber was learning at the side of an experienced industry veteran and was expected to one day assume control of the business unit. While the Liner business unit was known as a "bus service," the Ship Services unit was referred to as a "taxi service." Customers of Norton Lilly's Ship Services unit operated car carriers, tankers, and bulk cargo vessels that scheduled shipments to and from U.S. ports based on demand rather than a defined timetable. Therefore, operators of such vessels were on call to pick up shipments of goods when requested and deliver the goods to whatever port the shipper desired. Typical ship services offered by Norton Lilly included fueling vessels, providing crew transport to and from vessels, arranging crew medical services,

restocking vessels with supplies and provisions, handling cargo, and arranging tugs to navigate vessels in and out of port. The main difference in the services provided by the Liner and Ship Services divisions was that the Liner unit focused on the cargo whereas the Ship Services unit focused more on the vessel.

The company's Overseas division was managed by Dwain Denniston, another industry veteran with more than 30 years' experience. The Overseas division offered both liner and ship services to vessels entering and departing ports serviced by Norton Lilly that were outside the United States. Norton Lilly's Overseas division operated offices in ports throughout the Caribbean, including Panama, Trinidad, Puerto Rico, and Mexico. The Overseas division also operated offices in ports located in the Middle East, including ports in Dubai, United Arab Emirates; Amman, Jordan; and Umm Qasr, Basra, and Baghdad, Iraq.

PHASE 1 OF THE TURNAROUND: BUILDING THE FOUNDATION

Understanding his mandate and the company's recent performance, Jim Burton set about analyzing the business with an emphasis on quick wins that would contribute to developing the long-term "execution" foundation. As an industry outsider and former consultant, Burton knew he was dealing with seasoned industry veterans, each with deeply held beliefs and paradigms about the business—how it had been and should be run. In an effort to build confidence and gain acceptance among his senior peers, Burton knew he had to introduce ideas the group would be willing to accept and build on. It had to be an incremental approach.

With encouragement and support of the owners, Burton first formed an executive committee of nine, including the five business unit executives; the two owners, Win Thurber and John Rutherford; the chief administrative officer, Sumner Adams (the son-in-law of John Rutherford), who had joined the company in 2006 after having worked a number of years at a marine terminal; and himself. The objective in forming an executive committee was to begin decentralizing the decision-making process away from the two owners. While they would be members of the committee, the owners would not actively participate in committee sessions, but would instead attend summary reviews, at the conclusion of each meeting, to provide counsel and advice.

Burton knew if he was to transform the company and build the sustainable growth platform the owners wanted, it would be through the executive committee. In consultation with the owners, it was understood that bold action was needed, given the company's 2006 performance; however, long-term success would best be achieved through logical, step-change fundamentals wherein results could be both visible and tangible. As the committee saw improved results, their confidence in the approach would grow and help ensure their continued buy-in to even newer ways of running the business.

Identifying and Understanding Value-Creating Processes

Rather than rapidly changing the company's strategy, Burton focused on its execution and on helping Norton Lilly's executives understand the key processes that enabled good strategy execution and value creation. Burton explained, "We followed the executive committee formation by introducing process mapping, in hopes of helping everyone understand exactly how we delivered our services." Upon arrival, one of the things Burton first heard among employees at all levels was "Well, we've always done it this way." He continued to explain, "The challenge was to instill a mind-set that would allow for a critical examination of how the work was being done and developing better ways of working in the future." This change in mind-set would act as the foundation for a culture of operational discipline and continuous improvement.

Burton first launched process mapping in the Liner group, which operated in eight different U.S. offices. At the time, the Liner division offered a fragmented mix of services across its eight locations, with each location performing some activities more effectively than other locations and all locations failing to provide adequate service in some regard. The intended end-to-end service delivery model—from bill of lading preparation, cargo release, to freight collections—was not coordinated and consisted of nonstandard processes, leading to rework and, more important, financial penalties within the context of existing contracts.

By late 2007, mapping the key processes involved in delivering each type of service had helped management and key employees understand the underlying causes of service failures and begin to close performance gaps. In addition, management and employee understanding of processes led to improved process standardization, ended administrative procedures that duplicated work, improved customer satisfaction, and reduced fines and penalties from $325,000 to $283,000, by December 2007. (Fines and penalties had been reduced to $28,000 by 2010.) The success of process mapping in the Liner business unit created buy-in among executive committee members and helped Burton move the company toward the concept of continuous improvement.

Another early-2007 foundation-building step involved clarifying accountability, as it was unclear who was accountable for what. Burton recalled, "Everyone was accountable, yet no one really was." Using the results from process mapping, Burton identified operating-level objectives for each process; he called those objectives key performance indicators (KPIs). By the end of 2007, Burton had assigned responsibility for achieving KPI goals to individual managers and supervisors overseeing specific value-creating processes within the Liner division.

Implementing a Balanced Scorecard Performance Measurement System

Accompanying the KPI rollout was a balanced scorecard, which further focused managerial employees' attention on the performance of value-creating processes. Metrics included in the balanced scorecard system used at Norton Lilly included process KPIs, customer satisfaction, and financial performance. In terms of integrating customer satisfaction as a performance metric for the first time at Norton Lilly, Burton commented, "I remember asking one of our guys 'How do you know you're meeting customer expectations?' He said, 'If we're not, they'll tell me.' Well, that seemed a little too open-ended. The company needed a more consistent discipline (process mapping) for defining what we did [and] how we did it, and a proactive approach for engaging the customer to ensure what and how we did things aligned with the contract and their expectations of us."

In late 2007, Norton Lilly's balanced scorecard system was expanded to include a "dashboard" of performance indicators that could provide a quick overview of operational and financial performance at the business unit level. The dashboard indicators were first established for the Liner business. The initial dashboards contained a fairly limited collection of KPIs, such as revenue compared to budget, expense groupings compared to budget, capital expenditures compared to budget, and Top 10 customer profitability. Top 10 customer profitability listed the 10 most profitable customer accounts at any given time. The addition of KPIs to Norton Lilly's process mapping better enabled each business unit leader to understand cause-and-effect relationships between day-to-day activities and operating and financial performance.

By the end of 2007, Norton Lilly's business unit leaders were holding monthly meetings to review KPI status and propose corrective actions to resolve differences between expectations and actual performance. In late 2007, John Wade Thurber stated, "When these dashboards and KPIs were first introduced, I admit, I was skeptical. I didn't see how they would add value. Now, having worked with them and having seen them assist in our improved performance, I now see the dashboard as one of the most, if not the most, important management tools at my disposal."

Resource Allocation Policies

Other foundation-building actions undertaken in 2007 included the initiation of various policy changes. One such policy change involved the company's capital outlay policy, which was the first new policy established by the executive committee and required that all projects or investments be considered only after satisfactory due diligence had been performed and proposals evaluated by the executive committee. All project or investment funding would be granted only if solid evidence had been presented demonstrating the projected financial value. For non-project-related expenditures, an authorization for expenditure (AFE) system was implemented to ensure that each business unit leader saw and signed off all capital expenditure requests and understood the impact of the expenditure on the KPI targets.

The capital outlay policy came about after Burton discovered that the company had previously launched into a number of ventures without much success. In probing how those decisions came about, he found that no formalized due diligence existed. For example, Norton Lilly made a decision to buy into a warehouse in Long Beach, California. While warehousing was a logical extension of the company's business model, the company had no expertise in the area. Moreover, no single executive owned the business, the company overpaid for the warehouse, and within 18 months it had lost over $1 million operating the warehouse. Implementing the capital outlay policy created a formal process for evaluating proposed projects or investments greater than $10,000. The policy called for a nine-step due diligence process, thereby ensuring consistency in proposals coming before the executive committee. The nine steps were as follows:

1. Description of the opportunity.
2. Description of how the opportunity fit with Norton Lilly International's objectives.
3. Assessment of the competitive threats.
4. Assessment of the competitive landscape.

5. How success would be ensured.
6. Proposed exit strategy.
7. Business case.
8. Financial pro forma.
9. List of major assumptions and risks.

The capital outlay policy would ensure that decisions to enter into any business venture would be fully vetted, based on facts, not opinions. As Flemming Buhl stated after signing off on the capital outlay policy, "I guess this means we all must do our homework, together."

Building Managerial Talent

Throughout 2007, Norton Lilly focused on another important foundation-building element—management development. Burton introduced a leadership development program that matched a person's profile to a job. The program was based on the fundamental premise that managerial employees could be classified into one of four basic profiles: strategist, project director, networker (i.e., account manager), or external qualifier (i.e., salesperson). An individual's profile was determined by how the person responded on a survey containing items related to dominance (the need to be in charge); influencing (introvert versus extrovert); steadiness (ability to multitask versus working in linear fashion); compliance (ability to comply with rules versus being a rebel); motivators (e.g., knowledge, status, or money); and cognitive style. The results of the survey determined a person's profile and suggested how he or she might fit or perform within the context of a given job. For example, a project director who was highly focused on "how" might not fare well within a sales job.

After being tested and profiled, the 20 highest-ranking employees at Norton Lilly entered into workshops directed at helping members of the management team interpret each profile and respect and deal effectively with differing profiles. The process aided basic understanding of the strengths of each executive committee member and ensured better communication within the committee. By late 2007, the prior approach of assigning a friend or former colleague to a given role had been replaced by recruitment based on the managerial profiles.

PHASE II OF THE TURNAROUND: REINFORCING THE FOUNDATION

The efforts undertaken during Phase I of Norton Lilly's turnaround had produced a profitable fiscal 2007, which was the company's first profitable year since 2003. The annual net profit provided Jim Burton with the momentum to continue to push the turnaround forward and build on his early execution-related successes. During 2008, the company extended process mapping across other business units, including administrative and accounting units. In addition, information gathered from process maps helped Norton Lilly's management determine break-even pricing and proper staffing levels for various-sized cargo ships.

Improving Information Used for Decision Making

Dashboards were also expanded to all of Norton Lilly's business units—Liner, Ship Services, and Overseas—as well as the addition of financial measures such as cash flow and accounts receivable KPIs. The inclusion of financial KPIs on management dashboards helped the percentage of accounts more than 60 days past due in the Liner business unit decline from 7 percent in December 2008 to less than 1 percent in June 2010.

In early 2008, Sumner Adams assumed the treasurer role and became the process owner for all collection and cash management functions. Using his process maps, Sumner examined the disbursement accounts (essentially customer billings for services rendered) and collection processes and established a service-based cash conversion cycle KPI. Adams's philosophy behind developing the cash conversion KPIs was "The faster we invoice, the faster we collect, therefore improving our cash and liquidity positions." The baseline cash conversion cycle was 24 days in late 2008. By May

2010, the cash conversion KPI was 16 days and tracking toward a stated goal of 15 days. The company's current ratio improved from 0.88:1 to 1.51:1 over the same period.

Changing Financial Performance Expectations

Burton initiated another policy change in 2008, although less a stated policy than a mind-set. The concept of value creation was introduced at an executive committee meeting in late 2007 and became the basis for all 2008 budgeting. As part of the 2008 budget process, Burton determined Norton Lilly's internal cost of capital and established it as the proxy for value creation. Before this point, the collective view at Norton Lilly was that any positive budget or set of results was a good thing. In fact, the 2007 budget called for the company to make $163,000 on $41 million in revenue. At the time, Win Thurber stated, "If you can assure me we can make this, I'll call it a year right now."

The concept of earning a fair rate of return based on assumed risk didn't exist at Norton Lilly, so, as part of the 2008 budgeting exercise, each business unit leader was given a margin target. As the behavioral shift toward value creation and away from budget negotiation began to take hold, each business unit was given greater decision autonomy, but with clear accountability to achieve its assigned margin targets.

A New Approach to Forecasting Financial Performance

Norton Lilly examined its relative performance against budget and found that the company missed its budgeted performance in 2007 and 2008 by 90 percent and 63 percent, respectively. Because of general economic uncertainty that could not be fully factored into a static budget, the company decided to adopt a 12-month rolling forecast. This would (1) provide continual refreshing of the assumptions underlying the forecast and (2) provide the company a continual look at its next 12 months, regardless of how many months were left in the calendar year. The move to rolling forecasts helped managers improve forecasting accuracy to the extent that the company missed its financial projections by only 9 percent in 2009 and was on track to achieve 94 percent of projected financial performance in 2010.

THE STATE OF THE TURNAROUND GOING INTO 2011

By the close of 2009, Norton Lilly International had seen steady improvement in its performance. Despite the general decline in the industry, 2009 proved to be the company's most profitable year, and 2010 showed signs of being even better. The company was on track in 2010 to generate revenues of about $45.7 million (up 4 percent over 2006) and net income of $3.3 million (up 251 percent over 2007). Exhibit 1 presents Norton Lilly International's income statements for 2006 through 2009. The company's balance sheets for 2008 and 2009 are presented in Exhibit 2. Its financial projections for 2010 are presented in Exhibit 3.

The overall improvement in Norton Lilly's financial performance could largely be traced to the foundation that was begun in 2007, consisting of the following:

- Continuous improvement had become an accepted discipline throughout the company.
- Accountability for achieving KPIs assigned to a unit had become mainstream.
- Dashboards were included in the monthly financial summary package, which was distributed to each executive committee member.
- Value creation and use of a 12-month rolling forecast had also become mainstream. The budget process had been eliminated, and decision making had been decentralized to business unit leaders, with full decision authority but also with accountability for achieving margin and growth targets.
- The use of management development based on the proper matching of people to jobs.

EXHIBIT 1

Norton Lilly International's Consolidated Statements of Income, 2006–2009 ($ thousands)

	2009	2008	2007	2006
Revenues	$44,680	$53,576	$55,692	$43,902
Cost of revenues	2,684	2,761	2,755	2,740
Gross profit	41,996	50,815	52,937	41,161
Expenses				
General and administrative expenses	37,435	46,383	49,042	40,659
Depreciation and amortization	704	797	827	858
Total expenses	38,139	47,180	49,869	41,516
Operating income (loss)	3,858	3,635	3,068	(355)
Other income and expenses				
Interest and dividend income	120	162	203	205
Loss on disposal of assets and investments	(49)	(261)	(347)	(68)
Foreign currency transaction gain (loss)	0	(1)	(1)	2
Investment income (loss)	210	383	(412)	(776)
Interest expense	(494)	(541)	(758)	(585)
Total other income and expenses	(212)	(259)	(1,315)	(1,223)
Net income (loss) before income taxes and controlling interests	3,645	3,376	1,753	(1,577)
Provision of income taxes	514	560	501	564
Net income (loss) before noncontrolling interests	3,131	2,816	1,252	(2,141)
Noncontrolling interests in subsidiaries earnings	(102)	(185)	(313)	(459)
Net income (loss)	$ 3,030	$ 2,631	$ 939	($ 2,600)

Source: Norton Lilly International.

- Policies had been clarified and/or created that ensured decision-making rigor. In addition, resources allocation policies helped ensure that resources would be committed to opportunities that were best in line with the company's strategic priorities.

Despite this foundation, Jim Burton told the company's vice president of human resources, Larry Baldwin, that he still had concern about the company's ability to execute its strategy with the highest level of proficiency. The company's compensation system had yet to be retooled to closely link rewards for employees at all levels to organizational KPIs, and there were questions about to what extent the culture

change had been fully ingrained in the managerial mind-set. During the conversation, Baldwin had noted a deeply entrenched philosophy of managers "knowing only one way to grow— sell, sell, sell. They now need to understand the tools of growth beyond simple expansion. Someone will need to provide that creativity and leadership." The challenge going forward was to find ways of improving growth while maintaining the discipline to produce improved bottom-line results. Burton knew that revenue growth would be a high priority for Norton Lilly International's executive committee members in 2011 since projected revenues for 2010 still remained considerably below the company's peak revenues of nearly $53 million in 2007.

EXHIBIT 2

Norton Lilly International's Consolidated Balance Sheets, 2008–2009 ($ thousands)

Assets	2009	2008
Current assets		
Cash	$ 549	$ 1,407
Time deposit pledges	1,758	1,130
Accounts receivable	9,929	11,438
Notes receivable	0	2
Other nontrade receivables	0	203
Deferred tax assets	18	18
Prepaid income taxes	314	34
Prepaid expenses	765	903
Total current assets	13,334	15,135
Property and equipment (net)	1,340	1,835
Intangible assets (net)	9,095	8,767
Deferred tax assets	245	418
Loans to stockholders	663	599
Other assets	1,434	1,038
Total assets	$26,112	$27,792

Liabilities and Stockholders' Equity		
Current liabilities		
Bank overdraft	$ 392	$ 5
Accounts payable	8,699	8,046
Current portion of long-term debt	4,415	215
Current portion of capital lease obligations	78	173
Due to principals	13,377	21,793
Accrued expenses	1,669	3,005
Deferred income taxes	71	38
Deferred revenues	70	60
Seniority premium	188	179
Income taxes payable	72	182
Total current liabilities	29,031	33,694
Long-term debt (net)	1,577	1,582
Capital lease obligations (net)	10	88
Deferred income taxes	956	939
Noncontrolling interests	76	73
Stockholders' equity (deficit)	(5,538)	(8,585)
Total liabilities and stockholders' equity	$26,112	$27,792

Source: Norton Lilly International.

EXHIBIT 3

Norton Lilly International's Projected Consolidated Statement of Income, 2010 ($ thousands)*

	2010
Revenues	$47,845
Operating and general expenses	40,103
Contribution margin	7,743
Depreciation and amortization	(496)
Interest income/expense (net)	(982)
Noncontrolling interest earnings (losses)	407
Total other income (expenses)	(1,071)
Operating income	6,672
Provision for taxes	(351)
Net income (loss)	$ 6,320

*Projection is 8 months actual plus 4-month forecast.

Source: Norton Lilly International.

STARBUCKS' STRATEGY AND INTERNAL INITIATIVES TO RETURN TO PROFITABLE GROWTH

Arthur A. Thompson
The University of Alabama

Amit J. Shah
Frostburg State University

Since its founding in 1987 as a modest nine-store operation in Seattle, Washington, Starbucks had become the world's premier roaster and retailer of specialty coffees, with 8,812 company-owned stores and 7,852 licensed stores in more than 50 countries as of April 2010 and annual sales of about $10 billion. But the company's 2008–2009 fiscal years were challenging. Sales at company-owned Starbucks stores open 13 months or longer declined an average of 3 percent in 2008 and another 5 percent in 2009. Company-wide revenues declined from $10.4 billion in fiscal year 2008 to $9.8 billion in fiscal year 2009. During fiscal 2009, Starbucks closed 800 underperforming company-operated stores in the United States and an additional 100 stores in other countries, restructured its entire operations in Australia (including the closure of 61 stores), and reduced the number of planned new store openings by more than 200. Starbucks' global workforce was trimmed by about 6,700 employees. The company's cost-reduction and labor-efficiency initiatives resulted in savings of about $580 million. Exhibit 1 shows the performance of Starbucks' company-operated retail stores for the most recent five fiscal years.

In his November 2009 letter to company shareholders, Howard Schultz, Starbucks' founder, chairman of the board, and chief executive officer, said:

> Two years ago, I expressed concern over challenges confronting our business of a breadth and magnitude unlike anything I had ever seen before. For the first time, we were beginning to see traffic in our U.S. stores slow. Strong competitors were entering our business. And perhaps most troublesome, where in the past Starbucks had always been forward-thinking and nimble in its decision-making and execution, like many fast-growing companies before us, we had allowed our success to make us complacent.
>
> It was obvious to me, and to our leadership team, that Starbucks needed nothing less than a full-fledged transformation to return to profitable growth. Our blueprint for change was the transformation agenda: improving the state of our business through better training, tools, and products; renewing our attention to store-level economics and operating efficiency; reigniting our emotional attachment with customers; and realigning Starbucks' organization for the long term.

▶EXHIBIT 1

Selected Operating Statistics for Starbucks Stores, Fiscal Years 2005–2009

	Fiscal Years Ending				
	Sept. 27, 2009	Sept. 28, 2008	Sept. 30, 2007	Oct. 1, 2006	Oct. 2, 2005
Net Revenues at Company-Operated Retail Stores ($ millions)					
United States	$ 6,572.1	$ 6,997.7	$ 6,560.9	$ 5,495.2	$ 4,539.5
International	1,608.0	1,774.2	1,437.4	1,087.9	852.5
Operating Income at Company-Operated Retail Stores ($ millions)					
United States	$ 531.8	$ 454.2	$ 1,005.2	$ 955.2	$ 818.5
International	92.9	110.0	137.7	108.5	82.3
Percentage Change in Sales at Company-Operated Stores Open 13 Months or Longer					
United States	−6%	−5%	4%	7%	9%
International	−2%	2%	7%	8%	6%
Worldwide average	−5%	−3%	5%	7%	8%
Average Sales Revenues at Company-Operated Retail Stores					
United States	$938,000	$970,000	$1,048,000	$1,049,000	$1,004,000
United Kingdom and Ireland	870,000	924,000	958,000	925,000	853,000
Canada	835,000	910,000	918,000	870,000	829,000
China	549,000	537,000	508,000	460,000	447,000
All other international locations	678,000	681,000	663,000	633,000	605,000
Stores Opened during the Year (net of closures)					
United States					
Company-operated stores	(474)	445	1,065	810	580
Licensed stores	35	438	723	733	596
International					
Company-operated stores	89	236	286	240	177
Licensed stores	305	550	497	416	319
Total store openings (net of closures)	(45)	1,669	2,571	2,199	1,672

Sources: Management Presentation at Barclays Capital Retail and Restaurants Conference on April 28, 2010, www.starbucks.com, accessed June 8, 2010; 2009 10-K report, p. 19 and p. 76; and 2007 10-K report, p. 70.

Since then, we have worked through the multitude of challenges required to revitalize our brand and transform our company—all in the face of the worst global economic environment of our generation. Today, I am pleased to report that we have made and continue to make significant progress in transforming Starbucks and returning the company to sustainable, profitable growth while preserving our values and guiding principles.

With our progress over the past two years, we are now in a position to take advantage of the global opportunities for Starbucks.[1]

COMPANY BACKGROUND

Starbucks Coffee, Tea, and Spice

Starbucks got its start in 1971 when three academics, English teacher Jerry Baldwin, history teacher Zev Siegel, and writer Gordon Bowker—all coffee aficionados—opened Starbucks Coffee, Tea, and Spice in the touristy Pikes Place Market in Seattle. Sharing a love for fine coffees and exotic teas, the three partners believed they could build a clientele in Seattle that would appreciate the best coffees and teas, much like what had already emerged in the San Francisco Bay area. They each invested $1,350 and borrowed another $5,000 from a bank to open the Pikes Place store. The inspiration and mentor for the Starbucks venture in Seattle was a Dutch immigrant named Alfred Peet who had opened Peet's Coffee and Tea in Berkeley, California, in 1966. Peet's store specialized in importing fine coffees and teas and dark-roasting its own beans the European way to bring out the full flavors of the beans. Customers were encouraged to learn how to grind the beans and make their own freshly brewed coffee at home. Baldwin, Siegel, and Bowker were well acquainted with Peet's expertise, having visited his store on numerous occasions and listened to him expound on quality coffees and the importance of proper bean-roasting techniques.

The Pikes Place store featured modest, hand-built, classic nautical fixtures. One wall was devoted to whole bean coffees, while another had shelves of coffee products. The store did not offer fresh-brewed coffee sold by the cup, but tasting samples were sometimes available. Initially, Siegel was the only paid employee. He wore a grocer's apron, scooped out beans for customers, extolled the virtues of fine, dark-roasted coffees, and functioned as the partnership's retail expert. The other two partners kept their day jobs but came by at lunch or after work to help out. During the start-up period, Baldwin kept the books and developed a growing knowledge of coffee; Bowker served as the "magic, mystery, and romance man."[2] The store was an immediate success, with sales exceeding expectations, partly because of interest stirred by a favorable article in the *Seattle Times*. For most of the first year, Starbucks ordered its coffee beans from Peet's, but then the partners purchased a used roaster from Holland, set up roasting operations in a nearby ramshackle building, and came up with their own blends and flavors.

By the early 1980s, the company had four Starbucks stores in the Seattle area and had been profitable every year since opening its doors. But then Zev Siegel experienced burnout and left the company to pursue other interests. Jerry Baldwin took over day-to-day management of the company and functioned as chief executive officer; Gordon Bowker remained involved as an owner but devoted most of his time to his advertising and design firm, a weekly newspaper he had founded, and a microbrewery that he was launching known as the Redhook Ale Brewery.

Howard Schultz Enters the Picture

In 1981, Howard Schultz, vice president and general manager of U.S. operations for a Swedish maker of stylish kitchen equipment and coffee-makers, decided to pay Starbucks a visit—he was curious about why Starbucks was selling so many of his company's products. When he arrived at the Pikes Place store, a solo violinist was playing Mozart at the door (his violin case open for donations). Schultz was immediately taken by the powerful and pleasing aroma of the coffees, the wall displaying coffee beans, and the rows of coffeemakers on the shelves. As he talked with the clerk behind the counter, the clerk scooped out some Sumatran coffee beans, ground them, put the grounds in a cone filter, poured hot water over the cone, and shortly handed Schultz a porcelain mug filled with freshly brewed coffee. After taking only three sips of the brew, Schultz was hooked. He began asking questions about the company, the coffees from different parts of the world, and the different ways of roasting coffee.

Later, when he met with Jerry Baldwin and Gordon Bowker, Schultz was struck by their knowledge of coffee, their commitment to providing customers with quality coffees, and their passion for educating customers about the merits of dark-roasted coffees. Baldwin told Schultz, "We don't manage the business to maximize anything other than the quality of the coffee."[3] The company purchased only the finest arabica coffees and put them through a meticulous dark-roasting process to bring out their full flavors. Baldwin explained that the cheap robusta coffees used in supermarket blends burned when subjected to dark-roasting. He also noted that the makers of supermarket blends preferred lighter roasts because it allowed higher yields (the longer a coffee was roasted, the more weight it lost).

Schultz was also struck by the business philosophy of the two partners. It was clear that Starbucks stood not just for good coffee but also for the dark-roasted flavor profiles that the founders were passionate about. Top-quality, fresh-roasted, whole-bean coffee was the company's differentiating feature and a bedrock value. It was also clear to Schultz that Starbucks was strongly committed to educating its customers to appreciate the qualities of fine coffees. The company depended mainly on word of mouth to get more people into its stores, then built customer loyalty cup by cup as buyers gained a sense of discovery and excitement about the taste of fine coffee.

On his return trip to New York, Howard Schultz could not stop thinking about Starbucks and what it would be like to be a part of the Starbucks enterprise. Schultz recalled, "There was something magic about it, a passion and authenticity I had never experienced in business."[4] The appeal of living in the Seattle area was another strong plus. By the time he landed at Kennedy Airport, he knew in his heart he wanted to go to work for Starbucks. At the first opportunity, Schultz asked Baldwin whether there was any way he could fit into Starbucks. While he and Baldwin had established an easy, comfortable personal rapport, it still took a year, numerous meetings at which Schultz presented his ideas, and a lot of convincing to get Baldwin, Bowker, and their silent partner from San Francisco to agree to hire him. Schultz pursued a job at Starbucks far more vigorously than Starbucks pursued hiring Schultz. The owners were nervous about bringing in an out-

sider, especially a high-powered New Yorker who had not grown up with the values of the company. Nonetheless, Schultz continued to press his ideas about the tremendous potential of expanding the Starbucks enterprise outside Seattle and exposing people all over America to Starbucks coffee.

At a meeting with the three owners in San Francisco in the spring of 1982, Schultz once again presented his ideas and vision for opening Starbucks stores across the United States and Canada. He thought the meeting went well and flew back to New York, believing a job offer was in the bag. However, the next day Jerry Baldwin called Schultz and indicated that the owners had decided against hiring him because geographic expansion was too risky and they did not share Schultz's vision for Starbucks. Schultz was despondent, seeing his dreams of being a part of Starbucks' future go up in smoke. Still, he believed so deeply in Starbucks' potential that he decided to make a last-ditch appeal; he called Baldwin the next day and made an impassioned, reasoned case for why the decision was a mistake. Baldwin agreed to reconsider. The next morning Baldwin called Schultz and told him the job of heading marketing and overseeing the retail stores was his. In September 1982, Howard Schultz took over his new responsibilities at Starbucks.

Starbucks and Howard Schultz, 1982–1985

In his first few months at Starbucks, Schultz spent most of his waking hours in the four Seattle stores—working behind the counters, tasting different kinds of coffee, talking with customers, getting to know store personnel, and learning the retail aspects of the coffee business. By December, Jerry Baldwin concluded that Schultz was ready for the final part of his training: actually roasting the coffee. Schultz spent a week getting an education about the colors of different coffee beans, listening for the telltale second pop of the beans during the roasting process, learning to taste the subtle differences among the various roasts, and familiarizing himself with the roasting techniques for different beans.

Schultz made a point of acclimating himself to the informal dress code at Starbucks, gaining credibility and building trust with colleagues, and making the transition from the high-energy, coat-and-tie style of New York to the more casual, low-key ambience of the Pacific Northwest. Schultz made real headway in gaining the acceptance and respect of company personnel while working at the Pike Place store one day during the busy Christmas season that first year. The store was packed and Schultz was behind the counter ringing up sales of coffee when someone shouted that a shopper had just headed out the door with two coffeemakers. Without thinking, Schultz leaped over the counter and chased the thief, yelling, "Drop that stuff! Drop it!" The thief dropped both pieces and ran. Schultz returned to the store, holding the coffeemakers up like trophies. Everyone applauded. When Schultz returned to his office later that afternoon, his staff had strung up a banner that read: "Make my day."[5]

Schultz was overflowing with ideas for the company. Early on, he noticed that first-time customers sometimes felt uneasy in the stores because of their lack of knowledge about fine coffees and because store employees sometimes came across as a little arrogant or superior to coffee novices. Schultz worked with store employees on customer-friendly sales skills and developed brochures that made it easy for customers to learn about fine coffees. However, Schultz's biggest inspiration and vision for Starbucks' future came during the spring of 1983 when the company sent him to Milan, Italy, to attend an international housewares show. While walking from his hotel to the convention center, he spotted an espresso bar and went inside to look around. The cashier beside the door nodded and smiled. The barista behind the counter greeted Schultz cheerfully and began pulling a shot of espresso for one customer and handcrafting a foamy cappuccino for another, all the while conversing merrily with patrons standing at the counter. Schultz thought the barista's performance was great

theater. Just down the way on a side street, he entered an even more crowded espresso bar, where the barista, which he surmised to be the owner, was greeting customers by name; people were laughing and talking in an atmosphere that plainly was comfortable and familiar. In the next few blocks, he saw two more espresso bars. That afternoon when the trade show concluded for the day, Schultz walked the streets of Milan to explore more espresso bars. Some were stylish and upscale; others attracted a blue-collar clientele. Most had few chairs, and it was common for Italian opera to be playing in the background. What struck Schultz was how popular and vibrant the Italian coffee bars were. They seemed to function as an integral community gathering place, and energy levels were typically high. Each bar had its own unique character, but they all had a barista that performed with flair and established a camaraderie with the customers.

Schultz remained in Milan for a week, exploring coffee bars and learning as much as he could about the Italian passion for coffee drinks. Schultz was particularly struck by the fact that there were 1,500 coffee bars in Milan, a city about the size of Philadelphia, and a total of 200,000 in all of Italy. In one bar, he heard a customer order a *caffelatte* and decided to try one himself—the barista made a shot of espresso, steamed a frothy pitcher of milk, poured the two together in a cup, and put a dollop of foam on the top. Schultz liked it immediately, concluding that lattes should be a feature item on any coffee bar menu even though none of the coffee experts he had talked to had ever mentioned them.

Schultz's 1983 trip to Milan produced a revelation: the Starbucks stores in Seattle completely missed the point. There was much more to the coffee business than just selling beans and getting people to appreciate grinding their own beans and brewing fine coffee in their homes. What Starbucks needed to do was serve fresh-brewed coffee, espressos, and cappuccinos in its stores (in addition to beans and coffee equipment) and try to create an American version of the Italian coffee bar culture. Going to Starbucks should be an experience, a special treat, a place to meet friends and visit. Re-creating the authentic Italian coffee bar culture in the United States could be Starbucks' differentiating factor.

Schultz Becomes Frustrated

On Schultz's return from Italy, he shared his revelation and ideas for modifying the format of Starbucks' stores with Baldwin and Bowker. But instead of winning their approval for trying out some of his ideas, Schultz encountered strong resistance. Baldwin and Bowker argued that Starbucks was a retailer, not a restaurant or coffee bar. They feared that serving drinks would put them in the beverage business and diminish the integrity of Starbucks' mission as a purveyor of fine coffees. They pointed out that Starbucks had been profitable every year and there was no reason to rock the boat in a small, private company like Starbucks. But a more pressing reason not to pursue Schultz's coffee bar concept emerged shortly—Baldwin and Bowker were excited by an opportunity to purchase Peet's Coffee and Tea. The acquisition was finalized in early 1984, and to fund it Starbucks had to take on considerable debt, leaving little in the way of financial flexibility to support Schultz's ideas for entering the beverage part of the coffee business or expanding the number of Starbucks stores. For most of 1984, Starbucks managers were dividing their time between operations in Seattle and the Peet's enterprise in San Francisco. Schultz found himself in San Francisco every other week supervising the marketing and operations of the five Peet stores. Starbucks employees began to feel neglected and, in one quarter, did not receive their usual bonus due to tight financial conditions. Employee discontent escalated to the point where a union election was called. The union won by three votes. Baldwin was shocked at the results, concluding that employees no longer trusted him. In the months that followed, he began to spend more of his energy on the Peet's operation in San Francisco.

It took Howard Schultz nearly a year to convince Jerry Baldwin to let him test an espresso bar. Baldwin relented when Starbucks opened its sixth store in April 1984. It was the first Starbucks store designed to sell beverages, and it was the first located in downtown Seattle. Schultz asked for a 1,500-square-foot space to set up a full-scale Italian-style espresso bar, but Baldwin agreed to allocating only 300 square feet in a corner of the new store. The store opened with no fanfare as a deliberate experiment to see what would happen. By closing time on the first day, some 400 customers had been served, well above the 250-customer average of Starbucks' best-performing stores. Within two months, the store was serving 800 customers per day. The two baristas could not keep up with orders during the early-morning hours, resulting in lines outside the door onto the sidewalk. Most of the business was at the espresso counter, while sales at the regular retail counter were only adequate.

Schultz was elated at the test results, expecting that Baldwin's doubts about entering the beverage side of the business would be dispelled and that he would gain approval to pursue the opportunity to take Starbucks to a new level. Every day he went into Baldwin's office to show him the sales figures and customer counts at the new downtown store. But Baldwin was not comfortable with the success of the new store, believing that it felt wrong and that espresso drinks were a distraction from the core business of marketing fine arabica coffees at retail. Baldwin rebelled at the thought that people would see Starbucks as a place to get a quick cup of coffee to go. He adamantly told Schultz, "We're coffee roasters. I don't want to be in the restaurant business. . . . Besides, we're too deeply in debt to consider pursuing this idea."[6] While he didn't deny that the experiment was succeeding, he didn't want to go forward with introducing beverages in other Starbucks stores. Schultz's efforts to persuade Baldwin to change his mind continued to meet strong resistance, although to avoid a total impasse Baldwin finally did agree to let Schultz put espresso machines in the back of one or two other Starbucks stores.

Over the next several months, Schultz made up his mind to leave Starbucks and start his own company. His plan was to open espresso bars in high-traffic downtown locations, serve espresso drinks and coffee by the cup, and try to emulate the friendly, energetic atmosphere he had encountered in Italian espresso bars. Baldwin and Bowker, knowing how frustrated Schultz had become, supported his efforts to go out on his own and agreed to let him stay in his current job and office until definitive plans were in place. Schultz left Starbucks in late 1985.

Schultz's II Giornale Venture

With the aid of a lawyer friend who helped companies raise venture capital and go public, Schultz began seeking out investors for the kind of company he had in mind. Ironically, Jerry Baldwin committed to investing $150,000 of Starbucks' money in Schultz's coffee bar enterprise, thus becoming Schultz's first investor. Baldwin accepted Schultz's invitation to be a director of the new company, and Gordon Bowker agreed to be a part-time consultant for six months. Bowker, pumped up about the new venture, urged Schultz to make sure that everything about the new stores—the name, the presentation, the care taken in preparing the coffee—was calculated to elevate customer expectations and lead them to expect something better than competitors offered. Bowker proposed that the new company be named II Giornale Coffee Company (pronounced *il jor NAHL ee*), a suggestion that Howard accepted. In December 1985, Bowker and Schultz made a trip to Italy, where they visited some 500 espresso bars in Milan and Verona, observing local habits, taking notes about decor and menus, snapping photographs, and videotaping baristas in action.

About $400,000 in seed capital was raised by the end of January 1986, enough to rent an office, hire a couple of key employees, develop a store design, and open the first store. But it took until the end of 1986 to raise the remaining $1.25 million needed to launch at least eight espresso bars and prove that Schultz's strategy and business model were viable. Schultz made presentations to 242 potential investors, 217 of whom said no. Many who heard Schultz's hour-long presentation saw coffee as a commodity business and thought that Schultz's espresso bar concept lacked any basis for sustainable competitive advantage (no patent on dark roast, no advantage in purchasing coffee beans, no ways to bar the entry of imitative competitors). Some noted that coffee couldn't be turned into a growth business—consumption of coffee had been declining since the mid-1960s. Others were skeptical that people would pay $1.50 or more for a cup of coffee, and the company's hard-to-pronounce name turned some off. Being rejected by so many potential investors was disheartening—some who listened to Schultz's presentation didn't even bother to call him back; others refused to take his calls. Nonetheless, Schultz maintained an upbeat attitude and displayed passion and enthusiasm in making his pitch. He ended up raising $1.65 million from about 30 investors; most of the money came from 9 people, 5 of whom became directors.

The first II Giornale store opened in April 1986. It had 700 square feet and was located near the entrance of Seattle's tallest building. The decor was Italian, and there were Italian words on the menu. Italian opera music played in the background. The baristas wore white shirts and bow ties. All service was stand-up; there were no chairs. National and international papers were hung on rods on the wall. By closing time on the first day, 300 customers had been served—mostly in the morning hours.

But while the core idea worked well, it soon became apparent that several aspects of the format were not appropriate for Seattle. Some customers objected to the incessant opera music, others wanted a place to sit down, and many did not understand the Italian words on the menu. These "mistakes" were quickly fixed, but an effort was made not to compromise the style and elegance of the store. Within six months, the store was serving more than 1,000 customers a day. Regular customers had learned how to pronounce the company's name. Because most customers were in a hurry, it became apparent that speedy service was essential.

Six months after the first II Giornale opened, a second store was opened in another downtown building. In April 1987, a third store was opened in Vancouver, British Columbia, to test the transferability of the company's business concept outside Seattle. Schultz's goal was to open 50 stores in five years, and he needed to dispel his investors' doubts about geographic expansion early on to achieve his growth objective. By mid-1987, sales at the three stores were running at a rate equal to $1.5 million annually.

Il Giornale Acquires Starbucks

In March 1987, Jerry Baldwin and Gordon Bowker decided to sell the whole Starbucks operation in Seattle—the stores, the roasting plant, and the Starbucks name. Bowker wanted to cash out his coffee business investment to concentrate on his other enterprises; Baldwin, who was tired of commuting between Seattle and San Francisco, wanted to concentrate on the Peet's operation. As he recalls, "My wife and I had a 30-second conversation and decided to keep Peet's. It was the original and it was better."[7]

Schultz knew immediately that he had to buy Starbucks; his board of directors agreed. Schultz and his newly hired finance and accounting manager drew up a set of financial projections for the combined operations and a financing package that included a stock offering to Il Giornale's original investors and a line of credit with local banks. While a rival plan to acquire Starbucks was put together by another Il Giornale investor, Schultz's proposal prevailed and within weeks Schultz had raised the $3.8 million needed to buy Starbucks. The acquisition was completed in August 1987. The new name of the combined companies was Starbucks Corporation. Howard Schultz, at the age of 34, became Starbucks' president and CEO.

STARBUCKS AS A PRIVATE COMPANY, 1987–1992

The following Monday morning, Schultz returned to the Starbucks offices at the roasting plant, greeted all the familiar faces, and accepted their congratulations. Then he called the staff together for a meeting on the roasting plant floor:

> All my life I have wanted to be part of a company and a group of people who share a common vision. . . . I'm here today because I love this company. I love what it represents. . . . I know you're concerned. . . . I promise you I will not let you down. I promise you I will not leave anyone behind. . . . In five years, I want you to look back at this day and say "I was there when it started. I helped build this company into something great."[8]

Schultz told the group that his vision was for Starbucks to become a national company with values and guiding principles that employees could be proud of. He indicated that he wanted to include people in the decision-making process and that he would be open and honest with them.

Schultz believed that building a company that valued and respected its people, that inspired them, and that shared the fruits of success with those who contributed to the company's long-term value was essential, not just an intriguing option. His aspiration was for Starbucks to become the most respected brand name in coffee and for the company to be admired for its corporate responsibility. In the next few days and weeks, Schultz came to see that the unity and morale at Starbucks had deteriorated badly in the 20 months he had been at Il Giornale. Some employees were cynical and felt unappreciated. There was a feeling that prior management had abandoned them and a wariness about what the new regime would bring. Schultz decided to make building a new relationship of mutual respect between employees and management a priority.

The business plan Schultz had presented investors called for the new 9-store company to open 125 stores in the next five years—15 the first year, 20 the second, 25 the third, 30 the fourth, and 35 the fifth. Revenues were projected to reach $60 million in 1992. But the company lacked experienced management. Schultz had never led a growth effort of such magnitude and was just learning what the job of CEO was all about, having been the president of a small company for barely two years. Dave Olsen, a Seattle coffee bar owner whom Schultz had recruited to direct store operations at Il Giornale, was still learning the ropes in managing a multistore operation. Ron Lawrence, the company's controller, had worked as a controller for several organizations. Other Starbucks employees had only the experience of managing or being a part of a six-store organization. When Starbucks' key roaster and coffee buyer resigned, Schultz put Dave Olsen in charge of buying and roasting coffee. Lawrence Maltz, who had 20 years' experience in business and 8 years' experience as president of a profitable public beverage company, was hired as executive vice president and charged with heading operations, finance, and human resources.

In the next several months, a number of changes were instituted. To symbolize the merging of the two companies and the two cultures, a new logo was created that melded the designs of the Starbucks logo and the Il Giornale logo. The Starbucks stores were equipped with espresso machines and remodeled to look more Italian than Old World nautical. Il Giornale green replaced the traditional Starbucks brown. The result was a new type of store—a cross between a retail coffee bean store and an espresso bar/café—that became Starbucks' signature.

By December 1987, the mood of the employees at Starbucks had turned upbeat. They were buying into the changes that Schultz was making, and trust began to build between management and employees. New stores were on the verge of opening in Vancouver and Chicago. One Starbucks store employee, Daryl Moore, who had started working at Starbucks in 1981 and who had voted against unionization in 1985, began to question the need for a union with his fellow employees. Over the next few weeks, Moore began a move to decertify the union. He carried a decertification letter around to Starbucks' stores securing the signatures of employees who no longer wished to be represented by the union. He got a majority of store employees to sign the letter and presented it to the National Labor Relations Board. The union representing store employees was decertified. Later, in 1992, the union representing Starbucks' roasting plant and warehouse employees was also decertified.

Market Expansion Outside the Pacific Northwest

Starbucks' entry into Chicago proved far more troublesome than management anticipated. The first Chicago store opened in October 1987, and three more stores were opened over the next six months. Customer counts at the stores were substantially below expectations. Chicagoans did not take to dark-roasted coffee as fast as Schultz had anticipated. The first downtown store opened onto the street rather than into the lobby of the building where it was located; in the winter months, customers were hesitant to go out in the wind and cold to acquire a cup of coffee. It was expensive to supply fresh coffee to the Chicago stores out of the Seattle warehouse (the company solved the problem of freshness and quality assurance by putting freshly roasted beans in special FlavorLock bags that used vacuum packaging techniques with a one-way valve to allow carbon dioxide to escape without allowing air and moisture in). Rents were higher in Chicago than in Seattle, and so were wage rates. The result was a squeeze on store profit margins. Gradually, customer counts improved, but Starbucks lost money on its Chicago stores until, in 1990, prices were raised to reflect higher rents and labor costs, more experienced store mangers were hired, and a critical mass of customers caught on to the taste of Starbucks products.

Portland, Oregon, was the next market entered, and Portland coffee drinkers took to Starbucks products quickly. By 1991, the Chicago stores had become profitable and the company was ready for its next big market entry. Management decided on California because of its host of neighborhood centers and the receptiveness of Californians to innovative, high-quality food. Los Angeles was chosen as the first California market to enter, principally because of its status as a trendsetter and its cultural ties to the rest of the country. L.A. consumers embraced Starbucks quickly, and the *Los Angeles Times* named Starbucks as the best coffee in America before the first store opened. The entry into San Francisco proved more troublesome because San Francisco had an ordinance against converting stores to restaurant-related uses in certain prime urban neighborhoods; Starbucks could sell beverages and pastries to customers at stand-up counters but could not offer seating in stores that had formerly been used for general retailing. However, the city council was soon convinced by café owners and real estate brokers to change the code. Still, Starbucks faced strong competition from Peet's and local espresso bars in the San Francisco market.

Starbucks' store expansion targets proved easier to meet than Schultz had originally anticipated, and he upped the numbers to keep challenging the organization. Starbucks opened 15 new stores in fiscal 1988, 20 in 1989, 30 in 1990, 32 in 1991, and 53 in 1992—producing a total of 161 stores, significantly above his original 1992 target of 125 stores.

From the outset, the strategy was to open only company-owned stores; franchising was avoided so as to keep the company in full control of the quality of its products and the character and location of its stores. But company ownership of all stores required Starbucks to raise new venture capital to cover the cost of new store expansion. In 1988, the company raised $3.9 million; in 1990, venture capitalists provided an additional $13.5 million; and, in 1991, another round of venture capital financing generated $15 million. Starbucks was able to raise the needed funds despite posting losses of $330,000 in 1987, $764,000 in 1988, and $1.2 million in 1989. While the losses were troubling to Starbucks' board of directors and investors, Schultz's business plan had forecast losses during the early years of expansion. At a particularly tense board meeting where directors sharply questioned him about the lack of profitability, Schultz said:

> Look, we're going to keep losing money until we can do three things. We have to attract a management team well beyond our expansion needs. We have to build a world-class roasting facility. And we need a computer information system sophisticated enough to keep track of sales in hundreds and hundreds of stores.[9]

Schultz argued for patience as the company invested in the infrastructure to support continued growth well into the 1990s. He contended that hiring experienced executives ahead of the growth curve, building facilities far beyond current needs, and installing support systems laid a strong foundation for rapid, profitable growth down the road. His arguments carried the day with the board and with investors, especially since revenues were growing by approximately 80 percent annually and customer traffic at the stores was meeting or exceeding expectations.

Starbucks became profitable in 1990. Profits had increased every year since 1990 except for fiscal year 2000 (because of a $58.8 million in investment write-offs in four dot-com enterprises) and for fiscal year 2008 (when the sharp global economic downturn hit the company's bottom line very hard). Because of the economic downturn in 2008–2009, Howard Schultz believed that new strategic initiatives and rejuvenated strategy execution efforts were very much needed at Starbucks. Exhibit 2 provides a summary of the company's financial performance for fiscal years 2005–2009. Exhibit 3 shows the long-term performance of the company's stock price; the stock had split 2-for-1 five times..

STARBUCKS STORES: DESIGN, AMBIENCE, AND EXPANSION OF LOCATIONS

Store Design

Starting in 1991, Starbucks created its own in-house team of architects and designers to ensure that each store would convey the right image and character. Stores had to be custom-designed because the company didn't buy real estate or build its own freestanding structures; rather, each space was leased in an existing structure, making each store differ in size and shape. Most stores ranged in size from 1,000 to 1,500 square feet and were located in office buildings, downtown and suburban retail centers, airport terminals, university campus areas, and busy neighborhood shopping areas convenient for

▶ EXHIBIT 2

Financial Summary for Starbucks Corporation, Fiscal Years 2005–2009 ($ billions, except for per share amounts)

	Fiscal Years Ending[*]				
	Sept. 27, 2009	Sept. 28, 2008	Sept. 30, 2007	Oct. 1, 2006	Oct. 2, 2005
Results of Operations Data					
Net revenues:					
Company-operated retail store revenues	$8,180.1	$ 8,771.9	$7,998.3	$6,583.1	$5,391.9
Specialty revenues:					
Licensing	1,222.3	1,171.6	1,026.3	860.6	673
Food service and other	372.2	439.5	386.9	343.2	304.4
Total specialty revenues	1,594.5	1,611.1	1,413.2	1,203.8	977.4
Total net revenues	$9,774.6	$10,383.0	$ 9,411.5	$7,786.9	$6,369.3
Cost of sales, including occupancy costs	4,324.9	4,645.3	3,999.1	3,178.8	2,605.2
Store operating expenses	3,425.1	3,745.3	3,215.9	2,687.8	2,165.9
Other operating expenses	264.4	330.1	294.2	253.7	192.5
Depreciation and amortization expenses	534.7	549.3	467.2	387.2	340.2
General and administrative expenses	453.0	456.0	489.2	479.4	361.6
Restructuring charges	332.4	266.9	—	—	—
Total operating expenses	9,334.5	9,992.7	8,465.6	6,986.9	5,665.4
Income from equity investees	121.9	113.6	108.0	93.9	76.6
Operating income	$ 562.0	$ 503.9	$1,053.9	$ 894.0	$ 780.5
Earnings before cumulative effect of change in accounting principle	390.8	315.5	672.6	581.5	494.4
Cumulative effect of accounting change for asset retirement obligations, net of taxes	—	—	—	17.2	—
Net earnings	$ 390.8	$ 315.5	$ 672.6	$ 564.3	$ 494.4
Net earnings per common share—diluted	$0.52	$0.43	$0.87	$0.71	$0.61
Balance Sheet Data					
Current assets	$2,035.8	$ 1,748.0	$1,696.5	$1,529.8	$1,209.3
Current liabilities	1,581.0	2,189.7	2,155.6	1,935.6	1,227.0
Total assets	5,576.8	5,672.6	5,343.9	4,428.9	3,513.7
Short-term borrowings	—	713	710.3	700	277
Long-term debt (including current portion)	549.5	550.3	550.9	2.7	3.6
Shareholders' equity	$3,045.7	$ 2,490.9	$2,284.1	$2,228.5	$2,090.3
Cash Flow Data					
Net cash provided by operating activities	$1,389.0	$1,258.7	$ 1,331.2	$ 1,131.6	$922.9
Capital expenditures (net additions to property, plant and equipment)	$445.6	$984.5	$1,080.3	$771.2	$643.3

[*]The company's fiscal year ended on the Sunday closest to September 30.

Source: Starbucks, 2009, 2007 and 2005 10-K reports.

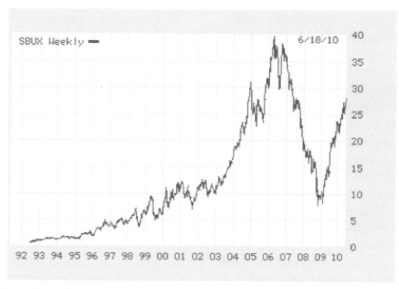

Source: *The Wall Street Journal,* http://online.wsj.com, accessed June 18, 2010.

pedestrian foot traffic and/or drivers. Only a select few were in suburban malls.

A "stores of the future" project team was formed in 1995 to raise Starbucks' store design to a still higher level and come up with the next generation of Starbucks stores. The team came up with four store designs—one for each of the four stages of coffeemaking: growing, roasting, brewing, and aroma—each with its own color combinations, lighting scheme, and component materials. Within each of the four basic store templates, Starbucks could vary the materials and details to adapt to different store sizes and settings (downtown buildings, college campuses, neighborhood shopping areas). In late 1996, Starbucks began opening new stores based on one of four formats and color schemes.

But as the number of stores increased rapidly between 2000 and 2003, greater store diversity and layout quickly became necessary. Some stores had special seating areas to help make Starbucks a desirable gathering place where customers could meet and chat or simply enjoy a peaceful interlude in their day. Flagship stores in high-traffic, high-visibility locations had fireplaces, leather chairs, newspapers, couches, and lots of ambience. The company also experi-

mented with drive-through windows in locations where speed and convenience were important to customers and with kiosks in supermarkets, building lobbies, and other public places. In recent years, Starbucks had begun emphasizing drive-through retail stores in order to provide a greater degree of access and convenience for nonpedestrian customers. At the end of fiscal 2009, Starbucks had around 2,650 drive-through locations.[10]

In June 2009, Starbucks announced a new global store design strategy. Each new store was to be a reflection of the environment in which it operated and was to be environmentally friendly. In 2010, Starbucks began an effort to achieve Leadership in Energy and Environmental Design (LEED) certification for all new company-owned stores. (LEED certification was a program that used independent third parties to certify that a building incorporated green building design, construction, operations, and maintenance solutions.)[11] Core characteristics of each new store included celebration of local materials and craftsmanship, a focus on reused and recycled elements, exposure of structural integrity and authentic roots, elevation of coffee and removal of unnecessary distractions, storytelling and customer engagement through all five senses, and flexibility to meet the needs of many customer types.[12] Exhibit 4 shows the diverse nature of Starbucks stores.

To better control average store opening costs, the company centralized buying, developed standard contracts and fixed fees for certain items, and consolidated work under those contractors who displayed good cost-control practices. The retail operations group outlined exactly the minimum amount of equipment each core store needed so that standard items could be ordered in volume from vendors at 20 to 30 percent discounts, then delivered just in time to the store site either from company warehouses or the vendor. Modular designs for display cases were developed. The layouts for new and remodeled stores were developed on a computer, with software that allowed the costs to be estimated as the design evolved. All this cut store opening and remodeling costs significantly and shortened the process to about 18 weeks.

Store Ambience

Starbucks management viewed each store as a billboard for the company and as a contributor to building the company's brand and image. The company went to great lengths to make sure that store fixtures, merchandise displays, colors, artwork, banners, music, and aromas all blended to create a consistent, inviting, stimulating environment that evoked the romance of coffee; that signaled the company's passion for coffee; that enhanced the mood and ambience of the store; and that rewarded customers with ceremony, stories, surprise, and a satisfying experience. The thesis was that every detail mattered in making Starbucks stores a welcoming and pleasant "third place" (apart from home and work) where people could meet friends and family, enjoy a quiet moment alone with a newspaper or book, or simply spend quality time relaxing.

To try to keep the coffee aromas in the stores pure, Starbucks banned smoking and asked employees to refrain from wearing perfumes or colognes. Prepared foods were kept covered so that customers would smell coffee only. Colorful banners and posters were used to keep the look of Starbucks stores fresh and to highlight seasons and holidays. Company designers came up with artwork for commuter mugs and T-shirts in different cities that were in keeping with each city's personality (peach-shaped coffee mugs for Atlanta, pictures of Paul Revere for Boston and the Statue of Liberty for New York).

In August 2002, Starbucks teamed up with T-Mobile USA to experiment with providing Internet access and enhanced digital entertainment to patrons at more than 1,200 Starbucks locations. The objective was to heighten the "third place" Starbucks experience, entice customers into perhaps buying a second latte or espresso while they caught up on e-mail, listened to digital music, put the finishing touches on a presentation, or surfed the Internet. Since the August 2002 introduction of Wi-Fi at Starbucks, wireless Internet service had been added at most company-operated stores in the United States. In an effort to better bridge Starbucks' "third place" coffeehouse experience with digital and social media, Starbucks announced that, beginning July 1, 2010, it would provide free Wi-Fi one-click Internet service through AT&T in all company-operated stores in the United States. There were also plans for a new online customer experience called the Starbucks Digital Network, in partnership with Yahoo, to debut in the fall of 2010 in U.S. company-operated Starbucks stores. This online experience would provide customers with free unrestricted access—via laptop, e-reader, or smartphone—to various paid sites and services such as *The Wall Street Journal*'s site (www.wsj.com), exclusive content and previews, free downloads, and local community news and activities.

Store Expansion Strategy

In 1992 and 1993, Starbucks developed a three-year geographic expansion strategy to target areas that not only had favorable demographic profiles but also could be serviced and supported by the company's operations infrastructure. For each targeted region, Starbucks selected a large city to serve as a "hub"; teams of professionals were located in hub cities to support the goal

▶ EXHIBIT 4   **Scenes from Starbucks Stores**

of opening 20 or more stores in the hub in the first two years. Once a number of stores were opened in a hub, then additional stores were opened in smaller, surrounding "spoke" areas in the region. To oversee the expansion process, Starbucks had zone vice presidents who oversaw the store expansion process in a geographic region and instilled the Starbucks culture in the newly opened stores.

In recent years, Starbucks' strategy in major metropolitan cities had been to blanket major cities with stores, even if some stores cannibalized a nearby store's business. While a new store might draw 30 percent of the business of an existing store two or so blocks away, management believed that a "Starbucks everywhere" strategy cut down on delivery and management costs, shortened customer lines at individual stores, and increased foot traffic for all the stores in an area. In 2002, new stores generated an average of $1.2 million in first-year revenues, compared with $700,000 in 1995 and only $427,000 in 1990. The steady increases in new-store revenues were due partly to growing popularity of premium coffee drinks, partly to Starbucks' growing reputation, and partly to expanded product offerings. But the strategy of blanketing metropolitan areas with stores had cannibalized sales of existing stores to such an extent that average sales per store in the United States had dropped to around $1 million annually. Starbucks' long-term profitability target for its retail stores in the United States was an operating profit margin in the high teens—the operating margin was 14.3 percent in fiscal 2007, but declining store sales and depressed economic conditions had driven the margins down to 6.0 percent in fiscal 2008 and 7.5 percent in fiscal 2009.

One of Starbucks' core competencies was identifying good retailing sites for its new stores. The company was regarded as having the best real estate team in the coffee bar industry and a sophisticated system for identifying not only the most attractive individual city blocks but also the exact store location that was best; it also worked hard at building good relationships with local real estate representatives in areas where it was opening multiple store locations.

Licensed Retail Stores   In 1995, Starbucks began entering into licensing agreements for store locations in areas where it did not have ability to locate its own outlets. Two early licensing agreements were with Marriott Host International to operate Starbucks retail stores in airport locations and with Aramark Food and Services to put Starbucks stores on university campuses and other locations operated by Aramark. Very quickly, Starbucks began to make increased use of licensing, both domestically and internationally. Starbucks preferred licensing to franchising because licensing permitted tighter controls over the operations of licensees.

Starbucks received a license fee and a royalty on sales at all licensed locations and supplied the coffee for resale at these locations. All licensed stores had to follow Starbucks' detailed operating procedures, and all managers and employees who worked in these stores received the same training given to managers and employees in company-operated Starbucks stores. As of 2009, there were 4,364 licensed stores in the United States and 3,439 licensed stores internationally.

International Expansion   In markets outside the continental United States (including Hawaii), Starbucks had a two-pronged store expansion: either open company-owned and -operated stores or else license a reputable and capable local company with retailing know-how in the target host country to develop and operate new Starbucks stores. In most countries, Starbucks used a local partner/licensee to help it recruit talented individuals, set up supplier relationships, locate suitable store sites, and cater to local market conditions. Starbucks looked for partners/licensees that had strong retail/restaurant experience, had values and a corporate culture compatible with Starbucks, were committed to good customer service, possessed talented management and strong financial resources, and had demonstrated brand-building skills. In those foreign countries where business risks were deemed relatively high, most if not all Starbucks stores were licensed rather than being company-owned and operated. As of September 2009, Starbucks had company-operated and licensed stores in 50 countries (see Exhibit 5) and expected to open 200 new stores internationally in fiscal 2010.

Starbucks' long-term profitability target for its international operations was an operating profit margin in the mid-to-high teens. But the margins in recent years had been far below the target: 8.1 percent in fiscal 2007, 5.2 percent in fiscal 2008, and 4.5 percent in fiscal 2009.

▶EXHIBIT 5

Company-Operated and Franchised Starbucks Stores

A. Number of Starbucks Store Locations Worldwide, 1987–March 2010 (selected years)

	Company-Operated Store Locations		Licensed Store Locations		
End of Fiscal Year*	United States	International	United States	International	Worldwide Total
1987	17	0	0	0	17
1990	84	0	0	0	84
1995	627	0	49	0	676
2000	2,446	530	173	352	3,501
2005	4,918	1,217	2,435	1,671	10,241
2006	5,728	1,457	3,168	2,087	12,440
2007	6,793	1,743	3,891	2,584	15,011
2008	7,238	1,979	4,329	3,134	16,680
2009	6,764	2,068	4,364	3,439	16,635
March 28, 2010	6,736	2,076	4,385	3,467	16,664

B. International Starbucks Store Locations at End of Fiscal Year 2009

International Locations of Company-Operated Starbucks Stores		International Locations of Licensed Starbucks Stores					
		Americas		Asia-Pacific		Europe/Africa/Middle East	
Canada	775	Canada	262	Japan	875	Turkey	123
United Kingdom	666	Mexico	261	South Korea	288	United Arab Emirates	91
China	191	Other	69	China	283	Spain	76
Germany	144			Taiwan	222	Greece	69
Thailand	131			Philippines	160	Saudi Arabia	68
Singapore	64			Malaysia	118	Kuwait	62
Australia	23			Indonesia	74	France	52
Other	74			New Zealand	42	Switzerland	47
Total	2,068					United Kingdom	46
						Other	151
						Licensed total worldwide	3,439

*Starbucks' fiscal year ended on the Sunday closest to September 30.

Source: Starbucks, 10-K reports, various years, and company records.

STARBUCKS' STRATEGY TO EXPAND ITS PRODUCT OFFERINGS AND ENTER NEW MARKET SEGMENTS

In the mid-1990s, thinking it was time for Starbucks to move out into mainstream markets, Howard Schultz led what proved to be an ongoing series of initiatives to expand Starbucks' product offerings beyond its retail stores and to pursue sales of Starbucks products in a wider variety of distribution channels and market segments. The strategy was to make Starbucks products more accessible to both existing and new customers where they worked, traveled, shopped, and dined and to find and promote new occasions for enjoying Starbucks products. The strategic objectives were to capitalize on Starbucks' growing brand awareness and brand-name strength and create a broader foundation for sustained long-term growth in revenues and profits.

The first initiative involved the establishment of an in-house specialty sales group to begin marketing Starbucks coffee products to restaurants, airlines, hotels, universities, hospitals, business offices, country clubs, and select retailers. Early users of Starbucks coffee included Horizon Airlines, a regional carrier based in Seattle, and United Airlines. There was much internal debate at Starbucks about whether it made sense for Starbucks coffee to be served on all United flights (since there was different coffeemaking equipment on different planes) and the possible damage to the integrity of the Starbucks brand if the quality of the coffee served did not measure up. It took seven months of negotiations for Starbucks and United to arrive at a mutually agreeable way to handle quality control on United's various types of planes. The specialty sales group also won accounts at Hyatt, Hilton, Sheraton, Radisson, and Westin hotels, resulting in packets of Starbucks coffee being in each room with coffeemaking equipment. Starbucks entered into an agreement with Wells Fargo to provide coffee service at some of the bank's locations in California. Later, the specialty sales group began working with leading institutional foodservice distributors, including Sysco Corporation and US Food service, to handle the distribution of Starbucks products to hotels, restaurants, office coffee distributors, educational and health care institutions, and other such enterprises. In fiscal 2009, Starbucks generated revenues of $372.2 million from providing whole bean and ground coffees and assorted other Starbucks products to some 21,000 food service accounts.

The second initiative came in 1994 when PepsiCo and Starbucks entered into a joint venture (now called the North American Coffee Partnership) to create new coffee-related products in bottles or cans for mass distribution through Pepsi channels. Howard Schultz saw the venture with PepsiCo as a major paradigm shift with the potential to cause Starbucks' business to evolve in heretofore unimaginable directions. The joint venture's first new product, Mazagran, a lightly flavored carbonated coffee drink, was a failure. Then, at a meeting with Pepsi executives, Schultz suggested developing a bottled version of Frappuccino, a new cold coffee drink that Starbucks had begun serving at its retail stores in the summer of 1995 and that quickly became a big hot-weather seller. Pepsi executives were enthusiastic. After months of experimentation, the joint venture product research team came up with a shelf-stable version of Frappuccino that tasted quite good. It was tested in West Coast supermarkets in the summer of 1996; sales ran 10 times projections, with 70 percent being repeat business. Sales of Frappuccino ready-to-drink beverages reached $125 million in 1997 and achieved national supermarket penetration of 80 percent. Starbucks' management believed that the market for Frappuccino would ultimately exceed $1 billion. The company began selling ready-to-drink Frappuccino products in Japan, Taiwan, and South Korea in 2005 chiefly through agreements with leading local distributors; the ready-to-drink beverage market in these countries represented more than $10 billion in annual sales.[13] In 2007, the PepsiCo-Starbucks partnership introduced a line of chilled Starbucks Doubleshot espresso drinks in the United States. Also in 2007, PepsiCo and Starbucks entered into a second joint venture called the International Coffee Partnership (ICP) for the purpose of introducing Starbucks-related beverages in country markets outside North America; one of the ICP's early moves was to begin marketing Frappuccino in China.[14] As of 2010, sales of Frappuccino products worldwide had reached $2 billion annually.[15]

In 2008, Starbucks partnered with Suntory to begin selling chilled ready-to-drink Doubleshot drinks in Japan. In 2010, Starbucks partnered with Arla Foods to begin selling Doubleshot products and Starbucks Discoveries chilled cup coffees in retail stores (as well as in Starbucks retail stores) across the United Kingdom.

In October 1995, Starbucks partnered with Dreyer's Grand Ice Cream to supply coffee extract for a new line of coffee ice cream made and distributed by Dreyer's under the Starbucks brand. By July 1996, Starbucks coffee-flavored ice cream was the number-one-selling superpremium brand in the coffee segment. In 2008, Starbucks discontinued its arrangement with Dreyer's and entered into an exclusive agreement with Unilever to manufacture, market, and distribute Starbucks-branded ice creams in the United States and Canada. Unilever was considered the global leader in ice cream, with annual sales of about $6 billion; its ice cream brands included Ben & Jerry's, Breyers, and Good Humor. Seven flavors of Starbucks ice cream and two flavors of novelty bars were marketed in 2010. Pints were available in the freezer sections at supermarkets for a suggested retail price of $3.99; the novelty bars sold for a suggested retail price of $2.49 and were also available in many convenience stores.

In 1997, a Starbucks store manager who had worked in the music industry and selected the music Starbucks played as background in its stores suggested that Starbucks begin selling the background music on tapes (and later

on CDs as they become the preferred format). The manager had gotten compliments from customers wanting to buy the music they heard and suggested to senior executives that there was a market for the company's hand-picked music. Research through two years of comment cards turned up hundreds asking Starbucks to sell the music it played in its stores. The Starbucks tapes/CDs proved a significant seller as an addition to the company's product line. In 2000, Starbucks acquired Hear Music, a San Francisco–based company, to give it added capability in enhancing its music CD offerings. In 2004, Starbucks introduced Hear Music media bars, a service that offered custom CD burning at select Starbucks stores. Later, Starbucks began offering customers the option of downloading music from the company's 200,000+ song library and, if they wished, having the downloaded songs burned onto a CD for purchase.

In the spring of 2008, Starbucks, in partnership with Apple's iTunes, began offering a Pick of the Week music card at its 7,000 stores in the United States that allowed customers to download each week's music selection at iTunes.[16] In 2010, Starbucks was continuing to offer CDs with handpicked music and new CDs featuring particular artists, all managed by Starbucks Entertainment in conjunction with Concord Music Group (which began managing the Hear Music Record Label in 2008); the CDs were typically priced at $12.95. Starbucks also had established a relationship with the William Morris Agency to identify books that it could offer for sale in its stores. Over the years, Starbucks' successes in music and books had included eight Grammy Awards and three number one books on the *New York Times* best-seller list.

In 1998, Starbucks licensed Kraft Foods to market and distribute Starbucks whole bean and ground coffees in grocery and mass-merchandise channels across the United States. Kraft managed all distribution, marketing, advertising, and promotions and paid a royalty to Starbucks based on a percentage of net sales. Product freshness was guaranteed by

Starbucks' FlavorLock packaging, and the price per pound paralleled the prices in Starbucks' retail stores. Flavor selections in supermarkets were more limited than the varieties at Starbucks stores. The licensing relationship with Kraft was later expanded to include the marketing and distribution of Starbucks coffees in the United Kingdom and Europe. Going into 2010, Starbucks coffees were available in some 33,500 grocery and warehouse clubs in the United States and 5,500 retail outlets outside the United States; Starbucks' revenues from these sales were approximately $370 million in fiscal 2009.[17]

In 1999, Starbucks purchased Tazo Tea for $8.1 million. Tazo Tea, a tea manufacturer and distributor based in Portland, Oregon, was founded in 1994 and marketed its teas to restaurants, food stores, and tea houses. Starbucks proceeded to introduce hot and iced Tazo Tea drinks in its retail stores. As part of a long-term campaign to expand the distribution of its line of superpremium Tazo teas, Starbucks expanded its agreement with Kraft to market and distribute Tazo teas worldwide. In August 2008, Starbucks entered into an agreement with PepsiCo and Unilever (Lipton Tea was one of Unilever's leading brands) to manufacture, market, and distribute Starbucks' superpremium Tazo Tea ready-to-drink beverages (including iced teas, juiced teas, and herbal-infused teas) in the United States and Canada. The Tazo line of ready-to-drink beverages was to become part of an existing venture between PepsiCo and Unilever (the Pepsi/Lipton Tea partnership) that was the leading North American distributor of ready-to-drink teas.

In 2001, Starbucks introduced the Starbucks Card, a reloadable card that allowed customers to pay for their purchases with a quick swipe at the cash register and also to earn and redeem rewards. In 2009, about 15 percent of customer purchases at Starbucks stores were made on Starbucks cards.

In 2003, Starbucks acquired Seattle's Best Coffee, an operator of Seattle's Best coffee shops and marketer of Seattle's Best whole bean and ground coffees, for $70 million. Starbucks continued to operate Seattle's Best as a separate subsidiary. As of May 2008, there were more than 540 Seattle's Best cafés in the United States (a number of which were in Borders book and music stores) and 86 Seattle's Best Coffee Express espresso bars. The Seattle's Best product line included more than 30 whole bean and ground coffees (including flavored, organic, and Fair Trade Certified coffees), espresso beverages, signature handcrafted JavaKula blended beverages, OvenSong bakery food and sandwiches, and select merchandise. Shortly after the acquisition, Starbucks expanded its licensing arrangement with Kraft Foods to include marketing and distributing Seattle's Best whole bean and ground coffees in grocery and mass merchandise channels in North America, with Starbucks to receive a royalty on all such sales. In 2009, Seattle's Best whole bean and ground coffee blends were available nationwide in supermarkets and were being served at more than 15,000 food service locations (college campuses, restaurants, hotels, airlines, and cruise lines). A new Seattle's Best line of ready-to-drink iced lattes was introduced in April 2010 in major grocery and convenience stores in the western United States; the manufacture, marketing, and distribution of the new Seattle's Best beverages was managed by PepsiCo as part of the long-standing Starbucks-PepsiCo joint venture for ready-to-drink Frappuccino products. In May 2010, Starbucks announced that it would relaunch Seattle's Best Coffee with new distinctive red packaging and a red logo, boost efforts to open more franchised Seattle's Best cafés, and expand the availability of Seattle's Best coffees to 30,000 distribution points by October 2010. By July 2010, freshly brewed and iced Seattle's Best Coffee drinks were being sold at 7,250 Burger King outlets in the United States, 9,000 Subway locations, and some 299 AMC movie theaters in five countries.

In 2004 Starbucks teamed with Jim Beam Brands to invent a Starbucks Coffee Liqueur that would be sold in bars, liquor stores, and restaurants; projections were for systemwide gross sales of more than $8 million annually. Launched in February 2005, Starbucks Coffee Liqueur was the number-one-selling new spirit product year-to-date through August 2005, according to Nielsen. In October 2005, again collaborating with Jim Beam Brands, Starbucks introduced Starbucks Cream Liqueur, a blend of cream, spirits, and a hint of Starbucks coffee. There were an estimated 22 million cordial consumers in the U.S. market, making the cream liqueur category nearly three times the size of the coffee liqueur category. Both Starbucks Coffee Liqueur and Starbucks Cream Liqueur were packaged in 750 milliliter bottles priced at $22.99.

In April 2005, Starbucks acquired Ethos Water for $8 million in cash. The acquisition was made to expand the line of beverages in Starbucks stores in the United States. Following the acquisition, the brand also became known for its campaign to raise $10 million by donating $0.05 of the retail price of each bottle sold to a charitable organization working to increase access to clean drinking water and conduct sanitation and hygiene education programs in developing countries in Africa and Asia; in 2010, more than $6 million had been raised.[18] The production, distribution, and marketing of Ethos water products was handled by PepsiCo, as part of its long-standing joint venture with Starbucks.

In response to customer requests for more wholesome food and beverage options and also to bring in business from non–coffee drinkers, Starbucks in 2008 began offering fruit cups, yogurt parfaits, skinny lattes, banana walnut bread (that was nearly 30 percent real banana), a 300-calorie farmer's market salad with all-natural dressing, and a line of "better-for-you" smoothies called Vivanno Nourishing Blends. Each Vivanno smoothie averaged 250 calories and consisted of one serving of fruit, 16 grams of protein, and 5 grams of fiber.[19] Additionally, in 2009, healthier, lower-calorie selections were included in the bakery cases at Starbucks stores, and the recipes for several other food items on the menu at Starbucks stores were reformulated to include whole grains and dried fruits and to cut back on or eliminate the use of artificial flavorings, dyes, high-fructose corn syrup, and artificial preservatives.[20]

In 2008, Starbucks introduced a new coffee blend called Pike Place Roast that would be brewed every day, all day in every Starbucks store.[21] Before then, Starbucks rotated coffees through its brewed lineup, sometimes switching them weekly, sometimes daily. While some customers liked the ever-changing variety, the feedback from a majority of customers indicated a preference for a consistent brew that customers could count on when they came into a Starbucks store. This reinvention of brewed coffee returned the company to the practice of grinding the beans in the store. Pike Place Roast was brewed in small batches in 30-minute intervals to ensure that customers were provided the freshest coffee possible. The Pike Place Roast was created by Starbucks' master blenders and coffee quality team using input from nearly 1,000 customers—it was smoother than any other Starbucks coffee and tasted great either black or with cream and sugar.

In the fall of 2009, Starbucks introduced Starbucks VIA Ready Brew—packets of roasted coffee in an instant form. VIA was made with a proprietary microground technology that Starbucks claimed represented a breakthrough.[22] Simply adding a packet of VIA to a cup of hot or cold water produced an instant coffee with a rich, full-bodied taste that closely replicated the taste, quality, and flavor of traditional freshly brewed coffee. Initially, VIA was introduced in Starbucks stores in the United States and Canada and select food service accounts; Starbucks stores held a four-day Starbucks VIA Taste Challenge promotional during which customers were invited to compare the difference between Starbucks VIA and fresh-brewed Starbucks coffee. During the 2009 holiday season, Starbucks VIA Ready Brew was one of the top-selling coffee products at Amazon.com. Encouraged by favorable customer response, in mid-2010 Starbucks expanded the distribution of VIA to include 25,000 grocery store, mass-merchandise store, and drugstore accounts, including Kroger, Safeway, Walmart,

Target, Costco, and CVS. VIA was available in three roasts—Colombian, Italian Roast, and Decaffeinated Italian Roast; the suggested retail price for Starbucks VIA was $2.95 for three servings and $7.49 for eight servings. Starbucks executives saw VIA as a promising vehicle for entering the instant coffee market and attracting a bigger fraction of on-the-go and at-home coffee drinkers. Instant coffee made up a significant fraction of the coffee purchases in the United Kingdom (80 percent), Japan (53 percent), Russia (85 percent), and other countries where Starbucks stores were located—in both the UK and Japan, sales of instant coffee exceeded $4 billion annually. Globally, the instant and single-serve coffee category was a $23 billion market. In March 2010, Starbucks made VIA available in all of its Starbucks stores in the UK. In April 2010, Starbucks introduced VIA in all of Japan's 870 Starbucks stores under the name Starbucks VIA Coffee Essence.[23]

The company's overall retail sales mix in 2009 was 76 percent beverages, 18 percent food items, 3 percent coffeemaking equipment and other merchandise, and 3 percent whole bean coffees.[24] However, the product mix in each store varied, depending on the size and location of each outlet. Larger stores carried a greater variety of whole coffee beans, gourmet food items, teas, coffee mugs, coffee grinders, coffeemaking equipment, filters, storage containers, and other accessories. Smaller stores and kiosks typically sold a full line of coffee beverages, a limited selection of whole bean and ground coffees and Tazo teas, and a few coffee-drinking accessories. Moreover, menu offerings at Starbucks stores were typically adapted to local cultures; for instance, the menu offerings at stores in North America included a selection of muffins, but stores in France had no muffins and instead featured locally made French pastries.

Starbucks' Consumer Products Group

All distribution channels for Starbucks products outside both licensed and company-operated retail stores were collectively referred to by Starbucks executives as "specialty operations." In 2010, Starbucks formed its Consumer Products Group (CPG) to manage all specialty operations activities. CPG was responsible for selling a selection of whole bean and ground coffees as well as a selection of premium Tazo teas outside Starbucks retail stores through licensing and distribution arrangements with Kraft, PepsiCo, Unilever, and others that covered both the United States and international markets. CPG also oversaw production and sales of ready-to-drink beverages (including bottled Frappuccino beverages, Starbucks Doubleshot espresso drinks, and Discoveries chilled cup coffee) as well as Starbucks superpremium ice creams and Starbucks liqueurs through the company's marketing and distribution agreements and joint ventures with PepsiCo, Unilever, and others. And it managed the sales of various Starbucks products to both food service accounts and the vast majority of the company's partnerships and licensing arrangements with prominent third parties.

Exhibit 6 shows the recent performance of the Consumer Products Group. Starbucks executives considered CPG's specialty operations attractive from the standpoint of both long-term growth and profitability. In fiscal 2007–2009, the company's operating profit margins from specialty operations were higher than the long-term target of 35 percent and vastly superior to the operating profit margins for the company's U.S. and international operations, as the following table shows:

	Operating Profit Margins		
	FY 2009	FY 2008	FY 2007
Consumer Products Group	39.6%	37.3%	35.9%
U.S. operations	7.5	6.0	14.3
International operations	4.8	5.2	8.1

▶**EXHIBIT 6**

Performance of Starbucks Consumer Products Group, Fiscal Years 2007–2009 (in $ millions)			
		Fiscal Year	
Consumer Product Group Operations	**2009**	**2008**	**2007**
Licensing revenues	$427.2	$392.6	$366.3
Food service revenues	322.4	355.0	326.1
Total revenues	$749.6	$747.6	$692.4
Operating income	$296.3	$279.2	$248.9
Operating income as a percent of total revenues	39.5%	37.3%	35.9%

Source: Starbucks, 2009 10-K report, p. 76

Advertising

So far, Starbucks had spent relatively little money on advertising, preferring instead to build the brand cup by cup with customers and depend on word of mouth and the appeal of its store-fronts. Advertising expenditures were $126.3 million in fiscal 2009, versus $129.0 million in fiscal 2008, $103.5 million in 2007, and $107.5 million in 2006. Starbucks stepped up advertising efforts in 2008 to combat the strategic initiatives of McDonald's and several other fast-food chains to begin offering premium coffees and coffee drinks at prices below those charged by Starbucks. In 2009, McDonald's reportedly spent more than $100 million on television, print, radio, billboard, and online ads promoting its new line of McCafé coffee drinks. Starbucks countered with the biggest advertising campaign the company had ever undertaken.[25]

Vertical Integration

Howard Schultz saw Starbucks as having a unique strategy compared to the strategies pursued by its many coffeehouse competitors. He observed:

> People sometimes fail to realize that almost unlike any retailer or restaurant, we are completely vertically integrated. We source coffee from 30 countries. We have a proprietary roasting process. We distribute to company owned stores, and finally serve the coffee. Others are resellers of commodity-based coffees.[26]

HOWARD SCHULTZ'S EFFORTS TO MAKE STARBUCKS A GREAT PLACE TO WORK

Howard Schultz deeply believed that Starbucks' success was heavily dependent on customers having a very positive experience in its stores. This meant having store employees who were knowledgeable about the company's products, who paid attention to detail in preparing the company's espresso drinks, who eagerly communicated the company's passion for coffee, and who possessed the skills and personality to deliver consistent, pleasing customer service. Many of the baristas were in their 20s and worked part-time, going to college on the side or pursuing other career activities. The challenge to Starbucks, in Schultz's view, was how to attract, motivate, and reward store employees in a manner that would make Starbucks a company that people would want to work for and that would generate enthusiastic commitment and higher levels of customer service. Moreover, Schultz wanted to send all Starbucks employees a message that would cement the trust that had been building between management and the company's workforce.

Instituting Health Care Coverage for All Employees

One of the requests that employees had made to the prior owners of Starbucks was to extend health insurance benefits to part-time workers. Their request had been turned down, but Schultz believed that expanding health insurance coverage to include part-timers was something the company needed to do. His father had recently passed away from cancer and he knew from having grown up in a family that struggled to make ends meet how difficult it was to cope with rising medical costs. In 1988, Schultz went to the board of directors with his plan to expand the company's health insurance plans to include part-timers who worked at least 20 hours per week. He saw the proposal not as a generous gesture but as a core strategy to win employee loyalty and commitment to the company's mission. Board members resisted because the company was unprofitable and the added costs of the extended coverage would only worsen the company's bottom line. But Schultz argued passionately that it was the right thing to do and wouldn't be as expensive as it seemed. He observed that if the new benefit reduced turnover, which he believed was likely, then it would reduce the costs of hiring and training—which equaled about $3,000 per new hire; he further pointed out that it cost $1,500 a year to provide an employee with full benefits. Part-timers, he argued, were vital to Starbucks, constituting two-thirds of the company's workforce. Many were baristas who knew the favorite drinks of regular customers; if the barista left, that connection with the customer was broken. Moreover, many part-time employees were called on to open the stores early, sometimes at 5:30 or 6:00 a.m.; others had to work until closing, usually 9:00 p.m. or later. Providing these employees with health insurance benefits, he argued, would signal that the company honored their value and contribution.

The board approved Schultz's plan, and starting in late 1988, part-timers working 20 or more hours were offered the same health coverage as full-time employees. Starbucks paid 75 percent of an employee's health insurance premium; the employee paid 25 percent. Over the years, Starbucks extended its health coverage to include preventive care, prescription drugs, dental care, eye care, mental health,

and chemical dependency. Coverage was also offered for unmarried partners in a committed relationship. Since most Starbucks employees were young and comparatively healthy, the company had been able to provide broader coverage while keeping monthly payments relatively low. Even when the company fell on lean times in 2008–2009, Starbucks refrained from making cuts in employee health insurance benefits; company expenditures for employee health insurance were $300 million in fiscal 2009, more than the company spent on its purchases of coffee beans.[27]

A Stock Option Plan for Employees

By 1991, the company's profitability had improved to the point where Schultz could pursue a stock option plan for all employees, a program he believed would have a positive, long-term effect on the success of Starbucks.[28] Schultz wanted to turn all Starbucks employees into partners, give them a chance to share in the success of the company, and make clear the connection between their contributions and the company's market value. Even though Starbucks was still a private company, the plan that emerged called for granting stock options to every full-time and part-time employee in proportion to his or her base pay. In May 1991, the plan, dubbed Bean Stock, was presented to the board. Though board members were concerned that increasing the number of shares might unduly dilute the value of the shares of investors who had put up hard cash, the plan received unanimous approval. The first grant was made in October 1991, just after the end of the company's fiscal year in September; each partner was granted stock options worth 12 percent of base pay. When the Bean Stock program was initiated, Starbucks dropped the term *employee* and began referring to all of its people as *partners* because every member of Starbucks' workforce became eligible for stock option awards after six months of employment and 500 paid work hours.

Starbucks went public in June 1992, selling its initial offering at a price of $17 per share.

Starting in October 1992 and continuing through October 2004, Starbucks granted each eligible employee a stock option award with a value equal to 14 percent of base pay. Beginning in 2005, the plan was modified to tie the size of each employee's stock option awards to three factors: (1) Starbucks' success and profitability for the fiscal year, (2) the size of an employee's base wages, and (3) the price at which the stock option could be exercised. The value of the stock options exercised by Starbucks partners was $44 million in fiscal 2009, $50 million in fiscal 2008, and $274 million in fiscal 2007. As of September 27, 2009, Starbucks partners held 63.6 million shares in stock option awards that had a weighted-average contractual life of 6.7 years; these shares had a weighted-average exercise price of $14.75 and an aggregate value of $442.4 million.[29]

Starbucks Stock Purchase Plan for Employees

In 1995, Starbucks implemented an employee stock purchase plan that gave partners who had been employed for at least 90 days an opportunity to purchase company stock through regular payroll deductions. Partners who enrolled could devote anywhere from 1 to 10 percent of their base earnings (up to a maximum of $25,000) to purchasing shares of Starbucks stock. After the end of each calendar quarter, each participant's contributions were used to buy Starbucks stock at a discount of 5 percent of the closing price on the last business day of the each calendar quarter (the discount was 15 percent until March 2009).

Since inception of the plan, some 23.5 million shares had been purchased by partners; roughly one-third of Starbucks partners participated in the stock purchase plan during the 2000–2009 period.

The Workplace Environment

Starbucks' management believed that the company's competitive pay scales and comprehensive benefits for both full-time and part-time partners allowed it to attract motivated people with above-average skills and good work habits. An employee's base pay was determined by the pay scales prevailing in the geographic region where an employee worked and by the person's job skills, experience, and job performance. About 90 percent of Starbucks' partners were full-time or part-time baristas, paid on an hourly basis. After six months of employment, baristas could expect to earn $8.50 to $9.50 per hour. In 2009, experienced full-time baristas in the company's U.S. stores earned an average of about $37,800; store managers earned an average of $44,400.[30] Voluntary turnover at Starbucks was 13 percent in 2009.[31] Starbucks executives believed that efforts to make the company an attractive, caring place to work were responsible for its relatively low turnover rates. Starbucks received 225,000 job applications in 2008 and 150,000 job applications in 2009.

Surveys of Starbucks partners conducted by *Fortune* magazine in the course of selecting companies for inclusion on its annual list "100 Best Companies to Work For" indicated that full-time baristas liked working at Starbucks because of the camaraderie, while part-timers were particularly pleased with the health insurance benefits (those who enrolled in Starbucks' most economical plan for just routine health care paid only $6.25 per week).[32] Starbucks had been named to *Fortune*'s list in 1998, 1999, 2000, and every year from 2002 through 2010. In 2010, Starbucks was ranked 93rd, down from 24th in 2009 and 7th in 2008.

Starbucks' management used annual Partner View surveys to solicit feedback from its workforce, learn their concerns, and measure job satisfaction. The 2002 survey revealed that many employees viewed the benefits package as only "average," prompting the company to increase its match of 401(k) contributions for those who had been with the company more than three years and to have these contributions vest immediately. In a survey conducted in fiscal 2008, 80 percent of Starbucks partners reported being satisfied.[33]

Schultz's approach to offering employees good compensation and a comprehensive benefits package was driven by his belief that sharing the company's success with the people who made it happen helped everyone think and act like an owner, build positive long-term relationships with customers, and do things efficiently. Schultz's rationale, based on his father's experience of going from one low-wage, no-benefits job to another, was that if you treated your employees well, they in turn would treat customers well.

Exhibit 7 contains a summary of Starbucks' fringe benefit program.

Employee Training and Recognition

To accommodate its strategy of rapid store expansion, Starbucks put in systems to recruit, hire, and train baristas and store managers. Starbucks' vice president for human resources used some simple guidelines in screening candidates for new positions: "We want passionate people who love coffee. . . . We're looking for a diverse workforce, which reflects our community. We want people who enjoy what they're doing and for whom work is an extension of themselves."[34]

All partners/baristas hired for a retail job in a Starbucks store received at least 24 hours training in their first two to four weeks. The topics included classes on coffee history, drink preparation, coffee knowledge (four hours), customer service (four hours), and retail skills, plus a four-hour workshop called "Brewing the Perfect Cup." Baristas spent considerable time learning about beverage preparation— grinding the beans, steaming milk, learning to pull perfect (18- to 23-second) shots of espresso,

▶ **EXHIBIT 7**

Starbucks' Fringe Benefit Program, 2010

- Medical insurance
- Sick time
- Dental and vision care
- Paid vacations (up to 120 hours annually for hourly workers with five or more years of service at retail stores and up to 200 hours annually for salaried and nonretail hourly employees with five or more years of service)
- Six paid holidays
- One paid personal day every six months for salaried and nonretail hourly partners
- A 30 percent discount on purchases of beverages, food, and merchandise at Starbucks stores
- Mental health and chemical dependency coverage
- 401(k) retirement savings plan—the company matched from 25% to 150%, based on length of service, of each employee's contributions up to the first 4% of compensation
- Short- and long-term disability
- Stock purchase plan—eligible employees could buy shares at a discounted price through regular payroll deductions
- Life insurance
- Short- and long-term disability insurance
- Accidental death and dismemberment insurance
- Adoption assistance
- Financial assistance program for partners that experience a financial crisis
- Stock option plan (Bean stock)
- Pre-tax payroll deductions for commuter expenses
- Free coffee and tea products each week
- Tuition reimbursement program

Source: Starbucks, "Careers," www.starbucks.com, accessed June 7, 2010.

memorizing the recipes of all the different drinks, practicing making the different drinks, and learning how to customize drinks to customer specifications. There were sessions on cash register operations, how to clean the milk wand on the espresso machine, explaining the Italian drink names to customers, selling home espresso machines, making eye contact with customers and interacting with them, and taking personal responsibility for the cleanliness of the store. And there were rules to be memorized: milk must be steamed to at least 150 degrees Fahrenheit but never more than 170 degrees; every espresso shot not pulled within 23 seconds must be tossed; never let coffee sit in the pot more than 20 minutes; always compensate dissatisfied customers with a Starbucks coupon that entitled them to a free drink.

Management trainees attended classes for 8 to 12 weeks. Their training went much deeper, covering not only coffee knowledge and information imparted to baristas but also details of store operations, practices and procedures as set forth in the company's operating manual, information systems, and the basics of managing people. Starbucks' trainers were all store managers and district managers with on-site experience. One of their major objectives was to ingrain the company's values, principles, and culture and to pass on their knowledge about coffee and their passion about Starbucks.

When Starbucks opened stores in a new market, it sent a Star Team of experienced managers and baristas to the area to lead the store opening effort and to conduct one-on-one training following the company's formal classes and basic orientation sessions at the Starbucks Coffee School in San Francisco. From time to time, Starbucks conducted special training programs, including a coffee masters program for store employees, leadership training for store managers, and career programs for partners in all types of jobs.

To recognize partner contributions, Starbucks had created a partner recognition program consisting of 18 different awards and programs. Examples included Coffee Master awards, Certified Barista awards, Spirit of Starbucks awards for exceptional achievement by a partner, a Manager of the Quarter for store manager leadership, Green Apron Awards for helping create a positive and welcoming store environment, Green Bean Awards for exceptional support for company's environmental mission, and Bravo! Awards for exceeding the standards of Starbucks customer service, significantly increasing sales, or reducing costs.

STARBUCKS' VALUES, BUSINESS PRINCIPLES, AND MISSION

During the early building years, Howard Schultz and other Starbucks senior executives worked to instill some key values and guiding principles into the Starbucks culture. The cornerstone value in their effort "to build a company with soul" was that the company would never stop pursuing the perfect cup of coffee by buying the best beans and roasting them to perfection. Schultz was adamant about controlling the quality of Starbucks products and building a culture common to all stores. He was rigidly opposed to selling artificially flavored coffee beans, saying that "we will not pollute our high-quality beans with chemicals"; if a customer wanted hazelnut-flavored coffee, Starbucks would provide it by adding hazelnut syrup to the drink rather than by adding hazelnut flavoring to the beans during roasting. Running flavored beans through the grinders would result in chemical residues being left behind to alter the flavor of beans ground afterward; plus, the chemical smell given off by artificially flavored beans was absorbed by other beans in the store.

Starbucks' management was also emphatic about the importance of employees paying attention to what pleased customers. Employees were trained to go out of their way and to take heroic measures, if necessary, to make sure customers were fully satisfied. The theme was "just say yes" to customer requests. Further, employees were encouraged to speak their minds without fear of retribution from upper management—senior executives wanted employees to be straight with them, being vocal about what Starbucks was doing right, what it was doing wrong, and what changes were needed. The intent was for employees to be involved in and contribute to the process of making Starbucks a better company.

Starbucks' Mission Statement

In early 1990, the senior executive team at Starbucks went to an off-site retreat to debate the company's values and beliefs and draft a mission statement. Schultz wanted the mission statement to convey a strong sense of organizational purpose and to articulate the company's fundamental beliefs and guiding principles. The draft was submitted to all employees for review, and several changes were made based on employee comments. The resulting mission statement and guiding principles are shown in Exhibit 8. In 2008, Starbucks partners from all across the company met for several months to refresh the mission statement and rephrase the underlying guiding principles; the revised mission statement and guiding principles are also shown in Exhibit 8.

STARBUCKS' COFFEE PURCHASING STRATEGY

Coffee beans were grown in 70 tropical countries and were the second-most-traded commodity in the world after petroleum. Most of the world's coffee was grown by some 25 million small farmers, most of whom lived on the edge of poverty. Starbucks personnel traveled regularly to coffee-producing countries, building relationships with growers and exporters, checking on agricultural conditions and crop yields, and searching out varieties and sources that would meet Starbucks' exacting standards of quality and flavor. The coffee-purchasing group, working with Starbucks personnel in roasting operations, tested new varieties and blends of green coffee beans from different sources. Sourcing from multiple geographic areas not only allowed Starbucks to offer a greater range of coffee varieties to customers but also spread the company's risks regarding weather, price

volatility, and changing economic and political conditions in coffee-growing countries.

Starbucks' coffee sourcing strategy had three key elements:

- Make sure that the prices Starbucks paid for green (unroasted) coffee beans were high enough to ensure that small farmers were able to cover their production costs and provide for their families.
- Use purchasing arrangements that limited Starbucks' exposure to sudden price jumps due to weather, economic and political conditions in the growing countries, new agreements establishing export quotas, and periodic efforts to bolster prices by restricting coffee supplies.
- Work directly with small coffee growers, local coffee-growing cooperatives, and other types of coffee suppliers to promote coffee cultivation methods that protected biodiversity and were environmentally sustainable.

Pricing and Purchasing Arrangements

Commodity-grade coffee was traded in a highly competitive market as an undifferentiated product. However, high-altitude arabica coffees of the quality purchased by Starbucks were bought on a negotiated basis at a substantial premium above commodity coffee. The prices of the top-quality coffees sourced by Starbucks depended on supply and demand conditions at the time of the purchase and were subject to considerable volatility due to weather, economic and political conditions in the growing countries, new agreements establishing export quotas, and periodic efforts to bolster prices by restricting coffee supplies.

Starbucks typically used fixed-price purchase commitments to limit its exposure to fluctuating coffee prices in upcoming periods and, on occasion, purchased coffee futures contracts to provide price protection. In years past, there had been times when unexpected jumps in coffee prices had put a squeeze on Starbucks' margins, forcing an increase in the prices of

EXHIBIT 8

Starbucks' Mission Statement, Values, and Business Principles

Mission Statement, 1990–October 2008

Establish Starbucks as the premier purveyor of the finest coffee in the world while maintaining our uncompromising principles as we grow.

The following six guiding principles will help us measure the appropriateness of our decisions:

- Provide a great work environment and treat each other with respect and dignity.
- Embrace diversity as an essential component in the way we do business.
- Apply the highest standards of excellence to the purchasing, roasting, and fresh delivery of our coffee.
- Develop enthusiastically satisfied customers all of the time.
- Contribute positively to our communities and our environment.
- Recognize that profitability is essential to our future success.

Mission Statement, October 2008 Forward

Our Mission: To inspire and nurture the human spirit—one person, one cup, and one neighborhood at a time.

Here are the principles of how we live that every day:

OUR COFFEE

It has always been, and will always be, about quality. We're passionate about ethically sourcing the finest coffee beans, roasting them with great care, and improving the lives of people who grow them. We care deeply about all of this; our work is never done.

OUR PARTNERS

We're called partners, because it's not just a job, it's our passion. Together, we embrace diversity to create a place where each of us can be ourselves. We always treat each other with respect and dignity. And we hold each other to that standard.

OUR CUSTOMERS

When we are fully engaged, we connect with, laugh with, and uplift the lives of our customers—even if just for a few moments. Sure, it starts with the promise of a perfectly made beverage, but our work goes far beyond that. It's really about human connection.

OUR STORES

When our customers feel this sense of belonging, our stores become a haven, a break from the worries outside, a place where you can meet with friends. It's about enjoyment at the speed of life—sometimes slow and savored, sometimes faster. Always full of humanity.

OUR NEIGHBORHOOD

Every store is part of a community, and we take our responsibility to be good neighbors seriously. We want to be invited in wherever we do business. We can be a force for positive action— bringing together our partners, customers, and the community to contribute every day. Now we see that our responsibility—and our potential for good—is even larger. The world is looking to Starbucks to set the new standard, yet again. We will lead.

OUR SHAREHOLDERS

We know that as we deliver in each of these areas, we enjoy the kind of success that rewards our shareholders. We are fully accountable to get each of these elements right so that Starbucks—and everyone it touches—can endure and thrive.

Source: Starbucks, "Our Starbucks Mission," www.starbucks.com, accessed March 7, 2010.

the beverages and beans sold at retail. During fiscal 2008, Starbucks more than doubled its volume of its fixed-price purchase commit- ments compared with fiscal 2007 because of the risk of rising prices for green coffee beans. Starbucks bought 367 million pounds of green coffee beans in fiscal 2009, paying an average of $1.47 per pound. At the end of fiscal 2009, the company had purchase commitments totaling $238 million, which, together with existing inventory, were expected to provide an adequate supply of green coffee through fiscal 2010.[35]

Starbucks and Fair Trade Certified Coffee   A growing number of small coffee growers were members of democratically run cooperatives that were registered with the Fair Trade Labeling Organizations International; these growers could sell their beans directly to importers, roasters, and retailers at favorable guaranteed fair trade prices. The idea behind guaranteed prices for fair trade coffees was to boost earnings for small coffee growers enough to allow them to invest in their farms and communities, develop the business skills needed to compete in the global market for coffee, and afford basic health care, education, and home improvements.

Starbucks began purchasing Fair Trade Certified coffee in 2000, steadily increasing its purchasing and marketing of such coffees in line with growing awareness of what Fair Trade Certified coffees were all about and consumer willingness to pay the typically higher prices for fair trade coffees. In 2008, Starbucks announced that it would double its purchases of Fair Trade Certified coffees in 2009, resulting in total purchases of 39 million pounds in 2009 (versus 19 million pounds in 2008 and 10 million pounds in 2005) and making Starbucks the largest purchaser of Fair Trade Certified coffee in the world. Starbucks marketed Fair Trade Certified coffees at most of its retail stores and through other locations that sold Starbucks coffees.

Best-Practice Coffee Cultivation and Environmental Sustainability

Since 1998, Starbucks had partnered with Conservation International's Center for Environmental Leadership to promote environmentally sustainable best practices in coffee cultivation methods and to develop specific guidelines—called Coffee and Farmer Equity (C.A.F.E.) Practices—to help farmers grow high-quality coffees in ways that were good for the planet. The C.A.F.E. Practices covered four areas: product quality, the price received by farmers/growers, safe and humane working conditions (including compliance with minimum wage requirements and child labor provisions), and environmental responsibility.[36] In addition, Starbucks operated Farmer Support Centers in Costa Rica and Rwanda that were staffed with agronomists and experts on environmentally responsible coffee growing methods; staff members at these two centers worked with coffee farming communities to promote best practices in coffee production and improve both coffee quality and production yields. During 2008–2009, approximately 80 percent of the coffee beans purchased by Starbucks came from suppliers whose coffee-growing methods met C.A.F.E. standards. In those instances where Starbucks sourced its coffee beans from nongrower C.A.F.E. Practices suppliers, it required suppliers to submit evidence of payments made through the coffee supply chain to demonstrate how much of the price Starbucks paid for green coffee beans got to the farmer/grower.

A growing percentage of the coffees that Starbucks purchased were grown organically (i.e., without the use of pesticides, herbicides, or chemical fertilizers); organic cultivation methods resulted in clean groundwater and helped protect against degrading of local ecosystems, many of which were fragile or in areas where biodiversity was under severe threat. Starbucks purchased 14 million pounds of certified organic coffee in fiscal 2009.

COFFEE ROASTING OPERATIONS

Starbucks considered the roasting of its coffee beans to be something of an art form, entailing trial-and-error testing of different combinations of time and temperature to get the most out of each type of bean and blend. Recipes were put together by the coffee department, once all the components had been tested. Computerized roasters guaranteed consistency. Highly trained and experienced roasting personnel monitored the process, using both smell and hearing, to help check when the beans were perfectly done—coffee beans make a popping sound when ready. Starbucks' standards were so exacting that roasters tested the color of the beans in a blood-cell analyzer and discarded the entire batch if the reading wasn't on target. After roasting and cooling, the coffee was immediately vacuum-sealed in bags that preserved freshness for up to 26 weeks. As a matter of policy, however, Starbucks removed coffees on its shelves after three months and, in the case of coffee used to prepare beverages in stores, the shelf life was limited to seven days after the bag was opened.

Starbucks had roasting plants in Kent, Washington; York, Pennsylvania; Minden, Nevada; Charleston, South Carolina; and The Netherlands. In addition to roasting capability, these plants also had additional space for warehousing and shipping coffees. In keeping with Starbucks' corporate commitment to reduce its environmental footprint, the new state-of-the-art roasting plant in South Carolina had been awarded LEED Silver certification for New Construction by the U.S. Green Building Council. Twenty percent of materials used in the construction of the building were from recycled content and more than 75 percent of the waste generated during construction was recycled. In addition, the facility used state-of-the-art light and water fixtures and was partly powered by wind energy. Some of the green elements in the South Carolina plant were being implemented in the other roasting plants as part of the company's initiative to achieve LEED certification for all company-operated facilities by the end of 2010.[37] In May 2010, Starbucks announced the opening of its first LEED-certified store in Asia. Located in Fukuoka, Japan, the new store was designed to serve as an extension of the existing landscape and to preserve the surrounding trees.[38]

STARBUCKS' CORPORATE SOCIAL RESPONSIBILITY STRATEGY

Howard Schultz's effort to "build a company with soul" included a long history of doing business in ways that were socially and environmentally responsible. A commitment to do the right thing had been central to how Starbucks operated as a company since Howard Schultz first became CEO in 1987. The specific actions comprising Starbucks' social responsibility strategy had varied over the years, but the intent of the strategy was consistently one of contributing positively to the communities in which Starbucks had stores, being a good environmental steward, and conducting its business in ways that earned the trust and respect of customers, partners/employees, suppliers, and the general public.

The Starbucks Foundation was set up in 1997 to orchestrate the company's philanthropic activities. Starbucks stores participated regularly in local charitable projects and community improvement activities. For years, the company had engaged in efforts to reduce, reuse, and recycle waste, conserve on water and energy usage, and generate less solid waste. Customers who brought their own mugs to stores were given a $0.10 discount on beverage purchases—in 2009, some 26 million beverages were served in customers' mugs. Coffee grounds, which were a big portion of the waste stream in stores, were packaged and given to customers, parks, schools, and plant nurseries as a soil amendment. Company personnel purchased paper products with high levels of recycled content and unbleached fiber. Stores participated in Earth Day activities each year with in-store promotions and volunteer efforts to educate employees and customers about the impacts their actions had on the environment. Suppliers were encouraged to provide the most energy-efficient products within their category and eliminate excessive packaging; Starbucks had recently instituted a set of Supplier Social Responsibility Standards covering the suppliers of all the manufactured goods and services used in the company's operations.

No genetically modified ingredients were used in any food or beverage products that Starbucks served, with the exception of milk (U.S. labeling requirements do not require milk producers to disclose the use of hormones aimed at increasing the milk production of dairy herds). In 2005, Starbucks made a $5 million, five-year commitment to long-term relief and recovery efforts for victims of hurricanes Rita and Katrina and committed $5 million to support educational programs in China. In 2010, the Starbucks Foundation donated $1 million to the American Red Cross efforts to provide aid to those suffering the devastating effects of the earthquake in Haiti; in addition, Starbucks customers were invited to make cash donations to the Haitian relief effort at store registers.[39]

In 2008–2010, Starbucks' corporate social responsibility strategy had four main elements:

1. *Ethically sourcing all of the company's products.* This included promoting responsible growing practices for the company's coffees, teas, and cocoa and striving to buy the manufactured products and services it needed from suppliers that had a demonstrated commitment to social and environmental responsibility. Starbucks had a 2015 goal of purchasing 100 percent of its coffees through sources there were either Fair Trade Certified or met C.A.F.E. Practices guidelines.

2. *Community involvement.* This included engaging in a wide variety of community service activities, Starbucks Youth Action Grants to engage young people in community improvement projects (in fiscal 2009, Starbucks made 71 grants totaling $2.1 million), a program to provide medicine to people in Africa with HIV, the Ethos Water Fund, and donations by the Starbucks Foundation. The company had a goal of getting Starbucks partners and customers to contribute more than 1 million hours of community service annually by 2015; service contributions totaled 246,000 hours in 2008 and 186,000 hours in 2009.

3. *Environmental stewardship.* Initiatives here included a wide variety of actions to increase recycling, reduce waste, be more energy-efficient and use renewable energy sources, conserve water resources, make all company facilities as green as possible by using environmentally friendly building materials and energy-efficient designs, and engage in more efforts to address climate change. The company had immediate objectives of achieving LEED certification globally for all new company-operated stores beginning in late 2010, reducing energy consumption in company-owned stores by 25 percent by the end of fiscal 2010, and purchasing renewable energy equivalent to 50 percent of the electricity used in company-owned stores by the end of fiscal 2010. Management believed that the company was on track to achieve all three targets.

In 2009, Starbucks became a member of the Business for Innovative Climate Change and Energy Policy coalition, which sought to spur a clean energy economy and mitigate global warming by advocating strong legislation by the U.S. Congress. Starbucks was also collaborating with Earthwatch Institute on replanting rain forests, mapping water resources and biodiversity indicators, and sharing sustainable agriculture practices with coffee growers. Starbucks had goals to implement front-of-store recycling in all company-owned stores by 2015, to ensure that 100 percent of its cups were reusable or recyclable by 2015, to serve 25 percent of the beverages made in its stores in reusable containers by 2015, and to reduce water consumption in company-owned stores by 25 percent by 2015. In 2009 the company made progress toward achieving all these goals but still faced significant challenges in implementing recycling at its more than 16,000 stores worldwide because of wide variations in municipal recycling capabilities.

4. *Farmer loans.* Because many of the tens of thousands of small family farms with less than 30 acres that grew coffees purchased by Starbucks often lacked the money to make farming improvements and/or cover all expenses until they sold their crops, Starbucks provided funding to organizations that made loans to small coffee growers. Over the years, Starbucks had committed more than $15 million to a variety of coffee farmer loan funds. The company boosted its farmer loan commitments from $12.5 million to $14.5 million in 2009 and had a goal to commit a total of $20 million by 2015.

In 2010, Starbucks was named to *Corporate Responsibility Magazine*'s list "The 100 Best Corporate Citizens" for the 10th time. The "100 Best Corporate Citizens" list was based on more than 360 data points of publicly available information in seven categories: Environment, Climate Change, Human Rights, Philanthropy, Employee Relations, Financial Performance, and Governance. In addition, Starbucks had received over 25 awards from a diverse group of organizations for its philanthropic, community service, and environmental activities.

TOP MANAGEMENT CHANGES: CHANGING ROLES FOR HOWARD SCHULTZ

In 2000, Howard Schultz decided to relinquish his role as CEO, retain his position as chairman of the company's board of directors, and assume the newly created role of chief strategic officer. Orin Smith, a Starbucks executive who had been with the company since its early days, was named CEO. Smith retired in 2005 and was replaced as CEO by Jim Donald, who had been president of Starbucks' North American division. In 2006, Donald proceeded to set a long-term objective of having 40,000 stores worldwide and launched a program of rapid store expansion in an effort to achieve that goal.

But investors and members of Starbucks' board of directors (including Howard Schultz) became uneasy about Donald's leadership of the company when customer traffic in Starbucks' U.S. stores began to erode in 2007, new store openings worldwide were continuing at the rate of six per day, and Donald kept pressing for increased efficiency in store operations at the expense of good customer service. Investors were distressed with the company's steadily declining stock price during 2007. Schultz had lamented in a 2007 internal company e-mail (which was leaked to the public) that the company's aggressive growth had led to "a watering down of the Starbucks experience."[40] In January 2008, Starbucks' board asked Howard Schultz to return to his role as CEO and lead a major restructuring and revitalization initiative.

HOWARD SCHULTZ'S TRANSFORMATION AGENDA FOR STARBUCKS, 2008–2010

Immediately upon his return as Starbucks CEO, Schultz undertook a series of moves to revamp the company's executive leadership team and change the roles and responsibilities of several key executives.[41] A former Starbucks executive was hired for the newly created role of chief creative officer responsible for elevating the in-store experience of customers and achieving new levels of innovation and differentiation.

Because he believed that Starbucks in recent years had become less passionate about customer relationships and the coffee experience that had fueled the company's success, Schultz further decided to launch a major campaign to retransform Starbucks into the company he had envisioned it ought to be and to push the company to new plateaus of differentiation and innovation—the transformation effort instantly became the centerpiece of his return as company CEO. Schultz's transformation agenda for Starbucks had three main themes: strengthen the core, elevate the experience, and invest and grow. Specific near-term actions that Schultz implemented to drive his transformation of Starbucks in 2008–2010 included the following:

- Slowing the pace of new store openings in the United States and opening a net of 75 new stores internationally.

- Closing 900 underperforming company-operated stores in the United States, nearly 75 percent of which were within three miles of an existing Starbucks store. It was expected that these closings would boost sales and traffic at many nearby stores.

- Raising the projected return on capital requirements for proposed new store locations.

- Restructuring the company's store operations in Australia to focus on three key cities and surrounding areas—Brisbane, Melbourne, and Sydney—and to close 61 underperforming store locations (mostly located in other parts of Australia).

- Coming up with new designs for future Starbucks stores. The global store design strategy was aimed at promoting a reinvigorated customer experience by reflecting the character of each store's surrounding neighborhood and making customers feel truly at home when visiting their local store. All of the designs had to incorporate environmentally friendly materials and furnishings.

- Enhancing the customer experience at Starbucks stores, including the discontinuance of serving warmed breakfast sandwiches in North American stores (because the scent of warmed sandwiches interfered with the coffee aroma) and a program to develop best-in-class baked goods and other new menu items that would make Starbucks a good source of a healthy breakfast for people on the go and better complement its coffee and espresso beverages. These efforts to improve the menu offerings at Starbucks stores were directly responsible for (1) the recent additions of fruit cups, yogurt parfaits, skinny lattes, the farmer's market salad, Vivanno smoothies, and healthier bakery selections, (2) the reformulated recipes to cut back on or eliminate the use of artificial flavorings, dyes, high-fructose corn syrup, and artificial preservatives, and (3) all-day brewing of Pikes Place Roast.

- A program to share best practices across all stores worldwide.

- Additional resources and tools for store employees, including laptops, an Internet-based software for scheduling work hours for store employees, and a new point-of-sale system for all stores in the United States, Canada, and the United Kingdom.

- Rigorous cost-containment initiatives to improve the company's bottom line, including a 1,000-person reduction in the staffing of the company's organizational support infrastructure to trim administrative expenses at the company's headquarters and regional offices.

- Renewed attention to employee training and reigniting enthusiasm on the part of store employees to please customers. In February 2008, Schultz ordered that 7,100 U.S. stores be temporarily closed for three regularly operating business hours (at 5:30 p.m. local time) for the purpose of conducting a special training session for store employees. The objectives were to give baristas hands-on training to improve the quality of the drinks they made, help reignite the emotional attachment of store employees to customers (a long-standing tradition at Starbucks stores), and refocus the attention of store employees on pleasing customers. Schultz viewed the training session as a way to help the company regain its "soul of the past" and improve the in-store Starbucks experience for customers.[42] When several major shareholders called Schultz to get his take on why he was closing 7,100 stores for three hours, he told them, "I am doing the right thing.

We are retraining our people because we have forgotten what we stand for, and that is the pursuit of an unequivocal, absolute commitment to quality."[43]

Schultz's insistence on more innovation had also spurred the recent introduction of the Starbucks VIA instant coffees.

Howard Schultz believed that the turning point in his effort to transform Starbucks came when he decided to hold a leadership conference for 10,000 store managers in New Orleans in early 2008. According to Schultz:

> I knew that if I could remind people of our character and values, we could make a difference. The conference was about galvanizing the entire leadership of the company—being vulnerable and transparent with our employees about how desperate the situation was, and how we had to understand that everyone must be personally accountable and responsible for every single customer interaction. We started the conference with community service. Our efforts represent the largest single block of community support in the history of New Orleans, contributing more than 54,000 volunteer hours and investing more than $1 million in local projects like painting, landscaping, and building playgrounds.
>
> If we had not had New Orleans, we wouldn't have turned things around. It was real, it was truthful, and it was about leadership. An outside CEO would have come into Starbucks and invariably done what was expected, which was cut the thing to the bone. We didn't do that. Now we did cut $581 million of costs out of the company. The cuts targeted all areas of the business, from supply chain efficiencies to waste reduction to rightsizing our support structure. But 99 percent were not consumer-facing, and in fact, our customer satisfaction scores began to rise at this time and have continued to reach unprecedented levels. We reinvested in our people, we reinvested in innovation, and we reinvested in the values of the company.

In 2010, as part of Schultz's "invest and grow" aspect of transforming Starbucks, the company was formulating plans to open "thousands of new stores" in China over time.[44] Japan had long been Starbucks' biggest foreign market outside North America, but Howard Schultz said that "Asia clearly represents the most significant growth opportunity on a go-forward basis."[45] Schultz also indicated that Starbucks was anxious to begin opening stores in India and Vietnam, two country markets that Starbucks believed were potentially lucrative.

Exhibit 9 is a letter that Howard Schultz sent to customers on the day he reassumed the position of Starbucks' chief executive officer. Exhibit 10 is a letter that Howard Schultz sent to all Starbucks partners three weeks after he returned as company CEO.

▶ EXHIBIT 9

Letter from Howard Schultz to Starbucks Customers, January 7, 2008

To Our Customers:

Twenty-five years ago, I walked into Starbucks' first store and I fell in love with the coffee I tasted, with the passion of the people working there, and with how it looked, smelled and felt. From that day, I had a vision that a store can offer a welcoming experience for customers, be part of their community, and become a warm "third place" that is part of their lives everyday and that it can provide a truly superior cup of coffee.

Based on that vision, I, along with a very talented group of people, brought Starbucks to life. We did it by being creative, innovative and courageous in offering coffee products that very few in America had ever tasted; by celebrating the interaction between us and our customers; by developing a store design unlike any that existed before; and by bringing on board an exceptionally engaged group of partners (employees) who shared our excitement about building a different kind of company.

(continued)

▶ **EXHIBIT 9** *(concluded)*

In doing this, we developed a culture based on treating each other, our customers and our coffee growers with respect and dignity. This includes embracing diversity, committing ourselves to ethical sourcing practices, providing health care and stock options to all of our eligible full- and part-time partners, supporting the communities we serve, and, most of all, ensuring that we are a company you can be proud to support.

I am writing today to thank you for the trust you have placed in us and to share with you my personal commitment to ensuring that every time you visit our stores you get the distinctive Starbucks Experience that you have come to expect, marked by the consistent delivery of the finest coffee in the world. To ensure this happens, in addition to my role as chairman, I am returning to the position of chief executive officer to help our partners build upon our heritage and our special relationship with you, and lead our company into the future.

We have enormous opportunity and exciting plans in place to make the Starbucks Experience as good as it has ever been and even better. In the coming months, you will see this come to life in the way our stores look, in the way our people serve you, in the new beverages and products we will offer. That is my promise to you. Everyone at Starbucks looks forward to sharing these initiatives with you.

Onward,

Howard Schultz

Source: Starbucks, press release, January 7, 2008, www.starbucks.com, accessed June 17, 2010.

▶ **EXHIBIT 10**

Communication from Howard Schultz to All Starbucks Partners, February 4, 2008

What I Know to Be True

Dear Partners,

As I sit down to write this note (6:30 a.m. Sunday morning) I am enjoying a spectacular cup of Sumatra, brewed my favorite way—in a French press.

It has been three weeks since I returned to my role as CEO of the company I love. We have made much progress as we begin to transform and innovate and there is much more to come. But this is not a sprint—it is a marathon—it always has been. I assure you that when all is said and done, we will, as we always have, succeed at our highest potential. We will not be deterred from our course—we are and will be a great, enduring company, known for inspiring and nurturing the human spirit.

During this time, I have heard from so many of you; in fact, I have received more than 2,000 emails. I can feel your passion and commitment to the company, to our customers and to one another. I also thank you for all your ideas and suggestions . . . keep them coming. No one knows our business and our customers better than you. I have visited with you in many of your stores, as well as stopping by to see what our competitors are doing as well.

It's been just a few days since my last communications to you, but I wanted to share with you

what I know to be true:

- Since 1971, we have been ethically sourcing and roasting the highest quality *Arabica* coffee in the world, and today there is not a coffee company on earth providing higher quality coffee to their customers than we are. Period!

- We are in the people business and always have been. What does that mean? It means you make the difference. You are the Starbucks brand. We succeed in the marketplace and distinguish ourselves by each and every partner embracing the values, guiding principles and culture of our company and bringing it to life one customer at a time.

(continued)

▶EXHIBIT 10   *(concluded)*

Our stores have become the Third Place in our communities—a destination where human connections happen tens of thousands of times a day. We are not in the coffee business serving people. We are in the people business serving coffee. You are the best people serving the best coffee and I am proud to be your partner. There is no other place I would rather be than with you right here, right now!

- We have a renewed clarity of purpose and we are laser-focused on the customer experience. We have returned to our core to reaffirm our coffee authority and we will have some fun doing it. We are not going to embrace the status quo. Instead, we will be curious, bold and innovative in our actions and, in doing so, we will exceed the expectation of our customers.

- There will be cynics and critics along the way, all of whom will have an opinion and a point of view. This is not about them or our competitors, although we must humbly respect the changing landscape and the many choices facing every consumer. We will be steadfast in our approach and in our commitment to the *Starbucks Experience*—what we know to be true. However, this is about us and our customers. We are in control of our destiny. Trust the coffee and trust one another.

- I will lead us back to the place where we belong, but I need your help and support every step of the way. My expectations of you are high, but higher of myself.

- I want to hear from you. I want to hear about your ideas, your wins, your concerns, and how we can collectively continue to improve. Please feel free to reach out to me. I have been flooded with emails, but believe me, I am reading and responding to all of them.

As I said, I am proud to be your partner. I know this to be true.

Onward . . .

Howard

P.S. Everything that we do, from this point on (from the most simple and basic), matters.

Master the fundamentals. Experience Starbucks.

Source: Starbucks, press release, February 4, 2008, www.starbucks.com, accessed June 17, 2010.

STARBUCKS' FUTURE PROSPECTS

In April 2010, halfway through the fiscal year, Howard Schultz continued to be pleased with the company's progress in returning to a path of profitable, long-term growth. Following five consecutive quarters of declining sales at stores open 13 months or longer (beginning with the first quarter of fiscal 2008), sales at Starbucks' company-operated stores worldwide had improved in each of the most recent five consecutive quarters—see Exhibit 11. Moreover, traffic (as measured by the number of cash register transactions) increased by 3 percent in the company's U.S. stores in the second quarter of fiscal 2010, the first positive increase in the last 13 quarters. Net revenues increased 8.6 percent in the second quarter of fiscal 2010 compared with the same quarter in fiscal 2009, while net income jumped from $25.0 million in the second quarter of fiscal 2009 to $217.3 million in the second quarter of fiscal 2010. In commenting on the company's earnings for the second quarter of fiscal 2010, Schultz said:

> Starbucks' second quarter results demonstrate the impact of innovation and the success of our efforts to dramatically transform our business over the last two years. Much credit goes to our partners all around the world who continue to deliver an improved experience to our customers. In addition, new products like Starbucks VIA, the opening of exciting new stores in Asia, Europe and the U.S., and expanded distribution outside our retail stores all represent opportunities for future growth.[46]

▶ EXHIBIT 11

Quarterly Sales Trends at Starbucks Company-Operated Stores, Quarter 1 of Fiscal 2008 through Quarter 2 of Fiscal 2010					

| | Five Quarters of Deteriorating Sales | | | | |
Sales at Company-Operated Starbucks Stores	Q1 2008	Q2 2008	Q3 2008	Q4 2008	Q1 2009
United States	(1%)	(4%)	(5%)	(8%)	(10%)
International	5%	3%	2%	0%	(3%)

| | Five Quarters of Improving Sales | | | | |
Sales at Company-Operated Starbucks Stores	Q2 2009	Q3 2009	Q4 2009	Q1 2010	Q2 2010
United States	(8%)	(6%)	(1%)	4%	7%
International	(3%)	(2%)	0%	4%	7%

In March 2010, Starbucks announced its first-ever cash dividend of $0.10 per share to be paid quarterly starting with the second quarter of fiscal 2010.

The company's updated targets for full-year 2010 were as follows:

- Mid-single-digit revenue growth world-wide, driven by mid-single-digit sales growth at company-operated stores open at least 13 months.
- Opening approximately 100 net new stores in the United States and approximately 200 net new stores in international markets. Both the U.S. and international net new additions were expected to be primarily licensed stores.
- Earnings per share in the range of $1.19 to $1.22.
- Non-GAAP earnings per share in the range of $1.19 to $1.22, excluding approximately $0.03 of expected restructuring charges and including approximately $0.04 from the extra week in the fiscal fourth quarter, as fiscal 2010 was a 53-week year for Starbucks.
- Capital expenditures were expected to be approximately $500 million for the full year.
- Cash flow from operations of at least $1.5 billion, and free cash flow of more than $1 billion.

Long term, the company's objective was to maintain Starbucks' standing as one of the most recognized and respected brands in the world. To achieve this, Starbucks executives planned to continue disciplined global expansion of its company-operated and licensed retail store base, introduce relevant new products in all its channels, and selectively develop new channels of distribution.

Schultz's long-term vision for Starbucks had seven key elements:

- Be the undisputed coffee authority.
- Engage and inspire Starbucks partners.
- Ignite the emotional attachment with our customers.
- Expand our global presence—while making each store the heart of the local neighborhood.
- Be a leader in ethical sourcing and environmental impact.
- Create innovative growth platforms worthy of our coffee.
- Deliver a sustainable economic model.

Schultz believed that Starbucks still had enormous growth potential. In the United States, Starbucks had only a 3 percent share of the estimated 37 billion cups of coffee served to on-the-go coffee drinkers, only a 4 percent share of the 25 billion cups of coffee served at home, and only a 13 percent share of the 3.7 billion cups of coffee served in restaurants and coffee-houses.[47] Internationally, Starbucks' shares of these same segments were smaller. According to Schultz:

> The size of the prize is still huge. We sell less than 10 percent of the coffee consumed in the U.S. and less than 1 percent outside the U.S. The momentum will come from

international. Slower growth in the U.S., accelerating growth overseas. The response to the Starbucks brand has been phenomenal in our international markets.[48]

Nonetheless, since his return as CEO in January 2008, Schultz had been mum about whether and when the company would aggressively pursue former CEO Jim Donald's lofty goal of having 40,000 stores worldwide.

ENDNOTES

[1] Starbucks, 2009 annual report, "Letter to Shareholders," p.1.

[2] Howard Schultz and Dori Jones Yang, *Pour Your Heart into It* (New York: Hyperion, 1997), p. 33.

[3] Ibid., p. 34.

[4] Ibid., p. 36.

[5] As told in ibid., p. 48.

[6] Ibid., pp. 61–62.

[7] As quoted in Jennifer Reese, "Starbucks: Inside the Coffee Cult," *Fortune*, December 9, 1996, p.193.

[8] Schultz and Yang, *Pour Your Heart Into It*, pp. 101–2.

[9] Ibid., p. 142.

[10] Starbucks, 2009 annual report, p. 3.

[11] Starbucks, "Global Responsibility Report," 2009, p. 13.

[12] "Starbucks Plans New Global Store Design," *Restaurants and Institutions*, June 25, 2009, www.rimag.com, accessed December 29, 2009.

[13] Starbucks, press releases, May 31, 2005, and October 25, 2005.

[14] Starbucks, press release, November 1, 2007.

[15] As stated by Howard Schultz in an interview with *Harvard Business Review* editor-in-chief Adi Ignatius; the interview was published in the July–August 2010 of the *Harvard Business Review*, pp. 108–15.

[16] Starbucks, "Starbucks and iTunes Bring Complimentary Digital Music and Video Offerings with Starbucks Pick of the Week," April 15, 2008, http://news.starbucks.com/article_display.cfm?article_id=93, accessed June 8, 2010.

[17] Starbucks, 2009 annual report, p. 5.

[18] Starbucks, "Starbucks Foundation," www.starbucks.com, accessed June 18, 2010.

[19] Starbucks, press release, July 14, 2008.

[20] Starbucks, press release, June 30, 2009.

[21] Starbucks, press release, April 7, 2008.

[22] Starbucks, press release, February 19, 2009.

[23] Starbucks, press release, April 13, 2010.

[24] Starbucks, 2009 annual report, p. 4.

[25] Claire Cain Miller, "New Starbucks Ads Seek to Recruit Online Fans," *New York Times*, May 18, 2009, www.nytimes.com, accessed January 3, 2010.

[26] Andy Server, "Schultz' Plan to Fix Starbucks," *Fortune*, January 18, 2008, www.fortune.com, accessed June 21, 2010.

[27] Beth Cowitt, "Starbucks CEO: We Spend More on Healthcare than Coffee," *Fortune*, June 7, 2010, http://money.cnn.com/2010/06/07/news/companies/starbucks_schultz_healthcare.fortune/index.html, accessed June 8, 2010.

[28] As related in Schultz and Yang, *Pour Your Heart Into It*, pp. 131–36.

[29] Starbucks, 2009 10-K report, p. 68.

[30] "100 Best Companies to Work For," *Fortune*, http://money.cnn.com/magazines/fortune/bestcompanies/2010/snapshots/93.html, accessed June 9, 2010.

[31] Ibid.

[32] Starbucks, press release, May 21, 2009, www.starbucks.com, accessed June 14, 2010.

[33] Starbucks, "Global Responsibility Report," 2008.

[34] Kate Rounds, "Starbucks Coffee," *Incentive* 167, no. 7, p. 22.

[35] Starbucks, 2009 10-K report, p. 6.

[36] Starbucks, "Corporate Responsibility," www.starbucks.com, accessed June 18, 2010.

[37] Starbucks, press release, February 19, 2009.

[38] Starbucks, press release, May 26, 2010.

[39] Starbucks, press release, January 18, 2010.

[40] "Shakeup at Starbucks," January 7, 2008, www.cbsnews.com, accessed June 16, 2010.

[41] Transcript of Starbucks Earnings Conference Call for Quarters 1 and 3 of fiscal year 2008, http://seekingalpha.com, accessed June 16, 2010.

[42] "Coffee Break for Starbucks' 135,000 Baristas," CNN, February 26, 2008, http://money.cnn.com, accessed December 28, 2009; and "Starbucks Takes a 3-Hour Coffee Break," *New York Times*, February 27, 2008, www.nytimes.com, accessed June 15, 2010.

[43] Quoted in Adi Ignatius, "We Had to Own the Mistakes," *Harvard Business Review* 88, no. 7/8 (July–August 2010), p. 111.

[44] Mariko Sanchanta, "Starbucks Plans Major China Expansion," *Wall Street Journal*, April 13, 2010, http://online.wsj.com, accessed June 10, 2010.

[45] Ibid.

[46] Starbucks, press release, April 21, 2010.

[47] Management presentation to Barclays Capital Retail and Restaurants Conference, April 28, 2010, www.starbucks.com, accessed June 21, 2010.

[48] Server, "Schultz' Plan to Fix Starbucks."

CASH CONNECTION: ARE ITS PAYDAY LENDER STRATEGY AND ITS BUSINESS MODEL ETHICAL?

A. J. Strickland
The University of Alabama

Tyler Chapman
The University of Alabama
MBA Candidate

After operating through years where the market growth seemed to have peaked due to the large number of rival companies, Cash Connection's president, Allen Franks, sat at his desk pondering new ideas on how to differentiate his firm from others in the short-term cash-lending business. In addition to rival companies, Cash Connection was also facing the looming influence of a financial czar designed by the federal government to heavily influence the operations of all companies within the financial services industry, primarily those within banking. The costs of audits that accompanied governmental regulations could be quite substantial for financial service companies. Franks believed that additional governmental restrictions would indeed take away from his company's ability to compete. He needed to find a way for Cash Connection to differentiate itself from its competitors so that it could gain the largest amount of market share possible in an attempt to weather the storm of the restrictions being imposed by the financial czar.

Allen Franks was born and raised in Shreveport, Louisiana. The son of a local veterinarian, Franks attended grade school in Shreveport and graduated from Jesuit High School. After high school, he attended Louisiana State University and graduated in 1979 with a degree in business administration.

While attending college, Franks purchased and remodeled rental homes in Shreveport. Upon completion of his degree, he owned and rented approximately 30 units and continued in the real estate industry until 1986, when he opened a check-cashing store in Shreveport. The first store of its kind in Shreveport, Franks's check-cashing store did quite well. After opening two more stores in Shreveport, however, Franks came to understand that the first store in a city was always more profitable than succeeding stores.

After this realization, he decided to open check-cashing stores only in cities that did not yet have one. After establishing stores in Jackson, Mississippi; Montgomery, Alabama; and Toledo, Ohio, Franks left real estate to work full-time in the check-cashing industry; his company became known as Cash Connection. In addition to providing payday advances and check cashing, Cash Connection expanded into offering bill payment services, prepaid phone cards, and money orders; its stores also served as Western Union agents to allow customers to transfer funds.

Throughout the mid to late 1990s, Cash Connection was one of several companies competing in an industry of substantial growth: short-term cash lending. Although the principle of extending short-term loans to borrowers in need has been around since the 18th century, much of the pioneering credit for making microloans to cash-constrained people living at or near the poverty level has been given to Muhammad Yunus, President of Grameen Bank, for his acts in the 1970s in Bangladesh. During this time Yunus began making microloans to impoverished people in Bangladesh to enable them to create their own fledgling business enterprise. Yunus hoped that such microloans for cash-constrained entrepreneurs would allow borrowers to become self-supporting and, ideally, to build sufficient wealth to exit poverty. Over the course of several years, Yunus was said to have loaned approximately $8 billion to some 8 million aspiring entrepreneurs in Bangladesh. As a result of his generous initiative, he was awarded the Nobel Peace Prize in 2006.

Payday advance services emerged in the early 1990s and grew as a result of robust consumer demand and changing conditions in the financial services marketplace, including the following:

1. The exiting of traditional financial institutions from the small-denomination, short-term credit market—a change largely due to the market's high cost structure.

2. The soaring cost of bounced checks and overdraft protection fees, late bill payment penalties, and other informal extensions of short-term credit.

3. The continuing trend toward regulation of the payday advance services, providing customers with important consumer protections.

As of 2010, industry analysts estimated that there were more than 22,000 payday advance locations across the United States, a higher number than the 9,500 banks spread throughout the country. Payday advances extended about $40 billion in short-term credit each year to millions of middle-class households that experienced cash shortfalls between paydays.

PAYDAY LOANS

Payday loans were short-term cash loans intended to cover the borrower's expenses until the borrower's next payday. Although repayment amounts could be very high, the loans were quick and convenient. The borrower typically wrote a postdated check that included the loan fees and was used as "collateral" for the loan; the borrower could also sign an Automated Clearing House (ACH) authorization to debit the borrower's account on payday.

The average payday loan amount was $300 and the term was typically for 14 to 30 days. Fees varied but averaged between $15 and $20 per $100. For a 14-day loan at $20 per $100, the annual percentage rate (APR) was an astounding 520 percent. That APR, as most payday

lenders were quick to point out, would apply only if the borrower had the loan for the whole year and paid $20 every two weeks. Payday loan fees were high because such loans carried a lot of risk for the company: many people who took out payday loans did not pay them back.

Throughout the United States, governments on every level were looking at payday loan outlets with increasing concern. Many people thought that they took advantage of low-income people in financial trouble. Some went so far as to say that payday lenders "preyed" on the poor. Those providing the loans argued that they were filling a need and not doing anything illegal.

The following situation illustrates why many people felt that payday loans worked against the favor of a large number of people: Suppose that you had an unexpected expense one month and took out a short-term loan to provide you with enough capital to solve your problem and allow you to get on with your life. Well, what if your next paycheck, after your budgeted expenses, wasn't enough to allow you to pay back the loan? If you came up short again, you could renew, or extend, your loan. This process was called a "rollover." If you rolled over your loan too many times, however, it could end up costing you a lot of money. Say you borrowed $100 for 14 days until your next payday. You wrote a check to the lender for $115 (the $100 in principal plus a $15 fee). The APR of that loan would be 391 percent! If you couldn't pay back the $115 on the due date, you could roll over the loan for another two weeks. If you rolled over the loan three times, the finances charge would reach $60 for the original $100 loan.

To avoid appearing to roll over the debt, some lenders asked the debtor to take out a "new loan" by paying a new fee and writing another check. Also, in a practice called "touch and go," lenders took a cash "payoff" for the old loan and immediately provided the borrower with funds from the "new loan." Irrespective of whether the repeat transactions were cast as "renewals," "extensions," or "new loans," the result was a continuous flow of interest-only payments at very short intervals that never reduced the principal. Given the high fees and very short terms, borrowers could find themselves owing more than the amount they originally borrowed after just a few rollovers within a single year.

The potential to recognize substantial profits through fees and interest charges, along with strong consumer demand, resulted in heavy saturation of payday lending companies throughout large cities and towns in the United States. Another reason for the high numbers of payday lending firms was that the start-up cost for an individual location was only approximately $130,000.

In addition to providing credit to many consumers, the payday loan industry had made significant contributions to U.S. and state economies (see Exhibit 1). The industry contributed more than $10 billion to the U.S. gross domestic product in 2007 and supported more than 155,000 jobs nationally; some 77,000 people worked in nearly 24,000 retail locations that made payday loans.

In 2007, the payday lending industry provided approximately $44 billion in credit to U.S. consumers. Between 2006 and 2007, there was a decrease of 2.5 percent in the number of payday

▶ EXHIBIT 1

Total U.S. Economic Impact of Payday Lending Industry in 2007			
Value Added to GDP	**Total Employment**	**Labor Income (Employee Compensation)**	**Tax Revenues Generated**
$10,212,730,000	155,581	$6,415,800,000	$2,630,000,000

Sources:: http://www.cfsa.net/downloads/eco_impact.pdf.

loan stores in the United States, from 24,189 to 23,586. There was no clear pattern for store closings. Some states experienced double-digit growth, and others experienced large drops in the number of stores per state. States with the highest growth in the number of stores in 2007 were South Dakota, Kansas, and Nevada. States with the biggest drops were Oregon, Indiana, and Minnesota.

Overall, the total labor income impact from the payday loan industry was $6.4 billion in 2007, as the industry helped generate over $2.6 billion in federal, state, and local taxes. Through direct employment, payday loan stores contributed $2.9 billion in labor income, which translated to approximately $37,689 per store employee. Suppliers to the payday lending industry contributed $1.4 billion in labor income as an indirect result of the revenues generated by the payday loan industry. Altogether, $2.1 billion was generated as payday loan store employees and supplier industries' employees spent their wages in local economies. In regard to the size of companies that served as industry players, any company with more than 51 branch locations nationwide was considered a national player. Cash Advance America, Check & Go, and Check America were examples of national players.

THE MARKET FOR PAYDAY LOANS

Policymakers, regulators, and consumer advocates had stakes equal to the industry's in getting a handle on the size and composition of the market for payday loans. If the near-term growth in demand by consumers who had never taken out a payday loan was insufficient to meet the industry's dramatically expanded capacity to originate them, the only way to make up the deficit in new demand was for lenders to encourage existing customers to borrow more frequently. This meant developing marketing and other strategies to convert occasional users of payday loans into routine borrowers.

Considerably less data was available on the aggregate size of the market for payday loans than on the characteristics of borrowers.

Analysts who closely followed the industry estimated that about 5 percent of the U.S. population had taken out at least one payday loan at some time. Community Financial Services Association of America, an industry trade organization, reported that more than 24 million Americans (10 percent of the population) said they were somewhat or very likely to obtain a payday advance. Taken together, these estimates suggested that the industry had penetrated about half its potential market and that there were substantial unrealized growth opportunities without having to entice existing customers to borrow more frequently.

Exhibit 2 shows the financial performance of Cash Connection from 2007 to 2009. The company's net income significantly decreased from 2007 to 2008, with additional declines in 2009. A large portion of the decline in performance could likely be attributed to the fast-growing number of firms competing in the payday lending industry while banks and other loan institutions were finding ways to differentiate themselves to be more appealing in attracting customers. Some industry experts felt the decline in income in the industry was due to the saturation of competitors and the overall decline in the economy.

PAYDAY LENDING INDUSTRY CUSTOMERS

Payday lending companies served the heart of America's working- and middle-class population. Customers came from hardworking families who had relationships with mainstream financial institutions. Although data on the demographics of payday loan borrowers were limited, many borrowers often faced severe credit restraints, had poor credit histories, and had bounced one or more checks in the previous five years. A 2001 study revealed the following demographic facts about payday advance customers:

1. They were of middle income.
    - The majority earned between $25,000 and $50,000.

▶ EXHIBIT 2

Cash Connection Profit & Loss Statement, 2007–2009

	Jan–Dec 31, 2007	Jan–Dec 31, 2008	Jan 1–Dec 27, 2009
Total Income	$6,348,544	$6,283,860	$5,768,805
Expenses			
Returned Items	389,147	690,003	847,310
401(k) Matching Funds	3,294	3,384	3,074
Advertising	142,160	176,939	187,294
Alarm Monitoring—Security	3,418	5,070	53,497
Armored Car Service	93,029	97,308	99,461
Auto Expense	62,123	72,072	59,545
Bad Debt	5,356	391	0
Check Cashing	4,050	3,885	5,505
Pay Day Loans	0	0	0
Total Bad Debt	9,405	4,276	5,505
Bank Charges	105,437	108,065	93,645
Cashier Errors	34,590	32,618	−3,225
Casual Labor	−52	0	113
Check Verification Expense	8,982	5,409	4,188
Collection Service	188	0	86
Consulting Expense	4,188	0	0
Depreciation	60,159	81,731	0
Donations	44	0	1,253
Dues, Subs & Directories	11,997	10,324	10,519
Employee Benefits	114,857	85,428	100,884
Fees, Permits & Licenses	34,745	30,969	30,570
Insurance			
Insurance—Operations	78,704	49,906	30,540
Insurance—Worker's Comp	13,648	9,522	10,668
Total Insurance	92,352	59,428	41,208
Interest	0	0	5,342
Interest—Investors	0	−1,133	21,594
Interest—Banks	242,574	114,859	111,093
Total Interest	242,574	113,726	138,029
Internet Provider	8,565	2,374	3,941
Management Fees	64,565	146,580	146,580
Meals & Entertainment	6,479	10,760	7,523
Miscellaneous	333	426	6,797
Money Order Expense	19,496	18,272	15,243
Outside Services	251,184	312,108	7,482
Pager	0	366	0
Postage	85,131	72,606	63,203
Professional Services			
Accounting & Audits	227,981	181,857	156,101
Legal	96,391	77,027	32,027
Legal—Collections	5,755	4,321	362
Payroll Service	0	0	10,434

(continued)

▶EXHIBIT 2   *(concluded)*

	Jan–Dec 31, 2007	Jan–Dec 31, 2008	Jan 1–Dec 27, 2009
Total Professional Services	330,127	263,205	198,923
Promotions	0	0	18,598
Rent			
Equipment	1,514	3,359	2,519
Storage	34,666	31,896	2,249
Building	400,156	417,872	443,285
Total Rent	436,336	453,127	448,053
Total Repairs & Maintenance	85,429	95,919	113,563
Salaries & Wages	0	138	0
District Management	255,959	202,163	209,622
Salaries allocated from CCC/CNI	0	0	251,696
Operations	1,438,701	1,550,049	1,686,903
Total Salaries & Wages	1,694,660	1,752,350	2,148,221
Software and Data Maintenance	0	0	40,592
Supplies	82,186	98,755	96,011
Supplies—Printing	7,296	14,554	3,404
Taxes			
Federal	−110	0	0
Payroll	156,353	160,934	174,544
Property	6,630	2,959	2,763
State	78,830	24,839	25,606
Total Taxes	241,702	188,732	202,912
Telephone	0	0	1,896
Land	148,166	135,562	143,463
Cellular	18,496	20,716	11,321
Total Telephone	166,663	156,279	156,679
Travel & Lodging	34,435	24,516	20,082
Utilities			
Gas & Electric	88,826	97,315	114,323
Water	1,126	3,791	4,332
Total Utilities	89,952	101,106	118,655
Total Expenses	5,017,173	5,488,623	5,569,912
Net Operating Income	1,331,371	795,237	198,893
Other Expenses			
Cherry Creek Ranch Income/Loss	0	344,586	0
Crime Loss	0	30,547	21,813
Monthly Accrued Payroll	0	0	0
Salary Expenses Accrued from Prior Year	−5,487	42,514	−94,880
7050 Settlements	241	34,900	0
Total Other Expenses	−5,246	452,548	−73,068
Net Other Income	5,246	−452,548	73,068
Net Income	$1,336,617	$ 342,689	$ 271,961

Source: Cash Connection.

2. They were of average education.
   - 94 percent had a high school diploma or better.
   - 56 percent had some college or a college degree.
3. They consisted of young families.
   - 68 percent were under 45 years old (only 3.5 percent were 65 or older).
   - The majority were married.
   - 64 percent had children in the household.
4. They were of the stable working class.
   - 42 percent owned homes.
   - 57 percent had major credit cards.
   - 100 percent had steady incomes.

Within these characteristics of customers, Cash Connection had two requirements that customers had to meet before they could receive loans. First, customers had to have a job that provided some source of income. Second, they had to have a checking account.

UNBANKED CUSTOMERS

Other prime users of the services provided by Cash Connection were "unbanked" or "underbanked." Unbanked individuals were those without an account at a bank or other financial institution for one reason or another. Underbanked, or underserved, individuals were those who had poor access to mainstream financial services. A recent study conducted by the Federal Deposit Insurance Corporation (FDIC) estimated that 10 million American households were either unbanked or underbanked. The fact that payday loans produced quick in-hand cash and offered easy repayment plans was reasons why these loans were so appealing for underbanked individuals. For unbanked individuals, who had no collection of funds in an account of their own and were at higher risk of nonrepayment, Cash Collection and other firms competing in this industry chose to provide only the service of check cashing.

In January 2009, the FDIC sponsored a special survey to collect national, state, and metropolitan area data on the number of U.S. households that were unbanked or underbanked, their demographic characteristics, and their reasons for being unbanked or underbanked (see Exhibit 3). Data for roughly 47,000 participating households were collected. The FDIC undertook this effort to address a gap in reliable data on the number of unbanked and underbanked households in the United States. Access to an account at a federally insured institution provided households with the opportunity to conduct basic financial transactions, save for emergency and long-term security needs, and access credit on affordable terms. Many people, particularly those in low- to moderate-income households, did not have access to mainstream financial products such as bank accounts and low-cost loans. Other households had access to a bank account but nevertheless relied on more costly financial service providers for a variety of reasons. In addition to paying more for basic transaction and credit financial services, these households could be vulnerable to loss or theft and often struggled to build credit histories and achieve financial security.

COMPETITION IN THE PAYDAY LENDING INDUSTRY

The relaxation of federal restrictions starting in the early 1980s led to increased competition in the payday lending industry. Increasing regulation in the loan servicing industry as well as the financial industry only heightened the ease with which new companies could enter the industry and remain competitive while protecting the revenue and profits of companies that were well established in the industry.

A barrier to entry was the level of industry competition. Large retail banking firms such as Bank of America, Wells Fargo, JPMorgan Chase, and Citigroup were major players in the loan origination industry. These companies had an increased ability to generate a portfolio of serviced loans. It was difficult for new companies to purchase loans from third parties and generate their own loan-servicing portfolios.

Individual company performance relative to other companies within the industry largely

▶**EXHIBIT 3**

Reasons Households Who Have Never Banked Are Unbanked

Reasons Household Is Unbanked	Number (000s)	Percent of Total
CUSTOMER SERVICE REASONS		
Banks have inconvenient hours	158	3.60%
There is no bank near work or home	153	3.49
There are language barriers at banks	293	6.68
Banks do not feel comfortable or welcoming	389	8.87
Banks do not offer needed services	149	3.40
Other/None of the above	3,041	69.37
Don't know/Refused	201	4.58
TOTAL	**4,384**	**100.0%**
FINANCIAL REASONS		
Minimum balance requirement is too high	540	11.98%
Service charges are too high	267	5.92
Bounced too many checks/had too many overdrafts	71	1.57
Banks take too long to clear checks	48	1.06
Do not have enough money to need account	1,581	35.06
Credit problems	139	3.08
Other/None of the above	1,606	35.62
Don't know/Refused	257	5.70
TOTAL	**4,509**	**100.0%**
OTHER REASONS		
Do not write enough checks	765	17.06%
Could not manage or balance account	162	3.61
Do not trust banks	268	5.98
Do not have documents to open account	235	5.24
Do not know how to open account	103	2.30
Do not see value of having account	530	11.82
Other/None of the above	2,105	46.96
Don't know/Refused	315	7.03
TOTAL	**4,483**	**100.0%**

Note: Figures do not always reconcile to totals because of the rounding of household weights to represent the population totals.
Households not involved in household finance are excluded from this tabulation. Total percentages may sum to more than 100 because respondents were permitted to choose multiple responses.

Source: FDIC National Survey of Unbanked and Underbanked Households, December 2009, http://www.fdic.gov/householdsurvey/full_report.

depended on the company's cost structure and services relative to other lending companies.

The performance of equity markets had affected both the demand for consumer lending and the quality of lending portfolios. A positive development in the stock market generally resulted in increased lending due to the wealth effect of rising share prices. Investors feeling wealthier felt more confident to undertake projects that increased their demand for credit. Rising stock prices also affected the quality of the lending portfolios because borrowers had an increased ability to meet repayments. Conversely, a fall in share prices had a negative impact on borrowers' ability to service debt, resulting in increased risk for those who extended the credit.

BANKING SERVICES

A 2008 study of the payday loan industry by Stephens Inc. projected that the payday loan market could encompass 10 percent of U.S. households. The substitute products for payday loans could have undesirable features for some consumers. Overdraft protection on a checking account was perhaps the closest substitute for payday loans, but its fees were on par with payday loan fees. Automated overdraft fees assessed by banks ranged from $10 to $38, with the average fee being $28.35, based on 1,024 banks in 364 cities. This average was an increase of more than $2.00 since the 2003 National Fee Survey was released. About one-fourth of the banks surveyed in the 2008 study also tacked on additional fees for accounts that remained in negative balance status. These fees were in the form of flat fees or interest charged on a percentage basis.

Bank service fees practically doubled in the eight years from 1995 to 2003, increasing from $16.4 to $32.6 billion. Fees from overdraft protection programs, also called nonsufficient funds (NSF) fees, had risen so dramatically that they represented the preponderance of all such fee income for banks and credit unions. NSF income for banks and/or credit unions could amount to as much as 50 percent of total consumer checking account revenue. One recent analysis estimated that NSF fees accounted for more than half, or roughly $18.8 billion, of the service-fee income derived by America's banks and credit unions. Another analysis estimated that banks collected $22 billion in overdraft fees in 2003.

The large majority of retail banks elected not to serve the needs of individuals who sought services such as payday loans. One recent study showed that 73 percent of banks were aware that significant unbanked and/or underbanked populations were in their market areas, but less than 18 percent of banks identified expanding services to unbanked and/or underbanked individuals as a priority in their business strategy. These depository institutions cited the lack of profitability as a significant barrier to serving unbanked and underbanked individuals. This was because banks tended to directly focus on the risk involved with conducting business with individuals who were not the most creditworthy of borrowers. Compared with that of payday loan companies, the lending structure of modern retail banks operated with loans of higher amounts over more extended terms after a background of credit was conducted on the consumers obtaining the loans. Many banks felt that collecting repayments, late fees, and default fees was highly unlikely in the event that short-term loans were placed in the wrong hands.

Exhibit 4 shows the impact of the recession on the banking industry in 2007 and 2008. Banks

▶ **EXHIBIT 4**

Recent Performance of Commercial Banking Industry in the U.S.		
	Revenue ($ millions)	Growth Rate(%)
2005	$585.9	7.7%
2006	640.1	9.3
2007	643.0	0.5
2008	542.7	−15.6
2009	489.0	−9.9

in those two years were attempting to increase fees to drive more income but were reluctant to move into new or different business segments. Exhibit 5 illustrates that the primary strategy at that time was building more branches.

CREDIT UNIONS

Credit unions were nonprofit organizations owned by and operated for the benefit of members. They generally were sponsored by

▶ EXHIBIT 5

Balance Sheet Statistics for U.S. Retail Banks, 2004–2008

	2008	2007	2006	2005	2004
Number of institutions reporting	7,086	7,283	7,401	7,526	7,631
ASSETS					
Cash from depository institutions	$ 1,041,800,469	$ 482,167,038	$ 433,022,250	$ 400,266,591	$ 387,555,301
Securities	1,746,324,740	1,590,804,716	1,666,232,385	1,572,272,561	1,551,101,104
Federal funds sold	688,071,175	646,116,706	529,562,658	443,397,239	385,239,490
Net loans & leases	6,681,762,460	6,537,222,244	5,912,241,523	5,312,245,715	4,832,865,517
Trading account assets	939,848,184	867,549,217	619,558,531	499,187,288	504,289,109
Bank premises & fixed assets	109,679,684	105,022,132	96,811,538	91,705,731	86,799,336
Other real estate owned	22,914,392	9,790,917	5,467,048	4,026,398	3,852,709
Goodwill and other intangibles	392,526,497	423,216,712	358,508,090	302,933,608	275,726,003
All other assets	685,929,531	514,200,896	470,136,854	414,258,899	388,186,394
TOTAL ASSETS	**$12,308,857,132**	**$11,176,090,578**	**$10,091,540,877**	**$9,040,294,030**	**$8,415,614,963**
LIABILITIES					
Total deposits	$ 8,082,183,258	$ 7,309,840,803	$6,731,419,422	$6,073,144,887	$5,593,174,725
Federal funds purchased	803,925,770	765,572,423	719,361,004	667,577,176	577,571,016
Trading liabilities	469,787,117	342,666,695	266,349,279	251,710,818	280,474,394
Other borrowed funds	1,275,166,890	1,114,956,388	869,841,343	755,848,619	738,096,866
Subordinated debt	182,987,299	174,904,850	149,794,691	122,236,763	110,137,664
All other liabilities	340,611,084	325,230,537	324,925,231	257,334,811	265,975,308
TOTAL LIABILITIES	**$11,154,661,418**	**$10,033,171,696**	**$9,061,690,970**	**$8,127,853,074**	**$7,565,429,973**
EQUITY CAPITAL					
Perpetual preferred stock	$ 6,391,140	$ 4,999,917	$ 5,122,235	$ 5,263,958	$ 6,237,011
Common stock	45,438,608	35,987,933	33,835,473	32,273,780	29,810,632
Surplus	851,008,910	738,886,871	625,617,888	529,798,223	493,501,576
Undivided profits	251,357,056	363,044,161	365,274,311	345,104,995	320,635,771
TOTAL EQUITY CAPITAL	**$1,154,195,714**	**$1,142,918,882**	**$1,029,849,907**	**$912,440,956**	**$850,184,990**

Source: http://www2.fdic.gov/SDI/SOB/.

an employer or association, so usually only employees or association members were eligible to join. Since there were no shareholders to answer to, they could often offer higher interest rates and lower fees than banks could; however, their services were more limited than those of banks. The size of the credit union could affect the variety of services offered. Smaller credit unions might offer only savings accounts and loans. Some credit unions focused on banking for low-income communities. Just like banks, credit unions collected deposits and made loans to their members. Deposits and loan payments often came from automatic payroll deposits that enabled credit unions to extend loans to their members at relatively low risk. A lower level of risk meant lower fees charged for services offered by credit unions. Since credit unions were nonprofit and paid no state or federal taxes, they often paid higher rates and charged lower fees than banks did. Any profit earned by a credit union was either invested back into the organization or paid out to members as a dividend. See Exhibit 6 for financial trends in federally insured credit unions.

The profile of a payday loan borrower suggested an individual who was capable of making rational decisions yet chose to do business with a payday lender instead of a credit union, for whatever reason. Somewhere between 10 and 20 percent of credit union members opted to do at least some of their business with payday lenders. Why? Perhaps it was the fear of being turned down, which in turn came from the knowledge that they had credit issues. Perhaps the credit union's hours and location weren't convenient when the member needed the loan. But more likely, it was because the credit union didn't have the right product—a small, short-term cash loan that could be accessed quickly and conveniently.

Why had credit unions shied away from payday-like loans? Perhaps credit unions feared that offering such loans placed them in the same category as a payday lender, which could be an unsettling feeling. However, credit unions were beginning to realize they could not ignore what it was costing their members to do business with payday lenders. Credit unions could offer a better-valued product that was both empowering for their members and sustainable for the credit union.

For credit unions, the national average NSF fee was $23.94, based on 519 locations in 253 cities. This represented an increase of nearly $3.00 since 2003. The national average returned-check fee charged by major merchants

▶ EXHIBIT 6

Financial Trends in Federally Insured Credit Unions, January 1, 2002–December 31, 2008

Highlights	Year	Number of Credit Unions Reporting	
		Federal Credit Unions	State Credit Unions
Assets increased $58.45 billion, or 7.74%, to $813.44 billion.	2002	5,953	3,735
	2003	5,776	3,593
Net Worth increased $2.80 billion, or 3.26%. The net worth to assets ratio decreased from 11.41% to 10.93%.	2004	5,572	3,442
	2005	5,393	3,302
	2006	5,189	3,173
Earnings as measured by the return on average assets decreased from 0.63% to 0.31%	2007	5,036	3,065
	2008	4,847	2,959
Loans increased $37.43 billion, or 7.08%. The loan-to-share ratio decreased from 83.58% to 83.10%.			

Source: "Payday Lending: The Credit Union Way," April 2008.

had risen by $1.44, to $26.64. The national high for bounced-check fees for both merchants and credit unions was $50.00. FDIC data suggest that more than 18,000 financial institutions and credit unions collected $32.6 billion annually in service charges from the 56 million checking accounts they serviced. Thus, these institutions annually derived $582 in service charges from an average checking account (see Exhibit 7).

Other sources of credit (e.g., pawnshops, auto title lenders, and subprime home equity) required borrowers to front collateral and were often not viewed by many consumers as suitable alternatives. For this reason, payday loans were often viewed as a valuable alternative source of credit for consumers.

CREDIT CARDS

Of all the instruments consumers used to obtain short-term credit, nothing was more commonly used than credit cards. In the fast-paced environment of the 21st century, U.S. consumers used credit cards for nearly 100,000 transactions per minute. Although the credit card industry had produced billions of dollars in profits, it had also produced trillions of dollars worth of debt, as Americans simply had not been able to pay back the amount of debt that had grown over the last 30 years. Throughout this time, banks had constantly changed terms on credit card usage and interest rates on individual consumers to appear as if they were locked in a game with these consumers. The use of credit cards also played a hand in the recent economic

Source: http://www.superiorpawn.com/gallery/signlg.jpg.

meltdown, as many consumers began to refinance their houses in order to help pay off their credit card debt. A large number of these individuals then turned around and quickly used up the amount of credit allotted on their cards.

One credit card company in particular whose name was synonymous with the tricks and traps that had entangled credit card customers over the last 20 years was Providian. Providian's downspin in reputation was believed to have started when the company began extending credit to the 35 to 40 million unbanked U.S. prospects that had low incomes, were bankrupt, or previously had not qualified for a credit card—that is, the riskiest

▶EXHIBIT 7

2008 Survey Data Regarding Overdraft or Nonsufficient Funds (NSF) Fees in the United States				
	Number of Vendors	**Number of Cities**	**Average Fee**	**Increase since 2003**
Bank NSF fees	364	1,024	$28.35	more than $2.00
Credit union NSF Fees	253	519	$23.94	$3.00
Merchant returned-check fees	342	—	$26.64	$1.44

Source: http://www.ncua.gov/Resources/Reports/statistics/Yearend2008.pdf.

of borrowers. Providian viewed these individuals as the ones who would generate the most profit for the company, and it soon began to generate nearly $1 billion per year through penalty fees and high interest rates. Providian's strategy was to get borrowers to pay back their transactions with the minimum payment so that it took longer for them to pay back the initial loan. By doing this, Providian generated larger profits. Borrowers could obtain cards from Providian with no activation fee but high interest rates and high penalty fees for late payments. Although Providian may have been the leading innovator of practices that many people would consider unethical, it was quickly followed by other credit card companies not long after the large profit margins were recognized. Exhibit 8 shows the late fees of credit cards in comparison with other similar late fees.

THE REGULATING ENVIRONMENT

The payday loan industry was regulated by a combination of state and federal laws and competitive market forces. As the payday loan industry matured over the past decade and consumers continued to demonstrate a desire for payday loans, the state and federal regulatory environment evolved along with the industry.

State Laws

Thirty-nine states and the District of Columbia explicitly allowed payday lending. However, via the Internet and telephone, payday lending was a de facto reality in virtually all states. Typically, states excused payday lenders from interest rate limits otherwise applicable to consumer loans in exchange for maximum fees and rollover limits. States also applied licensing regimes and conducted regular examinations. Twenty-two states did not permit immediate rollovers. Five states limited rollovers to three times. Some states allowed rollovers only if debt counseling was available. Only Georgia and Maryland explicitly prohibited payday lending in every form. The vast majority of states that permitted payday loans had established limits on the loan amount; many of those limits were set at approximately $500.

State laws usually prohibited lenders from threatening borrowers with criminal or civil action if the borrowers defaulted. In states where

▶**EXHIBIT 8** **Late Fees Expressed as an Annual Percentage Rate (APR)**

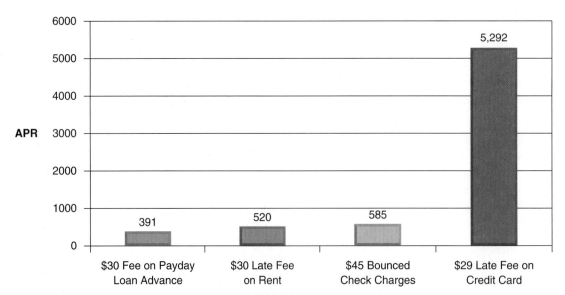

Source: "The Card Game," *PBS Frontline,* http://www.pbs.org/wgbh/pages/frontline/creditcards/.

payday lending was authorized, regulatory regimes existed to ensure that lenders were complying with state and federal laws, and that they were not financially vulnerable.

Federal Laws

The following laws regulating payday lending operations are just one example of ways in which the federal government was attempting to heighten its control over the financial services industry:

- *Truth in Lending Act:* This law required lenders to disclose loan APRs and finance charges. The Federal Trade Commission oversaw compliance with this legislation by nonbank payday lenders, and the FDIC generally enforced compliance for its insured banks.
- *Fair Debt Collection Practices Act:* While this legislation applied only to third-party collection, the industry best practices set out by the Community Financial Services Association (CFSA) suggested that members adhere to the Fair Debt Collection Practices Act.
- *The Federal Deposit Insurance Act:* Under Section 27 of the Federal Deposit Insurance Act, insured state-chartered banks (which were presently the only banks making payday loans) were entitled to charge nationwide the interest rates that applied in their home states. This law (and its analog with respect to national banks, Section 85 of the National Bank Act) had led a number of financial institutions to establish credit card banks in states without interest rate limits. Some payday lenders had agreements with Delaware- and South Dakota–based banks, by which the bank provided the loan by "exporting" the interest-rate laws of its home state. The CFSA's "best practices" placed restrictions on such relationships.
- *Gramm-Leach-Bliley Act:* This act's privacy requirements applied to payday lenders and were enforced by the Federal

Trade Commission with respect to non-bank lenders.

Federal and state regulators were also considering mandating interest rates and placing limits on the amount of funds available to be loaned to consumers.

Although a rational belief would be that many restrictions placed on payday loans would favor borrowers, several research studies have found that heavy regulations and bans on payday lending have left borrowers in greater financial distress. These studies found that, since their states eliminated payday lending, consumers in Georgia and North Carolina have bounced more checks, complained more about lenders and debt collectors, and have filed for Chapter 7 bankruptcy at a higher rate than before. In states that have been given some form of loan restriction, the most common option for consumers dealing with a financial constraint has been to pay late or not to pay at all. Of those who paid bills late or not at all, 10 percent had utilities disconnected, went without a prescription medication, or had a damaged credit rating, and 50 percent incurred late fees on charges, including those who said that their bill was turned over to a collection agency or that they faced repossession or bankruptcy.

BUSINESS OBJECTIVE

For companies that operated within the payday loan industry, a desirable main objective was to serve customers in compliance with the rules of the industry and better educate them on financial services and products. Alabama's Council for Fair Lending (CFL) was established in November of 2007 by a group of Alabama-based cash advance and title loan lenders that recognized a need to operate in a parallel style. While they expressed an understanding that the loans they offered served as a short-term solution for many consumers, they made a conscious effort to inform those consumers on the importance of wise borrowing. The CFL's Code of Fair Lending is shown in Exhibit 9.

► EXHIBIT 9

Alabama Council for Fair Lending's Code of Fair Lending

OUR CODE OF FAIR LENDING......

We, the members of this association, in order to best serve the citizens of this state, recognize and adopt the following operating principles:

1. All customers will be treated with concern in an honest & professional manner.
2. All customers will be fully informed of their borrowing rights & obligations.
3. We will promote the responsible use of credit and strive to educate our customers on their financial choices.
4. Our employees will treat all customers with courtesy, fairness & integrity and will respond to any complaint about our service promptly and directly.
5. We will protect our customer's rights to privacy with respect to personal information.
6. We will honor and respect members of active military & their dependents. The Department of Defense's regulations on loans will be strictly adhered to.
7. We will comply with city, county, state and federal laws and keep our customers informed of the regulations that govern our actions.
8. We will exercise compassion to cash advance customers when warranted by offering repayment options before proceeding with civil collections. Title customers whose vehicles are repossessed will be offered options to retrieve their vehicles.
9. We will offer reasonably affordable loans to customers on fixed incomes.
10. We will not allow customers to roll over a loan unless authorized by state law.
11. We will give our customers the right to rescind, at no cost, a new loan on or before the close of the next business day.
12. We will prominently display the Borrow Smart seal in all of our stores and adhere to the Borrow Smart Alabama Code of Customer Service.

Source: http://www.borrowsmartalabama.com/.

PAYDAY LENDING NATIONAL CUSTOMER SURVEY

In 2004, a survey was conducted by Cypress Research Group to examine the degree of customer satisfaction for individuals involved with a payday lending process. Two thousand payday advance customers were surveyed in an effort to examine industry performance from the customer's perspective; evaluate the long-term viability of the industry; and assess consumer confidence in, and satisfaction with, the payday advance service. The following are some of the findings taken from the survey:

- Most of these consumers had other financial options available, but payday advance could sometimes be a better financial decision and was quick and convenient.
- Two-thirds of customers had at least one option that offered quick access to money.

Source: Cash Connection of Tuscaloosa, AL.

- Half of customers had overdraft protection on their checking accounts.
- Fifty percent of customers had a major credit card(s). Thirty-five percent had a credit card(s) with available credit.
- In comparison to other credit products with which respondents had recent experience, customer overall satisfaction with payday advance (75 percent) was second only to check overdraft protection (83 percent). Payday advance also ranked higher than overall satisfactions with obtaining a home equity line of credit, a major credit card, a loan with a bank or credit union, and a car title loan.
- A large majority of customers cited the following reasons for taking a payday advance:

  1. Cover an unexpected expense (84 percent).
  2. Avoid late charges on bills (73 percent).
  3. Avoid bouncing checks (66 percent).
  4. Bridge a temporary reduction in income (62 percent).

More than three-quarters of customers were satisfied with the repayment schedule, the amount they could borrow and their ability to refinance or renew the loan if they chose to.

The rationale behind the boom in payday loans was perceived to be the high credit card rates and high bank fees for bounced checks charged by companies that operated as alternatives to payday lending firms. The immediate gratification offered by payday loans to the consumer was another driving force in the deferred deposit business, as there was nowhere a consumer could go for a small loan in an emergency. Banks did not offer very small loans, and loan companies were too slow and complicated. When looking at whether lenders or borrowers benefited the most from payday loans, a July 2007 study, "Expanding Credit Access: Using Randomized Supply Decisions to Estimate the Impacts," favored the borrowers. Individuals taking high-interest loans were less likely to be in poverty, less likely to be hungry or malnourished, and less likely to have lost their jobs.

With the federal government acting as a looming financial czar over many businesses in the private sector, especially those in the financial services industry, companies felt that they had to do everything within reasonable limits to give themselves an upper hand over competitors. In difficult times, the decisions of company leaders were crucial to future performance. Given the expected regulation by the federal government and expected moves by competitive firms, what could Allen Franks do to differentiate Cash Connection and make it the top choice for consumers attempting to receive a payday loan?

INDEXES

Organization

Name

a

b

c

d